Pershing

GENERAL OF THE ARMIES

Isabel Mangum

John J. Pershing

Donald Smythe

Pershing

GENERAL OF THE ARMIES

Indiana University Press

BLOOMINGTON

Chapters or parts of chapters of *Pershing: General of the
Armies* first appeared in various journals under the following titles:
"A.E.F. Snafu at Sedan" in *Prologue*, September 1973; "Five
Days in June" and "AEF Strategy in France, 1917–1918" in *Army
Quarterly and Defence Journal*, January 1974 and April 1985;
"Pershing after the Armistice, 1918–1919" in *Missouri Historical
Review*, October 1984; "Literary Salvos" in *Mid-America*, July
1975; "Pershing Goes 'Over There' " in *American Neptune*,
October 1974; "The Battle of the Books" in *Army*, September
1972; "The Pershing-March Conflict in World War I," " 'Your
Authority in France Will Be Supreme,' " and "St. Mihiel" in
Parameters, December 1981, September 1979, and June 1983;
"General of the Armies John J. Pershing" in Michael Carver, ed.,
The War Lords (Boston: Little, Brown & Co., 1976); "Portrait of
Pershing" in *Indiana Military History Journal*, October 1985.

Library of Congress Cataloging-in-Publication Data

Smythe, Donald. 1927–
  Pershing, general of the armies.

  Bibliography: p.
  Includes index.
  1. Pershing, John J. (John Joseph), 1860–1948.
2. Generals—United States—Biography. 3. United
States. Army—Biography. 4. World War, 1914–1918—
Campaigns—France. 5. United States. Army—History—
World War, 1914–1918. I. Title.
U53.P4S69 1986   355'.0092'4 [B]   85-42529
ISBN 0-253-34381-X
1 2 3 4 5 90 89 88 87 86

To the men of Rodman Hall

Contents

ILLUSTRATIONS

MAPS

ACKNOWLEDGMENTS

While it is impossible to thank all who helped with this book since its inception in 1970, it is a pleasure to single out certain people for special mention. In particular, I am indebted to my fellow historians and colleagues for advice and counsel: Sr. Serafina D'Alessio, M.P.F., Lloyd E. Ambrosius, Leonard S. Baker, Martin Blumenson, Elbridge Colby, Herman Duncan, Keith E. Eiler, Thomas R. English, Robert and Nancy Heinl, André Kaspi, Barbara Kraft, Bullitt Lowry, Tom Mahoney, Williamson Murray, Richard O'Conner, Edgar F. Raines, Jr., James W. Rainey, and Russell F. Weigley.

At John Carroll University Dr. Louis G. Pecek and the Committee on Research and Service furnished financial aid. Dr. Arthur J. Noetzel, then Academic Vice-President, gave encouragement and a summer grant. The History Department consented to my being absent for long periods and was unfailingly supportive, especially William J. Ulrich, Michael S. Pap, and George J. Prpic. Richard Klein and Susan A. Halderman served as research assistants. At Grasselli Library John Piety and his staff, especially William J. Balconi, Florence Krueger, Mary K. Sweeny, and Charles E. Wood, answered my many requests for help. Margie P. Wasdovich and Ethel Epstein typed the manuscript and Roy Drake, S.J., Donald F. Grazko, Terri Macejko, and Maura T. Sweeney saw it through the intricacies of a computer. Proofing was done by William M. Bichl, S.J., Mary Margaret Cooney, Daniel S. Gaul, Monica Holland, Paul J. Hulseman, Peg Mahon, Michelle M. Monnin, Daniel O'Neill, Michael Owendoff, John Riga, Joan Russell, Betty Skerl, Suzanne Walsh, Mary Ann Wiesemann, O.P., and especially Rosemary Malloy Hackman. Others at John Carroll or in the Cleveland area who helped were Roy and Florence Anderson, Lucien A. Aube, Thomas C. Biecker, S.J., Emmanuel Carreira, S.J., Robert Carver, Marilyn Coffee, Warren Daane, Dolores Kasper, George Qua, Robert Selzman, and Paula Wright.

For their help in the Manuscript Room at the Library of Congress I thank Charles Kelly, Gary Kohn, Ruth Nicholson, Marilyn Parr, and Carolyn Sung. At the National Archives I was ably served by Tim Nenninger, Judy Pratt, Richard Smith, and Leslie Waffen. My thanks to Ray Moseley and Harold D. Williams of the Washington National Records Center, Suitland, Maryland; to Richard N. Sheldon of the National Historical Publications and Records Commission; to Leslie H. Cross of the National Guard Association Library; to Dianne S. Tapley of the Infantry School Library at Fort Benning, Georgia, and to Laszlo Alfondi, Richard J. Summers, and the U.S. Army Military History Institute at Carlisle Barracks [Pennsylvania]; and to the faculty and staff of the Combat Studies Institute (CSI) at the U.S. Army Command and General Staff College, Fort Leavenworth, Kansas, who provided a gracious atmosphere in which to live and work for a year. At CSI

Donald L. Gilmore, Lawrence A. Yates, and Kay L. Sanders did the final proofing of the manuscript.

In the Washington, D.C., area, I was grateful for the help and support of Malin Craig, Jr., Carol Cutler, George and Sylvana Hinman, James and Isabel Mangum, Myrtle Montgomery, and Thomas North.

Others who helped in various parts of the country were Sr. Leona Eberhardt, Margaret Egeland, Nida Glick, Stephen J. Linsenmeyer, Russell J. Mittelstadt, Dana Stewart, William J. Weaver, Jr., Gladys Williams, and George V. Woodling.

One or more chapters of the book were read by Ernest Hillman, D. Clayton James, Jack C. Lane, and John D. Skilton. The book was read in its entirety by Daniel R. Beaver, Edward M. Coffman, I. B. Holley, Vada Hummel, Dolores Kratzer, Allan R. Millett, and Forrest C. Pogue.

To all who helped, my thanks.

DONALD SMYTHE
John Carroll University
Cleveland, Ohio

Pershing

GENERAL OF THE ARMIES

ONE

Selected to Command

(April–May 1917)

W HEN WAR BROKE OUT in Europe in 1914, the mood of the American people was well summed up by an editorial in the Chicago *Herald*: "Peace-loving citizens of this country will now rise up and tender a hearty vote of thanks to Columbus for having discovered America."[1]

Three years later the mood had changed. Addressing a throng in Times Square, Billy Sunday exclaimed: "If hell could be turned upside down, you would find stamped on its bottom, 'Made in Germany!' " Theodore Roosevelt thundered: "There is no question about 'going to war.' Germany is already at war with us." Demanded the New York *Tribune*: "Declare war!" On April 6, 1917, Congress did.[2]

If war meant some kind of American expeditionary force overseas, who would command it? The highest ranking American line officers, all major generals, in order of seniority, were Leonard Wood, J. Franklin Bell, Thomas H. Barry, Hugh L. Scott, Tasker H. Bliss, and John J. Pershing. Of these, only the first and the last were serious possibilities. Bell and Barry were in ill health; Scott and Bliss were both due to retire within the year. That left Wood and Pershing.[3]

Pershing was fifty-seven years old. Born in 1860 in Laclede, Missouri, he attended the U.S. Military Academy at West Point from 1882–1886. Although ranking a middling thirtieth out of seventy-seven academically, he proved himself a leader of men, being chosen first captain of cadets and president of his class.

From 1886–1891 he served as a frontier cavalryman at various posts in New Mexico and South Dakota, helping to put down an Indian uprising called the Ghost Dance Rebellion. In 1891 he began a four-year stint at the University of Nebraska as an instructor in military science, earning a law degree on the side in 1893. He had such success with the university's drill team that the students voted to change its name to the Pershing Rifles—the first of scores of such companies which exist today.

After several more years of frontier service and an assignment on the staff of Gen. Nelson A. Miles, Commanding General of the Army, Pershing went back to

West Point as a tactical officer (1897–1898). He got off on the wrong foot with the cadets. So unpopular was he—mainly because of excessive strictness—that they derisively nicknamed him "Black Jack," a reference to his having commanded black troops on the frontier. The name stuck.

In the Spanish-American War (1898) he did exceptionally well; a commanding officer said he was "cool as a bowl of cracked ice" under fire. The following year he sailed to the Philippines to begin the first of three tours there. Stationed in the southern island of Mindanao as a young lieutenant, he encountered a fierce, warlike people called Moros, with whom he had remarkable success in gaining their friendship and trust. They honored him, in fact, by naming him a *datto*, a native chieftain.

Still only a captain, he returned to the United States in 1903. The promotion system was so slow that he occasionally thought of resigning from the Army and practicing law. That year he met Helen Frances Warren, daughter of the wealthy and influential Senator Francis E. Warren of Wyoming. Almost immediately falling in love, he courted her for two years, during one of which he was a student at the new Army War College in Washington, D.C. They married in 1905.

Pershing spent his honeymoon in Tokyo where he was assigned as a military attaché. He also served in Manchuria as an observer during the Russo-Japanese War from 1905–1906. During the latter year he was suddenly promoted from captain to brigadier general, leapfrogging 862 senior officers. Since Senator Warren was chairman of the Senate Military Affairs Committee at the time, critics charged gross favoritism—a charge not altogether true, since Pershing had been recommended for such promotion by every general in the Army save one. But the Senator undoubtedly helped get the confirmation through the Senate.

That same year, 1906, some disgruntled officers circulated a story that Pershing had fathered several illegitimate children during his service in the Philippines. The story made both the Philippine and American newspapers, causing concern in the War Department. Pershing vigorously denied the charge, eventually securing sufficient affidavits to clear his name.

From 1907–1908 Pershing commanded Fort William McKinley near Manila, the largest American post outside the continental United States. The next four years, 1909–1913, he served again in southern Mindanao as governor of the Moro Province. During that time he fought several important engagements with rebellious Moros and further solidified American control of the southern islands.

Returning to America in 1914, he commanded the 8th Brigade with headquarters at the Presidio in San Francisco. Because of trouble along the Mexican border, he and the brigade were ordered to El Paso, where he remained the next two years. His wife, who by now had borne him four children—three girls and a boy—stayed in San Francisco.

On the night of August 26–27, 1915, a fire broke out at the home there, suffocating his wife and three daughters. Only the boy Warren survived. Pershing was utterly crushed. As he told a friend when promoted to major general in 1916: "All the promotion in the world would make no difference now."

That same year the Mexican bandit Francisco (Pancho) Villa, angered by American support of his rival, Venustiano Carranza, and goaded by the need for supplies, raided Columbus, New Mexico, killing eighteen Americans. Pershing led a hastily assembled Punitive Expedition, pursuing the bandit four hundred miles into Mexico. The expedition, which eventually numbered about eleven thousand men, stayed almost a year. Although it never caught Villa, the force broke up his band and killed a number of his subordinates. In February 1917 it withdrew. Thus Pershing was available for overseas service when the United States declared war on Germany in April.[4]

So also was Gen. Leonard Wood. A former Chief of Staff (1909–1913) and the current senior major general of the army, Wood was the best-known American officer in Europe before the war. He was a longtime friend of Gen. Hugh L. Scott, the Chief of Staff, who had offered his resignation to the President at war's outbreak, telling him to appoint Wood in his stead. On May 7, Wood wrote the Adjutant General: "I request assignment to duty with the first expeditionary force which is sent to France."[5]

But he had drawbacks, the first of which was physical. Years before, while military governor of Santiago, Cuba, after the Spanish-American War, he had severely injured his skull when he accidentally collided with a heavy chandelier while rising suddenly from his desk. Several brain operations failed to give him relief and he walked with an increasingly noticeable limp. (He died after a third operation in 1927.) While visiting Wood's camp at Plattsburgh, New York, in 1916, Secretary of War Newton D. Baker noticed that the General, in climbing a hill to get a view of a mock battle, "panted and labored so obviously that I came to the conclusion that his health was bad, and when I later came to make the decision between Pershing and Wood that recollection influenced the choice."[6]

A second consideration was Wood's lack of recent field experience compared with Pershing's. Third—and mainly—the Administration suspected Wood of being a political general, an officer who could not be trusted to carry out orders and who was ambitious to be President of the United States. President Woodrow Wilson still remembered that it had been Wood who had probably leaked to the press a confidential meeting about sending a fleet to the Pacific against Japan in 1913. "Personally," he told the Secretary of War in January 1917, "I have no confidence either in General Wood's discretion or in his loyalty to his superiors."[7]

Nor did the Secretary of War. In March of that year, despite explicit orders, Wood exasperated Secretary Baker by calling for war against Germany while addressing several large meetings. Although capable of arousing intense enthusiasm and loyalty in those under him, Wood was himself unable to manifest these same qualities toward those over him. He "had no conception whatever of loyalty to his superiors," said Secretary Baker; "[he] did not know the meaning of the word. He was the most insubordinate general officer in the entire army."[8]

That left Pershing. He ranked well in precisely those qualities which Wood lacked. He had shown himself physically fit and vigorous in the recent Mexican field campaign. Although a Republican, he was not thought to have political ambitions; and appointing a Republican would give a desirable non-partisan cast to the war effort. In Mexico, although hemmed in by vexatious restrictions of his own government, he had shown himself obedient and loyal. He inspired confidence. He could be relied upon.[9]

Without hesitation, Secretary Baker made the decision for Pershing. The Chief of Staff recommended him, as did the Assistant Chief of Staff. When Baker informally asked a young staff officer at the War Department named Douglas MacArthur whom he would pick, the latter answered unhesitatingly: "Pershing or [Peyton C.] March."[10]

Baker took his decision to President Wilson, who confirmed it orally. While Pershing's father-in-law was an influential senator, Baker said that Senator Warren "had no part, and sought no part in the selection of General Pershing for the overseas command. . . ." Pershing's record sufficed; he did not need political influence.[11]

Pershing ardently desired the command. The statement in his postwar memoirs ("I had scarcely given a thought to the possibility of my being chosen as commander-in-chief of our forces abroad") is simply not true. On the Punitive Expedition's return to the United States in February 1917, he had called together the newspaper correspondents and said: "We have broken diplomatic relations with Germany. That means that we will send an expedition abroad. I'd like to command it. Each of you must know some way in which you can help me. Now tell me how I can help you so that you can help me." On March 3 he wrote the Chief of Staff, requesting foreign service; in April, after praising the President's war message, he told the Secretary of War that he was "prepared for the duties of this hour."[12]

The first intimation that his hour had come was a telegram sent to his headquarters at Fort Sam Houston, Texas, from Senator Warren: "Wire me to-day whether and how much you speak, read and write French." Pershing had struggled through the language as a West Point cadet over thirty years before, but had brushed up on it for a few months in 1908 while he and his wife were in Europe. His French was really not very good, but the stakes were high, so he stretched the truth a bit and wired back: "Spent several months in France 1908 studying language. Spoke quite fluently; could read and write very well at that time. Can easily reacquire satisfactory working knowledge."[13]

He never did, at least not easily. For all important World War I conferences he depended on an interpreter, and he felt that his French was never very good. His confidante, Micheline Resco, said later that she tried unsuccessfully to teach the language to three generations of Pershings.[14]

On the other hand, Pershing wrote to his sister in December 1917 that he got along in the language "fairly well," and his letters to Mademoiselle Resco, written after the war, show some facility in writing the language. In 1924 he read Victor Hugo's *Lucrèce Borgia* and Jacques Bainville's *Histoire de France* in the original.[15]

That he would depend on interpreters for important meetings was natural and, at least one person suspected, may even have been Missouri canniness, to give himself time to think. He could follow a conversation in French and was aware of nuances which soften a criticism. Once, when talking with a French general, he remarked that people said that French troops were so habituated to the use of grenades that they forgot to fire at the enemy, even when he was out in the open a short distance away. "*Il dit* [he says]," the interpreter began. "No," Pershing interrupted, "*On dit* [they say]."[16]

The second intimation of future command was a telegram from the Chief of Staff, General Scott, alerting him that the War Department contemplated sending four regiments of infantry and one of artillery to France. They would be drawn from Pershing's Southern Department. "If plans are carried out, you will be in command of the entire force. Wire me at once the designation of the regiments selected by you. . . ."[17]

With the assistance of his Chief of Staff and former West Point classmate, Malvern Hill Barnum, Pershing selected the 16th, 18th, 26th, and 28th Infantry Regiments and the 6th Field Artillery. These, when joined by the 5th and 7th Field Artillery and other auxiliary units, were later to form the famed 1st Division, Pershing's favorite.[18]

Ordered to Washington, Pershing reported to the Chief of Staff on the morning of May 10. General Scott, who had begun his career in the 7th Cavalry as a replacement for a lieutenant killed with Custer at Little Big Horn, was nearing the end of his career and was due to retire in September. In many ways he was "over the hill." General Peyton C. March said rather uncharitably of him: "He was deaf; preferred to talk in grunts and the sign language; and he went to sleep in his chair while transacting official business." But he deserved well of the nation in standing like a rock for the draft and against a volunteer army when the question was being considered. He was sympathetic to Pershing and had warned him, while in Mexico, of rumors that he was speaking against the Administration. Pershing wrote an official denial, which cleared the way for his service overseas. He would command a division, Scott told him—twelve thousand men.[19]

Pershing's next meeting was with Secretary Baker. A former student of Woodrow Wilson's at Johns Hopkins University, Baker had spent most of his life in municipal affairs: as a lawyer for the city of Cleveland, as city solicitor, and as mayor. He had campaigned actively for Wilson in 1912. In 1916, just after retiring as mayor of Cleveland, Wilson invited him to be his Secretary of War.[20]

It was a most unlikely choice. As Baker said, "I had never played even with tin soldiers." He telegraphed the President that he would come to Washington and give him conclusive reasons why he should not be Secretary. He had a deep aversion to war and had been associated with various peace societies. He was considered, mistakenly, a pacifist. He knew nothing about military affairs, save what he had read about the Civil War years before.[21]

"I came to Washington," said Baker, "went in to see the President and gave him what it would seem to me were perfectly adequate reasons, and when I had finished my explanation, to which he listened with great patience, he said, 'Are you ready to be sworn in?' "[22]

Wilson chose better than he knew, for Baker is commonly considered one of America's better Secretaries of War. Well-read and well-bred, gifted with a clear and methodical mind, Baker was competence personified. His mind, said Raymond

B. Fosdick, was "one of those rare combinations in which swift perception is balanced by judgment, and clarity and sanity run hand in hand."[23]

A small, timid-looking man, who sat with one leg under his body and the other barely reaching the floor, Baker looked as if he ought to be teaching Latin in some girls' academy. A Cleveland newspaper called his appointment as Secretary of War "grotesque." But he could be remarkably strong, freewheeling, and innovative. He manfully resisted any attempt to appoint favorites to commissions, defended the General Staff against attempts by the supply bureaus to weaken it, and when the situation demanded, spent money which had not yet been authorized by Congress.[24]

One thing Baker had learned from his Civil War reading and from his father, who had fought in it, was that a Secretary of War ought to give his field commanders authority and let them fight the war without undue interference. His philosophy, as he expressed it after the war, was: "Select a commander in whom you have confidence; give him power and responsibility, and then . . . work your own head off to get him everything he needs and support him in every decision he makes."[25]

Baker not only preached that doctrine, he lived it. Some time after Pershing had been in France, a general whom he had sent home came to Baker with the request that he cable Pershing, asking why it had been done. Said Baker: "No, General, I will not do that and I will not only not cable him but I will not write him and if I happen to meet him, I will not ask him."

"I think I have a right to know," said the general.

"I think so too and as you know the Army Regulations authorize you to demand a court of inquiry; you have to demand that in writing and I have to grant it and then I have to fix the time of assembly of the court. So if you will write that letter, I will fix the time of assembly of the court as one month after the signing of peace."

"That is a little hard on me."

"That may be, but as long as General Pershing is in France he is to have absolute discretion in such matters. I do not intend to interfere with him; he can send everybody home, himself included, if he gets results. All I ask of General Pershing is results and what I hope to give him is unqualified support."[26]

He did. George C. Marshall, Jr., said to Pershing after World War I: "Though we have a hundred more wars, I do not think we will ever be so lucky in the choice of a Secretary. I cannot conceive of any future field commander ever being accorded the support you received."[27]

All this, of course, was in the future and Pershing could not have known the tremendous backing he would receive from Baker, a man he had never met, as he stood before him that day in May 1917; but he may have had an inkling when Baker said to him, either then or on another occasion: "I will give you only two orders—one to go to France and the other to come home. In the meantime your authority in France will be supreme."[28]

Baker impressed Pershing at their first meeting. "He was courteous and pleasant and impressed me as being frank, fair, and businesslike." During the war, there developed a mutual respect and affection which lasted until Baker's death on

Christmas Day, 1937. Speaking of him on an NBC radio broadcast a week later, Pershing said: "He stood the test of war, and will be remembered as the nation's ablest War Secretary."[29]

Several days after their initial meeting, Baker called Pershing in again and told him that the overseas project had been expanded from a single division to an indeterminate larger force. Pershing would command it. He was now head of the American Expeditionary Forces—the AEF.

On the afternoon of May 10, Secretary Baker called a conference on munitions. Present, along with Pershing, Scott, and several others, was an officer destined to have considerable influence on the war—Maj. Gen. Tasker H. Bliss, the Assistant Chief of Staff. A massive man with a domelike head, a drooping mustache, and a face resembling Bismarck's, Bliss had been one of Elihu Root's counselors when the General Staff was formed in 1903. Since Scott was absent from the country on a mission to Russia from mid-May to August 1917, and then retired in September, Bliss was virtually acting Chief of Staff from the early days of the war until his own retirement on December 31, 1917. Later he was to serve on the Supreme War Council and, after the war, as one of five American commissioners to the Versailles Peace Conference. Wilson found him "a wise counselor," and Pershing did too.[30]

Bliss's learning was tremendous. He would have ornamented any university faculty, provided the professors could get used to feeling second-rate in his presence. A scholar in uniform, he knew geology, French, Spanish, Italian, Latin, and Greek, which he read as easily as his native English—a language he wrote with clarity and spoke with force. A friend once found him reading a copy of Plato's *Republic* in the original Greek, having torn off the cover and substituted a different one, lest his staff think him high-hat for displaying his erudition.[31]

Secretary Baker, no mean intellectual himself, said of Bliss in 1934: "[He had] in a higher degree than anybody else with whom I have ever been in contact, the habit of deliberate and consecutive thinking. Nearly everybody else, including myself, thinks spasmodically . . . but Bliss's mind was a comprehensive card index and his method of using it was like one of those machines . . . where you feed in ten thousand cards with various data upon them and then read at the bottom of the machine the total number of cross-eyed persons in the ten thousand."[32]

At the May 10 conference Bliss wisely argued in favor of using Allied rifles and artillery rather than developing America's own, since with the Allies' manpower continually declining, they would have a surplus of weapons. Accordingly, the decision was made to adopt the British Enfield rifle and modify it to use American ammunition.[33]

Rifles are useless, of course, without men to operate them. Initially it had been assumed, based on the oft-repeated statements of Allied officials, both civil and military, that the United States would have approximately a year to train her men. America was cautioned not to throw troops into the fighting before they were ready, and to employ her small Regular Army to train the mass of raw recruits. She should not permit the Regulars to be decimated (as the British Regulars had been), leaving the nation without a sufficient nucleus to train her raw levies.[34]

A different view of things had emerged when Allied missions arrived in the United States during April. The British Mission, headed by Arthur J. Balfour, proposed that at least a brigade be sent at once for the moral effect of showing the flag, followed by a larger force in the fall. In general, however, the British advised against a separate American Army in France; it would make two more joints in the trench line, and joints were always the weak places. On April 30 Maj. Gen. G. T. M. (Tommy) Bridges, the British military attaché in Washington, told the U.S. Chief of Staff, "If you ask me how your force could most quickly make itself felt in Europe, I would say by sending 500,000 untrained men at once to our depots in England to be trained there, and drafted into our armies in France."[35]

The same plea for troops was made by the French Mission of René Viviani. He was accompanied by Marshal Joseph Joffre, the hero of the Marne, who admitted that French morale was low and asked that some force, say a division, be sent immediately to stiffen flagging spirits, along with fifty thousand other men for certain technical work. Even before Joffre's arrival, General Vignal, the French military attaché in Washington, began urging incorporation of American soldiers into French units for training purposes.[36]

Thus the amalgamation question, which was to vex Pershing all through the war, had raised its head even before he arrived in Washington. General Bliss warned Secretary Baker: "When the war is over it may be a literal fact that the American flag may not have appeared anywhere on the line because our organizations will simply be parts of battalions and regiments of the Entente Allies. We might have a million men there and yet no American army and no American commander. Speaking frankly, I have received the impression from English and French officers that such is their deliberate desire."[37]

Pershing too, once he was made privy to Allied suggestions, was decidedly against any amalgamation proposal. As he put it in his postwar memoirs, "It was definitely understood between the Secretary of War and myself that we should proceed to organize our own units from top to bottom and build a distinctive army of our own as rapidly as possible."[38]

Reflecting on the Anglo-French missions, Pershing noted signs of Allied disunity, which had hindered the war effort for three years. The two missions omitted common meetings in Europe before sailing, embarked on separate ships, arrived at different times, and had no common plan to present. Said Pershing: "The Allies would never win the war until they secured unity of action under some form of coordinated control." Out of this insight came his determination to push for a supreme Allied commander, which bore fruit in the spring of 1918 with the selection of Gen. Ferdinand Foch.[39]

The organized strength of the American military on April 1, 1917, was 127,588 Regular Army officers and men and 80,446 National Guard officers and men—a total of 208,034. The quality of the National Guard was dubious. Sen. John W. Weeks said on the floor of Congress on April 23, 1917: "When our men went to the border last year, a very considerable percentage—possibly as many as one-half—had never fired a rifle and nearly as large a proportion had never had an hour's drill." Before the war ended, the Army would need 200,000 officers and 4,000,000 men. Where were they to come from?[40]

For a year and a half Great Britain had tried to rely on volunteers before being compelled finally to resort to conscription. The U.S. War Department was convinced that it should avoid England's mistake and have a draft right from the start. Scott told Baker: "If you do not secure conscription now, you will already have lost this war."[41]

Like Scott, Pershing felt that conscription was absolutely necessary. While commander of Fort Sam Houston, he had persuaded the governor to use his influence with the Texas delegation in Congress to have it passed. Both Houses approved conscription in principle on April 28, but then got hung up for the next two and one-half weeks on whether to allow volunteers as well. The main volunteer everyone had in mind was Theodore Roosevelt who, even before war was declared, had petitioned Baker for permission to raise a division (later a corps) of volunteers for use against the Germans—a twentieth-century updated version of the Rough Riders.[42]

Pershing liked Roosevelt and was beholden to him for his 1906 promotion from captain to brigadier general, in which he had leapfrogged 862 other officers. But he was convinced that this was a war for professionals, not amateurs. The day of waving your hat, yelling "Come on, boys!" and charging up a hill was past. The Germans were not the Spanish. He felt Roosevelt's agitation for volunteer forces was so much grandstanding, and when Congress finally passed a draft bill with an optional provision for 200,000 volunteers if the President wished to call them, Pershing advised against it. No volunteers were called.[43]

Crucial to Pershing's determination to create a distinctive, effective army overseas was the condition of the General Staff in Washington, which was—or ought to be—the brains of the army. Just what could happen when the brain was not functioning, when it was not allocating resources and determining priorities, was illustrated during the very first weeks of the war. Arriving at the War Department one morning, Secretary Baker discovered the entire basement filled with cases of new typewriters, some twelve thousand of them. They all belonged to the Adjutant General, Brig. Gen. Henry P. McCain.

"What in the world are all those typewriters downstairs for?" he demanded. "Is this to be a typewriter war?"

"No, Mr. Secretary," replied McCain, "but I am on easy street. There is going to be the greatest competition in typewriters around here and I have them all. I have every free typewriter in the United States, I will not be caught short in typewriters."

Baker patiently explained that this would not do at all. The Navy might need typewriters, or the Quartermaster Department, or some other agency. "We cannot let you have them all. . . . Get some kind of board together and make an apportionment of this monopoly of yours and let everybody have as many typewriters as they need. . . ."[44]

The incident was typical of the condition of the Washington General Staff. In no way was it organized or prepared for war. Most of the functions of army administration were carried on by the bureaus (one of which was McCain's), which thought selfishly of themselves and steadfastly resisted attempts of the General Staff to make them pull in harness.[45]

England went to war with a General Staff numbering 232; Germany, 650. America went with only forty-one, and was further handicapped by a law which prohibited more than half being in the capital at any one time. Hence the General Staff in Washington, the very hub of the American war effort, numbered just nineteen. Before the war ended, 1,072 were found necessary.[46]

Improvement in quality as well as quantity was needed. George C. Marshall, Jr., said later that the General Staff "was a collection of old officers ... who had ceased mental development years before ... and were literally wholly unacquainted with any of the proper functions of a General Staff."[47]

Pershing agreed. He excoriated War Department delays and inaction, especially in the early days of the war. Writing in 1923, he jotted the following comments on a Departmental wartime memo: "not done," "too late," "merely a recommendation," "of course," "ought to have been done one year before."[48]

On May 18, the day the Draft Bill became law, Secretary Baker announced that an expeditionary force of one division would sail as soon as possible for France. Pershing faced the important task of choosing a suitable staff. The key position was AEF Chief of Staff, and for this he selected a fellow-cavalryman, James G. Harbord, then serving in Washington at the Army War College. Harbord had graduated from Kansas State Agricultural College in 1886 and, after failing to get an appointment to West Point, had enlisted in the army as a private in 1889. He had served two years in Cuba, twelve in the Philippines (over ten as an official in the insular government), and the remainder in the United States. Pershing had had various contacts with him in 1898, 1906, 1913, and 1915.[49]

A man of wit, imagination, and independent thought, Harbord was enormously competent. No one can read his *Leaves from a War Diary*, published in 1925, without being struck by his broad-ranging, liberally educated mind, which roamed freely and easily over art, architecture, and literature. The qualities Pershing praised in Harbord reveal the qualities he valued most: unselfishness, resourcefulness, energy, and, above all, loyalty. Pershing called him "the ablest officer I know."[50]

With Harbord's assistance, Pershing selected the rest of the staff. The criteria, both then and later, was efficiency and availability; it was not personal friendship or graduation from West Point. George C. Marshall, Jr., who later became Pershing's protégé, was a graduate of the Virginia Military Institute. Harbord, an enlisted man who worked his way up through the ranks, was a good friend of Pershing's rival, Leonard Wood, as were also Frank McCoy, James A. Logan, Edward Bowditch, Jr., John McAuley Palmer, George Van Horn Moseley, and William D. Connor, all of whom served on Pershing's staff eventually. Harbord's letters to

Wood from the Philippines in 1911 were quite critical of Pershing, although doubtless the latter never knew it.[51]

Where possible, Pershing tried to pick officers known to him, at least by reputation. Capt. James L. Collins had been with him in the Philippines and in Mexico. Maj. John L. Hines had been his adjutant during the Punitive Expedition, and 1st Lt. George S. Patton, Jr., had been his aide. Capt. Hugh A. Drum had been Assistant Chief of Staff of the Southern Department.[52]

In selecting the initial staff and in choosing men for responsible positions thereafter as the AEF grew, Pershing's long service and wide background furnished him with a fund of knowledge from which to draw. His years at West Point as a cadet had permitted him to size up graduates from the classes of 1883 to 1889. These furnished about 30 percent of the 474 general officers of the war. As a tactical officer at West Point immediately before the Spanish-American War, he had seen cadets from the classes of 1895 to 1899; these furnished almost 10 percent of the general officers. His experience had been broadened by service in Cuba in 1898 and in the Philippines from 1899 to 1913. His command of the Punitive Expedition in 1916–1917 and of the Southern Department furnished further opportunity for judging officer material.[53]

Pershing turned down a number of requests to accompany him, notably J. Franklin Bell, whom he judged too ill, and Theodore Roosevelt, whom he judged too unprofessional. The latter, when it was clear he would not go, made an eloquent plea for his sons Theodore and Archibald. Pershing could not take them with him, but promised to send for them later.[54]

It had been hoped that Pershing could get an early start to France, but the sailing was postponed several times. Although the War College Division had recommended that the AEF commander "should not be concerned with the detailed command or administration of the advance division," in point of fact he was. In 1917 the United States had no division it could pick up bodily and send to France. Pershing's last days in America were complicated by the need to plan for the future first division, as well as for his own AEF organization. By May 23, however, work was completed. Pershing handed in the list of men he wanted and requested that the necessary travel orders be drawn up.[55]

The following day, for the first and only time during hostilities, Pershing met President Wilson. He found him cordial, but was surprised that the President did not discuss the war or America's part in it, nor did he give instructions or outline the course he should pursue. Perhaps no field commander in history was ever given a freer hand to conduct operations than was Pershing by Wilson.[56]

Pershing went to Europe under two letters of instructions, both dated May 26. One, drafted by Harbord and himself, was signed by General Bliss, Acting Chief of Staff in the absence of Scott, who was with the Root Mission in Russia. The other, drawn by Brig. Gen. Francis J. Kernan, Acting Assistant Chief of Staff in place of Bliss, was signed by the Secretary of War. Although they both basically said the same thing, Kernan's letter, as General March delightedly pointed out later in *The Nation at War*, was a better piece of staff work, more inclusive in stating that Pershing's authority extended to continental Europe and not just France, and specifically provided for a "separate and distinct" American army, "the identity of which must be preserved." Both letters went to France, were put into a safe, and never consulted again. Perhaps their chief significance is in revealing the confused, disorganized condition of the General Staff in the early days of the war when apparently its right hand did not know what its left was doing.[57]

One may also note, in view of the fact that Pershing later held out against Allied pressure for amalgamation of American troops into their armies, that throughout the war he was simply doing what he had been ordered to do. Section 5 of the ruling letter, the one drafted by Kernan and signed by Baker, specifically provided for this. In preserving American troops under his own command (which many think was the great Pershing achievement), he was simply following a national tradition and the natural inclination of any commander. As S. L. A. Marshall commented: "He could hardly have acted otherwise."[58]

The Voyage Overseas

(May-June 1917)

THE SAILING OF PERSHING'S party—191 officers and men—was supposed to be a deep, dark secret. For two weeks, Harbord remembered, it tried to make itself inconspicuous around Washington, "avoiding its friends and looking mysterious when Europe was mentioned." Harbord informed two officers of their selection by having them come to his home in the dark of night.[1]

Newspapermen, whose business is to spread news, discreetly kept their mouths shut, while military men, supposed to be good at secrecy, blundered about like bulls in a china shop. All had been ordered to report at Governors Island, New York, on May 28 in civilian clothes; through a mixup thirty showed up in uniform. Others, even in mufti, wore army shoes and socks and carried their officer swords. Pershing's orderly, Sergeant Frank Lanckton, was afraid he might lose the General's handbags, so he put a large tag on each: "General Pershing, Paris, France." At Pier 60 in New York, War Department supplies lay for two days conspicuously labeled: "S.S. *Baltic*, General Pershing's Headquarters." And finally, lest any German spy somehow miss the event, the signal battery at Governors Island boomed out a farewell salute as Pershing departed.[2]

There was, of course, some attempt at secrecy. Rather than board the *Baltic* at Pier 60, Pershing and his group assembled at Governors Island, then took a tug to Gravesend and rendezvoused with the ocean liner as it headed out to sea. Not knowing of the plan to transfer ships, one of the soldiers bellyached as he stepped aboard the battered, old tugboat, "Hell, we can't go to France in this damned thing!"[3]

The *Baltic* was three hours late in appearing but finally, a little after 5:00 P.M., it headed out to sea. There was nothing romantic about the leave-taking, no inspiring view of the New York skyline, no Statue of Liberty to remember. It was dark and rainy, cold and foggy. Harbord wondered whether the raw weather presaged the expedition's future, or whether the adage was true that bad beginnings make for good endings?[4]

By far the most important work done on the trip was by certain boards of study, either conducted by Pershing or commissioned by him. The whole nature, scope, and effectiveness of the future AEF was determined by these studies which addressed themselves to important questions:

What size force should the AEF be eventually?

Where would the ship tonnage come from to transport and supply it?

What should be the composition and organization of Pershing's headquarters, the combat forces, and the services of supply behind the lines?

Should any amount of amalgamation into Allied forces be permitted?

What should be the American theater of operations?

When could American troops be expected to go into action?

Would expected German attacks influence this timetable?[5]

These were fundamental questions, demanding fundamental answers, for on them depended the course of America's contribution to the war. As time went on, the answers grew beyond anything imagined when the questions were first asked. To take but one example, early in the war Lt. Col. Amos A. Fries, Chief of the Gas Service, put in a requisition for forty thousand sheets of stationery. It was disallowed on the ground of being excessive; forty thousand sheets would last two years. Before one year had elapsed Fries was using three times that amount *during one week!*[6]

The most fundamental question was manpower—how big should the AEF be—for on this many other questions depended, like ship tonnage, supplies, port facilities. On board the *Baltic* tentative plans were made for an army of at least one million men. This too was to be an underestimation.[7]

On board the *Baltic* Pershing's expert on venereal disease, Dr. Hugh Young, gave several graphic lectures on the topic, intensifying Pershing's determination to fight VD in the AEF by every means he could. When Dr. Young later reported that British prostitutes sought out foreign troops because they had more money, Pershing cabled the War Department to withhold a portion of each soldier's pay. What a man didn't have, he couldn't spend on a prostitute. It was the first of a whole series of stern Pershing measures to keep the AEF clean.[8]

The closer the *Baltic* came to England, the greater the possibility of being torpedoed. Hardly an hour passed without an SOS from a sinking ship or from one fleeing a submarine. The *Baltic* responded to none of them, fearing that they were fake distress signals sent by a waiting sub. Fifteen ships went down in British waters while Pershing crossed the Atlantic.[9]

On June 8, nudged by tugs, the *Baltic* warped its way up to the dock at Liverpool, England. There to meet it were a few British dignitaries, some newspapermen, and a few curious spectators—not many, for the landing had been kept secret. Pershing inspected the honor guard, the Royal Welsh Fusiliers, stopping now and then when he saw a wound stripe to ask a pertinent question, and generally made a good impression. A British journalist thought him "stiff as steel to look at" and felt that his firm jaw indicated interior doggedness—which indeed it did. Seeking to establish good relations, Pershing mentioned that the Royal Welsh

Fusiliers had recently served with American forces in North China. He tactfully did not say anything about their ancestors shooting at Americans at Bunker Hill.[10]

The world had turned over many times since then and bygones must be bygones. In a hands-across-the-sea editorial, one British newspaper said that America and Britain had been separated in 1776 by "the Prussian policy of Lord North and George III" and now Prussianism had served again to reunite them. It called Pershing "the herald of the greatest and noblest family reunion from which the world has ever benefited."[11]

The *London Graphic* apotheosized Pershing by surrounding his photo with an image of a goddess holding a laurel wreath over his head. The caption said, "Now is the winter of our discontent made glorious summer by this sun of (New) York." No matter that he came from Missouri.[12]

The inspection completed, there was an hour's delay while the British removed the baggage, although Harbord felt that the Americans could have done it themselves in fifteen minutes. "The celerity with which the British handled it, however, quite surprised themselves, and I was given the impression that no foreigner landing in Great Britain had been handled with such suddenness since perhaps the late J. Caesar came ashore some time ago."[13]

During the delay Pershing held a press conference in the ship's lounge. He handled questions well (which is to say he dodged a number) and got off a quotable remark about himself and his command being "very glad indeed to be the standard bearers of our country in this great war for civilization." That same day he sent a cable to the War Department recommending severe restrictions on the press in the AEF.[14]

At 3:00 P.M. a special train carrying Pershing's party pulled into Euston Station in London. Heywood Broun, whom Pershing was to send home later for violating censorship regulations, remarked as the general stepped forth to the platform, "No man ever looked more the ordained leader of fighting men. He was tall, broad, and deep-chested, splendidly set up. . . ." Floyd Gibbons was more pithy: Pershing was "lean, clean, keen."[15]

Greeting him with outstretched arms, the American ambassador, Walter Hines Page, introduced Pershing to the waiting dignitaries: Lord Derby, Secretary of State for War; Field Marshal Sir John French, the first commander of the British Expeditionary Force in France; Vice Adm. William S. Sims, the American naval commander in England, and others.[16]

Before leaving the station, Harbord suggested that it would be good public relations for Pershing to thank the engineer and fireman for the speed and comfort of the train trip. "The grimy pair were ostentatiously brought up and he shook hands with them, ruining a new pair of gloves. At the request of the moving picture man the performance responded to an encore, the gloves were entirely put out of the running, and the camera immortalized the Chief's democracy."[17]

That night Brigadier Lord Guy Brooke, assigned as Pershing's aide-de-camp while in England, gave an informal dinner for the American commander and his staff. Afterwards everyone stood around and talked for two hours, standing because

Pershing was and he in turn standing because no one had asked him to sit down. No one seemed to know how to end the party.[18]

Both the British and Americans were unfamiliar with each other's uniform and were confused as to which insignia meant what. Harbord, a lowly major, was pleased to find himself regarded as a major general. When the British asked why silver outranked gold in the American insignia, Harbord told the truth. "None of us know," he said.[19]

At 10:30 A.M. on June 9, King George V received Pershing and his principal staff officers at Buckingham Palace. Although Harbord did not think he looked much like a king, Pershing said he had a good talk with him and found him on top of events. But King George had heard, incorrectly, that the United States expected to have fifty thousand planes in the air soon—not a surprising error in view of certain wild statements in America about her air capabilities. Actually, as Pershing explained to the King with some embarrassment, such reports were exaggerated. America had some fifty-five *training* planes. Of these, fifty-one were obsolete and four obsolescent.[20]

Despite such miserable aviation conditions, rumors continued to circulate about darkening the sun with American airplanes. As late as February 28, 1918, Pershing sent a strong cable of protest against such unfounded newspaper stories, pointing out that after almost one year of war there was not yet a single American-made airplane in Europe.[21]

Leaving the palace, Pershing visited the American Embassy where he presented his staff to Ambassador Page. An anglophile, Page told him he had been embarrassed by America's neutrality, and added, "Now I am able to hold up my head and look people squarely in the eye."[22]

At the Embassy Pershing was shocked by Admiral Sims's statistics on German sinkings of Allied shipping: 1,500,000 tons in April and May alone. At that rate there would not be British shipping to help bring the AEF to France or to supply it afterwards.[23]

Sims was a crusader for the convoy system and, with an assist from the British prime minister, David Lloyd George, he was instrumental in later initiating it. Its success was almost immediate, with the result that not a single convoyed vessel was lost on the voyage to Europe. Pershing well appreciated the accomplishment, and used to say when people praised the AEF, "Don't overlook the part the Navy played. . . . They did a magnificent job."[24]

On Sunday, June 10, Pershing attended services at Westminster Abbey and was much impressed. "This joint meeting there with the British . . . seemed to symbolize the unity of aims and purposes of our two peoples, through which, fighting shoulder to shoulder, we should one day achieve the victory." More prosaically, Harbord noted the money collection—"never forgotten in any church that I have ever attended."[25]

Accompanied by the Pages, Pershing lunched with the King and Queen at Buckingham Palace on June 11. After the meal the King showed them his garden where, instead of flowers, there now grew potatoes. Speaking bitterly of German air raids on London, he pointed to a statue of Queen Victoria just outside his window and exclaimed, "The Kaiser, God damn him, has even tried to destroy the statue of his own grandmother."[26]

Pershing later related the incident in the newspaper version of his memoirs but, ever sensitive to giving offense, thought it best in the book version to delete the phrase "God damn him." Even in the newspaper version he added the pious remark, "For a moment I was surprised at his words, but I quickly realized that it was a solemn expression of profound indignation and not profanity." To which the *Baltimore Sun* remarked that a raconteur ought to have the courage of his anecdotes, ought to realize that kings swear, and ought not to make a swear word sound like an excerpt from the Athanasian Creed.[27]

In the afternoon Pershing had a half-hour's talk with General Sir William (Wully) Robertson, Chief of the Imperial General Staff, a blunt, tough, square-jawed, plain-speaking man in his fifties, who had enlisted as a private and worked his way up to the top. Pershing considered the talk "very satisfactory," but neither man brought the other to his point of view. Robertson wanted the Americans to serve with or near the British, but Pershing's staff on the *Baltic* had already made a tentative decision for a zone of operations in Lorraine, to the right of the French and completely removed from the British. On the other hand, when Pershing spoke of the need of additional shipping to bring over the American Army in sufficient quantities to have an effect, Robertson said it was "entirely out of the question," the British having all they could do to find ships for their own needs. Thus on shipping, the crucial question of the whole AEF and of the war itself, there was a standoff from Pershing's first days in Europe. The matter was not to be resolved for over a year, with considerable bad feeling in the interim.[28]

Over Pershing's protests that they had come to work and not to socialize, Ambassador Page scheduled a formal dinner that night, a veritable Who's Who of the English-speaking world. Was Pershing awed by these famous people? "Not in the least," said John C. Hughes, his aide, who saw him up close. "Whether it was a king, queen, Foch, Pétain, Haig, etc., he never betrayed any nervousness when moving among the great of this world."[29]

Up at 5:00 A.M. on June 12, Pershing visited Brentwood in Essex to observe a British training camp. The course was a quick nine weeks, covering standard items like bayonet work, gas defense, trench mortars, hand grenades, and practice in following a rolling barrage. Pershing found the use of trench mortars and hand grenades "more realistic than anything we had so far seen in our own service." Harbord thought that the weak look of the troops ("runts, crooked, undeveloped!") was a sure sign that England was draining the bottom of the manpower barrel.[30]

That afternoon Pershing conferred with the prime minister, David Lloyd George. "He was cordial enough," said Pershing in describing his first impressions of a man with whom he was to have some ferocious fights and whom he later called, in private, "a son of a bitch." That past April Lloyd George had expressed the key to victory in three words: "Ships, ships, ships," but when Pershing spoke of the need of British tonnage to transport the AEF, the prime minister was no more amenable than Robertson had been the day before. The British, he noted, "were seriously alarmed regarding their own food situation."[31]

Pershing now saw that shipping was the key to success in the war. With present tonnage available in America, it would take at the *minimum* two and one-half years to transport 900,000 men to France, and it might even take as long as four years. The whole future history of the AEF rested on the question of ships.[32]

THREE

First Days in France

(June 1917)

Rising at 4:00 A.M. on June 13, Pershing's party boarded the cross-channel steamer *Invicta* and arrived at Boulogne, France, at 10:00 A.M. Everyone's eyes were a little moist as the ship approached shore and then nosed her way into the dock. Here was the American Army come to repay a debt to the fatherland of Lafayette and Rochambeau. All were conscious of participating in an historic event.[1]

Yet it had its comical aspects. "The band blared out 'The Star-Spangled Banner' and we stood to attention for several days it seemed to me," grumbled Harbord, "while they played it over and over. Even the General, who stands like a statue, growled over the number of times they played it. Then we had the 'Marseillaise' several times and then, our hands having broken off at the wrist, we stood up to the gangway while a dozen fuzzy little Frenchmen came up. Each saluted the General and made a little speech, then sidestepped and was replaced by another until each little man had said his speech." When the last man appeared—a brigadier general with only one arm—Harbord surmised that the man had lost his arm from atrophy at an earlier ceremonial, standing with his hand at his cap while the band played the national anthems.[2]

Joining Pershing at Boulogne was Lt. Col. Count Adalbert (Bertie) de Chambrun, a descendant of Lafayette, who had been born in the United States and was married to Representative Nicholas Longworth's sister. He spoke very good English (and very much of it) and was of some use as an aide, although his value was minimized by a tendency to flattery. He declared, for example, that Pershing spoke "the most perfect French," which was certainly a whopper. A long talk with him, observed one American, was like a big meal of soufflé.[3]

Because the French wished Pershing to arrive in Paris at the end of the working day when people were out on the streets and could provide a reception, he had to mark time in Boulogne. Walking around during the delay, Harbord remarked on the irony of Boulogne, currently a British debarkation port, having been in Napoleon's day the embarkation port for his projected invasion of England. "Other days; other alliances," he observed.[4]

The trip to Paris was uneventful, but the Gare du Nord was packed with people and the atmosphere was electric when the train pulled in at 5:20 P.M. Pershing appeared in the doorway, then stood erect and motionless as the band struck up a stirring "Star-Spangled Banner," followed by the "Marseillaise." "He was a statuesque figure there," said Charles H. Grasty of the *New York Times*, "the very impersonation and incarnation of West Point training and tradition and as fine a specimen of American style and physical manhood as could be found in a month's search from the Atlantic to the Pacific."[5]

There to greet Pershing was Paul Painlevé, Minister of War (soon to be Premier); Joffre and Viviani, both of whom had been on the April mission to Washington; Maj. Gen. Ferdinand Foch, the French Chief of Staff; American Ambassador William G. Sharp; and others. There were no speeches, just handshakes and informal introductions all around. There was, however, a certain amount of jockeying for positions for the honor of riding in the lead cars. Painlevé ended up with Pershing, while Joffre, a ceremonial figure and no longer a power, was bumped from carriage to carriage and ended up fourth in line.[6]

What followed next as the cortège moved out for the two-mile journey from the station to the Hôtel de Crillon cannot be adequately described. It had to be experienced to be appreciated and those who did never forgot it. Thousands of war-weary people, to whom the coming of the Americans meant hope and the promise of victory, responded from their inmost being with all the warmth and emotion of which the French are capable when deeply moved. It was almost hysterical—and some people actually were, weeping unashamedly. "Vive l'Amérique! Vive l'Amérique!" they cried, as they waved flags, handkerchiefs, and banners, threw flowers, blew kisses, caressed soldiers, and tried to climb into the automobiles. "Vive l'Amérique! Pair-Shang! Heep, heep, hourrah! Vive l'Amérique!" They were delirious—a people gone semi-mad, thirsting for victory and drinking deep draughts of the heady wine of hope. "Though I live a thousand years," said one participant, "I shall never forget that crowded hour."[7]

Normally the trip would have taken fifteen minutes; it took about an hour. Beyond control, the crowd inundated the automobiles which began to heat up from running so long in low gear. Quickly losing sight of cars in front and back, Harbord actually wondered whether, in the confusion, he had gotten out of line and was being mistaken for Pershing. "There were no streets," remembered Sgt. Carl Moline, "just a solid mass of people, noisy and hysterical people, and flowers, and kisses." Charles B. Shaw, a field clerk, said he almost lost his arm shaking hands with people. Someone with a bent for statistics figured out that, at one franc per flower (20 cents), five thousand dollars in flowers was thrown at the Americans that day. According to one who saw both events, the Pershing reception exceeded in warmth that accorded President Wilson after the war.[8]

Arrived at the Crillon, the AEF commander again and again was forced to appear on the hotel balcony overlooking the Place de la Concorde to respond to cheers from the crowd. Allied flags were clustered at each end of the balcony and, when a breeze blew the French tricolor in his direction, Pershing drew it to him and reverently kissed its folds. The French below went wild.[9]

When the day was done and the cheers had faded away, however, a heavy mood settled over Pershing as he reflected on his reception. "It was most touching and in a sense most pathetic," he wrote later. French hopes ran so high and he had so very little to fulfill them. "The Americans have come!" the Parisians cried. Yes, all 191 of them. The vast army that America needed and France expected was still in civilian clothes three thousand miles away across a vast ocean, utterly untrained for war. In B. H. Liddell Hart's words, America was "a giant armed with a penknife." The German comment on the day was snide, but very close to the truth: "The arrival of the General without an army was turned into a triumphal march. . . ." Pershing shuddered as he thought of Ambassador Sharp's remark at dinner that night: "I hope you have not arrived too late."[10]

As with the visit to England, a certain amount of obligatory ceremonial took place during the first few days in France. It began on June 14 with a morning visit to Napoleon's tomb in Les Invalides where Pershing, with an uncanny knack for doing the right thing in a dramatic way, made a tremendous impression. When an old French veteran offered him Napoleon's sword, he did not accept it, but bowed from the waist, hands stiffly at his side, and reverently kissed it. The French sucked in their breath. "Magnifique!" they exclaimed. "This will be told at every dinner table in Paris tonight."[11]

A similar incident occurred on June 16, when after a performance at the Opera Comique, Pershing made a hit backstage by offering a toast. "To France!" he said; "To *our* France!"[12]

Such incidents were typical of what observers noted about the American commander during these early days: He got off on the right foot. His fine physical presence and bearing, his knowledge of what to do or say (and when to keep quiet), his innate dignity—all made an impression socially and diplomatically. "He is America at its very best," wrote Charles H. Grasty, who thought he resembled Robert E. Lee in his tremendous dignity and authority. Three weeks after arrival, Harbord said of him: "He has captured the fickle Paris crowd . . . and could be elected King of France to-morrow if it depended on Paris."[13]

But France did not need a king; she needed rejuvenation. War weariness was everywhere. The will to fight was waning. Thirty-five months of combat and two million casualties had taken their toll. French soldiers had the worn, tired look of men driven beyond endurance, for whom no end of suffering is in sight. Dorothy Canfield Fisher, an old friend from University of Nebraska days who was living in France, told Pershing two days after his arrival: "There is a limit to what flesh and blood and endurance can stand . . . and . . . the French have just about reached that limit!"[14]

French depression was aggravated by the letdown after the disastrous Nivelle offensive the previous April. An arrogant, vain man, Gen. Robert Nivelle had predicted that he would "break the German front at will . . . in from twenty-four to forty-eight hours." Instead, what he broke was the flower of the French Army, sacrificing 120,000 men in a catastrophic offensive which had no chance of success.[15]

After that the French Army simply mutinied. In sixteen army corps, virtually at the same time, the cry went up: "We have had enough! Down with the war! We will not go into line!" In the whole French Army, said Painlevé, only two French divisions could be absolutely relied on to stand firm if the Germans launched a large-scale attack. One division even tried to march on Paris.[16]

At this point the French Army was saved by its new commander, Gen. Henri Philippe Pétain. He was everywhere, visiting everyone, listening to the grievances of all. He improved food, granted more furloughs (some men had not seen their families for three years), and redressed grievances. Mainly, however, he let it be known that there would be no more large-scale attacks such as Nivelle's; France did not have the men. "We must wait for the Americans," he said. Until they came, attacks would be minor and for limited objectives; Pétain made only two of them during the rest of the year.[17]

When Pershing arrived in France the mutinies were still going on, although the backbone of them had been broken and the worst was over. Pétain, a master military psychologist, a soldier's soldier, had saved France. Pershing, who had been shocked at the low French morale, said later that Pétain's appointment as commander of the French Army ranked in importance with Foch's appointment as generalissimo in achieving victory.[18]

The American commander met Pétain for the first time on June 16 at the latter's headquarters at Compiègne. In many ways the two men were remarkably similar. About the same age, both were strong men, ambitious, serious minded, determined to the point of ruthlessness, with a certain external frigidity which inspired awe and respect. Both were physically handsome, of commanding presence, attracting women and in turn attracted by them. Both were men of sound common sense, of great steadiness, of dogged determination, tempered by humanity and a knowledge of human weakness. Both were men of the possible, who knew that the grandest of schemes must be conditioned by finite human and material resources.[19]

When Pershing was ushered in, Pétain had many things on his mind (like mutinies) and met the American with great seriousness, even formality. Blue-eyed, blonde-mustached, erect of carriage, Pétain conveyed an impression of great energy and mental alertness. Extremely frank in speech, he was direct to the point of brusqueness. He had a sense of humor (as one must to stay sane in the grisly business of war), but he was a man of brooding silences too. During the luncheon that followed, he broke one of them by interjecting a remark which had nothing to do with the table talk. "I hope it is not too late," he said with great seriousness. The words made a deep impression on Pershing and brought home to him how close the war was to being lost.[20]

As time went on Pershing grew to have the deepest respect and admiration for Pétain. Mark Boatner, a Pershing aide, said he loved the man. They were simpatico. After the war, when Pétain came to America, Pershing held a private dinner in his honor, inviting select military men. During it he stood up, put his hand on Pétain's shoulder, looked the audience over as if to say he'd court-martial anyone who disagreed with him, and said, "I want it to be understood that this

Newton D. Baker, Secretary of War,
1916–1921. *Baker & Hostetler*

Tasker H. Bliss, Army Chief of Staff, 1917.
U.S. Army Military History Institute

James G. Harbord, AEF Chief of Staff,
1917–1918. *National Archives*

Henri Philippe Pétain,
French Commander in Chief.
U.S. Army Military History Institute

man is the greatest general of the war." Then, after a pause: "I want to repeat what I've just said. This general is the greatest of the war."[21]

Pétain reciprocated the friendship. He said on one occasion: "If ever the history of Franco-American relations, which has brought to light the friendship of Washington and Lafayette, adds that in their shadow lies the friendship of Pershing and Pétain, I shall be touched and happy."[22]

Thanks to the generosity of Ogden Mills, a rich American, Pershing had first-class accommodations in Paris throughout the war. Mills placed at his disposal the magnificent residence at 73 rue de Varenne, a large mansion of some forty-odd rooms dating back to the reign of Louis XIV, with a superbly landscaped garden in the back. Pershing settled in there on June 26, taking with him his chief of staff, inspector general, adjutant general, and personal aides. The rest of his command was left to find their own accommodations, frequently at high prices.[23]

In contrast to living accommodations, office facilities were cramped and confining: two private houses at 27–31 rue de Constantine. Harbord speculated that they may have been picked with the idea of making Pershing so uncomfortable that he would hurry to get out of Paris—which indeed was his desire, for too long a stay in the pleasure-loving capital would not make a good impression.[24]

Everything was new to the Americans: the city, the country, the language, the war. Everything and everyone clamored for attention: the French War Office, the Parisian authorities, the police, the U.S. Embassy, the Red Cross, the Lafayette Escadrille, and so on. The AEF had to adjust to French laws and customs, which were unfamiliar and oftentimes irritating, like their disregard for time or their system of graft. It was hectic. "The summer of 1917 was a difficult one for all of us," remembered Harbord.[25]

Questions originally considered on the *Baltic* had now to be considered in the light of knowledge gained by the visit to England and the first days in France. How big should the AEF now be? How should it be organized? On what fronts should it fight? How much supplies would it need? No large-scale shipment of troops was possible until answers were supplied.

Then there were the more practical, immediate questions. What ports would the AEF need right away, and would they need improvement? Where should the storehouses and shelters be built for the mountain of supplies which would be needed? How much timber could the French supply, and how much must the Americans cut for themselves? What railroads would have to be built to move equipment across France; what animals procured to move it to the front? What guns, munitions, and planes could be purchased in Europe, and what must be sent from home? What raw material must be shipped from America for the Allies to make into finished products in Europe? How many ships would be needed for transport, and where would they come from?[26]

All these questions came eventually to Pershing, and in the beginning, all the answers had to cross his desk. He checked everything very closely, even to the wording of what a year later would be a routine cablegram handled by a minor staff officer. While this could be abused, distracting him from more important issues, in the beginning it was probably a good thing, on the principle that "as the twig is bent, so shall the tree grow." "I'm looking to the details now while I can," said Pershing, "so that later, when I can't, my subordinates will know how my mind works."[27]

These were crucial days for the AEF, perhaps the most crucial of the war. Decisions made now—and made, be it noted, under the press of circumstances and with inadequate facilities and personnel—might be reversed later with great difficulty, if at all. A supply dump built at the wrong place would be extremely hard to move, whereas in the blueprint stage it simply meant erasing lines on a piece of paper. Like a maestro without an orchestra, Pershing worked hard, knowing that when the orchestra appeared its performance would be largely determined by what he did now. "Work hard and be inconspicuous," was his dictum. "After we have tried our metal, and I hope made good, then it will be time enough for the waving of flags and the sounding of trumpets at home."[28]

All agree that Pershing thought big. From the time he went to Europe, said Secretary Baker in retrospect, "he had the largest grasp of the situation and the truest and best informed imagination of what was necessary to win the war of anybody on either side of the ocean, civil or military, with whom I came in contact."[29]

His work had three aspects: economic, military, and political. He had to equip and supply an army, fight it against the Germans, and defend it against Allied incursions on its manpower. As the war went on, wearing three hats became increasingly difficult and, in truth, Pershing tried to wear them too long. But one result was to impress his mark on the AEF in a way similar to that of Robert E. Lee on the Army of Northern Virginia. As Allan R. Millett has remarked, Pershing created "not only an army, but a distinct cultural milieu within which that army's officers were to function until 1919."[30]

During his first month in France Pershing asked the War Department not to allow officers' wives to come to Europe. They would only increase transportation and subsistence problems, besides creating tension between officers and enlisted men. Secretary Baker was adamant in backing Pershing on this point, going so far as to threaten Mrs. William D. Connor that if she went to Europe as a Red Cross worker, he would send her home.[31]

Mrs. Theodore Roosevelt, Jr., who had gone to France before the prohibition took effect, remembered how seriously Pershing took it. During a dinner he was complimenting her on YMCA work (and also on her looks), when suddenly his face clouded. "How do you happen to be here anyhow?" he asked sharply. "No wives are allowed to come overseas. . . . I think you ought to be sent home!"

Mrs. Roosevelt stammered something about having come over before the rule was made, but Pershing didn't listen. A damper descended on the evening. But when they met several months later, he took her hands and apologized. "I'm afraid I must have hurt your feelings that night at dinner, but really I didn't mean to. I know about the work you're doing, and it's good. Can we be friends again?"[32]

Later that summer Pershing took time out from his busy schedule to write a statement for the American Bible Society to be inserted into the Testaments given soldiers as they left for Europe:

"To the American soldier:

"Aroused against a nation waging war in violation of all Christian principles, our people are fighting in the cause of liberty.

"Hardships will be your lot, but trust in God will give you comfort; temptation will befall you, but the teachings of our Savior will give you strength.

"Let your valor as a soldier and your conduct as a man be an inspiration to your comrades and an honor to your country."[33]

Pershing also took time to write a personal letter to a girl who had been a friend of one of his deceased daughters:

"My dear Little Mary:

"First of all, I want to take you in my arms and hug and kiss you. It is so splendid of you to have thought of me and have written me the very nice letter I have just received from you.

"I wish I could see you and tell you just what your letter means to me. It would be a delight, also, to go out with you and try your rifle and see how you look in military costume.

"You touch me very deeply when you say you would like to come over and be my little girl. Nothing in the world would give me greater pleasure than that, because you were so sweet to my own little girl."[34]

Of Pershing's working style, Harbord has left this contemporary portrait: "He thinks very clearly and directly; goes to his conclusions directly when matters call for decision. He can talk straighter to people when calling them down than any one I have seen. . . . He has naturally a good disposition and a keen sense of humor. He loses his temper occasionally, and stupidity and vagueness irritate him more than anything else. He can stand plain talk, but the staff officer who goes in with only vagueness where he ought to have certainty, who does not know what he wants, and fumbles about, has lost time and generally gained some straight talk. He develops great fondness for people whom he likes and is indulgent toward their faults, but at the same time is relentless when convinced of inefficiency. Personal loyalty to friends is strong with him, . . . but does not blind him to the truth."[35]

His great fault, from the viewpoint of his staff, was utter lack of any sense of time. He simply was oblivious of it. Left to himself, he would never be on time for a conference with a king, prime minister, or field marshal. His staff and aides had to be constantly nipping at his heels, so to speak, trying to usher him out of one meeting and get him on the road so he would not be unnecessarily late for another.[36]

He also over-invited people to dinner. Maj. Robert H. Bacon, former ambassador to France and commandant of the headquarters troop, never knew how many were coming. Consider a typical Sunday night dinner. On Saturday night the projected number was fourteen. Sunday noon Pershing was away, but the staff, talking among themselves and comparing notes, discovered that nineteen were expected. Everything was closed on Sunday, so it took a certain amount of frantic scurrying around to various hotels to make up the difference. Half an hour before the meal, in would come Pershing, all smiles, and blithely announce: "I saw so-

and-so this afternoon and tried to get him to come in to dinner to-night but he couldn't come. I did ask that stepdaughter of so-and-so, though. She said she would come." Twenty people were at the table. In time the staff learned that the solution was to take the number Pershing gave them and add three or four, on the supposition that he would probably invite that many extra.[37]

On June 26 Pershing conferred with Pétain on the location of an American front. When he asked for Lorraine, an area his staff had selected on the *Baltic*, Pétain readily agreed. The whole conversation did not last ten minutes, the two men having evidently previously conferred on the matter informally.

The reasons for selecting Lorraine were both negative and positive. The British were sensitive about the area covering the channel ports, and the French would not allow any other army but their own to defend the territory in front of Paris. Hence if the Americans wanted a front, they had to take what was left: the area east of the Argonne Forest, that is, Lorraine.

But Lorraine had positive advantages as well. American supply lines could be routed south of the channel ports and Paris, and thus would be less exposed in the event of a German advance. This was important in case the war went on for long, with the Americans carrying an increasingly heavy load.

Second, being less congested, Lorraine offered more areas for billeting and training than did areas to the west. Because troops had not been there as much, certain supplies would also be more obtainable locally.

In addition, Lorraine had fine offensive possibilities, perhaps the best on the western front. Straight east—in some cases less than forty miles from the battle line—a strategic German railroad ran northwest from Thionville, serving as a main line of communication and supply for German armies to the west. Cutting the railroad would seriously dislocate German plans and might cause a general withdrawal of the whole southern part of their line.

An advance would also carry the war to German soil, which the enemy would be reluctant to devastate as he had France the previous year, wantonly cutting down orchards as he retreated. Additionally, the freeing of Lorraine, one of the two lost provinces after the Franco-Prussian War, would give a tremendous psychological boost to France.

Finally, and most important of all, an advance from Lorraine would do tremendous economic damage to Germany. Less than fifty miles from the battle line (in many cases much closer) were the vitally important coal mines of the Saar and the iron mines of Longwy-Briey, estimated to produce about half of the raw material used in German munitions.

For these reasons Lorraine was selected as the tentative American sector, with an attack against the St. Mihiel salient scheduled as the first offensive to clear the way for subsequent operations against the German railroad and the coal and iron mines.[38]

The choice of the sector in part determined where the American line of communication would be. St. Nazaire, La Pallice, and Bassens, three deep-draft ports considerably south of the main Allied supply routes, became the main Amer-

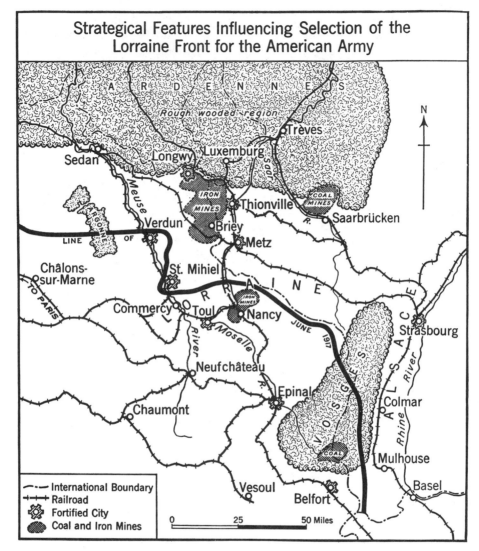

Strategical Features Influencing Selection of the Lorraine Front for the American Army

From American Battle Monuments Commission, *American Armies and Battlefields in Europe*, Washington, D.C., 1938.

ican ports for supplies, while Nantes, Pauillac, and Bordeaux were used for light-draft shipping. Le Havre and Cherbourg were pressed into service later, as were Marseille and Toulon, when the American effort increased. Brest served as a debarkation port for troops.[39]

On June 26 advance elements of the 1st Division—some 14,000 men—arrived at St. Nazaire. (Not until late September did the next major troop shipment arrive—

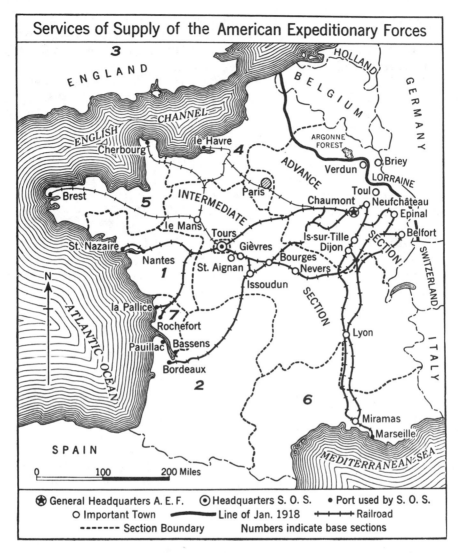

Services of Supply of the American Expeditionary Forces

From American Battle Monuments Commission, *American Armies and Battlefields in Europe*, Washington, D.C., 1938.

a delay of two months that Pershing must have found vexing, as people began to ask the inevitable question, "Where are the Americans?")[40]

Although Joffre had told the French that the first arrivals would be "excellent" troops and "very well-outfitted," they were far otherwise. Some gun companies not only did not have their weapons, but had never heard of them and had no idea what they even looked like![41]

The 1st Division was Regular Army, but its members were Regulars in name only. Half the company commanders had less than six months' experience. Ac-

tually, it was a pickup division, thrown together and sent over, with only a sprin-
kling of professionals who, it was hoped, would leave the mass of raw recruits.
The Regulars had been siphoned off, kept back in America to serve as nuclei in
the various new divisions which were being constituted.[42]

The soldiers were an undisciplined and nondescript lot. Leaning far out over
the ship railing and cupping his hands, one yelled, "Say, do they let the enlisted
men in the saloons here?" Another called out, "Say, where the hell is all this
trouble, anyhow?" When a French general approached an American sentry, instead
of standing at attention the disheveled soldier handed him his rifle and sat down
in a doorway to roll himself a cigarette. In truth, the men were pretty much as
they had come to the recruiting station, civilians in uniform with a minimum
amount of drill.[43] Pershing feared the bad impression the 1st Division must make
on the French. This was not an army; this was a rabble. The Germans would chew
such an outfit to pieces.[44]

He was also disappointed in the officer the War Department had made its
commander: Maj. Gen. William L. Sibert. Sibert was basically an engineer, promoted to general for his work in building the Panama Canal. He had never commanded combat troops, did not look much like a soldier, was not a "driver," and
was frankly a surprise as a commander.[45]

Yet there were some good future leaders in the new arrivals and in subsequent
1st Division contingents. Hanson E. Ely rose to command the 5th Division; George
B. Duncan, the 82nd; and Frank Parker, the 1st. Harold B. Fiske later took charge
of AEF training. Arthur L. Conger became an expert on the German Army Order
of Battle, and George C. Marshall, Jr., handled Operations for the American First
Army. John L. Hines and Charles P. Summerall became corps commanders; Robert
L. Bullard, an army commander; and Peyton C. March, Army Chief of Staff in
Washington.[46]

The 1st Division was billeted in a series of small villages near Gondrecourt,
some twenty-five to forty miles from the front lines. Living in barracks, or even
tents, would have been more comfortable, but was out of the question; wood and
cloth simply were not available, or had more important uses. Hence, six to fourteen
men parceled themselves out in each house or barn, the men generally in haylofts
and the officers in houses.[47]

The billets were crowded, miserable affairs, especially the haylofts and sheds,
which were dark, dismal, and without heat. The French didn't help matters by
their custom of piling wood in front of the only window open for ventilation.
Sometimes they even piled manure![48]

Inspecting a billet once, Pershing preceded Pétain up a rickety ladder to a
hayloft, then stood aside to make room for him. His eyes not yet adjusted to the
dim light, Pétain mistook Pershing for an NCO. "Sergeant, are your men content?"
he asked. Taken aback, Pershing replied, "Oui, mon général, nous sommes très
content." Pétain passed on, unaware of his mistake.[49]

After the inspection the two generals were riding along at a good clip when
their chauffeur came to a railroad crossing whose gates were carelessly open. At
that moment a train rapidly approached. The chauffeur hesitated, then accelerated,

and the car squeaked across just as the train roared by. During the danger, Pétain cast a quick glance at Pershing. Not a muscle of his face showed alarm.[50]

Training of the 1st Division, and of all subsequent divisions, was under an AEF staff training section headed by Lt. Col. Paul B. Malone. It was in three phases. In the first, which averaged one month, troops learned the use of basic weapons and engaged in various exercises. In the second, small units rotated up to the trenches as parts of a French division, supported by French artillery while their own artillery trained elsewhere. In the third, the whole division reassembled for one month's work with combined arms (artillery and aviation), after which it was considered ready to hold its own sector of the front under its own officers, but as part of a French corps.[51]

That was the ideal, but pressure of events often made a shambles of the schedule, particularly in the last days of the war. In August 1918 Gen. Douglas MacArthur's brigade received several thousand replacements. Of forty-three in one company, almost half had only three weeks' training and one man had only seven days.[52]

To assist in training, Pershing established over twenty schools on the division, corps, and army level. Probably the most crucial was the General Staff College at Langres under Brig. Gen. James W. (Dad) McAndrew. Its purpose was to provide the badly needed staff officers on which the AEF would depend. Instructors were American, although British and French officers did serve as advisors.[53]

By the end of June Pershing had a reasonably clear impression of conditions in France. They were bad. Journeying through the countryside, one saw only women, children, and an old man; France's youth was either at the front or in cemeteries. Alexandre Ribot, the prime minister, spoke of serious despondency among all classes. French politics was a can of worms, rumors circulating of a possible coup d'état. Pershing confided to James L. Collins, his aide, that matters could hardly be worse.[54]

Conditions were scarcely much better with the British. Since February 1, when the intensive German submarine campaign began, the average shipping loss per month (British, Allied, and neutrals) was 636,000 gross tons, whereas the British were building only 100,000 gross tons per month. On June 20 Admiral Sims called the submarine situation "critical." "The outstanding fact which cannot be escaped is that we are not succeeding . . . ," he said.[55]

Allied harmony was coming apart at the seams. The French resented the British who, they felt, were not pulling their weight in the war. With more men in their army than the French, the British occupied a front only one-third as long. Harbord reported a fight in a café between French and British officers, forty on a side, which took the police to quell. Ambassador Page reported friction between Australians and Canadians on the one hand and the British on the other. "Nothing could keep these nations together a week but dire necessity," he observed.[56]

Despite press stories about "brave little Belgium," both the British and French regarded its army with contempt. It did little, said Georges Clemenceau later, except issue communiqués. A French jibe ran: "We will fight until not a single Belgian remains on French soil."[57]

As for the Italians, they were almost universally considered beneath contempt. They provoked derision at an Allied meeting once by announcing complacently that they had no naval losses to report; all their ships were safely in port. When a British warship accidentally sank an Italian submarine in the Mediterranean, the French Chamber of Deputies was said to have applauded.[58]

Despite the many reasons for pessimism, Pershing never entertained doubts about ultimate victory. Asked to give a statement to the London *Sunday Times* at the beginning of the fourth year of war, he said: "Spirit and morale of Allied armies splendid. General situation better than at the beginning of any other year of war. Allies should look forward with full confidence to complete victory."[59]

His words were in no way justified by the facts.

FOUR

Getting Organized

(July-August 1917)

ALTHOUGH PARIS HAD seen Pershing and his staff, it had not seen many American troops, and the French authorities badly wanted some of them to march through to make an impression. On July 4, American Independence Day, Pershing reluctantly allowed a battalion of the 16th Infantry Regiment of the 1st Division, recently arrived at St. Nazaire, to parade through Paris from Les Invalides, site of Napoleon's tomb, to Picpus Cemetery, burial place of Lafayette. He was reluctant because he knew the inexperience of the recent arrivals and feared lest the French military judge that these men, known to be Regulars at least in name, represented the American soldier at his best.[1]

He judged correctly. The 16th Infantry looked exactly like what it was: civilians in uniform. One seasoned French veteran turned to his companion in the crowd and said: "And they send *that* to help us."[2]

But the civilian crowd, less discriminating and weary unto death with the war, was thrilled beyond measure. Here were the Americans, the "Sammies"; here was hope incarnate. The three-mile parade route was bedlam; women linked arms with the outer flanks of the soldiers, kissing them, weeping almost hysterically. Many dropped to their knees in reverence as the column passed. With wreaths around their necks and with flowers projecting from their hatbands and rifle barrels, the 16th Infantry looked from a distance like a moving flower garden. As far as the eye could see there were people, people, people, laughing, shouting, weeping, stirred to a frenzy of excitement by the crowd spirit, the martial music, and the fact that, in truth, the Americans did represent the salvation of France.[3]

The parade culminated at the grave of Lafayette, buried, according to his wish, in earth brought from America. Pershing laid a wreath of five hundred roses on the grave and delegated Col. Charles E. Stanton, who had command of French and a reputation of being an orator, to speak for him. Stanton gave a regular Fourth of July speech, waving his arms, pounding the podium, annihilating the Kaiser and the whole German army in purple-patched prose. The French loved it, wildly applauding, especially his final words: "Lafayette, we are here!" Thus was born

the most famous American quotation of World War I, a remark erroneously
attributed to Pershing because he was there and, despite his disclaimer, still attributed to him.[4]

Although he had not intended to speak, the French insisted, so Pershing made
a few remarks. Brand Whitlock, who had never seen him before, was impressed.
"He said a few words, very simply, very quietly, very dignifiedly; precisely the right
thing, in perfect taste."[5]

The following day, July 5, Pershing organized his General Staff. Based on
consultations with British and French counterparts, it eventually contained five
main sections: Administration, Intelligence, Operations, Co-ordination, and Training. It also embraced a Technical and Administrative staff composed of the chiefs
of some fifteen separate Departments, Corps, and Services (e.g., Inspector General
Department, Medical Corps, Air Service, etc.).[6]

The Administration Section, dealing with general matters of policy and organization, was under Maj. James A. Logan, Jr., an exceedingly able man who had
been stationed in France at the outbreak of the war. In August 1918 he was replaced
by Col. Avery D. Andrews, a Pershing West Point classmate.[7]

The Intelligence Section was capably commanded throughout the war by Maj.
Dennis E. Nolan, whose chewing gum cud and slow speech belied an exceedingly
sharp mind. Inconceivable as it seems, America entered the war with an Intelligence
Section of the General Staff numbering only four men: two officers and two clerks.
Under Nolan, AEF Intelligence expanded enormously, so that by the end of the
conflict Pershing felt that America had the best intelligence of any army in Europe.[8]

Lt. Col. John McAuley Palmer headed the Operations Section until sickness
forced him to give way in November to Col. Fox Conner, a West Pointer from
Mississippi, who became, next to Harbord, the man on whom Pershing relied
most. Fluent in French, frank-talking, extremely competent, and utterly loyal,
Pershing said of him, "I could have spared any other man in the A.E.F. better than
you." After the war he had a great influence on a young officer named Dwight D.
Eisenhower.[9]

Until April 1918 Lt. Col. William D. Connor headed the Co-ordination Sec-
tion, which dealt with matters of supply; he was replaced by Col. George Van
Horn Moseley, an equally capable officer. Lt. Col. Paul B. Malone headed the
Training Section.

The staff was a good one. Logan, Nolan, Conner, and Malone had all known
each other on a nickname basis for years, as had Frank R. McCoy, Secretary of
the General Staff, Harold B. Fiske, who replaced Malone in February 1918, and
Robert C. (Corky) Davis, the Adjutant General. So they got along well. Harbord
doubted that any commanding general was ever better served by his staff.[10]

The most important officer on the whole staff, of course, was Harbord himself,
the Chief of Staff, the man directly under Pershing and over the five main sections
and the fifteen technical sections. As the principal adviser and alter ego of the
commander, whom he accompanied to all important conferences, he supervised
and coordinated the work of all other staff heads. He relieved Pershing of much

that was burdensome, and was responsible for seeing that the whole staff worked together as a team. He fought for the staff's views with the commander, then turned around to justify and impose on the staff an adverse final decision. He was the neck of the bottle, everything flowing in and out through him. He was, in short, a tremendously important man.[11]

Harbord, who held this position during the first year of the war, found Pershing occasionally hard to understand. What the commander said was not necessarily what he meant; he threw out trial balloons to test reactions. Sometimes the reactions got a little hot, with raised voices and pounded desks. Overworked himself, Pershing tended to overwork his staff, especially in the early days. Once he suddenly asked Harbord what a certain staff officer was doing—in tones which indicated doubt that he was doing anything. In fact, he was doing a great deal and doing it efficiently.[12]

Pershing dominated his staff, impressing his own mark on it. He wanted its top officers to rotate as combat commanders, to remind them that they were dealing with human beings, not chessmen, when they made their plans. While the staff may not have been afraid of him, they generally stood on the defensive, knowing that he would not hesitate to relieve them if he felt the need. "I expect you to make mistakes . . . ," he told Colonel Connor in appointing him; "don't make too many of them."[13]

The AEF General Staff, usually graduates of the School of the Line and the Staff College at Fort Leavenworth, grew from three at the start of the war to over two hundred by the end. While the Allies consistently doubted its capacity to handle large groups of men, it eventually vindicated itself, although not without mistakes. Man for man, Pershing believed that the Leavenworth graduate and the professionally trained American soldier was the equal, if not the superior, of any in the world.[14]

The only trouble was there weren't enough good Leavenworth men to go around. Pershing early put in a request to Washington to build up his small nucleus, but it was like robbing Peter to pay Paul. As the War Department pointed out, "Frequently officers asked for by name cannot be sent without seriously interfering with operations here."[15]

On July 6 Pershing told the War Department it should plan on sending over "at least one million men by next May." The Department replied that, straining every effort, the most it could land in Europe by June 15, 1918, was approximately 635,000. Combined with elements of the 1st Division which had already landed at St. Nazaire, that made about 650,000, or 65 percent of Pershing's request. The discrepancy was notable and reflected the two contrary approaches to the manpower problem: Pershing thinking of what was needed; the War Department of what was possible.[16]

Two days later a situation which could have caused a serious problem was successfully met and handled. It arose out of the fact that on May 28, the day Pershing sailed for Europe, the War Department had appointed an independent twelve-man mission to go overseas, investigate the situation, and make an independent report on "the organization, training, transportation, operations, supply, and administration of our forces. . . ." The mission was not under Pershing's authority, was not even ordered to report to him, and could do considerable mischief. Historian Harvey A. DeWeerd called it "one of Secretary Baker's few unhelpful decisions in World War I." While it might be useful to have a second set of recommendations on AEF organization (on the theory that two heads are better than one), the mission's recommendations might also be drastically different from Pershing's. In that case the mission, being able to argue its conclusions face to face in Washington, would have considerable advantage over the AEF commander, three thousand miles away, who was forced to argue through a tortuous, and at times garbled, trans-atlantic cable.[17]

Fortunately, the head of the mission, Col. Chauncey B. Baker, was an old friend and West Point classmate ('86), who told Pershing he would like to meet with the AEF General Staff before he returned to America to make his recommendations. It was a courteous gesture, but also eminently appropriate. Since Pershing was the one who would have to fight the war, it would hardly be fair to saddle him with an organization with which he disapproved without giving him a chance to represent his views.[18]

On July 7–8 the Baker Mission and the AEF General Staff conferred. Pershing, who served as chairman, desired that both groups submit common recommendations to obviate the difficulty of the War Department's having to choose between them. In such cases, the temptation would be to split the difference in a spirit of compromise, or worse, to choose the mission's recommendations instead of his own. Perhaps to avoid this, he stacked the deck, bringing to the conference eighteen of his own people to outvote twelve of Baker's.[19]

Both groups agreed about most things, but a very serious difference about artillery developed between the Baker Mission's Artillery Section, headed by Col. Charles P. Summerall, and the AEF Operations Division, represented by Col. Fox Conner. Summerall, a strong personality who believed that the proposed AEF organization was undergunned and that men's lives would be needlessly sacrificed as a consequence, spoke out strongly against Conner and Pershing. In fact, said Harbord, he "carried his argument as nearly to the limit of courtesy as I have ever seen an officer go and escape unrebuked."

Pershing kept his temper, knowing he had no authority over Summerall and badly wanting to avoid a split in recommendations. When the vote was taken, the AEF General Staff position won out, 16 to 5.[20]

Summerall may have been right; Bliss said later that he felt that American divisions were underpowered in artillery. In combat a division's front was determined, not by the number of its infantry, but by its artillery. Yet the American division, while almost twice the strength of Allied divisions in personnel, was no stronger in artillery.[21]

Summerall impressed Pershing. A man who liked strong men, including those who stood up to him, he cabled the War Department, asking that Summerall be sent back to the AEF, where he consistently promoted him from one key position to another. When the war was over, he lauded him in words not used about any other American general. "An exceptionally able man in all respects," he said. "Possesses soldierly qualities instinctively. Thorough in his knowledge of his profession. Most loyal and reliable. Very energetic and determined. Inspires the highest ideals of service in his subordinates, and makes them feel that nothing is impossible. Brilliant in handling a command, none better. Would have been an army commander if the war had lasted. The highest type of man and soldier worthy of every confidence and able to fill any position."[22]

As Pershing had desired, the Baker Mission-AEF General Staff conference did produce a common set of recommendations. Known as the General Organization Project, it specified the organization for a field army of one million men (infantry, artillery, services, etc.), but added significantly, "Plans for the future should be based, especially in reference to the manufacture, etc., of artillery, aviation, and other material, on three times this force—i.e., at least three million men."[23]

Roughly speaking, those men were eventually organized into infantry units as follows:

Platoon: the basic unit, fifty-eight men, under a 2d or 1st lieutenant.

Company: six officers and 250 men, under a captain.

Battalion: four companies, about one thousand officers and men, under a major.

Regiment: three battalions and a machine gun company, about 3,800, under a colonel.

Brigade: two regiments and a machine gun battalion, about 8,500, under a brigadier general.

Division: two infantry and one field artillery brigades, one engineer regiment, one machine gun battalion, one signal battalion, and trains; 72 guns, 260 machine guns, 17,666 rifles, about 28,000 officers and men, under a major general.

Corps: two or more divisions, under a major general.

Army: two or more corps, under a lieutenant general.

Army Group: two or more armies, under a general.[24]

Probably the most controversial point of this organization was the size of the division—approximately 28,000 men—double that of any other army, allied or enemy. The decision was made after consultation with the British and French General Staffs who recommended a large division, saying that they would have it themselves except for a manpower shortage. Even apart from Allied advice, AEF planners inclined in this direction for several reasons.[25]

The first was "staying power." Once committed to combat, a division ought to be able to stay in line for some time, for only thus could it make its full weight felt, delivering really effective blows before needing to be replaced. Replacing a division always produced a certain loss of momentum, like shifting gears in a car. A big division was thought to be able to stay longer, hit harder, and endure more than a smaller one.[26]

Second, the AEF badly lacked trained men for command and staff work. By having large divisions the few available trained men could be concentrated at the top, whereas smaller divisions meant finding more trained commanders and staff—

people in short supply. Hence the decision for fewer divisions, which in turn meant larger divisions.

Third, AEF planners generally had a low opinion of National Guard commanders and staff. By concentrating U.S. troops in large divisions they could more easily be placed under Regular Army officers rather than left under National Guard leadership in smaller divisions.[27]

Not all of these reasons are convincing. If staying power justified large divisions for the AEF, why not for other armies? A manpower shortage—their supposed reason for not having them—could be overcome by simply concentrating available manpower in large divisions rather than smaller.

Granted that the sparse number of trained command and staff officers should be concentrated at the top, still no U.S. officer, including Pershing himself, had ever commanded in combat a normal-sized division, much less a double-sized one. It could not fairly be assumed that green American officers were more competent than their experienced French and British counterparts. The oversized division actually placed double the burden on command and staff. With inexperienced officers and men, one could argue that the situation called for keeping divisions small rather than big.[28]

In addition, the oversized divisions also had drawbacks. The Allies, within whose corps and armies the AEF fought for most of the war, were organized on a smaller divisional basis for supply, transport, and deployment in battle. Inevitable problems arose about road use, sector assignment, communications, and deployment.[29]

In the United States the oversized divisions threw cantonment construction, planned and actually begun with smaller divisions in mind, into a cocked hat. As Frederick Palmer remarked, it was "as if, after all plans had been made and material ordered for constructing a high office building, the owner had suddenly decided to add ten stories, put the elevators in different places, and reduce the height of the ceilings by a foot."[30]

On July 20 Pershing met Field Marshal Sir Douglas Haig, the British commander in chief, during a four-day visit to the latter's headquarters, and the American was much impressed. Both men had much in common: exact bearing, immaculate grooming, a certain reserve based on shyness. Both were cordial men, but not effusive. But Haig was a more sensitive man than Pershing, with a nervous system and a digestive tract more inclined to kick up under stress. He needed regular hours, careful diet, and a prescribed amount of sleep. Like Sir William Robertson, he suffered from an inability to communicate his ideas effectively, especially with his civilian superior, Lloyd George, who was not overfulsome in his regard for Haig.[31]

Both generals hit it off. Haig wrote in his diary: "I was much struck with his quiet gentlemanly bearing—so unusual for an American. Most anxious to learn, and fully realizes the greatness of the task before him. He has already begun to realize that the French are a broken reed."[32]

John Charteris, Haig's intelligence chief, thought Pershing would do well. "He has determination and goes at everything very thoroughly." Charteris did, however, note that the Americans were where the British had been in 1914 (green and untrained) and put his finger on what would be a key problem: "It will be a very difficult job for them to get a serviceable staff going even in a year's time."[33]

On August 1 Pershing inspected the 1st Division to see how it looked after a month in France and after two weeks of training with the crack French 47th Division, the *Chasseurs Alpin*. He was not pleased with what he saw. The men did not look like soldiers. Officers were nonchalant in bearing and dress. Enlisted men failed to salute or stand at attention. The drill was sloppy; the manual of arms and marching shoddy. Teamsters, chauffeurs, and isolated detachments were especially careless about military etiquette.[34]

Doubtless Pershing could be, and has been, faulted for his insistence on military discipline, on the externals of soldiering, on what was to be called "spit and polish." He sincerely believed that men were not soldiers, would not act as such, unless they looked the part, unless they adopted certain external mannerisms such as standing stiffly at attention, giving snappy salutes, and marching in close order precision. None of these things have to do with real soldiering, which is a matter of physical toughness, endurance, teamwork, resourcefulness, coping with fear, staying healthy in bad weather, knowing how to shoot and take cover, and in general (as Patton later put it) "making the other poor dumb bastard die for his country" rather than you.[35]

Pershing knew this, of course, but believed that imposing a certain exterior discipline on a man inculcated the proper interior mental attitude. "The prompt assumption of the position of attention," he claimed, "marks in the education of the soldier the first complete submission of his will to that of his superior, and is the foundation on which his future efficiency is to be built, and can not therefore be too strongly insisted upon." (Someone once said that Pershing's favorite soldier was the Biblical warrior Joshua, because he made the sun stand at attention.) Military etiquette, then, had as its purpose training a soldier to instant, unthinking, implicit obedience to the will of his superior. Only thus would the soldier be conditioned to go forward under command in the face of death.[36]

The point is arguable, and has been argued by those who contend that running an obstacle course involves the same amount of obedience and does a lot more good for the soldier than close order drill. Others, like S. L. A. Marshall, have pointed out that men fight, not because of any Pavlovian conditioning due to drill and saluting, but because of close, personal relationships established within a company of men. Thus one does his duty because he does not want to let his buddies down and fears to shame himself in front of them.[37]

In truth, no one can accurately predict the future conduct of a soldier in combat. One perfect in drill may be a Samson or a coward; one careless in salute may be a slacker or a raging tiger. Undoubtedly Pershing knew this, but felt that one had to have some standard to go on and, almost by default if nothing else, military discipline was as good as any. The Germans used it, and he had the greatest respect for them.

In any event, the 1st Division lacked discipline when Pershing inspected it and—no coincidence as far as he was concerned—also was deficient in other regards. Officers were lazy and careless in caring for their men; equipment and supplies were lacking; bayonet training was poor.[38]

Pershing blamed General Sibert. He was not sufficiently on top of things, did not get about among his men, did not inspire them to action. "He cannot stand the gaff," said Pershing. The contrast between Sibert and his men, and French generals and theirs, was striking. As one officer put it, "It all means death."[39]

Meanwhile, work went on apace at the rue de Constantine headquarters. It seemed endless; no matter what was done there was always more to do. Patton said it was like "a rat chewing an oak tree."[40]

Although airplanes had not performed well in the Punitive Expedition, Pershing now desperately wanted them. "Push American production program hard as possible . . . ," he cabled the War Department. "Also push American training program to the utmost. . . . Cannot have too many pilots or too soon."[41]

In August he contracted with the French air ministry for 5,000 planes and 8,500 motors, to be delivered by June 1918. The bill was sixty million dollars, more than Congress appropriated initially for the Spanish-American War. "He did it without winking an eye," observed Harbord, "as easily as though ordering a postage stamp. . . ." It was a somewhat bold move to make on his own, Pershing admitted, "but under the circumstances some one had to take the initiative. . . ."[42]

That same month he cabled Washington that, since America's entrance into the war had saved the Allies from defeat, "our position in this war [is] very strong and should enable us largely to dictate policy of Allies in future. . . . We need not hesitate [to] demand both aggressive naval policy and full share [of] Allied commercial shipping."[43]

By "aggressive naval policy" Pershing meant some sort of Allied naval movement against the U-boat bases, especially by the British. Nothing came of this suggestion, however, as the English admirals claimed that the submarine pens were impregnable. Privately, Harbord felt that the British declined to attack because their losses would make the American navy supreme after the war.[44]

About this time Pershing established an AEF chemical warfare branch, putting in charge Lt. Col. Amos A. Fries. When Fries protested that he didn't know anything about gas, Pershing responded, "That's O.K. Learn."[45]

Fries did. By the time of the armistice, American production of mustard gas was about ten times that of the German. Pershing was even prepared to drop gas bombs on civilians if the enemy did it first.[46]

Initially the AEF used the British gas mask which, while affording good protection, was uncomfortable, hard to carry, and difficult to see through. At Cantigny the following May Americans suffered nine hundred gas casualties in one night because they couldn't stand to wear the mask for twelve or more hours. Its tight nose clip and gaggy mouthpiece became unendurable.

Later, Fries took an experimental American-made mask to Pershing. He showed a lively interest, putting it on and doing calisthenics to see if it fogged or was uncomfortable. Eventually an American mask went into production without the objectionable nose clip and mouthpiece.[47]

Pershing's main problem now was organizing the supply of his future army. The AEF would eventually have almost two million men in France, consuming forty-five thousand tons of supplies a day. How was all this to be managed?

The basic supply system was created on August 13 in General Orders 20, which established the Line of Communications (LOC), which was divided into Base, Intermediate, and Advance Sections. Although not all were set up at once, in time there were eight Base Sections with headquarters respectively at St. Nazaire, Bordeaux, London, Le Havre, Brest, Marseille, La Pallice, and in Italy. The Base Sections maintained a forty-five day supply reserve; the Intermediate, thirty days; and the Advance Section, fifteen days.[48]

Building and stocking scores of supply depots was a problem because there were not enough goods to go around, and McCain's hoarding of typewriters in the War Department basement was being repeated overseas. American engineers and quartermasters were competing against each other in the open market, as well as against the British and French, sending prices skyrocketing and causing one group to have too much while another went wanting. The need to coordinate all this, to supervise procurement, and to check the scramble for supplies was apparent.[49]

In order to do this, Pershing established on August 20 a General Purchasing Board (GPB), doing so against the unanimous advice of a group of officers he had appointed to study the matter, who argued that a centralized purchasing agency was illegal. He waved aside the objection. "An emergency confronted us and it was no time to discuss technicalities," he said later.[50]

The GPB was a board of ten officers, representing all the purchasing departments of the AEF, together with the Red Cross and the YMCA. They met, made known their relative needs and stockpiles, and determined who should purchase what and where. This reduced competition for the same articles and allowed discounts through placing combined orders. The GPB also served as the liaison agency with the Allies for coordinating purchases with them.[51]

Pershing placed his old friend from University of Nebraska days, Lt. Col. Charles G. Dawes, in charge of the GPB. The latter was a civilian in uniform, having come to Europe with an engineer regiment in which he had wrangled a commission on the thin justification that, as a youth in Ohio, he had carried a surveyor chain for a month or two. Dawes was no engineer, but he was a man of eminent savvy and drive, a lawyer, and an outstanding businessman. (Later he would be vice-president of the United States under Calvin Coolidge, author of the Dawes Plan for European reparations, and American ambassador at the Court of St. James.) Harbord thought him "the most outstanding civilian in the American uniform," one of the dozen most influential men in the whole AEF.[52]

Dawes idolized Pershing. He had known him at the University of Nebraska in the 1890s and boasted a relationship with the general that few could match.

Fox Conner, AEF Chief of Operations.
National Archives

Charles P. Summerall.
U.S. Army Military History Institute

Sir Douglas Haig, British Commander in
Chief. *U.S. Army Military History Institute*

Charles G. Dawes, AEF General Purchasing
Agent. *U.S. Army Military History Institute*

Dawes was, for example, the only person Ralph A. Curtin, Pershing's secretary, ever heard call the general by his first name. Frequently he was an overnight guest at Pershing's chateau. In the morning the two men would rise early (Pershing rarely slept past 7:30, even after the most trying night) and stroll about the grounds in their pajamas, Pershing's arm around Dawes's shoulder or vice versa.[53]

Dawes performed valiantly, fired by his personal devotion to the commander in chief and backed by the latter's assurance that he would have virtually unlimited authority. Not only did Dawes centralize purchases, he broadened and extended them, scrounging all of Europe for supplies. Every item purchased there saved that much space on crowded ships bringing material from America. In a Europe supposedly stripped bare of material, Dawes rounded up an amazing ten million tons of supplies, compared to a total of some seven million tons sent over by the War Department.[54]

If, as Harbord said, Pershing developed great fondness for those he liked and tolerated their faults, Dawes was a prime example. Edward (Peter) Bowditch, Jr., another Pershing aide, recalled incidents where Dawes came to see Pershing and was told that the general was not to be disturbed. Dawes walked right in anyway. Rather than becoming angry, Pershing seemed amused.[55]

Dawes's "fault" was that he was not military; he cared not a whit about the military punctilio and discipline of which Pershing made so much. He either ignored it, or burlesqued it, or both. He thought nothing of riding down the Champs Elysées in uniform while dangling both feet outside the car, or of inviting enlisted men to dine with officers. To him, the military experience was a big lark, a game for little boys. Once, after a dinner in which Dawes was the senior officer present, Patton stood up, precisely military, and asked to be excused. When Patton rose, one of his subordinates did too, whereupon Dawes banged his fist down on the table. "Isn't that something!" he exclaimed, delightedly. "When Patton stands up, he flushes only a lieutenant. But when I stand up, everyone else here will have to too."[56]

Pershing once called Dawes "the most unmilitary human that ever lived." (A possible competitor would be Heywood Broun, whom Pershing once asked when he saw the newspaperman's disheveled appearance, "Did you fall down?") Spying Dawes's unbuttoned collar in public, Pershing would send an aide to button him up, or come and do it himself.[57]

In time, Dawes's unmilitary characteristics became a legend, prompting stories—some of which were undoubtedly apocryphal—which illustrated the point. According to one, Pershing entered a room where Dawes sat with a big, black cigar in his mouth. Dawes neither removed the cigar nor rose. Said the AEF commander: "It's customary when a superior officer walks into the room to at least shift the cigar from one side of the mouth to the other."[58]

Perhaps Dawes cultivated a sense of humor to keep himself sane in his dealings with French bureaus. If so, he needed it. First he would encounter a minor official who, after considerable wrangling, would agree to do something or other. Then Dawes would discover that the official had little or no authority and that his superior had vetoed the request. Next, the superior having been won over, Dawes learned that the man's office really did not handle such matters and so-and-so should be approached. At last, the proper office having been found, the answer was NO, the reason being (if there was one) that it had never been done before. At this stage, if the matter was important enough, it would go all the way up to Pershing who would take it up with some French official at the very top (like the prime minister, the war minister, or Pétain), who, exerting pressure, would eventually see that something was done.[59]

Take, for example, the problem of obtaining lumber, widely used for wharves, pilings, telegraph poles, fuel, railroad ties, cantonments—just about anything. At first the French said they could deliver the lumber needed for wharf construction. Later they reneged and promised only timber facilities (i.e., the standing trees), but no laborers or sawmills or equipment for transporting the cut lumber to railroads. Still later they reneged on even the trees, leaving the whole AEF effort "dead in the water." Without wood, wharves could not be built to unload the ships, nor railroads to transport material, nor buildings to store it. It took persistent pressure by AEF officials and finally the personal intervention of Pershing himself with Painlevé, the Minister of War (involving a letter, a conference, and subsequent telephone messages), to break, quite literally, the logjam.[60]

After encountering the system, Pershing marveled that the French had been able to survive three years of war. America was no stranger to red tape, but "the art of tying things up in official routine was in swaddling clothes in America as compared to its development in France," he said.[61]

FIVE

Chaumont

(September 1917)

"THE GENERAL WAS . . . raving mad . . . and swore he was going to get out of Paris as soon as possible . . . ," wrote Pershing's aide, Collins, after one month in France. Paris, with its social distractions and constant interruptions from visitors, simply was no place to work.[1]

For his new headquarters Pershing chose Chaumont, some 150 miles to the east, in the upper Marne. It was near the probable American sector, featured a large, four-story military barracks eminently suitable for headquarters, had ample billeting facilities for the officers, and suitable temporary barracks for the enlisted men. Pershing moved there on September 6.[2]

The move was supposed to be secret, but it was pretty hard to keep anything concealed in Paris—that city of gossip and intrigue—which was another reason for getting away from it. When a soldier, Francis R. Stoddard, inquired of American officers in Paris where Pershing was, no one would tell him. When he asked a man on the street, the latter replied, "Everybody knows. . . . He is at Chaumont."[3]

Pershing's personal residence was on the outskirts of town in a large house, garishly furnished in the style of the nouveau riche. "The damdest taste you ever saw . . . ," commented Patton, observing how the walls were lined with all sorts of animal heads, horns, and skins. "There is a huge crocodile fifteen feet long with gaping jaws who appears ready to spring on you when you enter the front hall. In Collins room two eagles are about to pounce on the bed while a wild boar threatens you when you eat. . . ."[4]

Until the AEF got its own wires strung, communication with Paris was by the archaic, exasperating French telephone system, in which a dozen or so operators had to plug in along the route. Phoning Paris sometimes took an hour, and often the user was cut off in the middle of a conversation.[5]

Soon after the AEF settled in at Chaumont, various foreign missions established themselves there. A mission was a group of officers, representing an Allied commander like Pétain or Haig, charged with liaison work. They kept their respective commanders informed of American plans, smoothed out difficulties, and generally acted as lubricant on the gears of the coalition's war machinery. It was quicker and more efficient, for example, to deal with the French Mission at Chaumont when a problem arose than to attempt to settle it by correspondence with Pétain's headquarters. Pétain's chief of mission at Chaumont was Brig. Gen. Camille M. Ragueneau; Pershing's with Pétain was Col. Paul H. Clark."[6]

On September 6, Pershing again inspected the 1st Division, this time with President Raymond Poincaré of France. Again, the division did not look very good. Scattered over 20–30 miles of countryside, some units did not learn of the inspection until the previous afternoon and arrived fatigued after an all-night march. Capt. George C. Marshall, Jr., the overworked division Acting Chief of Staff, unfortunately picked the review ground late the previous evening, not noticing in the fading light that it was irregular, churned up and muddy—unsuitable for precision marching. Since over one-half of the officers and two-thirds of the men were recruits, they were not much good at marching anyway. Moreover, under the tutelage of the French 47th Division, a crack unit known as the "Blue Devils," they had been concentrating, not on marching, but on practical combat work. The result then, as might have been expected, was a shoddy review. Poincaré's impression, said Pershing, "could not have been particularly favorable. . . ." Nor was his own; it was another nail in the coffin of General Sibert.[7]

Shortly afterwards Pershing received a letter from Secretary Baker, urging that American troops not be put on the firing line until they were fully trained and could give a good account of themselves. This was welcome news, particularly since Georges M. Clemenceau, while visiting the 1st Division with General Edouard de Castelnau on another occasion, had strongly insisted that it be put in without delay. America had been in the war for months and the French people wanted to know when they were going to see U.S. troops in action. Told that the Americans were not ready, Clemenceau answered that it was not a question of being ready (nobody is ever completely ready), but of helping France—which was exhausted, bled white, and needed relief. Clemenceau's contention, made more insistently when he became premier in November, was a recurring bone of contention throughout the war.[8]

Baker also mentioned that Scott would retire as Chief of Staff that month, and that he intended to appoint Bliss as his successor until November or December when the latter was scheduled to retire. He wondered whom Pershing would recommend after that. Baker inclined toward Maj. Gen. Peyton C. March. He had had War Department experience, was then in charge of the 1st Division artillery brigade, and was known as "a man of positive and decided character." By the end of the year he would have been in France about six months, would know the situation there, and would understand Pershing's needs and problems. A young, aggressive man, with a good record and with experience on both sides of the Atlantic, he seemed ideally suited to be Chief of Staff.[9]

Pershing, who took over two months to answer, recommended Maj. Gen. John Biddle, an engineer officer and a former superintendent of West Point. Like

Pershing's Residence at Val des Écoliers. *Madame de Rouvres*

Pershing's Office at Chaumont. *Ralph A. Curtin*

March, Biddle had had overseas experience. Pershing recommended March as second choice.[10]

Pershing misjudged his men here. At the time he wrote, November 13, Biddle had already returned from France and was serving as Acting Chief of Staff, since Bliss was in Europe on a mission. Before leaving France, Biddle had told Pershing frankly that he did not think himself suited for the job. Nonetheless, Pershing recommended him ahead of March, whom he had seen firsthand in France, knew was doing a bang-up job, and recently had promoted to Chief of AEF Artillery. Perhaps, knowing March's headstrong and irascible disposition, he thought that Biddle would be easier to deal with. If so, he was certainly right.[11]

On September 23 Bliss replaced Scott as Chief of Staff. He was all that Pershing could desire from the viewpoint of loyalty, personal friendship, unselfishness, and desire to serve. In fact, he considered his office subordinate to that of the overseas command. As he confessed to Pershing later, he conceived of himself as the "Assistant Chief of Staff to the Chief of Staff of the AEF"—in other words, subordinate to Harbord—a concept quite foreign to the General Staff reforms initiated by Secretary of War Elihu Root in 1903.[12]

Yet for all his good will and scholarly attainments, the War Department under Bliss did not function smoothly. Maj. Gen. Enoch Crowder, the Provost Marshal General, called Bliss "hopeless," "completely overwhelmed by his job." It was impossible to get a quick decision out of him, Crowder said; "he seemed dazed."[13]

Perhaps motivated by misguided charity, he permitted a number of General Staff officers in Washington to apply for overseas service, where the action was—and promotions. The result was that the War Department was shorthanded of experienced officers at a critical time, or had an inefficient turnover of them. Moreover, he did not sufficiently crack heads and stop the practice of circulating AEF requests to any bureau which might care to comment. It may have been a good practice in peacetime, but now speed was important. Some AEF cable requests quite literally were given the "run-around" in the War Department.[14]

For example, after careful calculation of requirements for construction of ordnance storehouses, the AEF cabled its plans to Washington. The Chief of Ordnance, unwilling to trust AEF recommendations (the bureaus frequently felt that Pershing was overestimating his needs), requested the French High Commissioner in Washington, André Tardieu, to obtain French views on the subject. Tardieu cabled the matter to his government, which turned it over to Pétain, who turned it over to Pershing, who naturally supported his original recommendation. "At times it seemed that the last refinement was being invoked to cause delay," he complained. "This endless chain should clearly indicate the necessity of handling such matters direct with my headquarters."[15]

Over Pershing's protests, supply contracts were initially made by War Department bureaus rather than by his own organization in France, sometimes with bad results. Issoudun, the first and largest American flying school in France, was chosen in Washington on the advice of French officers there. A slimy morass in wet weather and a sea of frozen mud in cold, it was, as one aviation student remarked, "a hell of a place."

"Strongly advise," Pershing cabled the War Department, ". . . that you do not make decision on advice foreign officers in Washington who are often not acquainted with latest developments here. There will be constant confusion if you so attempt have foreign advisers same subjects on which we are advising you from here. . . . You cannot use two sets advisers same time same subject."[16]

Pershing's irritation at the War Department's refusal to accept his estimates and follow his leads flowed from a threefold source. One was the fact that he was on the ground and therefore in a better position to know than any bureau chief three thousand miles away. Another was his determination to assert control over the traditionally recalcitrant bureaus. "This is going to be one American campaign where the tail does not wag the dog, and where the command actually commands," he asserted. Third, and most fundamentally, he felt that the AEF was a semi-autonomous command, virtually independent of the War Department and its bureaus. As he said in his memoirs, "In principle it was simply their duty to furnish the army overseas what it asked for, if possible, as otherwise we could not be held responsible for results."[17]

As we have noted, Bliss was quite willing to go along with this concept, as was Biddle, who replaced Bliss. But General March, who became Chief of Staff in March 1918, certainly did not. Much of the friction which resulted between Pershing and March was simply an attempt on the part of the latter to regain prerogatives that he felt had been unwarrantedly surrendered by his predecessors.[18]

In any event, Pershing's cables to the War Department during this period were a long litany of remonstrances about lack of secrecy, lack of information, lack of key men and material, false priorities, deficient material, and lack of planning. In one instance he actually compared the snafus to those during the Spanish-American War.[19]

For example, despite repeated requests to stop, the War Department continued to give information of troop sailings to the French before it did to Pershing, sometimes by as much as a week. It was "SECRET," of course, but in France little was secret. "Such methods do not command respect of . . . Allies and embarrass us in our dealings with them," Pershing warned.[20]

On the other hand, frequently no information from the War Department was forthcoming at all, directly or indirectly. Cables remained unanswered; letters received no reply. On June 27 Pershing requested certain draftsmen and specialists. Two months later he had heard no word about them.[21]

Without answers to cables and letters, it was impossible to plan, the AEF not knowing whether requests had been disapproved, approved but modified, or accepted in toto. Everything was at sixes and sevens; no one knew where he stood. Back in July Pershing had fired off a cable which said bluntly: "Delay answers my cables makes almost impossible necessary arrangements here. Must have immediate answers my numbers, 3, 4, 6, 10, 11, 16, 18, 20, 22, 24, 25, 26, 27, 28, and 29."[22]

So frustrated was Pershing by his inability to get answers to his cables (even a negative answer would be better than none) that on September 12 he sent a test cable dated 4:00 P.M., requesting a report on its exact time of arrival and also the exact time when the reply was filed. Back came the answer: Pershing's cable had arrived the next morning at 9:53 A.M. Washington's reply was dated one day later. The delay then was not in transmitting the cables, but in doing something about them after they arrived.[23]

Col. Harry Taylor, AEF Chief Engineer Officer, predicted catastrophe unless the War Department speeded up shipment of his equipment. One engineer regiment had no steam shovels, no pile drivers, and no other tools suitable for heavy work, although recommendations for them had been made on June 12, even before Pershing arrived in France. Taylor's men were supposed to move some 400,000 yards of fill and 75,000 of rock cut, construct a trestle 60 feet high and 600 feet long, build docks and then lay 80–100 miles of railroad track connecting the docks to the main lines. But they couldn't do such things with wheelbarrows and step-ladders. Knowing that pile drivers and steam shovels were absolutely necessary, Taylor cabled Washington: "Unless they are promptly sent my entire plans for port development will be upset. The effect of leaving us without proper ports cannot be realized in the United States. I can say that it will be nothing less than absolute disaster."[24]

So it went along the line—an insistent, repeated demand for equipment and workers of all kinds to build and maintain the line of communications necessary to support the combat divisions when they arrived. Pershing's Chief Quartermaster had only one stenographer in his supply division; he cabled for seventy-five more immediately and for another hundred during the next two months.[25]

Things were getting so bad that Hugh Drum, who was working on logistics, feared that troop shipments would have to be halted until sufficient labor troops were sent to build up the line of communications. In an unguarded moment, Assistant Secretary of War William M. Ingraham told newsmen in October that troops shipments *had* ceased. They would not be resumed, he said, "until they can be adequately cared for with supplies."[26]

Even when supplies arrived, they were frequently defective, useless, delayed, or packed haphazardly. The early gas masks were "faulty in almost every detail," said Pershing. One-third of the small arms ammunition sent prior to September was defective. When a division quartermaster opened a box of men's underwear, he was shocked to discover twelve dozen infants' nightshirts! In a consignment of rubber boots he found ladies or misses sizes—and small sizes at that. Engineers arrived without tools, wagons without wheels, trucks without motors, mules without harness. Frequently supplies arrived without proper identification, resulting in confusion, complication of records, and delay in distribution. Pershing was forced to give rather elementary instructions to supply departments as to how to label shipments.[27]

Some snafus would have been funny had the situation not been so serious. As it was, they were tragic. One ship arrived loaded with shavings for a cold storage plant, shavings which could easily have been obtained in abundance from the sawmills of France. Another carried 800 tons of sand for ballast on its return trip to America and then, instead of dumping it, brought it back to France again.

Exclaimed Harbord: "In the whole world just now, from our standpoint, there is no material thing or entity so valuable as shipping space to bring over material, men and munitions. . . . Think of the shoes, the toothpaste, cartridges, socks, etc., etc., crowded out by that 800 tons of French sand. Wow-wow, and then wow!!!!!!!!!"[28]

The worst abuse was summed up in a Pershing cable: "Recommend no further shipments be made of following articles. . . . Bath bricks, book cases, bath tubs, cabinets for blanks, chairs except folding chairs, cuspidors, office desks, floor wax, hose except fire hose, step ladders, lawn mowers, refrigerators, safes except iron field safes, settees, sickles, stools, window shades."[29]

But perhaps even this was topped when a shipment of seventy-foot piles arrived for a dock at Bordeaux. Those loaded on the deck were fine. Those in the hold had been cut into twenty and fifty foot lengths in order to stow them for the trip![30]

Describing what must have been in Pershing's mind, the war correspondent Frederick Palmer said, "Sometimes we thought of the effort in America as the effort of some gigantic piston hardly fast to its moorings, walloping about, as it drove through a tiny orifice what seemed driblets of supplies for us considering our vast requirements."[31]

Not surprisingly, Pershing blamed the War Department for these incredible snafus, mentioning them in his memoirs. In retrospect it seemed to him that there was "considerable lack of enthusiasm about the war" for the first six or eight months. Congress, for example, did not pass the appropriation bill for the Army until June 15, over two months after war been declared. And as late as July 1, only sixty-four officers were on General Staff duty in Washington.[32]

Not all the fault, however, rested with the War Department. It had, after all, been set up for a smaller operation: the workings of a peacetime army of some 125,000 men. Pouring the business of an army of two million through the neck of a bottle built for 125,000 was bound to result in some jamming.

Then too, even with an adequate, smoothly functioning system, operations under pressure made errors inevitable. (Washington was eventually handling 120,000 separate classifications of goods.) What War Department officers from the top down resented when Pershing published his memoirs was his repeated reiteration of foul-ups, almost as if they were typical of daily War Department work. "He saw his own problems," commented Secretary Baker, "but seems wholly to have failed to grasp ours."[33]

Some of Pershing's urgent requests were impossible to fulfill. He demanded priority shipment of badly needed piling for dock construction, then complained when a ship arrived loaded partly with piling, partly with other goods. "You can't load a given ship, which happens to be the only one available, with nothing but piling . . . ," explained a loading officer. "There are fixed hold spaces, and there are laws of bouyancy, so that a chief stevedore is restricted both as to the bulk and weight in his labors. His ship must be trim and it must have bouyancy if it is going to reach the other side. . . . Some of the requests sent over were literally impossible of exact fulfillment. . . ."[34]

Pershing's own AEF was responsible for some of the confusion in the War Department. Changes in requirements overseas dislocated planning at home, throwing programs out of gear and causing delays during retooling. Gantry cranes and horse boats were ordered, cancelled, then reordered—Pershing's cables leaving in their wake frustration and bewilderment. In July, with production ready to go on an eight-cylinder Liberty motor, Pershing cabled for a twelve-cylinder one instead. After American industry retooled and got set up, Pershing changed back to the eight-cylinder motor the following May.[35]

It was not always possible for units to arrive with transportation, a fact that Pershing should have known. Troop transports differ from cargo and animal transports. The War Department's efforts to send them simultaneously met inevitable delays because of the unavailability of proper ships. Pershing was partly responsible, because in July he had cabled that the French would furnish approximately seven thousand horses and mules, causing the War Department to temporarily suspend shipment of animals with units going abroad. Later Pershing cabled that the French could not furnish the animals after all. By this time the animal transports had been converted into cargo carriers and were en route to Europe. It was now necessary to find new ships, convert them into animal transports, and outfit them with guns— all of which took time, especially because of the crowded condition of the shipyards and the urgent demand of the Navy for ships of its own. Not until November was animal shipment resumed.[36]

The badly overworked Chief of Embarkation, Brig. Gen. Chauncey B. Baker, Pershing's West Point classmate, certainly desired to help his friend in any way he could. On September 26 he made the quite reasonable request that future complaints about inefficient ship loading include "specific information" to aid in fixing responsibility. Despite this, Pershing on October 10 complained of abuses without giving the names of ships or the dates of arrival. Such indiscriminate general criticism without specific facts was useless. As Bliss told Pershing: "To make satisfactory investigation of a specific case here we must know name of transport and time of arrival. Whenever I can fasten the facts on responsible parties they will be dismissed."[37]

In his memoirs Pershing excoriated those who shipped the lawn mowers, cuspidors, and floor wax, saying: "I have often wondered what manner of man was responsible for shipping such things, . . . thereby wasting tonnage, when winter clothing, building material, steel and any number of real necessities were being delayed."[38]

Part of the problem probably lay with AEF officials. In all probability the items listed were part of a routine list of commodities habitually supplied to a peacetime garrison. Some dozing AEF quartermaster probably requisitioned "Table of Supplies Number X," without bothering to check out what it included. This could easily happen, particularly in the hectic early days of the AEF, with everyone working a seven-day week and having too much to do. Much of the blame belonged in the AEF, not in the War Department, where Pershing placed it. Furthermore, as newspaperman Mark Watson noted, many Washington staff officers were understandably irritated "that this trifling piece of stupidity should be recorded as a typical thing rather than a single episode in the shipping of five million tons of munitions."[39]

Especially when one of the cuspidors complained of ended up doing duty beside Pershing's desk![40]

SIX

Into the Lines

(October 1917)

A T VARIOUS TIMES in October some fifteen major generals visited Europe as part of Secretary Baker's program to familiarize them with modern battle conditions so that they might better train their divisions on return to the United States. Touring the front lines and observing training and combat work, they spent thirty days overseas: twelve with the British, twelve with the French, and six with the AEF.[1]

Pershing met each general and stressed that training back home should concentrate on discipline, the use of the rifle, and instruction in open warfare. He later wrote a bad report on virtually all of them: "in bad shape," "should not be returned," "too old," "infirm," "very fat and inactive," "could not begin to stand the strain." None should be sent over, he said, unless "entirely fit."[2]

One exception was Maj. Gen. Hunter Liggett, one of the most respected men in the American Army. A graduate of West Point ('79), Liggett had commanded combat troops, officered a brigade, and commanded the Philippine Department. He had been associated with the Army War College as student, faculty member, and president. Level-headed, imperturbable in crisis, a student of military history, unselfish and loyal, Liggett was a good soldier.[3]

His only trouble was that he didn't look like one. Fat and dumpy, he resembled Colonel Blimp. He was also sixty, considerably over the age Pershing recommended for division commanders. A British general thought him "very much too old" for such command. Pershing recognized his abilities, however, and decided to keep him in Europe. In January he appointed Liggett commander of I Corps where less physical exertion was demanded than in a divisional command.[4]

On October 3 Pershing again inspected the 1st Division. Maj. Theodore Roosevelt, Jr., the former president's son and a battalion commander of the 26th Infantry, demonstrated a method of attacking an entrenched enemy, after which Pershing called on General Sibert for a critique. Sibert fumbled badly. So did one of his junior officers. At this point Pershing blew up and "just gave everybody hell," particularly Sibert, dressing him down in front of his own officers. When the division's chief of staff also gave evasive answers about matters he should have known, Pershing cut him off with a gesture of contempt and turned on his heel to leave.

Captain Marshall, who had come over with the division and who was loyal to Sibert, became visibly angry. Perhaps he remembered the miserable review of September 6, in large part due to his having selected unsuitable ground the night before, for which Sibert was blamed the following day. He knew that the chief of staff could not be expected to be up on facts, having recently arrived with the division, so he began an explanation. When Pershing, unwilling to listen, turned away, Marshall put his hand on his arm.

"General Pershing, there's something to be said here and I think I should say it because I've been here longest."

Pershing stopped and Marshall, in white heat, poured out a torrent of words, speaking animatedly, horrifying bystanders who watched him destroying his military career. When he finished, Pershing looked at him thoughtfully, then walked away. "You must appreciate the troubles we have," he said, ending the discussion.

Still angry, Marshall fired back: "Yes, General, but we have them every day and they have to be solved before night."

Marshall's friends expected him to be "fired right off," but he was not. On the contrary, when Pershing visited the 1st Division subsequently he often took Marshall aside and asked him about things. The general had that rarest of qualities: the ability to take honest criticism, to profit by it, and not to hold a grudge afterwards. Said Marshall: "He could listen to more opposition to his apparent view . . . and show less personal feeling than anyone I have ever seen. . . . He was the most outstanding example of a man with complete tolerance . . . , regardless of what his own personal opinions seemed to be. In that quality lay a great part of his strength."[5]

While Marshall took a step up in Pershing's estimation on this occasion, Sibert certainly did not. Pershing jotted down a devastating critique: "Sibert: slow of speech and of thought. . . . Slovenly in dress, has an eye to his personal interests. Without any ability as a soldier. Utterly hopeless as an instructor or as a tactician. Fails to appreciate soldierly qualities, possessing none himself. Loyal as far as it suits his purpose. Opinionated withal and difficult to teach. Has a very high opinion of his own worth but doesn't show that side to the casual observer."[6]

The following day, October 4, Pershing wrote a confidential letter to Secretary Baker. "I fear that we have some general officers who have neither the experience, the energy, nor the aggressive spirit to prepare their units or to handle them under battle conditions as they exist to-day." He enclosed a confidential memorandum, specifying which generals he had in mind. Sibert led the list.[7]

Besides Sibert, Pershing listed ten other generals he considered unfit for one reason or another. "All such should be kept at home," he told Bliss. "I cannot impress this upon you too strongly, General, and I hope you will aid me in getting the very best men for these jobs. . . ."[8]

Despite this, nine out of the ten (including the celebrated Leonard Wood) were sent to Europe that fall and winter. Three of them were already on the high seas when Pershing wrote in October, but he must have wondered about the sending of the six others. Maj. Gen. William A. Mann, for example, was virtually inactive when his 42d Division arrived in November. He had to be relieved the following month.[9]

Meanwhile, Congress had done something to make Pershing's rank more comparable to that of European commanders. Haig, Joffre, and Hindenburg were all field marshals, whereas the AEF commander wore only two stars, the rank of numerous division commanders in Europe. America had no field marshal, but on October 6 it gave Pershing its highest rank: full general (four stars) "for the period of the existing emergency only." Bliss, as Chief of Staff, was given the same temporary rank.

Acknowledging congratulations, Pershing wrote his sister that such honors "only increase one's responsibilities and make one feel more and more the weight of them. However, I am well and strong and working like a Trojan. . . ."[10]

On October 21 American soldiers entered the front-line trenches for the first time. Each regiment of the 1st Division sent one of its battalions for a ten-day tour with a French division in the Sommerviller Sector, a quiet area east of Nancy, in which there had been little action since 1914. American captains controlled their companies, but American battalion and regimental commanders were there only as observers.[11]

Late October can be cold in France, especially in the driving rain the 1st Division encountered when it was still in summer uniform. Pershing had sent no less than six cables concerning winter clothing and blankets, but the last he had heard was a War Department cable disallowing his initial requisition and drastically reducing subsequent allotments on the ground that such goods were needed to supply troops in the United States. "Weather conditions in France are far more severe than in southern part of United States," he cabled back in exasperation, "and zero weather frequent during the winter. Practically no winter clothing now in depots in France and troops not supplied."[12]

On October 23 the French launched the second of their two limited offenses undertaken since the Nivelle disaster of April. Directed against Fort Malmaison and the Chemin des Dames, it was a set-piece attack which depended on a tremendous concentration of artillery. For six days and nights French guns, one for every five yards, plowed and replowed the ground, reducing Fort Malmaison to rubble. French infantry then easily overcame the dazed German defenders, capturing 10,000 prisoners at a very low cost to themselves. Historian Correlli Barnett put it well when he called it a "clear-cut small victory: neat and compact and satisfying as a gift package; indeed a gift to cheer a tired and discouraged country." It was of little strategic importance, but it did provide a needed boost to morale.[13]

The Allies needed all the boost they could get, because the following day the Central Powers more than offset the French victory at Malmaison. Using tactics developed by General Oskar von Hutier at Riga the previous September, Austrian forces, supported by seven picked German divisions, ruptured the Italian lines at Caporetto, wiped out all the Italian gains of the war, advanced sixty miles, and took 300,000 prisoners, 3,000 artillery pieces, and immense stores of supplies.[14]

Hutier's tactics were the exact opposite of the French's at Malmaison. Instead of a long preliminary bombardment which announced what was coming, Hutier restored surprise to the battlefield. A short, violent bombardment, which included the use of smoke and gas, preceded the assault by picked combat teams, which were brought up by night marches and secretly concentrated toward the front. Heavily armed with machine guns, heavy grenades, and satchel charges, and trained to great audacity and boldness, they disregarded any attempt to keep their lines straight, but probed for weak places which they then penetrated. Assaulting machine gun nests from behind, under cover of the gas and smoke, they shot up flares to indicate where paths had been cleared through the defenses. Through these gaps waiting infantry poured, then fanned out to exploit the attack from flank and rear. Meanwhile, the storm troopers went on ahead to repeat the procedure against the next line of defenses.

In terms of images, Hutier's tactic was not like a closed fist, pushing with equal force against all parts of a line. It was like an open hand, the fingers spread out and encased in steel, probing and pushing their way into a soft substance, periodically closing and crushing out a segment of it.[15]

While demonstrating the success of Hutier's tactics, Caporetto also revealed the built-in limitation of any breakthrough. The problem was logistical. The farther the advance got from its initial line, the more difficult it became to supply it with food, ammunition, and artillery to keep it going. It was like a giant machine beating progressively on fewer cylinders. Inevitably it simply slowed and ground to a halt. On November 10 the Italians finally made a stand behind the Piave River, their front stiffened by five British and six French divisions sent to their aid.[16]

Hutier's method would, however, be used again successfully in the great German offensives of 1918—in March, April, May, and June. In July it would meet its match in Pétain's defensive arrangements: a very lightly held (false) front line, with the main line of resistance considerably to the rear, sometimes miles back. This capitalized on the built-in logistical problem of the offense, bogging it down before it could reach and tear open the real front.

While a disaster of the first magnitude, Caporetto had a few bright spots. French and British aid to Italy pointed up the need for inter-Allied cooperation. The Allies must hang together or they would all hang separately. From this catastrophe, and from the one which later befell the British in March, would come a surrender of national pride sufficient to result in the appointment of a supreme commander for all the Allies. Pershing was an early proponent of such inter-Allied cooperation.[17]

He believed that Hutier's success vindicated his own stress on open warfare. Vindicated too was his belief in the need to create an independent AEF transportation lifeline, as he saw existing rail facilities preempted by the British and French in their rush to get aid to Italy. Ane he was gratified that Dennis Nolan's intelligence section, recently given good marks by the British intelligence chief,

General Charteris, accurately predicted the Caporetto offensive—and this without an observer even being in Italy.[18]

Near the end of October Pershing made a five-day inspection trip of the Line of Communications. St. Nazaire, the principal port, was congested because the unfinished hull of the *Paris*, later one of the great ships of the French Line, cluttered up the harbor. Massive AEF efforts to get that hull removed during the war finally worked—one week before the armistice.[19]

Near Bordeaux Pershing saw what an excess of democracy can do to soldiers. A Russian brigade, serving on the French front at the time of the Russian Revolution, had gone Bolshevik, murdered some of its officers, and become so unreliable that the French had removed it from combat and confined it to a camp. Officers no longer had authority; everything was now decided by soldier committees which decided how much work to do, if any. Pershing called the camp "the vilest and most unsanitary place I have ever seen," and Patton related a French joke about how little could be expected of the Russians now:

"How far did the Russians retreat today?"

"Fourteen kilometers, and [they] will retreat the same tomorrow."

"How do you know?"

"That is as far as a tired German can walk."[20]

On the basis of what he saw on this inspection trip, Pershing decided to relieve the commander of the Line of Communications, Maj. Gen. Robert M. Blatchford. He put his old West Point classmate, Mason M. Patrick, temporarily in charge, while awaiting War Department approval to appoint Maj. Gen. Francis J. Kernan, commander of the 31st Division, then in France for a month's tour with other generals.[21]

Blatchford, a hard-working officer, was totally without experience in supply matters and quite unsuited to the work. To spare his feelings, Pershing called him into his office and pretended that he was simply returning him to line duty, an assignment he knew Blatchford desired. When Blatchford expressed regret that his work had not been better, Pershing rose, put his hand on the man's shoulder, and said, "Do not for a moment think that I am dissatisfied with your work; you have had a hard task and have done your job well and I thank you for it."[22]

After the war Blatchford believed that his reputation had been clouded by his relief as LOC commander. When he pushed the matter all the way up to the Secretary of War, Pershing, who was then Chief of Staff in Washington, wrote him:

"I have refrained from going into this because of my almost lifelong friendship for you and my reluctance to say anything that might be disagreeable. The truth is, however, that in the position to which you were assigned your services were not satisfactory and did not warrant your retention on the very important duty involved. . . . It might have been better to have advised you at the time."[23]

After ten days in the front-line trenches, the first battalions of the 1st Division came out. They had put their names in the record book: first gun fired, first man wounded, first prisoner captured (an orderly who wandered into their area by mistake). And they had no casualties.

These came very soon. During the night of November 2–3, the new battalions rotated in. It was dark and rainy. For several days the Germans had suspected that Americans occupied the trenches opposite them; this night they determined to find out.[24]

About three in the morning, the new battalions being in place less than six hours, the Germans unloosed a heavy box barrage on an isolated outpost occupied by a platoon of Company F, 16th Infantry Regiment (which had paraded in Paris on July 4). For about an hour shells rained down, cutting telephone wires leading back from the outpost and caving in communication trenches leading out to it. The barrage poured down on the outpost itself, forcing the defenders into their dugouts and shelters. Meanwhile, a raiding party of 213 officers and men from the 7th Bavarian Landwehr Regiment exploded bangalore torpedoes under the American barbed wire, blasting a hole sixty yards wide. The German barrage lifted as the raiders, outnumbering the outpost at least four to one, descended on it from two sides.

The next fifteen minutes was a wild melee of violence in which five Americans were wounded, twelve taken prisoner, and three killed: one was shot, one had his throat cut, and one had his skull bashed in.

As quickly as they had come, the raiders were gone. They had lost two dead, seven wounded, and one deserter. Said the leader of the raiding party: "The enemy was very good in hand to hand fighting. . . ." Nevertheless, the Americans were shaken. One who visited Company F later recalled their "agony of soul . . . evidenced in white, drawn faces and haunted eyes."[25]

The AEF had been bloodied. According to Henry Burke, who saw it, when Pershing received the news he wept.[26]

The French took charge of the funeral ceremony, sending a large military contingent headed by General Paul E. Bordeaux, in whose division the Americans were serving. He made an eloquent oration, so eloquent that George C. Marshall, Jr., paraphrased it thirty years later when, as Chairman of the American Battle Monuments Commission, he dedicated a memorial to the first Americans killed in France. Said General Bordeaux:

"We will, therefore, ask that the mortal remains of these young men be left here, be left to us forever. . . . The passerby will stop and uncover his head. The travelers of France, of the Allied countries, of America, the men of heart, who will come to visit our battlefield of Lorraine, will go out of the way to come here, to bring to these graves the tribute of their respect and of their gratefulness.

"Corporal Gresham, Private Enright, Private Hay, in the name of France, I thank you. God receive your souls. Farewell!"[27]

SEVEN

Bleak Prospects

(November 1917)

E VER SINCE HIS arrival in Europe, Pershing had been distressed by the lack of coordination between the Allies. "When one was attacking the other was usually standing still . . . ," he observed. "The Germans were thus left free to concentrate their reserves against the threatened point." The Allies badly needed a supreme commander to give over-all direction and unity to the war.[1]

But a supreme commander, a generalissimo, was out of the question in 1917. The French, contributing the largest number of combatants, would insist on a Frenchman, which the British would not tolerate. They still felt as they had in 1914 when Lord Kitchener told Sir John French, then commander of the British Expeditionary Force (BEF), "I wish you to distinctly understand that your command is an entirely independent one and that in no case will you place yourself under the orders of an Allied general."[2] It would take an utter disaster—the destruction of a British field army in March 1918—to alter this attitude.

A stopgap then was the Supreme War Council (SWC), formed after the Caporetto defeat at Rapallo, Italy, on November 7. Headed by the prime ministers of France, England, and Italy (America had no regular member since President Wilson could not attend), the SWC had for its mission "to watch over the general conduct of the war" and to coordinate military action on the western front. Its headquarters was at Versailles, where each nation had a permanent military representative.

While not enthusiastic over the creation of the SWC, Pershing did see it as a step in the right direction—toward unity of command, which he strongly believed in. For America's non-voting military representative, he recommended General Liggett, but the War Department appointed General Bliss, soon to retire as Chief of Staff. France's representative was General Ferdinand Foch, recently brought out of obscurity at Pétain's suggestion to become Chief of Staff, who had been rushed down to Italy after Caporetto with six French divisions. Italy's was General Luigi Cadorna, kicked upstairs after the Caporetto disaster when General Armando Diaz replaced him. England's was General Sir Henry Wilson.[3]

Tall and angular, with a face so ugly it looked as if it had been carved out of a gnarled tree, Wilson was a controversial figure. Considered by many a politician, he was as fluent in talk as Robertson and Haig, his rivals, were tongue-tied, and he enjoyed Lloyd George's confidence in a way that they did not. His appointment led many to believe that Lloyd George's purpose in forming the SWC was not just coordination of the war but a surreptitious effort to undercut the influence of Robertson and Haig. Both these generals were western front men, convinced that the war must be won there and not in peripheral efforts like Macedonia or Palestine, so dear to the prime minister's heart.[4]

In appointing Wilson as its military adviser to the SWC, the British government was actually creating a divided council for itself. The advisers of France, Italy, and America were all either their chiefs of staff or their deputies. Wilson was not. He could give advice totally at variance with that coming from Robertson. Instead of removing Robertson as Chief of the Imperial General Staff—a course sure to produce an uproar—Lloyd George chose the politically more acceptable course of leaving him in office and placing a rival as military adviser with the SWC, where he could undercut Robertson's positions. It was one reason, among others, why Harbord believed that the SWC had "infinite capacity for harm and . . . little utility for good." Critics called it the "Soviet" or the "Sanhedrin." Robertson, after limping along for a few months under this intolerable arrangement, resigned in February. Lloyd George immediately appointed Wilson as his successor.[5]

By November the AEF had four divisions in France: the 1st, 2d, 26th, and 42d. The first three were short 20,000 men. Since it was imperative to bring them up to full strength, it seemed logical to take the recently arrived 42d Division and break it up as replacements. General Mann, its commander, was unfit and scheduled soon to retire. It had not yet begun its training as a division, its artillery had not yet been assigned its material, and it was the only division of the four with complete personnel ready to feed into needy units. Accordingly, Fox Conner, Acting Chief of Operations, supported by Harbord, recommended classifying the 42d as a replacement division.[6]

The only trouble was, the 42d Division was Secretary Baker's personal creation. The previous summer he had remarked to Douglas MacArthur, who was on the War Department General Staff, that he "wished we had a division in which there were components from every State so that each State could take pride in the fact that some of its own boys were among the first to go." MacArthur suggested that many National Guard divisions had surplus units which might be joined together to form such a unit. When Baker added that he wanted them visually to cover the United States, MacArthur said, "Fine, that will stretch over the whole country like a rainbow." Thus was born the famous Rainbow Division. Maj. Gen. William A. Mann, Chief of the Militia Bureau, was enthusiastic about the project and became the division's first commander. MacArthur became its Chief of Staff.[7]

Arriving in France, however, the Rainbow found itself being cannibalized. Equipment, supplies, and clothing were taken from it to supply deficiencies in the

1st and 26th Divisions. Thirty-three of its finest officers, including the incomparable Summerall, destined to become a postwar Army Chief of Staff, were reassigned either to Chaumont or to other divisions. Mann and MacArthur protested vigorously, the latter going so far as to leak to newsman Herbert Corey a story which Chaumont subsequently killed.[8]

Officers at AEF headquarters knew that they had a hot potato on their hands. While a far from vigorous general, Mann was a very active politician with many influential friends in Washington because of his years there as Chief of the Militia Bureau. MacArthur had the respect of Secretary Baker and the ear of the press. The division itself, representing units from twenty-six different states and the District of Columbia, had received extensive publicity and acquired a widespread constituency concerned about its survival, not the least of which was one of its regiments, a rollicking group of New York Irishmen called "The Fighting 69th."[9]

To Chaumont, however, the 42d Division was a test case. By all the rules of logic, it should be the replacement division. If it was not, it would establish the precedent of allowing National Guard units special consideration, a policy fraught with danger. If National Guard units could not be used for replacements, then National Army units (those formed by the draft) must be. Since these were not expected in Europe for some time (the first did not arrive until April), AEF divisions would continue to be understaffed and underequipped. Fox Conner told Harbord that if they allowed the Rainbow to get away with their political maneuverings, it would become increasingly difficult to control National Guard divisions. There would not be one U.S. Army in Europe, but two.[10]

The Rainbow was indeed maneuvering. Mann, MacArthur, and others alerted influential friends back home, and before long the War Department received a barrage of letters and telegrams demanding that the division be saved. In Europe MacArthur collared Harbord, an old friend from Philippine days, and asked him personally to inspect the division and judge "whether such a splendid unit should be relegated to a replacement status."[11]

Harbord did and was impressed. He then drew up a list of reasons for Pershing, pro and con, about making the 42d a replacement unit. They were mostly con. Perhaps his most cogent reason was the last: "I much fear that if you used it for replacement without notice to the War Department that you would be reversed; on the other hand if you ask the War Department that you will not be permitted to do it." That settled the matter. Pershing designated the next division to arrive, the 41st (also National Guard troops) as the replacement unit. The Rainbow Division was saved. It became one of the best divisions in the AEF.

In general, however, Pershing had a low opinion of National Guard divisions, especially of their officers. In 1940 he remarked to Fox Conner that he had "not changed the opinion of these troops that I formed during the World War and since. To fit them for war will make it necessary to weed out a large number of worthless officers and to give those remaining considerable training. . . ."[12]

While the French limited themselves after the Nivelle offensive to two set-piece attacks, near Verdun in August and Fort Malmaison in October, the British were bogged down in the mud of Flanders in a disastrous campaign around Ypres which heaped up over 270,000 casualties. Surveying the terrain later, a British staff officer burst into tears and cried, "Good God, did we really send men to fight in that?"[13]

On November 20 Haig shifted his attention south and ruptured the German line in front of Cambrai. Omitting the usual long preliminary artillery bombardment and substituting an unusually heavy force of 300 tanks which ripped open the barbed wire and cleared out the machine gun nests, the British penetrated some four and one-half miles on a six-mile front. (Unfortunately, most of these gains were wiped out by a strong German counterattack ten days later.) Pershing, who was on the spot to observe the initial success of the British offensive, was much impressed. "An example to emulate," he said.[14]

The admiration was not mutual. Haig described Pershing as "a fine type of man, honest, . . . determined to do what he believes is right." But the British were concerned, not to say dismayed, by American slowness in making their presence felt on the western front. As one Britisher said, "You seem to be very deliberate."[15]

In truth, the American contribution to date had been minimal. On November 6 Fox Conner reported that none of the four U.S. divisions in France could be put into the front line other than for training purposes. Only one, the 1st Division, had been in the line at all thus far—and only part of it and then only in a quiet sector. In an emergency only the 1st Division could be used as a unit; the others would have to be thrown in "as a desperate measure" by battalions.[16]

What made this so depressing was the growing superiority of German forces on the western front. With Russia limping out of the war, German forces being transferred from the east would soon raise their strength in the west to perhaps 217 divisions. The most the Allies could muster was 169, exclusive of American strength which was decidedly weak.[17]

Back in July Pershing had asked for one million men in France by the following May, only to be told that the best that could be done was 650,000 men by mid-June. Now it appeared even that was not attainable. By using all possible facilities, American troops in France would number not more than 525,000 by May, including non-combat forces. Worse, having gotten them there, the United States lacked sufficient tonnage to supply and feed them. When Bliss mentioned this to Sir William Robertson, the latter "expressed grave apprehension."[18]

It was such facts which seriously concerned the Allies in the winter of 1917–1918, making them wonder if America realized the seriousness of the situation. "It is better that I should put the facts quite frankly to you," said Lloyd George on November 20 to a visiting American mission headed by Colonel Edward M. House, "*because there is a danger that you might think you can work your army up at leisure, and that it does not matter whether your troops are there in 1918 or 1919. But I want you to understand that it might make the most vital difference. . . .*"[19]

Bliss, who had come to Europe with the House Mission, realized the urgency of the situation. Even should shipping suddenly become available, it would take a full year to transport the force Pershing had in mind. So serious did Bliss consider the shipping problem that he felt the United States ought to calculate what tonnage it could furnish and ask the Allies to make up the difference. If they could not, then it made no sense to continue the war. On shipping hinged the question of whether America had raised an army at enormous expense, which was doomed never to cross the ocean in time.[20]

On November 15 Pershing stressed his desperate situation in identical messages sent to both the Secretary of War and the Chief of Staff: "It should be no longer a question of how much tonnage can be spared for military purposes, but only the most imperative necessity should permit its use for any other purpose."[21]

Meanwhile, even with existing shipping, the problems mounted, congestion threatening to ensnarl the AEF in one gigantic traffic jam, leaving it helplessly immobile. Material for constructing and operating the docks, repeatedly requested, had not arrived. Even ordinary things like ropes, cables, chains, and nets were in short supply, so that only two out of three, or three out of four hatches could be unloaded at a time. Transports were stacked up twenty-eight deep in St. Nazaire.

Because of such congestion, some troops were landed in England, but this in turn required finding ships to shuttle and convoy them across the channel, and French railway cars to move them out of crowded ports like Le Havre, Cherbourg, and Brest. But railroad cars were in short supply. Many were being used to ship men and material to Italy. Others, because of a hopelessly antiquated French railway system, were sitting on sidings all over the land without anyone knowing where they were. Thousands more stood idle for want of repairs.[22]

French officials, each a petty lord jealous of his domain, constantly laid obstacles in the movement of supplies. So bad was the situation, especially at St. Nazaire, which Pershing called "truly alarming," that he eventually addressed a personal letter to Clemenceau, now prime minister, asking that St. Nazaire, Bordeaux, and La Pallice be placed in "état de siège."[23]

But not all blame was on the French. Pershing complained that troops from the United States were still being sent without adequate transportation, or with none at all. Ships were still loading under 50 percent of capacity, and not loading well. For example, quartermaster supplies were packed on top of troop baggage, making it necessary for troops to stay on board the ships upon landing until the supplies were unloaded. "It is a mess . . . ," reported Brig. Gen. Mason M. Patrick, interim chief of the LOC. "Fool work in New York apparently."[24]

Shortages were developing everywhere. Although the French had promised to supply artillery ammunition, they now reneged because of America's failure to furnish the raw materials for making it. Pershing, who had considered the French allotment a temporary expedient until America could produce her own ammunition, was thunderstruck to receive a War Department cable in late October which said, "The French government must furnish it, for there is no other way of getting it. At the present time there is not in this country any actual output of ammunition of the types mentioned." The types mentioned were the 75-mm and 155-mm shells, the mainstay of divisional artillery. Pershing considered this "entirely inexcusable."[25]

So bad was the supply situation becoming that a board which had been convened to study troop movements said ominously, "It is a matter for examination and decision whether the flow of troops should not be checked until adequate supply arrangements have been made."[26]

Supply shortages overseas were paralleled by those at home. Camp Sherman at Chillicothe, Ohio, was short five thousand overcoats on a bitterly cold winter day. Camp Funston, Kansas, where Leonard Wood was training the 89th Division, had not a single modern rifle or field artillery piece. Without uniforms, the men trained in overalls, using wooden sticks to simulate guns.[27]

From all over the country came a rising tide of complaints about mix-ups, delays, snafus, incompetence, and inadequacies. So great was the uproar that in mid-December Congress launched an investigation, summoning camp commanders to testify about conditions. After hearing a recital of horror stories, Sen. George E. Chamberlain, the Democratic chairman of the investigating committee, dramatically summarized the findings: "The Military Establishment of America has fallen down . . . ," he said. "It has almost stopped functioning . . . because of inefficiency in every bureau and every department. . . ."[28]

Valley Forge

(December 1917)

WITH SOME TRUTH Frederick Palmer called the winter of 1917–1918 the Valley Forge of the AEF. A bitter cold, sharp and piercing, penetrated to the bone, with temperatures as low as seven below zero at Chaumont and still lower at the front near Verdun. In one of the worst winters France could remember, soldiers in inadequate clothing wrapped their feet in burlap and left trails of blood in the snow.[1]

Animals in the 1st Division, without forage, chewed up their rope and leather halters, and even gnawed at the wood of their stalls. During a maneuver so many of them dropped dead from exhaustion that it had to be called off.[2]

One division, spread out over an area five miles wide and ten long, had only two motor trucks to supply it. Like prisoners in a chain gang, infantrymen trudged the roads, carrying on their backs sacks filled with rock needed to prepare billets.[3]

Men never forgot that terrible winter. Which was worse: the awful cold which came through nicks and crannies of the barnyard billets, piercing summer uniforms? Or the heavy fetid air, pungent with the smell of unwashed bodies, of livestock milling about below, and of manure piles, dank and wet?[4]

Doughboys felt it only natural that Joan of Arc had come from Lorraine; she had been bred to fortitude by the climate. One soldier commented as he climbed into a chilly hayloft for the night, "I'd like to be a cloth and be wrapped around a steam-pipe until spring." An officer, shivering after bathing with cold water in a cold room, declared that he was not going to bathe again until he had blue mold on his back.[5]

Pershing was deeply concerned about these conditions and about the welfare of the men. As he traveled through village after village and saw men standing at attention, he asked himself, "What's behind their salute? What do they think? How do they feel?"

He discovered that Corinna Lindon Smith, who had come to France with her husband to do relief work among French children, had spent ten days in the Gondrecourt area talking with troops in their off-duty hours. "He fired inquiries at me about conditions affecting their comfort," she recalled, "insisting that I be frank and omit none of the bad spots. Had the rolling kitchens arrived? Was the food well cooked and served hot? Were the billets as bad as reported in parts of the Gondrecourt district? How about the bunks in the barracks?"

Pershing listened attentively as Mrs. Smith reported. "Inadequate planning," he commented, concerning food shortages. "Why did not someone tell me that fact?" he asked, concerning poor shelter. His jaw set, he determined to correct abuses and not wait for army red tape to "burn up from spontaneous combustion."[6]

Christmas was a feast of mixed emotions. "It was a pretty gloomy time and many of the men were homesick," a doughboy remembered. At Chaumont, Pershing celebrated with Harbord and the GHQ staff. After dinner an aide played a few rags on the piano, while Pershing and Collins tried to dance to them.[7]

A few days later, at Harbord's suggestion that the Belgians were a little "wobbly" (as disgusted with their Allies as the latter were with them) and that a visit would be good public relations, Pershing journeyed to Adinkerke to see King Albert. Unfortunately, the train arrived ten minutes early, catching Pershing only partly dressed. "General, we have arrived," announced his aide, Carl Boyd.

"I knew it only too well," Pershing said, "as the train had stopped and the royal band outside was playing the *Star Spangled Banner* in the usual mournful cadence common to foreign bands. . . . In another minute, when the orderly and I were struggling, this time with the left boot, Boyd again appeared and said in a stage whisper that was no doubt heard by the entire escort outside, 'Sir, the King is out there standing at the salute.'

"That was too much, the humor of the situation overcame me, and for an instant all of us, including the orderly, who rarely smiled, were convulsed with laughter. That did not help matters, of course, and meanwhile the band outside, which had already played the national air through three times, was dolefully beginning on the fourth, when I hurriedly descended the steps of my car opposite His Majesty, buttoning my overcoat with one hand and saluting with the other. At my appearance the band started afresh and, as though they had just begun, ran through our national anthem rather more vigorously, cheered up no doubt at last to see me in evidence."

Lunch with the king started stiffly, remembered Pershing, but later became relaxed, even gay, "especially when I became bold enough to air my dreadful French."[8]

In December Pershing decided that the time had come to relieve General Sibert. The 1st Division commander lacked the necessary push to make his unit the model division Pershing wanted it to be. As second senior officer in France, he might take over if anything happened to Pershing, putting the AEF in the hands of a man virtually without experience in commanding troops.[9]

Sibert probably knew that the ax was coming, but resented very much the way it fell. On December 13 Pershing issued a strongly worded letter against pessimism, based on information which had reached him from certain Americans visiting the training areas. They had reported "deep pessimism," "apprehension of undue hardships," "belief in the impregnability of [German] lines," and a feeling that the war was already lost. Such an attitude, said Pershing, "marks an unfitness for command of such an officer" and "it will constitute grounds for his removal without application." He sent a copy to Sibert and the following day relieved him.[10]

Actually the message was addressed not so much to Sibert as to Maj. Gen. Clarence Edwards, commander of the 26th Division, who received the same letter. Perhaps, having already decided to relieve Sibert, Pershing thought to throw the fear of the Lord into Edwards by writing identical letters to both men and then relieving one. If so, he was wrong. Whatever Sibert's deficiencies, he was no defeatist and should not have been tarred with a brush designed for Edwards. He was a capable officer who, on his return to the United States, did good work as director of the Chemical Warfare Service. Captain George C. Marshall, Jr., considered the relief unjust. Pershing's staff, he felt, was trying to outdo him in severity, without even knowing "what they were being severe about."[11]

As Sibert's replacement Pershing picked Maj. Gen. Robert Lee Bullard, a lean, tough Alabaman whom he had known at West Point as a cadet, at Fort Wingate, New Mexico, and in the Philippine Islands. Not a brilliant man, he was nonetheless endowed with hard common sense and a fighting spirit. Immediately on taking command he urged his officers to instill the spirit of hate in their men. The "watchword must be *kill, kill*, KILL the Boche," he said.[12]

Bullard did not particularly admire Pershing, considering him a little weak. When in November Pershing confided his intention to relieve Sibert, Bullard wrote in his diary, "Gen. Pershing is hardly strong enough to do this." "I don't believe [he] has the force. . . ." Recalling Pershing's conciliatory measures in the Philippines and the great lengths he went to avoid combat, Bullard wrote on December 3: "General Pershing is not a fighter; he is in all his history a pacifist and, unless driven thereto by the A.E.F., will do no fighting in France for many a day."[13]

Bullard misjudged his man, as he himself admitted later. Pershing had more iron in his soul than the Alabaman imagined. He also put the fear of God into Bullard, who wrote in his diary two weeks after assuming command: "He is looking for results. He intends to have them. He will sacrifice any man who does not bring them."[14]

By late December Generals Sibert, Mann, and Blatchford had all been sent home. Two out of four division commanders and the commanding general of the LOC were thus victims of Pershing's drive "for results."[15]

December was a bad month for the Allies. Russia was out of the war; enemy divisions from that front would soon be transferred to the west, giving Germany, according to the latest calculations, a possible 60 percent advantage in manpower. Italy was still reeling after Caporetto. England had just ended the disastrous campaign of Ypres and Passchendaele; her armies numbered 200,000 less than the year before. France, recovering from the Nivelle failure and the spring mutinies, had reached her manpower limit and was starting to break up battalions to keep up existing units.[16]

"We must wait for the Americans," Pétain had said. But where were they? Nine months after declaring war America had only 175,000 troops in France, including no more than four combat divisions in various stages of training. Canada, with a tenth of America's resources, had placed a division in line within six months and a corps in a little over a year. The Anzacs had sent two divisions to the Gallipoli campaign after eight months.[17]

"Do you yankees really want to know what Englishmen are saying about you at this moment?" said a British journalist to an American intelligence officer. "Well, it is this—that after more than eight months of being in the war, you haven't really fired a damned shot! When are you going to do something? It is all very well, this great help you're giving us, and the things you say you are going to do. But when is something actually to be done in the fighting line?"[18]

The French felt the same; some called the Americans boy scouts. "We expected to see two million cowboys throw themselves upon the Boches and we see only a few thousand workers building warehouses," they said. When an American accidentally ran over a Parisian with his automobile, the French jeered that the Americans were killing Frenchmen sooner than they were Germans. A disillusioned Clemenceau said that Pershing's "principal preoccupation" seemed to be to have dinner in Paris.[19]

In December, then, began in earnest what perhaps had never been far from Allied thoughts: attempts to amalgamate small American units into British and French ranks. There was much to be said for the idea. The Allies had the existing staffs for divisions, corps, and field armies; they lacked men to fill the units. America had the men, but lacked the higher organizations, and by the time she created them the war might well be lost under the massive German assaults anticipated for the spring and summer of 1918. The Allies may have been divided on many things, but they were united in believing they would fail unless American manpower were fed into their ranks, and soon.[20]

As far as the Allies were concerned, amalgamation—at least temporarily— made sense, even from the viewpoint of the AEF. Raw recruits would train better and faster if associated with veterans; consequently American casualties would be lower. Amalgamation would also eliminate the need to develop AEF higher staffs; hence America's weight could more quickly be brought to bear and the war ended sooner, which was to America's interest. Finally, amalgamation would relieve the tonnage problem, since it would not be necessary for the United States to bring over support troops (about 45 percent of the existing AEF was that) and impedimenta to sustain full divisions, corps, and armies.[21]

Always, in treating of amalgamation, the Allies spoke of an *eventual* American Army. Only for the present, only *pro tem*, would smaller units be trained and fought in larger Allied units. Later, after they were "bloodied" and proficient, American regiments would be gathered into their own divisions, American divisions into their own corps, and American corps into their own army. The advantage of this was that it was organic; it permitted the development of larger American units after they had grown to proficiency as smaller ones. In the meantime they would have the benefit of Allied tutelage and experience. How much better this would be, they contended, than for Pershing to commit a whole American army, virtually untried and untested, to a separate portion of the front. The Germans would surely tear it apart.

These were good arguments, irrefutable in the eyes of the Allies. Even so staunch a Pershing partisan as Harbord admitted that, were he French or English, "my views on amalgamation would have been the same as theirs."[22]

Pershing himself admitted that, had massive German offensives occurred during the fall and winter of 1917, instead of during the following spring and summer, he would have had no choice but to accede to amalgamation. But he was always suspicious of Allied talk about a separate and independent American army in the future, while clamoring for immediate amalgamation in the present. Such talk he considered so much "camouflage," "a downright piece of impudence." He observed that, with rare exceptions, the British had never thought to amalgamate Australians, Canadians, or Indians into British units; nor had the French attempted it with their Senegalese, Moroccans, or other colonials.[23]

The Allies might point out, however, that the Canadians and Australians had had time—three years of war—to develop their organizations organically. Furthermore, in their formation and development they had not been confronted with the crisis that loomed up now on the western front: a projected 60 percent manpower disadvantage during the coming German offensives.[24]

On the other hand, as Pershing continually pointed out, there were strong arguments against amalgamation: national pride, language difficulties in serving with the French, Irish-American antipathy regarding associating with the British, the downplaying of America's role in the war and the subsequent peace conference by having no army of her own in the field, and inevitable recriminations if American casualties were run up under bungling Allied commanders. Everyone knew that French and British generals had piled up stacks of corpses. Marshal Joffre admitted that it took ten to fifteen thousand infantry casualties to train a major general. Lloyd George so distrusted Haig's ability that he deliberately kept men in England, lest the BEF commander throw their lives away in futile offenses like Passchendaele.[25]

Thus there was something to be said on both sides. The whole question was charged with emotion and continued to be agitated almost to the day of the armistice. Some people felt Pershing spent as much time fighting the Allies as he did the Germans.

Lloyd George began the amalgamation controversy by proposing on December 2 that the United States bring over surplus American companies or battalions for temporary incorporation into corresponding British units, with the understanding that after the emergency they could be recalled for American divisions. As surplus troops, their temporary incorporation would not interfere with American plans for forming a separate army.[26]

Having made the proposal, Lloyd George exerted considerable diplomatic pressure in Washington to make sure it was accepted. The Germans, he warned on December 15, were planning "a knockout blow to the Allies before a fully trained American Army is fit. . . ."[27]

Concerned, Secretary Baker talked the matter over with President Wilson and on December 18 cabled Pershing as follows: "We do not desire loss of identity of our forces but regard that as secondary to the meeting of any critical situation by the most helpful use possible of the troops at your command." This was Pershing's basic position also, although Lloyd George came to believe that the General, impervious to "intelligence and common sense," preferred to build a separate American Army even at the cost of losing the war.[28]

The crucial phrase in Baker's cablegram was "critical situation." How critical must a situation be, and who was to decide? The answer was: Pershing. Baker's cable gave him "full authority to use the forces at your command as you deem wise. . . ."[29]

In effect, then, the United States was placing in the hands of its field commander the ultimate decision as to whether to amalgamate and, if so, under what circumstances. The effect was to focus and bring to bear enormous pressures on Pershing, the Allies knowing that if he could be persuaded, cajoled, intimidated, or in some manner won over, the fight was won. Washington, feeling that Pershing was on the spot and knew the situation firsthand, would concur in his decision.

With the exception of Lord Northcliffe, a British newspaper publisher, and Marshal Joffre, a sidelined general, the Europeans presented a united front against Pershing on this question. Prime ministers, chiefs of staff, field commanders, ambassadors—all made their pressure felt during the ensuing months, attempting to wear him down.[30]

Pershing resisted them all, at times fighting a rearguard action as he was pushed back by force of circumstance, reluctantly yielding ground that he tried immediately thereafter to recapture. If American troops went into Allied ranks, "very few of them would ever come out," he predicted. Furthermore, "no people with a grain of national pride would consent to furnish men to build up the army of another nation." His basic stand, held unswervingly throughout the coming months, was summed up in the declaration: "We cannot permit our men to serve under another flag except in an extreme emergency and then only temporarily."[31]

He ran a great risk, for the Allies might well be right. Nobody maintained that the Americans were incapable, given time, of providing skilled generals and staffs. But time was what was lacking. An inexperienced, untrained American Army was a gamble and if the Germans tore it apart, as they were to do to experienced Allied armies in the coming months, the result could be disaster. Harbord well said of Pershing, "He risked the chance of being cursed to the latest generation if, through his failure to co-operate, the War were lost."[32]

Replying to Baker's December 18 cable on January 1, 1918, Pershing admitted that Allied clamor for American entry into the lines was "very persistent," but added: "Do not think emergency now exists that would warrant our putting companies or battalions into British or French divisions, and would not do so except in grave crisis." This was his basic position, maintained steadfastly in the months to come.[33]

His objections, both then and later, were the loss of national identity, the problem of reclaiming contingents without disrupting Allied divisions, language difficulties with the French, hard feelings if American casualties resulted from Allied mistakes, and differences in training methods.[34]

Nonetheless, Pershing did allow Pétain to have four black regiments which had arrived in France without their brigade and divisional organizations, on the understanding that they were to be returned when called for and formed into the U.S. 93d Division. They were never called for, serving throughout the war as parts of French divisions. Despite Pershing's talk about language difficulties, they did quite well and the French thought highly of them.

In June Pétain asked for eight more black regiments, but Pershing refused. "The colored regiments are composed of American citizens" he said, "and I do not feel warranted in employing them on any basis other than that followed in the case of white regiments."[35]

One black division, the 92d, was formed in the AEF, and participated in the Meuse-Argonne campaign in September. While three out of its four regiments did well, the 368th Infantry Regiment disintegrated in battle and ran away. The result was to stigmatize the generally good record that black troops made in the war.

Part of the 368th Infantry's difficulty was its white field officers, a racially prejudiced lot, who blamed the regiment's failure on its junior black officers. The debacle confirmed their prejudice that blacks were not ready to be officers. Pershing more or less agreed. "It would have been much wiser," he later wrote, "to have followed the long experience of our Regular Army and provided these colored units with selected white officers."[36]

Pershing's objection to the Allies' training methods concerned what he considered an excessive emphasis on trench rather than open warfare. Trench warfare was as the name implies: oriented toward the taking and holding of trenches. According to an AEF combat memorandum, it was "marked by uniform formations, the regulation of space and time by higher command down to the smallest details, absence of scouts preceding the first wave, fixed distances and intervals between units and individuals, voluminous orders, careful rehearsal, little initiative upon the part of the individual soldier."

Open warfare, in contrast, was "marked by scouts who precede the first wave, irregularity of formation, comparatively little regulation of space and time by the higher command, the greatest possible use of the infantry's own fire power to enable it to get forward, variable distances and intervals between units and individuals, use of every form of cover and accident of the ground during the advance, brief orders, and the greatest possible use of individual initiative by all troops engaged in the action."[37]

It was this open type of warfare for which Pershing felt Americans had a special genius and in which he wanted them trained, especially in America where vast spaces permitted sweeping movements. Trench warfare was frontal assault warfare, for limited objectives, and it had not moved the lines on the western front more than ten miles in either direction since late 1914, while heaping up casualties by the millions. Open warfare was fluid, flexible, oriented to the earth's surface rather than its bowels. With men trained to fight on the earth rather than within it, he hoped to break open the front and win the war. Victory could only be won, he maintained, "by driving the enemy out into the open and engaging him in a war of movement."[38]

The dispute over training methods was epitomized in the rifle. In trench warfare it was not that important, since artillery did the preliminary work, while grenades and satchel charges did the mopping up. Pershing actually heard of cases where French soldiers were so habituated to using grenades that, encountering the enemy in the open, they instinctively threw grenades at them, rather than shot.

In open warfare, however, the rifle was the weapon *par excellence*; as the infantrymen moved forward, they hugged the ground, isolated strong points, and killed at a distance. Significantly, French target ranges were short, under one hundred meters. Pershing insisted that Americans be trained to shoot up to at least six hundred meters. To him the rifle was the essential infantry weapon, and he complained repeatedly that it was not sufficiently stressed in training at home. A flow of "teach them to shoot straight" cables went to the War Department, followed by complaints that they were not being complied with.[39]

They were not, because French instructors, sent to the United States to aid in training, taught trench, not open, warfare, and the War Department deferred to their experience. An American assigned to translate French training documents said that he "never once saw any mention of open warfare." At Waco, Texas, after a month of instruction devoted exclusively to trench warfare, an American asked one of the French instructors, "How shall we know what to do if we should ever have the Germans on the run?"

"This war will be fought out in the trenches," was the reply; "in this respect, it has been different, and will be different, from all previous wars."[40]

From the French viewpoint, the Americans had a lot to learn. The Yanks, after all, had not even fired a shot in anger until October, and were surely foolish if they did not follow French instruction, based as it was on three years of hard-fought combat. "If the Americans do not permit the French to teach them," said Clemenceau ruefully, "the Germans will do so. . . ."[41]

When Colonel House passed through Paris in late November, Pétain let it be known, with a deprecating shrug of the shoulders and nod of the head, that he did not think American training was all it ought to be. Pershing "was a good man but narrow," he said. "Most of the help proffered by the French had been curtly refused." Later, when Pétain's headquarters issued a manual on the conduct of large-unit offensives, Pershing ordered it suppressed in the AEF.

Pershing found out about Pétain's going behind his back to House and resented it. He told the Frenchman that, if he had complaints, they should be brought directly and not tattled behind his back. Pétain apologized and said it would not happen again.[42]

Thus divided, America and the Allies entered the year 1918.

NINE

The Robertson Proposal

(January 1918)

ON JANUARY 18 the 1st Division, the only American unit which had thus far had any experience in the trenches (ten days by battalions in October-November), went back into the front lines. Unlike the previous occasion, when they had been interspersed with French companies and backed up by French artillery, now the division was going it alone. For the first time the AEF was actually taking over a sector of the front for which it was responsible. Pershing considered announcing the event in the press, but Pétain warned that this might invite a strong German raid and that it was better to leave the enemy in the dark.[1]

In a cold, chilling rain that turned to ice and sleet, the 1st Brigade relieved a French Moroccan division in the Ansauville sector on the south face of the St. Mihiel salient. The men were benumbed, frozen to the skin, drugged with fatigue during a grueling march in the cold over slippery roads. "As one in a trance, my legs moved . . . ," remembered one veteran.[2]

Although roughshod, mules could not get a footing on the ice and refused to move. Wagons slid down the slope from the crown of the road and tumbled into ditches, where they had to be unloaded, hauled out, and repacked by hand.

During the night, the ice melted, the Meuse River overflowed, and the men marched nearly a mile across land buried under one to two feet of water. Occasionally some doughboys unwittingly stepped off the highway and disappeared in water up to their necks. That night they slept in wet clothes, without fires, exhausted and miserable.[3]

Since 1914 this section of the front had been quiescent, both sides sending mauled divisions here for rest and recuperation. But the terrain was deplorable, awash with water and mud. Cold, wet, and clammy, the doughboys cursed the previous occupants who had urinated and defecated in the trenches. They soon picked up their body lice and shuddered at the rats.[4]

The French took no chances on the untried Americans, retaining tactical control of the sector for the first fifteen days. Communications got fouled up, prompting Pershing to call down Edgar Russel, AEF Chief Signal Officer, and "very positively" inform him that he was holding him responsible for communication efficiency "from the base ports to the barbed wire."[5]

It didn't take the Germans long to discover who was in the French trenches. Within a short time they raided a listening post, killing two, wounding two, and capturing one. Sometime later they ambushed an American patrol in no-man's land, killing four, wounding two, and capturing two. "I am trying to have our people pull off a raid," wrote Hugh Drum in his diary. "We must do something to insure their morale. This thing of letting the Boche do it all is getting on the nerves."[6]

Having carried the brunt of the war since the Nivelle disaster the previous spring, and having been fearfully bloodied, the British regarded the future with dark apprehension. Already they had been forced to reduce the strength of some infantry divisions by 25 percent, with prospects of even greater reductions later. The Germans now had twelve more divisions on the western front than the previous year; with Russia out of the war they could easily bring forty more by May. In contrast, the Allies had eleven fewer divisions.[7]

In these circumstances Sir William Robertson made an important proposal. Meeting with Pershing on January 9–10, he pointed out that the United States was raising forty-five divisions, of which four were already in France, and part of a fifth. She hoped to have fifteen overseas by midsummer and thirty by the end of the year. That left fifteen extra, and it was these fifteen that Robertson proposed to do something with, lest they sit idle until 1919, when the war might well be lost.

Robertson suggested that the Americans break up some of these surplus divisions, just as the British had done in 1915, and bring them over to serve as battalions in the BEF. Shipping would be provided by the British. (In Lloyd George's proposal the previous month the Americans presumably furnished the ships.) By diverting tonnage normally allocated for food, the British estimated they could bring over 150,000 men for 150 battalions. These would be trained by Americans and then fed into British brigades for combat. When seasoned, they would be gathered together as American brigades in British divisions and, still later, completely consolidated as full American divisions. Robertson pointed out that his proposal concerned only surplus American troops, and hence would not interfere with Pershing's plans to regularly bring over full American divisions.

When Pershing objected that, if shipping was available, it would be better to bring over full divisions, not just infantry battalions, Robertson pointed out that it was precisely infantry battalions which were needed now and that they could be brought over about five times as fast as full divisions, which required their artillery, support troops, transportation, and other impedimenta. The British were willing to run the risk of a possible food shortage to bring over critically needed infantrymen; they were not about to starve to bring over hordes of typists, supply clerks, and stevedores.[8]

Looking back on Robertson's proposal in 1931, Pershing saw it as an example of British selfishness:

"The arguments General Robertson advanced clearly indicated that the British were playing for advantage to themselves in offering to transport our troops. In other words, they had the shipping to transport American battalions on condition that they would serve in the British armies. Their purpose was to build up their own units instead of aiding the cause in general by augmenting the number of complete combat divisions on the western front.

"The question that naturally arose in my mind was that if tonnage was available for this purpose, why had it not been offered to us some time before. . . ."[9]

This was not a fair appraisal. A good case can be made that the urgent need in January 1918 was for infantry battalions to be fed into existing trained divisions as an emergency measure, rather than full divisions which, with their impedimenta, took five times as long to transport and even longer to train. It is quite understandable that the British government would be willing to put its head on the block in risking a food shortage (about 80 percent of its wheat was imported) if the stakes were 150 fresh infantry battalions, and would not be willing for a few full American divisions, particularly in the light of serious criticisms made of AEF training thus far.[10]

That the British offered shipping when they did and not before was due, not only to their depleted manpower, but to greater success against the U-boats. In the first half of 1917 the British lost eighty-nine ships sunk or seriously damaged; in the second half, forty-eight; in the first half of 1918, fifteen. As Sir Frederick Maurice, Robertson's Operations Chief, explained it: "We could not have given the United States tonnage until we knew that we were on the way to master the U-boats, the greater part of our food supplies being sea-borne; and, as it was, our people had to make very real sacrifices to make shipping available."[11]

Perhaps because it concerned surplus troops who would not otherwise reach Europe before 1919, perhaps because the British consented to use their ships to transport them, Pershing looked more favorably on Robertson's proposal than he had on Lloyd George's in December. On January 13 he recommended it to the War Department. "This whole question seems to me to be one of necessity, and we must consider the probability of strong German attacks in early spring and summer. . . . The emergency requires this temporary supply of men for the British. . . ."[12]

Pershing was later to deny that he recommended Robertson's proposal, but clearly he did. As he wrote Secretary Baker on January 17: "Basically the question presented is, can we afford not to send over extra men to help our allies in what may be an emergency when the necessary extra sea transportation is offered and we have the spare men."[13]

There were conditions, however. It must be considered "a temporary measure to meet a probable emergency"; it must in no way interfere with regularly scheduled American shipments to build up a separate army; the amalgamated troops must be returned when called for; and the Allies must do what they could to keep up their own manpower. "When we make this concession," said Pershing, "the tendency is certainly going to be for them to relax and let the burden fall on us to the detriment of our own preparations for decisive action later."[14]

Communicating these conditions to Robertson on January 15, Pershing requested a full statement on British manpower. He knew that Lloyd George kept troops in England to prevent Haig from using them on futile offensives, or dispatched them to far-off places like Palestine and Mesopotamia, thereby reducing forces available for the western front. Robertson later admitted in his memoirs that there were nearly 1,500,000 men in England and 1,200,000 in distant theaters.[15]

In Washington Secretary Baker, noting that the proposal had the approval of just about everybody—Pershing, the French, and his own War Department advisers—recommended it to the President, who approved, but added a caution: "I have one fear about this. It is that, whatever they may promise now, the British will, when it comes to the pinch, in fact cut us off from some part of the tonnage they will promise us for our general programme in order themselves to make sure of these battalions; or will promise us less for the general programme than they would otherwise have given, had their plan for these reenforcements for their own front not been accepted."[16]

Accordingly, when Baker on January 21 cabled approval of the Robertson proposal to General Bliss, just arrived in Europe as American military adviser to the SWC, he told him to make very clear that U.S. approval was contingent upon the British living up to existing arrangements for helping to transport and supply a separate American Army. The project "has the approval of Pershing," Baker said, adding that Bliss should consult with the AEF commander before finalizing anything.[17]

Undoubtedly, Pershing regarded Bliss's appointment to the SWC with a certain apprehension. Their personal relations were good, but Pershing would have preferred General Liggett, a man less known than Bliss and whose selection would have left Pershing more dominant in Europe. Bliss was a former Chief of Staff, a full general, and a man whose opinions counted heavily with Baker. Bliss would have independent cable connections with the Secretary and his recommendations might well be contrary to those of the AEF commander. Harbord considered Bliss's appointment "pregnant with possibilities" for mischief.[18]

When Bliss arrived in London, the British lost no time in seeking his favor. Lord Reading talked to him for two hours from a sickbed about the need for 150 infantry battalions. The following morning Lloyd George went over the same ground, as did General Robertson and Lord Derby in the afternoon, and Bonar Law and Lloyd George again at dinner that night. "They all seem to be badly rattled...," Bliss reported. "They want men and they want them quickly."[19]

Bliss was disposed to grant their request, even though it delayed the formation of an independent American force. "If we do not make the greatest sacrifices *now*," he cabled Baker, "and, as a result, a great disaster should come, we will never forgive ourselves nor will the world forgive us."[20]

Meanwhile, Pershing was having second thoughts about Robertson's proposal. On January 21 he wrote Bliss, who had arrived in England only two days before, that "we should be very guarded in making any concessions to the British" and should finalize nothing until "the entire question" could be discussed in Paris.[21]

On January 25 Pershing and Bliss met Robertson in the French capital. The Britisher fully expected approval of his proposal, since Pershing had told him on January 15 that he had recommended its "serious consideration" to the War Department and since, at a meeting on the nineteenth between Pershing, Pétain, and Haig (the first such session where the three top commanders had been in the same room together), Pershing had said nothing contrary when it was more or less assumed that the proposal would go through. Robertson was accordingly thunderstruck to hear Pershing state that he did not favor the British plan. Instead of transporting 150 infantry battalions (150,000 men), he proposed instead that the British use their shipping to bring over the same number of men but as personnel of six complete American divisions—approximately 90,000 infantry and 60,000 other arms and services. They would train with the British and then reassemble and be used in American units.[22] Robertson pointed out that this would give the British only a little over half of the infantry battalions they desperately needed, but Pershing was adamant, so Robertson telegraphed Lloyd George for further instructions.

In London the British War Office was furious at this turn of events. That very day, January 25, it listened to extracts from a French report on the dismal state of the American Army, only one division of which, after almost ten months of war, had been in the trenches at all. Projections for the future were equally bad. By May 1919 only sixteen "trained" American divisions would be available, "trained" meaning capable of holding a quiet sector. Hence even after sixteen months more, said the French report, "the American Army will only constitute a comparatively weak asset."[23]

There was, however, one glimmer of hope. At the January 25 Paris meeting, to Pershing's consternation, Bliss had sided with the British. He had been impressed with the desperate state of Allied manpower and with the fact, recognized by all, that small battalions could be trained far quicker than large divisions.[24]

Back in Paris Pershing closeted himself with Bliss in an attempt to change his mind. Although Baker had given Pershing authority in his December 18 cable to decide how much to cooperate with the British and French, Pershing knew that the Secretary respected Bliss's judgment and would be put in a quandary if he had to choose between the advice of his two top generals. It would also look bad to have a disagreement on the first matter of importance since Bliss's arrival. So when Bliss proposed that they each cable Washington their opposing views and ask for a decision, Pershing said bluntly: "Well, Bliss, do you know what would happen if we should do that? We would both be relieved from further duty in France and that is exactly what we should deserve."[25]

Pershing said that they had a duty to get together and present a common recommendation; Bliss saw the truth of this. He saw less clearly the contention that bringing over six full divisions was preferable in the circumstances to bringing 150 infantry battalions. But Pershing talked long and hard, using his usual arguments against amalgamation. For example, while the infantry battalions might be trained under the Robertson scheme, their command and staff, their artillery and auxiliary troops would not be. He also used as ammunition a confidential talk he had had with Joffre, who contended that French and British manpower shortages were exaggerated, as was the threat of the coming German offensive. People talked about the Germans having 230 divisions to the Allies' 170; Joffre thought a truer figure was 190 to 170. Reinforcements coming from Russia would be of poor quality, since the Germans had for some time creamed off the best officers and men for the western front. In the fall of 1914, with a superiority of 300,000 men, the Germans had failed to break the Allied lines. Joffre thought their chances were "much less favorable now."[26]

Using these and other arguments, Pershing talked persuasively, as he was quite capable of doing on a man-to-man basis, especially when the stakes were high. At the end, Bliss said: "I think you are right and I shall back you up in the position you have taken."[27]

Years later, when Pershing's confidante, Micheline Resco, was asked if she had ever heard Pershing express particular satisfaction about something he had done, she answered, "Yes, when he won Bliss over to his point of view once." It was undoubtedly this occasion that Pershing had in mind.[28]

Meanwhile the British, still thinking Bliss was on their side, made plans to overcome the AEF commander. "We must force Pershing's hand . . . ," said Sir Henry Wilson. On January 29–30 he, Lord Milner (the new Secretary of State for War), Lloyd George, Robertson, and Haig converged on Versailles to meet with Pershing, who was accompanied by Bliss. Pershing stoutly opposed the Robertson proposal, skillfully turning back a number of the arguments in favor of it. For example, if the British were so terribly short of manpower on the western front, why had they so many men in Palestine? If the expected German offensive would take place before the end of March, how would 150 battalions help to stop it, since they would not arrive by that time?[29]

At times the argument grew heated. When Pershing commented that he agreed with Haig on a certain point, provided he "meant what he said," Sir Douglas replied somewhat testily that he understood the English language.[30]

Desperately seeking support, Lloyd George asked Bliss to state his views. "Pershing will speak for us," replied Bliss, "and whatever he says with regard to the disposition of the American forces will have my approval."[31]

Pershing was tremendously gratified. He described Bliss as "an able man, as square as a die, and loyal to the core." Loyalty (meaning loyalty to him, of course) was a cardinal virtue in Pershing's hierarchy.[32]

Faced with the solid front of America's two full generals and the confidence that Baker placed in them, Lloyd George knew he would have to accept Pershing's counterproposal. There was nothing else he could do.[33]

The British thereupon agreed to bring over the full personnel of six American divisions. This would amount to about 150,000 men (the number contemplated by the Robertson scheme), but only 90,000 of them would be infantrymen such as the British desired. The rest would be artillerymen and other troops needed to make up the basic, self-contained division. The infantry and auxiliary troops would be sent to the British for training, not fighting; the artillery would train with the French. Subsequently the infantry and artillery would be reunited as full divisions under American officers and staff, who, meanwhile, would have understudied with the British.[34]

The agreement was a compromise. Baker approved it, but felt that an even better scheme would have been if the British brought over six complete divisions— not just their personnel, but their cargo, artillery, transportation, and so forth. He supported Pershing's objections to the Robertson proposal and sent a strong statement about an independent American Army which fortified Pershing when the question came up again, as it did repeatedly: "We are willing to trust your judgment upon all points of training . . . , but advise that nothing except sudden and manifest emergency be suffered to interfere with the building up of a great, distinct American force at the front. . . ."[35]

In point of fact, a "sudden and manifest emergency" would skewer all Pershing's hopes for "a great, distinct American force." Under existing plans, American troops would be training with both the British and French. Should the Allies be attacked, doughboys could hardly stand by, pleading the excuse that they were there for training, not fighting. Pershing would have to commit them.

Leonard Wood

(February 1918)

W ITH A MASSIVE German attack imminent, no single Allied commander in chief yet existed to coordinate and direct Allied resistance. Nor did any general reserve exist which could be shifted to meet the point of greatest danger. Each Allied commander thought of his own army and his own fate. They were not hanging together; so, not surprisingly, they were hanging separately. No wonder Clemenceau said that he had lost respect for Napoleon's military reputation when he realized that the Little Corporal had made it fighting against coalitions.

A step toward remedying these deficiencies was taken on February 2 when the SWC agreed to create a general reserve for the whole western front and designated an Executive Committee of Foch (chairman), Wilson, Cadorna, and Bliss to oversee it. On February 6 the Executive Committee set the minimum number of divisions in the general reserve as thirty, asking the French to contribute thirteen, the British ten, and the Italians seven.[1]

Somewhat related to the question of a general reserve was that of the amount of front held by each army. The French occupied approximately 340 miles; the British, with about the same number of men, held only 110 miles. To repeated French attempts to get him to take over more of the line, Haig was deaf. It was quite out of the question, he said, claiming there were other considerations besides the length of front: the fact that the British defended certain indispensable ports and coal mines, and were exhausted from having borne the brunt of the fray during the past year. Privately, he thought that the expected German spring offensive would fall on him rather than on Pétain and, as events showed, he was right.[2]

Accordingly, Haig took a dim view of extending his line and *a fortiori* of committing ten of his divisions to an Allied reserve. He dragged his feet until March 2 when he simply reneged and said he couldn't commit them. He did, however, work out a sort of gentleman's agreement with Pétain, whereby each earmarked six to eight divisions to be sent to the relief of the other if hard pressed.[3]

Thus far nothing had been done about a supreme commander. Bliss's proposal to create one was voted down at the February 2 SWC meeting. The French insisted that he be a Frenchman, since they contributed most to the common effort, while the British saw all sorts of political reverberations if they handed over British troops to be killed by a foreign commander. Interestingly, in pressing for the Robertson proposal, they did not seem to mind asking the same thing of the Americans.[4]

Meanwhile, the supply problem, both at home and abroad, remained unsolved and was getting worse. Because of lack of berthing space and freight-handling facilities, and because convoys necessarily brought large groups of ships in all at once, the ports were congested in a terrible way. Even when they unloaded eight thousand tons a day, railway facilities could move out only three thousand. Sometimes goods remained unloaded for want of buildings to store them or railroads to move them. Some fifteen thousand railroad cars stood idle for need of repairs; the French had no men to fix them and American repairmen, repeatedly requested by cable, had not arrived.[5]

When things are going wrong, the natural tendency is to blame somebody else and Pershing was no exception. He blamed the French, but mostly he blamed the War Department, particularly the staff departments, for their recalcitrance, obduracy, and downright bungling.[6]

He should also have blamed himself. When George Rublee, Dwight Morrow, and others from the United States visited Chaumont in February to discuss the supply question, they discovered, said Rublee, "that Pershing didn't understand it at all." Brig. Gen. Mason Patrick, Pershing's West Point classmate and AEF Chief Engineer Officer, described a meeting that Pershing called concerning the ports. "He handled the matter rather poorly and haltingly—asked a few questions about docks available. Said he was not satisfied with progress being made, thought fault *might* lie with the organization. . . ." To Patrick, there was no doubt about it; the fault definitely lay with the organization, and Pershing was responsible.[7]

Chaumont headquarters was overstaffed and top-heavy. Some fifteen heads of departments, bureaus, and services were stationed there, in addition to the five General Staff chiefs, besides miscellaneous bodies like the press bureau and various welfare groups. Each chief was directly under Pershing or Harbord; just to see each of them for fifteen minutes would take five hours of a working day. Trying to manage all these administrative and staff bureaus, deal with his military associates like Pétain and Haig, skirmish with Clemenceau and Lloyd George over amalgamation, entertain important visitors, and make necessary inspections, Pershing was like a dog chasing its own tail. "He was getting so busy," said Harbord, "he had no time for his real job," which was command, not administration. W. D. Connor, Chief of the Coordination Section, said that the arrangement was "as faulty an organization as could have been set up," and that practically everyone was "simply bursting to have the whole headquarters reorganized. . . ."[8]

Pershing finally reorganized headquarters on February 16. He transferred eleven technical and supply bureaus to Tours and placed them under the commanding general of the Line of Communications, which was renamed Service of the Rear

(SOR) and, still later, the Services of Supply (SOS). Harbord said that Chaumont was like "a deserted village" after the change. Pershing now had more time to think; his aides were no longer glorified traffic cops, routing an endless stream of supply and technical chiefs in and out of his office.

Left at Chaumont, besides a few technical and administrative chiefs, were the five main sections of the General Staff, which were renamed G-1, G-2, G-3, G-4, and G-5. Their duties roughly corresponded to their former names (Administration, Intelligence, Operations, Coordination, and Training), but the new designation permitted dividing up the work more equitably without worrying about whether a certain task sounded like "Administration" or "Coordination."[9]

Between October and January, as part of Secretary Baker's program of familiarizing them with modern war conditions, thirty-two U.S. division commanders had visited Europe. After looking them over, Pershing on February 24 sent a confidential memorandum to the Secretary, asking that ten of them not be sent back. His reasons were age (eight were sixty or over), sickness, and lack of practical experience in commanding troops.

Pershing entrusted the memorandum to Gen. J. Franklin Bell, an old friend, who very much wanted to see action in Europe. Although Bell didn't know it, the memo listed his name as one not to be sent back. The fact that Pershing asked Bell to be, in a sense, his own executioner, delivering the document that killed his chances of returning, was cited later by Gen. Peyton C. March as an example of Pershing's "perfidy."[10]

Pershing knew, of course, that some of the men he vetoed would take it badly. With Baker and the War Department coming under fire in America, his own organization in Europe was bound to be criticized also. No doubt the canned generals would "get out their little hammers and join in the general anvil chorus," he speculated. The most dangerous was Leonard Wood.[11]

Before the war Wood was probably the best-known American military figure in Europe, a man many Europeans had expected to command the AEF. Even now reports circulated of Allied wonderment that he was not being used more prominently, either in Europe as a corps commander or as military adviser to the SWC, or in America as Army Chief of Staff.[12]

Wood's one-month tour of Europe, which began on December 28, came at a most crucial time concerning the amalgamation controversy. Ten days before Wood arrived in Europe, Baker had let the Allies know that he considered an integral American Army secondary to meeting "any critical situation," and that Pershing had authority to consent to amalgamation. During January both the French and the British had proposed it, Bliss appeared to go along, and Pershing seemed in danger of being isolated and overwhelmed by Allied pressures. He could not help but be sensitive at this hard-pressed time to anything which undercut his authority, impugned his ability, or made common cause with his adversaries on the amalgamation issue.[13]

Wood did just that. Stopping off in London on his way to France, he got off a number of very indiscreet remarks to important British officials, the sum and

Edward M. House.
U.S. Army Military History Institute

Robert L. Bullard.
U.S. Army Military History Institute

Sir William Robertson.
U.S. Army Military History Institute

Leonard Wood.
U.S. Army Military History Institute

substance of which was that the American Army was a bloody mess at home and abroad, training with broomsticks and wooden guns. To any and all willing to listen, he launched into a freewheeling attack on President Wilson ("that rabbit") and his administration, speaking of America's complete unpreparedness for combat. British eyebrows went up, salons and drawing rooms buzzed with gossip ("Did you hear what General Wood said about the American Army?"), and people were generally frightened and unsettled to discover, apparently from an inside source—a former Chief of Staff and America's best-known soldier—the inside story.[14]

Wood also had a few choice comments about Pershing, expressing grave doubts about his ability to do the job and wonder at President Wilson's selecting such a man for command. British listeners were shocked at what they heard, just as Sen. James Wadsworth was, when he invited Wood to luncheon after his return from Europe and heard him launch into "a lengthy and bitter criticism" of Pershing, substantially what he had said in London. "He went to such lengths as to shock me . . . ," said Wadsworth. "Literally, I gripped my chair in dismay and astonishment."[15]

Ironically, while Wood was creating an uproar with his loose talk, he seemed blissfully unaware of what he was doing. Perhaps he simply could not help himself. Perhaps, as even his friends surmised, his judgment had become impaired by his head injury. For example, he wrote in his diary on January 11 that he had spoken about "the grotesque fizzle" of Pershing's Mexican Expedition, "but did not go much into it as I was afraid it would be misunderstood as an attack on the present Commander in Chief here which would be rather unfortunate at this time, as we must have confidence if nothing else."[16]

When Wood later heard people say that he had criticized the Wilson administration in London, he wrote, "These stories evidently . . . were circulated for the purpose of making trouble, as I . . . was most careful to avoid anything which could be interpreted as criticism."[17]

In Paris Wood repeated his performance, leaving behind him a trail of shaken confidence in America's ability to contribute substantially to winning the war. When Bliss arrived in Europe on January 19, he no sooner stepped off the ship than he heard complaints from all sides about Wood's "reckless remarks." "He has done his best to discredit the United States here in Europe," Bliss cabled Baker. "He has told of everything that has not been done and nothing as to the things which have been done."[18]

The result was foreseeable and pernicious. Wood's talk reinforced European fears about the competency of a separate American Army, strengthened the movement for amalgamation, weakened Pershing's prestige, and raised the question whether he was the best man to command in Europe. As Bliss said, "It is going to make it much more difficult for us to negotiate about getting aid in shipping if people here believe that whatever sacrifices they make to give us additional tonnage is only for the purpose of bringing over an unorganized and undisciplined mob." Bliss said he would not be surprised to find a movement initiated very soon to oust Pershing and replace him with a general who saw things more through European eyes, namely, Wood. Lloyd George let it be known that he wanted to see Wood again as soon as the latter returned from France.[19]

Eventually news of Wood's remarks came to Pershing, who was understandably concerned. He paid Wood a courtesy call in the hospital when the latter was wounded by an accidental explosion of a trench mortar near the French front. But he'd be damned if he'd have such an officer in Europe under his command. At a Chaumont conference with Bliss and Peyton C. March, who was scheduled to return to America to be the new Chief of Staff, Pershing excoriated Wood's lack of loyalty, said the War Department had given him authority to return officers who did not fit into the AEF machine, and that if Wood ever came back to France after his inspection tour was over, he would send him right home again.[20]

The best solution, however, was not to have him sent to France again in the first place. To that end he included Wood in the February 24 list of ten officers he considered unfit for divisional command, giving as the reason Wood's head injury which left him "seriously and permanently crippled."[21]

To make doubly sure, however, he sent off that same day two "personal and confidential" memoranda, one for the Secretary of War, the other for the Chief of Staff, but both about Wood without mentioning his name.

"With reference to a certain general," he began, "he is very hostile to the administration and has criticized the War Department very freely. . . . His attitude is really one of disloyalty, in fact he is simply a political general and insubordination is a pronounced trait in his character. He is not in any sense true, and seemingly cannot control his overwhelming ambition for notoriety. . . . It would settle his pernicious activities if he could be retired and then recalled for some unimportant duty."[22]

Because of convalescing from the mortar injury, Wood stayed in Europe beyond the usual month's tour for visiting generals. George Van Horn Moseley, later AEF G-4, visited him in the hospital. "He spent the whole time of the visit criticizing Pershing," Moseley remembered.

To Pershing's chagrin, Wood tried to prolong his stay, for he was getting more attention in Europe than he ever would in America. "Think General Wood should expedite his movements," growled Pershing to Harbord. Wood was ordered home at the end of February, after being denied permission to go to London to have some clothes fitted, or to Italy in answer to an Italian request that he visit there.[23]

Before leaving, he warned Bliss that refusing the Italian invitation might lead to "an international situation," for the Italians had invited him "quite unsolicited" and might consider the American refusal "insulting." Bliss said nothing, but inside he was furious, for he knew that the Italian invitation was not unsolicited. Cadorna had told him that Wood had asked for a visit.[24]

When Baker learned of such conduct, he was more than ever convinced that Wood should not be allowed to return to France. While recognizing his great ability and the loyalty he elicited in others, Baker concluded that Wood himself had no concept whatever of loyalty to his own superiors. "He was the most insubordinate general officer in the entire army."[25]

The United States had now been at war for ten months, yet "it was depressing," said Pershing, to think that after all that time, with the nation's vast wealth, manpower, and supposed hustle, it had only one unit, the 1st Division, holding a front of its own, and that in a quiet sector. Even that division, in French opinion, would not be ready for four more months to withstand an attack, much less make one. When Paul H. Clark, a U.S. liaison officer at Pétain's headquarters, asked a French colleague, Major Rozet, what would happen if the anticipated German offensive struck where the 1st Division was, he answered, "It would be promptly taken out and sent to some part of the line which was relatively quiet." It was not individual American courage or valor which was deficient, said Rozet; the staff work was simply not adequate yet.[26]

Of the three other divisions, the 26th was probably furthest along. Commanded by Maj. Gen. Clarence Edwards, a West Pointer ('83) whom Pershing had known as a cadet, it went into line by battalions and regiments on February 6 for training with the French in a quiet sector. Pershing's relations with Edwards were friendly, but he was not one to let friendship interfere with military professionalism, and already bad reports were coming in on Edwards's division.[27]

The 42d Division, which went into the lines for its training period with the French on February 21, also had its problems. General Mann, its original commander, had been replaced in December by Maj. Gen. Charles T. Menoher, a Pershing classmate. He was a field artilleryman who knew little about infantry, and some on the AEF staff doubted whether he would make good. Collins, Pershing's aide, was impressed, however, by the division's Chief of Staff, a bright young chap full of get up and go. His name was Douglas MacArthur.[28]

As for the 2d Division, it was still being assembled and would not go into the front lines for its practice session until March 17.

In sum, the situation was not encouraging. "Here we were," said Pershing, "likely to be confronted by the mightiest military offensive that the world had ever known and it looked as though we should be compelled to stand by almost helpless and see the Allies again suffer losses of hundreds of thousands of men in their struggle against defeat."[29]

The Germans felt the same. "In only one way has the Entente been enriched by the entrance of America into the war," editorialized a German newspaper; "that is in hopes."[30]

Peyton C. March

(March 1918)

O N MARCH 4 the War Department received a needed shot of adrenalin when it got a new Chief of Staff: Maj. Gen. Peyton C. March. An experienced artilleryman, March had come to France in July 1917 to command the artillery training camp at Valdahon, and later all the AEF artillery. Pershing had known him for some years (first at West Point in the 1880s, later on the General Staff in Washington in 1903) and considered him "a very able man." When Baker requested him as Chief of Staff, Pershing said, "He will be difficult to replace but I feel that you need the best man we can find, so I cheerfully let him go."[1]

Before March left France, Pershing saw to it that he was thoroughly briefed on the whole AEF operation. March visited Chaumont to learn the general headquarters' viewpoint and method of operation, did the same with the supply headquarters at Tours, consulted with General Bliss about the SWC at Versailles, had a tour of the trenches to gain the doughboys' perspective, met Foch and Clemenceau, and spent some time with Pershing. "We went over together the entire military situation . . . ," said March.[2]

Saying goodby, Pershing wished March well and said he knew he would make good. After he left, one of Pershing's staff said to him, "That man is going to cause you trouble."

"I know that," Pershing replied. "But he is a capable officer."

James L. Collins, Pershing's aide, agreed that March was capable, but felt that he was also a vain autocrat who would permit no one to stand in his way. "I thought he would play General Pershing's game as long as it suited him, but not a day longer," Collins wrote in his diary.[3]

Pershing was to find that March's conception of the office of Chief of Staff—its nature and prerogatives—differed markedly from that of his predecessors. Bliss, by his own admission, felt that his job as Chief of Staff was to give Pershing everything he asked for. Except in name, he said, he was "Assistant Chief of Staff to the Chief of Staff of the A.E.F.," that is, to Harbord.[4]

March in no way believed this, nor, it might be added, did Elihu Root in setting up the American General Staff in 1903. Nor indeed is such an understanding tolerable to anyone who has a proper conception of general staff ideas, military hierarchy, and proper subordination. The Chief of Staff is the supreme military authority in the Army. He is not an assistant to anybody, except to his civilian superior, the Secretary of War. March intuitively and correctly grasped this. In August 1918 he explicitly expressed it in General Order #80 which stated that the Chief of Staff "takes rank and precedence over all officers of the Army."[5]

This was not Pershing's idea, nor was it Harbord's, who considered March's claims to supremacy an "hallucination." Both conceived of the AEF chief as virtually an independent commander, directly under the President and the Secretary of War, subject to no other soldier. March, they felt, had power over the War Department General Staff but over no one else, except insofar as he spoke for the Secretary of War, in which case he was simply a messenger boy transmitting orders. When March acted otherwise, Harbord considered it a case of a telegraph wire taking on airs because it carried an important message.[6]

When March took over, the war had been on almost a year, during which three Chiefs of Staff had come and gone: Scott, Bliss, and Biddle. During this time Pershing was the one constant factor in the War Department-AEF relationship. By the end of February 1918 he had consolidated his position as a virtually semi-independent, autonomous field commander, coequal to, if not supreme over, the Chief of Staff in Washington. When March, a strong personality, went into office with a different (and, be it noted, correct) conception of his role, there was bound to be friction.

Much of it was unnecessary and caused by Secretary Baker's faulty concept of general staff organization, his romantic idea of glorifying his field commander and allowing him virtually independent status. To Baker, a controversy over whether the Chief of Staff or the field commander was supreme was "purely technical" and "unimportant"—which speaks volumes about how well Baker understood basic general staff organization and principles.[7]

AEF generals, from Pershing on down, are virtually unanimous in praising Baker as a great Secretary of War. Historian James E. Hewes, Jr., has quite rightly suggested that one reason was because Baker let the AEF do pretty much as it wanted.[8]

The three wartime Chiefs of Staff before General March were not very effectual. Scott was out of the country most of the time, Bliss had his problems, and Biddle couldn't make decisions. The result, quite naturally, was that the Secretary of War turned for advice to bureau chiefs such as Maj. Gen. Enoch H. Crowder, the Provost Marshal General, and deferred increasingly to the overseas commander, Pershing. March accurately put his finger on the deficiency: "If a Chief of Staff is a weak man, and the results obtained by his supervision are not satisfactory to the Secretary of War, the remedy is not to break down his authority and invest subordinates with that authority. The answer is to get a new Chief of Staff who can handle the job."[9]

March certainly could handle his. A human dynamo, he "lived, breathed and slept efficiency," said one subordinate. "He took the War Department like a dog takes a cat by the neck, and he shook it," said another. March provided the energy that galvanized the department; it shuddered, coughed, blew out the black carbon and, like a great, magnificent machine, roared to life and began to hum.[10]

Up at 6:00 A.M., March was generally the first man in the office, took lunch at his desk, came back to work after supper, and stayed until midnight or 1:00 A.M. He cut through red tape like a hurricane. A subordinate summarized orally the content of papers, while March barked out "approved" or "disapproved," not even touching the documents. When a subordinate said, "I am not very familiar with this paper, General," March gave him a dirty look and snapped, "Take it back and get familiar with it."[11]

Before March took over, turnaround time for troopships was as high as sixty-seven days; under him it went down to an average of thirty-five. A month before his assignment, the United States shipped some 49,000 men to Europe; the month after, almost 120,000. In subsequent months the number skyrocketed to 245,000, 278,000, and 306,000.[12]

"I propose to get the men to France if they have to swim," March said, and he meant it. His basic idea was that troopships should be ferryboats, not trans-atlantic luxury liners. A ferryboat is uncomfortable, but the discomfort lasts only a short time and the boat gets you there. March packed the men in, quite literally, like sardines, with three men for each bunk in which they slept in shifts. On Pershing's recommendation he later cut the cargo allotment from fifty pounds per man per day to thirty pounds, saving cargo space and increasing the transport of men. By that summer he was pouring men onto the shores of France at the rate of almost 10,000 per day. Watching the endless stream of doughboys coming down the gangplanks, a German prisoner of war exclaimed tearfully, "Mein Gott in Himmel."[13]

Afraid of nobody, March was ruthless in achieving his ends. Once he received a letter from President Wilson expressing annoyance that a certain ship had been taken over for cargo service to France which he had personally promised the Secretary of the Treasury would be retained in America for carrying coal to New England. Knowing that Secretary Baker would be questioned about this at the cabinet meeting the next day, March put stevedores on a crash program of loading the ship around the clock, so that by the time of the meeting it was two-thirds full. As he expected, the President acquiesced rather than order the ship unloaded again.[14]

Ruthlessly efficient, March hewed mightily around him and let the chips fall where they might. "You cannot run a war on tact," he asserted, and he did not. Endowed with a positive genius for irritating everyone, he was described as a modern day Richelieu, *fortiter in modo* but not *suaviter*. Another put it more succinctly: "March was a real sonofabitch if there ever was one."[15]

Ernest Ginnetti, a barber at the Army and Navy Club in Washington, remembered the time an officer approached March in the barber chair to ask if he would be in his office for business later. March ignored him. Approaching closer, the officer repeated his question. At that March leaped out of his chair. "Yes, damn you!" he rasped. "But I'm not going to be in to see you!" It was not a quick remark, recalled Ginnetti, but spoken deliberately, with force and relish.[16]

Frederick Palmer said that when he met March on the street he expected to see a trail of horseshoe nails bitten in two behind him. Secretary Baker claimed that a large part of his working day was spent acting the Good Samaritan: pouring in oil and binding up the wounds of subordinates whom March had laid low in his relentless drive for efficiency. He was "arrogant, harsh, dictatorial and opinionated," said Baker. He ruled by a reign of terror, "riding rough-shod over everyone."[17]

Did that include Pershing? Hardly. Pershing was not the type of man anyone rode over. He did, however, have several set-tos with March that spring.

The first concerned promotions. Asked to recommend a list of names for general officer vacancies, Pershing sent it to Washington and was surprised to discover later that three of ten new major generals and over half of the brigadiers were not on his list. Irritated, and accustomed to having his recommendations followed, he cabled his disapproval, requesting that Baker be informed (which should, he thought, solve the matter), and that confirmation by the Senate be held up until he sent a new list.[18]

March's reply lectured Pershing like a schoolboy: "The American Expeditionary Force is only a part of the American army and whatever promotions to the grades of Major General and Brigadier General are necessary will be made ... from the entire army. You were directed to submit recommendations as were other general officers. ... Your recommendations are regarded as especially valuable as far as they are limited to the American Expeditionary Forces, but the efficiency of senior officers at home is determined by what there is actually accomplished here, based upon specific reports of inspectors and division commanders. ... There will be no changes in the nominations already sent to the Senate."[19]

When Baker later saw the cable, he wrote on the bottom of it: "An excellent illustration of the way *not* to send a message!"[20]

Pershing returned a soft answer, saying that it had not been his intention to try to limit army promotions to the AEF, which would be manifestly unfair and hurt officer morale at home, but to point out that service overseas was the acid test. There had been cases of officers promoted and then sent overseas, where they outranked tested AEF officers and then proved inadequate. He was trying to avoid that.[21]

The other disagreement was over the Sam Browne belt. An insignificant item of clothing, but with strong symbolic and caste overtones, the Sam Browne belt was an over-the-shoulder strap designed by a British officer of that name while serving in India in the 1870s. Originally it had served a practical purpose: to hold up the waist belt when it was heavily burdened with sword, revolver, binoculars, canteen, and other items. Later, when these were eliminated, the strap remained as part of the dress uniform, becoming eventually the distinguishing mark of the British officer. Pershing liked it, feeling it "set off" the uniform, giving a more

Pershing wearing the Sam Browne belt and March omitting it,
October 21, 1920. *Air University Review*

military look. Soon after landing in Europe in June 1917 he ordered the shoulder belt worn at AEF headquarters and subsequently prescribed it for all AEF officers.[22]

In the United States, however, it was prohibited. In view of the leather short-age, it seemed to March downright extravagant to use scarce material on these ceremonial belts which had no practical purpose and which were never used in the trenches, a pistol belt and suspenders being substituted instead. In May he suggested that Pershing do away with it. Pershing disagreed, and the belt stayed. Harbord considered March's view very "narrow" and said that going without the Sam Browne belt was like going out without one's pants![23]

The result was that every officer going to Europe had to purchase the belt. (March estimated total cost at two million dollars if the war had gone into 1919.) In time it became a caste symbol, setting off the AEF officer from both the enlisted man overseas and the officer at home—and universally detested by both.[24]

Despite these and other disagreements, relations between March and Pershing were generally good during the war. The so-called "feud" between the two men was, as historian Edward M. Coffman has pointed out, a product of the internecine "Battle of the Books" during the 1930s. During 1918–1919 the tone in cables and letters was cordial, even friendly. One reads the correspondence between the two men with the feeling that March attempted to be the more cordial.

Given the traditional rivalry between line and staff, the fact that the two men were separated by 3,000 miles, that each worked overlong hours, frequently in a crisis atmosphere, the wonder is that there were not more disagreements. Had the two been able to confer face to face, instead of by letter and cable, "there would have been no trouble . . . ," thought Douglas MacArthur.[25]

Part of the difficulty was that Harbord, who considered March ambitious and unscrupulous, kept whispering in Pershing's ear about him. On March 14, for example, March asked Pershing to send back to America thirty General Staff officers, to be replaced by thirty from home. The change would inject officers with the AEF viewpoint into the War Department and would give foreign service to home officers whose careers would otherwise suffer without it.[26]

Harbord saw all sorts of dark implications in the proposal. It was "a distinctly unfriendly act," he told Pershing. "It shows no consideration for your needs, and undermines your well-laid foundation, with what wild ambition in mind we can only guess. The best that could be said, if it is not hostile, is that it is selfish, inconsiderate, and ordered with no thought for your organization or intelligent comprehension of the task immediately before you."[27]

If March had proposed taking the officers only from Pershing's GHQ (thirty men out of a total of sixty-four), as Harbord thought, his objections would have had merit. But March realized this would be unfair and had explicitly stated that they could come from the whole AEF. It was a perfectly reasonable request, but members of Pershing's staff, which some felt poisoned him against March, misread its plain words and tended to see a conspiracy where none was involved.[28]

The incident is also instructive as illustrating the AEF attitude toward auton-omy. Harbord put it thus: "All you wish from America is such Staff Service there as will insure you a steady flow of troops and supplies. *You do not want there a*

Staff dealing with any phase of your business here." (My italics.) It would be hard to find a more concise statement of a field command desiring independence from General Staff control.[29]

Once Pershing correctly understood March's intent, he complied, but only halfheartedly. Of thirty officers sent back, only three were found suited for General Staff work. An exchange arrangement limped on, but Pershing was not about to let good men out of his hands, so pressed was he for General Staff officers. One effect of his policy was to foredoom General Staff officers in Washington to sitting out the war at their desks.[30]

Ever since arriving in France in June, Pershing had repeatedly expressed a strong desire that Secretary Baker visit the AEF, the better to comprehend its problems and accomplishments. Baker had delayed, partly because of complications in his own department which brought it under Congressional fire in December and January, and partly because he wanted to see the AEF when it had developed more. On March 10, however, he arrived in Paris. George S. Patton, Jr., who saw him, remarked: "He is a little rat, but very smart."[31]

Baker received a Cook's tour of the whole AEF from the base ports through the intermediate zone and up to the front lines, where he spent two days. At the flying school at Issoudun he craned his neck to watch some hair-raising turns done in the air by a young major named Carl A. Spaatz, who in World War II would command U.S. Strategic Air Forces in Europe. Visiting the Rainbow Division, he encountered a handsome Irishman of New York's "Fighting 69th" who wore a brand new French Croix de Guerre. When the division commander pointed out somewhat apologetically that the officer was wearing the medal without authority— the government not yet having authorized receiving foreign decorations—Baker interposed: "I give you executive authority to wear that cross. If anyone questions your right to wear it, refer them to me." The officer was William J. (Wild Bill) Donovan, who rose to command a regiment in the Rainbow Division and in World War II headed the Office of Strategic Services.[32]

Pershing, who accompanied the Secretary on part of the trip, made it a point to instruct him on the reasons behind the choice of ports, front, and line of communications. He explained his problem of getting men and material to construct the supply line necessary to maintain an ever-growing AEF, and also went into detail on relations with Allies. It was a thorough job of indoctrination, of putting his best foot forward and letting Baker see just what he had done in the months since they had first met. "You have the President's entire confidence," said the Secretary, "as you have my own. We will back you in every possible way."[33]

Meanwhile, the whole world waited for the expected German spring attack. Although the French and British were each convinced that the blow would fall on them, actually it was the British who were targeted, at the juncture where their armies joined the French. The Germans hoped to capture the key rail and supply center at Amiens, and even to roll the British all the way back to the coast, separating them from the French and hemming them in as they later did at Dunkirk in World War II. Being closer to the coast, the BEF had less room to maneuver and fall back on if hard pressed.[34]

Surprisingly (considering what was about to happen to him), Haig was confident, fearing that the Germans would be so impressed with his defenses that they would call off their attack, thus depriving him of the opportunity to kill a lot of them. He needn't have worried. Or rather, he should have, but about himself. He was short of men, for Lloyd George had kept thousands in England, supposedly to prevent invasion, but actually to keep Haig from frittering them away in disasters like Passchendaele. And the British Fifth Army, which in December had taken over twenty-five miles of front from the French, had not had time to organize defenses in depth; some of their "lines" were merely marks on the ground to indicate where future trenches should be dug. It was on this army that the attack would mainly fall.[35]

TWELVE

The German March Offensive

(March 1918)

THE GERMAN OFFENSIVE was Riga and Caporetto all over again, only worse. The same generals were there (Below and Hutier) using the same tactics to effect the same result: a "maneuver of rupture," as they called it, "very brutal."

Troops marched to the front at the last minute under cover of night or early morning fog, along routes not visible to observation balloons. Artillery moved into position by night and calculated ranges, not by firing, but by Pulkowsky's system of mathematical prediction.[1]

At 4:40 A.M. on March 21 the heaviest German bombardment of the war could be heard as far back as Pétain's headquarters at Compiègne, where Frederick Palmer compared it to the roar of a distant surf. An avalanche, a torrent, a hurricane of fire descended on the front and rear positions of the British Third and Fifth Armies—on the command posts, the gun positions, the bunkers, the trenches—sweeping like an angry god laying waste the landscape. In the forward area, shells fell five yards apart, with craters almost touching each other.

For five hours the deluge lasted. Then they came: picked storm troopers with light machine guns, satchel charges, flamethrowers, and stick bombs. Specially trained to probe weak spots, they pushed forward like water running downhill, flowing around obstacles and meeting behind them, an ever-growing torrent sweeping all before it.

Seventy-one German divisions hit twenty-six British divisions, some of them weak and recuperating. Suddenly the western front, which since October 1914 had scarcely moved ten miles in either direction, had a hole in it forty miles deep and forty wide. Before the offensive was over on April 5, the British would suffer 164,000 casualties, and lose 90,000 prisoners, 200 tanks, 1,000 guns, 4,000 machine guns, 200,000 rifles, and 70,000 tons of ammunition. It was a disaster.[2]

Refugees—"human leaves driven by war's storm," Frederick Palmer called them—crowded the vital railroad station at Amiens, where thousands of women and crying children tried to board every train that left. Others, clogging the foot-paths, vainly sought a ride from anyone heading to the rear.[3]

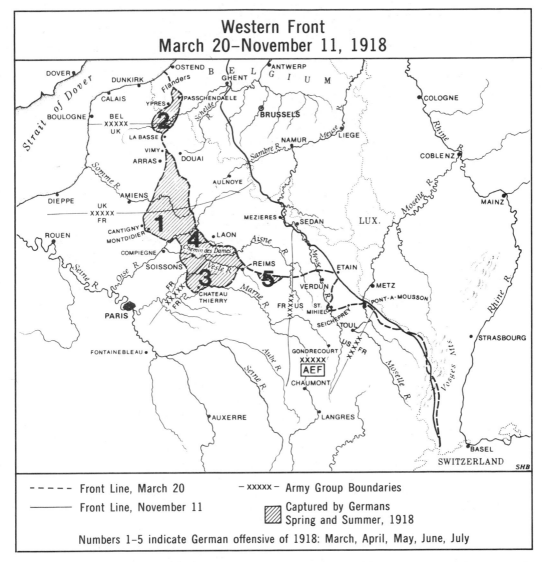

Western Front
March 20–November 11, 1918

- - - - - Front Line, March 20   – xxxxx – Army Group Boundaries
———— Front Line, November 11   ▨ Captured by Germans
                                             Spring and Summer, 1918

Numbers 1–5 indicate German offensive of 1918: March, April, May, June, July

Map by Samuel H. Bryant from *Memoirs of My Service in the World War, 1917–1918* by George C. Marshall. Copyright © 1976 by Molly B. Winn. Reprinted by permission of Houghton Mifflin Company.

Faced with catastrophe, each ally thought primarily of itself: the British to fall back and cover the channel ports, the French to cover Paris. Haig was asking for at least twenty French divisions to relieve pressure on himself. In Paris people talked of evacuating the government to Bordeaux again, as in 1914.

Privately, Pershing felt that the German breakthrough vindicated his ideas about open warfare. It had blown the front wide open. He noted with approval a British criticism of the stultifying effects of trench warfare on their own men:

"They get out into the open and act as though they were suddenly thrust naked into the public view and didn't know what to do with themselves, as if something were radically wrong and that there ought to be another trench somewhere for them to get into."

When a newspaperman asked what the United States would do if the Allies gave way, Pershing replied, "We're going to keep right on fighting if we have to go back to the line of the Pyrenees and fight there."[4]

At Compiègne, Col. Paul H. Clark, Pershing's liaison officer at Pétain's headquarters, watched the tension mount as the German offensive continued to gain ground day after day. By March 25 General de Barescut, French Chief of Operations, was pacing around his office like a caged tiger, stopping occasionally to study a large map on an easel, then thrusting a clenched fist into the air. Suddenly he spoke: "Go quickly to the telephone and tell your chief the situation. Urge him to give us without delay all the help he possibly can."

Clark hurried to the phone, got Pershing's principal aide, Carl Boyd, and heard him relay the message. In a moment Boyd's voice came back over the phone: "General Pershing will come to see General Pétain today."

When Clark relayed the message, Barescut reacted angrily. "Mon Dieu, why does he wait to come? Why doesn't he telephone what he will do?"

Disappearing into Pétain's office, he came out five minutes later, still in the manner of a caged tiger.

"Please go at once to the telephone and tell General Pershing not to come; General Pétain will likely be away and even were he here the imperative demands of the moment require his whole time and thought. He could not see anybody. Tell General Pershing very strongly not to come."

Clark got Boyd again, gave the message with as much forcefulness as he had received it, and heard him pass it on. Over the wire he heard Pershing's voice: "Tell Clark I will come to see General Pétain this afternoon."

Barescut was visibly displeased.

Afternoon came, but Pershing did not. Several times the French asked for news of him, but Clark had none. Pétain postponed dinner one hour, awaiting his guest. Still no arrival.

From late afternoon on Clark stationed himself outside in the courtyard in order to avoid dirty looks as the French passed by. "I could feel so much tension and displeasure among the French over the coming of General Pershing," he said.

At 9:00 P.M. one of Pétain's aides came outside. His nerves frayed with strain and fatigue, he spoke impatiently of Pershing's inconsiderateness: first in coming when he had been told not to, and then in not coming on time. He invited Clark inside to escape the chilly night air, but the embarrassed American thought it best to remain alone.

About 10:30 P.M. the aide came out again, asking for news. When Clark had none, the Frenchman exploded: "Doesn't he think we want to sleep at all! Does he not know that since March 20 we have been without sleep! He says he's coming! You tell him *not* to come! He replies that is IS coming! But he DOESN'T come! Mon Dieu! I'm going to get some sleep!"

He shot back into the house, slamming the door violently. Clark took no offense; the man's reaction was perfectly justified.

About 10:45 P.M. Pershing arrived, looking fresh and confident. "The roads," he explained, "are choked with troops and trains of automobiles and refugees to such an extent that much of the time I could not make any headway. I am sorry to have caused any inconvenience."

"They waited dinner for you and have been very impatient for you to come," said Clark.[5]

Pershing then went in and saw Pétain, who was shaken, worried, and pressed for time since he was about to transfer his headquarters to Chantilly to get farther back from the German advance. He was waiting with a map all spread out showing where he wanted American divisions to go into quiet sectors to relieve French divisions who would go to aid the British. "No time was wasted," Pershing remembered; "everyone talked fast."[6]

Pershing readily agreed to put all four of his divisions in line, but suggested that they be concentrated together to form a corps, rather than spread out. Pétain, who had enough troubles, quickly pointed out how inadvisable this was. A large section of the front held by such green troops would constitute a particularly tempting target for German attack which, if successful, would cause havoc, since French reserves were being taken away and sent to the battle in the north. Furthermore, in order to obtain more troops, Pétain might have to shorten his lines in the American area, and an untrained corps could well botch up the logistics of conducting such a movement.

Pershing, who desired to help and who realized how bad things were, acquiesced. Because the eruption on the British front seemed to preclude training there, he even seemed amenable to a French suggestion that American troops brought over by the British be fed into French units under a progressive arrangement whereby certain French divisions would eventually become American.[7]

The following day, March 26, Clemenceau, Foch, Pétain, Poincaré, Haig, Wilson, and Milner met together at Doullens. Pétain was in a blue funk; Haig thought that he had lost his nerve. Two days earlier Pétain had issued orders in anticipation of abandoning contact with the British and swinging the French left back to cover Paris. When Haig spoke of placing the British Fifth Army under Pétain, the latter replied: "There is very little of it left, and in strict truth we may say that the Fifth Army no longer exists."[8]

For his part, Pétain believed that Haig was licked. Pointing to him, he whispered to Clemenceau: "There is a man who will be obliged to capitulate in open field within a fortnight, and very lucky if we are not obliged to do the same."[9]

The one bright spot was Foch, who arrived in a whirl, full of fire, and dominated everything with his metallic, cutting voice. "You aren't fighting?" he exclaimed. "I would fight without a break. I would fight in front of Amiens. I would fight in Amiens. I would fight behind Amiens. I would fight all the time."[10]

High-strung, radiating nervous energy, Foch was aggressiveness personified. In the battle of the Marne, he had been quoted as saying, "My flanks are turned; my center gives way; I attack!" He never said it, but the remark typified his spirit.[11]

Looking at him, Haig thought him a man fit to overrule the pessimism of Pétain and save the day. It was now clear that there must be a supreme commander; the German breakthrough made that imperative. It must perforce be a French general, but this step, which previously no British government could have proposed and stayed in power, was now made necessary and inevitable by the very magnitude of threatening disaster. At Doullens therefore the British and French entrusted to Foch "the coordination of the military operations of the Allied armies on the Western Front."

Pershing called the choice of Foch an "accident." The Frenchman had headed the SWC's military advisory committee and happened to be available when needed. But, said Pershing, his selection "was certainly not because of any particular military ability he had displayed up to that moment."

Pershing could never quite warm up to Foch. He described him as cold and austere, "narrow," "haughty, Napoleonic, and moderately conceited." "Foch never seemed interested when I talked with him of our problems and I doubt whether at the time he ever thought, knew, or cared much about our organization, or our questions of transportation or supply."[12]

Meanwhile, Gen. Henry Rawlinson, who had replaced General Wilson as British military adviser to the SWC, had proposed that the advisers recommend incorporating American forces into Allied units during the emergency. Bliss asked that Pershing be allowed to state his views when the advisers met on March 27 to discuss the question.

Not surprisingly, Pershing opposed Rawlinson's proposal, suggesting as an alternative that the Allies consolidate their own weakened divisions into fewer ones and let full U.S. divisions replace them on the line as they arrived. When asked whether the Americans were capable of immediately going into battle as full divisions soon after getting off the ships, Pershing said yes. "I am prepared to put the American divisions on the line as fast as they arrive." In view of Pershing's delay in committing to the line the divisions which had heretofore arrived in France, that statement was indeed amazing.[13]

After Pershing left, Bliss remarked: "General Pershing expressed only his personal opinion . . . ; it is [we] who must make a decision."[14]

Bliss then proposed a resolution which was substantially that of Rawlinson's and which was unanimously adopted and sent to the SWC as Joint Note #18: "It is highly desirable that the American Government should assist the Allied armies as soon as possible by permitting, in principle, the temporary service of American units in Allied army corps and divisions. . . . In execution of the foregoing, and until otherwise directed by the Supreme War Council, only American infantry and machine-gun units [should] be brought to France. . . ."[15]

Bliss did add certain saving phrases that he thought Pershing would want. The proposed reinforcements were to come from America and not from American divisions already in France, which should be preserved intact. Also, amalgamated units "must eventually be returned to the American army." Nonetheless, Pershing was shocked at Bliss's resolution and considered himself somewhat undercut. It would stop practically all shipments of artillery, technical units, service of the rear, corps, and army troops—in other words, stop the formation of a separate American Army.[16]

Since Secretary Baker was still in Europe, Bliss presented Joint Note #18 directly to him in Paris. Baker was aware that Allied proposals for amalgamation, at least during the emergency, had considerable merit. Many patriotic Americans supported them, for example, Bliss, Wood, Sims, and House. House wrote the President at the end of March: "Pershing's feeling that an American army under his command should be established and made as formidable as possible is understandable. Nevertheless, the thing to be done now is to stop the Germans and to stop them it is evident that we must put in every man that is available."[17]

Baker must also have been aware of considerable Allied bitterness over America's meager manpower contribution after one year of war. "It was heart-rending to see our men being mown down unceasingly," Clemenceau was to write later, "while . . . large bodies of American troops remained idle, within earshot of the guns. . . . Pershing, with his tight-lipped smile, kept putting things off . . . while my country's fate was every moment at stake on the battlefields, which had already drunk the best blood of France."[18]

Accordingly, Baker overruled Pershing and on March 28 recommended that President Wilson approve Joint Note #18 "in view of the present critical situation." Shipments of infantry and machine-gun units would be given preference, even though this necessarily postponed organization and training of complete American divisions and thus delayed the formation of an independent American army. No specific numbers of troops were mentioned, nor the length of time that they would be given preferential shipment. On arriving in Europe, they would be directly under Pershing for training and use, and ultimately be gathered by him into a separate American Army.[19]

Bliss's refusal to support Pershing on March 27, coupled with Baker's siding with Bliss the following morning, may have chastened the AEF commander somewhat, suggesting that the crisis was really more serious than he supposed, justifying extreme actions. In any event, he showed up at Foch's headquarters at Clermont in the afternoon and got off one of those quotable quotes of which he was capable when deeply moved. Foch was so touched that he grabbed him by the arm and dragged him outside to where Clemenceau and Pétain were standing, asking him to repeat what he had said. With all eyes on him, Pershing sensed the drama of the moment, rose to it, and poured out in French an eloquent declaration:

"I have come to tell you that the American people would consider it a great honor for our troops to be engaged in the present battle. I ask you for this in their name and my own.

"At this moment there are no other questions but of fighting.

"Infantry, artillery, aviation, all that we have are yours; use them as you wish. More will come, in numbers equal to requirements.

"I have come especially to tell you that the American people will be proud to take part in the greatest battle of history."

Foch was visibly enthusiastic. Clemenceau's face flushed, his eyes lighting up with fire so vividly that Pershing understood why they called him "Le Tigre." Even

Pétain, normally so phlegmatic that he was nicknamed "the Sphinx," registered emotion. "They were all manifestly touched," Pershing observed, and so indeed was he, caught up in the excitement of the moment and their obvious approval of him and what he had said.[20]

Yet there were seeds of misunderstanding here. Given the context of Pershing's remarks, which came one day after Joint Note #18, which Bliss and Baker had supported and he had opposed, the French might well see in Pershing's "all that we have" offer his capitulation on the amalgamation question. They probably so understood it. Certainly their perfervid reaction was not justified by what Pershing had to hand over on the spot. He had little artillery or aviation. But he did have infantry and he had just said, "Use them as you wish." They most certainly did wish to use them—as replacements in their own depleted units.[21]

That, however, was probably not what Pershing had in mind. His opposition to Joint Note #18 on March 27 was quite compatible with his offer to Foch on March 28, for the former looked to troops to be sent over from America in the future and piecemealed out, whereas the latter referred to troops already in France which would serve as full divisions. A day or so later, Pershing confided to Clarence C. Williams, AEF Chief of Ordnance, his continued concern about holding American troops together and "having an American army under the American flag" as soon as possible.[22]

Of such misunderstandings are frustration and ulcers made. No wonder Clemenceau said that they "often parted with smiles that on both sides concealed gnashings of teeth."[23]

Practically speaking, Pershing's offer of March 28 had relatively little effect. The 1st Division was ordered from Lorraine to the front in Picardy, but was not used, the German drive having been blunted by that time. The 2d Division extended its front; the 26th and 42d Divisions relieved French divisions in quiet sectors, freeing them for active use. But the only Americans actively engaged were two engineer companies who happened to be attached to the British Fifth Army for railway work and got caught in the attack. They suffered seventy-eight casualties.[24]

On March 28, the day Pershing made his "all that we have" offer, the German offensive began to grind to a halt. An attack toward Arras was repulsed with heavy losses. The battle dragged on until April 5, but it soon became clear that the British line, while bent, was not going to break. The Germans were increasingly bothered by the difficulty of getting food, ammunition, and guns over a lunar-like landscape and keeping an offensive going with men increasingly worn down by fatigue. It was the old story: The avalanche of artillery which made possible the initial breakthrough became the very thing that hindered most a subsequent advance, for it demolished the terrain across which wagons and trains had to make their way.[25]

Meanwhile, the Allies were exerting every effort for a favorable American decision regarding Joint Note #18, which called for preferential shipment of infantry and machine-gun units only. Lloyd George fired off two cablegrams to Washington to Lord Reading, urging him to see President Wilson immediately and beg him to approve amalgamation during the crisis. France's reserves were at an end; England was scraping the bottom of the barrel. The draft age was being

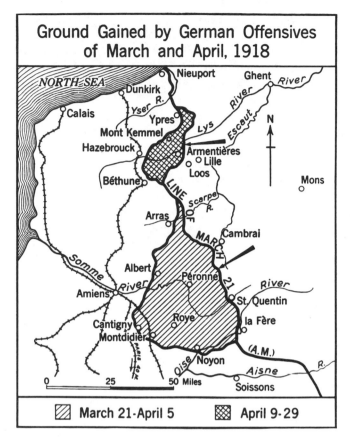

Ground Gained by German Offensives of March and April, 1918

Legend: ▨ March 21-April 5   ▩ April 9-29

From American Battle Monuments Commission, *American Armies and Battlefields in Europe*, Washington, D.C., 1938.

lowered to eighteen and raised to fifty, perhaps fifty-five. Conscription was even being contemplated for Ireland, something heretofore considered unworkable. "I beg you to press this . . . upon President Wilson with all the force you can," he urged. "For the present it is not material which is required, but man power to make good the losses in killed, wounded, and missing."[26]

Lloyd George sent a copy of his appeal to Winston Churchill, who happened to be in Paris, telling him to see Clemenceau at once and urge him "to support this appeal in the strongest manner," which the latter did. Foch also cabled the President that unless 600,000 American infantry were shipped in the next three months the war was lost.[27]

The President, urged on all sides to approve preferential shipment of infantry and machine-gun units, said yes. But at this point a failure of communication occurred. Joint Note #18, which Baker had recommended, said nothing about specific numbers or months. Lloyd George, however, in his plea to Wilson, specified 120,000 men per month during April, May, June, and July—a total of 480,000.

After seeing the President, Lord Reading cabled that Wilson had agreed to this specific arrangement.[28]

When Baker asked for a clarification as to what had or had not been agreed to with Reading, the President replied: "I told him that . . . we would send troops over as fast as we could make them ready. . . . That was all. The details are left to be worked out. . . ."[29]

Nonetheless, any arrangement looking toward preferential transportation of American infantry and machine-gun units implicitly bore on the amalgamation question, which is why Pershing opposed it. With a preponderance of such troops in Europe, he would have no choice but to allow them to be fed into Allied ranks as crisis followed crisis, as need followed need. Lloyd George told a cheering House of Commons that President Wilson's approval of Joint Note #18 meant that "American battalions will be brigaded with those of the Allies."[30]

The London Agreement

(April 1918)

O N APRIL 3, at a meeting convened at Beauvais, Foch's powers were further elaborated: "The British, French, and American governments . . . entrust to General Foch the strategic direction of military operations. The Commanders-in-Chief of the British, French, and American armies have full control of the tactical employment of their forces. Each Commander-in-Chief will have the right of appeal to his government if in his opinion the safety of his army is compromised by any order received from General Foch."[1]

The original draft had made no mention of an American army, since none existed, but Pershing was insistent that the wording be changed. "There may not be an American army in force functioning now," he argued, "but there soon will be, and I want this resolution to apply to it when it becomes a fact. The American Government is represented here at this conference and in the war, and any action as to the supreme command that includes the British and French armies should also include the American Army."[2]

One must not make too much of the Beauvais agreement or of Foch's later title: General Commander-in-Chief of Allied Armies in France. His authority was more moral than legal. As his later difficulties with Pershing demonstrated, he could not simply command. He had often to prod, suggest, or wheedle. Nor was his "strategic direction" more than just a general orientation, with subordinate commanders in chief working out the details. He had only a small personal staff, some twenty or thirty men, worlds removed from Eisenhower's SHAEF staff of World War II. Foch's influence was more personal and inspirational than organizational.[3]

The appointment of Foch as supreme commander over Allied manpower gave rise to thoughts of a similar generalissimo over Allied material. Certainly a case could be made for one. Due to declining supplies, French warehouses were more and more empty at the very time that the AEF, at considerable expense and tie-up of tonnage, was building more and more of them. Why build what the French already had and weren't using? Why not coordinate things? Why not pool facilities and supplies? What was true of warehouses might also be true of docking facilities, motor transport, freight cars and locomotives, civilian labor, munitions, coal, horses, gasoline, wagons, lumber, food, and so on.

Dawes, Chief of the AEF Purchasing Board, suggested the idea of pooling supplies to Pershing, who approved it wholeheartedly and commended it to Clemenceau, who wondered why no one had thought of it before. Eventually some pooling was worked out, more with the British than the French, but nothing like a wholesale, massive, throwing together of supply stocks. It was too much to ask of human nature, thought Harbord, too Christlike in its unselfishness, "almost utopian."[4]

Meanwhile, the Germans had launched their second great spring offensive, this time astride the Lys River, catching Haig off guard again. On April 9, German artillery crashed down violently on British command posts, strong points, trenches, and artillery, while German storm troopers moved forward under cover of gas and fog. An unreliable Portuguese division serving with the British gave way, neglecting to blow the Lys bridges and leaving a massive hole in the British lines. Twenty-seven German divisions swept forward on a twenty-four-mile front.[5]

Two days later, on April 11, Haig issued his famous "backs to the wall" order. "There is no other course open to us but to fight it out!" he said. "Every position must be held to the last man; there must be no retirement. With our backs to the wall, and believing in the justice of our cause, each one of us must fight on to the end. The safety of our homes and the freedom of mankind alike depend upon the conduct of each one of us at this critical moment."[6]

Pershing was with the Rainbow Division when a copy of Haig's order came in. Douglas MacArthur watched him as he read it and noticed a certain hoarseness in his voice when he spoke—a sign of being troubled. "We old First Captains, Douglas, must never flinch," he said.[7]

With Haig calling for help, Foch asked if the 1st Division was "ready to go." Pershing answered yes. On April 16 he gathered its officers, some 900 men, to speak a few final words. It was his favorite division. These men had been longest in France, had the most experience, and, by God, they were Regulars. Pershing caught the momentousness of the occasion, as did others. "You are going to meet a savage enemy, flushed with victory," he said. "Meet them like Americans. When you hit, hit hard and don't stop hitting. You don't know the meaning of the word defeat. When you go into battle forget all you have learned out of books. Use your head and hit the line hard."

Pershing stressed that they were well trained, should be confident, and should apply the immutable principles of war to ever-changing situations. He called for determination, aggressiveness, stamina, character, and above all, the "will to win." They should lead by example and take care of their men. Then came a stirring peroration, as Pershing, quite caught up, went beyond himself.

"I have every confidence in the 1st Division. . . . You have behind you your own national traditions that should make you the finest soldiers in Europe to-day.

We come from a young and aggressive nation. We come from a nation that for one hundred and fifty years has stood before the world as the champion of the sacred principles of human liberty. We now return to Europe, the home of our ancestors, to help defend those same principles upon European soil. . . .

"Our people to-day are hanging expectant upon your deeds. Our future part in this conflict depends upon your action. You are going forward and your conduct will be an example for suceeding units of our army. I hope the standard you set will be high—I know it will be high. You are taking with you the sincerest good wishes and the highest hopes of the President and all of our people at home. I assure you in their behalf and in my own of our strong belief in your success and of our confidence in your courage and in your loyalty, with a feeling of certainty in our hearts that you are going to make a record of which your country will be proud."[8]

It was a stirring speech. John L. Hines, commander of the 16th Infantry Regiment, thought that Pershing threw his whole personality into it. "Every officer," Hines said, "was inspired to do his best out of personal loyalty to such a chief, even if for no other motive."[9]

But beating the enemy would take more than fine phrases and the "will to win." Four days after Pershing's speech the Germans humiliated the Americans at Seicheprey.

The 26th (Yankee) Division, commanded by Maj. Gen. Clarence Edwards, held this area on the south face of the St. Mihiel salient. It was considered a quiet area, and well that it was, for it was one of the most miserable spots on the western front. Trenches were filled with soft, thick mud one to three feet deep.

At 3:00 A.M. on April 20 the Germans opened up with a tremendous barrage of high explosive shells and gas. For two hours it rained down, cutting telephone wires and destroying support positions. At 5:00 A.M. 2,800 Germans, including picked storm troopers, came over and hit two companies (approximately 510 officers and men) of the 102d Regiment of the 26th Division. They overwhelmed them. An American who came on the scene later was struck by the sight. "There they were, dead—in windrows almost, out in front of the fire trenches which by reason of the mud made poor places from which to fight."[10]

It was a wild, confused morning, with wires cut, runners killed or bogged in mud, and people not sure just what was happening. A counterattack was planned, then postponed, then ordered, and finally aborted by a major who refused to carry it out. When the Yankees finally advanced they found that the Germans had pulled back, after holding the captured trenches for twenty-four hours. American casualties, officers and men, totaled 81 killed, 187 wounded, 214 gassed, 187 missing or prisoners. It was the heaviest American engagement to date and, although General Edwards claimed that his 26th Division had given more than it had taken, it did not seem like an American success.[11]

Pershing was angry. This was no small thing like the raid on the 1st Division in November which killed three and captured twelve. This involved 669 casualties. Coming as it did, when the Allies were pushing for amalgamation and raising questions about American competence to handle divisions—much less larger formations—this had to be considered bad news. As Lloyd George commented soon afterwards, "This kind of result . . . is bound to occur on an enormous scale if a large amateur United States Army is built up without the guidance of more experienced [i.e., Allied] General Officers.[12]

Pershing's anger was probably unjustified. Most raids succeeded. They were surprise operations, hitting the defenders suddenly and unexpectedly with overwhelming numbers and an artillery avalanche. And Seicheprey was particularly vulnerable.[13]

While Pershing was considering disciplinary action, word arrived that General Passaga, the French corps commander, had liberally bestowed the Croix de Guerre on members of the division for their conduct during the attack. The rank and file certainly deserved it, for they had fought desperately and well, although without direction and support. It was the leaders whom Pershing felt had fallen down. But Passaga's move made disciplinary action seem inappropriate and none was taken. Pershing did request, however, that in the future no such foreign awards be bestowed without his prior assent.[14]

Meanwhile, Secretary Baker had returned to America and was having second thoughts about priority shipments of infantry and machine gunners. One must always keep in mind that Baker, like Pershing, was conditioned by events taking place on the western front. Neither man was inflexible on the amalgamation issue. Both maintained that, in an emergency, they would allow American troops to be fed into Allied ranks. The basic question, however, remained: how bad must a situation be to be an emergency? On this reasonable men could differ, and did.

On March 28, seven days after the first German onslaught, Baker had broken with Pershing and sided with Bliss in recommending to the President that he approve Joint Note #18, which provided for priority shipment of infantry and machine gunners. By April 7, however, when Baker and Pershing met British shipping representatives in Paris, the German attack was over and the danger passed. Baker was then as intransigent as Pershing in rejecting a British proposal of priority shipments of 120,000 infantry and machine gunners a month for four straight months. The agreement hammered out provided only for 60,000 such troops in British shipping and only for the month of April.

On April 9, the day after Baker sailed for America, the Germans launched their second offensive and two days later Haig issued his "backs to the wall" order. The situation again seemed precarious; the Germans were striking a hammer blow at an army barely recovered from the March attack. In such circumstances Baker reconsidered the British request. The situation seemed more an "emergency" than it had earlier in the month.

Baker was also influenced by British insistence that they were not just pulling numbers out of a hat in asking for a total of 480,000 men over four months. They themselves hoped to draft approximately that number as replacements for their army, but it would take approximately four months to train them, that is, until the end of July. Hence they asked for that number of Americans to fill in during the interval. And they wanted a definite commitment, so they would know where they stood and could plan accordingly.[15]

Baker decided to comply. On April 19, after consulting with President Wilson, he handed Lord Reading a memorandum in which the United States agreed to give preferential transport to 120,000 infantry and machine-gun units a month during April, May, June, and July, using both its own and British shipping. This decision was made because of "the exigencies of the present military situation." When transported, these troops were to be under Pershing's direction and trained and used at his discretion.[16]

The fat was in the fire. Pershing was to say later when he read the memorandum: "If this isn't amalgamation what is it?" Even though these troops were to be under his control, what else could he do with them except feed them into Allied ranks in an emergency? It was either that or sit out the war. He lacked the auxiliary and supply services to build up his own divisions, much less corps and armies.[17]

By some inexplicable quirk, the Administration failed to inform Pershing of Baker's important memorandum until April 26, one week after it had been given to Reading. Although Pershing heard a rumor of it through the British liaison officer at Chaumont, he disbelieved it.[18]

From April 22–24 Pershing and Harbord were in London, conferring with Sir Henry Wilson, Chief of the Imperial General Staff, and Lord Alfred Milner, who had recently replaced Lord Derby as Minister of War. Harbord thought Henry Wilson "a good deal of a politician," which he was, and thought Milner "the most difficult person to bring over," which, from the British viewpoint, might also have been said of Pershing.[19]

Wilson opened with a statement that the British expected to be able to bring over 750,000 American troops by the end of July, a remark which Harbord found "astounding" in its sharp contrast to all previous estimates and in view of the fact that, until recently, the British were claiming they did not have a spare rowboat. "Where has such an amount of shipping been?" he wondered. "Why has it needed a German menace to the Channel ports to make it available?"[20]

The British then produced their haymaker: a cable from Reading, quoting Baker's memorandum of April 19, promising 120,000 American infantry and machine gunners a month from April through July. Even though he had heard a rumor of this, Pershing was still taken aback and could not believe it, feeling that Reading had misunderstood Baker just as he had earlier misunderstood the President. He frankly said that such a concession could not possibly have been made and he would not be bound by it.[21]

Although the British gnashed their teeth at Pershing's refusal and were quite sure that he was wrong, they decided to come to terms with him. Even under the April 19 memorandum, he had something they very much wanted—discretion to decide where American troops went after they arrived in Europe. Thus far the British could expect only 60,000 under the previously mentioned agreement Baker and Pershing had concluded with them on April 7.

Accordingly, Milner signed an accord with Pershing on April 24 (known as the London Agreement), whereby during the month of May infantry and machine-gun units of six divisions would be brought over for training and service with the British. Artillery personnel were to be brought over next and, should any surplus shipping be available, it would be used to complete divisional, corps, and field army organizations and provide Service of the Rear troops.[22]

It was a return to the Six Division Plan approved by Pershing and Robertson in January. The only differences were that now Pershing consented to bring over the infantry and machine gunners first (rather than bring a complete division at a time) and the British agreed that, if they had any transportation left over, they would bring over whatever Pershing wanted to balance out his forces.

When Pershing returned to Chaumont, he was startled to receive a copy of Baker's memorandum of April 19, promising priority shipment of 120,000 infantry and machine gunners a month from April through July. Only then did he realize how far off base he had been at London. Whereas Baker had committed himself to a priority shipment of 480,000 infantry and machine gunners stretched over four months, Pershing had allowed the British only some 126,000, and this only for the month of May, exacting a promise that the British bring over artillery personnel and other troops "immediately thereafter."[23]

The question now was, which agreement would the United States honor?

By all rights, it should have been the Baker Memorandum of April 19, made by Pershing's superior, the Secretary of War. But Baker, once he learned of the April 24 London Agreement, decided to support it, perhaps thinking that, if the British were willing to agree to it, things were not as bad as they seemed. (In point of fact, the second German offensive petered out by April 26 and, although it had advanced about ten miles, was not as serious as the earlier one in March.) Furthermore, Pershing was on the scene. His London Agreement preserved American freedom of action, kept future options open, and did not so drastically postpone the formation of a separate American army.[24]

The fact that two separate and contradictory agreements had been made (the Baker-Reading Memorandum of April 19 and the Pershing-Milner London Agreement of April 24) brought home to Secretary Baker the inevitable confusion of trying to carry on negotiations simultaneously on both sides of the Atlantic. Accordingly, he strongly recommended to President Wilson that any future arrangements be made by Pershing, "so that we would have one agreement made at one place, rather than several agreements made in several places which were more or less irreconcilable in some of their terms." To their great vexation, the British and French ambassadors were told that Baker would make no further agreements with them concerning troop shipments; on this question the man to see was Pershing.[25]

During March and April the Allies had sustained two massive German assaults successfully. But there were strains on the coalition; cracks were beginning to show.

The French felt that the British, who held a shorter line, were keeping an excessive number of men in England. "They are crying all the time," said one

French staff officer, "telling us to hurry that they can't hold out any longer." During the German March and April offensives, the French sent approximately fifty divisions to the British front.[26]

"I know what I am talking about," Pétain told Major Paul H. Clark, Pershing's representative at his headquarters. "The British should have a million more men in France now than they have. . . . Look at the map. Here is the French front (indicating), here is the British front (indicating), the British have 48,000,000 people in England, Scotland, Wales and Ireland, and the French have 39,000,000 in France, and think of all the British colonies, and yet France can put 1,000,000 more men on the front than Britain. Why? Because we make more effort, because in England a man is excused from service upon slight cause, whereas in France he is not excused for slight cause."[27]

The British too had their grievances. Although the French held a longer front, much of it was inactive, requiring few defenders, while the British front was active, vulnerable, and had borne the brunt of the two recent German assaults. And French support, although forthcoming, had not always been as prompt as desired. "They always seem to be able to produce a very plausible reason for getting out of their promises when they want to," observed John Charteris, Haig's Chief of Intelligence, who believed the French were not men of their word.[28]

As for manpower, the British had other fronts to consider besides France, such as Palestine and Greece. England also maintained she was the industrial workshop of the Alliance, producing all sorts of munitions, coal, steel, and shipping that France used, but which necessitated exempting Englishmen from military service to work in critical civilian occupations.[29]

Although the Allies had their differences, one thing both could agree on was the poor American showing to date. In October Haig had expected that by now six American divisions would be capable of offensive action. Actually only one (the 1st) was ready, while three others (2d, 26th, and 42d) were fit only for service in quiet sectors. Three-fifths of the AEF were involved in Service of the Rear work, building installations behind the lines. American combat deaths after one full year of war totaled a whopping 163! In view of the crisis facing the Allies, Foch felt that American aid had been "too ineffective for words."[30]

The attack on the 26th Division at Seicheprey on April 20 seemed to bear out what the Allies had repeatedly said and what the AEF high command had to admit, that the men were better than their officers. The latter lacked command and staff experience, especially in handling large units. Less than 1 percent of all AEF captains had one year's military experience.[31]

Pétain told Foch that American divisions wore themselves out quickly in a sector due to lack of training. They also took two-to-four times greater casualties than the French while serving on the same front. Camille M. Ragueneau, French Mission chief at Chaumont, frankly doubted that America could train division and higher staffs in the time required.[32]

American units arriving in France, said a French memorandum of May 1, 1918, had "very incomplete instructions." They were good with the rifle, especially at sniping, in which they excelled, but were weak on specialties like grenades, mortars, and machine guns. Most of their officers "have either everything to learn, or only possess the elements of theoretical instruction." Training for open warfare, while laudable, was leaving the troops deficient in handling trench warefare, which they would immediately have to face.[33]

British GHQ, after looking over seven American divisions training with them, reported in late May, 1918: "The American Commanders and Staffs are almost wholly untrained, and without military experience so far as the majority of the Staff Officers are concerned." Haig thought it would be "criminal" to count on strong U.S. help that spring or summer. An independent U.S. army was at least two years away.[34]

FOURTEEN

Abbeville

(May 1918)

O N MAY 1, 1918, the fifth session of the Supreme War Council met at Abbeville. Everybody was there: the prime ministers, permanent military representatives, war ministers, chiefs of staff, army commanders, and others. As Harbord later remarked, in the rank of its participants and the importance of the subjects discussed, Abbeville was one of the great historic conferences of the war.

Clemenceau, French Premier and War Minister, was in the chair and in a black mood. The French were angry over the Pershing-Milner London Agreement of April 24, feeling that the British had stolen a march on them in obtaining all the American infantry and machine gunners to be brought over in May, none going to them. They contended that Joint Note #18 had implied that such troops would be divided up equally between the French and British. Now the British had pulled off this coup without consulting their ally or having a French representative present at the London meeting. It was typical of the British. With a rumored 1,000,000 men under arms in England whom they refused to send to France, they had now grabbed all available new American combat troops to do their dirty work for them. You could not trust them. "They always have an *arrière-pensée* [an ulterior motive]," said a French officer.[1]

Pershing's mood matched Clemenceau's. He had believed the manpower question settled by the London Agreement which he had taken care to explain to Foch afterwards, on April 26, and which he had thought that the Frenchman had accepted. Now the whole question was to be "sprung" on him again. Bliss had insisted that Pershing be invited to Abbeville to have a chance to defend himself, but the AEF commander did not relish being called down like a schoolboy to stand reprimand by his preceptors. "Pershing was black as thunder . . . ," observed Sir William Wiseman, a British participant. "He was very sulky."[2]

Clemenceau opened up with a salvo against the Pershing-Milner agreement of April 24:

"It had been understood at Versailles [when the SWC ratified Joint Note #18 on March 27] that America would send 120,000 men per month, which the French and British armies would share equally. Under the Milner-Pershing arrangement, it appears none are to go to France. The French have not been consulted. We might suppose that in compensation the American troops arriving in June would be given to France. But it now appears they are also to join the British. I wish to protest that this is not satisfactory."[3]

"There is no agreement between my Government and anybody else," replied Pershing darkly, "that a single American soldier shall be sent to either the British or French." All that existed, he said, was a private arrangement made between himself (not his government) and Lloyd George on January 30 to bring over six American divisions for training with the British, and another agreement between himself and Lord Milner on April 24 to give priority to the combat troops of these six divisions during May. President Wilson's approval of Joint Note #18 had specifically reserved to the American commander in chief the assignment of any troops brought over.[4]

Clemenceau having been derailed, Foch jumped in. The British army was exhausted, he said; ten divisions had been used up. The great need now was for American infantry and machine-gun units, without which they were lost. The London Agreement gave priority to them for May. "I am sure that General Pershing, with his generosity and his breadth of view, . . . will extend for June the agreement decided upon for May."[5]

"I do not suppose," replied Pershing pointedly," . . . that the American Army is to be entirely at the disposal of the French and British commands."

"Of course, this is not the intention," said Clemenceau.

"We must look forward to the time when we shall have our own army," said Pershing, going on the offensive. "I must insist on its being recognized. . . . As to the extension of the May agreement to June, I am not prepared to accept it. . . . We have the whole month of May ahead of us before deciding whether the emergency still exists. . . . I do not wish to commit the American Army so long in advance. If need be, I shall recommend the extension into June. I can see no reason for it now." On the other hand, "it is not too early to . . . declare the principle of an American Army under the American flag."

Lloyd George said that he agreed to a separate American Army in principle. "However, at the present time, we are engaged in what is perhaps the decisive battle of the war. If we lose this battle, we shall need tonnage to take home what there is left of the British and American armies."

Foch agreed. "Nobody is more for the constitution of an American army than I, for I know how much more an army is worth when fighting under its own commander and under its own flag. But now the needs are immediate; there is a battle to be won or a battle to be lost. I ask for the continuation of the May program."

At this point Foch suggested that he, Milner, and Pershing meet separately to see if something could be worked out for June. The three adjourned to an adjacent room and, for the next hour, went over again what had already been discussed in full conference for two hours.

The session was not very fruitful. Pershing argued, not entirely fairly, that they were asking him to bring over untrained men to fight in Allied units, saying that at minimum it took nine weeks to train a man even for trench warfare and this, coupled with transportation time, would take them into August when, by Allied admission, their own replacements would be ready. The Allies contended that there must exist in the United States many men near the end of their training who could be brought over. Even if only partially trained, the emergency justified throwing them into battle if it meant the fate of the war, which they maintained it did. Pershing had some rather extreme ideas on how much training was necessary, and as events were to prove, a unit such as the 3d Division, which he had not scheduled for active duty before mid-August, was to do well at Château-Thierry in May, despite never having been at the front, even in a quiet sector.

Said Foch in exasperation: "You are willing to risk our being driven back to the Loire?"

"Yes, I am willing to take the risk," Pershing replied. "Moreover, the time may come when the American Army will have to stand the brunt of this war, and it is not wise to fritter away our resources in this manner. . . . It would be a grave mistake to give up the idea of building an American army in its details as rapidly as possible."

Foch responded pointedly, and correctly, that the war might be over by the time that happened.

At this juncture the three prime ministers—Clemenceau, Lloyd George, and Vittorio Orlando of Italy—stuck their heads in the door to see how things were going. Milner walked over to Lloyd George and whispered, "You can't budge him an inch." Clemenceau groaned inwardly, seeing visions of millions of French corpses heaped up by the mule-headed intransigence of a Missouri general.

Then all five—Lloyd George, Clemenceau, Orlando, Foch, and Milner—sat down and bombarded Pershing with arguments he had heard over and over. Round and round they went, like an animal chasing its tail. Milner described it as a "dog-fight." They insisted, Pershing counterinsisted, they insisted still more. "Can't you see that the war will be lost unless we get this support?" asked Lloyd George, desperately.

Finally, after about forty minutes, Pershing banged the table with his fist and said with the greatest possible force: "Gentlemen, I have thought this program over very deliberately and will not be coerced." He stamped out of the meeting, anger written all over his face. All the way home in the car he swore.[6]

That ended the meeting. But Clemenceau said that it would be continued the next day.

When the SWC met on May 2, Foch asked permission to make a formal statement. Pershing found it a "rather grandiose dissertation," probably because it was such a telling indictment against his position and stated so clearly the fundamental issue.

"In all conscience," said Foch, "it is of the utmost necessity that there arrive each month in France from America, at least during the months of May, June, and July, on a priority basis, 120,000 American infantry and machine-gunners."

Even more were desired, if possible, for British losses during March and April had exceeded expectations. British manpower was exhausted and the French almost so. "I ask in the most positive manner that the Supreme War Council . . . declare itself on this request and that it submit it to the President of the United States."

While sympathetic with Pershing's desire to form a separate American army, and while admitting that the priority shipments would delay it, Foch added: "My imperative duty as a soldier and as General-in-Chief forces me to declare that, when the greatest German army opens the greatest offensive of this war . . . , [such] a delay cannot be taken into consideration when the very issue of the war may depend on [it]."

Lloyd George, of course, "seconded the motion." Since March 21, he pointed out, British casualties had totaled 280,000 and the French 60–70,000 more. England had called up "her very last men," taking boys of eighteen and old men of fifty. "If the United States does not come to our aid," he said, "then perhaps the enemy's calculations will be correct. If France and Great Britain should have to yield, their defeat would be honorable, for they would have fought to their last man, while the United States would have to stop without having put into line more men than little Belgium." Thus far the Americans had hardly put their little finger into the struggle.

That must have hurt, but Pershing kept his temper. In point of fact, American troops were then holding thirty-five miles of front, double that held by the Belgians and more than that held by the British during their first year of the war.

Then Pershing launched into what the Allies considered his *idée fixe*: "America declared war independently of the Allies and she must face it as soon as possible with a powerful army. There is one important point upon which I wish to lay stress, and that is that the morale of our soldiers depends upon their fighting under our own flag.

"America is already anxious to know where her army is. The Germans are once more circulating propaganda in the United States to the effect that the Allies have so little confidence in the American troops that they parcel them out among Allied divisions.

"The American soldier has his own pride, and the time will come when our troops, as well as our Government, will demand an autonomous army under the American High Command."[7]

Observing Pershing, Sir William Wiseman thought him "an odd man," supremely confident of his own judgment, while minimizing that of others. He seemed obsessed by two ideas: the creation of an autonomous American army, and the suspicion that the Allies were overstressing the present emergency in order to recruit for their armies. Many of Pershing's objections to amalgamation, Wiseman thought, were political rather military.

On the other hand, Wiseman felt a certain sympathy for Pershing. "He is much overworked and understaffed, and is called upon to discuss, indeed to decide, questions which should clearly be determined by civilian authorities."

In addition, Wiseman thought there was much to be said for Pershing's position, more indeed than the Allies cared to admit. The Germans had launched two massive attacks, but both had been stopped and with heavy casualties. The odds were against their obtaining another massive breakthrough as they had in March. Still, as Wiseman put it in summing up the basic European view of the case, "the stakes are too big to take chances, and we had better have too many than too few infantry at the crucial stage."[8]

Despite Pershing's apparent intransigence, he was not, nor could he afford to be, absolutely inflexible. The risks were too great. If the Germans succeeded in winning the war that summer, as the Allies feared, his plans for a separate American army would be tragically in vain. The name *Pershing* would go down in history as a synonym for a man who made grandiose plans while the ship was sinking beneath him. Foch's memorandum, with its call for a direct appeal to the President of the United States to overrule Pershing, showed that the Allies meant business.

At Abbeville Pershing was alone and isolated. Bliss was of no particular assistance to him. In keeping with his policy of arguing with Pershing privately but supporting him publicly, he said little during the conference, letting Pershing speak for them both. But the Allies were right in thinking that Bliss sympathized with their position and would have supported it.[9]

Accordingly, Pershing proposed a compromise. He would not agree to give priority to infantry and machine gunners during three months (May, June, and July), such as Foch demanded, but he would consent to allow the London agreement with Milner, which gave such priority in May, to be extended to June. But that was as far as he would go. He would make no provision for July, although he did consent to another meeting in early June to see how the situation looked then.

Although unhappy, the Allies accepted this arrangement, perhaps because they felt they could not do otherwise. They desired, if possible, to avoid an open rupture with Pershing who, after all, had authority to decide where American troops went once they were brought over—with the British, the French, or the AEF. President Wilson's approval of Joint Note #18 had specifically reserved that discretionary power to Pershing, and it served as a sort of trump card in his negotiations with the Allies.

As finally formulized on May 2, the Abbeville Agreement provided that 130,000 American infantry and machine-gun units were to be transported in British shipping during May, and 150,000 during June. American shipping would be used to transport artillery personnel, engineers, auxiliary, and other services suitable for building up a separate American army, which the SWC also committed itself to in a formal declaration.[10]

Pershing was satisfied with his conduct at Abbeville. His friend Martin Egan, who saw him immediately afterwards, thought he gave the impression of "greater force, greater grasp, greater clarity of mind" than formerly. "He is in splendid condition and is taking excellent care of himself."[11]

Pershing's cabled report on the conference to Secretary Baker was self-justifying and not altogether accurate. He presented it as a discussion "between the French on one side and the British and ourselves on the other" and explained away Joint Note #18, which called for preferential shipment of combat troops indefinitely, by saying it "was evidently made without considering the serious effect upon our plans. . . ." He represented the Allies as being satisfied. "I think we have fully and fairly met the situation. We have given the Supreme War Council all it asked at Abbeville."[12]

All these statments were highly debatable, to say the least.

The Supreme War Council in Joint Note #18 had recommended shipping *only* infantry and machine-gun units until further notice. The Abbeville Agreement provided for other troops. Pershing's position was that Abbeville represented the SWC's "latest view," revising and modifying its earlier one of March 27. This was not true and not fair reporting. More than ever, the SWC held to its earlier recommendation about priority for combat troops and accepted less than that only because of what Clemenceau called Pershing's "invincible obstinacy."[13]

Pershing's representation of Allied contentment at Abbeville was egregiously wrong. Lloyd George confessed himself bitterly disappointed with the agreement, adding that Foch was "intensely depressed and disgusted," Wiseman "very much upset," and Bliss in "complete disagreement with Pershing's attitude." Haig thought the AEF commander "obstinate and stupid." Pershing "is very obstinate," wrote Maurice Hankey, a British participant, on May 2, "and we had great difficulty in reaching a not very satisfactory agreement."[14]

Clemenceau condemned Pershing's stubbornness, forwarding a copy of Foch's strong statement of May 2 to Ambassador Jules Jusserand in Washington, asking him to commmunicate it to President Wilson. He also sent a French general to America, ostensibly on an inspection trip, but actually to lay the Allied case personally before the President.[15]

"It is maddening," said Lloyd George, "to think that though the men are there the issue may be endangered because of the shortsightedness of one General and the failure of his Government to order him to carry out their undertakings." The problem, as he saw it, was that Pershing was working out of his field; he was a soldier dabbling in statecraft. Had Colonel House been at Abbeville, matters would have been settled to everyone's satisfaction, including the Americans. In mid-May the British prime minister asked that House be sent over to attend the June meeting of the SWC as the President's personal representative.[16]

House was reluctant to go and the President to send him. Lord Reading confided to House his opinion that it would be a mistake for him to go "because it is so evident that what Lloyd George wants is someone to over-rule Pershing." House stayed home.[17]

Nevertheless, Allied complaints in Washington concerning the inadequacy of the Abbeville Agreement had an effect. On May 11 Secretary Baker cabled Pershing that the President "has been much impressed and disturbed by representations officially made to him here by French and British Ambassadors showing the steady drain upon French and British replacements and the small number of replacements now available. . . . General Foch may reopen this subject with you and the President hopes you will approach any such interview as sympathetically as possible. . . ."[18]

That message must have been somewhat disturbing. With everyone against Pershing in Europe, it revealed that his adversaries were making inroads with his immediate superiors in America. But it also contained a highly significant piece of news, which would serve as an ace in the hole in future negotiating with the Allies. The War Department revealed that, excluding three divisions about to embark, there were only 263,852 infantrymen ready for shipment. There was therefore a practical limit to America's trained manpower. Hence Pershing would be fortified in resisting Allied demands, using as an excuse that America simply didn't have the men to send.[19]

The Removal of Leonard Wood

(May 1918)

DURING THE FIRST week of May 1918 Pershing made certain AEF staff changes, some for reasons of health, some for efficiency, some in order to rotate staff and line. He invalided home Generals Benjamin Alvord and Alfred E. Bradley, replacing them as Adjutant General and Chief Surgeon with Robert C. (Corky) Davis and Merritte W. Ireland. Frank R. McCoy, Secretary of the General Staff, left for a brigade command, being replaced by Maj. James L. Collins, who had been with Pershing in the Philippines and Mexico. William D. Connor relinquished his G-4 position to Col. George Van Horn Moseley, and Col. LeRoy Eltinge took over as Deputy Chief of Staff, a newly created position.[1]

But the most important change was in the Chief of Staff. For some time Pershing had promised Harbord service with troops, and he now assigned him to command the Marine Brigade of the 2d Division. He spoke of the change as temporary, intending to bring him back to GHQ, but Harbord said he should not make such a promise. Harbord had never commanded more than a squadron of cavalry; should he fail, Pershing could not afford to bring him back. At the farewell Pershing broke the tension of parting with his good friend by remarking gruffly, "I'm giving you the best brigade in France and if things don't work out I'll know whom to blame."[2]

Harbord's replacement was Maj. Gen. James W. (Dad) McAndrew, whom Pershing had known at West Point (Class of '88) and who had been in charge of the AEF General Staff School at Langres. Less of a driver than Harbord, he was more reflective and was exceedingly loyal to his superior, a quality Pershing rated highly. McAndrew once said that he believed that Divine Providence gave Pershing to the country at its time of need.[3]

Meanwhile, events were occurring in the United States involving Leonard Wood which seriously embarrassed the Administration and embittered Wood against Pershing.

On returning to the United States in March, Wood had testified before the Senate Committee on Military Affairs, where he excoriated the War Department for falling down on the job, especially in matters of shipping, aviation, and ordnance. He said not a word of criticism about the AEF, mentioning Pershing's name only once, and that in passing. Wood then returned to Camp Funston at Fort Riley, Kansas, to complete training of the 89th Division, which was devoted to him. He fully expected to go to France with it and to rise high in the AEF command.[4]

All officers scheduled for overseas service had to take a physical examination. Knowing Wood's physical disability, Pershing anticipated that he would fail it, thus happily solving the problem of how to keep him in America without creating a fuss. Wood delayed the examination, claiming that the chairman of the board was personally inimical to him. A substitution was made, Wood took the exam and, to Pershing's consternation, passed![5]

"How in the hell any board could bring itself to believe that General Wood is fit for active service is more than I can understand," Pershing exploded. "He is a cripple and that is all there is to it, and there is no use in sending cripples over here to do men's work."[6]

Secretary Baker also was disappointed by the medical findings, for, having received reports of Wood's misconduct in Europe and Pershing's strong February recommendation against his return, he had determined to keep him in America. A bad medical report would have been a convenient excuse to do so. Baker consulted with General March and they decided to leave Wood with the 89th Division until it was ready to embark for Europe, then separate him from it and appoint a new commander.[7]

But they reckoned without bad luck, or more probably the enterprise of one of America's most forceful generals who was never at a loss for means to achieve his end, especially if it embarrassed a Democratic Administration. On May 21 the 89th Division began to move to the embarkation ports, a procedure which, because of the size of a division, ordinarily took some time. The advance detachment would not sail until June 4 and the last detachment until June 28. Normally a division commander stayed some time at the old station to ensure that the move was being made smoothly before moving to the new. March expected that Wood would still be at Camp Funston when he telegraphed him on May 24: "You are assigned to command Western Department. You will remain at Camp Funston until departure of last unit of 89th Division, when you will proceed to San Francisco, California, and assume command of Western Department...."[8]

But Wood had already left. Perhaps realizing that the administration might try to detach him from his division and that to do so once he had arrived on the east coast would be more difficult (removing a commander when he had one foot on board ship, so to speak), Wood left for the East on May 23, preceding his division rather than following it. March's telegram was forwarded to him in New York City.[9]

Understandably, Wood was furious. "His rage was Olympian," said a biographer. He immediately saw Colonel House, who advised him to see Secretary Baker and, if possible, the President.[10]

Descending on Washington, Wood first saw the Chief of Staff. Was his relief based on supposed physical disability, he demanded? March looked at the man: powerful, large-chested, a former football player, and an all-round athlete. Making a fist, he rapped Wood vigorously on the chest. "There is nothing the matter with you physically," he said.

Then why the relief, asked Wood.

"General Pershing has asked specifically that you be not sent to France, and the War Department is going to back him."

Wood was stunned. He had surmised that the opposition to him was political, coming from President Wilson. When March mentioned military opposition, Wood did not know what to say. It never occurred to him that any soldier could question his competence or not desire his services. Finally he asked if there was any objection to relating the news to some of his friends in Congress.

"What friends?" shot back March. "You understand clearly that no backfire on General Pershing will be permitted, and you should understand, as a military officer of high rank and experience, that we must either support General Pershing or relieve him, and we don't propose to relieve him."[11]

On May 27 Wood had an appointment with the Secretary of War. At the door he said to one of his two aides, "You stay outside. We had better not all go in. He will think we have come to kill him."[12]

The amenities exchanged, Baker informed Wood that he, along with other major generals, had been sent to France to view conditions firsthand and to be looked over by Pershing, that the AEF commander had a list of those he desired returned, and Wood's name was not on the list.

"Then I am to understand that my relief is due to General Pershing?" asked Wood.

"Yes. . . . General Pershing most positively does not want you in France; and frankly, General Wood, I must state that if I were commanding general in France I should not want you, as I fear you would not be subordinate."

"Then I am to understand that the reputation of any officer in the United States Army is placed in General Pershing's hands to make or break as he sees fit?"

"We will not send any officer to France nor keep any officer there against General Pershing's will. We must have a homogeneous working force."

From there the discussion rambled cross-country, Wood expressing surprise at Pershing's objection, since his own impression while visiting Europe was that Pershing was "very anxious" to have him there—an apt comment on Wood's inability to judge other people's feelings about himself.

Wood also mentioned the incident where Pershing had been publicly accused of fathering illegitimate children in the Philippines in 1906. The implication, thought Baker, was that since Wood had "covered" for Pershing in this personal matter (Wood had been commander of the Division of the Philippines then), a fitting reciprocation was due now. To Baker the bringing up of the Philippine scandal story was entirely irrelevant and unworthy of consideration. Finally, Wood asked to see the President, which Baker said he had a right to do.[13]

At 5:00 P.M. on May 28 Wood met the President. Earlier that day Wilson had addressed Congress, saying that "politics is adjourned" during wartime. Now there stood before him a man who had placed him in the embarrassing position of seeming to play politics, of shabbily treating a political rival by letting him come all the way across the country to be humiliatingly ordered back just as he was about to set foot on a ship for France.

The meeting was civil enough, Wood protesting his goodwill and loyalty and denying reports of criticizing the President. He did, however, bring up Pershing and the old Philippine scandal, whereupon the President, as he later told his secretary, Joseph Tumulty, remarked that "he did not care a god damn" what Pershing had or had not done, that he was now doing what they wanted.

The meeting ended noncommittally, Wilson saying he would take the matter under advisement. But on the way out Wood encountered Tumulty and unburdened himself from the strain of talking civilly with a man he hated by a violent denunciation of the way he was being treated, hinting at things about the President's morals which would be embarrassing if brought out, and Pershing's too, and suggesting that if the barrel were tipped over there would be quite a stink.[14]

The President, of course, had no intention of sending Wood to France. Editorial writers blamed him for playing politics at a time he said politics was adjourned, but this was to be expected. A cartoonist named Caesare published a famous drawing in the *New York Sun* showing a disgruntled Wood talking to a despondent Theodore Roosevelt about Woodrow Wilson. "Well, he kept *us* out of war," was the caption.[15]

During the uproar over Wood's relief Wilson confided to Richard Hooker, a personal friend and editor of the *Springfield Republican*, the reason for his decision. "In the first place, I am not sending him because General Pershing has said that he does not want him, and, in the second place, General Pershing's disinclination to have General Wood sent over is only too well founded. Wherever General Wood goes, there is controversy and conflict of judgment. On this side of the water we can take care of things of that sort, because the fighting is not being done here, but it would be fatal to let it go on at or anywhere near the front.

"I have had a great deal of experience with General Wood. He is a man of unusual ability but apparently absolutely unable to submit his judgment to those who are superior to him in command."[16]

On June 1 Wood went to Camp Mills, where his division was assembling, to say farewell to his men. He made a moving talk to his officers, many of whom choked up and were unable to speak as they shook hands and said goodby. On the way back to New York he sat silent in the automobile, occasionally brushing tears off his face. "I have never before realized in all my life," said a companion, "what a melancholy, helpless, ugly spectacle is the rugged figure of a man with the tears rolling down his cheeks."[17]

Frustrated and humiliated, Wood took his resentment out on Pershing. "My, how he hated him," remembered Alice Roosevelt Longworth, who heard Wood ranting and raving, spicing his denunciations with generous details about Pershing

WELL, "HE KEPT *US* OUT OF WAR."

Caesare's Cartoon of Leonard Wood and Theodore
Roosevelt which made a play on Wilson's 1916
campaign slogan: "He kept us out of war."
New York Sun

and Filipino women. "No one ever hated anyone as much as Wood hated Pershing. How he talked! There was nothing he didn't say about him!"[18]

For Pershing's part, whenever he heard rumors in Washington to discredit himself and his work, he suspected Wood. "You know how insidious are his methods," he told Senator Warren, whom he asked to be his watchdog in the capital. "You can always count on his being busy at all times in an endeavor to obtain some sort of advantage, mainly by running down others."[19]

In an attempt to quiet the furor caused by Wood's relief, Baker considered sending him to Italy as head of the first American contingent shipped there, but Pershing was unalterably opposed. "No matter what he promised, he would never be subordinate. . . . He is unscrupulous and I should have no confidence in him. . . . This war is no place for political generals. . . ."[20]

Wood sat out the war in the United States, a bitter and angry man.

SIXTEEN

Cantigny and Chemin des Dames

(May 1918)

BY THE END OF May 1918 the United States had been at war almost fourteen months and had 650,000 officers and men in Europe. While of some use in holding quiet sectors, they had participated in nothing bigger than the melee at Seicheprey, in which they had not exactly covered themselves with glory. Now, however, they were scheduled to make an attack. It was to be a limited one, on the regimental level (some 4,000 men), against Cantigny, a little village northwest of Montdidier, near the farthest point reached by the German March offensive.[1]

Cantigny was selected because it was on a low ridge which overlooked the American 1st Division and provided good observation posts for German artillery. More importantly, however, Cantigny was to be a test case, testing the capacity of the American command and staff to plan and carry off an offensive, albeit a minor one. If they could, it would reinforce Pershing's argument for an independent army in the near future. If they could not, it would reinforce the Allied contention that, for the moment, American troops could best be utilized in British and French formations. From the AEF viewpoint, it was important that the Cantigny operation succeed. As Col. Hanson E. Ely, commander of the assault regiment, remarked later: "General Pershing said that 'no inch was to be given up' when we attacked the place."[2]

While the 28th Infantry Regiment of the 1st Division was designated for the attack, the 1st Division staff, especially Campbell King and George C. Marshall, Jr., planned the operation, with assistance from the French X Corps and the French First Army. They reinforced the regiment with the divisional artillery and machine-gun battalions, with the machine-gun companies of two other regiments, with an engineer company, and two additional rifle companies from the 18th Infantry Regiment of the 1st Division. The French contributed 368 guns and trench mortars from corps and army artillery, twelve heavy tanks, flamethrower teams, and air cover. Most of the equipment amassed for the attack was foreign; the only American items were the rifle and the bayonet.[3]

Preparations for the assault were elaborate and meticulous, leaving nothing to chance. The French had taken and lost Cantigny twice; this must not happen now.

A mock Cantigny was laid out behind American lines on terrain similar to that of the real town. Jump-off trenches were marked out and each battalion practiced separately, in coordination with the tanks, exactly where it should go and what it should do. Men carrying boughs or flags (to represent the rolling barrage) preceded the assault troops who were instructed to "hug" the barrage, that is, stay within fifty to seventy-five yards of the exploding shells, so that they would be upon the Germans before the latter had time to recover from the shelling and come up out of their dugouts.[4]

A sand table, twenty by thirty feet, reproduced the contours of Cantigny and its environs. Houses and trenches were marked out and numbered by blocks. Instructions indicated where the doors were and which houses had cellars. Individual squads were designated to mop up particular dugouts or assault specific houses.

Officers and NCOs alternated between the sand table and the rehearsal terrain. The reinforced regiment walked through the attack, first as groups practicing individually, then as a whole in a dress rehearsal. It was practiced once, twice, three times, each time getting better, but still not perfect.

Meanwhile, on the real terrain, new jumping-off trenches were dug at night so that each of the regiment's three battalions should reach the enemy at approximately the same time. Dumps of ammunition, water, wire, grenades, sandbags, picks, and stakes were moved up.[5]

Everyone had drilled into him, from the division commander on down, that the attack must succeed and that terrain, once taken, must not be relinquished. Planners were confident that the artillery preparation would be so heavy that the initial assault would be no problem. The thing was to get in fast and get set before the counterbarrage hit and the counterattacks began. The Germans had orders to counterattack immediately, and if this failed, to bring up reserves and make a massive attack within six hours.[6]

By the morning of May 28 everyone was in position. Each soldier carried 220 rounds of ammunition, three sandbags, two hand grenades, one rifle grenade, two water canteens, two iron rations, one shelter half, two cakes of chocolate as emergency rations, plus one lemon and wads of chewing gum as thirst quenchers.

The actual attack was more precise and better carried out than any of the practices. It went off like clockwork, the French taking movies of it. Beginning at 4:45 A.M., divisional, corps, and army artillery pulverized the village with gas and high explosive shells. For two hours they rained down. Then at 6:45 A.M. the attacking forces moved out behind a smoke screen and a rolling barrage of artillery and machine guns.[7]

Taking the town was easy. The artillery, in Colonel Ely's words, had "smashed the place up." The village was a mass of smoke, debris, craters, and mangled bodies. Tanks, which these particular Germans had never seen before, helped flush and dispatch machine-gun nests. Flamethrowers did their grisly work against defenders hidden in dugouts. Clarence R. Huebner saw one German run out "just as I had seen rabbits in Kansas come out of burning straw stacks. . . . " He ran about fifteen yards and fell over dead.[8]

The attackers, losing only about fifty men, took about a hundred prisoners. Some they did not take. These were the last-ditch machine gunners, who fired until their ammunition was exhausted and then tried to surrender. For some dough-boys it was simply too much to see a buddy machine-gunned and then hear his killer yell "*Kamerad*" to escape retaliation. They killed the *Kamerad* with mixed feelings of grief and hate.[9]

During the morning Pershing showed up at division headquarters. He was elated at the early success, but warned General Bullard, the 1st Division com-mander, to beware of German counterattacks, which were sure to come. He stressed again that Cantigny must be held at all costs.[10]

Problems soon developed. During the preliminary bombardment, many Ger-mans had taken shelter in the basements; emerging now, they were behind Amer-ican lines which, in the initial assault, had pushed east of the town. House-to-house fighting occurred during the next three days. Reserve American platoons actually took more casualties than the frontline troops as they moved east to support them.[11]

More serious, however, was the sudden withdrawal of French artillery and air support. As luck would have it, the day before the Cantigny attack the Germans had launched a massive assault along the Chemin des Dames, rupturing the French front and heading for Paris. Accordingly, French corps and army artillery were diverted to meet this new German threat, and so were their planes. German aviation was soon strafing American trenches point-blank and directing massive artillery bombardments from the German "heavies"; in contrast, the Americans had only divisional artillery (mostly the short range 75s) with which to respond. At the time the 1st Division most needed counterbattery fire, it was denuded of it.[12]

"If you expect to keep me," taunted a captured German captain, "you better send me to the rear. My men will retake this place in two hours." The enemy launched some six or seven counterattacks, the first almost immediately after losing the village. One of the heaviest came around 6:00 P.M., when the German first wave got on the American side of the defensive barrage before it came down. The defenders beat them off with rifle and machine-gun fire, while the artillery barrage chewed up the second and third waves.[13]

Because German counterattacks were not properly coordinated with their artillery, Ely's men were able to repulse them. But the German artillery continued to rain down and American casualties mounted during the next two days, May 29–30. Losses approached nearly one-third of Ely's original force, most or three-quarters of them, he was convinced, due to enemy heavy artillery which was accurately directed by their planes which controlled the air. Many Americans were withdrawn to the safety of the Cantigny dugouts and basements, but the continuous German counterattacks and American orders that no ground should be relinquished kept a comparatively large number in the front lines and shell holes, where they were chewed up by artillery.[14]

Repeatedly, Ely called for artillery barrages to break up real or threatening counterattacks. When he apologized for calling for so many, General Summerall, the 1st Division artillery commander, responded, "That is what we are here for. . . . We don't criticize and [we don't] ask questions."[15]

Summerall's divisional guns had enough punch to break up enemy counterattacks, but lacked the range to reach the German heavy guns which were ranging in with terrible effect. "Front line pounded to hell and gone . . . ," Ely telephoned brigade headquarters at 8:55 P.M. on May 29. The entire front line must be relieved within twenty-four hours, he said, or he "would not be responsible."[16]

Ely remarked later that there is a vast difference between a man in normal circumstances of food, sleep, routine, and so on, and a man in battle where, in a sense, nothing is normal. Fearful, dirty, ears deafened by explosions, eating cold and unpalatable food or no food at all, without sleep or with insufficient sleep, nerves taut and overstretched, aghast at the carnage he sees all about him, especially of friends, his body overexerted and deadened with fatigue under heavy shellfire— all this conspires to make a man, in Colonel Ely's words, "half-crazy, temporarily insane." There are many more such in battle than people like to believe. "Very few of them are normal," he said.[17]

One dazed soldier came into a dressing station, his arm shot in two and hanging by the skin. Splinted and bandaged, he said, "Richard is himself again," and walked semiconsciously amid exploding shrapnel. Another, a berserk lieutenant, ran around crazily, shooting with his automatic at American runners scampering past. A German shell killed him.[18]

By the third day Ely felt that his men had had it. When a divisional staff officer suggested that they could still hold, Ely exploded: "Let me tell you one thing and you put it down in your notebook. These men have been fighting three days and three nights and have been successful, but five of them are *not worth now what one* of them was when he came in. . . . There are the three other regiments that have had their sleep right along and their loss is comparatively nothing. It is an *injustice* not to relieve the men who have been fighting so long." During the night of May 30–31, Ely's 28th Infantry came out and the 18th Infantry Regiment went in. Although German counterattacks ceased, the Americans took heavy shelling for a number of days.[19]

Said Ely of his exhausted men: "They could only stagger back, hollow-eyed with sunken cheeks, and if one stopped for a moment he would fall asleep." What it had cost the 1st Division fifty men to take, it had cost over 1,000 to hold—a high price to pay for an unknown village of relatively little value. But it was a test of wills and a baptism of fire for the Americans, and that gave it significance.[20]

Although the Germans who defended Cantigny were not the best troops (American intelligence rated them as third-class), Pershing was properly elated by the success. Dining with him and his staff shortly after the battle, Dorothy Canfield Fisher observed that "they all talked at the top of their voices . . . about what they thought had been the magnificent conduct of the American troops. . . . I remember particularly Pershing's banging his fist down on the table and shouting out 'I am certainly going to jump down the throat of the next person who asks me, "Will the Americans really fight?" '[21]

He cabled the War Department: "This action illustrates the facility with which our officers and men learn, and emphasizes the importance of organizing our own divisions and higher units as soon as circumstances permit. It is my firm conviction that our troops are the best in Europe and our staffs are the equals of any."[22]

When André Tardieu, recently French High Commissioner in the United States, ventured some criticism of AEF staff work, Pershing told him that he had "had quite enough of this sort of thing" and that if the French "would cease troubling themselves so much about our affairs and attend more strictly to their own we should all get along much better." French attempts to assume airs, or even to dictate, he said, "had reached the limit of patience."[23]

While Pershing was elated with the success in taking and holding against seven counterattacks a place the French had taken and lost twice, Thomas M. Johnson, a war correspondent, correctly pointed out that "compared with the giant struggle going on elsewhere it was just a little outburst. . . ." It is perhaps the saddest commentary on America's war capabilities that, one year and two months after commencing hostilities, at a time when the European powers were maneuvering and locking in battle divisions, corps, armies, and army groups, the greatest American combat effort was to capture an obscure village using one regiment, slightly reinforced. When one recalls that a regiment is only one-fourth of a division, truly the mountainous AEF had labored mightily and brought forth a mouse.[24]

The Big Show was some fifty miles to the southeast, along the Chemin des Dames, a fifteen-mile ridge running east of Soissons. There Gen. Erich von Ludendorff, chief strategist of the German High Command, who had launched two offensives against the British in March and April, now launched a third one in May, this time against the French. Its purpose was diversionary: to draw Allied reserves away from the British front and fix them farther south. Once this was achieved, Ludendorff planned to deliver a final blow against the British in the north, sometime in June or July.

Ludendorff selected the Chemin des Dames as his point of attack because it was a "quiet" sector, supposedly too strong to be assaulted. No action had occurred there since the French attack against Fort Malmaison the previous October. Both sides used it as a rest area. The Germans called it the "sanatorium of the west" and the French showed visitors around as an example of what a strong defensive position looked like.

The Germans concealed their intentions skillfully. They left thirty divisions in Flanders as a decoy, with heavy radio traffic and nightly signal fires to give the impression that they were about to resume their attack against the British. Meanwhile, other divisions quietly withdrew and concentrated behind the Chemin des Dames, approaching the front by night marches. If an Allied plane flew overhead, German officers ordered "about face," so that troops would appear to be marching away from the front instead of toward it.

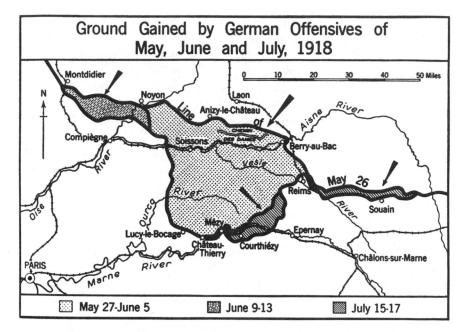

From American Battle Monuments Commission, *American Armies and Battlefields in Europe*, Washington, D.C., 1938.

German concealment was aided by French failure to take proper reconnaissance measures. For two months no aerial photographs had been taken behind the German lines on this front, and for one month no observation plane had flown over it at all. Considering the fact that French intelligence could not locate forty-five German divisions, this was surprising.[25]

But the German deception was not completely successful. At Chaumont a young American intelligence officer, Samuel T. Hubbard, located some fifteen German divisions behind the Chemin des Dames. Taking as his principle that the enemy would attack at the point least expected and knowing that the area was lightly held (some British divisions mauled in the March offensive had been sent there to recuperate), Hubbard concluded that the Germans would attack on this front sometime between May 25 and 30. He convinced his superior, Col. Dennis Nolan, who sent him to warn French GHQ about May 20. The French were not terribly impressed, especially General Denis Duchêne, commander of the French Sixth Army, who believed Hubbard wrong and who felt that his defenses were adequate.[26]

In fact, they were not. Duchêne crowded his troops into the front lines—the worst possible thing to do. The best intelligence pointed increasingly to lightly held front lines as the best defensive tactic, with the main position being several miles to the rear. German artillery could always pulverize the front lines, whereas it had increasing difficulty getting forward to reach subsequent defensive positions, especially over ground cratered by its initial bombardment.

With one minor exception, the French had never before encountered the Hutier tactics. When the British had given way in March, and again in April, the French had chalked it up to poor generalship, inefficiency, lack of planning, and so forth, similar to the Russian failure at Riga and the Italian at Caporetto. Now it was their turn to be humiliated.

At 1:00 A.M. on May 27 the Germans laid down a tremendous artillery barrage along a twenty-four-mile front. In some places they concentrated forty batteries per mile, nearly twice the concentration used against the British in March. Much of this bombardment was gas, extending twelve kilometers behind the French lines and causing considerable disorganization and paralysis. German artillery crashed down on the crowded frontline trenches, on the French forward and rear area artillery positions, and on defensive barbed wire entanglements. After almost three hours of shelling, German storm troops swept forward behind a rolling barrage. Seventeen German divisions, with six in immediate support, hit six Allied divisions, with four in reserve.

By 11:00 A.M. the Germans were at the Aisne River, the French second line, and still going strong. By night they had reached the Vesle River, making a first-day gain twelve miles deep and almost thirty miles wide. What had started out to be a diversion suddenly became the most dramatic breakthrough of the war.[27]

Next day they were across the Vesle and heading for the Marne. General Bliss said later that "the Germans could not have proceded more rapidly if it had been a peace maneuver." Soissons fell. French divisions, thrown in piecemeal as they hurried up to the front, "evaporated immediately like drops of rain on white-hot iron," said a French staff officer.[28]

At the end of three days the Germans had advanced thirty miles, captured 650 guns, 2,000 machine guns, 60,000 prisoners, and vast stores of ammunition, supplies, and rolling stock. On the fourth day, May 30, they were at the Marne River, with outposts across it.[29]

"It was nothing less than a rout," said Frederick Palmer, who saw it. Panic and despair were far worse, he thought, than during the German drive of 1914. When Gen. Jean J. Mordacq, Clemenceau's Chief of Staff, encountered Gen. Joseph Degoutte, a corps commander who was retreating before the onslaught, he found him weeping silently over a tattered map. "I left him with no hope of ever seeing him again," said Mordacq.[30]

On May 30 Pershing took breakfast with Haig, who criticized the French for their lack of success in standing up to the Germans. In view of the British record during the past two months, Pershing found this criticism "rather remarkable."[31]

Later that day he took supper with Foch at the generalissimo's headquarters at Sarcus. "It would be difficult to imagine a more depressed group of officers," he related. "They sat through the meal scarcely speaking a word as they contemplated what was probably the most serious situation of the war."[32]

Allied reserves were so far away that it would take three to four days to get them to where they were needed right now. And what if the Germans unleashed another attack elsewhere, say against the British in the Arras-Amiens area once it was uncovered? No doubt about it, the situation was *"très serieuse,"* as the French admitted.[33]

Not surprisingly, Foch again urged bringing over only infantry and machine-gun units from America. In what must be one of the world's most inappropriate remarks, considering that the war was about to be lost, Pershing later faulted Foch on this occasion for failing to see "the urgency of bringing over men to relieve the extraordinary strain on our supply system."[34]

Two U.S. divisions, the 2d (Omar Bundy) and the 3d (Joseph T. Dickman), were within reach to throw into the path of the advancing Germans, and they were ordered forward. To the west, the 1st Division, still at Cantigny, extended its front to the left to relieve a French division sent to the fray. George C. Marshall, Jr., organized the division's noncombatants into two scratch battalions, and his assistant gave them their orders: "You are to die east of the railroad. That is all the order you need."[35]

SEVENTEEN

Versailles and Belleau Wood

(June 1918)

I N THESE CIRCUMSTANCES, not knowing whether this meeting would be the last or whether the next would be "in the Pyrenees," as Clemenceau said, the Supreme War Council met at Versailles on June 1–2, 1918. Ten miles away in Paris people were fleeing the city by the hundreds, and the government was packing up its papers preparatory to doing the same.

With the war about to be lost, people's emotions surfaced. They said what they thought about each other and about the issues. This was no time to mince words; the stakes were too high. The main agenda concerned the use of American troops and Clemenceau requested Bliss to ask Pershing to be present. This time, once and for all, the Allies intended to state the case for temporary amalgamation with such forcefulness that even the stubborn Missourian would see it. They meant to compel full compliance with Joint Note #18, passed by the SWC back in March.[1]

Stressing the crisis, Foch called for shipping only infantry and machine-gun units from America for the indefinite future. To Pershing this was intolerable. It meant postponing indefinitely the formation of a separate American army which, it seemed to him, was always being postponed, however much the Allies agreed to it in principle, as at Abbeville.

Pershing pointed out that his London and Abbeville concessions had already put him considerably behind schedule in forming a balanced and integral American army. His supply problem was becoming acute, as was his transportation. Railway repair workers, for instance, were urgently needed to repair French rolling stock, without which supplies would pile up at the ports, and without supplies his forces would stagnate. Already, under existing agreements, he was some 205,000 men short for his Services of Supply (SOS).

Foch was unmoved. The Germans were on the Marne; the Fatherland was in peril. He kept waving his hands excitedly and repeating, "The battle, the battle, nothing else counts."

At this point Mr. Graeme Thomson, a British transportation expert, supported Pershing by remarking that it would be a very serious mistake to permit American rail transportation to further degenerate, it being already in bad condition. Thomson's words had no more effect on Foch, said Pershing, "than if they had not been uttered." Waving his hands, the generalissimo said everything else could be postponed. "*La bataille, la bataille, il n'y a que ça qui compte.*"[2]

Pershing then played his ace in the hole, the card given him by the Chief of Staff in Washington, who had cabled on May 11 that the number of trained men in the United States was getting quite low. Hence there was a limit to the number America could send, even if the Allies had ships. It was quite impossible, Pershing declared, to send over only infantry and machine-gun units to the extent Foch demanded: 250,000 men each for June and July, a total of 500,000. Apart from three divisions ready to embark, only 263,852 trained men remained in the United States.[3]

Foch promptly trumped Pershing's ace. Send them anyway, he said in effect, even untrained men. The situation required it. "*La bataille, la bataille!*"

To Pershing the proper course was not to bring over untrained infantrymen, but to bring over the trained infantrymen available and use the shipping surplus to bring over the auxiliary arms, like artillery and SOS personnel, corps and army troops. Clemenceau had shrugged his shoulders helplessly when Pershing had revealed the shortage of infantrymen. "Then we can practically expect nothing from the United States after the present schedules are completed," he said. "That is a great disappointment."

"Not at all, Mr. Prime Minister," replied Pershing. "Every ton of available shipping will be used to bring over the SOS troops that are absolutely needed, as well as divisional and corps troops that are needed to complete the American combat organizations. In the present crisis I consider this essential."[4]

Foch waved his arms and called for "the largest possible number of troops, trained or untrained." Pershing pointed out that untrained combat troops could not be used for two months anyway, so why not leave them in the United States and use shipping to bring over what was needed to complete existing units and build up his SOS organization? Foch said that men learned quicker in France. Lord Milner, the British War Minister, jumped in with the remark that "we form a coalition and must make concessions"; therefore Pershing ought to consider sending untrained infantrymen.[5]

Later, when Pershing suggested calling up earlier the latest class of French youth, Lloyd George interrupted, "Why, General Pershing, you surely would not put those mere boys into the trenches?"

"Mr. Prime Minister," Pershing rounded on him, "you have suggested that we put American boys not as well trained as the French boys you refer to into the trenches. I cannot see the distinction."[6]

Pershing then complained that the Allies, despite promises, were not meeting existing commitments to supply and maintain American troops. Shortages existed in artillery, transport, and other facilities. He did not blame them for conditions over which they had no control, but the deteriorating situation pointed up the need to build up the SOS organization sufficiently to handle the American Army when it came into being.

Foch was adamant. "He saw no reason," said Pershing, "why we should not fill up ships in July with men called to the colors in May."[7]

Suggesting an adjournment, Pershing walked out in the yard with McAndrew, his Chief of Staff. He was willing to do everything reasonable to help the Allies in their plight, he told him, but could not see shipping untrained men, who could not be used for at least two months, when so many other men (non-combat support troops) were needed immediately. Up until May 1, 1918, the War Department had drafted only about 116,000 men a month because of limited shipping facilities. With shipping suddenly available for 250,000 a month, an infantryman shortage had now developed. This would be remedied in time (in May, 373,000 men were drafted), but in the interval it seemed the path of wisdom to bring over trained non-combatant troops rather than untrained combat troops. The former could build up the structure necessary to receive the latter when they came; otherwise the influx of infantrymen would cause the American organization, in Pershing's words, to "go to smash."[8]

When the meeting resumed, everyone was keyed up. Tempers were short, exacerbated by the fact that eighteen people were crowded into a tiny unventilated room and were hot and uncomfortable.

"You are willing to risk our being driven back to the Loire?" Foch queried, repeating the question he had asked at Abbeville the month before.

"Yes," responded Pershing most positively, "I am willing to take the risk."[9]

"Well, we will refer this to your President," said Lloyd George.

"Refer it to the President and be damned," answered Pershing hotly. "I know what the President will do. He will simply refer it back to me for recommendation and I will make to him the same recommendation as I have made here today."[10]

Later, when Pershing remarked that he considered Foch his superior officer, the conference reporter noted that Foch "made a short remark which was not intelligible." It was probably just as well; it probably could not have been printed anyway.[11]

"The whole discussion was very erratic," remembered Pershing, "as one of the Allies would take exception to nearly every statement made by the other." Even among the British themselves disagreement occurred over the number of Allied divisions available. Milner exclaimed with some exasperation that it was useless to talk about their resources to meet the German threat when they could not even agree as to what they had. He entered a formal protest against all figures used in the discussion.[12]

Pershing knew that the Allied leaders had little confidence in him, his AEF organization, and its ability to function as an equal. They had kept harping, all the way up to President Wilson, about the untried American higher command and staff, warning that its inexperience invited disaster. The French in particular said that, for the moment, the Americans should attempt nothing larger than divisional organizations. Corps, armies, or groups of armies were out of the question.[13]

At the conference Lloyd George actually proposed that Pershing relinquish control over American divisions training with the British, so that Haig, rather than himself, would determine when their training was complete and when they should be sent into battle. "I held my temper," Pershing wrote in his diary, "but very firmly objected . . . and stated I could not, should not and would not surrender my prerogatives in this manner."[14]

Only a few days after the Versailles Conference, General Jan Christian Smuts made the extraordinary suggestion of taking the American Army away from any American general and giving it to someone more capable of using to best advantage its first-class material, namely, himself. "Pershing is very commonplace," he wrote Lloyd George confidentially, "without real war experience, and already overwhelmed by the initial difficulties of a job too big for him. It is also doubtful whether he will loyally co-operate with the Allied Higher Commands. He could not get together a first-class Staff either. I fear very much that with the present Higher Command the American Army will not be used to the best advantage; and victory for us depends on squeezing the last ounce of proper use out of the American Army." Pershing, he suggested, could be retained behind the lines, to handle bases, supplies, training camps, transport, and so forth.[15]

That such an extraordinary suggestion could actually be made, one so offensive to American national pride, so farfetched, and so unlikely of ever being accepted by any people with any sense of their military worth, may be taken as a measure of Allied opinion of Pershing.

As the conference deadlocked, Pershing suggested that he, Milner, and Foch see if they could work out something privately. When the three closeted themselves, Foch remained adamant until his Chief of Staff, General Maxime Weygand (whom some said was the brains behind Foch) remarked that perhaps it might be best to leave untrained combat troops in America a while longer, since they could not be used in Europe for several months anyway. Pershing had been saying the same thing over and over without effect, but once Weygand said it, Foch immediately agreed.[16]

An agreement was accordingly signed between Foch, Milner, and Pershing which, on the assumption that 250,000 men could be transported in each month, gave priority to 170,000 combat troops in June and 140,000 in July, a total of 310,000. The rest for each month would be the support and supply troops Pershing desired, a total of 190,000. Any surplus above 250,000 a month would be combat troops.[17]

The agreement was a victory for Pershing, embodying his contention that untrained combat troops should not be used and that the surplus shipping available during the two months should bring over trained support troops. The agreement had far-reaching effects on an American army, for it is hard to see how it could have functioned without the concession about support troops won from the Allies in the Versailles agreement. Even as it was, the AEF was plagued by personnel shortages in the fall.[18]

Nonetheless, all agreements were conditioned by what the Germans did. As S. L. A. Marshall later remarked: "Not Allied pressure, but the remorseless grind of events" would determine the fate of a separate American army. "If Allied defeat continued, the feeding of U.S. divisions into the line piecemeal as they arrived must perforce continue. There could be no choice in this matter. But if the tide could be stemmed, . . . Foch could build up his margins, and as the reserve swelled, the constituting of a separate U.S. Army would be to general advantage."[19]

At that very moment the tide was being stemmed. On May 30 the U.S. 3d Division (Dickman) was ordered toward Château-Thierry. The motorized machine-gun battalion got there on May 31, followed by the infantry the next day. They blew up the main bridge over the Marne, spread out along the river to the east for ten miles, and repulsed all German attempts to cross.[20]

Much was made of it later, but as S. L. A. Marshall pointed out, the action was not that big. The German thrust was more an exploratory probe, made by light forces, rather than a massive crossing. Blowing the bridge, while preventing a crossing to the south, also prevented one to the north, thus effectively securing the German flank against a counterattack. Furthermore, the Germans did not have to cross the Marne at this point to reach Paris; that was already open to the west.[21]

Elsewhere the U.S. 2d Division (Bundy), originally scheduled to relieve the 1st Division at Cantigny, had been hastily diverted, moved by motor trucks, and rushed pell-mell up the Paris road to fan out west of Château-Thierry. One of its brigades was made up of Marines (Harbord); the other, Regular Army (Edward M. Lewis).[22]

Approaching the front through Meaux, some twenty miles northeast of Paris, the Americans encountered a sea of humanity fleeing the German advance. Harbord saw "men, women, children hurrying toward the rear; tired, worn, with terror in their faces. Some riding on artillery caissons or trucks. Many walking, an occasional woman wheeling a baby carriage with her baby in it. Sick people resting by the side of the road in the fields. Some driving carts piled high with their little properties including all kinds of household effects, one old woman leading two poor little goats while she trudged along the crowded driveway. Little flocks of sheep, occasionally a led cow, sometimes a crate of chickens on a cart. Everything that a frightened peasantry fleeing before a barbarian invader would be likely to think of bringing from among their little treasures was to be seen on that congested highway. I have never seen a more pathetic sight."[23]

The Americans encountered French soldiers too, but with one exception they were all going the wrong way. "They were tired and demoralized," Harbord observed. They came back, not in large units, but fragmented—three or four men in a group, every man for himself. It was a beaten, routed army.[24]

The vandalism inflicted on deserted villages and farms confirmed it. French troops, some of them drunk from despoiled wine cellars, had looted everything not nailed down, leaving the dwellings looking as if a tornado had hit them. The Americans saw dresser drawers and clothes closets emptied on the floor, their contents helter-skelter, clothing torn, mirrors smashed, books ripped apart, farm animals slaughtered. Disshevelled bed sheets bore the muddy imprint of poilus who had flopped down on them. In one instance, when a French peasant remonstrated with the troops, they tied him to a chair and beat him.[25]

Walking wounded now appeared, heading for the rear, heads bandaged, arms in slings, tell-tale reddish brown stains showing through the bandages. The French seemed heartened by the sight of fresh Americans heading for the battle, but what would happen when they got there? "The Boche are coming," the poilus said, and when the Americans responded, "We're here," the French repeated, "Ah, oui, but the Boche, he is *still* coming."[26]

On June 1 the 2d Division, Harbord's brigade on the left and Lewis's on the right, deployed across the Paris-Metz highway west of Château-Thierry, behind two French divisions which gradually fell back and passed through American lines. The Germans, who had been going hell-bent for election since May 27, moved into Belleau Wood, Bouresches, and Vaux as their artillery pounded the Americans on their front.

The 2d Division artillery fired back, its 75s barking a sharp staccato, its 155s a deep-throated roar. Fired rapidly, the gun barrels glowed with heat at night, and in the dark the exploding flashes from their muzzles resembled a multitude of fireflies shining in the forests and fields.

Harbord received orders from a French general to hold the line "at all hazards," shortly followed by another message to dig some trenches behind "just in case." "We will dig no trenches to fall back to," replied Harbord. "The Marines will hold where they stand."[27]

Holding was not really that difficult, for the German offensive, in its sixth day when the 2d Division deployed, had in many ways "shot its bolt." All World War I offensives tended to peter out after a week because of difficulty getting men and matériel forward across devastated terrain in sufficient quantities and speed to keep the offensive going. Then too the French, while giving away at the center, had held firm at the shoulders of the salient, at Reims on the right and west of Soissons on the left. Holding at the shoulders necessarily limited advance in the center and would eventually make the salient very vulnerable.[28]

Nevertheless, the 2d Division's stand across the Paris highway had important effects at the time, for French troops, fleeing the Germans, were crying "*la guerre finie*" to the advancing Americans as they passed. As Harbord said, "When the Second Division went into line on the afternoon of June 1st on both sides of the Paris-Metz highway, the French had been retiring along the whole Reims-Soissons front from one to ten miles a day for five days. No unit along the whole front had stood against the German masses. The first unit to stand was the Second Division and it not only stood but went forward."[29]

The effect was tremendous, all out of proportion to the numbers involved. According to Bliss, Foch felt that the 2d Division practically saved Paris. Speaking of the surge of Americans to the east when all else was retreating to the west, Jean de Pierrefeu, an officer on Pétain's staff, wrote, "We all had the impression that we were about to see a wonderful transfusion of blood. Life was coming in floods to reanimate the dying body of France...."[30]

On June 6 Harbord ordered his Marine Brigade against Belleau Wood. "Come on, you sons-o'-bitches," yelled Sgt. Dan Daly. "Do you want to live forever?" The Marines swept forward and a knock-down, drag-out fight that endured for twenty days was on.[31]

Belleau Wood was a natural strong point. Heavily forested, rugged, and rocky, with tangles of dense undergrowth, it was a defender's dream. Massive boulders from some antediluvian upheaval, some as big as freight cars, afforded excellent protection for machine-gun nests, making them impervious to artillery fire except by direct hits. As usual, the Germans skillfully emplaced these nests so that they mutually supported each other.

Into the maelstrom went four future commandants of the Marine Corps: Wendell C. Neville, Thomas Holcomb, Clifton B. Cates, and Lemuel C. Shephard, Jr. There also went a newspaperman named Floyd Gibbons, who lost an eye that first day of battle, along with 1,087 Marines who lost their lives. It was the single most costly day in Marine Corps history until World War II.

The next nineteen days were pure hell. Charles G. Dawes, who visited Belleau Wood afterwards, wondered that anybody came out alive. Long, almost unbroken lines of ambulances headed back along the Paris road, carrying men racked by disease, diarrhea, thirst, exhaustion, wounds, bad weather, and gas. The gas casualties were particularly pitiable; many were delirious, nearly all were blind, crying, moaning, and thrashing about.

The shelling, which never seemed to stop, produced its grisly effects. Harbord saw the dismembered bodies of seven or eight men who had been struck by a 155-millimeter shell. One of them was hanging grotesquely from the crotch of a tree some ten or twelve feet in the air.

Extraordinary heroism was ordinary. Men dashed out under shellfire, sometimes through hundreds of yards of danger, to rescue fallen buddies. Runners with broken legs dragged themselves across the ground to deliver messages. Men with a hand or foot shot off continued to fight until they were ordered to the rear or collapsed from shock and loss of blood. Men stepped on grenades to shield their comrades, losing a foot. Others drove ammunition trucks in broad daylight down a highway where high explosive shells were dropping like rain.[32]

And for what? A woods named Belleau and two villages named Bouresches and Vaux. In all history, nothing important had happened in these places, nor has anything since. As S. L. A. Marshall pointed out, Belleau Wood "was not a key position but a blind alley." It led nowhere. It was not on the vital Paris road.[33]

The importance of Belleau Wood was not strategical, or even tactical, but psychological. General Böhm, commander of the German 28th Division, one of the four which defended it, pinpointed the issue: "It is not a question of the possession or nonpossession of this or that village or woods, insignificant in itself; it is a question whether the Anglo-American claim that the American Army is equal or even the superior of the German Army is to be made good."[34]

It was a test of wills. Even Ludendorff recognized the consequences when on June 8 he ordered that any American units encountered "should be hit particularly hard in order to render difficult the formation of an American Army."[35]

And so it went on, both sides slugging away, fighting for inches of ground which would later be lost, retaken, lost again. To a Marine colonel Belleau Wood became a "dark, sullen mystery." At one point Harbord described his men as one step removed from "complete physical exhaustion." They were withdrawn for a time, then sent back in again.[36]

During the month the Germans used four divisions against the Marines. Two were fourth-class, but two others (the 10th and 28th) were rated among the better German divisions. Captured prisoners said: "It was decided to use picked men against the Americans. . . . The purpose of . . . the 28th Infantry Division was to prevent at all costs the achievement of success by the Americans—especially a moral success."[37]

On June 26, after an all-day artillery preparation, the Marines drove into Belleau Wood and finally came out on the other side. "Woods now U.S. Marine Corps entirely" read the message sent to headquarters. The cost of the 20-day battle was high: some 5,000 casualties—over 50 percent of the Marine Brigade of the 2d Division.[38]

Was it worth it? Certainly the land had little military value. It just happened to be at the farthest point of the German May offensive, which had slowed down and was officially considered over by June 6, the day the Marines hit Belleau Wood for the first time.

The Marines thought it was worth it in June 1918, and still do today. Battle is more than just taking terrain; it involves a psychological factor too (what generals call "establishing moral ascendency"). The Germans thought it important to establish this by retaining Belleau Wood; the Marines, by taking it. And the Marines did.

The Germans were impressed with the 2d Division, as well they might be. "The 2d American Division may be classified as a very good division, perhaps even as assault troops," wrote a German intelligence officer on June 17, 1918. "The various attacks of both regiments on Belleau Woods were carried out with dash and recklessness. The moral effect of our fire-arms did not materially check the advance of the infantry; the nerves of the Americans are still unshaken.

"The individual soldiers are very good. They are healthy, vigorous and physically well developed. . . . The troops are fresh and full of straightforward confidence. A remark of one of the prisoners is indicative of their spirit: 'We kill or get killed.' "[39]

Through several censorship slips the Marines got more publicity for their exploits than they actually deserved. AEF policy was to allow newsmen to mention service branches such as infantry and artillery, but not specific units. During the Belleau Wood fight, correspondents asked if they might mention the Marines, since it was known that the Germans had identified them as such. The censor said yes, on the principle that no military information was being given that the enemy did not already have, and also on the principle of letting newspapermen put in as much detail as was consonant with military security. Then too it seemed that "marines" were just another category, like infantry and artillery. It slipped his mind that in all of France there was but one group of Marines, the Marine Brigade of the 2d Division. These accordingly got a tremendous amount of publicity for their action, whereas the other brigade (Regular Army) got none at all, they being classified as "infantry," of which there were thousands in France. Thus when the army brigade captured Vaux in a splendid attack, they got no attention; it was just "American infantry" that took the town.[40]

Considerable hard feeling resulted from such slips, not only within the 2d Division, but with the 3d Division which had opposed the Germans at Château-Thierry. Floyd Gibbons had been with the Marines during their initial attack on June 6, and been erroneously reported as dead. Prior to the action he had filed a skeleton dispatch, intending to fill it out later with details. The dispatch mentioned the Marines and, since no one in America had ever heard of Belleau Wood, he named the place they were near, Château-Thierry. The Paris censor, a friend of Gibbons, thinking he had "gone west" and that this was the last thing he could do for "poor old Floyd," released the dispatch. Thus in America the Marines got credit for action not only at Belleau Wood but at Château-Thierry, which they hadn't been within miles of.[41]

Soon after the fighting Pershing visited the hospitals. These were French, since American divisions were serving in French corps and armies. Pershing moved among the cots, stopping to chat, asking about the food, being cheerful, speaking words of encouragement and appreciation. The doughboys made it clear that they did not like French hospitals and wanted to be in their own. They didn't speak French, didn't know the word for water, and said that when they made drinking motions they frequently got some bitter-tasting stuff, a saturated solution of epsom salt. Arrangements were soon made to transfer American patients to their own hospitals as soon as they were fit to travel.[42]

Sometimes the hospital scenes produced chuckles. Pershing asked a fine young soldier where he was wounded—meaning, of course, what part of his body. The reply was: "Do you remember, Sir, just where the road skirts a small grove and turns to the left across a wheatfield, and then leads up over the brow of the hill? Well! Right there, Sir."[43]

But sometimes the scenes were pathetic, for example, men standing at salute beside their cots with bandaged eyes that would never see again, doomed to a world of darkness. In a surgical ward, Pershing came to the bed of a soldier named Jimmie, who had been operated on the day before and who remarked apologetically through parched lips: "I cannot salute you, sir." Pershing noticed the dent in the sheet where the right arm would normally be. "No," he replied, running his hand lightly through the boy's tousled hair, "it's I that should salute you."[44]

On one occasion Pershing's cheerfulness during a hospital visit gave way to tears later in the privacy of his automobile. He told Dawes, who was with him, that he had great difficulty controlling his emotions at seeing men who were maimed as the result of his orders. He hoped that God would be good to them.[45]

The 100-Division Program

(June-July 1918)

THE SUCCESS OF the 1st Division at Cantigny, of the 3d Division at Château-Thierry, and the 2d Division at Belleau Wood, Bouresches, and Vaux, strengthened Pershing's determination to cut loose from Allied tutelage. "Do they patronize you?" he asked General Bullard around the time of Cantigny. "Do they assume superior airs with you?" When Bullard said no, Pershing replied vehemently, "By —! They have been trying it with me, and I don't intend to stand a bit of it!"[1]

Although he had about 800,000 troops in France, not one American division was tactically under an American corps; they were all under British and French command. American corps exercized control only over administration and supply. Hence Pershing was concerned to concentrate his divisions into progressively larger units: first corps, then armies. "The fact is," he told Secretary Baker, "that our officers and men are far and away superior to the tired Europeans."[2]

Beginning in April and continuing through early June, with one exception, every U.S. division arriving in Europe had been assigned to the British for training. They numbered ten in all. The British fed them, equipped them, and had the assurance that, in the event of a German onslaught, they could be thrown into battle.

The one exception was the 92d Divison, composed of black troops. To Pershing's surprise, the British objected to receiving them. "These Negroes are American citizens . . . ," he protested to Haig. "Naturally I cannot and will not discriminate against them." To avoid making an issue of the case, the War Department scheduled the 92d Division for training with the French, who were happy to have them.[3]

Doughboys did not like service with the British, or with anyone else for that matter. The British ration was smaller and different: tea and jam instead of coffee and sugar. When sick or wounded, they ended up in British hospitals, feeling isolated, lonely, and homesick, their roommates not knowing who the Brooklyn Dodgers were and they knowing nothing about cricket and caring less. They missed recreation facilities like the YMCA. They also thought the British talked funny.

A truck was a "lorry"; a railroad car was a "truck." Irish-Americans in particular found fault with anything British and fomented ill-feeling.

Lloyd Griscom, AEF liaison officer with the British, said that, after only two weeks, "our men were quickly abusing everything British and enquiring where was the American Army they had come to fight in?" Griscom, who had been a diplomat before he became a major in the 77th Division, warned that, while a crisis might justify amalgamation, "I can assure you there will be trouble if it lasts long."[4]

The recent German offensive provided an occasion to withdraw some of these doughboys from the British. With the Germans back on the Marne, Foch on June 2 asked that five of the ten U.S. divisions be sent south to quiet sectors on the French front, relieving French divisions for combat. Haig was miffed when Pershing approved the request, because he had hoped to retain the ten divisions for some time and derive use from them. The remaining five divisions were actually one less than the British expected to have when they concluded the Six Division arrangement with Pershing back in January.[5]

Five American divisions (35th, 77th, 82d, 4th, and 28th) were therefore transferred out of the British zone. The last two were halted en route to the Vosges and placed on the west face of the recently created Marne salient near Château-Thierry. Together with the 2d and 3d Divisions, which had been at the tip of the salient since late May, and the 26th and 42d Divisions, which were sent to the general vicinity, that made six American divisions grouped around the Marne salient, forming a possible nucleus for the future American Army.[6]

"There was, perhaps, no branch of the service that gave us more trouble than aviation," Pershing wrote in an early draft of his memoirs—then deleted it, following his policy of not giving offense. He did say, however, in the final published version, "Jealousies existed among them, no one had the confidence of all the others, and it was not easy to select from among the officers of the corps any outstanding executive." In its first year, the Air Service had no less than six different commanders.[7]

Because aviation was spectacular, bringing more rapid promotion and higher pay, it was subject to a certain amount of envy and jealousy by non-flyers. The aviation people, in their turn, reflected a certain disdain for outsiders and non-professionals. The latter might be Regular Army and have rank, but they didn't know airplanes. Harbord, for example, called an airdrome a place where planes were "stabled" and a cavalry officer referred to propellers as "fans."[8]

The dispute between the flying and non-flying officers was epitomized in Benjamin D. Foulois and William B. (Billy) Mitchell. Foulois was himself a pilot, having flown one of the early test flights with Orville Wright in 1909. But the staff officers he brought over with him to France in November 1917 were not. According to Mitchell, they displaced flying officers in the Zone of the Advance (Mitchell's bailiwick) who were trained and experienced and running a working organization. In their place Foulois substituted non-flying officers of superior rank. The training section of the Air Service was under a colonel with no practical flying knowledge.[9]

Foulois conceded this, but contended that there simply weren't enough flying officers to build up the Air Service to its contemplated size—larger than the whole Regular Army in 1914. What was needed, he believed, was a cadre of non-flying Regular Army officers with organizational and executive ability who would command things initially until enough flying officers could be trained. Mitchell, however, maintained that such non-flying officers were exercising command in areas they knew nothing about, such as training and tactics.[10]

During January and February 1918 friction developed between Mitchell and a Foulois subordinate over their respective authority in the Zone of the Advance. In March, and again in April, Mitchell publicly criticized Foulois, his organization, and his subordinates. In May Pershing confessed that aviation was causing him "great anxiety," with "everyone running around in circles." It badly needed straightening out.[11]

To do the job, Pershing on May 29 appointed his West Point classmate Mason M. Patrick as Chief of Air Service, AEF. Patrick, an excellent administrator, replaced Foulois, who became Chief of Air Service, First Army. Mitchell became Chief of Air Service, I Corps. Foulois was still Mitchell's superior, but Patrick was over both of them to shake their heads together and make them pull in tandem.[12]

In June Mitchell and Foulois had a spat which was more worthy of fishwives than professional soldiers. The new arrangement designated Mitchell's old office in Toul as Foulois's new headquarters. When Foulois showed up to take command, Mitchell claimed that practically everything in sight pertained to Air Service, I Corps, and therefore he was taking it with him: the entire office staff, office furniture, maps on the wall, clocks, and even the telephone. Foulois would be moving into a bare room and have to conduct business seated on the floor or on orange crates.[13]

Foulois complained to I Corps commander, Hunter Liggett, who sent a staff officer to Toul to tell Mitchell to leave Foulois what he needed to carry on. But Foulois was absolutely incensed, asking for Mitchell's immediate relief and return to the United States. Mitchell's conduct, he said, was "extremely childish"; he could not work with such an officer.[14]

Pershing talked matters over with Patrick. Mitchell, he knew, was hard to get along with, but he was a damned good airman and it would be a shame to lose him. Even Foulois admitted that Mitchell had few superiors in the tactical use of airpower. Pershing called in Mitchell, laid down the law, and told him he must go to Foulois and make up. He also told Foulois that when Mitchell came he should meet him more than half way. "We must put aside absolutely all questions of personality . . . ," he instructed.

The meeting was cordial and from that time on Foulois thought Mitchell's attitude showed "a marked improvement." Eventually, Foulois recommended Mitchell as his replacement for Chief of Air Service, First Army.[15]

The Germans had now launched three major offensives in 1918, one a month during March, April, and May. Two of them (March and May) had made giant salients, like two huge breasts projecting into Allied lines. On June 9 the Germans attacked again, in an offensive designed to eliminate the "cleavage." Unless this were done the Marne salient would be particularly vulnerable, for it had only one main line of communication, through Soissons, which was close to the French lines and therefore open to a flanking attack.

The new offensive (June 9–13), while gaining some ground, soon broke down and was called off. The Marne salient still remained vulnerable and the Allies would hit it a month later.[16]

Pershing happened to be with Clemenceau on the day the German drive opened. Initial reports credited it with considerable success and Pershing asked what would happen if Paris fell? Clemenceau said they would fight on. "Above Paris is France, and above France is civilization."

"Well, Mr. President," Pershing responded, "it may not look encouraging just now but we are certain to win in the end."

Clemenceau clung to his hand and said plaintively, "Do you really think that? I am glad to hear you say it."

It was the first (and only) time Pershing realized that the premier had doubts.[17]

Contacting Foch the same day, Pershing asked the same question and received the same answer. Foch repeated it with such force, however, that Pershing, who could be an emotional man when moved, felt impelled to jump up and shake hands with him. "I told him he could count on us to the last," he wrote in his diary, "and that I wanted to be near him in this fight, to share it with him and live his life."[18]

Despite the Frenchmen's brave words, Pershing knew that the monthly German attacks had shaken the Allies. French morale, especially among the lower ranks, was very low. On June 17 Foch asked Pershing to consider turning over to the French the five divisions remaining with the British, to be assigned to twenty tired French divisions, one regiment per each division. The reason, said Foch frankly, was morale. The French were asking, "Where are the Americans, and what are they doing?" Inserting American regiments would be like a blood transfusion, putting the divisions on their feet and giving them again *envie de marcher*."[19]

Pershing seriously considered it, which is noteworthy in view of his known opposition to amalgamation. That he did consider it illustrates his flexibility; he was much more fluid on the amalgamation question than people have given him credit for. All along—and Pershing was consistent in this—he maintained that, should the emergency require it, he would do whatever was necessary, even to the extent of putting doughboys into Allied ranks by companies. "We cannot afford to allow their morale to become too low," he wrote General March two days after Foch's proposal, "as there is danger of their breaking at the wrong time." He told Secretary Baker that he contemplated granting the French request in order "to give them courage."[20]

Eventually, however, Pershing decided against the proposal. Americans would do "twice as much," he felt, if concentrated in large units under their own leaders; associating with tired divisions, far from emboldening the French, would only dispirit the Americans.[21]

Yet Pershing knew that something must be done to help. "The Allies are done for," he wrote Colonel House on June 19, "and the only thing that will hold them (especially France) in the war will be the assurance that we have force enough to assume the initiative." America must exert herself mightily to win the war in 1919 or not at all. The Allies would probably quit after that, the Germans would be able to recruit new manpower from their Russian possessions, and America herself would become increasingly tired of a long war. "The burden of the war from now on is practically upon our shoulders," Pershing told Theodore Roosevelt.[22]

From mid-June on, therefore, Pershing began to upgrade the size of the American Army required for victory. On June 18 he told his supply and staff chiefs to plan for an AEF of three million men. (Its size was then approximately 800,000.) The following day he cabled a recommendation to the War Department for 66 full divisions in France by May 1, 1919, saying it was "the least that should be thought of."

He asked the War Department to draft 400,000 men a month for the next five months (July through November), a total of two million. By April 1 all of them would have had at least four months training and most of them could be in Europe swelling the American Army for a massive spring offensive to knock Germany out of the war. If tents or cantonments were insufficient for these draftees, said Pershing, let them be billeted in private homes, as they were in France.

"We are face to face with the most serious situation that has ever confronted a nation," he told Secretary Baker, "and it must be met at any sacrifice and without any delay. . . . There is nothing so dreadfully important as winning this war. . . ."[23]

Four days later, on June 23, Pershing upped the ante. After talking with Foch, he and the generalissimo sent a joint recommendation to the War Department calling for 80 divisions in France by April and 100 by July.[24]

It is hard not to fault Pershing for irresponsibility here. Why 100 divisions? It sounds like a good round number, pulled out of a hat, rather than a carefully calculated figure. And why such an increase in just four days: 66 divisions up to 100, a fantastic increase!

Pershing explained that his June 19 recommendation had been conditioned by lack of cantonments in America, lack of equipment, and lack of shipping. But this is lame. He had already spoken of billeting to both Baker and March when recommending his earlier program, and he had also spoken of the Allies making up American equipment and shipping deficiencies.[25]

Rather than being based on good reasons, Pershing's 100-division recommendation appears to have been inspired by a spur-of-the-moment impulse to have as many divisions as possible and by the knowledge that he would probably get less than he asked for. Brutally put, ask for 100 and hope to get 66. Pershing admitted as much after the war. Even 80 divisions, he conceded, would probably overtax AEF transportation and supply facilities. "I was willing to ask for the greater numbers, feeling, however, that the War Department would do wonders if it could carry out even the 66-division plan."[26]

And just how many men did 100 divisions involve? Each combat division numbered approximately 28,000 men, but since corps and army troops had also to be allowed for, the AEF as a rule of thumb calculated a division at 40,000. Thus 100 divisions would total 4,000,000. One must, however, also include replacements (because of casualties) and Services of Supply troops. Hence Pershing thought he was asking for "at least 5,000,000 men."[27]

Considering that the Allies already had almost 3,000,000 men on the western front to oppose the Germans' 3,500,000, it was absurd to contend, as Pershing and Foch did in their June 23 recommendation, that Allied numerical superiority "can only be obtained" by the increment of 100 U.S. divisions. Pershing's AEF would almost be big enough to take on the Allied and Enemy armies combined.[28]

A 100-division program would have enormous consequences. It was not just a question of shipping so many men to France; with British shipping that might be practicable. But supplies must be shipped to maintain them, railway rolling stock to transport them, horses to move supplies on the battlefield, and forage and grain to feed the horses. Even as it was, the AEF was beginning to be seriously imbalanced (because of the crash program of infantry and machine-gun shipments) regarding the proportion of supplies to men. For the moment, the deficiency was being made up by the British agreement to feed, and if necessary clothe, American troops training with them. But what would happen when Pershing withdrew them from the British, as he was beginning to do?[29]

It was a serious problem, not met by Pershing's airy assurances to the War Department that "we can and will handle anything and everything" it could send over. Even now ships were unloading matériel at ports faster than it was being evacuated. An increase in cargo transport could only make this bottleneck worse.[30]

The War Department cautioned both Pershing and Bliss not to hold out any hope to the Allies for the 100-division program until they could study the proposal and make a judgment on America's capacities. It soon developed that the program was far beyond them. Shipping was simply unavailable to supply that number of divisions in the time allotted. Furthermore, not enough berths existed in France, even if all those used by the British and French were taken away from them and given to the AEF, to supply 100 U.S. divisions. Pershing and his staff might be excused for being ignorant of America's shipping capacities, but French berths, their number and capacity, were matters one would expect them to know something about, they being on the scene. Pershing's 100-division recommendation therefore meant that he had gone off half-cocked.[31]

In Washington General March concluded that, while 100 divisions was absolutely impossible for 1919, 60 divisions was a certainty and 80 divisions a possibility, something to shoot for. But it would mean extending the draft age to cover 18 to 45, appropriating billions of dollars to arm and equip the extra troops, borrowing Allied heavy artillery until America could produce her own in quantity, and continuing reliance on Britain to transport and supply the AEF. On July 23 March cabled Bliss that they would attempt an 80-division program by June 30, 1919. Surprisingly, March did not cable Pershing, perhaps thinking that Bliss would relay the information to him. The AEF commander continued to think in terms of 100 divisions.[32]

On July 10 Pershing conferrred with Foch about bringing together American divisions scattered throughout France to finally form an American Army. Foch repeated what he had said at the Abbeville Conference in May: that he knew that troops fought best under their own flag and that he wanted a separate American Army as soon as possible.[33]

This sounded good but, as Pershing noted in his diary, when pressed for details Foch became very vague. "He said he did not see how we could proceed till we see what the Germans are going to do, that if they attack we would have to do so and so; if not, we would perhaps do so and so, or so and so. He did not have definite ideas on any of these so and so's."[34]

Pershing also wanted a decision on an American sector, without which it was impossible to plan for the American Army. His first choice was Lorraine, for reasons which he and Pétain had agreed on the previous summer and which he explained again to Foch. In general, it meant east of Verdun. As a second choice, however, he would agree to the Marne salient, since U.S. divisions were already at or near there. The big thing was to have a decision, and soon.

Foch objected to Lorraine because it put the American Army too far away from the British and French. All three armies, he felt, should line up side by side in the same general region and push straight ahead, the spirit of competition urging each to greater effort. Because of the channel ports the British front would naturally be from the coast to Amiens; because of the need to cover Paris, the French would run from Amiens to Reims; the U.S. front then, in order to be in the same vicinity, should run from Reims to the Argonne Forest. This would put the American Army west of Verdun rather than east, in Champagne rather than Lorraine, where the AEF had been building warehouses, depots, railways, and other facilities for over a year.[35]

Listening to Foch, Pershing must have wondered just how good a strategist he was? Lining three armies up side by side would not necessarily produce emulation. It was not like a racetrack where one contestant could see another. And what of difficulties in terrain, which made such a contest unequal?

Rather than three runners on a track, the situation was more like three men attempting to cross a river. They would more likely confuse the enemy by crossing at different points, especially simultaneously, than by grouping in the same area.[36]

On July 21 Pershing saw Pétain and got his support for forming an American army near the Marne salient, where a number of American divisions already were. Pershing told him he expected to take personal command of the army, a statement which surprised Pétain in view of Pershing's other duties at GHQ and with the SOS. Pershing replied that "all this was arranged so as to go on with very little supervision from me"—a strange remark in view of the fact that one week later he would remove the SOS commander for inefficiency. It was again a manifestation of Pershing's tendency to try to do too many things at once.[37]

Commencing in March, the Germans had launched one offensive per month; they now planned their July operation. It was to be directed east and west of Reims, having as its purpose the capture of that city and the enlargement of the salient around Château-Thierry by reaching the Marne at Épernay and Châlons. Hopefully, it would draw off and use up French reserves from the north, so that Ludendorff could resume his attack against the British in Flanders.

The Germans cleverly selected Monday, July 15, for the attack. July 14 was Bastille Day but, as was the custom when this fell on Sunday, Monday was also a holiday. Thus, after a long weekend with much celebration and inebriation, the French by Monday, July 15, would be suitably set up to be "smashed" even more than they were.[38]

But the French got wind of it. As early as June 28, their Fourth Army, located east of Reims, captured prisoners who told of the impending attack. Foch accordingly reinforced that army, as well as the French Fifth and Sixth Armies, located west of Reims, and brought up reserves behind the front.

General Henri Gouraud, commanding the French Fourth Army, made excellent defensive arrangements. His front line was a "false front," lightly held by the fewest of defenders. Not knowing this, the Germans would waste their heavy preliminary bombardment on it. The real line of defense was a second position, strongly held, some distance back beyond the range of most German artillery, and a third position, even farther back, in case the enemy broke through. When the German infantry attacked, the defenders in the first (false) line were to send up warning flares and rockets and then evacuate. French artillery would then fall on the front trenches and decimate the Germans as they came on toward the second (main) position. When (and if) they reached the second line, they would be met by fresh, strongly entrenched defenders, while they themselves would have been badly chewed up in the process of getting there.[39]

Defensive arrangements in the French Fifth Army (Henri-Mathias Berthelot) and the Sixth Army (Joseph Degoutte) were less satisfactory. Neither French general believed in a false front, and so they crowded troops into the front line where they would bear the brunt of German artillery.

But even here luck was with the French. On July 14 a raiding party captured German prisoners who revealed the exact hour for the attack: midnight for the start of the artillery preparation, 4:00 A.M. for the infantry assault.

Approximately 30 minutes before midnight French and American artillery laid down a furious cannonade on crowded German frontline positions, as well as on road approaches, artillery emplacements, ammunition dumps, and assembly points. It caused tremendous havoc, putting some German units out of action before the attack began.[40]

At midnight the German artillery opened up. By now approximately 5,500 guns were in action on both sides. "The whole sky seemed to be torn apart with sound . . . ," said Fr. Francis P. Duffy of New York's Fighting 69th. Men could

Peyton C. March, Army Chief of Staff,
1918–1921. *U.S. Army Military
History Institute*

Ferdinand Foch, Allied Commander in
Chief. *National Archives*

Hanson Ely.
U.S. Army Military History Institute

Joseph T. Dickman.
National Archives

not make themselves heard in the din; orders had to be written to be understood. The guns became so hot they had to be swabbed out after each shot.[41]

For four hours the shelling continued, gas and high explosives dropping on Gouraud's false front and on the crowded first lines of Berthelot and Degoutte. Then about 4:00 A.M. gray-clad shock troops moved forward. In Gouraud's zone they easily swept over the first line (the false front), killing the few defenders (suicide troops) who had survived the bombardment. But from that moment on, for approximately one and one-half miles, they came under French and American shellfire all the way to the second (main) line. Douglas MacArthur, who watched them, said: "When they met the dikes of our real line, they were exhausted, uncoordinated, and scattered, incapable of going further without being reorganized and reinforced." The attack east of Reims bogged down.[42]

To the west of Reims, against Berthelot's and Degoutte's armies, the Germans did better. Encountering no false front, German artillery chewed up the front line; their infantry crossed the Marne and penetrated in one place as far as five miles.

Dickman's 3d Division, however, serving in Degoutte's Sixth Army east of Château-Thierry along the Marne, dug in its heels and resisted furiously, earning its sobriquet, "The Rock of the Marne." As soon as the Germans got pontoon bridges across the river, the Americans blew them up. But the Germans kept coming and some got across. In the grainfields down by the riverbank Dickman's men, lying in semicircles, let the Germans get within thirty steps and then cut them down en masse. "Never have I seen so many dead men," said a German officer, "never such frightful battle scenes."[43]

Said Dickman later: "No German soldier crossed the road [south of the Marne] . . . except as a prisoner of war, and by noon of the following day (July 16) there were no Germans in the foreground of the Third Division sector except the dead." In one regiment this ran above ninety percent.[44]

The 3d Division paid for it, however. Fighting in three directions at once, infantry and machine-guns losses in some instances reached fifty percent. Many who survived were mentally undone. Said a medical officer: "Some of them cursed and raved and had to be tied to their litters; some shook violently . . . some trembled and slunk away in apparent abject fear of every incoming shell, while others simply stood speechless, oblivious to all surroundings."[45]

The same was true in the 42d Division, which had fought as part of Gouraud's Fourth Army east of Reims. Douglas MacArthur, its Chief of Staff, was haunted by "the vision of those writhing bodies hanging from the barbed wire" and "the stench of dead flesh."[46]

On July 17 the German High Command called off the offensive. It was simply not worth continuing for the slight gains it was making at such terribly high cost.[47]

NINETEEN

Soissons: The Turn of the Tide

(July 1918)

WITH THE GERMAN attempt to enlarge the Marne salient bogged down, Foch moved to eliminate it. It was obviously vulnerable. As early as May 30, when the salient was being formed by the breakthrough at Chemin des Dames and the push to the Marne at Château-Thierry, Pershing had suggested a counterattack against the flanks, offering American troops. Foch said he had such a move in mind and during June ordered Pétain to prepare for it.

The logical place to attack was the west face of the salient, near Soissons, through which ran the main highway leading to Château-Thierry and the Paris-Soissons railroad. Should these be cut, or at least interdicted by artillery, the Germans would have to withdraw from the whole salient. It was as simple as that.

The attack was entrusted to Gen. Charles Mangin's French Tenth Army, specifically to the XX Corps composed of the American 1st Division (of Cantigny fame), the American 2d Division (of Belleau Wood, Bouresches, and Vaux), with the 1st Moroccan Division sandwiched in between them. The Moroccans were tough as nails (the famous French Foreign Legion was part of them) and everyone was afraid of them, perhaps even the French. They were considered the best assault troops in the French army; the Americans would be in select company. But Pershing was putting his best men forward with his two most experienced Regular Army divisions. The attack was scheduled for dawn on July 18, with Mangin's main thrust being supplemented by similar attacks around the salient on the part of the French Sixth, Ninth, and Fifth Armies.

Both the 1st and 2d Divisions had new commanders, appointed July 15. The 1st Division was now under Maj. Gen. Charles P. Summerall, who had commanded its artillery brigade. Ruthless, hard-driving, efficient, he was rated by Pershing as his top commander. Summerall replaced Bullard, who was promoted to command III Corps.[1]

The 2d Division got Harbord, who had commanded its Marine Brigade. The former commander, Bundy, was sent into limbo, being used later as a decoy corps commander in the Belfort Ruse in September. Pershing had been disappointed

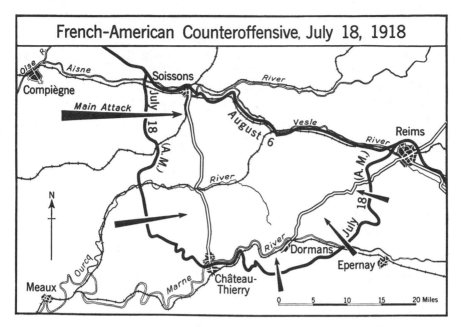

French-American Counteroffensive, July 18, 1918

From American Battle Monuments Commission, *American Armies and Battlefields in Europe*, Washington, D.C., 1938.

with him; "he lacks the grasp," he said. When someone remonstrated against removing Bundy, arguing old ties and friendship, Pershing replied: "I don't care. Men's lives are involved."[2]

The Moroccans were already on the scene, but the two U.S. divisions moved in at the last minute in order to maintain secrecy: the 1st Division coming down from Picardy; the 2d Division coming up from the Château-Thierry sector. For the doughboys the moves were almost as harrowing as the battle which followed.

The problem was that, although administratively the 1st and 2d Divisions were under the U.S. III Corps, commanded by Bullard, tactically they were under the French XX Corps (Pierre E. Berdoulat), whose staff officers issued orders in rather freewheeling fashion without bothering to explain to the Americans what they were doing. Harbord in particular was vexed. "A Division of twenty-eight thousand men, the size of a British or French Army Corps, [was] completely removed from the knowledge and control of its responsible Commander, and deflected by truck and by marching through France to a destination uncommunicated to any authority responsible for its supply, its safety·or its efficiency in an attack but thirty hours away. General Berdoulat and his people were unable to say where it would be debussed or where orders could reach it which would move it to its place in time."[3]

The time factor was important because, unlike the usual attack, there was to be no artillery preparation, just a rolling barrage which was scheduled to begin at 4:35 A.M. on July 18 and then move forward at so many yards per minute. Should the infantry be late, the rolling barrage would be wasted. The Germans would then have time to come up out of their dugouts and have a clear field of fire at the Americans as they attacked.

The approach to the battlefield was via the Forest of Retz, a dense, dark area through which roads proceeded like tunnels through gloom. To Marvin Taylor, an officer in the 2d Division, July 17 was a night such as he had never experienced before and hoped never to experience again. The road through the forest was literally crawling with men and equipment: a double stream of vehicular traffic in the center (trucks, artillery, wagons, caissons) with infantry on either side. It was a madhouse, men staggering forward in the dark, wretched in the rain, holding on to the man in front to keep from getting lost. Sometimes the line would jam and buckle and grind to a halt; other times one ran headlong in the darkness trying to keep up. Because of the rain, mud, darkness, congestion, and confusion, progress was one mile an hour, if that.

Occasionally there was a halt while extra bandoleers of ammunition were issued, or wrecked artillery and carcasses of horses hit by a German shell were dumped off the road. Though tired, the men did not sit down because sitting in mud would have made them more miserable than they already were.[4]

Harbord was frantic to get his men up on time. Not knowing the whereabouts of a single unit of his division, save the artillery, he had had to make out his attack order in the dark and had scheduled some units for the first wave which, it now turned out, were considerably in the rear. Changing the attack order now would only compound the confusion, so Harbord could do nothing except put his military police on the road with orders to hurry up the crucial units.

Some of these had been marching all that night, all the previous night, and the day in between. Some had been without food and almost without water. Some were disoriented. "I was completely at sea," said Marvin Taylor. "I had no idea where we were and did not even know the direction of the enemy."[5]

Incredibly, miraculously, most of the units got to the jump-off line on time. One brigade of the 1st Division reached it with only five minutes to spare. A lead battalion of the 2d Division ran the last ten minutes to reach the front, arriving out of breath and exhausted. Hanson Ely's 3d Brigade of the 2d Division jumped off with its telephone and wireless units lost somewhere in the rear, hopelessly snarled in a massive traffic jam in the darkness. Some machine-gun units never made the deadline and were sorely missed.

Precisely at 4:35 A.M. the rolling barrage began. "It seemed that every piece of artillery in France had fired simultaneously," observed one soldier. French and American artillerymen frantically worked their guns, deluging the German front lines.[6]

Watching from a plane as the rolling barrage crept toward German trenches on another occasion, Eddie Rickenbacker never forgot the harrowing sight. "Some gigantic hand seemed to be tearing up the earth in huge handfuls, opening ugly yellow holes from which sprang a whirling mass of dirt, sticks, and dust. And nearer and nearer to the line of trenches this devastating annihilation was coming. To know that human beings were lying there without means of escape—waiting there while the pitiless hailstorm of shrapnel drew slowly closer to their hiding places—seemed such a diabolical method of torture that I wondered why men in the trenches did not go utterly mad with terror."

Eventually the barrage reached the German line. "A first shell fell directly into the trench in front of me, tearing it open and gutting it completely for a space of thirty feet. The next instant a Boche soldier sprang out of the trench alongside this point and flinging down his rifle proceeded to run for all he was worth back to a safer zone in the rear trenches. Hardly had he gone ten yards when a high explosive shell lit in front of him. Before I saw the burst of the shell I saw him stop with his arms flung over his head. Next instant he was simply swept away in dust and disappeared, as the explosion took effect. Not a vestige of him remained when the dust had settled and the smoke had cleared away."[7]

In the American trenches, lieutenants cried, "Forward," but could not be heard above the din. They gave hand signals and led their men over the top.

The rain had ceased; the sun was just lightening the sky. The attackers plodded forward across a sodden landscape, picking their way around shell holes which had become miniature lakes in the rain. When they hit the first German trench, they kept on going. It was filled with corpses, casualties of the rolling barrage.

Almost four hundred tanks were in the attack. The soldiers stayed close, using them for protection as bullets rat-a-tatted off their hides, and blessed them as they ran over a machine-gun nest or blasted it out of existence.

Men began to be hit. Some stumbled to the rear, holding their wounds, gritting their teeth, their faces contorted in pain. Others fell prostrate in wheat fields where, because the grain was waist-high, they could easily be overlooked and slowly bleed to death. Good Samaritans stopped momentarily to stick the fallen man's rifle in the ground, bayonet first, and hang his helmet on its butt, so it would be noticed by a medical corpsman when he passed by.

Prisoners also began to appear, heading for the rear. Their captors had cut suspenders and belts, thus handicapping the enemy, and sent them rearward with well-directed kicks.

In a wheat field Ben H. Bernheisel of the 1st Division encountered a German not one foot away. The man sprang up, hands in the air to surrender, but the American instinctively brought up his rifle and had its bayonet right at the man's throat. "His eyes stuck out like marbles and his face was ghastly," said Bernheisel. He grabbed the German's canteen, made him drink from it to be sure it wasn't poisoned, then kept it himself and kicked the enemy as a signal to move on.[8]

From time to time the Americans saw the Moroccans on their flanks. They made no attempt at formation, but went forward in groups, sitting down occasionally under a tree to eat some of their black bread or take a swig of wine from their canteens. Their rifles were mostly slung rather than carried, but they flashed some exceedingly wicked-looking knives.

Several villages were on the line of advance, with the inevitable, terrible street fighting. "We struggled forward in groups made up of men of all outfits—infantrymen, Marines, and Moroccans—in a strange hodge podge," remembered one soldier. "Sweating; panting for breath; straining at the obstructions; cursing in as many languages and dialects as there were sections represented, appealing profanely to God for assistance in the mighty effort to kill the enemy who were, no doubt, equally as profanely seeking aid from that same Diety in still another tongue."[9]

Across a plateau, across a wheat field, down a ravine, up the other side, house-to-house fighting through a village, on they went—1st Division, Moroccans, 2d Division—flanks sometimes in the air, units intermixed, confused, fatigued, men spending and being spent.

The day was fearfully hot. The sun bore down, thirst became extreme, and men stripped the dead—friend and enemy alike—of their canteens. Although knowing better, they filled them from little pools of stagnant water, pushing aside the green scum. The water was obviously germ laden, but they were just too damned thirsty to care.[10]

Men went over the top together, but soon broke up into small groups and became quite separated. Wherever he looked, the soldier saw open spaces with a few men here and there, heard the rat-a-tat of machine guns and the noise of a shell going overhead. "You are alone and feel alone," said one veteran. Looking for a helmet to use, a doughboy picked one up, began to brush the dirt out, then stopped. Inside was the top of a man's skull—a mass of matted, bloody hair.[11]

On the way to a dressing station Ben Bernheisel saw a disabled French tank, its front all blown in, and looked inside out of curiosity. The back wall was covered with a bloody splash and a body lay crushed on the floor.[12]

Atop a hill Marvin Taylor encountered a dead German machine gunner seated at his weapon, his hand still on the trigger. He was slumped over, a bullet hole in his forehead and a bayonet thrust in his throat. The gun had an excellent field of fire, and many Americans had died approaching it. Taylor was a humane man, but he laughed aloud at seeing the corpse; it seemed a fit retribution for what the gunner had done to others.[13]

By the end of the day the 1st Division had advanced some three miles, the Moroccans slightly more, and the 2d Division some four and one-half miles, more than any other division in the four French armies attaching that day.

Everyone was dog tired. Men at the front dug shelter holes for themselves with their mess knives and helmets. They took turns watching at night but, said one, "we were so dead tired I believe the entire German army could have advanced unseen."[14]

To the rear, hospital facilities were entirely inadequate. "The scene was indescribable," said Dr. Hugh Young. One little field hospital with two hundred beds was inundated with over three thousand cases during five days. Clothes cut away, men lay outside on flagstones, cold and wet from the night air. Many who might have been saved died from shock, exposure, and lack of attention. There was blood over everything, as all, friend and foe, were "leveled in the common democracy of suffering and death."[15]

Pershing was deeply disturbed when he heard of inadequate care for the wounded. It was a "damned poor piece of staff work," he said. All future French plans involving U.S. divisions, he insisted, must give sufficient advance warning to allow the American medical corps time to set up hospitalization and evacuation facilities.[16]

On the second day, July 19, the attack continued. The first day surprise and strong artillery support had brought great gains with relatively slight losses, but from now on it was just the opposite. Surprise was gone, and American artillery could not locate the position of advance units because the doughboys were deficient in plotting their front lines for the observation planes. It was hard spreading out white panels on the ground when someone was shooting at you.[17]

Less molested by artillery, German machine guns hidden in caves or in ravines took a heavy toll. So also did German airplanes which appeared over the 2d Division and began strafing the foxholes, flying so low that the Americans could clearly see the pilot's faces and the black fourchée crosses on the wings. Completely unopposed, they roamed at will. One doughboy said later that he doubted that he or his comrades would ever forgive American aviators for not putting in an appearance.[18]

In truth, American flyers had many problems at this time. Recently transferred from the Toul sector, which had been quieter, Billy Mitchell's fighter pilots suddenly found themselves in the big time. Not only were they outnumbered, but they were up against some of the finest fliers in the German Air Force—Baron von Richthofen's Flying Circus. Flying in larger formations, the Germans took a heavy toll on the less experienced Americans.[19]

By dark on July 19 the 2d Division was used up and was withdrawn during the night. In two days it had advanced seven miles, captured almost 3,000 Germans, 75 guns, hundreds of machine guns—all at the cost of some 5,000 killed and wounded. Battalions, normally more than 1,000 men at full strength, marched back with only several hundred men; companies, 250 at full strength, came back with 25 or 30 men. In the rear areas they learned for the first time where they had been. Newspapers showed a cartoon of the Marne salient being cut off by a large pair of pincers in the hands of General Foch.[20]

Pershing encountered Harbord as his division came back and congratulated him warmly. Even if the 1st and 2d Divisions never fired another shot, he said, they had "made themselves and their commanders immortal."[21]

For two more days the 1st Division slugged ahead, casualties mounting to 7,300 as Summerall pushed his men. When a battalion commander reported that he was stopped at such and such a place, Summerall rejoined: "You may have paused for reorganization. If you ever send another message with the word *stopped* in it, you will be sent to the rear for reclassification."[22]

When asked by a corps staff officer if his division were capable of another attack after the heavy losses sustained, Summerall was reputed to have said: "Sir, when the 1st Division has only two men left they will be echeloned in depth and attacking toward Berlin."[23]

By the night of July 21, when it was relieved, the 1st Division had cut both the Soissons-Paris railroad and the Soissons-Château-Thierry highway, and captured nearly 3,400 Germans and 75 guns.[24]

The French were delighted. Colonel Paul H. Clark reported that the Operations Section of Pétain's GHQ was acting like schoolboys. One Frenchman impersonated Ludendorff receiving news of the July 18 counterattack. Two others, convulsing everyone with their gestures, impersonated Ludendorff relaying it to the German Crown Prince. A third mimicked the Kaiser as he received the news. They excitedly posted messages about the XX Corps advance and shook Clark's hand. "*Superbe! Magnifique! Épatant!*" they said. "Without the Americans this would never have been possible. We owe it all to you. . . ."[25]

The French officers' shenanigans about German reactions contained much truth. The battle of Soissons was the turn of the tide. Having had the initiative since March, the Germans had now lost it and would never regain it again. Reserves which they had scheduled for the attack against the English in Flanders had to be diverted south to protect their withdrawal from the Marne salient. Field Marshal Paul von Hindenburg, the German Commander, was depressed. "How many hopes, cherished during the last few months, had probably collapsed at one blow! How many calculations had been scattered to the winds!"[26]

The German Chancellor, George von Hertling, summed it up best in one paragraph:

"At the beginning of July, 1918, I was convinced, I confess it, that before the first of September our adversaries would send us peace proposals. . . . We expected grave events in Paris for the end of July. That was on the 15th. On the 18th even the most optimistic among us knew that all was lost. The history of the world was played out in three days."[27]

While the cutting of the Soissons railroad and highway rendered the salient untenable, the German withdrawal from it was by no means precipitate. They wanted time to remove their huge store of matériel and they gained it by conducting a skillful retreat, contesting every foot of ground and making stands at the Ourcq and Vesle rivers. For the next two weeks the Germans moved slowly backwards under pressure from French and American forces pushing in against the salient's apex and sides. The Marne salient slowly contracted like a huge deflating dome.

The Germans were nobody's fools when it came to fighting defensive actions. Moving up in the dark at night, a small American unit encountered some men and heard a challenge in English. "Halt!" it said.

"Americans," responded the doughboy in charge.

"*Feind* [Enemy]!" came the reply, and the next moment a German machine gun wiped out virtually the whole unit.[28]

At one point the Germans converted a cemetery into a defensive works by throwing the bodies out of the vaults and using them for dugouts. At another point they defended one small hill by ringing it with seven consecutive circles of machine guns.[29]

The village of Sergy changed hands eleven times before the 42d Division finally took and held it on July 29. The Americans sobbed when they came out of line and encountered their dead lying like cordwood on the slopes around Meurcy Farm.[30]

Advancing beyond Sergy at night, Douglas MacArthur encountered the dead so thick "we tumbled over them. There must have been at least 2,000 of those sprawled bodies. . . . The stench was suffocating. Not a tree was standing. The moans and cries of wounded men sounded everywhere."[31]

Used at critical points during this operation (known officially as the Aisne-Marne Counteroffensive, July 18-August 6) were the U.S. III Corps (Bullard) and I Corps (Liggett), with the U.S. 3d, 4th, 26th, 28th, 32d, and 42d Divisions. After a slow start, the AEF was now making its presence felt in a decisive way.[32]

But American inexperience took its toll. The doughboys made the initial advances in good form, but after that they tended to bunch up in groups, making it easier for machine guns to mow them down. They attacked like lions, said a French officer, but they were *très imprudents*," for they frequently charged frontally instead of from the sides or rear. When halted, they often did not bother to dig even a shallow trench which might have provided some protection from the inevitable counterbarrage.

Casualties mounted because replacements, rushed over during the massive summer shipments, were frequently terribly untrained. Although two months' training was considered the minimum necessary for combat, men were arriving with only three weeks'. In an extreme case, one man had only one week. "Cannon fodder, if there ever was any," commented a veteran.[33]

Commanders, some with little more experience than their men, made mistakes by crowding them up into the front lines, increasing supply difficulties and running up casualties. Instead of pulling their men back and smothering the Germans with artillery when they encountered stiff resistance, they ordered a second or third infantry assault. They took the objective, but at great cost—sometimes more than it was worth.

During the offensive very little attention was paid to burying the dead. Many lay for days without being interred; others were improperly buried or only partially buried in shell holes. Some ten percent were never identified; in many cases no attempt was even made. When Pershing heard about these conditions, he gave strict orders for the future.[34]

If the Americans lacked experience, they made up for it in *élan*. General Walther Reinhardt, Chief of Staff of the German Seventh Army, which opposed the Americans, called it more important than training or experience. It was something that could not be taught, but must be inborn: the will to attack, to kill or be killed. With the entry of America into the war, he said, the French obtained once more what they had once had and lost after three years of combat: troops who could be relied on to give everything that was in them to take an objective, or die in the attempt. "They may not look so good," said Reinhardt, "but hell, how they can fight!"[35]

Taking part in the counteroffensive were Pierre Teilhard de Chardin, later a renowned Jesuit anthropologist and philosopher; Henry J. Reilly, who became a noted military writer; Fr. Francis Duffy of New York's "Fighting 69th"; William J. (Wild Bill) Donovan, head of the Office of Strategic Services during World War II; Charles L. Bolté, later Vice Chief of Staff of the Army; Theodore Roosevelt, Jr., TR's son and the only general to land with the first-wave troops on D-Day in 1944; Troy Middleton and Clarence R. Huebner, both corps commanders in World

War II; and John L. Hines, Charles P. Summerall, Douglas MacArthur, and Malin Craig, Army Chiefs of Staff respectively from 1924–1939.[36]

Also taking part were the poet Joyce Kilmer and Theodore Roosevelt's son, Quentin, both of whom were killed. When Pershing heard of the latter's death, he wrote the father: "Quentin died as he had lived and served, nobly and unselfishly, in the full strength and vigor of his youth, fighting the enemy in clean combat. You may well be proud of your gift to the nation in his supreme sacrifice."[37]

Pershing's kindness and consideration on this occasion meant much to the former president. Recalling the general's own personal tragedy when his wife and three children died in a fire at the Presidio in 1915, Roosevelt replied: "You bore it with splendid courage and I should be ashamed of myself if I did not try in a lesser way to emulate that courage."[38]

Profoundly moved by his son's death, TR wrote a stirring editorial for *Metropolitan* magazine, part of which was later carved in stone on the Theodore Roosevelt monument in Washington, D.C.: "Only those are fit to live who do not fear to die," he said; "and none are fit to die who have shrunk from the joy of life and the duty of life."[39]

On August 6 the campaign ended with the Marne salient eliminated and the two opposing forces facing each other on either side of the Vesle River in a straight line from Soissons east to Reims.

TWENTY

The Goethals Proposal

(July 1918)

O N JULY 24, Marshal Foch, in a good mood, called his three higher commanders together: Pétain, Haig, and Pershing. As the generalissimo saw it, things were on the upswing. The July German offensive, recently stopped, had been turned into a defeat by the Franco-American offensive then in progress. American manpower had now brought the Allies equal to the enemy in numbers, with the prospect of superiority in the future. In addition, the Allies already had a decided superiority in tanks and aviation and, to a lesser extent, in artillery. The tide had turned and the Allies now had the initiative.

For the immediate future Foch proposed eliminating two key German salients: that of the Somme (caused by the March 21, 1918, offensive), which threatened the Paris-Amiens railroad, and that of St. Mihiel, which threatened the Paris-Nancy railroad. Some important mining regions in northern France should also be recaptured. Beyond that it was impossible to plan, except to seek to end the war in 1919. Reduction of the St. Mihiel salient was entrusted to the American Army whenever it came into being.[1]

That same day, July 24, Pershing formally issued orders creating the American First Army, to take effect on August 10.

How successful it would be in large part depended on logistics, on its supply lifeline, and here evidence was mounting that not all was well. From July 1 onward the AEF was falling steadily behind in finding sufficient berthing space for incoming cargo ships and sufficient transportation to move material out once it was landed. Statistics showed that week by week the amount of supplies landed at the ports was more than the amount moved inland. What was happening therefore was the creation of a massive bottleneck at the ports that an increase of cargo ships would only make worse.[2]

Despite this, Pershing kept reassuring the War Department that all was well, or soon would be. "You get the men and supplies over here and we will do the rest," he wrote General March on July 19. In his postwar autobiography he admitted that "any expression of doubt on our part about handling cargo would probably cause a slowing down at home, from which it might be impossible later to recover. . . ."[3]

Pershing was playing it safe, but in doing so he manifested a lack of confidence in the War Department, as well as a certain irresponsibility. Things *were* piling up at the ports. To carry out the 100-Division program, which he had recommended so strenuously, the docks would have to unload almost *three times* the highest previous daily average.[4]

In Washington the feeling grew that Pershing was trying to do too much, attempting to wear too many hats. Sir William Wiseman, who had the ear of both Colonel House and President Wilson, warned that the AEF was heading for a supply crisis and that something must be done about it. After talking to Wiseman, House wrote in his diary: "He thinks Pershing is getting 'the big head' and that it will continue to grow until something happens to reduce it. He considers him an able man but not a great one. He believes he has too much to do."[5]

House agreed. Even back in December, when he had visited Europe, he felt the AEF commander was overworked and urged him to transfer diplomatic matters to someone else's shoulders. "If you train and fight our army and defeat the enemy, you will have done all that the Nation expects of you," he counseled. "You should be unhampered to do the greater work."[6]

On June 3, 1918, House suggested to the President that Pershing "be relieved from all responsibility except the training and fighting of our troops . . . He should be relieved of all questions of policy except where his opinion is asked. There should be no need for him to be in consultation with the Prime Ministers and Foreign Secretaries of England, France and Italy. He should be in touch with Foch and Foch should be in touch with these."[7]

General March wrote to the same effect on July 5, stating that almost certainly a subdivision of Pershing's work would be made "in the near future." Privately, he told Dwight Morrow that Pershing had more to do "than any one man in this world could accomplish. . . ."[8]

Secretary Baker too approved the idea of freeing Pershing from all tasks except military. He contemplated putting Vance McCormick in charge of diplomacy overseas and General George W. Goethals in charge of logistics.[9]

Builder of the Panama Canal, Goethals had an international reputation as an administrator. He had been an instructor at West Point when Pershing and March were cadets, and later served with them on the first General Staff. Pershing liked him, calling him a "man after my own pattern." As Director of the Purchase, Storage and Traffic Division, he was the No. 2 man in the War Department and a good choice to succeed March if anything happened to the Chief of Staff. He was brilliant at handling supplies and saving space. Before the war a commercial bale of hay occupied 220 cubic feet; through special compresses, Goethals condensed it to about 80 cubic feet, which was not only almost three times smaller but also more impervious to moisture.[10]

On July 6 Baker wrote Pershing that he planned to send Goethals to Europe to handle supplies and that, in order to free Pershing to devote full time to training and fighting his army, Goethals would be in a coordinate, rather than subordinate, position.[11]

Pershing gagged on the letter, which arrived July 26. To him an independent supply chief violated a fundamental military principle—unity of command. In all the major armies the field commander also controlled the supply lines. Only thus could military operations and their logistical support be properly coordinated.[12]

Fortunately for Pershing, Baker's proposal was only a suggestion. As always, the Secretary was extraordinarily deferential to his field commander. "Will take no action until we are in perfect accord . . . ," he promised. "My whole purpose in this matter is to get all of the data before you and rather to aid you to come to a right conclusion than to impose my own."[13]

To tell the truth, Pershing knew that his supply organization needed shaking up. Its head, Maj. Gen. Francis J. Kernan, was inefficient and Pershing had already planned to replace him. At first he thought of Brig. Gen. Henry L. Rogers, AEF Chief Quartermaster, but by July 19, having been forewarned by friends in Washington of the Goethals proposal, he had decided on his close friend, James G. Harbord.[14]

Harbord had been with the AEF from the beginning and his recent service with the 2d Division gave him the feel of the troops and their impressions of how well the SOS was "delivering the goods." He had drive, imagination, initiative and, above all, loyalty. "I am his man," Harbord had once remarked of Pershing; "he can send me to Hell if he wants to."[15]

On July 26, while Harbord was still resting up from the ordeal at Soissons the week before, his phone rang with orders to hurry down to GHQ at Chaumont. When he arrived, Pershing was waiting for him and, after the briefest of salutations, told Harbord about his dissatisfaction with Kernan, Baker's proposal about Goethals, and his desire to appoint Harbord instead. Sleep on it, he said, and let me know in the morning.

Harbord was thunderstruck. He had done well as a brigade and division commander, and envisioned himself as a future corps, even army, commander. And now this: the supply lines! It was hot that July night, Harbord remembered, "and what was going on made it no cooler."

Harbord said there was no need to sleep on the matter. He was Pershing's man, grateful to him for his previous appointments at GHQ and with the 2d Division. He said that he would "go anywhere . . . and on any kind of duty."[16]

The following day, July 27, Pershing appointed Harbord as Chief of Staff of the SOS, and sent off a confidential cable to the Secretary of War marked RUSH RUSH RUSH RUSH. The supply system, he said, "includes transportation up to the trenches and is intimately interwoven with our whole organization. The whole must remain absolutely under one head. Any division of responsibility or coordinate control in any sense would be fatal. The man who fights the armies must control their supply through subordinates responsible to him alone. The responsibility is then fixed and the possibility of conflicting authority avoided. This military principle is vital and cannot be violated without inviting failure. It is the very principle which we all urged upon the Allies when we got a supreme commander. . . . I very earnestly urge upon you Mr. Secretary that no variation from this principle be permitted."[17]

Later that day Pershing sent another cable, asking Baker to postpone a decision until a letter on the subject could reach him. He also urged the Secretary to visit Europe again "just as soon as possible." Pershing was obviously worried by what he considered a threat, in the person of Goethals with coordinate authority, to his AEF organization.[18]

The following day Pershing wrote a letter repeating his arguments, especially that of unity of command and responsibility. Still later that day he wrote again, suggesting that if Baker felt strongly on the matter, Goethals could be sent to Europe to look things over, but with no promise of command. Pershing could ascertain his attitude and decide if he would fit in. He was insistent, however, that it must be as a subordinate.[19]

Two cables and two letters within 48 hours; the Secretary had certainly touched a sensitive nerve!

Baker undoubtedly realized this. He agreed with Pershing's arguments about unity of command, accepted Harbord as SOS chief "for the present," but reserved judgement for the future. As builder of the Panama Canal, Goethals certainly had more experience with supply work than Harbord.[20]

Having put Harbord in charge of supplies, Pershing thought it a good idea to make a rapid inspection tour of the SOS with him to see how things really were. They met at Tours, SOS headquarters, and, using the Commander in Chief's special train, began a flying tour of the principal ports and bases. With them went McAndrew, the AEF Chief of Staff, Col. William J. Wilgus, the Deputy Director General of Transport, and a few others. They saw much requiring attention. At Bassens freight was piled up so heavily on the docks, due to the inability to move it inland, that people feared they might sideslip into the river.[21]

On the other hand, some stations like Gièvres, the largest U.S. depot on the main supply line, were impressive and running smoothly. At 8:15 A.M. one day an order was received for 4,596 tons of supplies, including 1,250,000 cans of tomatoes, 1,000,000 pounds of sugar, 600,000 cans of corned beef, 750,000 pounds of tinned hash, and 150,000 pounds of dried beans. By 6:15 P.M. that evening it was all loaded and on its way to the front.[22]

The inspection trip lasted a week. Pershing used the occasion to build up morale, telling the stevedores, laborers, and railroad men how important their work was, and how they shared in the recent victory at Soissons. He could be very good at stump speeches like this; the men cheered him and went back to work with renewed energy.[23]

The trip completed, Pershing sent Secretary Baker a glowing, somewhat exaggerated report on August 7, designed to forestall the Goethals proposal. "Everything is working so well and so in accordance with our plans that any change in organization now could but have very serious and far reaching effects in an untoward way," he said. Harbord "has taken hold in splendid fashion."[24]

In point of fact, Harbord had been on the job only a week and had spent it, as Pershing had, in a sightseeing tour of the installations.

Nonetheless, Baker decided to drop the Goethals idea. He was won over by Pershing's arguments against divided authority and realized that Goethals, while extremely competent, was not an easy man to work with, while Harbord worked well with Pershing and had his entire confidence. Urged on by Baker and by House, whom Pershing had contacted, President Wilson decided that "nothing would be done contrary to Pershing's wishes." Rarely has an overseas commander received greater support from his superiors.[25]

Harbord did a good job with the SOS, partly through correcting certain structural defects in the organization, partly through his own driving personality. Kernan, his predecessor, had been hobbled by Pershing's tendency to keep too many things in his own hands. All SOS cables, for instance, even those concerning routine supplies, had to be sent up to GHQ at Chaumont, approved there, and then sent out. It meant a useless extra step in the chain of command and at times involved weeks of delay. Harbord persuaded Pershing to allow him to communicate directly with the War Department on SOS matters.[26]

Another structural defect was an arrangement whereby Brig. Gen. William W. Atterbury, formerly vice-president of the Pennsylvania Railroad and now AEF Director General of Transportation, insisted on being in charge of the stevedores at the ports, even though it created divided authority which led to friction and inefficiency. Atterbury's transportation officers commanded the stevedores only when they were actually working during the day. At all other times they were under the base commander, who was responsible for their shelter, clothing, subsistence, pay, instruction, and discipline. The base commander had no responsibility for (and therefore little interest in) the quantity or quality of their work, since he received no credit for it. The transportation officers had nothing to say about how the stevedores spent their off-work hours, although what happened then would certainly influence the condition in which they reported for work.

Quite obviously the proper arrangement was for the transportation officer to be on the staff of the base commander and under him, just as medical officers were, even though they belonged to a separate corps. Base commanders did not try to tell a doctor how to perform an appendectomy, but Atterbury feared they would try to tell his men how to run a railroad. He consistently opposed subordinating his transportation officers to the base commanders. Ironically Pershing, who opposed the Goethals proposal because it violated unity of command, tolerated such divided command in the SOS. It was not until August 1918, after considerable friction, misunderstanding, and pulling at cross-purposes, that Harbord was able to persuade Atterbury to have his transportation officers placed under the base commanders, thus creating one authority for stevedore performance around the clock.[27]

In addition to these organizational changes, Harbord brought to his task imagination, force, and efficiency. "My business," he said, "is to put steam into the existing boilers and try to speed things up."[28]

General Kernan, his predecessor, had rarely moved from his desk at Tours, made few inspections, and had never seen whole segments of the vast SOS enterprise. When Kernan did inspect, he had gone by motorcar, which limited his travel to the daylight hours, reduced his staff to perhaps a single aide, and lost time on the road as far as work was concerned.

Harbord changed all that. The first day in office he ordered a special train so that he could travel at night, inspect during the day, and range far and wide over his entire command. The train contained sleeping, eating, telegraph, telephone, and other facilities, which enabled him to keep in touch with Chaumont, Tours, and various SOS stations. Two automobiles, carried on the train, gave him wheels for side trips. Said Harbord: "The car is comfortable; the cook is good; we are quite independent of local people for meals and transportation, and we do business!!!!!!!!!!!!!"

Intuitively, he understood that there was nothing like a commander being seen to keep subordinates on their toes. And seeing things firsthand himself was indispensible for judging situations and making corrections on the spot. He took with him his Quartermaster, the Director of Transport, the Chief Surgeon, the Director of Construction and Forestry, the Motor Transport officer, the Chief Engineer—or their delegates if they were obliged to stay at Tours. With such a staff he could accurately judge and correct any difficulty on the spot: a shortage of cars or trucks or clothing or food, a broken bridge or fallen pier, bad sanitary conditions, and so forth. Nothing boosted morale in the SOS like seeing a chief who got around, found out what was wrong, and did something about it—right away![29]

During Harbord's first one hundred days as SOS commander, he spent fifty-five nights on the train. Stevedores and laborers to whom the SOS chief had been only a name in far-off Tours suddenly found him in their midst, asking questions, listening to gripes, cutting red tape, remedying abuses, chopping off heads, and getting things done fast. Floyd Gibbons nicknamed him "toot sweet" [tout de suite] Harbord, and André Brewster, AEF Inspector General, observed that "in the twinkling of an eye" a great change came over the whole SOS. "It was as if some great force had suddenly awakened from slumber. . . ."[30]

Harbord understood men in a way that Pershing did not. The AEF commander promised stevedores that, if they did good work, he would give them an opportunity to go up to the front as combat troops—a hell of a reward, thought many. One black corporal told Pershing's aide, Colonel Boyd, to please inform the general that he was "very well satisfied" where he was.[31]

Harbord, on the other hand, offered men leaves to the Riviera and a place on the first ship home after the war. He put into effect a competition called "The Race to Berlin," in which ports competed with each other in upping the percentage of cargo they unloaded. Statistics were reported weekly, posted in every port, printed in the Stars and Stripes, and flashed on newsreel screens. Stimulated by the competition, and by musicians playing fast ragtime while they worked, the base ports increased the tonnage unloaded by approximately 20 percent.[32]

One upshot of the plan to send Goethals over was to bring to a head certain AEF suspicions concerning the Chief of Staff in Washington. From June 1918 on, stories had been circulating that General March wanted Pershing's job. Some of Pershing's staff, Harbord in particular, saw the Goethals proposal as a step towards this. It was more than a step; it was a plot.

It was inconceivable, reasoned Harbord, that Baker had made the proposal without consulting the Chief of Staff, who must have told him to do it. The proposal envisioned "a perfectly impossible situation from any military standpoint except that which might desire the failure of the expedition and incidentally of Pershing; or perhaps I ought to say 'of Pershing' and not necessarily of the expedition. A divided control here in France would mean nothing but disaster."[33]

Not necessarily. In World War II Lt. Gen. Brehon B. Sommervell proposed putting supplies for all theaters under one head, who would be located in the United States. He would establish priorities and be responsible for the purchase, storage, transport, and delivery of goods right up to the zone of operations, being directly under the War Department and not under any theater commander. It was no conspiracy, simply a proposal for efficiency which had advantages and drawbacks. Theater commanders understandably opposed it and it was not adopted. But it was not a plot.[34]

Pershing was not so sure. After explaining to Colonel House that SOS conditions were better than people in America thought, he added: "Confidentially, in view of the facts, one is inclined to suspect that this erroneous impression has been circulated for a purpose."[35]

Pershing was also concerned with what he considered "a very curt tone" in March's recent cables which gave "a distinct impression of unfriendliness." Furthermore, he acted as if he was Pershing's military superior. He was, of course, but Pershing never admitted it, preferring to think of himself as directly under the Secretary of War.[36]

Finally, there was the promotion question. In May 1918 the War Department had asked Pershing's recommendations for six major generals and thirty-three brigadier generals. When the promotions were made in July, Pershing was furious. Men whom he had *not* recommended, like Douglas MacArthur, were promoted over scores of others who had served longer and were, he felt, more efficient. Others whom he *had* recommended were passed over. These included some of his top GHQ officers like LeRoy Eltinge, Dennis E. Nolan, and Fox Conner, as well as top regimental commanders like Frank McCoy and Paul B. Malone.[37]

"The question of promotions," Pershing wrote in his diary, "involves some transactions on the part of the Chief of Staff in Washington which I am afraid would not look well in the light of an honest investigation."[38]

"It is an outrage . . . ," Harbord said, suggesting that it was probably no accident that all five of those who had been passed over had had differences with General March when he was commander of the artillery camp at Le Valdahon in the early days of the AEF. Since it was unlikely that the Secretary, normally so cooperative, would disregard Pershing's recommendations, the culprit must be the Chief of Staff.[39]

On July 17 Harbord told Pershing of the very bad impression the new promotions had made, and warned: "You are held responsible as the channel through which the merits of the men who serve under you must be made known to the Secretary of War. Once your people think you do not reward merit by your recommendations, or that your recommendations are not followed by the War Department, your influence is on the wane."[40]

Actually, Pershing himself was partly to blame for what had happened. Because he had announced the policy of rotating officers from staff to line, it could happen that a colonel was promoted to brigadier general while serving temporarily on the General Staff and then, when he went out to line duty, such as McCoy and Malone had done, have disproportionate rank over other regimental commanders who were normally colonels or lieutenant colonels. Hence March's reluctance to promote such people. He explained this to Pershing and asked him for the names of men he expected to keep permanently at GHQ and whom he wanted promoted. These March promoted the next time around.[41]

Nonetheless, Pershing was still aggrieved. The proposal to send over Goethals with independent command, the tone of superiority in March's recent cables, and the objectionable July promotion list—all seemed to indicate a pattern of hostility on the part of the Chief of Staff. On August 17 Pershing wrote Secretary Baker a very frank letter, setting forth what he considered a lack of "satisfactory teamwork with us over here" and suggesting that "some of the personnel" in Washington might not be "entirely satisfactory." He had March in mind, although he did not mention him by name. But the meaning was clear, and Pershing implicitly suggested it. The War Department would probably never run smoothly, he said, until someone was put in charge "who has actually gone through this organization here from beginning to end. . . . All this comes to my mind following the idea of an occasional change, of which you spoke when here as being your intention."[42]

Baker, who appreciated March's qualities, was not about to relieve him, nor did he show him Pershing's letter. Had he shown it, "there certainly would have been a showdown," said March later. Pershing, he complained, "wanted a rubber stamp for Chief of Staff at home, so he could be entirely independent of any supervision or control."[43]

March was partially right. Pershing did consider the Chief of Staff a rubber stamp. He acknowledged the Secretary of War as his own military superior, but since Baker in practice, and almost by policy, deferred to his field commander, who knew this, Pershing became virtually independent.

In August 1918 March tried to correct this by issuing War Department General Order #80, which stated that "the Chief of Staff by law . . . takes rank and precedence over all officers of the Army. . . ." But it was too late. Pershing had become so entrenched in privilege and so enjoyed the confidence of the Secretary of War, that practically this status of the Chief of Staff was never attained. Secretary Baker permitted March to raise himself to a coordinate position with Pershing, but not superior.[44]

Significantly, when Pershing later became Chief of Staff in 1921, he saw to it that he was superior to any other officer in the army. But then, of course, the shoe was on the other foot.[45]

TWENTY-ONE

The American First Army

(August 1918)

D URING AUGUST PERSHING was tremendously busy. "From the number of phone calls everyone in France wanted to see the Commander-in-Chief personally," remembered James L. Collins. Visitors were often a nuisance, even when they were important people like Franklin D. Roosevelt, Assistant Secretary of the Navy, who arrived with his party, eager for a tour of the front. "Like everybody else," commented an observer, "they wanted to get shot at with a guarantee against a hit and smell dead men and horses."[1]

Although busy, Pershing thrived on the work, buoyed up with the success of his troops and anticipation of consolidating them into an American army. "I never saw General Pershing looking or feeling better," wrote Charles G. Dawes in his diary on August 25. "He is sleeping well. He is tremendously active. He will soon strike with his field army."[2]

By August, the battle against amalgamation was virtually won. Although Albert Thomas, ex-minister of Munitions and Armaments and a member of the French War Committee, proposed that month that one hundred American regiments be incorporated into one hundred French divisions to maintain them at full strength, Clemenceau told Pershing on August 13 that, although he had disagreed initially about amalgamation, he had now changed his mind. According to Pershing's notes, Clemenceau said that "I was right and that every one who was against me on this proposition was wrong."[3]

In August a change occurred in American training methods which, up to now, had proceeded in two phases. During the first, American troops served by battalions in Allied divisions in the front lines. Subsequently, the three battalions of a regiment were gathered together and the experience was repeated by regiments, again serving in Allied divisions. In the second phase, the four American regiments were gathered together, joined to their American artillery which had been training separately, and formed into an integral division under its own American commander and his divisional staff.

In May, however, the 3d Division had been rushed to the Marne because of the Chemin des Dames emergency without having gone through the first phase. It did quite well, especially during its magnificent stand as "The Rock of the Marne" against the German attack on July 15. Accordingly, from around July onward, the first phase was dispensed with and new American divisions were sent intact, as divisions, directly into the front lines, usually in a quiet area such as the Vosges.[4]

Another reason for the change was Pershing's conviction that service with tired Allied troops was "of little value." In some cases it was "a positive detriment." Harold B. Fiske, his Chief of Training, felt that Allied tutelage was actually "a serious handicap."[5]

By August the AEF had dispensed with all French instructors, considering them useless or detrimental. McAndrew tried to put a good face on the matter by telling the French the reason they would not be needed was that the AEF hated "to deprive the French army of so many of its highly trained officers and men," but the point was clear. The AEF wished to be free of all tutelage, handling its own training in all details.[6]

Similarly, Pershing told Foch that some British instruction had been "a detriment," and hence he did not intend to send any more divisions to them for training. He also asked the War Department to cancel the use of British and French instructors in a proposed course for higher commanders in the United States. American training methods were better, he asserted, and all Allied instruction in the United States should be withdrawn.[7]

Meanwhile, to the north, the British had attacked the Somme salient (formed by the German breakthrough of March 21, 1918) with telling effect. On August 8, using massed tanks, General Henry Rawlinson's Fourth Army ripped open the German line, penetrating seven miles along a fifteen-mile front. It captured 400 guns and 27,000 prisoners, at a cost of only 10,000 casualties. Ludendorff called August 8 the "black day of the German Army"; it was the greatest German defeat of the war.[8]

Although British gains were slower on subsequent days, as surprise was lost and the enemy was able to bring up reserves, the effect was profound. A number of supposedly battle-worthy German divisions collapsed. Retreating troops jeered at the reinforcements, calling them "prolongers of the war." Troop trains heading for the front bore the furtive but ominous chalk words: "Slaughter Cattle for Wilhelm & Sons." One week after the attack the Austrians told their German allies that they could not hold out over the winter, that the war must be ended as soon as possible.[9]

Since the British had used one regiment of the U.S. 33d Division in their Somme attack, and undoubtedly planned to use more of the five U.S. divisions training with them, Pershing judged that the time had come to recall them before they got too involved in British operations. As early as July 10 he had asked Foch to take this matter up with Haig, but the generalissimo, recalling the hard feelings from American recall of the first five divisions in June, passed the buck and asked Pershing to do it himself.[10]

Pershing treaded warily. On August 12 he visited Haig's headquarters and had lunch with the Field Marshal, "during which we chatted about everything except the object of my visit." Afterwards, however, when they retired to Haig's office and Pershing stated that he was planning an offensive and would need three out of the five U.S. divisions training with the British, the conversation turned unpleasant. Haig "hit the ceiling," said Pershing. The Field Marshal pointed out that these divisions had been transported by the British, fed by the British, clothed by the British, and trained by the British. They had been sent to fight with the British, and now they were being withdrawn without participating in a battle!

Pershing responded that he intended to form an American army and would not consent "to have my troops used here, there and the other place at the will of any allies." All this had been set down very clearly in black and white. The divisions were there for training and, if necessary, for combat in an emergency. But they were not on indefinite loan. "We are all fighting the Germans . . . ; the best way at present for my troops to fight the Germans is in my army."

Haig, who had seen enough of Pershing to know when argument was futile, finally said, "Pershing, of course you shall have them, there can never be any difference between us." But he was seething inside and wrote in his diary, "What will History say regarding this action of the Americans leaving the British zone of operations when *the decisive battle* of the war is at its height, and the decision still in doubt!"[11]

Haig's reluctance confirmed what Pershing had always suspected: that, for all their protestations, the British would try to keep U.S. divisions for a long time. He had been right in thinking that it was easier to deny them men in the first place than to attempt to withdraw them later.[12]

Because Foch requested it and because relations with the British were already strained, Pershing consented to leave the last two divisions (27th and 30th) with the British "temporarily." (In point of fact, they remained throughout the war.) But the U.S. 33d, 78th, and 80th Divisions left the BEF to join the American Army forming up for an attack on the St. Mihiel salient.[13]

As Pershing began to gather in his divisions, the British showed a corresponding reluctance to transport and supply U.S. troops. Notwithstanding their assurances in July that America could count on their shipping "till the end of the year," the British now began to draw back.

On August 2 Lloyd George announced that cargo transport would have to cease and troop transport be considerably reduced. The alleged reasons were ship losses to submarines, workers idle in England because of lack of raw material like cotton, and coal shortages affecting munitions manufacture and naval transportation.[14]

But the underlying reason was the British feeling that, having brought so many Americans to Europe, they had a claim on their use which was not being honored. As Lloyd George told Clemenceau earlier, "Because of the sacrifices made to furnish this shipping our people have the right to expect that more than five divisions of the twenty-eight American divisions now in France should be put in training behind our lines." Now that U.S. divisions with the BEF were down to two, *a fortiori* the British were reluctant to continue the sacrifices.[15]

Since the 80-division program, not to say the 100-division one, was contingent on British assistance, the Americans were considerably alarmed and irritated at what seemed British unreliability. "How characteristic after urging the 100 division programme!" exclaimed President Wilson. "Would that we were dealing with responsible persons!"[16]

The British change on shipping further clouded an already murky question: How many Americans would be in Europe by July 1919? It was murky because differences existed as to how many men were in a U.S. division, how many divisions were planned on, and whether such plans had any real hope for success.

As was mentioned earlier, on June 23, 1918, Pershing had recommended 100 divisions in France by July 1919. After a study the War Department concluded that this was impossible and that the best it could hope to achieve was 80 divisions, so informing Bliss on July 23. Pershing certainly knew about Washington's decision the first week of August when Lloyd George cabled Clemenceau that America had abandoned the 100-division program and was shooting only for 80. Clemenceau gave a copy of the cable to Pershing a few days later.[17]

Yet he continued to urge the 100-division program as a *minimum*. "This is very least American force that will insure our victory in 1919," he cabled Washington on August 17. Where there's a will, there's a way, seemed to be his attitude. Make the great leap; dare the great dare. Instead of worrying whether cargo ships would be available to supply such great numbers of men, send the men and then some way will be found to supply them because we have to. "The task will prove much easier than it is made to appear."[18]

The War Department thought otherwise and finally got around to telling Pershing by cable that 80 divisions was the approved and *maximum* program. That was on September 25, over two months after the decision had been made.[19]

And what was meant by "a division"? Was it a combat division, or did it also include what was called a depot division, which provided replacements to keep a combat division going? On August 20 Pershing told his staff that the 80-division program meant 80 combat divisions. With the necessary depot divisions to go along with them (one for every five combat divisions), that made a total of 96.[20]

The War Department was not thinking this way and confusion was being confounded. Pershing was calling for 100 divisions as a "minimum," without expecting to get them or even possibly believing they were needed. The War Department was planning on 80 divisions, without, however, telling its field commander, who was officially in the dark for two months after the decision was made. And that same field commander, knowing unofficially through Bliss and Lloyd George that 80 divisions was the official program, tried to hedge by stating that 80 was really 96.[21]

Furthermore, different people calculated differently as to the numbers in a "division." For Foch, Clemenceau, and Bliss 100 divisions meant 4,160,000 men; for March, 4,260,000; for Pershing, "at least 5,000,000 men."[22]

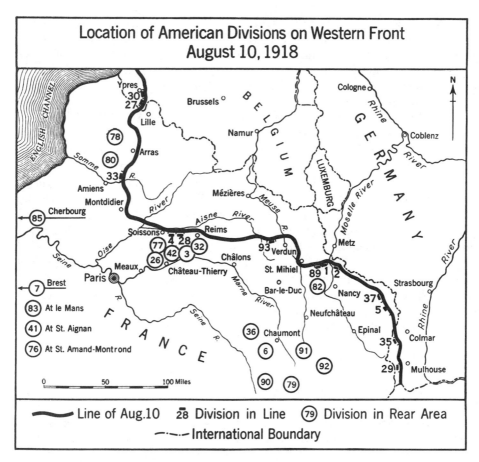

Location of American Divisions on Western Front
August 10, 1918

- —— Line of Aug.10　㉘ Division in Line　㉙ Division in Rear Area
- —·—·— International Boundary

From American Battle Monuments Commission, *American Armies and Battlefields in Europe*, Washington, D.C., 1938.

It was a strange way to run a war.

By August 6 the Aisne-Marne counteroffensive was over, the Château-Thierry salient eliminated, and the front stabilized along the Vesle River, where it stayed until early September. Accordingly, Pershing abandoned his plan to form his army along this front (it had been a temporary expedient anyway, conceived when the front was active) and reverted to his original intention to form it in Lorraine, with reduction of the St. Mihiel salient as its first objective.

On August 10 the American First Army came into official existence, with Pershing himself as its field commander. He thrilled that morning at 11:00 when he took command. Finally, after a year of planning, trouble, and frustration, the American Army was a reality.[23]

How good it would be remained to be seen. The French had misgivings about its staff and wondered whether its services would be able to "walk alone."[24]

On August 29 First Army headquarters moved to Ligny-en-Barrois, twenty-five miles southeast of St. Mihiel. The French, in turning over the sector, presented Pershing with two large volumes, each about 150 pages, containing their offensive and defensive plans for the area. In contrast, Pershing's staff had drawn up an offensive plan of six pages and a defensive one of eight.[25]

Then came a bombshell. On August 30 Foch showed up at Ligny with a radically different proposal for Pershing and the American Army, based on a concept suggested to him by Haig a few days before.

Up to the present the Allies had been attacking, or were planning to attack, separate and isolated German salients like that at Château-Thierry (July 18-August 6), Amiens (the current British Somme offensive), and St. Mihiel (the contemplated American attack). This had some value in shortening the front, driving back the invader, and opening railway lines, but the attacks were directed toward no overall objective, save that of pushing the enemy out of France. But look at the map, said Foch. The whole front line, bulging out as it did into France, could be considered one huge salient extending from the North Sea down to Verdun. Why not then attack it as one normally did a salient, pushing in from the shoulders? The British Army, engaged in the Somme offensive since August 8, was already exerting pressure on what could be considered the left shoulder of this massive salient. What remained was for the French and Americans to exert pressure on the right, by launching an attack up from the south in the direction of Mézières to correspond with the BEF thrust toward Cambrai.[26]

In this strategy the coming American attack against the St. Mihiel salient made relatively little sense, since it went nowhere. It was outside the larger overall salient which Foch saw when looking at his map. While it should be reduced (its elimination would open the Paris-Nancy Railway), its reduction was not that important compared to an attack towards Mézières, which would cave in the right shoulder of the massive salient. Yet the Americans were making big plans for the St. Mihiel operation.

The thing to do, said Foch, was to de-emphasize the St. Mihiel operation, which headed east, and concentrate American strength, in conjunction with the French, in a northerly push toward Mézières between the Meuse and Aisne rivers. Tracing his finger on the map from east to west, Foch projected an attack by the French Second Army between the Meuse River and the Argonne Forest, an attack by the American First Army between the Argonne Forest and an area west of the Aisne River, and an attack by the French Fourth Army to the west of that. Since the French Second Army was weak, he envisaged four to six American divisions reinforcing it. They would be under French army command, although, of course, under their own corps commanders.

One effect of Foch's plan would be a certain fragmentation of American forces: one group, relatively small, in Lorraine operating against the south face of the St. Mihiel salient, another group with the French Second Army, and the main body astride the Aisne River—each with French groups in between. Foch intended to remedy this somewhat by putting the American divisions assigned to the French Second Army on its left flank so that, after they passed the Argonne Forest, they could angle to the left and connect up with the main American body. Still, it was a far cry from what Pershing thought he had before Foch walked into the room: a compact American army concentrated around St. Mihiel.[27]

"I realize," said Foch, "that I am presenting a number of new ideas and that you will probably need time to think them over, but I should like your first impressions."

They were distinctly unfavorable.

"Marshal Foch, here on the very day that you turn over a sector to the American Army, and almost on the eve of an offensive, you ask me to reduce the operation so that you can take away several of my divisions and assign some to the French Second Army and use others to form an American Army to operate on the Aisne in conjunction with the French Fourth Army, leaving me with little to do except hold what will become a quiet sector after the St. Mihiel offensive. This virtually destroys the American Army that we have been trying so long to form."

Actually, it did not. But it shifted it considerably to the west at the last minute, away from American railroads, depots, hospitals, and other installations which had been located in anticipation of the St. Mihiel attack, and it did put a number of Americans under foreign command in the French Second Army.

Foch regretted this, but did not see how it could be avoided. "The fate of the 1918 campaign will be decided in the Aisne region and I wish to limit the Woëvre [St. Mihiel] attack so that the Americans can participate in the Meuse offensive, which will produce still greater results."

Pershing felt that if they were going to hit the St. Mihiel salient at all, they ought to hit it hard and from both sides, not just the south, but Foch feared lest the Americans become too deeply involved there and use up forces needed for the northward offensive scheduled shortly after. Since Pershing would be tied up in the St. Mihiel operation, some other commander would be temporarily needed to plan the attack of the American Army forming astride the Aisne. Foch suggested a French general, Degoutte, who was familiar with the region and who could set things in motion until the time Pershing arrived to take over when the St. Mihiel operation was finished.

This set poorly with Pershing, who felt that many American lives had been needlessly sacrificed while serving as part of Degoutte's Sixth Army on the Vesle that month. Besides, "this was only a round-about way of attempting to assign General Degoutte to command our forces."[28]

Pershing was willing, although reluctant, to form an American Army astride the Aisne, but dead set against sending four to six divisions to serve in the French Second Army east of it. Couldn't the French find reinforcements from their own men? French soldiers held the Aisne region now, so why not send them when the Americans moved in? No, said Foch, these men would be needed for the French Fourth Army. Without U.S. support, the French Second Army lacked sufficient divisions to attack.

The discussion became very heated.

"Do you wish to take part in the battle?" demanded Foch, challenging.

"Most assuredly," Pershing shot back, "but as an American Army and in no other way." He did not want to appear difficult, but "the American people and the American government expect that the American Army shall act as such and shall not be dispersed here and there along the Western front. Each time that we are on the point of accomplishing this organization, some proposition is presented to break it up."

As the argument heated up, Foch made a slighting reference to American inadequacies in artillery and other services. To Pershing this was a low blow. For months the French—Foch among them—had insisted over and over that America transport only infantry and machine-gun units, knowing this would dislocate the AEF organization, but promising repeatedly to make good any deficiencies until the United States could supply them. "Fulfill these promises," demanded Pershing.

Foch returned to the attack, pushing his plan, citing lack of time for any alternative and appealing to Pershing's pride as a soldier. "Your French and English comrades are going into battle; are you coming with them?"

Pershing exclaimed angrily: "Marshal Foch, you have no authority as Allied Commander-in-Chief to call upon me to yield up my command of the American Army and have it scattered among the Allied forces where it will not be an American Army at all."

"I must insist upon the arrangement."

"Marshal Foch, you may insist all you please, but I decline absolutely to agree to your plan. While our army will fight wherever you may decide, it will not fight except as an independent American army."[29]

Both men rose from the table. Blazingly angry, Pershing for one wild instant thought of hitting Foch, but concluded this was not the way to treat a generalissimo. Foch, pale and drained, gathered his maps and papers, handed Pershing a memorandum of his proposal, and paused at the door to suggest that, once Pershing had thought more about it, he would consent.[30]

There was not a chance.

The meeting had lasted two and one-half hours. "We had a very long, outspoken and unsatisfactory conversation . . . ," Pershing wrote in his diary. Later he added that he was "firmly convinced that it was the fixed purpose of the French, and perhaps of the British, that the formation of an American Army . . . should be prevented if possible. Perhaps they did not wish America to find out her strength. . . ."[31]

Confronted by a crisis, Pershing ordered James McAndrew and Fox Conner up to Ligny at once. The next morning, after consulting them, Pershing wrote a formal reply to Foch. Either the St. Mihiel operation should be carried off as scheduled (attacks on both faces) or dropped altogether. While acknowledging Foch's supremacy in planning strategy and while approving the proposed offensive northward toward Mézières, Pershing insisted that "there is one thing that must not be done and that is to disperse the American forces among the Allied armies; the danger of destroying by such dispersion the fine morale of the American soldier is too great, to say nothing of the results to be obtained by using the American Army as a whole. If you decide to utilize American forces in attacking in the direction of Mézières, I accept that decision, even though it complicates my supply system and the care of sick and wounded, but I do insist that the American Army must be employed as a whole, either east of the Argonne or west of the Argonne, and not four or five divisions here and six or seven there."[32]

That afternoon Pershing talked to Pétain, who thought that Foch had over-stepped his authority in telling Pershing to attack only the southern face of the St. Mihiel salient. Foch had strategic authority, not tactical. He could tell where to attack, but not how.

Pétain also appreciated Pershing's objection to having his forces used piece-meal. For over a year now Lorraine had been considered the future American sector, and installations set up with that in mind. Logically the ideal solution would be to retain that sector and expand west. This would keep all U.S. forces side by side instead of dividing them by having the French Second Army in between, as Foch envisaged. The push toward Mézières would thus find an American Army between the Meuse River and the Argonne Forest. The only difficulty was that this operation was scheduled so soon after the one at St. Mihiel that it was doubtful that American forces could undertake both, which is why Foch's plan assigned the Meuse-Argonne operation to the French Second Army (reinforced by four to six U.S. divisions) and placed the American force astride the Aisne to the west, where an attack was scheduled later and over easier terrain. Hence, under the present time schedule, either the St. Mihiel attack would have to be dropped or the Meuse-Argonne attack delayed.[33]

Pershing and Pétain presented these considerations to Foch at his headquarters at Bombon on September 2. Pershing was quite willing to cancel the St. Mihiel operation and concentrate on the offensive west of the Meuse that Foch wanted, but because of transportation difficulties, was not sure he could be ready by September 15, the date Foch insisted on. The American Army, after all, was just in the process of collecting itself, and had been geared up to an attack against St. Mihiel some sixty miles to the east. Planning a new battle and moving men and matériel to a new front would take time, perhaps until September 20 or 22.

To Foch this was waiting too long "without doing anything." Could not Pershing in the meantime execute a limited operation against St. Mihiel, wiping out the salient, and then stop, all the while preparing for the big push west of the Meuse? If so, the timetable for the latter operation could be pushed back, say to September 25.

Pershing agreed to this, and thus committed himself to what was really too large an undertaking. An American Army, untested and in many ways untrained, was to engage in a great battle, disengage itself, and move to another great battle some sixty miles away, all within the space of about two weeks, under a First Army staff that Pershing admitted was not perfect and, as of this date, had no inkling that an operation west of the Meuse was even contemplated. Army staffs normally required two to three months to form a fully articulated battle plan with all its technical annexes; this staff—and, again, it must be emphasized that it was new, inexperienced, and untested—would have about three weeks. It was a for-midable commitment, not to say impossible, and it is not clear that Pershing should have made it. Two of his four army corps had just been organized, while the army staff had no experience as yet working as a team.

The alternative, however, was to leave the St. Mihiel salient bulging in the Allied lines, menacing the flank and rear of any army operating west of the Meuse. Its reduction would open up the Paris-Nancy Railway, and eliminate the last German salient on the western front. Besides, and perhaps this was the major consideration, the Americans were all set to attack it. Everything was ready to go.

In sum, then, Pershing was to execute the St. Mihiel project (an eastern thrust) without getting too involved, then move his army for the more major operation west of the Meuse (a northwest thrust). In order to keep Pershing's army together and avoid parceling it out among French forces, Foch consented to the Americans extending their line westward from the St. Mihiel region to the Argonne Forest, taking on forty-eight miles of additional frontage, making a ninety-mile line in all.[34]

On September 3, 1918, Foch gave orders for the concentric attack against the massive German salient he had described to Pershing on August 30. The British were to advance in the general direction of Cambrai-St. Quentin; the French and Americans in the general direction of Mézières, sometime between September 20 and 25. Prior to this, between September 10 and 15, the Americans were to crush out the St. Mihiel salient.[35]

TWENTY-TWO

St. Mihiel

(September 12–16, 1918)

THE ST. MIHIEL salient (Foch called it a "hernia") was a huge triangle jutting into the Allied lines. It cut the Paris-Nancy Railway and served as a jump-off line for a possible German flanking attack against Verdun to the west or Nancy to the east. It also served as an effective German bulwark against any Allied advance against Metz or the vital Briey iron mines.

Reducing the salient had long been an American dream. Pershing spoke of it to Pétain on first meeting him in June 1917. A strategical study in the fall of that year by GHQ staff officers recommended that it be the first U.S. operation; Fox Conner reconfirmed this view in February 1918, and on June 24, 1918, when Foch met Pershing, Haig, and Pétain to plan future offensives, the generalissimo assigned reduction of the salient to the Americans.[1]

The St. Mihiel salient was approximately twenty-five miles across and sixteen miles deep, with its apex at St. Mihiel and its base anchored at Haudiomont and Pont-à-Mousson. It had been a quiet zone for most of four years. The Germans had settled down, planted vegetable gardens, and fathered children by local women.

They also had had time to construct some formidable defensive works: four or five zones with elaborately constructed trenches, shelters, barbed wire entanglements, machine-gun nests, and artillery emplacements. The barbed wire seemed endless; in one place it ran 13 rows, some as deep as a room. The fact that, after two strong but futile attacks in 1915, the French had been content thereafter to leave the salient alone may be taken as a measure of its strength. Pershing called it "a great field fortress."[2]

To be sure, it had some weaknesses. Like all salients, it was vulnerable to converging attacks from the sides. Perhaps because the salient had been quiet for so long, the Germans manned it with second- or third-class troops. Of the eight and one-half divisions assigned to its defense, one had recently arrived from Russia and was, by the Germans' own admission, "not reliable." Another was "completely worn out." A German noncom wrote home: "The men are so embittered that

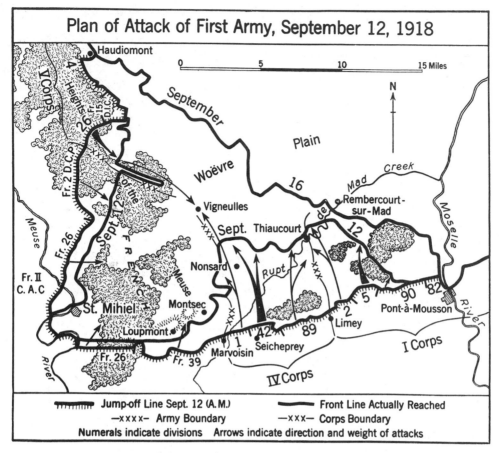

From American Battle Monuments Commission, *American Armies and Battlefields in Europe*, Washington, D.C., 1938.

they have no interest in anything and they only want the war to end, no matter how."[3]

Despite this, considerable pessimism existed in the Allied high command concerning the coming U.S. attack. Sir Henry Wilson told Lloyd Griscom that he viewed the "premature" formation of the American Army with "great concern." Although individual doughboys were brave, American staff officers suffered from "incapacity and inexperience." One of two things would surely happen: The Americans would encounter heavy resistance and be stopped with "cruel losses," as the French had been; or encountering light resistance, they would pursue and fall into a trap. Since the Americans were sure to make a mess of it, jeopardizing the cause, Wilson sent a special messenger to Foch to get him to cancel the operation. Foch refused to, although he did admit that the American Army was "inexperienced and immature."[4]

Planning for the St. Mihiel operation, which was scheduled for September 12, went on at both First Army headquarters and at GHQ. Since Pershing was busy as commander of both headquarters, he delegated much responsibility to the First Army Chief of Staff, Hugh Drum, a brilliant, 38-year-old officer of wide staff experience, who had been on his staff at Fort Sam Houston before the war. Fox Conner, AEF Operations Chief, loaned the First Army George C. Marshall, Jr., 37, who had the reputation for hard work, being on top of things, and doing well whatever he did. Conner, Drum, and Marshall were graduates of the Command and General Staff School at Fort Leavenworth, understood the same language, and worked well together.[5]

The material buildup for the St. Mihiel operation had begun in August and was formidable: 3,010 guns, 40,000 tons of ammunition, 65 evacuation trains, 21,000 beds for the sick and wounded, 15 miles of reconstructed roads using 100,000 tons of crushed stone, 45 miles of standard gauge and 250 miles of light railways, 19 railhead depots for distributing food, clothing, and equipment, 120 water points which furnished 1,200,000 gallons per day, a 38-circuit central switchboard with separate nets for command, supply, artillery, air service, and utilities, and so forth. Maps alone for the operation weighed fifteen tons.[6]

Much of what was furnished had to be borrowed from the Allies, since the spring and summer priority shipments of infantry and machine gunners had thoroughly imbalanced the American Army in matters of artillery, transportation, and needed services. Not one of the 3,010 guns was of American manufacture, nor were any of the 267 tanks. The French provided virtually all the transportation and nearly half the artillerymen, tank crews, and airplanes. The air force, under Col. Billy Mitchell, had 1,400 planes—the largest armada ever assembled to that time—but not one was American-built.[7]

To use this mass of matériel some two-thirds of a million men—550,000 Americans and 110,000 Frenchmen—moved into position around the salient. Pershing gathered his troops from all parts of the front: from the BEF, from the Château-Thierry area, from the Vosges—all joining Americans who had been stationed near the salient. Finally, at long last, eighteen months after the nation declared war and over a year after beginning its training and service with various Allied units, the American Army was coming into being as a living, working organism.[8]

The movement was difficult, for it had to be made secretly and at night. In the dark the roads swarmed with men, animals, trucks, guns, caissons, tanks, and every kind of impedimenta. During the day the men hid in woods or billets and tried to catch what sleep they could. At night they were on the road again, without lights, struggling forward in the direction of the salient. The American Army was moving up!

Or rather, slogging up. The mud was incredible and the continuing rain kept making more of it. Elmer Sherwood, a Rainbow Division veteran, speculated that the only vehicles making their usual speed were the airplanes. Another soldier suggested that the American high command ought to substitute "submarines for tanks, ducks for carrier-pigeons, and alligators for soldiers." Grimy, slimy, wet and cold, the troops cursed the mud which got into clothes, hair, food, drink, and equipment. It was one of the agonies long remembered. Sunny France![9]

Pershing's Order of Battle, from right to left, was as follows: the U.S. I Corps (Hunter Liggett) with the 82d, 90th, 5th, and the 2d Divisions. Then came the U.S. IV Corps (Joseph T. Dickman) with the 89th, 42d, and the 1st Divisions. The two corps lined up on the south face of the salient.

At the apex was the French II Colonial Corps with three French divisions (39th, 26th, and 2d Dismounted Cavalry).

On the west face of the salient was the U.S. V Corps (George H. Cameron) with the 26th Division, part of the 4th, and the French 15th Colonial.

Against the German salient, then, Pershing was sending four corps, composed of four French and eight and one-half U.S. divisions.[10]

Strategically, the most important corps were those of Dickman and Cameron. Entrusted with the veteran 1st and 42d Divisions, Dickman was to hit from the south face and drive hard for Vigneulles where, hopefully, he would be met by Cameron driving in with the veteran 26th Division from the west face. The juncture of the two U.S. forces should close the salient and bag the Germans inside it.

The primary attack was thus on the south face by the IV Corps (Dickman), coupled with a secondary attack three hours later by the V Corps (Cameron) on the west face, with supporting attacks by the I Corps (Liggett) on the right shoulder and the French corps at the apex.

Besides the First Army staff, which was new and untried, Pershing was gambling on two new corps commanders and on four untested divisions. The new corps commanders were Dickman and Cameron, both promoted from divisional command after the Aisne-Marne campaign in July; they had had less than a month to organize their headquarters and prepare for battle.

The four new divisions were the 5th, 82d, 89th, and 90th. Two of them (5th and 89th) were commanded by Pershing's old West Point classmates, John E. McMahon and William M. Wright, while the 90th was headed by Henry T. Allen, who had been with Pershing in the Punitive Expedition. These three divisions had had frontline training, either in the Vosges or near the salient. William P. Burnham's 82d, however, which had trained in the rear with the British, had had no frontline experience. None of the four, of course, had seen active combat operations yet.

The other five divisions were workhorses on whom Pershing knew he could depend. The 1st and 2d had spearheaded the Soissons counteroffensive on July 18; they were ranked "excellent" as to training, equipment, and morale. The 4th, 26th, and 42d Divisions had seen hard fighting in the drive from Château-Thierry to the Vesle River. They too ranked high.

The 1st Division was under the capable Charles P. Summerall, a commander without peer; the 2d under John A. Lejeune, former commander of its Marine Brigade; the 4th under John L. Hines, Pershing's adjutant during the Punitive Expedition, who had come with him to Europe on the *Baltic*; the 42d was under Charles T. Menoher, another Pershing West Point classmate; and the 26th was under Clarence R. Edwards. Although Edwards was beloved of his men, many officers on Pershing's staff had serious doubts about his competence. Lejeune and

Hines were new commanders, replacing Harbord, who had gone to the SOS, and Cameron, who had moved up to command the V Corps.[11]

In using the 1st, 2d, 4th, 26th and 42d Divisions, Pershing was calling upon the very best he had. Hoping to ensure the success of the St. Mihiel operation, he was leaving the cupboard quite bare of experienced frontline troops for the coming Meuse-Argonne operation. He knew the risk, but there was little he could do about it. The decision to employ these experienced divisions had been made before Foch sprang the Meuse-Argonne operation on him on August 30 and before he agreed to it on September 2. By that time these divisions were so thoroughly committed to St. Mihiel that they could not be changed.[12]

In planning the attack the First Army had counted on borrowing 300 heavy tanks from the British and 500 light tanks from the French, but when the time came the British could not spare the "heavies" and the French could furnish only 267 "lights," about which they were pessimistic. The muddy terrain, they said, would probably bog down the machines, which were none too reliable, and the deepest German trenches were eight feet across, two feet wider than the tanks were able to cross.

But Brig. Gen. Samuel D. Rockenbach, AEF Chief of Tank Corps, and Lt. Col. George S. Patton, Jr., a tank brigade commander, were convinced the tanks could advance, provided the mud didn't get worse. Even though the small Renaults could not cross the deepest German trenches, they could effect an initial surprise, crush the wire, and lead the infantry up to the first line of trenches, which, if they were too wide, could be crossed with the aid of pioneers. "You are going to have a walkover," Rockenbach assured Pershing.[13]

On September 10, two days before the attack, Pershing held a conference with his corps commanders and key members of their staffs. Liggett and Dickman wanted no artillery preparation in order to achieve tactical surprise. The only exception would be if the rain continued, inhibiting the use of tanks. Cameron wanted a four-hour barrage. Maj. Gen. Edward F. McGlachlin, Jr., First Army Chief of Artillery, was undecided, but inclined to a twenty-two-hour barrage. Lt. Cols. George C. Marshall, Jr., and Walter S. Grant, both on loan to First Army from Chaumont, urged an eighteen-hour preparation.[14]

Pershing postponed a decision. It had been raining off and on all day, sometimes quite hard. That night he decided initially on no artillery preparation, then reversed himself the next morning, September 11, and ordered a four-hour preparation on the southern face and a seven-hour on the western. The preparation fire would disconcert the enemy, give a psychological boost to the attackers, and damage the wire in case tanks couldn't do it.

It kept raining on September 11. Pershing wrote in his diary, "Luck seems to be against us," although all his corps commanders said they were ready and confident of success. He worked in the office all day, waiting for the attack.[15]

The night of September 11 was jet black with steady rain. The artillery was in position, in some cases almost hub to hub, ominously silent, like sphinxes. The troops were moved into the front lines at the last possible minute to achieve surprise. Sgt. William L. Langer, carrying ammunition in the trenches, found them practically empty at 8:00 P.M., but a short time later they were crowded with infantrymen, waiting apprehensively for the dawn.

Precisely at 1:00 A.M. on September 12 thousands of cannons fired simultaneously. Light belched from their muzzles, flaming out so continuously up and down the line that one soldier read the *Stars and Stripes* newspaper by the glare. Sergeant Langer compared the noise "to what one hears beneath a wooden bridge when a heavy vehicle passes overhead."[16]

Watching the preliminary bombardment, Pershing found the scene both "picturesque and terrible." He exulted that, now at last, after eighteen months of effort, an American Army was a living reality, "fighting under its own flag." Yet how many men would die today—American, French, German—the tragedy of it all.[17]

In the trenches, cold, wet, and miserable, men huddled over their rifles, shocked by the thunder of cannons, gazing with frightened fascination at the weirdly illuminated landscape, lit up as they had never seen it before. "Will I still be alive a few hours from now?" each one wondered.

The artillery fire was directed at German command posts, rail lines and junctures, trenches, and wire. It was not terribly effective, but it did, as Pershing hoped, give a psychological boost to the waiting infantrymen, especially those who had not heard so much artillery before.

At 5:00 A.M. the whistles blew. All along the front men took a tight grip on their rifles, clambered up the wood ladders out of the trenches, and went "over the top."

Watching from a commanding height at old Fort Gironville, Pershing could not see clearly because of the drizzling rain and mist, but followed the advance by watching the explosions of the rolling barrage. He hoped the infantry was right behind.[18]

The first thing they encountered was the barbed wire. The artillery had taken out some of it, but not much, because of the shortness of the preliminary bombardment. But trained teams of pioneers and engineers were in the lead, armed with axes, wire cutters, and bangalore torpedoes (long tin or sheet-iron tubes containing TNT). Fortunately, German counterbarrage fire was weak, giving them time to cut holes in the wire.

The infantry rushed through the gaps or, where there were none, used American ingenuity to pass. Leading platoons carried chickenwire which, thrown across the top, formed a bridge for crossing. Where this was lacking, and where the wire was thick and low, the doughboys simply vaulted up on top of it and ran across, somewhat like a kid crossing a stream by jumping from rock to rock.[19]

The advance went well, especially on the south face, paced by the veteran 1st, 2d, and 42d Divisions, which Pershing had assigned to the open terrain so they could flank the wooded areas, which were assigned to the four new divisions.

"Get forward, there," Wild Bill Donovan yelled to his Rainbow Division men; "what the hell do you think this is, a wake?"[20]

It almost was for Terry de la Mesa Allen of the 90th Division. Shot in the mouth, teeth missing, blood running down his face, he helped wipe out a machine-gun nest before loss of blood sent him to a first aid station. In World War II Allen would command the 1st Division in North Africa and Sicily.

Some incidents were bizzare. Sgt. Harry J. Adams of the 89th Division saw a German run into a dugout at Bouillonville. The American had only two shots left in his pistol, so he fired them both through the door and called for the man to surrender. The door opened and the German came out, followed by another, and another, and another, and another, and another—some 300 in all! Amazed, Adams marched the whole contingent back toward the rear, covering them with his empty pistol. Americans who saw them coming thought at first it was a German counterattack.

Some incidents seemed unbelievable. The 2d Division captured prisoners from fifty-seven (!) different German units—an impossible mélange. It was found that they were from all over the western front, sent to Thiaucourt to attend a machine-gun school there.[21]

Much of the ease with which the Americans advanced was due to the German decision to evacuate the salient, orders having been given to that effect on September 10. Some matériel had already been withdrawn and more was in the process of moving when the Americans struck.

The attack thus caught the Germans embarrassingly *in via*. Some German units had practically no artillery in position; those which did were almost out of ammunition. The German defenders were certainly not of the diehard type, as Sergeant Adams discovered when he marched in his 300 prisoners with an empty pistol. Thus it was Pershing's luck to attack a salient that the Germans were just about to hand over to him anyway, capturing without heavy losses positions which, if stoutly defended, would have heaped up American corpses. A wag described St. Mihiel as the battle "where the Americans relieved the Germans."[22]

By the afternoon troops on the southern face of the salient had reached their objectives; by evening they were one day ahead of schedule. On the west face progress was slower, the 26th Division being retarded by the failure of the French 15th Colonial to keep up on its left.

On its right, however, some units of the 26th had projected a long finger into the German lines pointing toward Vigneulles, a town through which ran the main road of escape out of the salient. Getting on the phone, Pershing ordered Cameron and Dickman to move toward Vigneulles "with all possible speed."

Pushing hard under "Hiking Hiram" Bearss, a regiment of the 26th Division reached Vigneulles at 2:15 A.M.; some four hours later a regiment of the 1st Division marched in from the east. The main road out of the salient was now cut; the mouth of the bag was squeezed shut.

On September 13 the advance continued from the south and west, wiping out the salient and stopping at the line agreed upon by Pershing at his September 2 conference with Foch. Local operations continued until the 16th, consolidating positions for defense while the First Army prepared to pull out and head for the Meuse-Argonne operation. It had captured 450 guns and 16,000 prisoners, at a cost of only 7,000 casualties.

The operation reduced the salient, restored two hundred square miles of French territory, freed the Paris-Nancy Railroad, opened water transportation on the Meuse, and protected the right flank of the First Army for its coming operation in the Meuse-Argonne. It also paved the way for a possible future attack against Metz, the Briey-Longwy industrial complex, and the crucial railroad supplying the Germans to the northwest.[23]

Finally, and perhaps most important, it demonstrated that the American Army was able successfully to handle an operation of some magnitude. As the British *Manchester Guardian* put it: "It is as swift and neat an operation as any in the war, and perhaps the most heartening of all its features is the proof it gives that the precision, skill, and imagination of American leadership is not inferior to the spirit of the troops."[24]

Actually, American success came a bit too easily at St. Mihiel, engendering perhaps an unwarranted optimism and confidence similar to that which afflicted the South after winning the battle of Bull Run. Knowing that the salient was scheduled to be evacuated anyway, German soldiers abandoned their positions more easily than they might have done. Even as it was, they delayed the First Army long enough to allow most of the defenders to escape before the jaws of the pincers closed.[25]

On the afternoon of September 13, Pétain came to Pershing's headquarters and together they visited the town of St. Mihiel. Ecstatic at their deliverance after four years of German occupation, the people—mostly women, children, and old men—crowded around them waving little French flags, saying every few seconds, "Bon jour, monsieur." They wept with joy but also with sorrow, for the Germans had taken with them all males between sixteen and forty-five. (Fortunately, after ten miles, the Germans let the prisoners go.)

Graciously, Pétain explained to the people that, although the French had taken the city, they served as part of the American First Army, whose soldiers had made victory possible by their attacks on the shoulders of the salient.

One of the town officials told Pétain that the Germans had treated them well, but that a number of the young women had behaved badly. Enticed by the prospect of better food, clothing, and more firewood, they had lived with German soldiers. Perhaps two hundred babies had been born of these liaisons, most of them later killed by being thrown into wells. Pétain listened sympathetically, then remarked that the villagers should not be too severe in judging these women. After he left, however, French soldiers rounded them up, packed them tightly in standing positions in trucks, and drove them off. Dr. Hugh Young, who saw them, said they looked "the picture of desperation."[26]

Tremendously elated by the victory, Pershing felt it vindicated his insistence on building a separate American Army. "We gave 'em a damn good licking, didn't we?" he remarked. That evening (September 13), when receiving the congratulations of Dennis Nolan, he rose from his desk and, pacing up and down, gave the most eloquent tribute to the American soldier that Nolan had ever heard. Going back into history, he remarked "how wave after wave of Europeans, dissatisfied with conditions in Europe, came to this country to seek liberty; how . . . those who came had the will-power and the spirit to seek opportunity in a new world rather than put up with unbearable conditions in the old; that those who came for that reason were superior in initiative to those, their relatives, who had remained and submitted to the conditions; that in addition to this initial superiority in initiative they had developed, and their children had developed, under a form of government and in a land of great opportunity where individual initiative was protected and rewarded. . . ." The consequence, was that "we had developed a type of manhood superior in initiative to that existing abroad, which given approximately equal training and discipline, developed a superior soldier to that existing abroad."[27]

Flushed with success, with an American Army in being and growing daily more important, Pershing faced the future with confidence and also with ambition. With American soldiers flooding into France at the rate they were, the day would not be far off when the American Army would be larger than either the French or British. "And when that time comes," he told George Van Horn Moseley later, "an American should command the Allied Army."[28]

The St. Mihiel victory left Pershing in a jaunty mood. When Lloyd George telegraphed his congratulations from a sickbed, saying that the news was better than any physic, Pershing answered: "It shall be the endeavor of the American Army to supply you with occasional doses of the same sort of medicine as needed. . . ."[29]

The witty Harbord pointed out in his congratulatory message that nearly three hundred years before on the same date, September 13, Oliver Cromwell had led his Ironsides into battle quoting Psalm 68. It seemed remarkably apropos to Pershing's recent success: "Let God arise and let His enemies be scattered; let them also that hate Him. Like as the smoke vanishes so shalt thou drive them away."

Pershing answered: "Your old division might well be termed The Ironsides, though I doubt whether they went to battle quoting Psalm 68."[30]

German reaction to the American victory was of the "sour grapes" variety. Newspapers and the official German communiqué pointed out that Germany had planned to evacuate the salient anyway, and that the troops had retired in good order to previously prepared positions.[31]

Privately, however, the German High Command was considerably upset. Though intending to evacuate, they had not wished to do so until absolutely necessary. Although most of the defenders had gotten out, considerable stores were either captured or had to be destroyed. General Max von Gallwitz, the Army Group Commander, had warned Lieutenant General Fuchs, commanding Army Detachment C, opposite Pershing, "not to concede an easy success, particularly since we are dealing with Americans." Despite this, the Americans had wiped out a four-year salient, twice unsuccessfully attacked by the French, in forty-eight hours.[32]

Ludendorff was terribly disturbed. A German officer who visited him the night of September 12 found him "so overcome by the events of the day as to be unable to carry on a clear and comprehensive discussion." Field Marshal Paul von Hindenburg, the titular German Commander in Chief, called September 12 a "severe defeat" which rendered Gallwitz's situation "critical."[33]

In later years a number of people believed that the Americans might have achieved an even greater victory had the First Army been allowed to keep going east. Douglas MacArthur was one such. On the night of September 13–14, MacArthur, a brigade commander in the 42d Division, stole through the enemy lines in the direction of Mars-la-Tour and with binoculars studied the key German fortress at Metz, ten miles to the east. From this reconnaissance and from interrogating prisoners, he concluded that Metz was "practically defenseless." Its garrison had been temporarily withdrawn to fight on other fronts. MacArthur immediately asked to attack Metz with his brigade, promising to be in the city hall "by nightfall."[34]

The request was denied. The St. Mihiel attack, after all, was a limited operation and had already achieved its objective. Further advance ran the risk of overinvolving the American Army, already committed to a new and even greater operation on a different front some two weeks hence.

MacArthur believed that this failure to push on toward Metz was "one of the great mistakes of the war." Pershing felt the same subsequently, although at the time he believed he had no other choice but to keep St. Mihiel a limited operation in order to be on schedule for the Meuse-Argonne attack he had committed himself to on September 2.[35]

The decision to stop was undoubtedly sound. Apart from the fact that it might have immeshed the First Army in a fight from which it could not readily disentangle itself in time to meet its Meuse-Argonne commitment, and apart from the fact that Pershing had already, with Pétain's permission, pushed beyond Foch's original boundaries for a "limited offensive," the American Army was as yet a new and largely untested machine. Better to take one sure step with success than fall on one's face by attempting to do too much. The very day MacArthur recommended a further advance his division's Chief of Staff was complaining that, because of logistical problems, the men were not being adequately fed and clothed.[36]

Hunter Liggett put the matter in its plain and correct light when he said that taking Metz was possible "only on the supposition that our army was a well-oiled, fully coordinated machine, which it was not as yet." Even doing its damnedest, the First Army "had an excellent chance of spending the greater part of the winter mired in the mud of the Woëvre, flanked both to the east and the west."[37]

Liggett, the I Corps commander in this operation and later First Army commander, knew what he was talking about when he said the Army was not well-oiled and coordinated. American infantry fired at their own planes. When encountering machine-gun nests, they seemed to have no sense of how to take cover. Instead of hugging the ground and crawling forward, they charged recklessly across open spaces or fell back walking bolt upright.

Artillery fired too slowly during the rolling barrages, holding up the infantry, and then delayed in moving forward, so that the infantry outstripped it during the advance. Despite the fact that the terrain furnished excellent observation posts and battery positions, the artillery fired by map rather than by direct observation, using ammunition extravagantly and inefficiently.

Discipline was lax. When halted, men tended to get out of ranks and disperse, becoming stragglers. Pilfering of prisoners was almost universal. Animals were misused, abused, or not used at all. During traffic jams, instead of dismounting and resting both horses and men, the riders slouched in the saddles for hours. Animal-drawn ambulances, vitally needed at the front for transportation over muddy roads which were impassable for motor transport, were in one division used for evacuating field hospitals in the rear. And when telephone lines went dead, instead of using a horse relay system which would have provided quick, practical service over roads impassable to vehicles, commanders simply remained out of touch.

Command headquarters were too far back and inadequately marked. One staff officer carrying an important message wandered for hours before he could find either one of a division's two brigade headquarters, although he was not far from either.

Divisions issued wordy orders, full of contingent clauses and appendices, repeating information available in standard manuals and prescribing detailed formations, even down to battalion level. Most subordinates probably never even read them.[38]

The traffic jams were monumental. Patton's gas trucks took thirty-two hours to cover nine miles on September 13. Two days later Clemenceau was caught in a jam so huge that it confirmed all his fears about U.S. incapacity to handle large forces. "I had warned them beforehand . . . ," he wrote in his memoirs. "They wanted an American Army. They had it. Any one who saw, as I saw, the hopeless congestion at Thiaucourt will bear witness that they may congratulate themselves on not having had it sooner."[39]

Far from being impressed by the American effort, many felt that it revealed serious deficiencies which boded ill for the future. "The Americans have not yet had sufficient experience," said a German intelligence report, "and are accordingly not to be feared in a great offensive. Up to this time our men have had too high an opinion of the Americans. . . ."[40]

And the Meuse-Argonne operation was less than two weeks away.

TWENTY-THREE

Meuse-Argonne:
September 26, 1918

THE MEUSE-ARGONNE sector assigned to the American First Army was probably the most strategically important area on the western front. All supply of German forces in Northern France was dependent on two great railroad networks: one through Liège in the north, the other through Thionville in the south. The mainstay of the southern line was a four-track railroad between Carignan, Sedan, and Mézières, over which reportedly some 250 trains moved a day. Should the First Army cut that line, say at Sedan, it would have serious consequences on all German forces serviced by it. Two-thirds of the German supply and evacuation facilities from Verdun to the Sambre River were dependent upon this railroad, and one-third from Verdun to Holland. Severing this line would throw an intolerable burden on the other main artery through Liège. Beset by massive Allied offensives, such as Foch envisioned, the Germans would be seriously hampered in supplying and reinforcing their troops in Northern France and, in the event of any Allied breakthrough, might not be able to evacuate them in time.

Foch had designated two armies for the Meuse-Argonne offensive: the American First Army (Pershing) east of the Argonne Forest and the French Fourth Army (Gouraud) west of it. Driving northwest, they were to cut the Thionville-Lille Railroad, or at least interdict it by artillery, in the vicinity of Sedan-Mézières.[1]

The terrain was highly defensible. Bordered on the east by the unfordable Meuse River and on the west by the hilly, heavily wooded, and all but impassable Argonne Forest, the area was virtually a tunnel 20 miles wide and 13 miles long, running southeast to northwest. Up the center ran a massive hogback, with high points at Montfaucon, Romagne, Cunel, and Barricourt, dividing the area into two sub-tunnels or defiles. Pershing's troops would have to force their way through this relatively narrow area, all the while being under observation and artillery fire from the Argonne Hills to the west, the Heights of the Meuse to the east, and

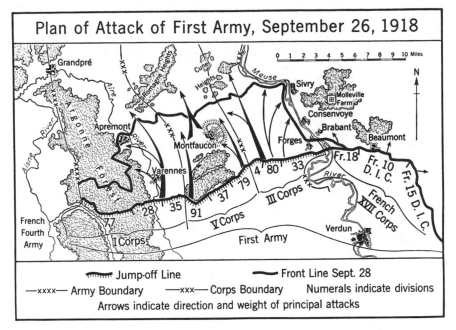

From American Battle Monuments Commission, *American Armies and Battlefields in Europe*, Washington, D.C., 1938.

the hogback in the center, which had a field of fire in both directions. In addition, the area was dotted with hills and heavy-growth woods, making progress difficult.

It was a defender's dream, an attacker's nightmare. Hugh Drum, First Army Chief of Staff, called it "the most ideal defensive terrain" he had ever seen or read about. Hunter Liggett, who subsequently commanded the First Army, called it "a natural fortress beside which the Virginia Wilderness in which Grant and Lee fought was a park."[2]

What nature had begun, the fertile German mind had intensified with every imaginable man-made defense: flanking and parallel trenches, concrete dugouts, fortified strong points, and a seemingly endless number of well-placed, concrete machine-gun emplacements. In addition, swirls of barbed wire, much of it concealed by vines and brush which had grown up over a four-year German occupation, crisscrossed the terrain. Harbord believed it was "probably the most comprehensive system of leisurely prepared field defense known to history." From Pershing's viewpoint the elaborate defenses were almost devilish; fittingly, the Germans had named their three main positions (*stellung*) after three Wagnerian witches: Giselher, Kriemhilde, and Freya.[3]

Because of the formidable terrain and strongly constructed defenses, the area was lightly held with five understrength German divisions. They could, however, bring up reinforcements rather rapidly. Fifteen enemy reserve divisions, added to the five already there, coupled with the naturally defensive terrain and the strong fortifications, made the position virtually impregnable.

Having committed his most experienced divisions at St. Mihiel (1st, 2d, 26th, 42d), Pershing lacked them for the coming attack. Of the nine frontline divisions scheduled for it, four had seen combat (4th, 28th, 33d, and 77th), but the five others (35th, 37th, 79th, 80th, and 91st) were almost totally without experience. Two of them (the 79th and 91st) had been in France only two months, during which they had never been in the front lines, even in a quiet sector.

Even supposedly experienced divisions like the 77th contained large numbers of replacements. Some 4,000 arrived just before the attack, completely green, only six weeks in the army and most of that spent in traveling. Incredibly, some had never handled a rifle![4]

To make matters worse, four of the nine divisions lacked their own artillery and would have to go into battle with substitutes with whom they had never worked. In addition, right before the battle the staffs of the five inexperienced divisions were "scalped" to provide students and instructors for the General Staff College at Langres so that the next class might start on schedule. "The amount of confusion and mismanagement resulting from this was tremendous," said George C. Marshall, Jr.[5]

Moving the First Army into position for the coming offensive was a task that would have taxed the most experienced staff. Only three roads led to the front, none of them particularly good, each barely adequate for transporting the mass of men and matériel which must flow in either direction.

Using just these three roads, the French Second Army, which was vacating the sector, had to march out two corps headquarters, corps troops, eleven divisions, and other army units, while the American First Army, which was taking over, had to move in three corps headquarters, corps troops, fifteen divisions, and assorted army troops—all under the cover of darkness.

The magnitude of this may be gathered from the fact that to move the personnel alone of a single AEF division required one thousand trucks strung out in a line of traffic four miles long! And this is not to mention the divisional baggage trains, artillery caissons, ammunition wagons, and other supply vehicles—all of which extended each division's "tail" to twenty miles! Nor the establishment of nineteen railheads, thirty-four evacuation hospitals, and more than eighty depots for supplies of all kinds—ordnance, quartermaster, medical, signal, engineer, motor, and tank.

The man designated to plan and execute this vast movement of men and supplies was a GHQ staff officer on loan to the First Army, Colonel George C. Marshall, Jr. By a combination of intelligence, drive, hard work, patience, understanding, flexibility, good sense, and knowing when to throw the book away, he pulled it off. But it was not easy. Most of the men came from the St. Mihiel sector, which meant that even while that battle was in progress, men and equipment had simultaneously to be withdrawn and routed toward a new battlefield sixty miles distant. Some units, for example, had to be moved from east of the Moselle River, at right angles to the drive at St. Mihiel.

Marshall designated one road as a motor highway and the other two for foot troops and animal-drawn vehicles. He worked out march tables, but things always went wrong. Trucks designated to carry infantry arrived late, causing gaps in the march line, which Marshall tried to fill by hurried calls to some nearby unit to get on the road "immediately." The delayed trucks would, of course, subsequently cause a traffic jam somewhere down the road, as they intersected another column crossing at right angles and which, in the original timetable, had had a clear line of march. To avoid this, Marshall would have to make sudden, ad hoc arrangements—for example, shifting horse-drawn transport to the motor road.

The doughboy, of course, cursed the "damned fool staff officers" who didn't plan things better, who had him out in the rain when he was cold and hungry, or who were ordering him back on the road, dead tired, when he thought the day's march was over. Some staff officers were damned fools, certainly, but Marshall was not one of them. Like the doughboys, he was a victim of circumstances. Horses dropped dead in their tracks, artillery scheduled to move to the new sector had to be retained on the St. Mihiel front, traffic snarls delayed French camions scheduled for use by the Americans. Marshall never knew more than twenty-four hours in advance which units would be ready to move. His work was a mixture of planning and improvisation, like juggling balls in the air.[6]

But he performed brilliantly, earning the nickname "Wizard." With justifiable pride he wrote of his work: "Despite the haste with which all the movements had to be carried out, the inexperience of most of the commanders in movements of such density, the condition of the animals and the limitations as to roads, the entire movement was carried out without a single element failing to reach its place on the date scheduled. . . ."[7]

Col. Charles Repington, a former British officer and correspondent for the *London Morning Post*, called the transfer of the American First Army from St. Mihiel to the Meuse-Argonne one of the most difficult staff operations of the war. In his judgment, "it was a fine piece of Staff work and no other Staff could have done it better."[8]

So the French Second Army moved out and the American First Army moved in, extending its front westward from the St. Mihiel sector to the western edge of the Argonne Forest. Its line now ran ninety-four miles, or about one-third of the active front from the North Sea to the Moselle River.

Pershing envisaged the offensive in four stages:

1) An initial, massive, and lightning-like thrust some ten miles north to the northern edge of the Argonne Forest at Grandpré. This would outflank the forest, leave German defenders there isolated and cut off, and ensure juncture with the French Fourth Army at Grandpré.

2) A second giant step, again ten miles, to the front Le Chesne-Stenay. This would outflank the German defenders fighting the French Fourth Army north of the Aisne, compelling their withdrawal. The French forces would come abreast on the left, protecting the American left flank.

3) An attack east of the Meuse against the heights there, driving the German artillery from their commanding positions and protecting the First Army's right flank.

4) A final thrust against the Sedan-Mézières Railroad.

Of the four steps, the most crucial was the first. By throwing nine double-strength American divisions against five understrength German, Pershing hoped to effect a quick breakthrough, permitting him to advance up to and through the Kriemhilde Stellung, the main enemy position (also called the Hindenburg Line), before the Germans could occupy it in force. To do this he was depending on surprise and numbers (First Army outnumbered the enemy about four to one). What was done, had to be done quickly. American intelligence knew that the Germans could bring up reinforcements of four divisions on the first day, two on the second, and nine on the third.

Success was a long shot, and the odds were against it. Pershing scheduled the whole ten-mile initial advance for the first day, a distance no American division had ever yet made, not even the experienced divisions in the successful St. Mihiel attack, which had advanced only about half that distance.

The plan of attack called for an assault by three corps: I (Liggett), V (Cameron), and III (Bullard) on a twenty-mile front. Cameron had the toughest assignment, bucking up the hogback in the center, especially against the strongpoint at Montfaucon, which in any man's book was an appalling challenge. Hopefully, Liggett would have easier going in the valley on the left and Bullard in the valley on the right, and would be able to drive two salients in the German lines, which would assist Cameron in outflanking Montfaucon and unhinging the Giselher Stellung. Then Cameron could drive straight ahead in a power thrust against the Kriemhilde Stellung with its strongpoints at Romagne and Cunel, all the while protected on the flanks by Liggett and Bullard, whose artillery was charged with suppressing enemy guns from, respectively, the Argonne on the left and the Heights of the Meuse on the right. But all this had to be done quickly, in a day or at most two, before German reinforcements arrived. Colonel Drum felt that if they did not penetrate the Kriemhilde Stellung by the second day, the operation would fail and they would be bogged down in attrition warfare.[9]

Pershing counted not only on the weight of superior numbers, but on the element of surprise. The First Army had recently attacked on a different front, St. Mihiel, and could well be expected to do so again, since Metz and the nearby iron and coal regions were tempting targets, which the enemy could not afford to leave unprotected. Of eighteen frontline divisions opposite the First Army, only five were west of the Meuse, indicating that the Germans expected a renewal of the St. Mihiel drive east of it.

At the last minute, however, some Germans divined American intentions. Although U.S. officers had worn French uniforms in their early reconnaissance of the sector, and although U.S. troops were not to be moved into the front lines until the last possible moment, on September 24, two days before the attack, German commanders in the Meuse-Argonne region concluded that the next AEF move would be against them. To foil the coming American artillery barrage they pulled back their outpost troops to their main line of resistance, and they started reinforcements on the road to the threatened area even before the attack had commenced.[10]

On the afternoon of September 25 Pershing visited corps and division head-quarters, speaking a word of encouragement to the commanders. "They were all alert and confident," he said, "and I returned feeling that all would go as planned." No judgment was ever more wrong.[11]

On the night of September 25 the last of the assault troops moved up into line. Running from left to right, that is, from the Argonne Forest to the Meuse River, they were as follows:

I Corps (Hunter Liggett): 77th Division (Robert Alexander), 28th (Charles H. Muir), 35th (Peter E. Traub).

V Corps (George H. Cameron): 91st (John A. Johnston), 37th (Charles S. Farnsworth), 79th (Joseph E. Kuhn).

III Corps (Robert L. Bullard): 4th (John L. Hines), 80th (Adelbert Cronkhite), 33d (George Bell, Jr.).

East of the Meuse the French XVII Colonial Corps (Claudel) and IV Corps (Joseph T. Dickman), located in the old St. Mihiel sector, were scheduled to make strong artillery demonstrations and raids on September 26, seeking to mask as long as possible the main point of American attack.[12]

With 850 French and U.S. planes, the Air Service of the First Army, under the command of Col. Billy Mitchell, outnumbered the enemy almost three-to-one. On the ground 189 light tanks, under Lt. Col. George S. Patton, Jr., were unopposed, since the Germans in the area had no tanks. Fearful of running out of gas again, as he had at St. Mihiel (and was to do later in World War II), Patton had stockpiled twenty thousand gallons of fuel for use after the first day. He also ordered each tank to carry two full gas cans on its tail, dangerous though it would be if a bullet struck.[13]

To the new, inexperienced U.S. divisions, and even to some older ones, the opening artillery barrage on September 25 seemed incredible. Beginning at 11:30 P.M. and crescendoing as the night wore on, almost 4,000 guns of all calibers, none of them made in America, rained an incessant fire on German rear areas, communication zones, assembly points, frontline trenches, and barbed-wire entanglements. Flying before dawn, Eddie Rickenbacker had the impression that every gun on the ground below was firing at once, lighting up the whole horizon "with one mass of jagged flashes." It was as if a giant switchboard had suddenly lit up with thousands of electric lights.[14]

Another pilot, Lt. Lansing C. Holden, Jr., sucked in his breath, thunderstruck at what he saw below. "The myriad of flashes extended in a line as far as one could see. The fire was incessant. Huge jets of flame from the big guns, with red pinpricks from the 75s, and then the enormous trench mortars bursting into a great fountain of sparks, leaving a glow in the white mist that was weird and ghostly." It all seemed unreal, like some Fourth of July celebration in a dream. Although Holden thought it was "the most gorgeous thing imaginable," he knew that soldiers were dying by the hundreds on the ground below, and he asked himself, "Have all men gone mad?"[15]

At 5:30 A.M. on September 26 the infantry climbed out of the trenches and started forward. Progress at first was good. Although a heavy morning fog interfered with American cohesion, creating feelings of isolation and loneliness, it permitted the attackers to get close to German positions before being seen. When James L. Collins visited Operations headquarters before noon, he reported that "everything was going along beautifully"—a fact that seemed quite "marvelous," considering that almost half the assault divisions had never been in combat before.[16]

Before long, however, problems began to develop. Confused by the fog and hampered by inexperience, the attacking troops lost liaison and began to lose cohesion. Although they took the German first positions in comparatively good order, they afterwards became, in the words of George C. Marshall, Jr., who studied the operation, "disorganized or confused to a remarkable degree."[17]

Mistakes noted at St. Mihiel were repeated. Men attacked in bunches, rather than singly, permitting a machine gun to winnow a whole platoon in one sweep. Failing to mop up as they moved forward, the attackers soon found themselves surrounded, with Germans in the rear as well as on their front. During temporary halts they neglected to dig in, so that after capturing a strong point, especially a hill, they were easily "blown off" it by enemy artillery and had to capture it all over again.

Divisional artillery performed badly. Too slow in moving up, it persisted in repeating the stereotyped barrages of the initial assault, firing blindly rather than by direct observation, wasting shots and leaving the infantry to assault machine-gun nests with rifle, bayonet, and bare flesh.

Tanks, badly needed at the front against such nests, lagged behind, clogging up the roads. When they finally got forward, the doughboys refused to accompany them, fearful of the heavy shelling directed against the metal monsters. So the tanks went out alone and were soon knocked out one by one as Germans approached from their blind side and dropped grenades through the portholes. In several instances tanks took towns but, without infantry support, were unable to hold them and were soon disabled. Then the same towns had to be retaken, this time by the infantry alone, without tank support.

Traffic control was poor, as was road discipline. In one case two artillery regiments bivouacked right on the road, completely blocking it as a communication artery. Some units in the rear looted kitchen wagons intended for the front, causing food shortages there.[18]

During the first day some serious mix-ups occurred, especially in Cameron's crucial V Corps, which was supposed to break through the German center. In an attempt to maintain control (some would say overcontrol) First Army planners had directed that, on reaching corps objectives, the divisions were to hold and await further orders before advancing toward army objectives. Unfortunately, V Corps, stalled before Montfaucon, held up III Corps on its right, with the result that for five hours men of its 4th Division sat waiting for an order to advance, during which the Germans occupied the Bois de Brieulles which had been empty, and rushed into Nantillois, which the 4th Division might have taken. Neither Montfaucon nor Nantillois were captured until the following day. The result was, as historian Allan R. Millett, has well remarked, that in that twenty-four hours the Meuse-Argonne campaign "turned from a sprint to a slugging match."[19]

In Liggett's I Corps on the left, messages from whatever source (telephone, radio, pigeon, runners, airplanes, liaison officers) were extremely few, and even then they were garbled, erroneous, and contradictory. Its 35th Division (Traub) was in the dark as to where its front line was, and the other two divisions of the corps were not much better off. Muir's 28th Division had airplane reports putting his front lines so far forward as to be impossible; Muir thought the Germans were dressing themselves up as Americans and laying out false display panels on the ground. But he really had no idea; his telephone wire had given out and he was out of touch with his regiments. Alexander's 77th Division was staggering around in the Argonne Forest, a mad area that had somehow been overlooked at creation when level ground was being passed out. Despite compasses, units assigned to the right flank ended over on the left, and vice versa. After one day the 77th was a mess and Alexander spent the next day straightening out the reins.[20]

On September 26, when the Meuse-Argonne attack began, General Max von Gallwitz, who commanded the German army group opposite the American First Army, thought it might be a diversion to cover a strong American attack along the old St. Mihiel front where, he knew, Pershing had veteran divisions. Nevertheless, he ordered more reserves into the Meuse-Argonne area as a precaution and these, coupled with the American failure to take Montfaucon on the first day and communication and transportation problems on subsequent days, put the Germans in good shape. "On the 27th and 28th," said Gallwitz, "we had no more worries. . . ."[21]

The American attack resumed on September 27 and did not go well. Almost universally, the rolling barrage outstripped the infantry. The Germans holed up in their dugouts and trenches until the barrage passed over, then rose up to pour a withering fire into the advancing troops, who again foolishly charged in bunches, bolt upright. The Germans cut them down like a scythe felling weeds. Said the doughboys: "Every goddam German there who didn't have a machine gun had a cannon."[22]

Using the elastic defense that the French had used so successfully against them on July 15, the Germans fought back with tenacity and skill. When cut off and surrounded, they came forward yelling "*Kamerad*," then suddenly threw bombs, and in the ensuing disorder yelled in English, "Retire! Retire!" as if American officers were ordering it.[23]

German artillery fire from the Argonne foothills on the left and the Heights of the Meuse on the right was simply devastating; Lieutenant Maury Maverick, later a Texas Congressman in the 1930s, described it thus: "There is a great swishing scream, a smash-bang, and it seems to tear everything loose from you. The intensity of it simply enters your heart and brain, and tears every nerve to pieces."[24]

On September 27 Pershing wrote in his diary that he was "not very much pleased" with First Army progress, attributing its failure to the inexperience of the division and brigade commanders and to their "lack of push." The following day he visited all three corps commanders and some division commanders, attempting to stir things up. At I Corps headquarters he had its Chief of Staff, Malin Craig, phone each division commander (77th, 28th, and 35th) and in Pershing's name "tell him that he must push on regardless of men or guns, night and day."

Liggett, whose I Corps had lagged behind the other two, tried to give his superior some notion of the difficult terrain, the formidably prepared defenses (manned in one area by the crack German 1st Guard Division), and the inexperience of both officers and men. The 35th Division, for instance, had just a few days before the battle received a new chief of staff, two new brigade commanders, and three out of four new regimental commanders. Pershing said that he appreciated all of this, but it may be doubted that he really did.[25]

En route to visit the corps commanders, he had stopped his automobile and, standing up, made an impassioned appeal to some of the men of the 35th Division, stressing the importance of the battle and the absolute necessity of their breaking through. Significantly, because of road blocks and traffic difficulties, it took him ninety minutes to cover just two and one-half miles on this trip. Logistical problems such as this, rather than a lack of push in his commanders, prevented the desired breakthrough.[26]

Pershing probably overestimated the power of élan in conquering obstacles and underestimated the difficulties that Liggett mentioned and that his soldiers had to face firsthand in all their terrifying intensity. The will to win is important and, victory being possible, has frequently brought it about. But it is not irresistible and some obstacles are insuperable, at least for the moment. The proverb, "Where there's a will, there's a way," is not always true; sometimes there is no way.[27]

During the battle, for example, moving artillery forward became increasingly difficult, and without artillery support so did further advance. Across no-man's-land and beyond, for approximately five kilometers, the three roads were so destroyed by shellfire as to require complete rebuilding. This took time, during which corps and divisions frantically called for artillery support. Unfortunately, the big, heavy 155s were started forward before the roads were ready, chewing them up and making it impossible for anything else to get by.

By now the First Army was attempting to move men, animals, guns, wagons, and all sorts of equipment over a landscape which was cratered, quite literally, like the surface of the moon. Some craters were fifteen feet wide and equally deep, and until they were filled in or bridged over, nothing moved, including the wounded, whose cries of agony and despair were heartrending. The engineers performed valiantly in the heavy rain, grabbing whatever came to hand to make or repair a passable road, but they were frequently as frustrated as everyone else. When someone complained that a portion of the road was not wide enough or good enough, an angry soldier cursed and said, "I've put a whole God-damn church in there."[28]

After visiting the corps and division commanders, Pershing wrote in his diary on September 28: "I . . . certainly have done all in my power to instill an aggressive spirit in the different Corps headquarters." He may have, but the next morning the First Army went out and promptly got hit a stiff clout in the snoot.[29]

Almost from the start the American attack went badly. The Germans actually counterattacked Traub's 35th Division, which they caught in the process of withdrawing in broad daylight, threw it into a panic, and stampeded it. The men simply

American infantry attempting to move across a cratered battlefield.
National Archives

ran away. "For a while," said the German Third Army war diary for September 29, "the entire American front between the Aire and the left wing of the [German Third] army was moving back. Concentrated artillery fire struck enemy masses streaming to the rear with an annihilating effect."[30]

While instances of individual heroism existed, organizationally the 35th Division dissolved into chaos. The men were demoralized and the chain of command was in shambles, as it had been during the four-day engagement. On one occasion a regimental commander got lost and wandered over the battlefield a full twenty-four hours, ending up with another division. His replacement could find neither the regimental command post nor the regiment itself, nor did brigade or division headquarters have any idea where they were.

Traub conducted the battle as if the ground were coming out from beneath him. He went for four days (September 26–29) without sleep, lived on cigarettes and coffee, wandered around the battlefield and almost into the German lines, was frequently out of touch with both his command post and his units, got gassed, and on one occasion, so it was said, personally tried to form up his attacking troops as if he were a young second lieutenant. By his own admission he had "a hell of a time" and at the end of the day hundreds of his officers and thousands of his men were missing.[31]

The debacle of the 35th Division was an extreme case, but it was symptomatic of the condition of the First Army. A situation report on the afternoon of September 29 revealed that "troops do not seem to be making an organized attack, or to be making an advance." Furthermore, unless the line could advance in the Argonne, "it may be found necessary to draw back the line of resistance south of Montfaucon and eventually to our old positions"—in other words, to where the First Army originally started.[32]

By September 29 the First Army attack had ground to a standstill. It had been stopped by a tenacious German defense, which made excellent use of terrain, and by its own command and logistic problems. Whether because of incompetence or inexperience or both, the First Army was wallowing in an unbelievable logistical snarl. It was as if someone had taken the army's intestines out and dumped them all over the table.[33]

Whatever the cause, the effect was the same. The First Army was dead in its tracks, "paralysed" in the words of General Weygand, helpless in the face of what Sir Frederick Maurice called the worst traffic jam of the war. Nothing moved, not even a horseman or a cyclist. What the Allies had feared and warned about had come to pass.[34]

Col. Paul H. Clark, AEF liaison officer with Pétain's GHQ, reported many I-told-you-so remarks among the French, who correctly pointed out that two major operations like St. Mihiel and Meuse-Argonne, scheduled so close together, were simply too much for an inexperienced American staff, and even, they admitted, for most French staffs.

Clark also reported that during the four days of battle (September 26–29) Pétain's operations map of the American front became so disfigured from constant erasures and corrections caused by conflicting reports of where the First Army was or was not, that the map's printing wore off. The French finally lost confidence in American reports and ceased making any changes.[35]

Visiting Pershing, General Jean-Henri Mordacq, Clemenceau's Chief of Staff, felt the American had been taught a lesson. "I could read clearly in his eyes that, at that moment, he realized his mistake. His soldiers were dying bravely, but they were not advancing, or very little, and their losses were heavy. All that great body of men which the American Army represented was literally struck with paralysis because 'the brain' didn't exist, because the generals and their staffs lacked experience. With enemies like the Germans, this kind of war couldn't be improvised."[36]

All armies, of course, have congestion and confusion in time of battle. Pershing stoutly maintained that the amount in his Army was exaggerated, which it probably was, but it was also far worse than he hoped or anticipated.[37]

As luck would have it, Clemenceau, who had been caught in a traffic jam behind Thiaucourt two weeks before, chose this time to attempt to visit Montfaucon, captured by the 79th Division on September 27. On September 29, while five miles away from Montfaucon, he found his car stopped by a tremendous backup of vehicles and impedimenta. After inching forward for a while, Clemenceau finally became "very much incensed" and ordered Capt. Charles de Marenches, whom Pershing had assigned to accompany him, to clear the way. Marenches strove mightily, but the road was so narrow, the area on each side so pockmarked with craters filled with water, and ammunition wagons so bunched up all around them that, despite everyone's willingness to cooperate, nothing could be done. Some drivers said that for two whole nights they had been scarcely able to advance more than a few yards.

Exasperated, and in a great hurry because he desired also to visit the French Fourth Army, Clemenceau jumped out of his car and started walking rapidly across the fields, telling Marenches to do what he could to get the car forward. The captain tried fruitlessly for half an hour, then gave up, and followed cross-country to where Clemenceau had gone about a mile ahead to a high hill, where he had a panoramic view of the congestion. He used "some strong language," said Marenches. Then, stalking back to the car, which was turned around "with great trouble," he drove off to visit the French.[38]

Rightly or wrongly, the hopeless congestion, coming back-to-back with what he had seen two weeks previously, could not but impress the French premier. Was the First Army capable of planning and conducting a large-scale, sustained offensive? It would seem not.

TWENTY-FOUR

Meuse-Argonne: October 4, 1918

LTHOUGH THE AMERICANS had taken Montfaucon on the second day (which Pétain said they would be lucky to do before winter) and although they had advanced at one point as far as eight miles, in terms of what had been planned and hoped for (advancing ten miles and piercing the Kriemhilde Stellung), the September 26 attack was a failure. Montfaucon had held long enough to hold up the whole advance. The Germans had brought up their reserves (six fresh divisions by September 30, with five more in close support), slammed the door tight on the Meuse-Argonne tunnel, and were leaning on it hard.[1]

Meanwhile, the whole western front had burst into flames. Thanks to massive American reinforcements, the Allies now had numerical superiority, and Foch intended to strike a series of successive, devastating blows all along the line, designed not to achieve a breakthrough but to exhaust German reserves. Unlike Ludendorff, Foch had the genius to finally see that a decisive, war-winning breakthrough was chimerical, for the defense could always move its reserves by rail and truck more quickly than the offense could move by foot, especially over devastated ground. The result was always the same: a salient, perhaps a massive one such as at Château-Thierry, but one unable to be exploited because held by increasingly exhausted troops who were always met by increasingly fresh reserves. Since exploitation in depth was impossible, the proper course was a series of offensives, each having the initial advantage of firepower that offensives always had, each compelling Ludendorff to use up his reserves in a stopgap, disorganized fashion. Like Grant facing Lee, Foch planned to apply pressure at all points simultaneously until the German war machine, oppressed from all sides and given no time to recoup, came crashing down.[2]

Accordingly, Foch had scheduled four great attacks for four successive days along the whole front from the Meuse River to the North Sea:

September 26: a Franco-American attack by the French Fourth Army (Gouraud) and the American First Army (Pershing) between the Meuse River and Reims.

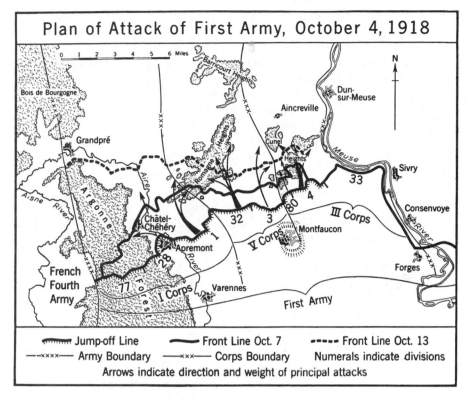

From American Battle Monuments Commission, *American Armies and Battlefields in Europe*, Washington, D.C., 1938.

September 27: An attack by the British First and Third Armies in the general direction of Cambrai.

September 28: A combined Allied attack in Flanders east of Ypres.

September 29: A Franco-British attack in the vicinity of St. Quentin.[3]

In contrast to Pershing's attack, the other offensives had gone well. The Allies drove the Germans back in Flanders and in the center drove through the Hindenburg Line during the first week.[4]

Surveying the American Army, Foch was "very disappointed," for it "continued to mark time" while others were advancing. Although its individual soldiers were brave, he believed its command and staff were logistically and tactically incompetent. They had overcrowded the front lines with assault troops (the French would have used about half the number Pershing used), clogging the arteries and causing traffic jams. Then, instead of sending up road repair units, the Americans had sent forward the heaviest vehicles, which tore up the already poor roads, rendering them impassable. In some cases nothing moved in either direction for 16–18 hours.[5]

By the end of September Foch was convinced that the Americans were too densely packed in both the Meuse-Argonne corridor and along the old St. Mihiel front. To relieve congestion and to make best use of all available manpower, he determined to withdraw some of those surplus American divisions and send them where they could be better used: two or three divisions to the French XVII Corps east of the Meuse, two or three divisions to the French XXXVIII Corps west of the Argonne Forest. He also planned a change in the command structure: Pershing to command the Franco-American forces on both sides of the Meuse River, and a French general the Franco-American forces on both sides of the Argonne Forest. He wrote this out as an order on September 30 and sent Weygand to communicate it to Pershing the following day.[6]

Pershing, who saw Clemenceau's hand in the order, objected. Not only would this place American divisions in French corps, which he tried to avoid, but it seemed to complicate the logistic problem still further, for, under the proposed arrangement, the same road east of the Argonne Forest would have to be used to supply both the American and French armies. Besides, contended Pershing, he was planning to resume the attack in the existing Meuse-Argonne sector in a day or two anyway.[7]

Faced with Pershing's recalcitrance, Foch decided to drop his order and leave the command arrangement alone. He did insist, however, on a condition, namely, "that your attacks start without delay and that, once begun, they be continued without any interruptions such as those which have just arisen."[8]

Pershing hit the ceiling over this. "The Marshal quite overstepped his bounds of authority in writing such a letter to me," he wrote in his diary. "His functions are strategical and he has no authority whatsoever to interfere in tactical questions. Any observations from him as to my way of carrying out my attack are all out of place. I will not stand for this letter which disparages myself and the American Army and the American effort. He will have to retract it, or I shall go further in the matter."[9]

A good case can be made that Foch was quite within his rights in insisting that the attacks start "without delay" and continue "without any interruptions." He was, after all, charged with strategical direction of the war and in strategy the timing of an attack is important. Indeed, one fault which Pershing found with the Allied conduct of the war before the appointment of a generalissimo was precisely this failure to coordinate operations, one Ally attacking while the other stood still, permitting the enemy to reinforce the threatened point. Foch was not, as Pershing claimed, attempting to tell him how to carry out the attack, which would indeed be a tactical question. He was insisting that an attack take place and that the pressure be kept up, which is strategic.[10]

But because Pershing was quite obviously miffed, and because Foch's practice was to persuade rather than to order, he returned a soft answer to the American's angry remonstrance, especially since Pershing planned an early resumption of the attack anyway. Foch's point had been made, however: the Americans should get going.[11]

By October 4, the First Army had regrouped and was ready to resume the advance. The objective was basically that of September 26: to reach and penetrate the Kriemhilde Stellung. The flank divisions were the same, but the Army's center had been bolstered by removing four inexperienced divisions (35th, 91st, 37th, and 79th) and replacing them with three veteran divisions: the 1st (Charles P. Summerall), 32d (William G. Haan), and 3d (Beaumont B. Buck). To avoid one corps being held up by another, as had occurred during the earlier attack, orders specified that each was to advance independently, without stopping at any pre-determined objective.[12]

At 5:00 A.M. on October 4 the First Army attacked. There was no preliminary bombardment, lest the Germans be forewarned, but there might just as well have been, for the Germans were ready and waiting. They had used the four-day lull to bring into line a number of fresh divisions who brought with them all the tricks of the trade.

During the assault American artillery concentrated its fire against the tree lines at the tops of hills because that, after all, is where any sensible defender would emplace his machine guns. Alas, when the Americans started forward they were mowed down by machine-gun nests hidden on the open face of hills. Or they were cut to pieces by machine guns planted in the center of woods which arched their fire over the treetops down onto the open fields. In neither case had American artillery officers thought to fire there.[13]

As with earlier attacks, the U.S. infantry charged bravely, even foolishly, compelling the admiration of enemy soldiers, who nevertheless mowed them down with gusto. It was just "one damn machine gun after another," complained the doughboys as they inched their way forward. Even a hundred-yard gain was an accomplishment.[14]

Flying overhead, Billy Mitchell marveled at the repeated, uncoordinated, and disorganized American attacks. It was like a man butting his head against a wall, he observed. Alexander's 77th Division had a detachment cut off by the Germans (the Lost Battalion), then fired on it by accident and also on the French on his left.[15]

There were, of course, instances of daring initiative and extraordinary heroism. In I Corps, Liggett and his brilliant chief of staff, Malin Craig, launched a boldly conceived "sideways attack" with one brigade of the 82d Division on October 7 and 8. It compelled German withdrawal along the front of the 77th and 28th Divisions, rescued the Lost Battalion (which was neither lost nor a battalion), and helped to clear the Argonne Forest, which was in American hands by October 10. During this attack a former conscientious objector named Alvin C. York single-handedly killed 28 Germans, captured 132 others (including a major and two lieutenants) and 35 machine guns.[16]

On October 8, in an attempt to suppress the killing fire from German batteries on the Heights of the Meuse, the First Army attacked east of the river. The operation was under Claudel's French XVII Corps, composed of two French divisions and two American: the 29th (Charles G. Morton) and the 33d (George Bell, Jr.)

Initially successful, the attack soon bogged down, as the Germans brought up reinforcements and pounded the XVII Corps with high explosives and poison gas. Bell's 33d Division, which had been in the original September 26 jump-off, remained almost a month in line before Pershing took the men out on October 21. They had suffered more gas casualties (over 2,000) than any other U.S. division, their clothes were in tatters, and the men were exhausted. Filthy dirty, unable to wash or change clothes for much of the period, their smelly skin stuck to their socks as they peeled them off.[17]

By October 10 Liggett's I Corps had cleared the Argonne, Cameron's V Corps was butting its head against the heights of the Bois de Romagne, Bullard's III Corps was still taking heavy fire from the Heights of the Meuse, and east of the river Claudel's XVII Corps was boxed in a pocket short of the Heights and would remain penned in for the rest of the month. Nowhere had Pershing pierced the Kriemhilde Stellung significantly, save for a short distance in Bullard's corps.[18]

Pershing said later that the first two weeks of October were the worst time of the war, both for the First Army and himself. The weather was terrible: cold, drizzly, and depressing. Constant rain and heavy traffic churned the yellow clay into a desolate, swampy quagmire, all but impassable. The land—naked, scarred, and burnt—reflected the mood of the men. Trees, their branches sheared off and their trunks shattered as if by some giant sledgehammer, stood gaunt against the dull, gray sky.[19]

The attacks were not going well and the whole world knew it. On the first day of the offensive, September 26, the First Army had advanced eleven kilometers with relatively light losses, but since then, during the next three weeks, it had advanced only five kilometers with very heavy losses. One AEF division, moving up in support, suffered 5,000 casualties from German artillery without firing a shot. In one attack by the 1st Division, over 12,000 men went in; only 2,000 came out.[20]

Pershing's friend Pétain warned him that Foch was "impatient," even "violent" on the subject of the American delay. When the generalissimo confronted Pershing at his headquarters at Bombon on October 13, he stated very flatly that the Allies were making "very marked progress on all fronts except the Americans," and again called for an advance. "No more promises!" said Foch. "Results!"

Pershing, who felt that no troops in the world could have done better under the circumstances, blamed the difficult terrain and the tenacious German resistance, especially the machine guns echeloned in depth. But Foch cut him off. "Results are the only thing to judge by.... If an attack is well planned and well executed, it succeeds ...; if it is not ... there is no advance." Since the Americans were not advancing, obviously something was wrong with their planning and execution.[21]

The distinguished French military historian, André Kaspi, has pointed out that Foch himself bore a large part of the blame for the poor U.S. showing, both in insisting on priority shipment of infantry and machine gunners in the spring, which impoverished the AEF logistically, and in suddenly changing the AEF theater of operations at the end of August. Pershing himself undoubtedly felt this, but that was poor consolation when so many things were suddenly going wrong.[22]

Manpower shortages, for instance. As more and more doughboys were killed, wounded, gassed, shell shocked, captured, missing, and straggling, the cry for more men to feed into the maelstrom became acute. On October 3, with three combat divisions short 80,000 men, Pershing cannibalized two recently arrived divisions to provide replacements, and he reduced infantry companies from 250 to 175 men. As the offensive ground on, he eventually skeletonized seven divisions for replacements to keep the attack going.[23]

But prospects for the future were bleak, as influenza suddenly broke out, with over 16,000 new cases in the AEF during the first week of October. In America more than 200,000 were down with the disease, causing General March to suspend nearly all draft calls, quarantine nearly all camps, and considerably reduce training.[24]

Supplying the AEF became increasingly difficult, compounded by the ongoing battle and the fact that priority shipments of infantry and machine gunners during the spring and summer had logistically unbalanced it. During the summer, Railway Transportation was 20 percent short of its tonnage allotment, the Medical Corps 23 percent, the Chemical Warfare Service 51 percent, the Signal Corps 52 percent, and Motor Transport a crippling 81 percent![25]

The transportation problem was such that, quite literally, the AEF threatened to become immobile! A huge mass of men and matériel, it would soon be like a giant turtle tipped over on its back, floundering helplessly, unable to move. Every man who set foot in France (and Pershing was now asking for 300,000 a month) simply aggravated the crisis. So too did the eight divisions recalled from the British, who were without transportation facilities since the BEF no longer furnished them.

To carry out the St. Mihiel operation, Pershing had borrowed transportation from the French and the SOS, but now, with offensives all along the western front, the French had their own needs and the SOS was approaching a breakdown. "We have reached the point where we can no longer improvise or borrow," Pershing cabled the War Department in October. "The needs of the S.O.S. must be met now—not months from now. Unless supplies are furnished when and as cabled for our armies will cease to operate."[26]

Especially in horse transportation was the problem severe. In September 1918, two U.S. divisions scheduled to go into line were unable to move; one had only 200 horses, the other none. No animals were shipped from America in August, only 1,839 in September, and only 2,570 the following month. By October Pershing was frantic. He needed at least 31,700 horses a month—more, if possible. He was short 106,263 animals, or 43 percent of his needs.[27]

In desperation he pleaded with Foch for 25,000 or 30,000 horses—with little success. He told Clemenceau that, unless some French help was forthcoming, the American Army "will shortly be unable to go forward." The premier responded that, since the French were short of horses themselves, the Americans would have to get them from home. Yet the latest word from Washington was that shipping 30,000 animals a month was impossible, except by diverting tonnage from what was considered essential. On October 9 Col. Avery D. Andrews, Pershing's G-1, reported "the animal situation will soon become desperate."[28]

So bad was the supply and transportation problem, so disproportionate the strength of combat troops to the services necessary to maintain them, so burdensome to the French was the incessant First Army "borrowing," pressed as the French were to maintain their own armies, that on October 8 Pétain proposed to

Foch that, unless the situation radically improved, Pershing's First Army should be dissolved and the American effort limited to corps and divisions until such time as the Americans could provide the support services to maintain a field army. In the meantime, divisions which they were unable to support should be distributed "among the French armies."[29]

In addition to all his other problems, Pershing was having difficulties with General March in Washington. AEF censorship policy was to keep the location of American divisions secret until the Germans definitely identified them. March, however, was giving out such information to the press, despite being asked not to, thereby jeopardizing operations and endangering lives.[30]

Another problem was an old one: promotions. Despite Pershing's earlier remonstrances, when a new list appeared in October, men were promoted in the AEF whom he had not recommended, others he had recommended were not promoted, and half the promotions went to men still in America. As before, Pershing blamed March. When Hanson Ely of Cantigny fame, a new major general, thanked Pershing for his influence, the latter replied, "Don't say that. A lot of people think it's no advantage to be a friend of mine."[31]

Faced with all these troubles—the battle going badly, the influenza epidemic, shortages of men, supplies, and transportation, security leaks, and what seemed to be a lack of support at home—and with prospects of all these problems coalescing into one, titanic, insoluble mess, Pershing was understandably fatigued and depressed. "I feel like I am carrying the whole world on my shoulders," he moaned.[32]

At the end of the day, after visiting corps and division commanders, he would return to his train and study reports and pore over maps until early in the morning. Outside he could hear the distant swish-swish of French stretcher bearers carrying the sick, the wounded, and the dying. Weary and worn, his hair whitening, his face lined and aching from overwork and overtaut nerves, not quite knowing what to do that he hadn't done, he felt indescribably saddened and alone.[33]

One day, driving toward the front, he suddenly bent forward, buried his face in his hands, and sobbed his dead wife's name. "Frankie . . . Frankie . . . my God, sometimes I don't know how I can go on. . . ."[34]

On October 12 James L. Collins noted in his diary that the General was "not looking so well the last few days." Foch was wondering whether Bliss could step in and take over in case Pershing was incapacitated.[35]

Despite how he felt, Pershing knew that, above all, war is a contest of wills. In the appalling carnage, victory would finally go to the side that had that last extra push, to the side which, after being bloodied perhaps even more than its opponent, came back for more and continued exerting pressure. Victory would come when one side, losing ground and exhausting resources and manpower, eventually lost the will to continue.

"Things are going badly," he told Maj. Gen. Henry T. Allen, commander of the 90th Division. "We are not getting on as we should. But by God! Allen, I was never so much in earnest in my life and we are going to get through."[36]

George C. Marshall, Jr., said later that Pershing's decision to keep pushing, despite all difficulties, was for him one of the high points of his AEF experience.

"With distressingly heavy casualties, disorganized and only partially trained troops, supply troubles of every character due to the devastated zone so hurriedly crossed, inclement and cold weather, flu, stubborn resistance by the enemy on one of the strongest positions of the Western Front, pessimism on all sides and the pleadings to halt the battle made by many of the influential members of the army, you persisted in your determination to force the fighting over all difficulties and objections. . . . Nothing else in your leadership throughout the war was comparable to this."

Marshall also remembered advice that Pershing gave him, namely, that a commander, no matter how weary, should never be seen burying his head on his desk, lest someone interpret it as a loss of hope. He must always give the impression of optimism.[37]

In Pershing's "Dark Night of the Soul" he received considerable support from Secretary Baker who had arrived in France for a second visit on September 7 and stayed about a month. A sensitive, humane man, Baker was aware of the pressures under which his commander operated and bent over backwards to encourage him. Baker too was a man subject to pressures, some quite unreasonable. "What a country we are!" he exclaimed to Walter Lippmann, an intelligence officer. "Do you know that I have a petition about a mile long asking me not to move supplies on Sunday!"[38]

Visiting the front lines and rear areas, Baker was greatly impressed with what he saw. The AEF had grown tremendously since his visit in March, and although it had its problems, it was engaged in operations the magnitude of which dwarfed anyone's earlier expectations. One SOS dock, for example, was four-fifths of a mile long, with adjoining warehouses and railroad tracks, and this was only one of many docks.[39]

The Baker visit presented an occasion to bring up the difficulties with General March, which Harbord, still Pershing's right-hand man despite his absence from Chaumont, took care to do while escorting the Secretary around SOS installations. Baker was surprised to hear the rumor that March wished to replace Pershing. He would set that at rest, he said, by telling the Chief of Staff that, in the event of the death or disability of Pershing, his replacement would come from someone in Europe. He also promised to see that Pershing's promotion recommendations were followed in the future. (Unfortunately, no new lists were made before the Armistice, at which time all promotions ceased.)[40]

Baker's prime purpose in coming to Europe was not just to look over the AEF, but to do something about the shipping situation. As was mentioned, the priority shipments of infantry and machine-gun units in the spring and summer had seriously dislocated the proper balance between service and combat troops. Where it should have been about one man in three in supply work, the actual ratio was closer to one man in five. The SOS was short over 150,000 men. It was also short on all kinds of equipment. To bring these over required ships, which the British had reneged on in August. Hence Baker's visit.[41]

The Secretary performed manfully. In October he got a British agreement to divert 200,000 tons of shipping from their cereal-import program. Baker promised that if a food shortage developed in the winter, the United States would come to Britain's aid with her own shipping, which by that time would be in good supply.[42]

During Baker's visit a problem surfaced which had been submerged throughout the summer: the 100-Division program. In June Pershing and Foch had signed a statement that in order "to win the victory in 1919" it was necessary to have 100 American divisions in France by July 1919. Having studied the matter, March concluded that 80 divisions was the maximum possible number and so informed Bliss on July 23, 1918, who apparently informed Pershing, who went right ahead in planning on a 100-division program.[43]

When Baker arrived in France he was surprised to find Pershing calculating on having many more divisions by July than the War Department was planning. Informed of this, March cabled Pershing on September 25 that the latter's program was absolutely impractical. The 80-division program meant 80 divisions *total*, both combat and depot, a division being calculated (counting its quota of complementary corps and army troops) at 40,000 men. "This 80-Division in France program is the official program," said March bluntly, "and you will give instructions . . . to correspond therewith."[44]

But Pershing was not through yet. In a bit of sleight of hand, he cabled back that he was indeed planning on only 80 divisions and calculating a division at 40,000 (the division itself, with proportionate corps and army troops), but was also figuring in the SOS troops to support them (800,000) and the necessary replacements (600,000)—a total of 1,400,000 extra men. Counting the requisite SOS and replacement troops, 80 divisions averaged out closer to 52,000 per division than 40,000. "The figures you give as to strength of divisions are in error . . . ," said Pershing.[45]

Exasperated, March laid down the law. "The demands for tonnage made upon Great Britain were not based upon divisions or other units but upon the number of men which we propose to transport and the necessary cargo tonnage to supply that given number of men." That maximum figure was 3,360,000 men, and no more. You will plan your operations accordingly, he stated.[46]

As it turned out, neither 80, 96, or 100 divisions would be needed in Europe by July 1, 1919, although few realized it. When someone asked Pershing around October 8 when the war would end, he answered, "I do not know."[47]

But Foch had premonitions. The Allies had the initiative everywhere, the Central Powers were beginning to crack, and one had only to observe him swinging down the street at Bombon, his cap set at a jaunty angle and his stick over his shoulder, to know that the war was going well.

Encountering him there, Col. T. Bentley Mott remarked that it looked like the Germans were taking a licking. "He came up close to me," said Mott, "took a firm hold on my belt with his left hand, and with his right fist delivered a punch at my chin, a hook under my ribs, and another drive at my ear; he then shouldered his stick and without a single word marched on to the chateau. . . ." No need to ask how the war was going.[48]

Just before returning to America in early October, Baker asked Foch how many American divisions he needed in Europe to win in 1919. Expecting to hear a number like 80 or 96 or 100, he was startled to hear the generalissimo answer, "Forty." Thinking the interpreter had mistranslated, Baker repeated the question, only to receive the same answer. When Baker remonstrated that there were almost that many divisions already in France and that Pershing was insisting on 100 divisions, Foch said flatly: "I win the war with forty."[49]

Since only a little over three months before Foch had loudly called for 100 divisions and signed his name with Pershing to a statement demanding it as a minimum, Harbord suspected that the generalissimo was deliberately trying to embarrass Pershing with his civilian superior. That need not have been the case. The tide of the war had simply changed that much in three months. Foch, charged with an overall view of the front, saw it, whereas Pershing, heavily engaged in the Meuse-Argonne and making little progress, did not. He still wanted all the men he could lay his hands on.[50]

TWENTY-FIVE

Meuse-Argonne: October 14, 1918

O N OCTOBER 14 the First Army returned to the attack under three new corps commanders. Dissatisfied with Cameron, whose center V Corps had lagged behind during the initial September 26 advance, Pershing had replaced him on October 12 with Charles P. Summerall, the former 1st Division commander, an aggressive leader and a man after Pershing's own heart. He was pleased also with Liggett and Bullard, both of whom moved up to higher commands. Liggett's replacement in the I Corps was Joseph T. Dickman, who had been commanding the IV Corps in the quiet area near the old St. Mihiel battlefield. Bullard's successor in the III Corps was John L. Hines, who had done well as commander of the 4th Division.[1]

For the coming attack Pershing had on hand some good divisions. The III Corps on the right was all Regular Army: the 3d Division (Beaumont B. Buck), 4th (George H. Cameron), and 5th (John E. McMahon). The V Corps in the center had the magnificent 42d Division (Charles T. Menoher) and the solid 32d (William G. Hahn) which had done good work in the Aisne-Marne campaign. The I Corps on the left, comprising the 77th Division (Robert Alexander) and 82d (George B. Duncan), had a holding mission.

Pershing placed great hope on the 42d and 5th Divisions, which were scheduled to drive deep salients on either side of the Bois de Romagne and the Bois de Bantheville, flanking and pinching off the Côte Dame Marie, the linchpin of the Kriemhilde Stellung. Both divisions were fresh and experienced.[2]

Pershing would need good divisions for this attack because most of the First Army was still short of the Kriemhilde Stellung, which it was attempting to penetrate. The terrain was still indescribably difficult: thick woods, deep ravines, high ridges, tangled underbrush—all fortified and bristling with armaments. Dead bodies, victims of previous attacks, littered the landscape, providing ominous warnings of what was likely to befall the assault troops.

The weather, as usual, was miserable, and so were the men, some of them still in summer uniforms, with no overcoats and only one blanket, who rose from sleeping in the mud to attempt a dawn attack.[3]

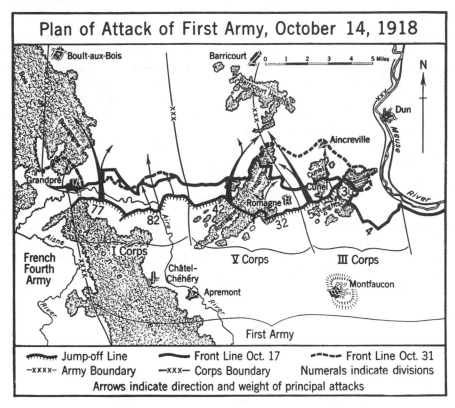

Plan of Attack of First Army, October 14, 1918

From American Battle Monuments Commission, *American Armies and Battlefields in Europe*, Washington, D.C., 1938.

The assault did not go well. The Germans counterattacked violently, forcing the Americans to take and retake the same area over and over. "Hope for better results tomorrow," Pershing wrote in his diary that day, October 14, and added significantly: "There is no particular reason for this hope except that if we keep on pounding, the Germans will be obliged to give way...." On the contrary, one might rejoin that the Americans would be obliged to lay in a massive supply of pine boxes.[4]

Things went not much better the following day. McMahon mishandled his 5th Division, crowding all his troops into the front lines, where they became disorganized, jammed up, and attacked without reserves.[5]

As day followed day the Germans fought back tenaciously, pounding both attacking and support troops with artillery and gas. They stood their ground until cut off and completely surrounded; only then did they surrender, and many did not. Even when they retreated, they exacted a bitter price. As F. Scott Fitzgerald said later, they "walked very slowly backward a few inches a day, leaving the dead like a million bloody rugs."[6]

One must never forget that the struggle was more than battle flags on a map or names in communiques. Each doughboy in khaki, each German in field gray, was caught up in a frighteningly violent, bizarre world, a living nightmare. Second Lieutenant Robert J. Franklin, who fought in the Meuse-Argonne campaign, may serve as a case in point. Going "over the top," he saw a friend turn and yell, "We are going to give them hell, aye, Bob?" The next moment a German shell made a direct hit, obliterating the man. There remained not "a drop of blood to show where he had been standing," said Franklin.

Later, running to escape heavy enemy shelling, Franklin fell into an open grave in the darkness and found himself tangled up with a human skeleton. Just then a shell hit topside, burying him alive with his macabre companion.

Still later, Franklin encountered a French artilleryman who came upon a dug-out, out of which ran a German soldier yelling "*Kamerad!*" His whole attitude indicated eagerness to surrender. "He was the happiest man I ever saw," said Franklin. When the German gestured that there were still eleven of his comrades inside who also wished to surrender, the Frenchman smiled. He pointed to something in the distance and, while the German was distracted, stuck a grenade in his pocket and knocked him down the dugout steps. A loud explosion followed. "One more, Monsieur," said the Frenchman, throwing another grenade. Afterwards, when Franklin went down the dugout steps, he saw the head of the man who had first run out. "I shall never forget the look on that face," he said.[7]

So it went, day after day.

During the battle Pershing visited corps and division commanders, pushing them to advance, although he admitted to Liggett that they had already been crowded to the limit and that many of them "were well used up." Pershing himself, of course, was being pressed in turn by Foch and Pétain.[8]

The doughboys did their damnedest. Against all expectations the 32d Division took Côte Dame Marie, the key position in the Kriemhilde Stellung, and Douglas MacArthur's brigade of the 42d Division captured the Côte de Chatillon, another strong point. But the cost was terrible. One unit went into battle with 1,500 men; it came out with only 300.[9]

By October 19 Pershing gave up attacking on a broad front, since the heavy losses were disproportionate to the ground gained. But the success of the 32d and 42d Divisions had at last broken through the ugly Kriemhilde Stellung. Three weeks after the initial attack of September 26 the First Army, by dint of sheer bulling ahead, had finally arrived where it had hoped to be that first day.[10]

During the battle Pershing sacked three division commanders: Beaumont B. Buck, John E. McMahon, and Clarence R. Edwards. When Pershing visited Buck's 3d Division headquarters at Montfaucon on October 15, he found the troops mixed, disorganized, and apparently disheartened. On October 18, he replaced Buck with Brig. Gen. Preston Brown. He tried to let Buck down gently, however, by suggesting that his return to America was part of a policy of rotating officers in order to give home units experienced commanders.[11]

Pershing's West Point classmate McMahon also was relieved on October 18. For the past month he had been declining physically, did not seem alert, and in the recent attack had lost control of his 5th Division. When Pershing asked about the condition of his men, McMahon replied that they were "very tired." As they had only been in line a short time, Pershing replied with emphasis that "it was probably the division commander who was tired." McMahon's replacement was Maj. Gen. Hanson E. Ely, of Cantigny fame, who was as aggressive as McMahon was lethargic.[12]

Undoubtedly the most controversial dismissal in the AEF was that of Maj. Gen. Clarence R. Edwards, a West Pointer, a charismatic personality, and a man beloved of the 26th Division, whose New Englanders called him "Daddy" and swore they would go through hell and high water for him. That might be, but Pershing would have preferred it if his men had done a better job of going through Germans. Ever since the division had come to France there had been disquieting reports about its poor discipline and efficiency, and its commander's habit of criticizing those in higher authority.

Back in April, when Edwards's division had relieved the 1st Division, GHQ staff officers reported that its "march discipline could hardly have been worse." That same month, after the German raid on Seicheprey, Edwards denied any losses and claimed absurd numbers of enemy killed. In July, despite orders to move only at night in preparation for the Aisne-Marne counteroffensive, Edwards moved openly and continuously during the day. He established headquarters other than where he was told to, neglected to bury his dead, and left four kilometers of his front completely unguarded.

Rarely, if ever, did he launch attacks at the prescribed hour. At no time during the Aisne-Marne counteroffensive could anyone learn, either from Edwards or from his brigade and regimental commanders, an accurate—or even an approximate—idea of where their commands were located. Despite the 26th Division having been in France longer than almost any other, Hunter Liggett felt that they had never received so much as basic training.[13]

Edwards knew that bad reports were continually being made about him and his division, but discounted them as motivated by prejudice. "Pershing is down on us," he told his staff, "because we are National Guard."[14]

Edwards was right; Pershing was down on him. But not because the 26th was a National Guard division. In a postwar evaluation he gave this pencil portrait of Edwards: "A thoroughly conceited man with little ability to base it on. In no sense a loyal subordinate, and hence does not inspire that quality in others. Ambitious, but not willing to obtain advancement by merit. A politician on principle; was so as a cadet. Opposes every order and undertakes to win popularity by assuming to know more than those above him and sides with his subordinates in any attitude they display of being imposed upon. Never should have been given a division. Spoiled one of the best ones we had."[15]

What triggered the removal of Edwards is not clear. Pershing may have been in a "busting" mood, after having sacked Cameron, Buck, and McMahon, and the reports against Edwards went back almost a year. Some of his soldiers had recently fraternized with Germans who told them that they felt the war was lost and they did not intend to fight any more. The implication was, if they didn't, maybe the Yankee Division shouldn't either. Liggett blew up when he heard about it on October 19, and may have mentioned it to Pershing the following day. In any event, on October 20 Edwards got sent the identical letter that Buck had, telling him that his services were urgently needed back in the States for training new divisions.[16]

The removal was unfortunately timed, because Edwards's division was in line and actually fighting. Although the letter was nicely phrased, it was a demotion and Edwards considered it such. He was angry, and so were his beloved Yankees. The bitter feelings engendered by this removal would last many years after the war.[17]

Pershing's dissatisfaction with some of his generals was matched, if not exceeded, by Allied dissatisfaction with him. It had taken over three weeks for the First Army to get where it had hoped to be at the end of the first day. On October 12 Lloyd George told Lord Reading, in briefing him for his return to America, that Pershing had been "most difficult" and that his army had been "quite ineffective." Referring to Haig's plan for a massive pincer movement on the western front, he added: "One side of the claw of the crab has not been working. The American Staff has not got the experience. . . . Wilson should know these facts, which are being withheld from him.[18]

Later that month Clemenceau told Colonel House that Pershing was handling his men badly and causing unnecessary casualties. He "is not making the progress he should and that which the other allies are making." The premier added that he himself had seen firsthand, near Thiaucourt on September 15 and Montfaucon on September 29, how chaotic was the American effort.[19]

So exasperated was Clemenceau with Pershing that he drafted a strongly worded letter to Foch, demanding that he do something about "the inaction of the American troops." The fault, as he saw it, was that Pershing refused to obey orders and Foch to insist on them, for example, his order of September 30 relieving Pershing of command of the Meuse-Argonne area and reassigning him to command the Franco-American forces on both sides of the Meuse. "It is our country's command that you command," Clemenceau told the generalissimo angrily.

Shown a draft of the letter, President Poincaré thought it far too strong (it called the American Army "paralysed") and advised against sending it. Clemenceau wrote a second toned-down version, which Poincaré still thought too strong, but the premier, angry and frustrated, decided to send it anyway. French soldiers were lying in heaps on the field, he asserted, because of Pershing's persistence in not acting and Foch's in not commanding.

Dated October 21, Clemenceau's letter spoke of "the crisis" existing in the American Army caused by its lack of organization. Due to Pershing's "invincible obstinacy," it had been "marking time" ever since September 26, while the British and French armies, at great cost, had moved forward. "Nobody can maintain that these fine [American] troops are unusable; they are merely unused."

Since Pershing had disobeyed orders, said Clemenceau, the time had come, or soon would, for "a radical solution" of the problem, namely, "to tell President

Wilson the truth and the whole truth concerning the situation of the American troops."[20]

Foch, whose relations with Clemenceau were never too good at best, reacted adversely to the letter. Now it was his turn to defend the Americans, using many of the very arguments that Pershing had used in defending them against Foch's own criticisms.

The First Army, Foch contended, had not been marking time, but attacking frequently, albeit unsuccessfully, over difficult, well-defended terrain, with losses estimated at 55,000. One could not go forward any faster simply by ordering it. "One might as well join battle with the elements. Don Quixote was animated by the same feelings when he tilted against windmills."

Many of the American difficulties, asserted Foch, were due not just to Pershing, but to the newness and inexperience of his staffs and commanders. Changing the First Army commander would not remedy this overnight, and an appeal to Wilson to relieve Pershing, even were it granted (which was by no means likely), would produce a great amount of American ill will.

Foch pointed out that, of thirty American divisions fit for combat, ten were with Allied armies and twenty were under Pershing's direct control. Whenever circumstances permitted, he planned to increase the ten and decrease the twenty. "It is by manipulation of this sort that I expect to diminish the weakness of the [American] High Command, rather than by orders." In other words, Pershing would retain command of the American First Army, but would have fewer divisions to mess up with.[21]

Meanwhile, the First Army did in fact have a new commander. With over 1,000,000 men under his command (135,000 of them French) and a front 83 miles long, Pershing's army was becoming too large and unwieldy. Accordingly, on October 12 he split his forces into two field armies, creating the American Second Army and assigning it an area to the east—roughly at the base of the old St. Mihiel salient. Maj. Gen. Robert L. Bullard took over as commander, with Col. Stuart Heintzelman as Chief of Staff.

The rest of the front—roughly the Meuse-Argonne battlefield—remained under the First Army, now commanded by Maj. Gen. Hunter Liggett, Pershing's most experienced corps commander, who took over on October 16. Hugh Drum stayed on as First Army Chief of Staff, and headquarters remained at Souilly. Pershing now became an Army Group commander with headquarters at Ligny-en-Barrois.[22]

The First Army which Pershing turned over to Liggett was in many ways a badly mauled army. Col. Thomas De W. Milling, who later served as Chief of its Air Service, called it "a disorganized and wrecked army." Although there were little or no shortages of food and ammunition, horse transportation was so desperately short that First Army artillery was practically immobile. Stragglers were all over the map; Liggett estimated that there were 100,000 of them. In the 3d and 5th Divisions, mishandled by Buck and McMahon, only a small proportion of the men could be found, estimated respectively at 4,000 and 5,000. Others wandered around the rear or hid in dugouts. Military Police had to search out key areas like aid stations, kitchens, and dugouts, round up the recalcitrants and send them forward, sometimes with the words "Stragglers from the Front Line" scrawled in placards on their backs. Preston Brown, the tough new commander of the 3d Division, authorized throwing bombs into dugouts if men refused to come out.

Liggett believed that the First Army needed "tightening up." With artillery virtually immobilized, further attacks with tired and/or depleted divisions stood little chance of success and would only raise casualties. The situation called for a breathing spell to give the Army time to rest, recoup, and refit. It also needed time to prepare for a big push which, hopefully, might achieve a breakthrough.[23]

For approximately the next two weeks, therefore, Liggett gave the First Army time to recover, ordering no new attacks except limited ones designed to gain ground advantageous as a jump-off for the coming offensive. He relieved tired divisions like the 4th, which had been in line since the initial September 26 offensive, and the 32d, which, because of casualties and straggling, was down to less than 2,000 armed effectives. He strengthened the staff by bringing in Col. Leon B. Kromer as G-1 and George C. Marshall, Jr., as G-3. He also began daily meetings with the Chiefs of Artillery, Air Service, and Engineers.[24]

In addition, he also manfully resisted any efforts by Pershing these two weeks to get him to attack before he was ready. Liggett's aide, Pierpont Stackpole, reported that initially Pershing kept "hovering around" First Army headquarters at Souilly, changing his mind many times "and worrying everybody with endless talk." Finally Liggett told him that since the First Army was too chewed up to undertake a major operation in the near future, he should "go away and forget it."[25]

Pershing was undoubtedly discouraged that the First Army had not done better under his immediate direction. Save for a short campaign against the St. Mihiel salient, which the Germans were planning to evacuate anyway, the record had not been particularly successful, especially when compared with striking Allied gains on other parts of the western front.

On the other hand, Pershing's troubles were not unique. Gouraud's French Fourth Army on the left had not broken through either, and in Flanders an Anglo-French-Belgian army group under General Degoutte had bogged down in mud, with transportation problems similar to those of the Americans.[26]

Faced with the fact that no spectacular breakthrough had occurred and that other Allied armies, particularly the British, had made greater headway elsewhere, Pershing and First Army partisans later emphasized the crucial nature of the front they were attacking (covering the Thionville-Lille Railroad) and argued that by attracting German divisions there they indirectly contributed to Allied successes elsewhere. During the first three weeks of the Meuse-Argonne offensive they estimated that the number of German divisions opposing the First Army had grown from five to thirty-three, two-thirds of them first- or second-class divisions.[27]

Just how many German divisions were actually attracted is impossible to state accurately, because figures differ. In the pell-mell rush to get up reinforcements, especially during the final days of the campaign, the Germans were forced to lay hands on whatever units were available, even fragmented ones, and send them into line. One should also note that by late October interdicting the key German railroad was less important than it had been. By October 31 British and French armies to the northwest had gone beyond it, in some cases to a depth of fifteen miles. This was a full week before the Americans reached it at Sedan.[28]

As Foch had planned, the incessant Allied attacks up and down the western front kept the Germans off balance, used up their reserves, and slowly wore them down. As he had predicted, eventually they became disorganized and demoralized, frantically sending up to the front exhausted units to plug holes in the line. Their defense became stopgap and disjointed, as decimated divisions were thrown back in without time to recoup or reorganize. What the German army needed badly was time to rest and recover; Foch was giving it none.[29]

On September 29, the fourth day of Foch's four-part offensive which exploded up and down the western front, the German High Command called for an immediate end of the war. "There is now no longer any possible hope of forcing peace on the enemy," Hindenburg told the German chancellor. "The situation grows more desperate every day. . . ."[30]

By October 14, the day the 32d Division took Côte Dame Marie, Ludendorff said that "our best men lay on the bloody battle-field."[31]

On October 16, the day that MacArthur's brigade captured Côte de Chatillon, a German company commander wrote: "Clouded prospects wherever one looks. Really has everything been in vain? Such a piteous finish. . . ."[32]

Five days later Maj. Gen. Baron von Quadt, commander of the German 76th Reserve Division, which had been in line on September 26 and was now being assaulted by the Americans at Grandpré, told his weary men they could expect no relief from the front. Even if relieved, he predicted, "the division would immediately be sent into line at another point, and most likely a worse one."[33]

On October 24 the *Arbeiter Zeitung* pointed out that every day 10,000 fresh, well-fed, and well-equipped Americans crossed the sea, 300,000 of them a month. "Do the people wish to continue war under such circumstances," it asked, "to sacrifice the lives of many hundred thousand men thereby destroying the remainder of the Nation's manhood and imperiling their future?"[34]

By the end of the month German soldiers were mutinying in some divisions and refusing to go into the line. Turkey surrendered on October 30; Austria-Hungary four days later. Bulgaria had been out of the war for over a month.[35]

With peace talk in the air, Foch called a conference of the supreme commanders at Senlis on October 25. Its purpose, he said, was not to decide whether an armistice should be granted or not, but to determine, if one was, what the precise terms should be.[36]

Speaking first, Haig said that the Germans were hurt, but not beaten. When hit, they struck back hard, inflicting heavy casualties, and they generally retired in good order and with great skill. As they retreated, their lines and front would shorten, permitting them to make a very strong stand. The Allies, on the other hand, "were pretty well exhausted." The British and French armies were short about 250,000 men, with no replacements. The American Army "was not yet organized, not yet formed, and had suffered a great deal on account of its ignorance of modern warfare. . . ." It "cannot be counted upon for much." Hence armistice terms should be relatively lenient, such that the Germans would easily accept.[37]

Foch took issue with Haig's statement that the German Army was not beaten. Since July 15 it had been steadily pushed back, losing 250,000 prisoners and 4,000 guns, and it was retreating now on a front of 400 kilometers. It was "an army that has been beaten every day for three months, . . . an army that is, physically and morally, thoroughly beaten."[38]

Pétain felt that the Germans both expected and deserved severe terms, such that if the armistice ceased the Allies would resume hostilities in a most favorable position.[39]

Pershing, who asked to speak last, agreed with Foch and Pétain. He thought that the military situation was "very favorable" and that "there should be no tendency towards leniency." Among other armistice terms, he wanted the surrender of all U-boats and their bases.

When Pershing mentioned submarines, Haig interrupted: "That is none of our affair. It is a matter for the Admiralty to decide." Pershing responded that the American Army's supply line was three thousand miles long, that submarines menaced it, and therefore their surrender was of vital importance. Foch thought Pershing's point well taken.[40]

Because Foch had called the meeting only to discuss armistice terms and not alternatives to an armistice, Pershing did not bring up a matter he felt very strongly about—that there should be no armistice terms offered at all, but unconditional surrender demanded instead. Like Foch, he believed that the Germans were thoroughly beaten. American intelligence reported that in the last four months twenty-nine German divisions had been disbanded and fifty had reduced the number of companies in a battalion. Replacements were being sent to the front with little or no training; wounded were being rushed from the hospitals direct to the firing line with no time for convalescence. Old men and young boys were staffing artillery units. Infantry was being kept in line excessively long. This being so, it was foolish to grant an armistice rather than demand unconditional surrender. "It is the experience of history," Pershing believed, "that victorious armies are prone to over-estimate the enemy's strength and too eagerly seek an opportunity for peace."

Furthermore, an armistice had certain drawbacks. It would give the Germans time to regroup, reorganize, reconstitute. It would break Allied momentum which had been steadily building since the July 18 counteroffensive and which, once broken, would be difficult to regain again should the enemy decide to resume fighting. Finally, it would deprive the Allies of "the full measure of victory."[41]

Although he felt strongly on the matter, Pershing said nothing about unconditional surrender in reporting the October 25 meeting to the War Department. He simply summarized the proposed armistice terms. On October 27, Secretary Baker cabled back, giving the President's reaction to each of the proposed terms. But he also included this very significant sentence: "The President directs me to say that he is relying upon your counsel and advice in this matter, and . . . he will be glad to have you feel entirely free to bring to his attention any consideration he may have overlooked which in your judgment ought to be weighed before settling finally his views."[42]

Baker and the President were thinking about modifications in the armistice terms. But Pershing took the message to mean he was authorized to suggest modifying the basic approach, that is, to propose surrender rather than an armistice.

Pershing did not receive Baker's cable until October 29, just one day before the SWC was to meet to discuss armistice terms. Time was short and, as bad luck would have it, Pershing was confined to bed with a bad case of the grippe and unable to talk over his ideas about surrender with Colonel House, who was in Europe and with whom he had been told to confer.[43]

Feeling that the matter was both important and urgent, Pershing summarized his arguments against an armistice and for unconditional surrender and on October 30 sent them to the SWC, simultaneously sending a copy to the War Department. He also gave a copy to Colonel House on his way into the SWC meeting.

During the meeting House read Pershing's document carefully and then handed it to the Allied prime ministers for their comments.

"Political, not military," snorted Lloyd George. "Someone put him up to it."

"Theatrical," snapped Clemenceau, "and not in accordance with what he has said to Marshal Foch."[44]

House was dismayed. The prime ministers were right. It was a political question, not a military one. While Pershing was in his rights to suggest specific armistice terms when requested to do so, he was obviously out of his element when suggesting that the war should be terminated on an entirely different basis, especially when unasked. President Wilson had determined on an armistice, as had the Allied leaders. Pershing was meddling where he didn't belong; he was that worst of all things: a general mixing in politics.

"I cannot understand General Pershing's extraordinary communication . . . ," House wrote in his diary. "Everyone believes it is a political document and a clear announcement of his intention to become a candidate for the Presidency in 1920."[45]

That night House dropped Pershing a note, asking whether his views were shared by any other Allied general. Pershing replied orally through his aide, Col. Carl Boyd, that he didn't know, since the question of surrender had never come up. From the way House grilled Boyd as to just what the general had in mind in submitting such a document, Pershing gathered that he was in trouble. So he hastened to send Boyd back with a note that "the reasons are of course purely military," that he had had no opportunity to present his views on unconditional surrender and that he felt it his "duty" to do so.[46]

House was still dissatisfied. "I wonder whether he actually knows that he is dealing with a political rather than a military question? It is something for the President and Prime Ministers to determine whether to treat with Germany for an armistice."[47]

Seeking support for his surrender proposal, Pershing sent a copy of his October 30 SWC document to Foch via his liaison officer, Colonel Mott. "Tell General Pershing not to give himself any uneasiness," replied the generalissimo. "What I am exacting of the Germans will be the same thing as what he suggests."[48]

On October 31 House asked Foch whether he thought the war should continue or an armistice be offered. Foch answered: "I am not waging war for the sake of waging war. If I obtain through the Armistice the conditions that we wish to impose upon Germany, I am satisfied. Once this object is attained, nobody has the right to shed one drop more of blood."[49]

Bliss too favored an armistice, on the assumption, shared by Foch, that the Germans would be powerless to resume the war afterwards. Otherwise, he said, it would be the equivalent of saying, "No, we haven't killed enough of you, there are some more towns we want to burn."[50]

While motoring together on November 2, House and Pershing had a chance for a good "heart-to-heart" talk. Pershing apologized for not having consulted House before sending his document to the SWC. "He said he was wrong and was sorry . . . ," reported the Colonel. "We . . . agreed that we would not allow mischief makers to cause trouble between us."[51]

Meanwhile, Pershing's copy of his October 30 document, together with House's report of its unfavorable reception, had reached Washington, producing consternation. Both March and Baker overreacted. The Chief of Staff suggested that Pershing had political aspirations and that his statement was not only at variance with the President's instructions, but also contradicted his report of the October 25 meeting with the commanders in which "he advised [armistice terms] and injected no political advice." Said Baker to the President: "He is obviously on record one way with you and another way with the Supreme War Council! It is really tragic."[52]

That Pershing had political aspirations in 1918 is questionable. It is true that his First Army had not done exceptionally well and that, had the war ended on October 30, its laurels would have been somewhat dimmed, but to suggest that Pershing wished the war to continue in order to have time to redeem his reputation, gain greater glory, and thus foster a future political career, is to attribute motives unworthy of the man.[53]

Nor is it true, as March asserted, that Pershing's October 25 and October 30 statements contradicted each other. The context of the earlier document was, as Foch said in opening the meeting, what should armistice terms be *if there is an armistice*? The context of the latter was, *should there be an armistice*?

March was right, however, in contending that Pershing had not followed instructions. He had been told in the October 27 cable that if he had any other ideas he was to communicate them to the *President*, and he was also urged to confer with Colonel House who was on the spot. Pershing did neither of these things. He sent his ideas directly to the SWC and let the President know about it afterwards, and he did the same with House, merely handing him a copy of his document on his way into the meeting. On both points he was clearly out of order.[54]

Called upon by Baker to explain his letter to the SWC, Pershing cited the Secretary's October 27 cable authorizing him to "feel entirely free" to bring up other considerations. Baker was unsatisfied. "A bad matter is made much worse by this . . . ," he said, and drew up a letter of reprimand, stressing that political matters were outside military jurisdiction. On the President's advice, however, he decided not to send it. The war, after all, was almost over.[55]

TWENTY-SIX

Meuse-Argonne: November 1, 1918

B Y THE END OF October, Liggett was ready to resume the First Army attack. He coordinated plans with Gouraud, whose French Fourth Army had advanced somewhat more successfully than the Americans since September 26. Liggett would jump off on November 1 and Gouraud the following day.

Extremely anxious that the attack succeed, Pershing told McAndrew and Conner to drop all other duties and devote full time to examining transportation, coordination, and communication questions, which had previously caused trouble. "Leave nothing undone that might cause us delay or failure," he insisted. He also wrote each corps commander, stating that he would personally hold him responsible for the success or failure of his troops.[1]

Everyone worked hard. Behind the lines, service troops rebuilt roads and moved up stockpiles of ammunition, equipment, and supplies. For the first time since the St. Mihiel operation on September 12, the First Army had time to prepare an offensive with some deliberation. As an added fillip, the weather, which had been miserable, turned reasonably pleasant.

The terrain was similar to that of the initial September 26 jump-off: river on the east (Meuse), woods on the west (Bois de Bourgogne), with heights in the center (Barricourt Ridge). The plan of battle called for a power drive straight ahead by Summerall's center corps to capture the Barricourt Ridge, then a thrust to the west to flank the Bois de Bourgogne and join up with the French Fourth Army at Boult-aux-Bois.

Liggett lined up seven divisions for the attack. On the right, touching the Meuse, was III Corps (Hines), with the 5th Division (Ely) and 90th (Allen). In the center, entrusted with delivering the main blow, was V Corps (Summerall), with the 89th (Wright) and 2d (Lejeune). On the left, touching the Bois de Bourgogne, was I Corps (Dickman), with the 80th (Cronkhite), 77th (Alexander), and 78th (James H. McRae). All four divisions in Hines's and Summerall's corps (5th, 90th, 89th, and 2d) were veterans of the St. Mihiel operation. In Dickman's corps two out of three divisions had been in the initial September 26 attack (80th and 77th),

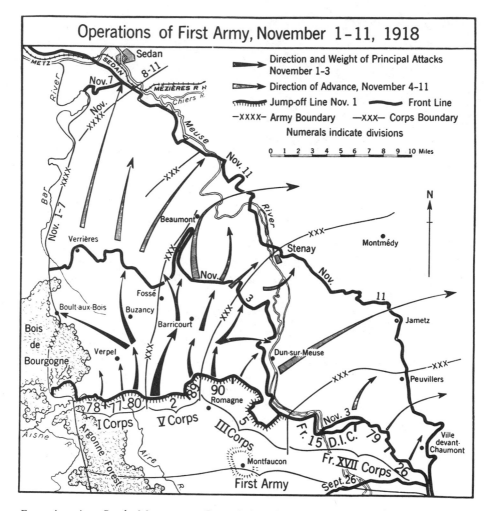

From American Battle Monuments Commission, *American Armies and Battlefields in Europe*, Washington, D.C., 1938.

while the third division (78th) had been in combat since October 16. Hines had in corps reserve the 3d and 32d Divisions; Summerall the 1st and 42d; Dickman the 82d. Every single division, both in line and in reserve, was a veteran division. Liggett was thus going into battle with a very strong bench.[2]

Opposing them were seven German divisions, four of which had been in line for quite a while, while three had recently reentered after a short rest. "All were weak," said Gallwitz.[3]

Although five hundred tanks were wanted for the attack, only eighteen were available and were assigned to the 2d Division in Summerall's corps. In his memoirs Pershing later bemoaned the fact that America, supposedly an industrial wizard, could, after eighteen months of war, furnish only eighteen of these "mechanical contrivances" so useful in saving infantry lives.[4]

Infantry-artillery cooperation had been a problem throughout the campaign, and still was, although less so. Priority shipments of infantry and machine gunners in the spring and summer had left the AEF short of artillery personnel, forcing the First Army to borrow French gunners and/or interchange American artillery brigades among various divisions. The result was that artillery and infantry commanders lacked experience in working together. Only three of the seven assault divisions had their own artillery.

By late October everything was ready. Day after day Summerall went among his battalion commanders, giving them pep talks like a football coach before the big game. "There is no excuse for failure," he said. "No man is ever so tired that he cannot take one step forward." "The best way to take machine guns is to go and take 'em! Press forward."[5]

During the week before the attack, three batteries of huge 14-inch naval guns mounted on railroad cars searched out enemy railway communications and crashed 1,400-pound shells into them from twenty-five miles away. Two days before the attack, the artillery drenched the eastern edge of the Bois de Bourgogne with mustard gas, turning it into a choking, agonizing hell and knocking out nine of twelve German batteries hidden there.[6]

The final, violent artillery preparation opened at 3:30 A.M. on November 1. The night, which would have been dark because of clouds and no moon, lit up like daylight. Men could stand anywhere and read the small print of a newspaper by the incessant flash-flash-flash of American guns. As barrels heated up and glowed like coals, artillerymen splashed buckets of water against them, the liquid turning instantly to steam.[7]

Dense and accurate, and heavily supplemented by a tremendous barrage from massed machine guns, American fire crashed down on enemy crossroads, strongholds, dumps, batteries, and sensitive points. Under it the greatest American Army ever sent to battle moved out to the assault at 5:30 A.M.

Just before the attack Lejeune pulled his 2d Division troops back five hundred yards from their own trenches and started the rolling barrage there, wiping out German machine gunners hidden in no-man's-land. Wright concentrated his 89th Division troops, not at the obvious jump-off line along the edge of a woods, but in an open field in front of it, where they escaped German counterbattery fire against the woods. The Americans had been in France a good many months now and had learned a few tricks of their own.[8]

For once, things went right. The 2d and 89th Divisions followed closely their massive barrage, heartened by the low-flying American planes which strafed the enemy, while high-flying bombers blasted his rear installations. By nightfall the 2d Division had gone five miles and reached its objectives on the heights of Barricourt. The 89th had gone almost as far. "For the first time," exulted Pershing, "the enemy's lines were completely broken through."[9]

On the right, Hines's III Corps also reached all its supplementary objectives. On the left, except for part of the 80th Division, Dickman's I Corps advanced little.

It didn't matter. Summerall's V Corps had thrust so far up the middle as to imperil the Germans on its left. They abandoned Bois des Loges and Champigneulles, which they had bitterly contested on November 1, and evacuated north, going so far and so fast that Dickman, using trucks, could not catch up with them. Their withdrawal exposed the flank of the corps opposing the French Fourth Army, which had been stalled on November 1, causing that corps also to withdraw.[10]

On November 2 the advance continued. "The roads and fields," said Pvt. Rush Young, "were strewn with dead Germans, horses, masses of Artillery, transports, ammunition limbers, helmets, guns, and bayonets." The Germans, demoralized, were withdrawing, while the Americans, exhilarated by a breakthrough after weeks of attrition warfare, were bounding forward with dash and imagination.[11]

At dusk on November 3, the 9th Infantry Regiment of the 2d Division reached the southern edge of the Bois de Belval. The men were tired, but their officers believed lives would be saved if they could get through the woods before the Germans, recently shelled out of it, had time to come back. So, bone weary, the 9th Regiment marched four miles right through thinly held enemy lines (they could hear Germans in the woods on both sides of the road), digging in at the far side at 10:45 P.M. In the process they captured some small German units, almost seized a division commander, and lost not one man.[12]

No doubt about it, things were going well. Although there was the inevitable congestion, and although some troops had to eat "goldfish" (as they called the canned salmon) until the rolling kitchens caught up, the First Army had considerably improved its communications and logistics since September 26. In contrast to former attacks, in which a fairly good first-day advance was followed by increasingly smaller ones, this attack was different. The third day's gains *exceeded* those of the first. The Army not only had an initial punch; it had reached the point where it could keep going.[13]

At First Army headquarters at Souilly, newspaperman Thomas M. Johnson watched happy staff officers who "almost capered before the wall map as the thumb-tacks and red string went forward to places that had seemed once as far away as Berlin."[14]

At Pétain's headquarters, Gen. Edmond Buat, the chief of staff, complimented Colonel Clark on the American effort. "That is work of the first order; it is superfine...." Buat, who knew the ground over which the First Army had been operating and how difficult it was to advance with inexperienced soldiers against a skilled enemy, had sympathized with American difficulties during October. Now he said: "I tell you there are no other troops in the world who could have done half what you did under all the circumstances."[15]

To Gallwitz the situation was hopeless. "All of the front line commanders report ... that the [German] troops are fighting courageously but just cannot do anything." The only recourse was to withdraw behind the Meuse immediately, he thought.[16]

But even that security was denied him. On November 3, 4, and 5, Ely's 5th Division, in a maneuver that Pershing termed "brilliant," forced its way across the Meuse on a wide front. The operation was difficult and showed the skill and tenacity of the attacking troops, for they had to cross an open plain, an 82-foot river, another open plain, and a 60-foot canal—all under enemy fire.[17]

Gallwitz was in despair on November 6 as he stood with field glasses watching Ely's men coming through the woods between Murvaux and Fontaines. On his desk were orders just received from Supreme Headquarters to prevent further crossings "at all costs" and, if possible, to drive the Americans back across the Meuse. They were already two miles east of it.[18]

Pershing was delighted with the progress. James E. Mangum, a field clerk, remembered typing out an order directing the First Army to capture certain points by a certain time. The phone rang; it was Col. George C. Marshall, Jr., reporting that troops had already passed the farthest point called for in the order Mangum was typing. The First Army was running off the map![19]

Foch was happy over American success, but on November 5 asked Pershing for six American divisions to be incorporated into Gen. Charles Mangin's French Tenth Army for a surprise attack in Lorraine on November 14. (He may have been thinking of his scheme of "increasing the 10 and diminishing the 20," which he explained to Clemenceau when the latter complained about U.S. inaction on October 21.) Pershing consented to furnish the six divisions, but insisted that they constitute a separate American Army. He had long suspected what a later study by Fox Conner confirmed: that where U.S. divisions served in French commands, American deaths were greater. Said Conner: "Under American Command identical divisions advanced farther against greater resistance in less time, and suffered less casualties."[20]

While Pershing was pleased with First Army progress, two problems were about to cause considerable trouble. The first concerned the so-called "Race to Sedan."

Sedan, of course, was a prime target of the Franco-American offensive, which aimed at the Sedan-Mézières Railway. It was also a city which had strong emotional associations for the French, for it was here, during the Franco-Prussian War, that the Germans had defeated a French army and captured the French emperor, Louis Napoleon III, as a result of which they deprived the Motherland of Alsace and Lorraine. The French burned to capture Sedan and erase the humiliation of the earlier defeat. For this reason the boundaries between the French Fourth Army and the American First Army, which intersected near Sedan, had been changed to place the city clearly within the French zone.[21]

Incredibly, considering French feeling about Sedan, Pershing wanted the First Army to capture the town and present it to the French in a sort of hands-across-the-sea gesture. It would be as if General Rochambeau had shouldered General Washington aside at Yorktown in 1781 and said, "Here, let me accept Cornwallis's surrender!"[22]

On November 3 Pershing met with Gen. Paul Maistre, commander of the French Group of Armies of the Center, under whom Gouraud's French Fourth Army was operating. As luck would have it, the First Army after the November 1 breakthrough was outdistancing the French Fourth Army on its left and might reach Sedan first, in which case, said Pershing, the Americans ought to take it. Maistre gave his consent.[23]

On November 5 Fox Conner went to First Army headquarters at Souilly and, in conjunction with Hugh Drum, the chief of staff, dictated the following order to Dickman and Summerall: "General Pershing desires that the honor of entering Sedan should fall to the First American Army. He has every confidence that the troops of the First Corps [Dickman], assisted on their right by the Fifth Corps [Summerall], will enable him to realize this desire.... Boundaries will not be considered binding.[24]

That last sentence was to occasion all sorts of trouble, although it should not have. Pershing obviously was thinking of the boundaries between the American First Army and the French Fourth. He was not thinking of those between I and V Corps, that is, he did not intend that Summerall should cut across Dickman's front and attempt to take Sedan on his own. Summerall was only to assist, as the order stated, by swinging his corps to the left, as Dickman also did, in order to keep contact in the American lines. It was a rather elementary tactic and should not have caused any difficulty, had not vanity and selfish glory-seeking entered in.[25]

Summerall, however, decided to convert his secondary mission into a primary one. On November 6 he ordered the 1st Division, which he once had commanded and which was on the leftmost flank of his corps, to immediately capture Sedan. He did this despite the fact that Dickman, with whom relations were not good, had not asked him for any such help and would certainly have opposed it, since it meant marching the 1st Division across the front and rear of the two divisions in Dickman's corps, the 77th and 42d, and this in the dead of night and without telling Dickman about it.[26]

What followed can only be called folly, an action unworthy of any army. The 1st Division, under Brig. Gen. Frank Parker, injected itself into the area of another corps, disrupting communications, snarling traffic, and generally creating chaos. Confused doughboys shot at each other in the dark. 1st Division troops, encountering Douglas MacArthur, a brigade commander in Menoher's 42d Division, and eyeing his sloppy garrison cap and non-regulation muffler, concluded he was a German spy masquerading as an American officer. They captured him at gunpoint.[27]

Menoher called the situation "intolerable." Alexander of the 77th Division, who was easily confused anyway, reported detachments of the 1st Division "going in every direction."[28]

The French, who had overcome their difficulties and come storming up, panting to take Sedan, were mad as hell. So also was Liggett, who when he heard about what had happened, ordered all 1st Division troops out of Dickman's area immediately and descended upon Summerall, demanding an explanation. Summerall quoted the November 5 memorandum ("Boundaries will not be considered binding") and said he was simply following orders, an explanation which Liggett found unsatisfactory, as did Dickman, who wanted both Summerall and Parker court-martialed.[29]

Hugh Drum, First Army Chief of Staff.
National Archives

George S. Patton, Jr., in command of the
Tank Corps School near Langres.
U.S. Army Military History Institute

Hunter Liggett. *National Archives*

Douglas MacArthur as "German spy."
MacArthur Memorial, Norfolk, Virginia

Liggett, however, decided to let the matter drop. The Germans, in the last stages of collapse, had been unable to take advantage of the American debacle and no great harm had resulted, except incredible confusion. In addition, the war ended almost immediately and, in the euphoria of victory, he hesitated to disgrace Summerall, who had made such a fine record otherwise.[30]

Pershing too made light of the incident, which illustrates how far he would go in tolerating deficiencies in those he admired. The 1st Division was his favorite; it had been commanded successfully at Soissons and St. Mihiel by the magnificent, aggressive Summerall.

If the shoe had been on the other foot, that is, if a National Guard division had marched across the front of a Regular Army one and not vice versa, Pershing would have blown up, all his prejudices confirmed about the "goddamn militiamen" and their lack of professionalism. But the blunder was committed by a Regular Army division which happened to be Pershing's favorite, under the orders of a fellow West Pointer whom Pershing considered his best commander—and that made the difference. According to Pershing, the 1st Division march was not, as Liggett called it, "an atrocity," but a "misconception of orders." Within two weeks of the event he had so far forgiven and forgotten it as to take the extraordinary step of praising the 1st Division in AEF general orders, Parker still in command. No other division in the entire war was so praised.[31]

If the Sedan farce was a minor, albeit controversial, crisis, the supply problem was a major one. Ever since spring, when priority shipments of infantry and machine gunners had disrupted a proper proportion of combat to supply personnel, the SOS had been limping along, robbing Peter to pay Paul, being in turn robbed by the First Army to supply its emergency needs during the summer and fall campaigns. One can only live this way so long, and there were increasing signs that the SOS, even under Harbord's outstanding leadership, was approaching a crisis.

Overseas shipments had fallen from fifty-three pounds per man per day in February to twenty-two pounds in October. Horses were in such short supply that in one division men actually took their places, hitching themselves to wagons and pulling them to the front. Medical personnel were so overworked that Dr. Merritte Ireland, AEF Chief Surgeon, warned that they were at "the breaking point." By November 11, 1918, the Transportation Corps had only 61 percent of its necessary personnel, 73 percent of its locomotives and only 32 percent of its cars.

Harbord said later that if the armistice had not come when it did, the AEF would have had to cease fighting until the supply problem could be solved. Only the armistice saved the AEF from a logistical disaster.[32]

On November 8 Marshal Foch, representing the Allied armies, and Sir Rosslyn Wemyss, representing the Allied navies, met German representatives in a railway car in the Compiègne Forest to negotiate a cease-fire. Because of congestion and disorganization behind enemy lines, the Germans were twelve hours late. Foch was harsh and ungracious, forcing them explicitly to ask for an armistice and making it clear that they were the ones requesting it, not he.[33]

The armistice terms were strong, as Foch, Pétain, and Pershing thought they should be. Among other things, they called for German retirement to certain places by certain dates, provided for Allied occupation of bridgeheads across the Rhine River, and demanded surrender of weapons and other means of war, such as locomotives and cars. The enemy considered the terms so harsh as to wonder whether Foch deliberately made them so, hoping that they would reject them and he could continue the war.[34]

The Germans protested that their army was in such an "unimaginable" state that they would have difficulty meeting any timetable for evacuation. They also objected to being forced to surrender thirty thousand machine guns, since with Bolshevism infecting the homeland, they might need them to fire on their own people. When Foch countered that they could get machine guns for riot control from their reserve divisions, the Germans revealed that they had no reserve divisions. Every division they had was in line![35]

Foch refused to grant a provisional armistice while the enemy considered the terms, or to allow more than seventy-two hours for a final decision on them, that is, until November 11. A courier left for Germany with a copy of the terms and the war went on.[36]

The next day, November 9, Bullard's Second Army, which had held a defensive sector in Lorraine since its formation on October 12, finally jumped off, making limited gains. Liggett's First Army made similar attacks. The Germans retreated, leaving behind small rearguard units with light machine guns, who made a stand at each successive ridge, forcing the Americans to deploy, at which the gunners retreated to the next ridge. All the while their engineers were blowing up bridges and culverts, and also laying mines, some set to explode as late as January, during Allied occupation.[37]

Moving up toward the front as an observer, Lloyd Griscom encountered a dead German soldier lying beside the road, very young, blond, and handsome. An American truck lurched through a puddle, spattering his white face with mud. Other trucks followed, each doing the same, until finally his face was entirely obscured. Watching what was happening, Griscom felt the hatred he bore the man as a German drain from him. "Here was a boy," he thought, "as nice as any American or English boy, dragged into this war without knowing what it was all about."[38]

Everyone knew of the armistice rumors, but until the Germans signed, nothing was definite, and they could well refuse. The deadline was 11:00 A.M. on November 11. The night before, Brig. Gen. John H. Sherburne, commanding the 92d Division's field artillery brigade, heard that the armistice had been agreed upon and that fighting was to stop the next day. Since an attack was scheduled for the morning, he phoned division, corps, and army headquarters, asking if it should be carried out. In each case the answer was yes; the attack order had not been countermanded.

On November 11 the men went over the top, took casualties, and a few hours later the war was over. "I cannot express the horror we all felt," said Sherburne, thinking of the waste of human life. The French on his right refrained from attacking on the eleventh, and even the tenth, saying they would do nothing until armistice negotiations were settled one way or the other.[39]

German acceptance of the armistice terms was received the night of November 10; Foch and the German delegates stayed up until dawn finalizing and then signing them at 5:10 A.M on November 11. The generalissimo immediately sent a message by wire and phone to the Allied commanders: "Hostilities will cease on the entire front *November 11th at 11:00* A.M. French time." In Foch's presence, Matthias Erzberger, head of the German delegation, read a bitter statement, protesting the harshness of the terms which, he claimed, threatened the German people with famine and anarchy. "A nation of seventy millions suffers but does not die," he said defiantly. On this sour note, so ominous for the future, the war ended.[40]

Word of the signing reached First and Second Army headquarters at 6:30 A.M., but they ordered no halt in operations. Fighting went on, in some instances right up until 11:00 that morning. The men who died or were maimed in those last few hours suffered needlessly and their mishandling provoked a Congressional investigation after the war.[41]

At Chaumont Pershing stood in front of the large wall map and watched the hands of the clock approach 11:00. He was glad the war was over (he would dance a jig that night), but he was also fiercely competitive and he still had his eyes on the Briey-Longwy region. "I suppose our campaigns are ended," he remarked, "but what an enormous difference a few days more would have made!"[42]

Pershing felt that the armistice was a mistake. "We shouldn't have done it," he commented shortly afterwards. "If they had given us another ten days we would have rounded up the entire German army, captured it, humiliated it. . . . The German troops today are marching back into Germany announcing that they have never been defeated. . . . What I dread is that Germany doesn't know that she was licked. Had they given us another week, we'd have *taught* them."[43]

Pershing was right about the German attitude. On November 11 General von Einem, commander of the German Third Army, told his troops, "Firing has ceased. *Undefeated* . . . you are terminating the war in enemy country." A decade later Adolf Hitler was propagating the same error.[44]

Reactions to the armistice varied. In the village of Tremont women gathered in their doorways as the village crier read an announcement of the armistice. "There were no loud cheers and there seemed to be more of sadness than of gladness in their voices," observed John McAuley Palmer. When he asked a woman if she was not glad the war was over, she replied, "Yes, yes, monsieur, but my three brothers will not return."[45]

Some doughboys were too tired, dirty, and miserable to do much; they took the news in stunned silence. Some Germans burst into joyful singing. Observing the two groups, one might wonder who won the war.[46]

In time, however, every American celebrated, few more exuberantly than the high-strung airmen of Eddie Rickenbacker's 94th Squadron. "Pandemonium broke loose," he reported. Shouting like mad, falling over one another, the airmen grabbed anything that could shoot—pistols, machine guns, flares, rockets, Very lights, star shells—and dashed outside to light up the night in one delirious, semihysterical orgy of noise, laughter, and light. Setting gasoline drums afire, they danced around them holding hands. *"I've lived through the war!"* shouted one man as he pirouetted around in a mudhole. Another grabbed Rickenbacker by the arm and shouted into his ear, almost in disbelief, *"We won't be shot at any more!"*[47]

Paris, quite literally, went mad with joy. As if under orders, people took to the streets *en masse*: Frenchmen, Belgians, Americans, British, old men and young, women with sleeping babies in their arms, flag-waving children, soldiers in uniform who were continually pounced upon, embraced, and kissed. (To remain unkissed, said one soldier, you had to find a cellar and hide.) At first the crowd washed back and forth, crescendoing the magnificent "Marseillaise." Then someone cried, "To Strasbourg! To Strasbourg!" and, as if with one will, the people headed for the Place de la Concorde where they surrounded the statue of Strasbourg, tore away the black crepe which had enveloped it since 1871 when the Germans took the city after the Franco-Prussian War, and covered the statue with flowers and wreaths. Then, said Dorothy Canfield Fisher, "we shouted as we had not done before, the great primitive, inarticulate cry of rejoicing that bursts from the heart too full."[48]

Coming into the Place de la Concorde, Pershing was almost immediately recognized. People stopped his car, climbed on the running boards, hood, and roof, and began to squeeze inside. Finally some passing American soldiers rescued him, clearing a path, a yard or two at a time, until they finally got the automobile across the Place. It took two hours.[49]

Pershing was not the demonstrative type, but he was profoundly moved in his own quiet way. A tremendous burden had been lifted from his shoulders. Later he spent a quiet hour with Joe and Corinna Smith, during which he said with great emotion: "A year ago it was hope and faith, today it is realization!" Several times he repeated proudly, "The men were willing to pay the price."[50]

A few days later Pershing encountered Clemenceau. "We fell into each other's arms," related the American, "choked up and had to wipe our eyes. We had no differences to discuss that day."[51]

Commented Harbord: "The armistice thus ended two wars for us—the one with our friends, the other with our enemies."[52]

How substantial was America's contribution to the victory? During the whole of 1918, out of every 100 artillery shells fired, the French shot 51, the British 43, and the Americans only 6. On Armistice Day, out of 6,287 airplanes in the AEF, only 1,216 were of American manufacture, and all but three were of the type known as "Flaming Coffins." Out of 2,012 75-millimeter guns, few, if any, were American made, and none of the 155-millimeter howitzers. Except for shrapnel, almost no American-produced artillery ammunition reached the front. Only one-third of the automatic rifles were of American make and virtually none of the tanks. As Pershing admitted, "We were literally beggars as to every important weapon, except the rifle."[53]

In frontage the AEF eventually held 134 kilometers, compared to 113 for the British and 343 for the French. In numbers the Americans had approximately

2,000,000 men in France, comprising 31 percent of the manpower on the western front, compared to 28 percent for the British and 41 percent for the French.[54]

Highlights of the American contribution to victory were the morale lifter at Cantigny on May 28, 1918, the action of the 2d and 3d Divisions in blocking the road to Paris after the Chemin des Dames breakthrough in late May, the 1st and 2d Division spearhead of the Allied attack against the Marne salient on July 18, the subsequent elimination of that salient during late July and early August involving 300,000 American troops, the attack on the St. Mihiel salient on September 12 with 550,000 American troops, and the final 47-day Meuse-Argonne Offensive which began on September 26 and achieved a breakthrough on November 1, employing an army of over 1,000,000 men, 135,000 of them French. At the end of the offensive the American First Army had captured 26,000 prisoners, 874 cannon, 3,000 machine guns, and large stores of matériel. It had inflicted approximately 100,000 casualties, at a cost of 117,000 to itself.[55]

In addition, there was the moral contribution: the hope given the Allies by the ever-increasing numbers of reinforcements from America and the discouragement caused Germany by the realization that, for it, the manpower ratio could only grow worse.[56]

On November 11, 1918, a French staff officer at Pétain's headquarters said to Colonel Clark, "Let me say from my heart that we French, we will feel an eternal gratitude to Americans, for without your aid we would today be Boche provinces instead of a free people. You came not one hour too soon. We were nearly finished."[57]

In a sense then it is true to say that "America won the war," provided one understands that the same statement could also be made about France or Great Britain. All three won it; none could have achieved victory alone.[58]

As commander of the AEF, Pershing played an important role in the victory. A careful rather than a brilliant or great commander, he worked hard in planning an army on a scale sufficient to tip the balance. It was largely the tremendous American influx that converted an Allied deficit of 324,000 riflemen on March 21, 1918, to a 627,000 superiority on November 11, 1918.[59]

Captain B. H. Liddell Hart, whom Pershing thought was prejudiced against him, wrote in Reputations Ten Years After: "It is sufficient to say that there was perhaps no other man who would or could have built the structure of the American army on the scale he planned. And without that army the war could hardly have been saved and could not have been won."[60]

In the amalgamation controversy, Pershing took great risks. A man who throughout life had stressed preparedness and the fact that in modern war one could not improvise overnight, he nonetheless seemed impervious to Allied arguments concerning the need for priority shipments of infantry and machine-gun units in the face of expected German attacks during the spring and summer of 1918. As Pershing admitted, he was willing to take the risk of the British being pushed into the sea and the French driven back beyond the Loire. History has been kind to him, in that he ran the risk successfully. But he was like a man playing

Russian roulette. He lived through it, but he was lucky he didn't blow his head off.

The very same argument that Pershing was deaf to when used by the Allies (the need to plan ahead), he advocated himself when arguing for larger draft calls in the spring of 1918, and he criticized Baker for being deaf to it. "I insisted that the number of troops we were likely to need be called out immediately, when he rather contended that we should not take men away from work on the farms until it was absolutely necessary. . . . The result, of course, might have been very disastrous, and I think he made an error in this respect."[61]

Pershing's refusal to ship infantry and machine-gun units to France might have been equally disastrous, and the Allies, without doubt, thought he made an error in this respect.

On the other hand, even conceding that he might at times have been unnecessarily obstinate and failed to see the gravity of successive crises, he nonetheless guessed correctly in estimating that they were not as severe as the Allies represented them and that the Germans would not in fact break through and win the war before an American army could be trained and fielded. He may have been lucky, but the fact is that he guessed correctly. The Allies did not need as many priority shipments of American infantry and machine-gun units as they said they did.

Concerning the controversy about rifle training for open warfare, Pershing wrote in his postwar memoirs: "Ultimately, we had the satisfaction of hearing the French admit that we were right, both in emphasizing training for open warfare and insisting upon proficiency in the use of the rifle." He did this despite the fact that a research assistant, having searched the writings of Clemenceau, Foch, Pétain, Mangin, Degoutte, and Debeney, told him that he could find no original source supporting such a statement.[62]

Was Pershing right? It may well be doubted.

Frederick Palmer, who liked Pershing and wrote his biography, said later: "On Salisbury field and at Aldershot in 1914 I heard the same talk about the value of the rifle that I heard later in our training camps in Lorraine; and I saw it put in practice not only by the Canadians, who are our neighbors in western individualism and frontier marksmanship, and by the Australians, but by the British themselves, without being able to go through the trench line to open warfare."[63]

Liddell Hart said of Pershing: "He thought he was spreading a new gospel of faith when actually it was an old faith exploded. . . . He omitted but one factor from his calculations—German machine guns—and was right in all his calculations but one—their effect."[64]

Harvey A. DeWeerd, an American military writer, felt that the secret of advancing against multiple defensive lines lay not in rifle marksmanship, but in a combination of artillery, tanks, and innovative infiltration methods such as the Germans had used at Riga and Caporetto. "The A.E.F. learned to fight through bitter experience," he said, "not through any legerdemain with the rifle."[65]

The key weapon in World War I was not the rifle, but the machine gun, which killed many, and artillery, which probably killed more. Against them the

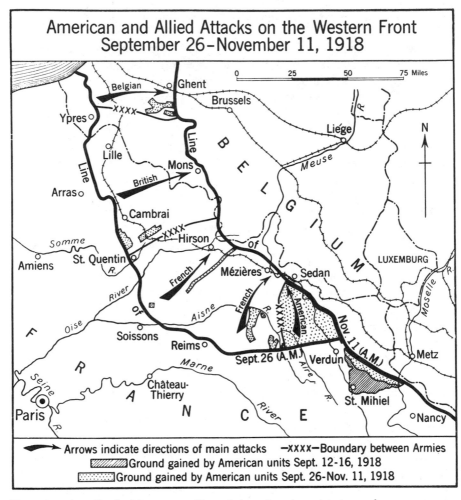

From American Battle Monuments Commission, *American Armies and Battlefields in Europe*, Washington, D.C., 1938.

American infantryman pitted raw courage, enthusiasm, inexperience, guts, some support from his auxiliary arms, and his own blood.[66]

As for open warfare, it is questionable how much the AEF actually engaged in it, especially during the Meuse-Argonne campaign. Day after day the First Army butted its head against stubborn German resistance, inching its way ahead from September 26 until November 1 when it finally achieved a breakthrough. In truth, it might be argued that the war was eventually won, not by the introduction of any tactic like open warfare, but simply by attrition, by the fact that one side ran out of men and equipment before the other—in other words, by exhaustion. At the armistice the Germans had not one division left in reserve. If they had, the war might still have gone on and Pershing, like Nivelle, might have been removed from command for ordering foolhardy assaults entirely incommensurate with the ground gained.[67]

Even as it was, he barely escaped ending the war under a cloud. Had the war ended on October 31 instead of eleven days later, his reputation would have been quite diminished. One has only to look at a war map dated October 31 to see how little the First Army had advanced under his leadership in comparison to its Allies. The First Army breakthrough on November 1, under Liggett, provided a happy ending to the AEF experience, producing a euphoria similar to that caused by Andrew Jackson's victory at New Orleans at the end of the War of 1812. People forgot the earlier failures and concentrated on the final success.[68]

That the First Army was able to break through on November 1 was due not to any new method like open warfare, nor even to the Army's growing competence, but in large part to the steady deterioration of its enemy. Had the German Army been in the fall of 1918 what it had been earlier, the First Army, for all its rifle marksmanship, open warfare tactics, or whatever, probably would have failed again. George C. Marshall, Jr., said, "Many mistakes were made in the Argonne which the Germans at that time were unable to charge to our account. . . ." Had they been able to, said Liddell Hart, it would have been a second "Nivelle massacre." Hunter Liggett, who ought to know, spoke the devastating truth when he wondered how the AEF would have done against the German Army of 1914, and answered, "Not so well."[69]

For all of Pershing's talk about the advantage of open warfare training and his indictment of the Allies for their defensive mentality and stress on trench warfare, the fact remains that during the last five months of the war, when the Germans were gradually pushed back all along the front, the British advanced farther and faster than the Americans. In addition, they captured twice as many guns and almost four times as many prisoners.[70]

Confronted with this fact, Pershing would later argue that the Americans were pushing against the most sensitive part of the German line, the pivot that the enemy had to hold lest he lose vital rail communication to his armies in the northwest, compelling him to withdraw all along the line. Since Hindenburg called the Meuse-Argonne "our most sensitive point" and said that "the American infantry in the Argonne won the war," there is something to be said for this. Which is why the argument still goes on.[71]

TWENTY-SEVEN

Portrait of Pershing

(1917–1948)

FOR MANY DURING World War I, Pershing was a remote, awesome figure—aloof, austere, unfeeling, unsympathetic, humorless, forbidding. He was, as some doughboy said, "that sonuvabitch [who] roared past our column in his big staff car, spattering every one of us with mud and water from head to foot."[1]

R. Ernest Dupuy, who knew Pershing only from a distance, said he couldn't imagine anyone ever relaxing in his presence. Harbord, as close to Pershing as any man, said that never in his wildest dreams did he ever think of calling him by his first name. Bullard, one of his army commanders who knew him from cadet days at West Point, regarded him as "a cold, intellectual, unhuman sort of a man of little sympathy or interest in anything or anybody outside of himself."[2]

A certain amount of aloofness, of course, is inherent in any high command, especially the military, where a commander must steel himself to make and execute difficult decisions which would tear him apart emotionally if he dwells on them. Sending men to their deaths is never easy, but at times it must be done.

Pershing knew of his reputation as a cold, unemotional martinet, and wished later that his men could have known him better. "For that [type of person] is not John Pershing as I have known him all my life," he said with a smile. "He is quite a different fellow, with many a soft spot in his make-up." He was, as many must be, two decidedly different men: remote and austere in his official life, warm and human in his personal.[3]

In his work he was a prodigious laborer, capable of sustained and effective effort over long periods of time. During the early days of the war he edited every cable, every order, squeezing every minute from the day. Callers, ushered into his office, found that he paid no attention to them until they had crossed the rather large room and stood, sometimes uncomfortably, at his desk, waiting for him to finish a line, sign a letter, or otherwise attend to some pressing business before looking up.[4]

A very busy man, he disliked wasting time in pointless talk or fruitless digressions. He also resented being interrupted. When the newspaperman Westbrook

Pegler walked in unannounced one day and asked for a statement, he got one. "Pegler, get the hell out of my office!"[5]

In transacting business he was honest, hardworking, and direct. His mind went right to the heart of things, cutting through nonessentials. James E. Mangum once overheard him commenting aloud as he read through a memorandum prepared by one of his officers. "Nonsense!" said Pershing at the end of the first paragraph. "Nonsense!" he repeated at the end of the second. At the end of the third, he exclaimed, "That is exactly right! Why in the hell couldn't he have said that in the first place?"[6]

Endowed with remarkable drive, discipline, and doggedness, he demanded these qualities in others and had little patience for those who tried to excuse failure by blaming circumstances or environment. "Success," he maintained, "depends upon determination regardless of environment." He gave as his one big rule of happiness "to have something worthwhile to do, and to do it with all there is in me—no matter what the circumstances."[7]

Some people got along with Pershing and some people didn't. The reason frequently was whether he felt they were mastering circumstances or letting circumstances master them.

At a press conference in the fall of 1917 a reporter raised the question whether the western front could be broken, since the Allies had failed to do it in three years. Pershing fixed him with a cold, hard stare, and replied icily, "Of course the western front can be broken. What are we here for?"[8]

Pershing drove his staff hard, too hard, thought Patton, who complained that Sundays at GHQ during the war were just like any other day. In time, Pershing ordered offices closed on Sundays so that people could take a break. Whenever he was absent from Chaumont, noted Patton, the pace slowed down.[9]

Although he drove his staff, they were generally at ease with him, particularly the lower levels and the enlisted men. (But a young intelligence officer named Walter Lippmann found him "a terrifying individual" who "never unbent.") Garfield Kass remembered that when Pershing passed through headquarters and the staff started to rise, Pershing waved them down and said to go on working. Patton felt that Pershing tried to do too much himself, especially in the early days of the war. But once he delegated a job, he left subordinates free to do it their own way.[10]

Pershing rarely lost his temper, but when he did he had quite a command of the English language to express his displeasure, which was generally proportionate to what the situation called for. He especially disliked inefficiency, bad judgment, wishy-washiness, and ignorance in one who should know the facts. Those who sought to curry favor by agreeing when they secretly disagreed incurred his special wrath when he discovered their deception. He wanted a man's true views, even if, and especially because, they disagreed with his own.[11]

On one occasion when a staff member brought something up, Pershing replied, "I know all about that matter and I've made my decision and I don't want to hear any more about it."

Sensing that the general had been misinformed, the officer checked out his facts and brought the matter up again the next day.

"Dammit," interrupted Pershing, "I've told you I didn't want to hear any more about this matter."

"General," the officer replied, "I'm sure there are some facts that have not been presented to you and I think I have a right to be heard out—that I have a responsibility to inform you and that you have a responsibility to listen."

Pershing listened, agreed that the new facts changed the matter, completely reversed his decision, and commended his subordinate.[12]

Knowing Pershing's passion for facts, subordinates became wary of making recommendations without having fully studied the matter. Once Pershing handed Mangum a written recommendation that someone had made. "What do you think about that?" he asked.

"I don't know, sir; I would have to think about it. I need more information."

"Well, what would you guess?"

"I wouldn't guess."

Pershing nodded approval, then said: "Suppose I said I wanted you to make me a guess right now. Then what would you guess?"

"My guess, General, is that this thing needs a lot more study."

Pershing gave a hearty laugh and said, "That is what I guess too. Take it and study it and let me know what you think about it."[13]

Possessed of a prodigious memory, especially for names and faces, Pershing would often appear to make snap judgments, whereas he remembered many of the facts of a case without the need to call for documents. On crucial matters he suspended judgment until he had all the facts or had a chance, as he said, "to sleep over it." Frequently he would discuss things with Collins, his aide, clarifying his own ideas by talking them out.[14]

Since he tried to clear his desk each day before retiring, his labors sometimes took him to the wee hours. Bright B. Butz, a staff member, had to remind him to quit work long after midnight in order to get a little rest before a trip scheduled to start early the next day.[15]

On such trips he was notoriously late, taking an oversanguine view of the time required to get somewhere. Although not bothered by being late for others, he was quite irritated when people were late for him.[16]

He gave little time to introspection, to regrets over the past or worries about the future. When the workday was over, he quit and left his work at the office. "I don't let anything worry me," he told Charles H. Grasty of the *New York Times*. "I try to do a good day's work, and when it is finished I go to bed. And what is more, I go to sleep." To make sure, he employed a masseur who gave him a good rubdown at night before retiring. The ability to sleep, he knew, was a prime requisite for a general.[17]

With the exception of Generals March and Wood, his mind was generally unburdened by prejudices or petty jealousies. Like Lincoln, he realized that holding grudges exacts a terrible price, both on one's time and nervous system. "He was not the type to waste time disliking any one individual," said J. Thomas Schneider, his aide. "He was too big a man."[18]

Mark S. Watson felt that whether one got along with Pershing or not was largely determined by how well one did one's job. "If the job was well done, there was no trouble. If it was poorly done, there was a great deal of trouble." Someone quoted Pershing as saying, "If they don't produce, throw them on the scrap heap." Dawes spoke of him as "a wild lion unloosed if one does not make good."[19]

While this may have been generally true, there were exceptions. The legend of Pershing as completely ruthless is overdrawn. He retained on his staff several officers and enlisted men who were not particularly efficient, but whom he liked for their earlier service with him. And even when removing a man, he tried to do it gently, as in the case of General Blatchford.[20]

When Joseph Cummings Chase came to paint Pershing's portrait, the headquarters staff suggested that he not depict him as grim as photographs seemed to, for he was not that way. He was solicitous for the staff, for men like John McAuley Palmer, who became ill and required extra attention, and James L. Collins, who said of Pershing, "He was anything but a cold machine to those who really knew him." Edward Bowditch, his aide, considered him "a good friend." Ralph Curtin, his secretary, found him "a very warm personality." Hugh Drum called him "the most companionable man I ever knew." George Eller, his chauffeur, said, "I won't say I liked him more than my father. I liked him in a different way, but I do think I liked him in a way comparable to my father."[21]

He was an interesting conversationalist, especially with his staff and small groups of friends. With people he trusted, he would pace up and down, talking animatedly, pounding his fist, and saying things strongly. With others, however, he was reserved. "You have to be cautious," he remarked.[22]

He had a good sense of humor, a warm smile, and a hearty laugh. John Hughes, his aide, recalled him "roaring with laughter" when reminiscing with Harbord and Bowditch about some incident during their Philippine days.[23]

He enjoyed telling stories on himself. On one occasion, while visiting a division close to the front, he encountered a black sentry who failed to call out the guard at his approach.

"Why didn't you call out the guard?" he demanded.

The sentry turned and yelled, "Officer ob de day!"

When a head appeared at the flap of a nearby tent, he yelled, "General Pershing's here!"

"That's what you should have done when you first saw me," said the general. "It's too late now, calling out the guard."

Whereupon the sentry turned and yelled again, only louder.

"Officer ob de day! Nebber min' now. General Pershing's only foolin'!"[24]

As a public speaker, he was effective in small, informal situations, where he could speak extemporaneously for a short time. But in larger, more formal situations, he was not. The very thought of a formal talk "makes me shiver," he said.

He constantly revised his text right up to the last minute, and the result was not very good.[25]

Socially he was poised, moving with easy assurance and a pleasant, gracious manner among all kinds of people. Like many an old cavalryman, he was a superb dancer, and as one of the world's most eligible bachelors, was much sought after by women. Strongly sexed, he seems to have taken a number of them, but without any thought of marriage.[26]

He enjoyed good-looking women and had a way with them. When an attractive French girl asked him to autograph her Golden Book, he wrote in it, "To my fair Ally!!!!" and signed his name.[27]

In dealing with the French he always used an interpreter, but on occasion he was emboldened, as he put it, "to air my dreadful French." Once he tried it out on a little six-year-old girl, who looked at him blankly, unresponsive to his questions. "Comprenez-vous?" he finally asked.

"Non," she replied bluntly, much to the amusement of Pershing's staff.[28]

His personal habits were abstemious. Occasionally he enjoyed a glass of wine before a meal, but generally he drank very little. Only once in thirty years could Ralph Curtin recall him feeling his liquor.[29]

He ate relatively little. When he first settled in at Ogden Mills's house in Paris in 1917, the French chef, anxious to show what he could do, inquired what the general wished for lunch.

"Tea, toast, and grapes," Pershing replied.

Taken aback, the chef asked about dinner.

"Grapes, toast, and tea."[30]

His use of tobacco was sparing. Instead of smoking, he normally cut off a little plug from a cigar and stuck it in the back of his mouth when working alone or riding horseback. Although he attempted to remove traces of it afterwards, eventually his teeth picked up an unattractive yellow cast.[31]

Although he rarely smoked, on one occasion he borrowed a cigarette from someone, lit it, took a few puffs, and then put it out. But first he inquired of a lady who was present if she would mind if he smoked. Since one of his staff had previously lighted up without so inquiring, this was Pershing's way of administering a polite rebuke.[32]

He was very much a "sound mind in a sound body" man. For exercise, he usually rode horseback, generally with a companion. Sometimes he walked the six kilometers from his office at Chaumont to his residence or, near the end of the war, alongside the headquarters train parked near Souilly, again with a companion. Weather was no deterrent. Observers remember Pershing walking in a hard rain for an hour or so, or running outside in the morning snow.[33]

"No matter how late he worked," said Patton, "and he usually did work well into the night, he always took a violent (no other word describes it) walk for half an hour before retiring. In the morning he took twenty minutes sitting up exercises before breakfast."[34]

As a result he enjoyed excellent health, both physical and mental. Although he was fifty-eight in 1918, doctors found that he had the heart and arteries of a man of thirty-five and the eye lens crystal of a boy of eighteen. "Physically and mentally he seemed almost tireless," said Earl Thornton, commander of Pershing's headquarters train.[35]

He was very conscious of his body and proud of it. He looked the part of the supreme commander. Beside him all other generals, Allied and American, suffered by comparison. Quick of step, alert of eye, he radiated "presence." Although he was only five feet, nine inches tall, people thought of him as above six feet. One Rainbow veteran said he was "of towering height." "He looked hard as nails," said Daniel A. Poling, later editor of the *Christian Herald*. "He was the perfect picture of the indomitable high commander," observed S. L. A. Marshall, "tailor-made for monuments." He posed for photographers instinctively: back straight, chest out, one foot slightly ahead of the other.[36]

His uniforms, London-made, never had anything in the pockets, so as to produce a trim, sharp look. He modified the standard Army uniform, introducing the Sam Browne belt and extending the cap visor, both innovations borrowed from the British. He liked the World War I uniform with its boots, belt, and high choke collar, and wore it as long as he could, believing that it looked more military than subsequent Army uniforms.[37]

Legend to the contrary, he was much more tender and compassionate than people gave him credit for. At Christmas 1917 he sent flowers and "a big hug and several kisses" to Dorothy Canfield Fisher, an old friend from University of Nebraska days. In July 1918, right before the last major German offensive, he left Provins about 10:00 P.M. and drove three hours to arrive at Chaumont, where he was scheduled to appear the next morning for the distribution of prizes at the lycée. "Would have stayed overnight on road," said his diary, "but did not want to disappoint the children."[38]

After the armistice, groups of French schoolchildren frequently visited his headquarters train as it moved about on the final inspections of divisions before their return home. Time permitting, he gave them a personally conducted tour of part of the train.[39]

Although not a very religious person, in the sense of being a regular churchgoer, he did believe in God, Providence, and an afterlife. In difficult situations he prayed for divine guidance.[40]

He was a man of principle, for whom the West Point motto, "Duty, Honor, Country," was the guiding beacon of his life. He was also a proud man: proud of himself, his army, his country.[41]

Yet he always retained a basic modesty. After the war he desired a quiet personal homecoming. Throughout life he rarely displayed the many awards and medals he had won, usually wearing only the Distinguished Service Medal.[42]

George P. Eller, Pershing's chauffeur, felt that he grew on one. "You couldn't be with him more than a month without respecting the man, without admiring him. Everything about him was American: the way he talked, the way he carried himself, the way he acted. He just commanded your respect. You couldn't help it. He was everything you would want to be yourself if you could."[43]

Harbord considered serving with him the greatest experience of his life. Charles G. Dawes, who met many strong men in his day, both in business and government, called Pershing the strongest man he ever met. Hanson Ely considered him the fairest commanding officer under whom he had ever served. George Van Horn Moseley admired the way he delegated authority to subordinates and then backed them up. "He was *fine*," said Moseley, his voice vibrating with emotion.[44]

He created and organized his own army, fashioning it in his own image and likeness. He epitomized the AEF; it found its highest embodiment in him. As Frank H. Simonds said: "When you stumbled upon a lost American doughboy in a God-forsaken Lorraine hamlet, his bearing, the set of his tunic, his salute, all authentically recalled the general who sat in Chaumont."[45]

Ralph Curtin, who knew Pershing for thirty years, felt that his strong points were sound common sense, the ability to pick a good staff, and the determination to see that, once a job was given, it was done—or else. Not the least of his merits, added Curtin, was that he was at all times conscious that, as head of the AEF, he carried the good name of the United States.[46]

TWENTY-EIGHT

Peace

(December 1918-April 1919)

ESPITE THE ARMISTICE, Pershing was about as busy as he had
been before, although the pressure was less. His aide, James L.
Collins, thought it "astounding" how the general kept up, considering the pace he had been going at since his arrival in France
almost two years before. McAndrew, Davis, Nolan, Conner, Mo-
seley, and others at GHQ looked like "a lot of squeezed out oranges," said Collins,
but Pershing went on day and night, being refreshed by social activities late in the
evening for work the next day.[1]

Part of that work concerned the American Third Army, which Pershing had
ordered formed in early November and which came into being after the armistice
as an occupation army. Marching to the Rhine River, it took up positions in the
American bridgehead at Koblenz under its commander, Maj. Gen. Joseph T. Dickman, who was still fuming about the Sedan débâcle. A competent, well-trained
officer, he inclined to be pompous and took himself very seriously. By May 1919
Pershing was dissatisfied with him and replaced him with Hunter Liggett.[2]

German reaction to the American occupation was generally friendly. Field
hands went out of their way to put American troops on the right road; housewives
lent them their cooking utensils, and even their food, when doughboys arrived
ahead of their rolling kitchens. Almost universally people were kindly, helpful,
and courteous.[3]

The Americans responded in kind. They ruled with such a light hand that the
French complained that the Americans treated the Germans better than their fellow
Germans did. In contrast, the French, who could neither forgive nor forget what
the Germans had done to them during four terrible years, inclined to stern measures
which the Americans considered unnecessarily harsh.[4]

Before long, relations between the French and Americans began to deteriorate.
The more the doughboys saw of the disciplined, clean, friendly Germans, the more
they preferred them to the French whom they regarded as slipshod, temperamental,
exploitive, and dirty. (Alexander Woollcott observed that the French never learned
to use a toothbrush.) In December Pershing warned Dickman about growing pro-

German, anti-French feeling in the American Third Army, and in January he wrote in his diary that unless the trend was reversed, many, if not most, American soldiers would go home with "more respect for the Germans than the French."[5]

Pershing himself was acutely aware how vexing the French could be, for he had a number of tête-à-têtes with Foch after the armistice which convinced him that the French were deliberately trying to slight the AEF. For example, when Colonel Mott, his liaison officer at Foch's headquarters, suggested that the French could make a "beau geste" by inviting American troops to share some of the triumphal entries into Alsace, he was told that it was unfortunately too late. Mott was convinced that it was not too late if the French had really desired it.[6]

Another example occurred when Foch, under guise of stressing the "inter-Allied nature of the occupation," ordered French divisions into both the British bridgehead at Cologne and the American at Koblenz. When Haig protested, Foch backed down, but when Pershing did, the marshal took the ground that if Pershing had any objections, he should have presented them sooner and that it was now too late to change plans. Later Foch reduced the size of the American bridgehead from sixty to thirty-five kilometers, which Pershing considered a "slight to the American Army."[7]

Pershing felt that Foch was guided by political considerations, attempting to impress the Germans with French presence everywhere. Once, while visiting the American bridgehead, Pershing was informed that Foch would be passing through and that the French had suggested a salute in his honor and had ordered German authorities to report to him. "I do not consider that the French have any jurisdiction whatsoever in this area," Pershing stated, countermanding the order.[8]

The Pershing-Foch relationship grew increasingly frosty, as Pershing opposed the marshal on the number of U.S. troops to be kept in Europe, the duration of their stay, and the use to be made of them. He refused to allow what he thought were French political agitators into the American bridgehead, and forced Foch to withdraw French troops from the grand duchy of Luxembourg, where Americans were garrisoned, under threat of revealing how the French were scheming to annex it.[9]

He opposed Foch's desire to use American troops as laborers to rehabilitate France by filling in trenches, removing barbed wire, and doing road and construction work. "It would be unjust and even criminal ... to use our soldiers as laborers," he said. Furthermore, the men would not stand for it.[10]

Pershing may have erred here. France needed rehabilitation. The average doughboy, as long as he had to remain in France anyhow, probably would have preferred doing something constructive, like helping people rebuild their homes, than following boring AEF training schedules, which had him sticking bayonets into gunny sacks. After all, Pershing himself admitted that the resumption of hostilities was highly unlikely. And he had given Herbert Hoover permission to draft men from the Army for relief work.[11]

Irked that the French "had never once said a word of thanks or complimented the American troops on what they had done," Pershing told Haig that Americans would never forget "the bad treatment which they had received from the French and that it was difficult to exaggerate the feeling of dislike for the French which existed in the American Army."[12]

On December 13 President Wilson arrived in Europe. Pershing had hoped that one of the President's first acts would be to visit the First Army, review a division around the battlefield at Montfaucon, and address the whole AEF through that division. It would provide the occasion for a great speech like Lincoln's Gettysburg Address.

Wilson, however, was not very interested in visiting the front, pleading lack of time. He did consent to a Christmas visit, not to Montfaucon, but to Langres, which had never been an AEF battlefield.

December 25 was raw, cold, and wet. The reviewing field was ankle deep in mud, and everyone, troops and spectators, probably wished they were somewhere else. James L. Collins thought the President's speech "lacked fire and fell flat." He said the right words but without any heart in them. The troops were as unmoved as he seemed to be. After visiting some billets of the 26th Division in the afternoon, the President begged off a scheduled dinner at night on the grounds that he had to leave for London.

The day's formalities over, Pershing and his staff celebrated a relaxed Christmas at his Chaumont chateau. "The general was in fine spirits," noted Collins. He presented candy and other gifts, "making a little speech to every man that was just apropos." Collins had the impression that Pershing felt good, not just because the day's events were over, but because he felt "that he appeared well and had not suffered in any respect by comparison with the President. . . ."[13]

Pershing's troubles with Foch, together with what seemed slighting references to American victories in the French press in the final days of the war, convinced Pershing that the French were trying to downplay the American contribution to victory. To counteract this, as well as to instill what he considered justifiable pride in the U.S. soldier, he selected nine hundred doughboys who in civilian life were editors, writers, or publishers, and sent them on a special two-week tour of the AEF, so that when they returned home they could tell people of American accomplishments. He also commissioned Hugh Drum, Willey Howell, and George C. Marshall, Jr., to make lecture tours of divisional camps to tell the AEF side of the story.[14]

Of the three, Marshall was probably the most effective. On April 20, when he gave a lecture at Chaumont to visiting members of the House Military Affairs Committee, he was so full of his subject and spoke so rapidly that stenographers assigned to take notes could not keep up with him. Pershing was most impressed. He had had his eye on Marshall for some time and a few days later asked him to become his aide. For the next five years Marshall stood at Pershing's right hand as personal adviser, secretary, and executive.[15]

Marshall, who found the experience invaluable, saw a lighter, more human side of Pershing than most people knew. In the early 1920s, when both were traveling on a train together and enjoying a bottle of Scotch, Pershing suggested that they ought to offer a bit to Sen. George Moses in the next car. Pouring a little into a water glass, they proceeded to where Pershing thought the senator was sleeping in a Pullman.

"Senator Moses," whispered Pershing, scratching the closed green curtain of a berth.

When there was no answer, Pershing raised the curtain a little, only to discover, not Senator Moses, but an angry, apprehensive woman who said sharply, "What do you want?"

Startled and scared, Pershing dropped the curtain and bolted down the aisle like a frightened schoolboy, jostling Marshall and spilling the scotch. "I had a hard time keeping out of his way," said the aide, "because he was running right up my back. But we got to the stateroom and got the door shut. Then he just sat down and laughed until he cried."

Finally, wiping his eyes, Pershing noticed that a little Scotch still remained in the glass and mischievously suggested that Marshall go back, alone this time, and try it again. Not on your life, Marshall replied in effect. "Get another aide."

Yet, for all his humanness, the general could be quite distant, even with a man like Marshall. The latter noticed, for example, that when the train trip was over and they had both got back into uniform, "he was just as stern as though we had never been together at all." In truth, there were two different Pershings.[16]

Marshall came to admire Pershing tremendously, especially for his hard common sense, his backbone, and his ability to take criticism dispassionately. On one occasion when Pershing was Chief of Staff of the Army he changed a War Department procedure, mainly, suspected Marshall, because Peyton C. March had initiated it. When Marshall wrote up a memorandum criticizing the change, Pershing sent for him. "I don't take to this at all," he said. "I don't agree with you."

Thinking he had not stated his objections clearly, Marshall went back and wrote up a second memorandum, this one in greater detail. When Pershing read it, he said, "I don't accept this."

Once more, a third time, Marshall rewrote his criticisms, explaining why the old procedure was preferable to the new. This time Pershing slapped his hand on the desk in an uncharacteristic gesture. "No!" he said angrily. "No, by God, we will do it this way."

At that, Marshall, who had first come to Pershing's attention by telling him unpleasant truths he did not like to hear, said forthrightly: "Now, General, just because you hate the guts of General March you're setting yourself up . . . to do something you know damn well is wrong."

Pershing studied his aide thoughtfully, then handed back the memorandum. "Well, have it your own way," he said.[17]

Pershing liked Marshall and wrote efficiency reports on him which were prescient for the future: "This officer should reach high rank and is capable of filling any position with ability and good judgment—a very exceptional man."[18]

One of Pershing's major problems after the armistice was the fact that almost every doughboy now had only one thing in mind: When do we go home? As days turned into weeks, and weeks into months, many began to paraphrase the remark attributed to Pershing on his arrival in France: "Lafayette, we are *still* here." Others groused: "We've paid our debt to Lafayette; who the hell do we owe now?"[19]

In these circumstances, the last thing in the world soldiers wanted was the strenuous training program that Pershing inaugurated in December 1918. To be sure, he had good reasons for it. An armistice is not a peace; hostilities might resume, in which case troops must be ready for action. Many soldiers, rushed over during the summer of 1918, were only partially trained. Even were hostilities not resumed, a training program would keep the men occupied and would provide the nation with a large body of experienced soldiers should war break out again in ten to fifteen years.[20]

Unfortunately, most men didn't see it that way. "No human enterprise goes flat so instantly as an Army training camp when war ends," observed Dwight D. Eisenhower. "Everything that sustains morale—peril to the country, imminent combat, zeal for victory, sense of importance—disappears. The only thing that counts for a citizen soldier is his date of discharge."[21]

The cement that held the AEF together began to crumble on November 11, 1918. After that men went through the motions, but in many cases that's all they did. Bored to tears, artillerymen who had fired thousands of shells in the Meuse-Argonne listlessly rammed empty shell casings into a gun for hours at a stretch, training the sights on a nonexistent enemy. "They seem to wilt under it," observed Raymond B. Fosdick.[22]

Frequently the winter weather was terrible, yet the men were marched out into rain and snow, five hours a day, to perform the prescribed exercises. George C. Marshall, Jr., believed that Pershing's good intentions suffered at the hands of stupid, overzealous martinets at the lower level who inflexibly applied his general directives.[23]

Whatever the cause, men who were without a change of dry socks or underwear after being out in inclement weather performing meaningless exercises became soured in mind and heart. "They were embittered in a way they never forgot," said Marshall. More than one who had seriously considered an army career angrily withdrew his application.[24]

In January Raymond B. Fosdick, chairman of the Commission on Training Camp Activities, reported that the morale situation was "little short of desperate." Earlier that month when Pershing's picture appeared on a movie screen, the soldier audience hooted and hissed. "Everybody had a bellyful of the damn Army," said one veteran.[25]

Pershing was understandably concerned about the deteriorating situation. He summoned Corinna Lindon Smith, whom he had used before on an informal fact-finding mission concerning soldiers' attitudes. "He seemed discouraged," she remembered, "and, with a very sad expression, remarked, 'Never has an army come into a war with such ideals as ours brought—are our soldiers losing them, and is it my fault, bad leadership?'" The next day Mrs. Smith left to talk to doughboys. "Confine your activities to the out-of-the-way villages and towns difficult of access," he instructed, "and handle the boys as you did before...."[26]

In time Pershing relaxed the training schedule, substituting for it other activities—recreational, educational, athletic—to occupy men's time. The soldiers especially appreciated a well-organized athletic program in which units competed against one another. In April, for example, Pershing attended the AEF championship boxing bouts in Paris, where the doughboys lustily cheered a light-heavyweight boxer from the SOS. His name was Gene Tunney.[27]

Much of Pershing's time from January to April was spent visiting, inspecting, and saying goodby to virtually all AEF units that were returning home. Some two million men were going back into civilian life, where they would have an important influence, and Pershing wanted to say certain things to them.[28]

Pershing inspected rapidly, his sharp eyes missing nothing. Spotting a wound stripe, he would frequently stop and ask where the soldier had been wounded, whether he had received good hospital care, and whether he was fully recovered. "Son, we're proud of you," he'd say, shaking hands.[29]

At one inspection S. L. A. Marshall, who later became a famous military writer, played a joke on Pershing without the general realizing it. Marshall, a young officer, had inherited a very poor company which had been shabbily treated by its previous captain. To restore spirits he ruled with a light hand, putting many men on leave, reducing guard and fatigue duty, improving food, and generally making very little of discipline. When word came that Pershing was to inspect, Marshall called the men together, reminded them of how well he had treated them over several months, and suggested that now was the time to spruce themselves up as a way of showing gratitude. At the inspection Marshall's company was one of the sharpest looking outfits in the division. Pershing noticed it, stopped, and asked what accounted for such smartness.

"Discipline!" said Marshall, knowing what the general liked to hear.

"I knew it!" exclaimed Pershing enthusiastically. "Discipline does it every time!"[30]

Periodically Pershing would inquire of a random soldier concerning his billets, food, clothing, training, athletics, recreation, and so forth. Whether by coincidence or not, a number of soldiers noticed that a short time after such inspections living conditions improved.[31]

One question put to officers always concerned venereal disease, for it was Pershing's endeavor, he told Secretary Baker, to send the army home "clean physically and clean morally." He himself had had gonorrhea twice in his younger days and knew the effects of such disease. A typical questioning went like this:

"How many cases of V.D.?"

"Only one, sir."

"One too many."[32]

Although one man in twenty who entered the army during the war already had V.D., Pershing was determined that none should leave the army with it. He ordered medics to carefully inspect at all re-embarkation camps and to detain anyone with such disease. Medics also conducted examinations on shipboard and again when they docked at home. No one left the army with V.D. Pershing returned to America the cleanest army in the history of the world.[33]

After reviewing a division, Pershing assembled its officers and gave a ten-minute talk, stressing the role that America had played in winning the war and the pride they should feel in having been a part of it. A typical speech, given at Brest in January 1919, went in part like this:

"The American soldier, as has been demonstrated in this war, is unequaled by any other soldier in the world, and the American Army . . . has no equal in Europe or anywhere else, and I doubt whether there will ever again be an American Army equal to the one of which you form a part. . . . [The Allies] can all say what they please, . . . but America won the war, and the American Army did it.

"You have formed a part of an expedition which is unique in history, and it has been a splendid part, and that part is something that each man should carry home as a treasure in his heart. . . .

"May I say just one word about the moral side? . . . It should be our ambition to maintain the splendid record for morality that has existed in the Army. . . . It is my very great ambition that not a single case [of V.D.] among the American Expeditionary Forces shall arrive in the United States. I think this is a goal that we all ought to work for. . . .

"I wish you one and all a pleasant journey home and all the success which your splendid service here has entitled you to."[34]

When he finished, the men applauded, sometimes enthusiastically, sometimes perfunctorily. Occasionally the speech was a dud. Some men did not feel the idealism Pershing thought they did, especially when they had been up at dawn and waiting for him for hours in a cold rain, some of them in puddles over their shoe tops.[35]

On one occasion, when Pershing mentioned that a unit was scheduled to return home soon, pandemonium broke out and he could not continue. On another, surely an extreme case, Pershing was booed and hooted down with cries of "We want to go home!" As it was apparent that the men had been sorely mistreated, Pershing inflicted no punishments, removed the camp commander and sent in Brig. Gen. Paul B. Malone, formerly of his training staff, who within forty-eight hours began to improve conditions.[36]

But these occasions were the exceptions; in general, the reception was good. Pershing was a legendary figure, a man whom soldiers had heard about but never hoped to see. Many of them were thrilled by that final inspection and would remember it for years. Said one veteran ten years later: "Seldom if ever have I been so impressed by one man's personality, seldom have I been so inspired merely by looking at a man."[37]

Although Pershing had become a national hero, he was subject to sniping attacks and whispering campaigns. There was no public criticism, just an undercurrent of talk. Washington "seethed" with it, reported Frederick Palmer.[38]

People said that Pershing had disobeyed Foch. He was not an administrator. He was not seen by his troops, nor popular with them. He surrounded himself with a Leavenworth and West Point clique, who, like him, were overtailored and pompous. He lacked personal magnetism and was jealous of men who possessed it, like Leonard Wood, whom he kept out of France. He was down on the National Guard and had removed Clarence Edwards because he stood up for it. He had cost the 35th Division seven thousand casualties in the Argonne because of lack of artillery and air support. He was a martinet, forbidding men to turn up their coat collars in a downpour of rain. He had had a mistress in the Philippines. He was glory mad.[39]

Why this undercurrent of criticism? Partly it was the postwar letdown; the enemy having been defeated, Americans could indulge in the luxury of fighting among themselves. The long-standing National Guard-Regular Army antipathy also had something to do with it. Wood and Edwards were popular officers, with devoted followers. A number of snafus had occurred in the AEF, and who better to blame than its commander in chief?

Partly too the criticism was political, inspired, thought Frederick Palmer, "by gentlemen with their own lightning rods out," who saw in Pershing a political rival. Both Edwards and Wood were running for president. Henry J. Allen, Governor of Kansas, who made the charge about the 35th Division being mishandled in the Argonne, was Wood's political ally and placed his name in nomination at the 1920 Republican Convention.[40]

Pershing discounted the criticisms. He thought Edwards's candidacy "a flash in the pan" and doubted whether "any sane body of men" would elect Wood. He told Secretary Baker that he was frankly surprised to hear that there was much bitterness against the AEF and thought that such reports were "very much overstated."[41]

As always, Baker stood by Pershing. It was his duty, as well as his pleasure, he said, to protect the general back in America. He squelched talk of investigating the AEF, although he did suggest to Pershing that it might be wise to line up certain key officers who could be sent home to testify if necessary.[42]

Pershing was correct in thinking that the criticisms would soon blow over. While he had enemies, he also had success and, as one Congressman put it, investigating him would be like "investigating the Duke of Wellington after the Battle of Waterloo."[43]

Nonetheless, in April Baker came to Europe, ostensibly on a business trip, but actually, Pershing suspected, to look him over and the AEF as well. The Secretary was pleased with what he saw. Certain bad conditions, such as the much criticized, semi-chaotic living arrangements at Camp Pontanezen, outside of Brest, had now been corrected. They had existed temporarily during the interim period when the AEF was shifting gears from rushing men into Europe to rushing them out of it.[44]

While Pershing was glad to see Secretary Baker, he was even happier to see his traveling companion: the general's nine-year-old son, Warren Pershing. With exquisite graciousness, Baker had brought the boy over, dressed in a miniature sergeant's uniform, hoping it would be a surprise.[45]

Pershing and his son Warren with some of the headquarters staff, May
25, 1919. L-R: Capt. John C. Hughes, Maj. Gen. James W. McAndrew,
Lt. Col. James G. Quekemeyer, General Pershing, Warren Pershing,
Lt. Col. Edward Bowditch, Maj. Gen. James G. Harbord, Capt. Frank
Pershing, Brig. Gen. Robert C. Davis, and Col. James L. Collins.
U.S. Army Military History Institute

Seeing Warren, Pershing was plainly moved. "Nothing was said particularly,"
said George P. Eller, Pershing's chauffeur, who choked up in remembering the
incident, "but you could see it in the general's eyes—the pride, the love, the feeling
that Warren was his and the only thing that he had left."[46]

Although Pershing had not seen his son in two years, the boy had not been
out of his thoughts. In the fall of 1917 he had asked his sister May to have an
educator draw up a course of reading for Warren. "I want him to get the habit
of reading things—not trashy stuff, but good, wholesome things put in child-lan-
guage. I am also thinking of having him study French. Of course I do not want
to crowd him too much, but I think he could do some studying outside of his
regular school work."[47]

He had also urged his brother Jim to visit Warren occasionally. "I do not
want him to grow up to be a 'sissy,' which is possible if a boy grows up without

any man around." To provide male influence, Pershing had had the boy spend the summer of 1918 at Senator Warren's ranch in Wyoming. Lest Warren become spoiled, the general forbade his picture being taken by the press.[48]

Clad in his sergeant's uniform, the boy accompanied Pershing on his final AEF inspection trips. He played soldier, but learned that a soldier's life makes certain demands. When Warren unbuttoned his jacket on a hot day, Pershing commanded sternly, "Button up that uniform or take it off."[49]

Baker's visit in April, like his earlier visits during the war, provided Pershing an occasion to talk over a number of things which were troubling him. The most serious was promotions, which General March had stopped with the armistice and which Pershing felt had worked a number of injustices. During the Meuse-Argonne campaign many division commanders had been so heavily engaged as not to have time to make recommendations for promotions. In addition, because of heavy casualties, many officers had performed tasks above their rank, for example, a captain had done the job of a major. It seemed only simple justice that the captain ought to end the war as a major, that a man like Fox Conner, whom Pershing considered indispensable, should wear more than one star, and that Harbord, who had revitalized the SOS, should wear more than two.

Pershing opposed the promotion stoppage, asking that he be authorized to make such promotions as he considered merited. The expense would be negligible, he declared, and men would leave the service in a better frame of mind, feeling that their accomplishments had been rewarded, a fact important in postwar America where any hope of universal military training would depend on the goodwill of veterans and their families.[50]

But General March, who was in the process of overseeing a reduction in manpower from 3.7 million men to about 200,000, didn't see it that way. He thought that what was called for was not promotions but complete demobilization of the army, followed by whatever promotions were necessary for men to have the proper rank in the new peacetime army. He suggested that Pershing could reward his officers by giving them the Distinguished Service Cross or Distinguished Service Medal or a promotion in the Reserve Corps.[51]

To Pershing's chagrin, Baker sided with March on this question. All Pershing could do therefore was to write letters of appreciation to his chief subordinates, explaining that he had recommended them for promotion, but that the War Department had ruled otherwise. He continued to feel, however, that men like Harbord, Liggett, Bullard, Dickman, McAndrew, Marshall, Summerall, MacArthur, Wright, Conner, and Moseley had been unjustly deprived of the proper recognition due them.[52]

His own top officers cut off from promotion, Pershing opposed any post-armistice promotion for March. When the question arose in January 1919 of making the Chief of Staff a permanent general, Pershing told Senator Warren that such a promotion would meet "with the absolute disapproval of every man who has served the country in Europe." While conceding that March had been "more or less successful" at home, "it has been his ambition to interfere with the organization which I established here. In this, fortunately, he was frustrated, but his cooperation has been entirely forced and . . . he is entitled only to the credit of doing what he did under compulsion."[53]

The promotion question continued to produce ill feeling, not just between Pershing and March, but between overseas and home officers. AEF commanders, lacking units to command as the army returned home, found themselves demoted almost as soon as they stepped off the ship. Home officers, however, many of them junior to their AEF counterparts, continued to retain their high rank. Charles D. Rhodes, busted down from major general to colonel on his return, summed up the typical AEF attitude: "Everywhere, I find much discontent. . . . All of Pershing's generals, with but few exceptions, have been promptly demoted, while all good army jobs continue to be filled with 'March adherents,' with officers of the field artillery 'running strong.' "[54]

In fairness to March, it should be noted that he did make an effort to integrate AEF officers into the home force. James W. McAndrew returned to become Commandant of the General Staff College. Two corps commanders, William G. Haan and William M. Wright, took over the War Plans Division as Director and Executive Assistant respectively. Another corps commander, Charles H. Muir, headed the Command and General Staff School at Fort Leavenworth. Douglas MacArthur became superintendant of West Point.[55]

But Pershing was still miffed.

TWENTY-NINE

The Return Home

(May-November 1919)

FOR PERSHING, as well as for the thousands who marched and the millions who watched—some of them sleeping overnight on the sidewalks to have a good view—the Paris Victory Parade of July 14, 1919, was one of life's memorable events. George C. Marshall, Jr., who saw a number of victory parades in his day, called it the greatest he had ever seen.[1]

It began early in the morning on a solemn note, as one thousand blind, lame, and mutilated veterans walked in procession. But then came the military pageantry: the massed colors, the martial music, the splendidly disciplined troops from every Allied nation, marching row upon row, behind their world-famous commanders. It stirred the blood and set the heart beating, as all, participants and spectators, were caught up in the spectacle, realizing that they were sharing in one of the world's great events. It was like the great triumphal processions of ancient Rome.[2]

Foch and Joffre led off, carrying their marshal's batons, accompanied by a small escort. Then came the military contingents—1,500 men or less—from the principal Allied nations, marching alphabetically: the Americans, Belgians, British, Czechs, Greeks, Italians, Japanese, Portuguese, Romanians, Serbs, Poles—with the French capping the procession at the end.[3]

A stunning figure on horseback, Pershing headed the American contingent. Behind him an officer bore his large, silk, four-starred flag, and behind the flagbearer rode Harbord, Pershing's alter ego, back at his old position as Chief of Staff. Ten yards behind, riding abreast, came Pershing's three aides, George C. Marshall, Jr., John G. Quekemeyer, and John C. Hughes, followed by Henry T. Allen, commander of the American Forces in Germany, and John L. Hines, destined to succeed Pershing later as Army Chief of Staff. Then, eight abreast, at ten-yard intervals, rode four lines of American generals—thirty in all. Next came the AEF Band, "Pershing's Own," leading the magnificent Composite Regiment, a select group of Regular Army officers and men, all six-footers, chosen from the best American troops in Europe. Those who saw them can never forget the tremendous impression of manliness, precision, and sheer physical power they conveyed. "The finest body of troops I have ever seen in my life," Pershing called them, and they undoubtedly were. With at least ninety American and regimental flags in their ranks, the blaze of color was breathtaking as they marched up the Avenue de la Grande Armée, through the Arc de Triomphe, down the Champs Elysées, by the Place de la Concorde, to the Boulevards and the Place de la République.[4]

Beside themselves with excitement, two million people cheered wildly, wave after wave of sound breaking over the boulevards along the seven-mile route. "It was a sight never to be forgotten . . . ," said Harbord. "There could have been nothing more impressive . . . ," said Pershing.[5]

Yes, there could. When the parade had passed, when the cheering had stopped, a long line of French civilians walked single file through the Arc de Triomphe, each silently dropping a single flower on the casket of the Unknown Soldier lying there. All afternoon they passed, and into the night—fathers, mothers, brothers, sisters, wives, sweethearts—commemorating their loved ones who would never be coming back. At the end the casket was covered with a mound of flowers. Lying there alone in the silent darkness, that flower-covered casket was the most impressive sight of the day.[6]

Five days later the superb Composite Regiment marched again in the London Victory Parade. Witnessing it in action, Winston Churchill reputedly commented, "What a magnificent body of men never to take another drink."[7]

In England Pershing received a sword of honor and the freedom of the City of London, honors which he took in good stride. A year earlier he had been knighted, but when Senator Warren somewhat facetiously began a letter with the words, "My dear Sir John!" Pershing responded, "Please have the goodness to forget it. . . . Such things . . . are undemocratic and unAmerican and run off my back like water off a duck."[8]

By the fall of 1919 the AEF was a shadow of its former self, with only a small force in Germany and a still smaller one in France. Pershing realized that the time had come to return home. As he prepared to leave, he remembered Memorial Day that year, the first since the war had ended. He had visited the little village of Beaumont where some 1,200 American soldiers, casualties of the Meuse-Argonne operation, lay buried. Walking down the long line of white crosses, he had encountered the village mayor and a group of small French children decorating the graves with wild flowers. In a few simple words the mayor had told him that the people would always care for the graves of these young men "sleeping so far away from their homes." Tears had rolled down Pershing's cheeks and, despite his troubles with Foch, he had answered that there were no people to whom he would rather entrust these comrades than "the dear people of France."[9]

That afternoon at Romagne, the largest American cemetery in Europe, where 10,000 were already buried and 4,200 more would later be added, Pershing had given a moving Memorial Day address. It was short, only two and one-half pages, but he had spent a whole day working on it, attempting to say in words what he felt so deeply inside: admiration for the soldier who had fallen, sorrow that he must be left behind. His peroration resembled Lincoln's Gettysburg Address:

Doughboys celebrating the Armistice. *National Archives*

Victory Parade in Paris, July 14, 1919. *National Archives*

"It is not for us to proclaim what they did, their silence speaks more eloquently than words, but it is for us to uphold the conception of duty, honor and country for which they fought and for which they died. It is for us the living to carry forward their purpose and make fruitful their sacrifice.

"And now, Dear Comrades, Farewell. Here, under the clear skies, on the green hillsides and amid the flowering fields of France, in the quiet hush of peace, we leave you forever in God's keeping."[10]

On September 1 Pershing embarked for home on the *Leviathan*, taking with him top AEF personnel and the Composite Regiment. In taking ship he realized that he was leaving behind the great episode of his life, one that would never be repeated and would exist henceforth only in memory. As Foch came aboard to say goodby, Pershing became deeply moved, forgetting for the moment all his disagreements with the marshal and remembering only all that they had been through together. "I never saw him show so much feeling . . . ," said Foch afterwards, much touched.[11]

Although Pershing knew that a tremendous reception awaited him upon his arrival back in America (which he frankly would have preferred to omit), even he was surprised by its magnitude. At 7:00 A.M. on September 8 he was awakened by the whistles and sirens of all manner of shipping which came out to accompany the *Leviathan* as it approached New York harbor. Tugs circled the great ship, tooting their horns and spraying jets of water wildly in the air. About 8:00 A.M. a destroyer came alongside bearing Secretary Baker, General March, Congressmen, and a number of former GHQ officers. Another vessel carried the Mayor of New York, Pershing's two sisters, his nephew, and the families of his officers, like Mrs. Fox Conner. Pershing was "frankly overwhelmed" at the size and enthusiasm of the welcome, as the *Leviathan*, the world's greatest ship, nosed its way toward Pier 4 amid tugs, destroyer escorts, water jets, overhead airplanes, salute guns, whistles, horns, and general pandemonium.[12]

Docking, Pershing met Secretary Baker, who led him to a small stand where he made a formal address of welcome and presented his commission as permanent general in the Regular Army. Pershing modestly replied that the reception was not for him alone, but "for all those Americans whom I had the honor to command."[13]

The presentation of Pershing's sword of permanent rank as a full general was the culmination of almost a year of political infighting. He had sailed for France in May 1917 as a major general (two stars) and in October 1917 had been promoted to full general (four stars) "for the period of the existing emergency only," which meant that he would revert to two-star rank when the emergency was over, that is, when the AEF went out of existence. Congress desired to reward him with a permanent full general commission, but balked when the Administration, in submitting Pershing's name for the honor, also submitted General March's, whom it disliked. When Pershing's name was read out, the entire House rose to its feet, applauding and cheering. When March's name was added, a number of Congressmen groaned, hurriedly took their seats, and called out, "No. No. Sit down, sit down."[14]

Many Congressmen had personal vendettas against March for his ruthless treatment of them. When one of them had asked for a draft exemption for a constituent, March had replied acidly, "I am here to get men across to France, not to keep them from going." There was no way that that Congressman would vote to honor March. Others, like Fiorello La Guardia, were simply ignorant of how important the Chief of Staff was in waging modern war. La Guardia protested against rewarding anyone with permanent high rank who had not earned it "on the field of battle"—as if Pershing, miles behind the front lines at Paris, Chaumont, Souilly, or Ligny, was any more in danger than March in Washington.[15]

Pershing showed little more appreciation for March's tremendous work than the Congressmen. When Senator Warren sent him a copy of Baker's letter to Sen. James Wadsworth, arguing that Pershing's and March's work was "complementary" and that "together they wrought the . . . victory," Pershing observed that Baker failed "to appreciate the relative importance" of each man's duties. Besides, he added, March came into office late and, while he did good work, the reward of permanent rank had traditionally been reserved "for actual service in the field, and I do not think the policy ought to be changed."[16]

Nor was it. Congress voted permanent rank for Pershing and refused it for March.

Pershing's commission, dated September 3, 1919, and signed by President Wilson before his ill-fated western tour, appointed him, not just "General," but "General of the Armies of the United States." In view of the fact that a general wears four stars and that the World War II commanders like Eisenhower, whose rank was "General of the Army," wore five stars, the question later arose whether Pershing was equivalently a six-star general, the only one in U.S. history? General of the *Armies*, it would seem, outranks General of the *Army*, just as an army group commander outranks an army commander.[17]

Actually, as Col. Frederick B. Wiener has conclusively demonstrated, "General of the Armies" was a purely personal, honorific title, and, in granting it, Congress meant only to appoint Pershing to the highest ranking position at that time, that is, general. For all practical purposes "General" and "General of the Armies" meant the same thing.[18]

New York City's Victory Parade took place on September 10: a three-hour procession of the 1st Division and the Composite Regiment from 110th Street to Washington Square. (By special permission, the officers wore their AEF Sam Browne belts.) Pershing was a magnificent sight on horseback before crowds which cast roses and laurel in front of his path. At a halt on 57th Street in front of St. Patrick's Cathedral, he dismounted to greet Belgium's Cardinal Mercier on its steps.[19]

Then followed a whirlwind of social and ceremonial events. Fifty thousand children greeted Pershing in Central Park, waving American flags. New York City extended him its freedom. Theater crowds rose to their feet at his entrance, applauding continuously and trying to shake his hand. Over two thousand telegrams arrived during his first few days in America, most from cities and clubs, asking that he visit them. His personal mail, most of which contained similar invitations, ran several hundred letters a day.[20]

The last great victory parade was in Washington, D.C., on September 17. A repetition of the New York experience, it was, in the words of Josephus Daniels, Secretary of the Navy, a tribute "such as the capitol had never seen." The following day a joint session of Congress formally tendered Pershing the nation's thanks. "We honor ourselves in honoring him," said Champ Clark, his fellow Missourian.[21]

Pershing replied with a short ten-minute speech, interrupted by applause over twenty-five times. The war experience had benefited America's citizen soldiers, he said. "They have returned in the full vigor of manhood, strong and clean. In the community of effort, men from all walks of life have learned to know and to appreciate each other. . . . They will bring into the life of our country a deeper love for our institutions and a more intelligent devotion to the duties of citizenship."[22]

For the next six weeks Pershing disappeared from view and had his first real rest in four years. He spent three weeks at William Cameron Forbes's estate on the island of Naushon, off Cape Cod, and then three further weeks at Brandreth, a 27,000-acre camp in the Adirondack wilderness which belonged to Fox Conner's father-in-law. Reaching camp at sunset, Pershing took one look at the placid lake reflecting the gorgeous sky, entered the old log house, threw down his hat and coat, and announced: "I'm never going back!"[23]

But he had to. Congress was holding hearings on the Army Reorganization Bill (called the Baker-March Bill), which provided for an army of approximately 500,000 men, and called for universal military training (UMT) for three months for all nineteen-year-olds. It provided for a strong General Staff, which would clearly dominate the bureaus, for promotion by selection, and for retention of new services created during the war, such as the Air Service, Tank Corps, Motor Transport Corps, and so forth. It did, however, abolish the Chemical Warfare Service, because of March's conviction that the use of gas was immoral.[24]

The bill aroused strong Congressional opposition, both for its UMT provision and for what many considered an excessively large standing army. Why, asked Sen. Hiram Johnson, "when we are facing an era of universal peace," should America have an army five times larger than ever before? Sen. Harry S. New of Indiana said: "It smacks too much of that very militarism which is righteously abhorrent to our national ideals and which we have denounced from every stump and housetop in the country." Sen. George E. Chamberlain called the bill "militarism run mad."[25]

During the fall of 1919 a whole procession of witnesses testified before the Senate and House Military Affairs Committees: Baker, March, Wood, Bullard, corps and division commanders, general staff officers, bureau chiefs, and enlisted men. Very few of them supported the War Department bill, but the most devastating criticism probably came during the two-day testimony of Col. John McAuley Palmer, who had been Pershing's Chief of Operations during the early months of the AEF. "In my opinion," said this respected military thinker, "the War Department bill proposes incomplete preparedness at excessive cost and under forms that are not in harmony with . . . American institutions."[26]

Although he was on vacation, Pershing closely followed the Congressional hearings, knowing he would be called upon for his own testimony. So great was his prestige, in fact, that Secretary Baker, in submitting the Army bill, refrained from formally endorsing it, since Pershing had not yet been consulted. He submitted it, he said, "only as the basis of hearings."[27]

In late October Pershing returned to Washington and spent two days interviewing some twenty bureau chiefs and General Staff officers in order to orient himself for his own testimony which, he knew, would have great weight. He also knew that the Baker-March bill was, for all practical purposes, dead.[28]

On October 31, with George C. Marshall, Jr., and Fox Conner sitting by his side, Pershing began a three-day testimony before the House and Senate Military Affairs Committee. The House Office Building Caucus Room was crowded, as Congressmen, absent from other meetings, came for this special occasion to hear what the General of the Armies had to say.

Pershing opened with a prepared statement, the very first paragraphs of which opposed the Baker-March bill. "In discussing preparedness it is to be remembered that our traditions are opposed to the maintenance of a large standing army." Arguing that a large standing army would cost too much, he proposed an army of 275,000 or 300,000—virtually half the size of that suggested by the War Department.[29]

Like John McAuley Palmer, whose views he implicitly endorsed, he envisaged a small professional army whose task would be to train a large civilian reserve force. "Our wars have practically all been fought by citizen soldiery," he said. Accordingly, he proposed six months' universal military training.[30]

Universal military training was about as popular as the plague and brought Pershing under some sharp, albeit respectful, questioning. One senator pointed out that in the recent war America had trained soldiers in approximately three months, not six. Why then this elaborate scheme for drafting everyone, disrupting their lives, against the possible contingency of another war? Another remarked that the costs of training such large numbers of men would probably approximate the cost of the large standing army which Pershing opposed.[31]

Speaking to the first objection, Pershing said: "I would emphasize . . . the educational and school features of this system more than I would the military features. We are now confronted with serious social problems resulting from the presence of large masses [of] ignorant foreigners in our midst, who are highly susceptible to . . . bolshevic proposals. . . . Universal military training is the only means I see available for educating this foreign element. . . ." As to the cost, Pershing admitted that he had not given that matter much thought.[32]

Reading Pershing's testimony, one gains the impression that, despite his following the hearings during vacation and despite his many interviews just before his own testimony, Pershing had not thought very deeply about Army reorganization. His lack of any idea about what a program of universal military training would cost is a case in point. Sen. James W. Wadsworth rated Pershing's testimony behind that of John McAuley Palmer, John F. O'Ryan, and Leonard Wood, and added: "We gathered the impression that he... had not had time to study the problem thoroughly...."[33]

But his basic approach, for what it was, was closer to Palmer than March: reliance on a citizen army rather than a large professional one, which Congress, in its present financial mood, would never endorse. If Palmer had delivered the death blow to the Baker-March bill, Pershing buried it.[34]

THIRTY

Marking Time

(December 1919-June 1920)

ONCE PERSHING FINISHED his vacation, Secretary Baker was somewhat at a loss to know what to do with him. Theoretically, he
remained still an overseas commander, with AEF headquarters no
longer in Paris or Chaumont, but in Washington, ten blocks away
from the War Department. But with the AEF ever diminishing,
it was only a question of time before he would be a commander without any
troops to command.[1]

Temporarily, the Secretary solved the problem by giving Pershing special proj-
ects to do, such as writing up the AEF final report. For this project he was given
office space and clerical assistance at the Old Land Office Building at 7th and E
Streets, and the retention of key staff officers like Davis, Connor, Brewster, and
Marshall, who helped in the writing.

Issued in December 1919, Pershing's *Final Report* was dull and impersonal,
a disappointment to anyone who hoped for a close, intimate view of the war as
seen by the American high commander. It lacked life, warmth, color, and names.
One reviewer noted that in ninety-five pages Pershing mentioned only ten officers,
whereas U. S. Grant, in a report almost twenty pages shorter, mentioned seventy-
six. Unpleasant events like Seicheprey were not mentioned, while heroic ones like
Ulysses G. McAlexander's 38th Regiment's stand as the "Rock of the Marne"
were treated impersonally—no mention of McAlexander or the 38th—it was just
"a regiment." New weapons like tanks and airplanes received hardly a mention,
being confined to two short paragraphs in a section entitled "Supply, Coordination,
Munitions, and Administration." In fact, religious activities got about as much
space as tanks and planes combined.[2]

When the *Final Report* was completed, Baker next suggested an inspection
trip of U.S. cantonments and military establishments for the purpose of recommending which should be retained and which closed. Besides giving Pershing something to do, the trip would open his eyes to what had been done in America in
his absence.

Starting in Washington and zigzagging across the country through thirty-two states, the trip lasted from early December to mid-February. With Pershing went many of his old AEF standbys: Nolan, Conner, Moseley, Davis, Brewster, plus aides like Marshall, Quekemeyer, and Edward Bowditch, and assistants like Ralph A. Curtin, J. Thomas Schneider, and George Adamson. Malin Craig joined en route.[3]

At each army post Pershing and his staff inspected the troops, physical plant, hospital and recreational facilities, and terrain for training and maneuvers. Fay W. Brabson, former Chief of Staff of the 88th Division in France and then executive officer at Camp Jackson, South Carolina, was struck by "the meticulous interest" Pershing showed in supply arrangements, training schedules, and the troops themselves. "In particular, General Pershing liked our idea of Americanization: of placing boys of different states in the same tent."[4]

In many instances Pershing found training and morale poor. Pay was low, housing bad, and installations considerably understaffed, causing extra paper work for officers and extra guard duty for men. In some instances noncommissioned officers (NCOs) were doing sentry duty; in one case a second lieutenant was standing guard. The famous 2d Division was down to 2,000 men and having trouble getting recruits.[5]

Pershing's visit to Fort Benning, Georgia, coincided with a tremendous deluge of rain which, in the post's history, became known as "The Pershing Flood." When he returned three years later and another deluge did too, he remarked that Benning might be a good place to locate a combined army-navy school.[6]

Besides being an inspection, the trip was also a sort of triumphal tour for America's hero, with parades, receptions, and speeches in major cities, in which Pershing preached preparedness and the need for universal military training. Speaking was not his strong point, and after one of his efforts a veteran came up close and whispered in his ear, "General, you fight better than you speak."[7]

Perhaps that is why he later adopted a clever tactic at a Williams College luncheon for honorary degree recipients, at which one would normally be required to speak. When introduced, he stood up, waited calmly until the ovation subsided, and then silently, without a word, gave one of his snappiest West Point salutes and immediately sat down. Said Dorothy Canfield Fisher who beheld it: "Then you had better believe the audience applauded! They took the roof off!"[8]

Because each community wanted to treat Pershing royally, he and his staff soon discovered that they were eating the same banquet meal over and over: chicken (which was considered the luxury of that day) and thousand island dressing (which was apparently the "in" thing), served at a head table presided over by local "big shots" and their overweight wives. When one community wrote ahead to ask if Pershing had any special requests, Marshall wired back an emphatic YES. "Do not have chicken or thousand island dressing and go fifty-fifty with pretty girls at speakers table." Said Moseley afterwards: "They had steak, and every other girl at the speakers table was a knockout."[9]

Parades, receptions, dinners, speeches, ceremonies—all can get pretty head-turning, especially if they go on for almost three months. But Pershing kept his feet on the ground. "The accolades that continued to be piled upon him never puffed up his ego," said J. Thomas Schneider.[10]

On the trip Pershing impressed both his staff and the public with his graciousness, tact, modesty, and affability. "This isn't to be a formal occasion," he said at a Daughters of the American Revolution meeting in Lincoln, Nebraska, as he moved easily around the room meeting old friends and new. He conversed easily with a cub reporter in Charleston, S.C., and pushed his way through a crowd at Fort Lewis, Washington, to greet a veteran whose First Army overcoat he recognized. In Laclede, Missouri, his hometown, he left $150.00 to be distributed to old Negro friends he had grown up with.[11]

Particularly was he good with children. One little girl in Chillicothe, Ohio, remembered Pershing's reaction when someone introduced her as "the little girl whose mother is so ill." With that "the General bent down and kissed me on the cheek, and removed a white carnation from his lapel and gave it to me." She saved the flower for the rest of her life.[12]

On another occasion, while traveling with Governor Milliken of Maine on an automobile tour of eleven counties, they saw up ahead of them on the road a little country schoolhouse with children outside holding flags.

"Are we going to stop there?" inquired the general.

"We hadn't planned on it," responded the governor.

"I guess we'd better stop. They're expecting us," said Pershing.[13]

With the exhausting inspection trip behind him, Pershing wrote a report, dated March 23, 1920, listing those military installations he thought most important to retain. In it he also recommended a decrease in paper work and the skeletonizing of certain units in order to increase personnel in others, supported the growth of ROTC in both colleges and high schools, recommended increased pay for officers and NCOs, suggested improved housing facilities, and advocated adjustment of rank to correct the recent demotions whereby junior officers retained emergency rank over former AEF officers.[14]

Indeed, promotions still remained a sore point with Pershing. Hugh Drum, Stuart Heintzelman, and Malin Craig, all brigadier generals during the war as Chiefs of Staff of the First, Second, and Third Armies respectively, all decorated by the British, French, and Belgium governments, all key men in the AEF success, had been busted down to majors. So also had Preston Brown, commander of the 3d Division, whom Pershing had recommended, less than a month before the armistice, for promotion to major general. He was now ranked by 23 major generals, 42 brigadier generals, 1,200 colonels, and 1,224 lieutenant colonels—none of whom had ever commanded a division in combat. Dennis E. Nolan, formerly a brigadier general and AEF G-2, was now also a major, ranked by a colonel on duty in the War Department who had been relieved from Nolan's office for inefficiency.[15]

Meanwhile, Congress had been debating the bill on army reorganization, attempting to work out a substitute for the now defunct Baker-March bill. Although both March and Pershing had called for universal military training (UMT), this seemed less and less appealing as Congressmen heard from their constituents. UMT cost money, threatened to "prussianize" America, interfered with people's lives, and might worsen America's already troubled race relations. "I know nothing so irresponsible," asserted a Virginia Congressman, "as a young negro boy rigged out in brass buttons and with a gun." When rumors circulated that the Democrats were about to drop UMT and might make an issue of it in the coming election, Republicans abandoned it too. They simply could not afford to be associated with this albatross.[16]

As finally passed and signed by the President on June 4, 1920, the new bill (The National Defense Act) provided for an army of almost 300,000 men, precisely what Pershing had called for. But he envisaged this army as a training force for a larger citizen army which would be provided by UMT, and in eliminating this provision, Congress had emasculated the integral military policy advocated by Palmer and Pershing. As a makeshift substitute, the War Department authorized the establishment of training centers where "volunteers" might come and be instructed by a Regular Army cadre. But in practice the volunteers were not forthcoming, the training centers were expensive (especially when trainees were lacking to train), and in time the army itself, hard pressed by budget cuts, recommended that they be dropped.[17]

By accepting one part of the Palmer-Pershing scheme (a small regular army whose main purpose would be the training of a citizen reserve) and rejecting the other (universal military training, to provide the reserve), Congress created an anomaly—a military structure, sound in principle, resting ultimately on a body of trained citizens, but eliminating the only sure means of providing that body. In practice, therefore, as historian Forrest C. Pogue has remarked, "The Army lost its position at the core of a citizen organization and reverted to a skeleton combat force which in case of war would again have to try to flesh itself out largely with another generation of raw recruits."[18]

A sign of the times and a token of what was to come was the army appropriation bill for 1920. Although Congress had debated extensively and in its wisdom finally authorized an army of almost 300,000, it appropriated funds to maintain fewer than 200,000. In subsequent years funds were further reduced. The training centers were dropped. National Guard units, dependent on federal funds, languished for want of equipment and training. Despite the high hopes of Palmer, Pershing, and others for effective army reorganization, the military establishment, as D. Clayton James has remarked, was by 1922 "almost worthless even as a nucleus for mobilization."[19]

By the spring of 1920 the problem of what to do with Pershing had become acute. The once great AEF was winding down into oblivion. In Germany only sixteen thousand men remained as an occupation army under Gen. Henry T. Allen. In Washington Pershing commanded the AEF General Headquarters (twenty-six officers beside himself), but this arrangement was scheduled for extinction by the fall.[20]

That Pershing should serve under General March in the War Department was unthinkable. Not only were the two men temperamentally incompatible, but March, because Congress had refused to make permanent his emergency rank as general, was now outranked by Pershing, two stars to four.[21]

The logical solution, one proposed to Secretary Baker by Harbord as early as April 1919, by President Wilson in June, and by Senator Wadsworth's colleagues in January 1920, was to make Pershing the Army Chief of Staff. It was also the solution Pershing himself wanted.[22]

Baker opposed this. He was loyal to March, whom he felt had served well and had been badly treated by Congress, as indeed he had been. March's term had only one more year to run under the Wilson administration; if Pershing were appointed now, the next president might not choose to continue him in office. Furthermore, Pershing might *be* the next president.[23]

The solution, it seemed to Baker, was to keep Pershing on active duty status, available to advise the President or the Secretary of War, with most of his time free to write "the final history" of the war and thus "preserve the experience of this war for our future guidance."[24]

No writer, Pershing was not happy with the suggestion and prepared to return to private life. He was not sure what he would do, but he did have a law degree, earned while Professor of Military Science at the University of Nebraska in 1893, and although he had never practiced, the name *Pershing* would grace any big New York law firm. Offers in this direction were not wanting.[25]

On June 7, 1920, Pershing wrote Baker that he planned to resign from the army sometime within the next few months in order "to engage in something more active." The timing of the letter, released to the public at the very moment when the Republican Convention in Chicago appeared to be deadlocked, led some newspapers to speculate that the general was standing tall in hopes that presidential lightning might strike him. Be that as it may (and this will be considered shortly), the fact remains that Pershing's position was indeed, as he put it, "peculiar," and that, as Forrest C. Pogue has remarked, he had "come to the end of the period when he could plausibly function as a quasi-independent field commander."[26]

THIRTY-ONE

Pershing for President

(1920)

U P UNTIL WORLD WAR I every major American conflict had catapulted a military hero into the presidency. The Revolutionary War had given America President George Washington; the War of 1812, Andrew Jackson and William Henry Harrison; the Mexican War, Zachary Taylor; the Civil War, U. S. Grant; the Spanish-American War, Theodore Roosevelt; and, looking ahead, World War II, Dwight D. Eisenhower. By all the laws of probability, therefore, Pershing should have been elected president in 1920.[1]

Pershing could not have been unaware of this, nor could his politically astute father-in-law, Senator Warren. Quite literally, from the moment Pershing set foot in Europe in June 1917, newspapers began printing stories about him as a future presidential possibility.[2]

Immediately, the Senator warned him about being beguiled. "Don't let the Presidential bug get to boring into your topknot, as it is sometimes worse than moths, caterpillars, and other things that make a bad mess of things. If it ever does come, let it come entirely unexpectedly, and let it make you feel and say, like the prudish girl when the question is popped, 'This is so sudden! I am terribly surprised!' "[3]

The Senator's sentiments were very much Pershing's own. "I should consider myself very much of an ass if I gave it one moment's consideration," he replied in July 1917. "I am here expressly to carry out the wishes of the President and the administration to the best of my mediocre ability. . . . If I fail, it will not be because I have any bug in my head." Privately, he asked the Senator to do all he could to discount such "perfectly ridiculous" talk and to let both the Secretary of War and the President know he deplored it.[4]

Throughout the war, both publicly and privately, Pershing disclaimed any political ambitions. Stating that in wartime all Americans should patriotically sacrifice petty politicking, and knowing that any political talk could only hurt him with the administration, he said, "I am for President Wilson until the end of this war and as long thereafter as he wants to be President."[5]

After the armistice, like flowers popping out of the ground following the spring rains, a new crop of presidential rumors burst forth. The International News Service wanted to know Pershing's political affiliation. The Republican Publicity Association invited his views on public questions. The former governor of Texas boosted Pershing for the presidency. A prominent Minneapolis Republican was confident Minnesota would go for Pershing at the national convention. The Vice-President of the National Republican League foresaw Pershing winning all but ten states in 1920 and doing for the Republican Party what General Grant had done for it after the Civil War. In Akron, Ohio, ex-Senator Charles Dick announced plans to form the Pershing Republican League to work for his nomination and election. Going him one better, ex-Senator Elmer J. Burkett, an old friend and a member of Pershing's law class of 1893, called for *both* parties to nominate the AEF commander. "Everybody wants to vote for him . . . ," he asserted.[6]

Again, Senator Warren counseled Pershing to sit tight. "Do not let your head get swelled. Do not invest extravagantly your funds, your talents, or your imagination. . . . As the Irish say, 'Far off cows wear long horns.' "[7]

Again, Pershing took the advice. Both publicly and privately, he repeatedly stated that while he appreciated friends' interest, he had no political ambitions and had more than enough to do in Europe overseeing demobilization of the AEF. His disclaimers, however, were undercut by his brother Jim, a businessman who, impelled by family pride and a sense of his own importance, publicly touted him for president. Pershing pleaded with him to stop. When he did not, when he accepted an invitation to be the main speaker in Cincinnati during its "Pershing Day," the general wrote him angrily on December 27, 1918:

"May the good Lord deliver us from fool friends and more foolish relatives. . . . I am not a candidate for anything and don't expect to be, but if I were, with you running around the country like a blatant ass making speeches whenever some bunch of advertisers desire to have you do so, it would not be long before we should all go the the scrap heap as a family of fools. . . . If you want to ruin my reputation as a soldier you couldn't go about it in a better way. . . . Oh, I am perfectly furious about it, after all the talking I have done. If you were here, this is not one-tenth of what I would say. . . . I ask you again to comply with my request and do not accept these invitations and keep your mouth shut."[8]

Senator Warren also did what he could to bank the fires on any Pershing boom. He told Charles Dick that Pershing had "several times assured him in the strongest language" that he "could not and would not be a candidate for the presidency, nor could he accept the nomination," as he had no ambitions except along military lines.[9]

Meanwhile, another soldier, Leonard Wood, was running hard for the nomination, spreading the word that Pershing was unpopular with his men. George Patton feared for Pershing if Wood's bid was successful. "You will command the Island of Guam," he predicted ruefully.[10]

Pershing thought Wood's election unlikely, but realized that his candidacy was a real danger because, even if he did not gain the nomination, he might have sufficient influence at the convention to bargain for a position in the new administration like Secretary of War or Chief of Staff. And if that happened, Pershing might well find himself exiled to Guam.[11]

It was therefore a politically wary Pershing who returned to the United States on the *Leviathan* in September 1919. Several days before his arrival Representative Guy E. Campbell had stood up in Congress during the voting which gave Pershing his permanent commission as general and said: "I would like to see the people of this country and this House put aside our partisanship . . . and make him the unanimous choice of the conventions that assemble next year and elect him President of the United States." The House applauded.[12]

Back in America, Pershing maintained a discreet silence, following the advice of both Senator Warren and Colonel House. When people popped the inevitable question, "Would you accept the nomination if it is offered?" he dodged and replied, "I never yet have accepted anything that was not offered me."[13]

Charlie Dawes, who knew Pershing better than nearly anyone, said in October that he saw practically no signs that the general was afflicted with the "political itch." In December, when an old friend named Sally Frier asked if he were going to run for president, Pershing answered, "Sally, do you think I'm a damned fool?"[14]

Down deep, however, despite all external disclaimers, Pershing felt an attraction for the presidency, although he was reluctant to show it unless the honor seemed reasonably within grasp. Possessed of a strong sense of dignity, he feared to repeat the mistakes of Adm. George Dewey after the Spanish-American War, who campaigned greedily and ended up looking ridiculous. But Pershing had been ambitious all his life and it is unlikely that he would not be attracted to this most ambitious of all American offices. As he had written to Senator Warren earlier, "If, when a time comes, there should be an [*sic*] unanimous demand over the country for such a thing, I do not see how any man can decline it."[15]

He was probably secretly glad, therefore, when old Nebraska hands like Dawes, Burkett, and Mark Woods decided to boom him for president as Nebraska's favorite son. In December Woods formed a "Pershing for President Club" and a "Nebraska University Alumni Pershing for President Association." Later a "Soldiers and Sailors for Pershing Club" was organized in Omaha. Woods predicted a fifth ballot victory in the Republican Convention.[16]

These events coincided with Pershing's inspection tour from December 1919 to February 1920. With the cheers of Victory Parades in New York and Washington recently in mind, with his Final Report written and the inspection trip coming to an end, with Baker opposing his appointment as Chief of Staff, and with no suitable or congenial work on the horizon which would engage his energies, Pershing began seriously to nibble at the bait his Nebraska friends were dangling before him.

The circumstances made it almost irresistible: a triumphal tour through most of the states during an election year, royal receptions by large and enthusiastic crowds, his picture and speeches splashed across the front pages and on newsreel screens. By the time he reached Camp Lewis in Washington State in January, he was kissing babies, an action entirely out of character. When a political delegation came from Tennessee and George Marshall, Jr., on his own sent them back home, Pershing's anger revealed how deeply he had been bitten by the political bug.[17]

When the inspection trip ended, Pershing returned to Washington still saying that he was "not a candidate for any important public office," but privately hoping that the call would come. He turned over his extensive scrapbooks to Frank Barrow, who planned to write a series of articles favoring him. Meanwhile, his Nebraska friends kept up their campaign of press releases, newspaper advertisements, and heavy mailings (reputedly as high as 200,000 letters)—all looking to capture delegates for the general in the April 20 Nebraska primary.[18]

Unfortunately, approximately ten days before that date, Michigan held her primary and a small group, against the wishes of Pershing's Nebraska backers, entered his name on the ballot. With no state organization or campaign, he did poorly, coming in a distant fifth behind Hiram Johnson, Leonard Wood, Frank Lowden, and Herbert Hoover. His 18,000 votes were only one-third of what Hoover got, and Hoover was fourth![19]

A few days later, concluding that he would never reach the altar if he acted too much like a reluctant virgin, Pershing finally spoke out. Addressing a Washington, D.C. reception given in his honor by the Nebraska Society on April 14, he said of the presidency: "While in no sense seeking it, I feel that no patriotic American could decline to serve in that high position if called to do so by the people." *The Washington Post* printed the announcement on page one: "PERSHING WILL RUN IF HE IS NOMINATED." It was not quite accurate. Pershing was not running; but he was quite willing to be caught, that is, to be drafted.[20]

Any likelihood of this received a dramatic setback on April 20 when results came in from the Nebraska primary. Of the state's 93 counties, only Lancaster (Lincoln) went to Pershing, and by the slimmest of pluralities, 35 percent. Hiram Johnson carried the state with 47 percent of the vote, Leonard Wood was second with 32 percent, and Pershing, "Nebraska's Favorite Son," had only 21 percent.[21]

The election was a disaster, the result of a combination of factors: Pershing's reluctance to campaign openly, his support of an unpopular cause like universal military training, a poorly managed campaign run by amateurs, and a general public which was fed up with war and austerity and was much more concerned with local issues and a desire for "normalcy."[22]

That same week a *Literary Digest* poll, reporting early returns on an extended mail canvass of eleven million voters, showed Pershing running well behind eight Republican leaders. In subsequent weeks he did even poorer. Final count gave him only 13,660 votes, less than one-twentieth the total of the front-runner, Leonard Wood.[23]

His candidacy now completely dead, Pershing went off to Panama during May for a brief inspection trip of the Canal Zone. Despite the Michigan and Nebraska primary disasters and the *Literary Digest* poll, he still remained hopeful, convinced through letters and other contacts that, in the event of a deadlock, the convention might turn to him. He considered this "more than a possibility" and urged Dawes to have someone ready "at the proper time to spring it."[24]

On June 7, the day before the convention opened, he cut short a tour of Maine, returned to Washington, and wrote the letter to Secretary Baker which was mentioned in the previous chapter. Promptly issued to the press, the letter stated that he planned to resign from the army and "return to civil life."[25]

The Republican convention met in Chicago and, as Pershing had hoped, deadlocked, with Leonard Wood, Frank Lowden, and Hiram Johnson as the chief contenders. But Pershing's name was never "sprung" on the convention and, after ten ballots, the weary delegates nominated Warren G. Harding.

For Pershing, the result was bittersweet. Although disappointed at his own personal loss, he rejoiced at the defeat of Leonard Wood. "The victory is ours," he telegraphed Dawes. "I die content."[26]

Except with people like Dawes, who knew better, Pershing continued to maintain the fiction that he had never had political ambitions in 1920. "The political situation is entirely to my satisfaction," he wrote a friend after Harding's nomination. "As you know I never wished to be in political life and never shall. I did object to some others posing as saviors of the world, but . . . I always remember that The Savior appeared about two thousand years ago, and all the rest of the so-called saviors, including some of our particular acquaintances, have been mere pikers."[27]

Serving as marshal of President Harding's inaugural parade on March 4, 1921, Pershing was deeply moved at the pitiable condition of the outgoing president, Woodrow Wilson. He hobbled over to a chair with the greatest difficulty. His eyes, pain-glazed, glared at bystanders like a wounded eagle's. Pershing called it "the most pitiable and tragic spectacle that I have ever in my life witnessed." Wilson, once so vigorous and commanding, once considered a demigod by millions, was now "entirely and completely broken."[28]

When the Republicans came back into power in 1921, rumors circulated that Pershing would be offered some important new position like a cabinet post or ambassadorship. The obvious post, and the one he wanted, Chief of Staff, was precluded when the new Secretary of War, John W. Weeks, decided to retain General March in that position, at least for the time.[29]

Faced with this situation, Pershing and his friends began to think of creating an entirely new office for him, that of Commanding General of the Army, a post supposedly abolished by Elihu Root in 1903 when he created the General Staff. Secretary Weeks went along with the idea and on April 21, 1921, announced that Pershing would command an Army GHQ, wholly separate from March's General Staff, having its own Chief of Staff, assistant chiefs, and bureau representatives. It would be charged with preparing war plans and would be ready to take the field instantly in time of war.[30]

There was something to be said for the idea, but not much. Before the war Marshal Joffre had prepared a skeleton headquarters which took the field instantly and was of some value. But the scheme created more difficulties than it solved, as even so staunch a partisan as Harbord pointed out to Pershing:

"The Chief of Staff is charged under the law with certain of the things you suggest that a G.H.Q. should undertake. . . . If the law were changed it would so minimize the position of Chief of Staff that the right sort of man would not wish to accept the position, for it is easy to see that it would mean that you and the

G.H.Q. would run the Army except as to purely administrative and supply functions in the War Department. It is wrong in principle to change an organic law to fit an individual case."[31]

Harbord was right. On May 13, 1921, Secretary Weeks concluded that it was better to appoint the man for the job than create the job for the man, and took the obvious step. He appointed Pershing Chief of Staff.[32]

THIRTY-TWO

Chief of Staff

(1921–1924)

ETTLED IN AT the War Department with Harbord as his executive assistant on July 1, 1921, Pershing promptly made it over in the image of the AEF. Within one week he ordered all officers to wear the Sam Browne belt—symbol of the overseas officer. He abolished General March's General Staff organization and replaced it with the AEF system: G-1 (Personnel), G-2 (Intelligence), G-3 (Operations), G-4 (Training), and a War Plans Division, which was charged with preparing plans in peace and executing them as a field army headquarters in war. He made it quite clear that in any future wars it would be the field commander and not the Chief of Staff in Washington who was superior.[1]

The command arrangement that Pershing established as Chief of Staff was quite anomalous. In peacetime he conceived of his office as exempt from routine military administration, which devolved upon the Deputy Chief of Staff, Harbord, who, interesting to note, occupied not his own office, but the old Chief of Staff office of General March. Pershing, Chief of Staff in name, occupied a massive three-room suite in another part of the State-War-and-Navy Building (the "General of the Armies" office), where his work was to oversee broad questions of military policy. In wartime, however, he would immediately take the field as commander of the field army, as in the AEF, with the War Plans Division as his ready-to-go general headquarters.

In effect, then, Pershing envisaged himself as two different men with two different functions, depending on the circumstances: Chief of Staff (in name, but not function) in time of peace; commanding general of a field army (in both name and function) in time of war. Since by law the Chief of Staff was the head of the army, Pershing was supreme whether in Washington or overseas. As Deputy Chief of Staff, Harbord remained subordinated to him, even though he sat in the Chief of Staff's office and did the Chief of Staff's work.

It was an awkward arrangement, totally unsuited to a multi-theater World War II type conflict, which scrapped it, but reflecting the World War I single-theater experience and Pershing's belief that the field commander was supreme over the Chief of Staff in Washington.[2]

Taking over the War Department in 1921, Pershing inherited a controversial superintendent of West Point, Brig. Gen. Douglas MacArthur. Appointed in June 1919 with orders to "revitalize and revamp the Academy," MacArthur had moved mightily to do just that. During the war he had been dismayed by what he considered an unhealthy rigidity in a number of West Point graduates in dealing with citizen soldiers. Like March, who appointed him, he believed that the Academy was years behind the times, and he meant to do what he could to help it catch up—fast.

The result was a series of whirlwind changes touching all aspects of the Academy from the curriculum to sports, all designed to liberalize cadet life. They were based on MacArthur's conviction that military education must be less parochial, more oriented toward the social sciences, producing officers more acquainted with the civilian world and thus better able to understand and lead the civilian soldiers of the future.[3]

Not surprisingly, a howl of outrage arose from the conservatives, both faculty and alumni. One alumnus, Mark L. Hersey, wrote Pershing of the poor impression he had received during graduation week, when grounds were "unkempt and littered" and cadet officers appeared in bathrobes and "all sorts of nondescript dress. One man reported out as naked as he was born wearing only a feather fan that he had accumulated from his best girl the night before." While admitting that such conduct might be merely graduation exuberance and not typical, Hersey still shook his head. Discipline was not what it had been in the good old days.[4]

Pershing, who inclined to be conservative, had heard reports like this for some time. Soon after assuming office, he informed MacArthur that this would be his last year as superintendent, giving as his reason that he was due for overseas service. As his successor he appointed Brig. Gen. Fred W. Sladen who tried, not completely successfully, to turn the clock back on a number of the changes MacArthur had made.

Because Sladen was a conservative, some people interpreted his appointment as Pershing's attempt to undo MacArthur's West Point reforms. Such was not necessarily the case. Like MacArthur, Pershing personally felt that previous Academy training had been too narrow, not allowing sufficient contact with the civilian world with which graduates would have to deal. He wrote Sladen in 1923, "I hope as liberal an attitude may be taken as is consistent with the high standard of discipline which we wish to maintain."[5]

Pershing's relations with MacArthur were complicated by the fact that just two weeks before the War Department announced that MacArthur's term at West Point would end and he would go overseas, the latter had become engaged to Mrs. Louise Cromwell Brooks, a woman with whom gossip connected Pershing romantically.

The daughter of Oliver E. Cromwell, a rich New York lawyer and yachtsman, and the stepdaughter of Edward T. Stotesbury, a Philadelphia banker whose fortune reputedly exceeded one hundred million dollars, Louise had known Pershing during the war when she and her husband, Walter Brooks, a wealthy Baltimore contractor, lived in Paris. Charming, attractive, and witty, she was a natural partner and Pershing, who liked good-looking women, enjoyed having her around.

In 1919 her marriage foundered and thereafter she was courted by Colonel John G. (Harry) Quekemeyer, Pershing's handsome bachelor aide. Since she served at times as Pershing's hostess when he returned to Washington after the war, and since the General was himself perhaps the world's most eligible bachelor, loose-tongued people spoke of an impending marriage.

Nothing could have been more unlikely. Physically attractive, Louise was also unstable. Just one week before she announced she would marry MacArthur, she told Quekemeyer that she would marry him. During her lifetime she had four husbands, one of whom was Lionel Atwill.[6]

On January 14, 1922, Louise announced her engagement to MacArthur, and on January 30, two weeks later, Pershing announced MacArthur's assignment to the Philippines. Jumping to conclusions, shallow-minded people said that Pershing was "exiling" MacArthur because he had beaten his time with the same girl.[7]

Scatterbrained, Louise fostered such rumors by foolish statements. "Jack wanted me to marry him. When I wouldn't, he wanted me to marry one of his colonels. I wouldn't do that—so here I am packing my trunks."[8]

There is not a word of truth in this. On November 22, 1921, almost two full months before Louise announced her engagement, Pershing had written Mac-Arthur: "I am writing now to advise you that at the end of the present school year [1921-1922] you will be available for a tour of service beyond the limits of the United States."[9]

As Forrest C. Pogue has pointed out, such foreign service was regularly required of officers, and MacArthur was number one on the list. The following year Pershing sent his former aide, George C. Marshall, Jr., to China under the same rule, without anyone suggesting that Marshall was somehow being punished or "exiled." Regular service overseas (usually Hawaii, the Philippines, China, or the Canal Zone) was standard War Department practice for officers.[10]

Queried about MacArthur's supposed exile, Pershing answered in exasperation, "It's all damn poppycock without the slightest foundation and based on the idlest gossip.... If I were married to all the ladies to whom the gossips have engaged me I would be a regular Brigham Young."[11]

Pershing must have thanked his lucky stars not to be married to such a vexatious woman and probably wondered how long MacArthur could get on with her. In point of fact, the marriage broke up in about seven years.[12]

One might mention here that Pershing's relations with MacArthur throughout life were externally cordial, but not overly friendly. He spoke well of MacArthur, once telling Bernard Baruch that he was "the greatest commander of troops we had." Although he opposed MacArthur's appointment as Chief of Staff in 1930, that was because he had his own candidate, Fox Conner, whom he unsuccessfully pushed for the job. He appreciated MacArthur's stand before a Senate Hearing on government economy in 1933, in which the Chief of Staff defended Pershing's special pension of $18,000 a year, pointing out that his British counterpart, Sir Douglas Haig, received almost $40,000 a year, plus a family trust fund of $500,000 through three generations. In 1942 MacArthur offered Pershing's son Warren a place on his staff.[13]

On the other hand, Pershing could never bring himself to accept what he considered a certain amount of posturing in MacArthur: the corncob pipe, the crumpled cap, the nonregulation uniform, the hand in the pocket. MacArthur's excessive ego, so obvious later in his *Reminiscences*, could not but repel him. Corinna Lindon Smith recalled a social event at which both men were present, with MacArthur monopolizing the conversation. When the event was over and the others had left, Pershing turned to her and asked, not in harshness but in amused amazement, "Was anybody else in the war?"[14]

Probably the best way to express the relationship between the two men is to say that Pershing respected MacArthur professionally, but disliked him personally.[15]

Pershing served as Chief of Staff from 1921 to 1924. Although he took no important part in the Washington Disarmament Conference of 1921–1922, which was primarily naval, he had strong feelings about disarmament, provided it was mutual. The lessons of the previous decade, he said, ought to convince everyone of the folly "of nations striding up and down the earth armed to the teeth." Unless something is done, he said presciently, "we may well ask ourselves whether civilization does really reach a point where it begins to destroy itself." At the conference he urged outlawing chemical warfare, calling it a "cruel, unfair and improper use of science."[16]

Part of his duties as Chief of Staff were ceremonial. In 1921 he marched behind the caisson of the Unknown Soldier, as the body was taken to Arlington National Cemetery for interment there. That same year he journeyed to France to lay the Congressional Medal of Honor on the tomb of France's Unknown Soldier.

Probably his main task, however, was to serve as the Army's spokesman in combating the postwar surge of pacifism. In personal correspondence, in magazine articles, in testimony before Congressional committees, and in speeches to private groups, he labored, as he put it, to keep the army's body and soul together and to stave off further manpower cuts.[17]

Asserting that no "blind belief in the benevolence of peoples will prevent wars," he called for "reasonable preparedness." He pointed out that the American army had been engaged in some kind of military operation every eighteen months of its existence, and in a major war every twenty or thirty years. "Is human nature going to change?" he asked. "Are conditions in the world any different from what they have been in the last fifteen or twenty centuries? Are wars becoming less frequent or any less severe?"[18]

He was fighting a losing battle. After all, "the war to end all wars" was over, the world had been made safe for democracy, and many Congressmen thought the army superfluous, except for riot duty. Said William M. Wright, former commander of the 89th Division: "The Army is like a yellow dog running down the street with a tin can tied on it, and everybody on the sidewalk throwing rocks." Despite Pershing's great personal popularity, said George C. Marshall, Jr., "I saw the Army . . . start rapidly on the downgrade to almost extinction. . . . His views didn't count at all."[19]

The problem was money. An economy-minded Congress, responding to the public mood, voted cuts, cuts, and more cuts. Although authorized an enlisted strength of 280,000, the Regular Army was reduced successively to 175,000, 150,000, 125,000, and in Pershing's last year as Chief of Staff about 111,000—only 11,000 more than the Treaty of Versailles allowed a conquered and disarmed Germany.[20]

It was not Pershing's fault. Washington, Grant, Sherman, Sheridan, and Pershing combined could not have altered matters, given the mood of the country and the Congress.

Faced with drastic manpower cuts which clearly made carrying out the 1920 army reorganization plan (National Defense Act) impossible, Pershing received conflicting advice from two of his closest advisers. John McAuley Palmer urged him to cut down the number of Regular Army divisions, but keep them at full strength, ready for immediate service in an emergency. He also advised keeping the training centers provided for in the 1920 Act, where the Regular Army in peacetime would train the citizen soldiers who would form the army's main reliance in a major war.[21]

James G. Harbord, on the other hand, suggested absorbing the manpower cuts by skeletonizing the nine divisions called for in the 1920 Act and by abolishing the training centers. The latter had low promotion possibilities; conversely, keeping the number of divisions large, even though skeletonized, created the need for more rank. One needed nine major generals to command nine divisions, even though skeletonized, but only four major generals to command four full strength divisions.[22]

To Palmer's chagrin, Pershing sided with Harbord. The training centers were dropped. The Regular Army became a small skeletonized combat force which limped through the 1920s and 1930s and fleshed itself out in World War II, as the AEF had done earlier, with hordes of raw recruits.

All things considered, Pershing's decision was probably right. There were not that many volunteers applying to the training centers anyway, and in the lean interwar years the army needed all the inducements it could to retain a quality officer corps. Rank was one of them. While in theory Pershing supported Palmer's citizen army idea, he recognized that harsh realities made it impossible. He was, above all, a realist.[23]

Although Pershing had very much wanted to be Chief of Staff when he took over in 1921, within one year he thought of retiring. After the exciting AEF days, being head of a peacetime, retrenched army was anticlimactic. While he stayed on the job until his retirement in 1924, one gains the impression that he did not work too hard at it. During the winter of 1923–1924, for example, he left America for six months, turning over the War Department to his deputy, John L. Hines, who had replaced Harbord in 1923 and who handled important matters like testifying before Congress concerning the army's needs.[24]

Pershing meanwhile was in Paris, trying to be incognito in order to have time to work on his memoirs. At first people knew he was there and bothered him, so he left town for Monte Carlo, remained a few days, and then returned quietly without telling anyone. Near the end of his stay he encountered Gen. Henri Gouraud, who said, "What luck you have had, General, by not staying here this winter; it has been very cold. I have not been able to ride horseback." Pershing had not only been there, but had been riding horseback every day.[25]

On September 13, 1924, Pershing retired as Chief of Staff. He told Gen. William D. Connor that he felt that he was leaving the War Department "in better working order . . . than ever before," and that he had, to a certain extent, "saved the country from the pacifistic slump." Both opinions are debatable, but a third one was clearly wrong when he said, "I believe that our people generally, as never before, have begun to appreciate the necessity of some sort of foresight." George C. Marshall, Jr., was much closer to the truth in his comment: "When it comes to appropriations in piping times of peace, I don't think America will ever learn its lesson. . . ."[26]

Evaluating Pershing, R. Ernest Dupuy, the noted military writer, remarked: "He was neither the greatest nor the worst Chief of Staff. He didn't have the finesse to get things out of Congress."[27]

He did, however, give the army the General Staff that carried it through World War II. And as historian Mark S. Watson said, "He did more than any other man since Root to build up the school system for the Army"—the branch, technical, and service schools, which, with the Command and General Staff School and the Army War College, provided a hard core of military talent sufficient to leaven the mass in World War II. The school system, said Watson, was "Pershing's most enduring gift to the country and his most enduring monument."[28]

In Retirement

(1924–1930)

PERSHING HATED the idea of retirement. In 1923 he had written Harbord: "Do you realize that I have just about one more year to serve before I become a wheedling, ossified, doddering old mendicant knocking at the doors of my friends here and there for a few kind words and crumbs? Sad to contemplate. Very!"[1]

Yet he was anything but doddering. Damon Runyon, who interviewed him soon after his retirement, was impressed by the clear, even voice, the steady hand, the brisk step. "Here was a man physically hale and hearty, and mentally hitting on all cylinders. . . ." His hair was thinner and he was putting on a bit of weight, but his skin was tight, clear, and unwrinkled. A physical exam revealed him as remarkably fit. James Mangum, who encountered Pershing stripped down to his trunks in 1924, was struck by his powerful physique. "He could outwalk, both in distance and in the time it took, many people who were half his age," said Mangum.[2]

Although he was sixty-four, the sap still flowed in his veins. Being fitted for a cape, he twirled around, studied himself in a mirror, and asked smilingly, "Do you think the girls will like me?" Making light of his age, he commented: "A woman is as old as she looks, and a man is old when he stops looking."

As perhaps the nation's No.1 eligible bachelor, rumors circulated from time to time about a possible Pershing marriage. In 1919, for example, soon after returning from France, a story went the rounds that he would marry Annie Boyd, widow of his former aide, probably because he had brought her and her daughter to Washington for the Victory Parade and put them up at the Shoreham Hotel. "What a despicable thing this is," he wrote her, "to think that one cannot be nice to one's friends, especially to one whom I hold so dearly to me, without being subjected to this sort of thing."[3]

For recreation Pershing rode horseback, which he did consummately well, or played golf, which he did indifferently. An afternoon on the links with Harbord and Dawes was apt to be hilarious, with much joshing and guttural profanity. Occasionally he sat in on a poker game with Washington friends.[4]

A rare photograph of a smiling Pershing.
National Archives

Pershing, in retirement, on one of his annual voyages to France.
Micheline Resco

Asked about his plans, Pershing said he had no interest in politics, although people were constantly urging him that way. In 1922 he had declined to run in Missouri for the U.S. Senate, and in 1924 he squelched talk of a vice-presidential candidacy. "I am not a candidate," he said, "and if by any chance the nomination should be offered to me I should decline to accept it."[5]

In 1925 President Coolidge asked Pershing to be chairman of a plebiscite commission to settle a boundary dispute between Chile and Peru over a region called Tacna-Arica. Although not particularly keen about such work, Pershing said yes as a public service, feeling the plebiscite would help world peace and improve U.S. relations with Latin America.[6]

Tacna and Arica were two small provinces adjoining Chile and Peru. Called the "Alsace and Lorraine" of South America, they had caused hatred and intrigue ever since 1879, when Chile occupied them after defeating Peru in a war. A promised plebiscite to determine their future had not been held and for decades relations between Chile and Peru had been poisoned by a dispute over the area. Finally, in the mid-1920s Chile consented to a plebiscite under the chairmanship of an American. On August 2, 1925, Pershing arrived in Tacna to conduct it.[7]

He had his work cut out for him. The Chileans, who had controlled the territory for more than forty years, owned the railroad, filled the administrative posts, and had the place swarming with secret agents and police. One member of Pershing's staff calculated there was about one police officer for every five inhabitants. Another, who had been through the Soviet Union, said, "This is as bad as anything I saw in Russia."[8]

There was, in fact, a reign of terror going on. The Chilean overlords were systematically intimidating the populace, deporting Peruvians, and causing a number of "unexplained disappearances." When Pershing held open hearings on these matters, so intimidated were Peruvians that only the most courageous would testify.

The situation was complicated by the question of who should vote in the plebiscite. Should it be those presently living in the disputed area, the normal procedure? Or, since the Peruvians claimed they had been driven out by terrorism, should it include those who had once lived there? If so, how long ago? Conversely, since Chile claimed Peru was sending in settlers to pack the ballot boxes, should it exclude those who had recently arrived? If so, how recently? The whole question was one big can of worms.

Given goodwill, such questions might possibly have been resolved, but goodwill was precisely what was lacking. "The bitterness, the antagonism, the animosity that exists between these two people is almost beyond comprehension," Pershing wrote after six weeks on the spot. "It is almost as if they were actually at war at this moment. Neither side will approve of anything suggested by the other and seriously I do not see what the end is to be."[9]

The end, it eventuated, was to be a sort of crucifixion for Pershing. "Difficulty multiplied by an infinitive would hardly give expression to how bad it is," he said.[10]

Convinced that the proper atmosphere for a vote simply did not exist, Pershing sent one of his staff, Harold W. Dodds, later president of Princeton University, back to Washington to tell the State Department that a fair plebiscite was impossible. The best that could be made of a bad situation, he suggested, was to split the territory along lines that Chile was willing to accept. Washington said no. A split had been considered and rejected; the plebiscite had been scheduled and must be held.[11]

Pershing refused. To him it was not a question of holding a mere *pro forma* plebiscite; it was a question of creating "a plebiscitary atmosphere" in which Peruvians could campaign for reannexation without fear and in which the final election would be truly free. It was a question of maintaining one's own honor.[12]

Although the Chileans accused him of being inflexible and autocratic, although feeling against the American delegation became so strong that it was not safe to go out on the streets at night, although the State Department pressured him to hold the plebiscite anyway no matter what the atmosphere, Pershing held his ground. Said Dodds, who saw him in action: "I came to have a tremendous respect for him. . . ." "My deepest impression . . . was [of] his integrity and honesty."[13]

For six months Pershing sweated out the antagonisms, the pressure, and the heat. As his anger and frustration mounted, so did his blood pressure. "The only way to handle such people is with a stuffed club . . . ," he grumbled. Finally, in January 1926, fed up with wasting his time and suffering from abscessed teeth and deteriorating health caused by tension and overwork, he packed up and sailed for home without conducting the plebiscite.[14]

His replacement, Gen. William Lassiter, had no better luck. It was not until 1929 that the problem was finally solved, not by plebiscite, but by Chile and Peru splitting the disputed territory along lines that Pershing had suggested.[15]

During Pershing's stint in Latin America an event occurred at home which might have raised his blood pressure still more had he been there: the court martial of Brig. Gen. William (Billy) Mitchell.

Flashy and colorful, brimming with energy and confidence, Mitchell had for years been a prophet, a man of vision. During World War I—in fact, on the very first day that Pershing arrived in France—he had sent GHQ a memo calling for an independent strategic bombing command to pulverize the German war effort behind the lines. If properly applied, he claimed, it "will have a greater influence on the ultimate decision of the war than any other one arm." Here was "Victory Through Air Power" in its embryo stage.[16]

Like Leonard Wood, Mitchell was a propagandist. In letters, articles, books, speeches, and public appearances, he harped on the unrealized potential of air power. In 1921 and 1923, to the chagrin of conservatives in both the Army and Navy, his planes had demonstrated their power by sinking obsolete battleships. Although skeptics pointed out that the ships were not in motion and not fighting back, as they would be in real combat, his demonstration was nonetheless impressive.

As time passed, Mitchell grew increasingly outspoken and vitriolic. In September 1925, following the crash of a navy dirigible, he issued a strong statement to the press, indicting the War and Navy Departments for "incompetency, criminal negligence, and almost treasonable administration of the National Defense." Convinced that this time Mitchell had gone too far, the War Department summoned him to stand trial on eight charges, especially "conduct prejudicial to good order and military discipline" and "conduct of a nature to bring discredit upon the military service."[17]

Shortly before the trial opened in October, Pershing wrote his views about the use of air power to Dwight W. Morrow, chairman of the president's aviation board. In general, he felt that air enthusiasts' claims were "extravagant." In World War I, for example, bomber pilots returned from their missions with glowing reports of destruction that later inspection revealed were quite exaggerated. He opposed a separate air force, stating that aviation should remain a separate branch *within* the army and be used, as was field artillery and other auxiliary arms, to "assist the infantry in gaining the victory." Finally, he felt that Mitchell's recent statements subverted military discipline and that there should "be no political claptrap about giving him his medicine without sugar coating." He undoubtedly approved the court's decision to convict Mitchell on all eight counts.[18]

Later generations have faulted Pershing for failing to appreciate a new weapon like the airplane, but it must be remembered how unproved this weapon was at the time. The World War I airplane was a rickety contraption of wood, wire, and canvas (which, incidentally, tended to come off the wings of the Nieuport fighter in a dive). Aviation was not that decisive in World War I, nor as decisive in World War II as Mitchell had predicted it would be. Furthermore, as Russell Weigley has remarked, in the 1920s Mitchell's theories "were utterly disproportionate to the military aircraft available."[19]

Returning from Tacna-Arica in late January 1926, Pershing spent the first weekend with his son Warren at the Waldorf in New York. He had not seen his sixteen-year-old boy for almost eighteen months and was amazed at how he had grown. "He seemed to be in the very picture of health and is really too good looking not to have a lot of trouble later on . . . ," Pershing wrote his sisters. "We had a little talk about girls. . . ."[20]

Pershing was concerned that Warren not grow up a snobbish kid, the spoiled son of a famous father. He urged attendance at a summer training camp, both to see what military life was like and, more importantly, to mix with a different class of person than he was encountering at a private boys' school.[21]

The next year, when Warren went off to Yale University, Pershing kept a tight rein on him, requiring each month an itemized expense account down to the smallest detail, with the exact date for each item, for example, twenty cents for a soda, fifty cents for haircut, seventy-five cents for taxi, and so forth.[22]

Like many fathers, Pershing complained about not hearing from his son when he was away. "I hope you are still in the land of the living," he wrote in one letter, "but I received no assurance to this effect from you. . . . I wrote you some time ago, . . . but all of my letters and requests seem to roll off you like water off a duck's back. I am quite put out about it all, but that doesn't seem to matter."[23]

On one occasion, probably the college years, Warren was driving his father and Aunt May from Lincoln to Cheyenne in a heavy rainstorm. Although he never learned to drive himself, Pershing considered himself an expert and peppered his son with suggestions and criticisms on the trip. Finally Warren turned and said, "Why in hell don't you stop telling me what to do? After all, I'm driving the car."

"Yes, but it happens to be *my* car."

"But I happen to be the only one who can drive *your* car."

After that, a frosty silence ensued. But when they reached the hotel, Pershing poured out a glass of brandy from the flask he always carried on such journeys and said, "I think it's about time you and I had our first drink together." To Warren, this was his father's way both of apologizing and of acknowledging his son's reaching maturity.[24]

He was proud when Warren graduated from Yale, voted by the senior class as "most likely to succeed." He was also ranked third among its "best looking" men.[25]

Although Pershing had declined an offer to be U.S. senator from Missouri in 1925, his name kept cropping up politically, especially after President Calvin Coolidge's remark, "I do not choose to run," had thrown open the 1928 presidential race. Editorials favoring the general's candidacy appeared in the *Nashville Banner* and the *New York Sun* in December 1927.[26]

As in 1920, Pershing repudiated overt candidacy. When a speaker in 1928 introduced him with the words, "Ladies and Gentlemen, I give you the next president of the United States," a bystander thought Pershing was going to hit him. "He got up and repudiated the whole idea in quite strong and definite terms."[27]

Privately, however, his feelings were otherwise. Ralph A. Curtin, his secretary during these years, felt that Pershing "would not have been against being president if it could have come to him like a ripe plum dropping into his hand. But he was not the type to go out and openly campaign, to engage in the rough and tumble of politics, battling it out against other politicians, barnstorming the country, and making speeches. It was not like him. If this was necessary to be president, then the general did not want to be. But if the question is simply, would he have liked to be president (without inquiring about how this could be achieved), the answer is yes."[28]

Dawes, who knew Pershing as well as any man, felt that he had the "presidential bee" in 1928. With Pershing's tacit approval, John Callan O'Laughlin, editor of the *Army and Navy Journal*, brought out a campaign biography that year. "He is in heart and mind a civilian," said the Preface, " . . . and his proudest boast is that he is a plain American citizen." The frontispiece showed Pershing in a business suit.[29]

As in 1920, Pershing hoped there might be a deadlock, causing his name to be presented to the 1928 Republican Convention. Three days before it opened in Kansas City in June, he returned from Europe, where he always visited from three to six months each year, to be available if the delegates turned to him. He and his brother Jim rented a suite at the Waldorf-Astoria in New York, with a direct telephone line to the convention. While Jim talked with an unidentified person at the other end of the line, Pershing would occasionally ask, "Any news, Jim?" The answer was always no.[30]

When the Convention nominated Herbert Hoover, Pershing kept up the fiction that he had never been interested. "I am quite happy that it came out as it did," he wrote his sister Bess. "You all know that I have never been at all keen on the political side of life."[31]

Two years later, in a statement given out on his seventieth birthday, Pershing elaborated on the non-political public image he maintained of himself.

"I can say with all sincerity that nothing gives me more happiness than that I have never been drawn into political life. I have watched what happens to holders of high political office. I have seen their every word distorted and twisted to find some hidden meaning. I have seen their political supporters picture them as prodigies of wisdom and statesmanship, while their opponents at the same time set them out as stupid scoundrels. And I have known them, and known that they were neither the one nor the other—just average Americans."[32]

In 1929 Marshal Foch died, as did Bishop Charles H. Brent, Chief Chaplain of the AEF. "And so, Charlie," Pershing wrote Dawes, "we are all going on, getting a little older every day, and the ranks are becoming thinner and thinner, and as the days go by we cherish more fondly the friendships of the past."[33]

Just about this time Pershing pulled a *faux pas* with his great friend Harbord. When the *Army and Navy Journal* printed a cigarette ad featuring Gen. Robert L. Bullard, Pershing, who disapproved of an officer commercializing the uniform, sent it to Harbord with a sharp comment about "one of our comrades [who] appears in all his glory as an advertisement for Lucky Strike cigarettes."[34]

Within a week, to his dismay, Pershing was reading the *Saturday Evening Post* and there, besplattered with medals, was a picture of Harbord in connection with the Simmons mattress! Chagrined and embarrassed, he immediately wrote his friend, apologizing and adding, "If you consider this apology insufficient, I stand ready to go as much further as you wish."[35]

As it turned out, the picture had been published without Harbord's consent, and so no feelings were hurt. But the incident illustrated Pershing's concern, in the twilight years of his life, to keep an old and valued friend.[36]

THIRTY-FOUR

My Experiences in the World War

(1931)

ALL THROUGH THE 1920s—in fact, even during the World War itself—publishers were after Pershing for the rights to his wartime memoirs. He delayed writing them, partly because of the press of other business, partly because he felt that they would reflect unfavorably on people still living. "If I publish a book now," he predicted, "it would probably cause another war."[1]

In 1921 he began gathering notes for a book, using as his starting point the wartime diary kept either by himself or his aide, Carl Boyd. This diary, together with letters, memoranda, and miscellaneous data, served as the raw material on which Pershing worked intermittently for about ten years.[2]

In 1924 he penned a first draft. Really only an outline, it came forth painfully and slowly. Pershing considered it "quite banal and stupid" and said he was "not satisfied with any of it." But when someone suggested he turn over his material to his friend, Dorothy Canfield Fisher, and commission her to write for him, he replied, "I've got to do this myself. Somebody else could do it better, but it just wouldn't be me."[3]

After retiring as Chief of Staff, he worked on the manuscript desultorily, "at odd moments and in varied places, in fact whenever I had spare time and felt the urge." But the urge was rare. Nearly two years passed in which he did not write a line. Crossing the Atlantic on his annual trips to France (he was always there for Memorial Day), he occasionally tinkered with the manuscript, but his tinkering probably made it worse. Mrs. J. Borden Harriman, who read one of the earlier drafts, found it much better written, much more colorful and interesting. Col. James E. Mangum felt that, while the revisions generally made the text more concise, "they also took some of the spontaneous flavor out of it."[4]

As the book developed, it tended to become not just *My Experiences in the World War* (his final title), but everyone's, for Pershing set himself to tell the story of virtually the whole AEF. This entailed a tremendous amount of research and so, around 1929, he enlisted the aid of various men in the Historical Section of the American Battle Monuments Commission who were working on monographs of the war. With Pershing issuing directions, they did pick-and-shovel work, researching and even writing various drafts of his book.[5]

Even with such assistance, the work was burdensome. Not a natural writer (if there is such a thing), Pershing found writing progressively more burdensome. After a while, nothing looked good. "It is the worst and most difficult job I have ever undertaken . . . ," he said. "I should prefer to go through the war again to writing about it."[6]

Although Pershing said later that he "felt like throwing it into the waste basket" many times, by 1930 the book was done. Competition to publish it was nothing short of tremendous, as twenty book publishers, eleven magazines, and sixteen newspapers or newspaper syndicates all tried to obtain the rights. Pershing finally signed with Frederick A. Stokes Company for the book rights ($50,000 in advance, with a 20 percent royalty) and with the North American Newspaper Alliance ($270,000), which serialized the story in seventy installments during the first three months of 1931. The book appeared in March in a two-volume format, selling for ten dollars. Stokes printed fifty thousand in the first edition, with expectations of another fifty thousand later on.[7]

It soon appeared that such expectations were wide of the mark, for sales lagged badly. With the depression deepening into its second year, many considered it a waste of money to pay ten dollars for a book they had already read for free in their local newspapers. By June it was selling for half-price. The following year, although it won the Pulitzer Prize, it was down to two dollars a set, with only half of the original fifty thousand printing sold.[8]

What sort of book was *My Experiences in the World War?*

It was a meticulously researched book, a valuable first-hand account of the American military effort written with special stress on American unpreparedness, disagreements with the Allies, and the fighting qualities of the AEF. Like its author, it was restrained, temperate, and fair.

It was also a book which had a lot wrong with it. The work was cold and passionless, lacking in warmth and human interest. It was dull, repetitious, finicky, and overly wrought. Pershing worked on it too long and with too much help.

One major defect was that the manuscript was organized around diary entries. Instead of concentrating a topic like aviation in a unified section or chapter, Pershing spread it all over the lot, treating aviation only when it appeared in his chronological diary entries. Thus, if aviation matters occurred in January, April, July, and October, Pershing separated them by hundreds of pages, all treating other matters like tanks, artillery, venereal disease, mail, recreation, and so forth. Each of these, in turn, was also fragmented, since, like aviation, they were pegged to the diary entries. The result was that the reader could not see the forest for the trees.

Somewhere in writing his book Pershing considered the question of organization and decided that the diary approach, although being "sort of choppy," would give the best idea of just how things took place. He wavered in this decision just once, when he was dissatisfied with the St. Mihiel and Meuse-Argonne chapters and asked a young officer on the American Battle Monuments Staff, Dwight D. Eisenhower, to rewrite them. Abandoning the diary format, Eisenhower rewrote them as straight accounts. Although initially pleased, Pershing later decided to take George C. Marshall, Jr.'s advice and stick with the diary scaffolding in order to be consistent throughout the book.[9]

Actually, the diary as it appeared in the book was fictitious. Instead of being the one kept during the war, it was a composite formed by combining the wartime diary with other headquarter records.[10]

A comparison will make the difference clear. The following is the actual headquarters' diary for June 18, 1917, as found in the Pershing Papers at the Library of Congress:

"June 18. Went to office about 10:00 A.M. Lunched alone at Crillon. Very busy during afternoon, going over various matters with members of staff. Mr. Harjes, of the Morgan, Harjes bank, and Mr. Grasty, of the New York Times, called during afternoon. Remained at office until about 7:00 P.M. On return to the Crillon member of French Senate called and chatted with Major Bacon and myself. Dined in sitting room of hotel with Captain Collins."[11]

The following is the entry as it appeared in the book:

"(Diary) Paris, Monday, June 18, 1917. Our headquarters are temporarily at 27 and 31 rue Constantine. We have scanty accommodations but sufficient for our probable brief stay in Paris.

"Harjes, of Morgan, Harjes Bank, called to-day. I spent the afternoon in conference with staff.

"Basically the Allied situation appears to be worse than reported."[12]

As far as factual accuracy was concerned, it probably was immaterial that the book entries were fabrications, since they ultimately rested on historically verifiable documents, generally dated around the time of the fictitious entries. But it is ironical that Pershing, who moved mountains to verify the historical accuracy of each little detail, should so lightly have made up fictionalized diary entries. He did so because his book's organization was pegged to a diary scheme, and he found the original diary too dry and restricted to bear the weight of the AEF story he intended to impose on it. One has the impression that the diary was, in many ways, the tail that wagged the dog, and that Pershing would have been better served if he had kept no diary at all or lost it, for he would have been freer psychologically to organize his material thematically.

Perhaps one reason the book was not more interesting is that Pershing failed to treat controversial matters like the keeping of Leonard Wood in America or the removal from command of Generals Cameron, Blatchford, Edwards, Buck, Bundy, McMahon, and Sibert. He said not a word about any of these things. The decision not to treat controversial matters was, of course, itself controversial. Pershing's inclination was to avoid hurting anyone's feelings. He was disgusted at the plethora of war memoirs, each attacking someone else and proving everyone was wrong except the writer. "It is a mess," he said. "I hate the whole thing. Sometimes I wish I never had anything to do with the war." Commendably, he spared people's feelings, but he did so at the price of a less interesting manuscript.[13]

Pershing the writer. His *My Experiences in the World War* (1931) won a Pulitzer Prize.
Micheline Resco

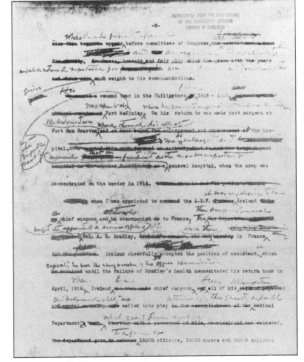

A sample page of the Pershing manuscript, showing how much he fretted over the text in revising it.
Library of Congress

Indeed, the book was quite dull, even the battle accounts, which were the poorest parts of the book. Partly this was due to Pershing's desire to give "equal time" to everyone. Near the end of his writing he had assistants go through the manuscript and tabulate the number of times each person, division, corps, and SOS unit was mentioned, so that the text would contain "a generally well balanced mentioning of units." (One staff memorandum read: "4th Infantry. Only regiment in 3d Division not mentioned. Can be mentioned in [Chapter] XLIX, p 4, line 5— its final clearing of the Bois de Forêt, Oct. 23d.") This attempt to "balance" everything, this concern to mention names (almost as if paying off political debts or running for office), this tendency to try to say something good about everybody (to mention all the division commanders and all the divisional actions, whether important or not) contributed to dulling the book, confusing the reader, and submerging important events under a mass of minor details. It produced a text that read like a phone book.[14]

In particular the Meuse-Argonne campaign, to which the whole book led and which should have climaxed the AEF story, was badly done. Pershing devoted page after page to it, and he had his research staff grub up details and check out all kinds of little facts for accuracy (names of commanders, who took what town, on what date, etc.), but the end result was a mishmash. "The whole chapter reads like an operations report rather than the title, *My* Experiences . . . ," said a friend. George C. Marshall, Jr., remarked that the Meuse-Argonne account was too detailed for the general reader and not detailed enough for the military student. "In endeavoring to mention each town and division and division commander, the battle has been made to appear a confused mass of little events, and from my point of view the big picture has been lost."[15]

Reviewing the book for the *American Historical Review*, the historian T. H. Thomas called it "in every way disappointing." "There is little or no arrangement of subject matter; in a single chapter a wide variety of topics often follow one upon another without transition. The reader is given a glance at everything only to be pulled away without seeing it, and the fault is by no means one of literary composition. As in so many official reports of the war-time period the text moves rapidly over the surface of the subject as if to escape from, rather than deal with, the essential matter; taking up points of substance only to elude them by swift generalizations, omissions, sweeping claims, or well-rounded covering statements. No little skill is shown in this protective treatment of thorny topics; for example, the crisis in the affairs of the S.O.S. is discussed at some length without disclosing in the least what happened. The result is a carefully defensive narrative; and in the end the real problems faced in France, the real results achieved, have not been set before the reader.

"These faults are particularly marked in the chapters dealing with military operations, which may fairly be termed a negative contribution to the subject. The Meuse-Argonne emerges in a thoroughly rationalized version. . . . The A.E.F. deserves a better memorial. . . ."[16]

Although Pershing tried to avoid hurting people's feelings, a number were miffed by his memoirs. Gen. Hugh L. Scott felt that they contained "unwarranted strictures" of the War Department that Pershing had "lugged in by the ears." Newton D. Baker, although congratulating Pershing on the work, was secretly saddened by what he considered a lack of generosity in recognizing other people's difficulties and achievements. "He saw his own problems," he told General March, "but seems wholly to have failed to have grasped ours." Much of the supply problem, said Baker, resulted from the "inability of the overseas men to get ships unloaded and supplies evacuated away from the docks in France, thus prolonging the turn around time of the ships we did have and in effect diminishing the amount of available tonnage. Was that not the chief reason we considered sending General Goethals over? Well this seems to me more serious than our sending over a couple of lawn mowers."[17]

The strongest reaction came from Peyton C. March, who was mentioned in the book only six times and whose picture Pershing had originally planned to omit, although he reproduced just about everyone else's, including a Canadian general's. "Everyone of importance concerned with the war knows of your hostility toward General March . . . ," Marshall had warned when the book was being written. "But, to me, the fact remains that there was not another man, saving yourself, and possibly General Wood, who could have filled the terribly difficult position of Chief of Staff in Washington. . . . He did a remarkable job, in my opinion, which you should in no way belittle."[18]

Pershing's treatment of March in the book was complimentary, but minimal. He described him in France as "a strong man," "a good executive," "an energetic and alert commander," "difficult to replace." After March returned to the United States, Pershing said: "With General Peyton C. March as Chief of Staff, the General Staff and the supply departments began to exert more energy." And that was the sum total of Pershing's comments in seven hundred pages. Nothing critical, nothing explicitly attacking March, but pretty close to a classic case of damning with faint praise.[19]

When March read the book he nearly had apoplexy. He considered it "the veriest blah," "perfidy," "very distressing to those who know the facts." The book should be called *Alone in France*, he said.[20]

According to March, when he visited Washington in February 1931 to deliver a lecture at the Army War College, he found people "completely disgusted with the Pershing attacks on the Department" and "his wholesale abuse of everybody." When Secretary of War Patrick Hurley urged him to tell his side of the story, and when Douglas MacArthur, the Chief of Staff, offered an office in the War Department, together with stenographers and clerical assistance in hunting documents, March agreed to write his memoirs, moving to Washington in the fall to begin work.[21]

An extremely aggressive personality, March was, if anything, even more outspoken and contentious than he had been during the war. The mild-mannered Baker once said of him, "If I had ever been the father of so obstreperous a child, I think I would have been driven either to putting him into an institution or going into one myself. . . ." When such a personality set pen to paper, there was bound to be fireworks.[22]

Baker, who liked both March and Pershing, attempted to head off a fight. The best approach, he told March, was simply for him to tell his own story, straightforwardly and without formally contradicting anyone. The readers could compare it with Pershing's account and draw their own conclusions. March was no more able to follow this advice than to fly.[23]

Writing rapidly, March finished his book by mid-February 1932, save for the final polishing. Called *The Nation at War* (in contrast to *Alone in France*), it consisted of one volume of 376 pages. When his publisher suggested postponing publication until the depression eased, March adamantly refused, insisting that it appear while people were still alive and could answer it.[24]

Although March disclaimed any animus against Pershing (he refused to allow the chapters criticizing him to be serialized separately or out of sequence), the animus was there and reviewers noticed it. Mark Watson thought that "the assault on Pershing was the main objective" of the book. Another reviewer commented: "'The Nation at War' was not written on asbestos paper with burning vitriol for ink, but, after a few such scathing comments as General March puts forth [about Pershing], one wonders how the book can be preserved from spontaneous combustion. March is angry, and his book's an angry book."[25]

Specifically, March accused Pershing of lacking sufficient training as a general, of being afraid of big men, of being insubordinate. He said Pershing had overlarge divisions, excessively delayed committing men to combat, and kept changing his mind about airplanes, throwing production schedules into turmoil. He ordered cavalry to France when obviously it couldn't be used, and made "preposterous" demands for huge shipments of men and matériel when the war was virtually over. He wanted a "rubber stamp" in Washington for Chief of Staff and his attacks on the War Department demoralized the army.[26]

When Pershing read March's book he was furious. "That son of a bitch!" he exploded. "One feels like using a club in reply."[27]

Though strongly tempted to retaliate in print, Pershing recognized that such a course would only draw attention to March's book and increase his sales. Following the advice of friends like Harbord, he kept quiet. But inside he was smoldering. Friends described him as "hopping mad," "exasperated," and "infuriated."[28]

Later, he began to have second thoughts about keeping quiet. Future historians, he reasoned, might look back on the fact that March had written a book criticizing him which was never answered and conclude that it could not be answered. To gather material for a refutation Pershing asked Drum, Conner, and Nolan to go over March's text and write out a list of errors or distortions. He then turned this material over to Harbord and asked him to write a book refuting March.[29]

Harbord hurriedly went through the material and concluded that it was impossible to use it without considerable embellishment, for it was just a string of statements against March and would do nothing except perhaps revive interest in his work. He therefore proposed an alternative: to write a book on the history of the AEF, in the course of which he would use occasions to set the record straight. Thus he would treat Pershing's fitness for command, his efficiency as an administrator, military diplomat and combat leader, and so forth—all impugned by March. This method of handling March, he told Pershing, ought to "worry him sick."[30]

Baker, who deplored March's attacks on Pershing, advised Harbord to play down the personal and controversial. He felt that both Pershing and March had performed magnificently during the war, that there was glory enough for both, and that nothing good would be accomplished by a "battle of the books."[31]

Harbord generally took this advice. His *The American Army in France, 1917–1919*, published in 1936, treated many of the points controverted by March, but rarely mentioned him by name. As with Pershing's book, allusions to March were minimal—some six index references in almost six hundred pages. Yet some of them so infuriated March that he wrote Harbord's publisher in protest.[32]

THIRTY-FIVE

Micheline Resco

(1917–1948)

W HEN PERSHING HAD sailed to Europe in May 1917, he was in love with, and engaged to, Miss Anne (Nita) Patton, the sister of his aide, George. A newspaper that summer printed her picture, with the caption that she was to be Pershing's bride after the war. But it was not to be. Pershing was in France for more than two years, during which the relationship cooled. But there was another, stronger reason: Micheline Resco.[1]

A Rumanian who had become a naturalized French citizen, Micheline was in 1917 twenty-three and something of a child prodigy, with training in art, piano, and violin. Thirty-four years younger than Pershing, she had studied at the Julian Art School, had been one of the youngest students accepted at the Beaux Arts School, and, possibly because of connections, had been selected by the French government to paint Pershing's picture.

Short, blonde, and bright-eyed, Micheline was a person of great winsomeness and charm. Attractive, but not beautiful, she possessed a pleasant smile, a winning laugh, and a sweet spontaneous gaiety. All observers agree that she was "very feminine." She had a "fragile air," said one. Instinctively modest and very sensitive to any sort of vulgar sensationalism, she inclined toward the conservative in art, dress, and public proprieties. She was probably spoiled somewhat in her early years, and was something of a coquette. Very soft and feline, she was a person who delighted in being waited on (up to a point, for she waited on her mother with great devotion) and a person who needed someone to cling to.[2]

Pershing met Micheline at a reception given in his honor at the Crillon Hotel the first day he arrived in Paris, June 13, 1917. Although neither spoke the other's language very well, they enjoyed each other right from the start—there are other ways of communicating besides words. By July, three weeks after arrival, Pershing was writing her affectionate letters. By September they were lovers.[3]

That month Pershing moved his headquarters to Chaumont, but kept in touch by letter, suggesting that they write each other at the same time of the day. Whenever he came to Paris he visited her surreptitiously at night. Several of his chauffeurs remembered how he sat up front with them in the dark, rather than in the rear, and ordered the two windshield signs which identified him—the U.S. flag and the four stars—to be put down where they would not be seen.[4]

Micheline's apartment at 4 rue Descombes served as a haven of peace for Pershing in the midst of heavy wartime work. He and Micheline sat in front of the fire, holding hands, neither saying anything, or saying very little, for long periods. When they talked, it was of everything in general and nothing in particular, the way friends do: what they had done that day, what they'd seen or read or heard. Almost never did Pershing speak about the war, although once he said with a little sigh, "I feel like I am carrying the whole world on my shoulders."[5]

But usually it was light, warm banter and lover's talk. Pershing tried to teach Micheline how to pronounce his name correctly: Per-shing, rather than Pear-shing, which was the usual French way. She said it wrong, he corrected her, she said it wrong again—until finally, with a warm smile which was so ingratiating, she changed his name and made it something she could pronounce: "General Darling."[6]

Marriage was out of the question during the war, but afterwards, when it was possible, Pershing seemed content to leave the relationship as it was. "I seriously doubt as to whether I shall ever change my present status," he said in November 1918 concerning rumors that he was engaged.[7]

In September 1919 Pershing returned to the United States—alone. Although he made plans for Micheline to come to America, these were delayed—first by his cross-country inspection trip lasting several months, then by his Panama Canal trip, both of which militated against seeing her and also against helping launch her artistic career in America, which he wanted to do.[8]

Meanwhile, he kept in touch by letters, which were ardent enough: "Ah, my dear, how I miss you each day and each night. I pray for you, for your presence, for your kisses, for the many ways you show your tenderness. The first time we get together again I am sure that we are going to die. I am going to just eat you all up, as I am going to kill you with love, with the greatest passion in the world. It is uncontrollable. It is *mad!*"[9]

Pershing also visited Micheline in France during the fall of 1921, beginning the first of what later became annual pilgrimages.

In 1922 Micheline finally came to America and opened a studio in New York. An innocent abroad, she was interviewed by the press, in the course of which she remarked that the American face, from the viewpoint of an artist, was the finest in the world. This was later reported in the newspapers under a headline like FRENCH ARTIST PREFERS AMERICAN MEN. Acutely averse to journalistic sensationalism, she was horrified. "I could have died," she said.[10]

Pershing commissioned her to paint him again and recommended her to friends like Harbord and Bullard, pointing out that she had successfully painted Foch, Sims, King Alexander of Yugoslavia, Faisal I of Iraq, and other famous people.[11]

Although living in different cities, New York and Washington, the couple saw each other on weekends, where they went for walks and excursions, and were entertained in private homes by friends. Lavish parties, of the kind given by Elsie

De Wolfe and Elsa Maxwell, had no appeal for them, nor had famous restaurants. "Neither of us cared for that sort of thing," said Micheline.[12]

The question of marriage again arose, but never got very far. People talked of the romance; some gossipy reporters picked up the story and printed it, usually in an unfavorable light. Pershing, after all, was old enough to be Micheline's father. It somehow just didn't seem right, especially in those days where public propriety counted for more than now, for the wife of the Army's top soldier to be a foreigner so many years his junior and so much younger than all the other top Army wives.[13]

Micheline and her friends maintained later that Pershing wished to marry her, but she refused. "Anything that would have tarnished his image and been a source of embarrassment for him would also have been for me," she said. "It would have made him unhappy, and me also. The marriage thus would have been the cause or occasion for pain, for hurting the General, and I did not want that."[14]

On the other hand, Ralph Curtin, who didn't particularly like Micheline and who never could understand her close association with priests and nuns while carrying on a clandestine relationship with the General, felt that she would have married him in an instant had he said the word.[15]

In any event, a marriage probably would have weakened the veneration in which Pershing was held by millions of Americans. Had it been known, the clandestine relationship with Micheline would have weakened it even more, but this was a well-kept secret, limited to a relative few. Perhaps sensing this, Pershing elected to keep the relationship as it was, at least while he was Chief of Staff (1921–1924) and so much in the public eye.

When Micheline went back to France during that period, the relationship continued to be what it was: an informal, quasi-common-law marriage, taken very seriously by Micheline, for whom the General was the one great love of her life, and less seriously by Pershing who, separated from Micheline at least six months of every year and surrounded by women only too eager to give themselves to him, may not have been as faithful as he would have liked.[16]

Micheline said later that, in her young inexperience, she did not realize how many temptations would come to Pershing when they were separated or how strong his needs were as a man. She was surprised, therefore, when he did not seem to be as completely hers as she was his.[17]

Although there may have been other women from time to time, Micheline clearly occupied the prime place in Pershing's life. He sent her a regular monthly check, named her as beneficiary on a $25,000 life insurance policy in 1926, and established a life income trust fund for her in 1938. He also constantly assured her of his affection and fidelity.[18]

"Here I am installed since Wednesday in this old morgue—The Metropolitan Club," he wrote her in 1926, "safe and secure against the wiles of any of the opposite sex, and for further protection and as an inspiration to be good, if any were necessary, I have two of your photographs on the mantle."[19]

Separated by the Atlantic Ocean six to eight months a year, the couple kept in touch by letter and cablegram. A discreet man, Pershing usually wrote his letters on plain paper or hotel or shipboard stationery, and sent his cables in code. A sample went like this: CHELINER. AURORA VELOURS. BEATRICE.

CHELINER was the code name for Micheline. AURORA meant "my beloved one, my own dear one"; VELOURS, "take good care of yourself, my treasure." The cables were signed with a common first name like BEATRICE, as in this case, which meant "May God protect you, my treasure; I pray for you every minute." Other commonly used names were BERNARD (write more often), CLAUDE (answer by cable), MIREILLE (millions of kisses), PATRICIA (don't forget all that I have said about love), ROSEMARY (my adored, my life, my love).[20]

From four to six months every year Pershing lived in France, variously working on his memoirs, overseeing American Battle Monuments Commission work, vacationing, and seeing Micheline. In Paris she entertained for him, giving small receptions at her studio to which she invited interesting people—artists, diplomats, and writers. Almost every evening he dined with her at her exquisitely furnished apartment at 5 rue des Renaudes, which he helped to supply with mementos from his Philippine days.[21]

Occasionally they took excursions together. On the way to visit Lourdes in the 1930s a woman in their party, a non-believer, remarked to another: "I hope the General won't smile at what he sees at Lourdes." Far from smiling, Pershing was deeply moved when he entered the grounds and encountered a great concourse of people from all over the globe, row on row of the sick, lying and sitting. Tears welled up in his eyes and flowed down his cheeks. "He was visibly moved by this mass of suffering humanity," remembered Micheline, "moved by their faith and by the religious atmosphere of the place."[22]

As lovers do, he was sometimes completely wasteful of time and money, doing some foolish, extravagant thing merely to show his affection. Once, when he had much dental work done, he lost a gold tooth in the upper part of his mouth which Micheline had liked. When he appeared with his new dentures, she said jestingly, "Oh, no, chéri, where is my little gold tooth? It's gone." Sometime later the gold tooth reappeared. Pershing had gone back to the dentist and had him redo the work.[23]

There were some who felt that Pershing eventually tired of Micheline and would have been happy to end the relationship, but feared to lest she rush into print about their affair. Such speculation is belied by the evidence. Not only was Micheline not a vengeful person (if injured, she was more likely to go into the corner and cry), but Pershing's letters to her through the years indicate a continued affection.[24]

In 1938 he wrote her: "I have just heard on the radio the wonderful music you taught me to love—Lohengrin and marching into Valhalla that we so enjoy together on our little phonograph at our little home—just you and I listening together. Can the memory of love like ours ever die? Does it not go on forever?"[25]

In 1948, on the day after Pershing's death, Warren delivered to Micheline a letter his father had written years before and saved for this occasion. Dated December 20, 1929, it said:

"My Dear Michette:

Micheline Resco's portrait of Pershing, December 1918. This sketch was the frontispiece of Volume II of Pershing's *My Experiences in the World War*.
Micheline Resco

Micheline Resco, holding a portrait she sketched of Warren Pershing in 1919.
Myrtle Montgomery

"What a beautiful love has been ours! How perfect the confidence and the communion! How happy have been the days we have spent together! At the twilight of my life God sent you to be near me. In my hours of sadness you have been my strength. In my moments of triumph you have been there to share them with me. Ever since we first met you have been in my thoughts by day and my dreams by night. . . . I fain would think your presence, unseen perhaps, has always filled my heart. As my dear companion in life you will be with me through eternity. I cannot but believe, chérie, that together we shall pluck the flowers that grow in some fairer land. So, do not weep, be brave, say not goodbye, but say goodnight, and in some brighter clime bid me good morning, where you will hold me in your dear arms, and I shall be your own. In all the future the lingering fragrance of your kisses shall be fresh on my lips."[26]

THIRTY-SIX

Awaiting the Bugle's Call

(1932–1948)

L IKE MANY OLDER MEN, Pershing lived increasingly in the past. He was a conservative—politically, economically, socially. Organized labor was a "damned outfit," Samuel Gompers, "a worthless whelp." Direct election of senators was a mistake. Newspapermen were busybodies. Franklin Roosevelt was "an upstart," a menace to the nation. America was wise in staying out of the League of Nations and the World Court. Congress did well to reject the Ludlow Amendment, which called for a national referendum before a declaration of war. "Congress is better qualified than the people to pass upon any such question," Pershing asserted, especially when the "people" were ethnics who were not fully Americanized.[1]

Troubled by rheumatism and increasingly bothered by colds as he grew older, Pershing began to spend the winters in Tucson, Arizona. His best friends were Harbord, who, after leaving the army in 1923, had become President and later Chairman of the Board of RCA, and Dawes, vice-president under Coolidge and later American ambassador to the Court of St. James. Both of them tried to coordinate their vacations with Pershing's Tucson stay.[2]

Another friend, George C. Marshall, Jr., received Pershing's special support and affection. When Marshall's wife died suddenly and unexpectedly in 1927, Pershing, who had lost his own wife and three daughters without warning in 1915, wrote him: "No one knows better than I what such a bereavement means, and my heart goes out to you very fully at this crisis in your life. It is at such moments that we realize that our reliance must be placed in the Father who rules over us all."[3]

Marshall responded: "The truth is, the thought of all you had endured gave me heart and hope."[4]

When Marshall remarried three years later, Pershing was his best man. The bride, an attractive widow named Katherine Tupper Brown, planned a quiet ceremony, sending out no invitations and merely telling close friends that they were welcome if they cared to come. Despite this, the church was packed, with a large crowd overflowing onto the sidewalks. Said the bride: "My friends were greatly outnumbered, I fear, by those curious to see General Pershing."[5]

In 1936, with Pershing's support, Marshall became a brigadier general and in 1938 Chief of the War Plans Division in Washington. The following year, when the Chief of Staff position opened up, Pershing switched his support from Hugh Drum, whom he had recommened four years earlier, to Marshall. Coming back from a meeting with President Roosevelt at the White House, Pershing remarked, "You know, I think I made George Marshall Chief of Staff today." He didn't— at least, not alone—but his support undoubtedly helped. A short time later Marshall got the job.[6]

Despite his doctor's remonstrances (for he had almost died the year before), Pershing went to Europe during the summer of 1939. He found the French very apprehensive about Hitler, with everyone talking about war being just around the corner. On September 1 Hitler invaded Poland. World War II was on.

"Right up to the end he found it impossible to believe that it would happen again," remembered Micheline Resco. "World War I seemed to him too recent. He couldn't believe that all that bloodshed and effort had been in vain."[7]

While Pershing hoped that America could stay out of the conflict, he did not see how she could stand by and permit the great western democracies, England and France, to be destroyed. "Practically the same reasons exist today for our entry into the World War that existed in 1917," he told Dawes.[8]

Poland fell rapidly, but combat on the western front was so minimal that Pershing thought that both sides, sobered by the frightful loss of life involved in modern war, would negotiate.[9]

In the spring of 1940, when the Germans blitzed into Norway, Denmark, Holland, Belgium, and France, Pershing believed that the time had come to join the Allies. But in the fall, as he reflected on Hitler's strength and America's weakness, he realized that America was "wholly unprepared" for war. She should use what time remained to prepare for the inevitable conflict by instituting a peacetime draft, by giving aid to Britain, and by repealing her "asinine" cash-and-carry law.[10]

With Britain at bay, President Roosevelt proposed trading fifty overage destroyers for the lease of British bases in Newfoundland and the Caribbean. It was a risky proposal, especially in an election year, and much public sentiment existed against it. With the approval of the President and the support of a group of influential men dedicated to the cause of Britain, Herbert Agar asked Pershing to make a nationwide radio speech favoring the destroyer-bases proposal. Pershing declined. He was not in the best of health (he had had a relapse in Europe the previous summer) and his physician had explicitly advised him against such engagements. "You'll have to get someone else," he said.

"General," responded Agar, "there's nobody in the United States that can do it except you."

Pershing pondered. As the former commander of the AEF, no one else could take such an authoritative position on military matters as himself; no one else had his prestige. When Agar said that, if Pershing declined, the whole radio address idea would simply be dropped, the latter responded, "If that is the case, then I must do it."[11]

With Agar and Walter Lippmann helping, Pershing wrote a speech called "The Security of the Americas." Broadcast nationally on August 4, 1940, on all major networks, it undoubtedly had an influence in swinging public opinion toward the President's proposal. Pershing's mail ran almost four-to-one in favor of his speech.[12]

That fall Franklin Roosevelt ran for an unprecedented third term. Although Pershing had originally looked on the New Deal with some sympathy in 1933, by now he was thoroughly disillusioned and considered FDR a man who broke promises, kowtowed to labor, and appealed "to the rabble by swearing at business."[13]

Despite Pershing's opposition to Roosevelt, the President offered him the ambassadorship to France after the election. Although gratified, Pershing felt he had to decline. The situation in France would be awkward, what with the Germans, his old enemies, partially occupying the country. Then, too, he was eighty years old.[14]

In May 1941 Pershing checked out of the Carlton Hotel, where he had been living, and checked into Walter Reed Hospital in Washington, setting up quarters in the officers' wing. The move had no particular significance, he told a friend. "It is simply a case of being where the medicos can more easily make their checks."[15]

But he was definitely slowing down. He stood all through the christening of Warren's son in June that year, but the experience so exhausted him that he had to cancel a trip to West Point for the fifty-fifth reunion of the Class of '86. The class, now down to 25 percent of its original strength, had fifteen members present, to whom Pershing talked by telephone from his suite in Walter Reed, speaking first a general message to all, then a personal message to each individual.[16]

Living in Walter Reed, Pershing passed the time as many retired men do. He slept late, dallied over breakfast and the morning paper, wrote letters, did some light reading, played cards, lunched with friends, rested, enjoyed the warmth of the sun roof, listened to the radio, and entertained visitors like Harbord, Dawes, Bernard Baruch, and John Callan O'Laughlin. Occasionally some stranger would drop in, like a middle-aged woman from Nebraska, whose group had planted some trees in Pershing's honor and wished to tell him about it.

"Is she good looking?" asked Pershing, who found such visits increasingly burdensome.

"Passable," said the nurse.

"Tell her my doctor will not allow me to have visitors," Pershing responded.[17]

Unable to ride horseback any more, he enjoyed automobile drives through the parks around Washington, and into the countryside. In quiet areas where he could be alone, he got out and walked on foot, something he could not do around the hospital grounds, where he was frequently stopped and engaged in conversation. "He was not, in his later years at least, a very gregarious person and he found it difficult to unbend to strangers," said his doctor, Shelley U. Marietta.[18]

Like most Americans, Pershing was shocked by the Japanese attack on Pearl Harbor on December 7, 1941. Three days later he wrote President Roosevelt, offering his services "to the last ounce" of his strength. "You are magnificent," the President responded. "You always have been—and you always will be. . . . Your services will be of great value." But he did nothing about accepting the offer and Pershing was right in thinking that World War I generals would be bypassed, just as the older officers had been back in 1917.[19]

His influence on World War II was minimal. During it he wrote letters to influential people supporting universal military training after the war and opposing a rumored transfer of General Marshall from Washington to England. Occasionally he was trotted out for a ceremony, like an Armistice Day celebration in Arlington National Cemetery, where, blanketed and clothed in his old World War I uniform, he listened to President Roosevelt speaking at the tomb of the Unknown Soldier.[20]

But mostly he sat out the war, ignored and neglected. His main contribution was whatever inspiration remained in the memories of officers who had served under his command in the earlier conflict. In the case of men like Marshall and Patton, this was considerable.[21]

Patton went out to see him in the fall of 1942, just before sailing for the invasion of North Africa. "He looks very old," Patton wrote in his diary afterwards. "He said that at the start of the war he was hurt because no one consulted him, but was now resigned to sit on the sidelines with his feet hanging over. He almost cried. It is pathetic how little he knows of the war."

Before leaving, Patton got down and asked for his blessing. Pershing squeezed his hand. "Goodbye, George. God bless and keep you and give you victory."

Rising, Patton saluted. Pershing rose too and returned the salute, smartly. "Twenty-five years seemed to drop from him," said Patton.[22]

In 1944 the question arose of giving top American commanders five-star rank, ostensibly to pair them with their British counterparts. Under this proposal, Marshall would become "General of the Armies," a title previously held by Pershing alone. Although Marshall opposed it in deference to his former commander, eventually, with the Navy pushing, the proposal went through. But by changing the title to "General of the *Army*" Pershing's "General of the *Armies*" rank remained unique.[23]

In September 1944 Pershing had a stroke. Dr. Marietta expected him to die within several months, but by December he had staged a remarkable comeback. In April 1945 he had another setback, and Warren flew in from Europe to be with his father. By now he was bedridden, paralyzed on his left side, unable to use his left arm or leg. He spent the day in bed, getting up to eat the main meal in his living room.[24]

George Siefert, Jr., who was sent up as a special orderly after the September stroke and served for the next fourteen months, was impressed by the general's demeanor, even in his semi-helpless condition. "At no time during the fourteen months that I associated with him did I ever see him lose his dignity," said Siefert. "It seemed inherent with him. He never said anything foolish or silly. Sometimes he would be confused, e.g., about where he was, but he *knew* he was confused. Then he would simply keep still and not say anything."[25]

Peggy Cummings, a special nurse, was similarly impressed. Semi-paralyzed, at times the general was incontinent and would wet the bed. On one occasion another nurse rather tactlessly told him she wanted to change the sheets for this reason. "Get out!" exclaimed Pershing angrily, waving his good arm. "And don't ever come back!"

When faced with the same problem, Peggy suggested that, as the weather had been hot and he had been perspiring, Pershing might feel more comfortable if he had a bath. "I can still see his sharp eyes fixed on me, studying my face for any sign of levity or betrayal of what I really had in mind. He permitted the bath. He knew what I wanted, of course, but the point is that he was tremendously conscious of his dignity and would not stand for being put in an embarrassing position."[26]

V-E Day brought back many memories as Pershing listened to the news over the radio that Germany had surrendered on May 8, 1945. From Europe Dwight D. Eisenhower cabled: "As the commander of this second American Expeditionary Force, I should like to acknowledge to you, the leader of the first, our obligation for the part you have played in the present victory." Citing Pershing's work in reorganizing and expanding the army school system, Eisenhower said: "The stamp of Benning, Sill, Riley, and Leavenworth is on every American battle in Europe and Africa. The sons of the men you led in battle in 1918 have much for which to thank you."[27]

Although Pershing had been a bit miffed that Eisenhower had gone to Europe in 1942 without saying goodby, he appreciated the message, which was by no means *pro forma*. "It voices my honest convictions," Eisenhower said in a covering message to Marshall.[28]

The days came and went. Living day after day in the same room, time took on a different meaning for Pershing, as it does for any sick person. A meal, a radio program, a visit, the evening paper—all assumed a far bigger importance than for the average person, becoming highlights of the day. Pershing did not chafe at his illness, but accepted it with good grace. "Without any reservation," said one of his orderlies, "I can say that in all the time I was with him, I never saw or heard anything that didn't make me like or admire him more."[29]

Like any patient, especially an older one, Pershing had his good and bad days. Many times his mind would be confused, sometimes for as much as ten straight days, but then he would snap out of it and be keenly alert.[30]

At times he got depressed. "Why should I eat my breakfast?" he would ask. "What good is it doing?"

"I can assure you, General Pershing," answered Dr. John T. King, "that some 160 million Americans have an interest in whether you eat your breakfast or not."

Smiling, Pershing would pick up his fork and eat.[31]

"His last years could have been made much happier," said Dr. G. R. N. McClary, "if any of us had only realized that to be made to feel needed is the greatest therapy we can offer our elderly people."[32]

Pershing's sister, May, who had moved into the guest house at Walter Reed, helped oversee his care. She read to him, suggested changes in his menu, helped answer his mail, and tucked him into bed at night. Proud of him, she was very concerned that he always be "The General" and make a good impression.[33]

Micheline Resco, who had come to America with her mother when war broke out in Europe in 1939, visited him daily. When others were present, she called him "General" and he called her "Miss Resco," but occasionally expressions of affection popped out. "Look, Chéri, what I have been knitting for the orphans of France," she would say. Pershing, for whom her visits were probably the high points of his day, would beam from ear to ear.[34]

Micheline read to him, made light conversation, and helped pass the time by playing poker for trivial stakes, which he much enjoyed. But almost never did she visit when May Pershing was around. "She was very jealous," remembered Micheline. "It was sad, because there was no need for it."[35]

May's hostility took the form of trying to prevent Micheline's visits by saying that the car which normally picked her up was needed for some other business, or claiming that the visits unnecessarily tired the general. At one point Dr. Marietta intervened, saying that he wanted Micheline to continue visiting because the general's health was better for it.[36]

On September 2, 1946, Micheline and Pershing were secretly married in Walter Reed Hospital by Fr. Jules A. Baisnée. A closely guarded secret for many years, the marriage was only gradually revealed by Micheline near the end of her life, and then only to very close friends.[37]

The days passed, the shadows lengthened. Visitors were restricted. Dr. Marietta advised Harbord against asking to see his old friend. "The General is failing very fast and there would be no happiness for either one . . . at such a meeting." On August 20, 1947, Harbord, who had remarked that he had "more friends in Arlington than I have in Washington," died quietly in his home. Lying unused among his papers was a three-page eulogy of Pershing that he had written to be used at the latter's death.[38]

That same year only ten telegrams arrived for Pershing on Armistice Day, in contrast to hundreds delivered years before. The times had changed. It was nearing the hour to move on.

On July 14, 1948, Pershing went into a coma and never regained consciousness. The following day at 3:50 A.M., he slept peacefully away. He was eighty-eight years old.[39]

For two days Pershing's body, clad in a late 1920s uniform, lay in state, first at Walter Reed, then in the Capitol rotunda. The great and not so great filed by. President Harry Truman, former captain of Battery D, 149th Field Artillery, walked slowly past. Secretary of State George C. Marshall, Jr., was visibly moved.[40]

"I saw the general once, when I was a kid," said Tony Sidlowski, a World War II veteran on crutches, who had waited from 9:00 A.M. to 3:00 P.M. for the doors to open and was the first in line. "We put on a show in St. John's Home. That's an orphanage in Brooklyn. Well, we invited the general and he came. . . . I guess that's what brought me here today. . . ."[41]

"I should be home grading term papers," said a summer school teacher. "But I met him once, and he was old then, but so strong, so straight, that—I don't know, but I just couldn't stay away."[42]

Pershing lying in state in the capitol rotunda, July 18, 1948.
Department of the Army

Sixteen American generals marching in the Pershing funeral procession,
July 19, 1948. *Ralph A. Curtin*

The funeral was memorable. Some 300,000 lined the streets to watch the procession from the Capitol, down Constitution Avenue and 23d Street, across Memorial Bridge, and into Arlington Cemetery. In contrast to President Roosevelt's funeral three years earlier, where people had wept openly, the crowd, three to five deep along the curbs, was silent, attentive, and respectful. For many of them Pershing was a far-off legendary figure. He belonged to another era, about which they knew little, but they somehow sensed that a great man was passing by and they stood in place, despite a sudden summer downpour on a hot, muggy day.[43]

Caught in the downpour, General Eisenhower turned to General Omar Bradley to query him about taking refuge in the limousines provided for just that purpose.

"Brad, what do you think?"

"For Black Jack Pershing I think it would be proper if we walked in the rain."[44]

As the cortege approached Arlington, an artillery battery began a measured nineteen-gun salute. In the amphitheater behind the Tomb of the Unknown Soldier, some 1,500 specially invited guests attended a short Episcopal ceremony. President Truman was there. So were cabinet members, Supreme Court justices, members of Congress, and a Who's Who of World War II: Dwight Eisenhower, Omar Bradley, George C. Marshall, Jr., Jacob Devers, Mark Clark, Courtney Hodges, Leonard Gerow, Walton Walker, William Leahy, and others. Peyton C. March was there, as were Avery D. Andrews and Charles P. Summerall.[45]

Burial was in a plot Pershing had selected years before, in the midst of a World War I section. According to Maj. Gen. John L. DeWitt, then Quartermaster General, who accompanied him, Pershing said, "Here let me rest among the World War veterans. When the last bugle call is sounded, I want to stand up with my soldiers."[46]

The remark may well be apocryphal, but the sentiment is admirable.

So too was the simple headstone erected later by Warren—an ordinary G.I. stone that the army provides for any of its veterans and their spouses, no matter how lowly. In sharp contrast to the monoliths of some of his subordinate generals, Pershing's simple tombstone, of no greater height or width or depth than any other in Arlington, standing alone on a crest of a hill and distinguished only by the wide swath of grass surrounding it, is impressive in its simplicity, calling attention to itself perhaps more than any other headstone in Arlington.

It was July 19, thirty years to the day that the 1st and 2d Divisions, with the Moroccans, had spearheaded the counterattack at Soissons, beginning the turn of the tide.

"The march of another soldier is ended," said Chaplain Luther D. Miller. "His battles are all fought and his victories all won and he lies down to rest while awaiting the bugle's call."[47]

NOTES

Abbreviations

#	Box numbers in manuscript collections	CEM	Charles E. Magoon
		CFF	Charles F. Farnsworth
A-	War Department Cable to Pershing	CG	Commanding General
		CGD	Charles G. Dawes
AB	Arthur Balfour	*CH*	*Chicago Herald*
ABMC	American Battle Monuments Commission	Chap.	Chapter
		CHM	Charles H. Muir
ADA	Avery D. Andrews	CIGS	Chief of the (British) Imperial General Staff
ADC	Aide-de-camp		
ADD	A. Draper Dewees	CinC	Commander in Chief
AEF	American Expeditionary Forces	CLS	Corinna Lindon Smith
		CMH	Center of Military History, Washington, D.C.
AF	Arthur Frazier		
AG	Adjutant General	*CN*	*Chicago News*
ANJ	*Army Navy Journal*	CO	Commanding Officer
ANR	*Army Navy Register*	*CO*	*Current Opinion*
APT	Arthur P. Terry	CofS	Chief of Staff
Autobiog	Autobiography	Corres	Correspondence
AWB	André W. Brewster	CPS	Charles P. Summerall
AWC	Army War College	*CR*	*Congressional Record* (see U.S. Congress[1])
BAP	Benjamin A. Poore		
BB	Bernard Baruch	CRE	Clarence R. Edwards
BDF	Benjamin D. Foulois	CTM	Charles T. Menoher
BEF	British Expeditionary Force	DCF	Dorothy Canfield Fisher
		DCS	David C. Shanks
BHB	Benjamin H. Bernheisel	DDE	Dwight D. Eisenhower
BP	Bess (Elizabeth) Pershing	DEN	Dennis E. Nolan
BS	*Baltimore Sun*	DH	Douglas Haig
BSP	*Boston Sunday Post*	Div.	Division
Cable A-	War Department Cable to Pershing	DLG	David Lloyd George
		DM	Douglas MacArthur
Cable P-	Pershing Cable to the War Department	DS	Donald Smythe, or documents in his possession
CBS	Charles B. Shaw		
CC	"Candid Comment on the American Soldier of 1917–1918 by the Germans" (1919)	DWM	Dwight W. Morrow
		EB	Edward (Peter) Bowditch
		EBH	Edith B. Helm
		EFM	Edward F. McGlachlin, Jr.
CDR	Charles D. Rhodes	EHC	Enoch H. Crowder

EMH	Edward M. House	JEM	James E. Mangum
FA	*Foreign Affairs*	JFB	J. Franklin Bell
FAS	Frederick A. Stokes	JGH	James G. Harbord
FC	Fox Conner	JJP	John J. Pershing
FDR	Franklin D. Roosevelt	JLC	James L. Collins
FEW	Francis E. Warren	JLH	John L. Hines
FF	Felix Frankfurter	JMP	John McAuley Palmer
FG	Floyd Gibbons	JNW	John N. Wheeler
FL	Frank Lanckton	JP	James Pershing
FLP	Frank L. Polk	JT	Joseph Tumulty
FP	Frederick Palmer	JTD	Joseph T. Dickman
FPK	Frederick P. Keppel	JWM	Joseph W. McAndrew
FR	*Foreign Relations* (see U.S. Department of State[1])	JWW	James W. Wadsworth
		LC	Library of Congress
FWP	F. Warren Pershing	LCG	Lloyd C. Griscom
FWP Papers	A collection of Pershing family papers which were consulted when F. Warren Pershing had them at his summer home in Southampton, N.Y. They have since been given to the Library of Congress.	*LD*	*Literary Digest*
		LE	Leroy Eltinge
		LOC	Line of Communications
		LR	Lord Reading (Rufus Isaacs)
		LT	*Louisville Times*
		Ltr	Letter
		LW	Leonard Wood
GA	Gordon Auchincloss	MAD	Maynard A. Dominick
GC	Georges Clemenceau	MC	Malin Craig
GCM	George C. Marshall, Jr.	ME	Martin Egan
GEA	George E. Adamson	MHT	Marvin H. Taylor
GHQ	General Headquarters	MLH	Mark L. Hersey
GPB	General Purchasing Board	MMP	Mason M. Patrick
GPE	George P. Eller	MP	May Pershing
GS	General Staff	MR	Micheline Resco
GSP	George S. Patton	MS	Manuscript
GVHM	George Van Horn Moseley	MTH	Myron T. Herrick
		MWI	Merritte W. Ireland
GWG	George W. Goethals	NA	National Archives, Washington, D.C.
HAD	Hugh A. Drum		
HCC	Henry C. Corbin	NCO	Noncommissioned Officer
HEE	Hanson E. Ely	NDB	Newton D. Baker
HH	Hermann Hagedorn	No.	Number
HJR	Henry J. Reilly	NOO-D	"Notes on Operations–D" (Meuse-Argonne)
HL	Hunter Liggett		
HLS	Hugh L. Scott	NPRC	National Personnel Records Center, St. Louis
HPP	Henry Philippe Pétain		
HTA	Henry T. Allen	NRO	"Notes on Recent Operations" (1918)
IG	Inspector General		
Intvw	Interview	NYC	New York City
JCH	John C. Hughes	*NYES*	*New York Evening Sun*
JCO	John Callan O'Laughlin	NYHS	New York Historical Society
JD	Joscphus Daniels		

NYHT	*New York Herald-Tribune*	SS	Secretary of State
NYT	*New York Times*	Sup.	Supplement
OHRO	Oral History Research Office, Columbia University	SW	Secretary of War
		SWC	Supreme War Council
		TAG	The Adjutant General
P-	Pershing Cable to the War Department	TBM	T. Bentley Mott
		THB	Tasker H. Bliss
PB	Preston Brown	TR	Theodore Roosevelt
PBM	Paul B. Malone	UMT	Universal Military Training
PCM	Peyton C. March	USAMHI	U.S. Army Military History Institute, Carlisle Barracks, Pennsylvania
PHC	Paul H. Clark		
PI	*Philadelphia Inquirer*		
PLS	Pierpont L. Stackpole	USAWC	U.S. Army War College, Carlisle Barracks, Pennsylvania
PP	Pershing Papers at the Library of Congress		
PPL	*Philadelphia Public Ledger*	USAWW	*United States Army in the World War I* (see U.S. Department of the Army[2])
PR	Press Review		
RA	Robert Alexander		
RAC	Ralph A. Curtin	USDA	U.S. Department of the Army
Remin	Reminiscence (at Oral History Research Office, Columbia University)		
		USMA	U.S. Military Academy, West Point, N.Y.
Rept	Report	USWD	U.S. War Department
RF	Raymond Fosdick	VF	Vincent Flaherty
RG	Record Group at the National Archives	Vol.	Volume
		WAW	William Allen White
RL	Robert Lansing	WCD	War College Division
RLB	Robert L. Bullard	WD	War Department
RMB	Ralph M. Brown	WDC	William D. Connor
RSB	Ray Stannard Baker	WHP	Walter Hines Page
SDR	Samuel D. Rockenbach	WM	William (Billy) Mitchell
Scrpbk.	Scrapbook	WP	*Washington Post*
SEP	*Saturday Evening Post*	WRR	William R. Robertson
Ser.	Series	WS	Willard Straight
Sess.	Session	WS	*Washington Star*
SI	"Summary of Information"	WSM	Walter S. McNair
		WSS	William S. Sims
SOR	Service of the Rear	WW	Woodrow Wilson
SOS	Services of Supply		
SOW	"Survey of the War, 1914–1918: Some Effects of American Participation".		

Notes

A word of explanation about the format of these Notes:

Manuscripts are cited as concisely as possible, e.g., NDB-PCM, 1/13/18, PCM #4, which means: letter of Newton D. Baker to Peyton C. March, January 13, 1918, in the Peyton C. March Papers, Box 4. Since the Bibliography lists the location of all document collections, I have not repeated it in the Notes. If there are several collections of the same person, however, the Notes specify the location. Where I had to choose between citing a manuscript collection and the same source in a published work, I have cited the latter on the ground that it would be more readily available to the reader.

Interviews (intvws) are cited by the last name only, e.g., Bliss intvw. The full name and the interview date are in the Bibliography. If several interviews occurred, the Notes specify the date, e.g., Curtin intvw, 3/28/60.

Correspondence (corres) is similarly cited, e.g., Jones corres. The full name of the writer and the date appear in the Bibliography. Where the author received several letters, the Notes specify the date, e.g., Allen, 9/28/60.

Army War College (AWC) talks follow the same pattern, with the Bibliography giving the full name of the speaker and the date of his talk. Where several talks were given, the Notes specify the date, e.g., Conner AWC talk, 1/6/25.

Reminiscences (remin) are from the Oral History Research Office at Columbia University. Since the Bibliography lists the full name, the Notes cite only the last name and page number of the reminiscence, e.g., Albright, p. 118.

Films are from the National Archives. Since their titles are listed in full in the Bibliography, I cite them in the Notes only by their call number and record group, e.g., Film H-1336, RG 111.

Books, Articles, Theses, and Dissertations are very abbreviated. I give only an author's last name and a page number, e.g., Adams, p. 324. The reader must consult the Bibliography for fuller information. Where the author has published a number of titles, I list each of them in the Bibliography, followed by an abbreviation for citing them in the Notes, e.g., (Ambrose[1]). If there is no author, I cite only the first few words of the title, e.g., "An Account of Rivalry." For the convenience of future researchers, the Bibliography lists the Library of Congress call number for most of the works cited.

1. Selected to Command (April-May 1917)

1. Sullivan, p. 32.
2. O'Connor, p. 145.
3. *Army List*, p. 9.
4. For details of Pershing's pre-World War I career, see the author's *Guerrilla Warrior*.
5. Harbord[3], pp. 193–94; Harbord[8], p. 132; LW-TAG, 5/7/17, HLS #29; Bowditch and Moseley intvws; Hagedorn, 2:222.
6. F. Palmer[9], 1:165; March, pp. 59–60; Harbord[3], p. 34; Bowditch intvw; Hagedorn, 1:210–11 and 2:60–61, 85–86 & 481.
7. F. Palmer[9], 1:163 and 165; WW-NDB, 1/13/17, NDB #4; RSB memo of intvw with Josephus Daniels, 3/20/29, RSB #28, Series 1.
8. Beaver[1], p. 42; memo of intvw of NDB by RSB and A. Howard Meneely, 4/6/28, RSB #20, Series 1 (cited as Baker-Meneely memo). See also F. Palmer[9], 1:164 and Cramer, pp. 114 & 116.

9. Smythe[7], pp. 217–82; Beaver[1], p. 44; NDB AWC talk, p. 5; FP-JJP, 2/2/18, PP #153; Hagedorn, 2:222–23.

10. NDB-PCM, 4/5/32 and 4/6/32, NDB #155; NDB-FP, 3/10/31, NDB #184; NDB AWC talk, p. 5; Hagedorn, 2:488; NDB-HH, 11/2/29, HH #23; Frothingham, xx–xxi.

11. Baker-Meneely memo; NDB-Paul Gallagher, 7/25/29 and NDB-GVHM, 9/29/29, GVHM #9.

12. Pershing[9], 1:13; JJP-TBM, 1/25/17, PP #141; S. L. A. Marshall[1], p. 205; S. L. A. Marshall intvw, 6/13/61; JJP-HLS, 3/3/17, HLS #28; JJP-NDB, 4/10/17, PP #19.

13. Pershing[9], 1:1–2; *BSP*, 2/2/19, p. 33; Smith corres, 6/26/63; "Pershing Tells."

14. C. Kelly intvw, 11/14/62; Resco intvw, 4/15/66; Ginsburgh (Nov. 1928), p. 54; JJP-H. Carnal, 9/3/24, FWP Papers.

15. JJP-MP, 12/8/17, FWP Papers; JJP-MR, 8/5/24, author's file; Grasty[2], p. 65; J. C. Hughes diary, 7/24/18, Hughes Papers.

16. F. Palmer[5], p. 152.

17. HLS-JJP, 5/2/17, PP #158; Pershing[9], 1:2.

18. Pershing[9], 1:3; Patch, p. 6.

19. Coffman[9], pp. 22–23; Pershing[9], 1:15; Scott, pp. 532 & 559–60; JJP-HLS, 3/3/17, PP #372; PCM AWC talk; Mott, p. 201.

20. Cramer, pp. 13–75; Beaver[1], pp. 4–8; Coffman[9], p. 21.

21. NDB AWC talk, pp. 2–3; Baker-Meneely memo; Keppel[2], p. 503; Cramer, pp. 80–82.

22. NDB AWC talk, p. 3.

23. Coffman[9], p. 21; GCM-JJP, 11/24/30, PP #354; Scott, p. 558; Fosdick, pp. 158–59 & 241; M. Watson[2], pp. 59 & 62.

24. NDB AWC talk, pp. 6 & 9–10; Baker-Meneely memo; "Newton D. Baker," p. 246; "A Pacifist Secretary," p. 701; F. Palmer[9], 1:118–19, 122 & 131–33; Cramer, pp. 79–80; Scott, pp. 531 & 566.

25. NDB-JJP, 8/3/19, PP #19; Baker-Meneely memo; Frothingham, xxii–xxiv; NDB AWC talk, pp. 8–9.

26. NDB AWC talk, p. 9. The general in question was probably William L. Sibert. See FP-JJP, 2/2/18, PP #153.

27. GCM-JJP, 11/24/30, PP #354.

28. F. Palmer[9], 1:180. I have paraphrased Baker's quotation.

29. Pershing[9], 1:117–18; Mangum intvw, 7/10/63; Curtin intvw, 7/17/63; Smythe[23], pp. 38–45. The radio text, 1/2/38, is in PP #19.

30. Pershing[9], 1:18 & 26; JJP diary, 5/10/17, JLC Papers; JGH AWC talk, 4/49/33, pp. 14–15; March, pp. 299, 301 & 309; F. Palmer[9], 1:143–44. Secretary Baker once asked Bliss how long the war would last. "Thirty years," he answered, explaining that the current war would end in a year or two, followed by a respite, economic competition, military buildup, and then another war. This, of course, is exactly what happened in the period 1914–1945. Bliss was off in his thirty-year estimate by only one year. Cramer, pp. 127–28.

31. NDB-FP, 7/30/34, NDB #184; Cramer, pp. 126–27; F. Palmer[9], 1:161.

32. NDB-FP, 7/30/34, NDB #184.

33. F. Palmer[3], pp. 151 & 153; Pershing[9], 1:26.

34. Carver, p. 33; F. Palmer[3], pp. 152–53.

35. Towne, pp. 9–87; Malcomb, pp. 49–56; Pershing[9], 1:32–33; *NYT*, 4/23/17; Bridges, p. 180; Lloyd George, 6:1678–79.

36. Joffre, 2:571; Notes d'un témoin, pp. 43–275; Viviani, pp. 11–262; F. Palmer[3], pp. 146 & 169–70; F. Palmer[9], 1:153–54. See also Halsey and Tessan.

37. F. Palmer[3], pp. 153–54.

38. Pershing[9], 1:33.

39. Ibid., 33–34.

40. U.S. Congress[9], p. 936; Harbord[3], p. 28; Coffman[9], p. 55.

41. Scott, p. 559.

42. Kraft, pp. 54–62; Leary, pp. 100–17; Pershing[9], 1:13–14; "Correspondence of Theodore Roosevelt," pp. 22–25, 62–65; Harbord[11], pp. 9–13, 40–42.

43. JJP-FEW, 4/17/17, FWP Papers; JJP-Guy Preston, 5/18/17, PP #164; Pershing[9], 1:21–22.

44. NDB AWC talk, pp. 6–7.

45. Hewes[2], pp. 70–71.

46. March, pp. 45–46; Coffman[9], p. 23.

47. GCM-JJP, 11/24/30, PP #354.

48. JJP annotation of TAG memo, 3/8/23, PP #364.

49. R. S. Baker[1], 7:75; Harbord[3], xiii and 44; Harbord[4], pp. 5–6; Gauss, pp. 28–29 and 62.

50. GEA-JGH, 8/12/35, JGH Papers, NYHS. See also the Harbord entries in the Bibliography.

51. Smythe[7], p. 157.

52. ANR, 6/16/17, pp. 697–98, gives the background of JJP's staff. Of the principal twelve who moved with him in the early days in Europe, four were non-West Pointers: James G. Harbord, André Brewster, Merritte W. Ireland, and Nelson E. Margetts. On Hines, see Peake, pp. 226–35.

53. Harbord[3], p. 40; JGH AWC talk, 4/29/33. Forty-two divisions eventually served under Pershing in France. Thirty were commanded by men whom he had known as cadets at West Point from 1882–1886 and several others by cadets he had known as a tactical officer there from 1897–1898.

54. Smythe[14], pp. 34–51; Pershing[9], 1:23; JGH-TR, 5/22/17, JGH Papers, NYHS.

55. USAWW, 1:117; Pershing[9], 1:36; FP-JJP, 10/19/21, PP #353; Chief, WCD-CofS, 5/10/17, PP #353; TAG-CofS, 3/8/23, PP #364.

56. Pershing[9], 1:37; JJP undated jotting #11 in 1920s, PP #355; Vandiver[2], pp. 69–76.

57. Pershing[9], 1:38–40; Harbord[3], pp. 63–64 & 67; Harbord[4], p. 15; Harbord[8], p. 3; PCM-NDB, 4/22/32, NDB #155; JGH-JJP, 11/17/31, PP #88; March, pp. 244–50.

58. March, pp. 247–48; S. L. A. Marshall[1], p. 207; F. Palmer[9], 1:175–76.

2. The Voyage Overseas (May-June 1917)

1. Harbord[2], p. 71; Harbord[8], p. 4.

2. Pershing[9], 1:42; R. Reynolds, p. 50; Hubbard, p. 4; Harbord[8], p. 4; JJP-THB, 6/7/17, PP #26; Ginsburgh (Nov. 1928), pp. 14–15.

3. HAD diary, 5/28/17, HAD Papers; HAD-JJP, 1/9/30, PP #354.

4. G. Marshall[3], p. 3; Harbord[8], pp. 4, 6 & 8; Smythe[2], pp.41–42; Grasty[3], pp. 1–2.

5. Details of the study boards are in Folder 655, File 1003, Box 3110, AEF/GHQ, G-3 repts, Gen. Corres, RG 120, NA. For a sample of a study board on ports, see E. Johnson, pp. 200–06.

6. Amos A. Fries, "History of Chemical Warfare in France," n.d., pp. 4–5, PP #351.

7. Pershing[9], 1:43.

8. Young, pp. 274, 310–12.

9. R. Reynolds, p. 52; Harbord[3], p. 75; Pershing[9], 1:43; Young, p. 271; Hubbard, pp. 6–7. Fuller details on the *Baltic* trip are in Smythe[17], pp. 262–77.

10. Gibbons[3], pp. 31–32; JJP diary, 6/8/17, JLC Papers; "Pershing in London," p. 2; CBS diary, 6/8/17, Shaw papers; Film H-1320, RG 111; Pershing[9], 1:44–45; Smythe[5], pp. 193–202.

11. "America's Advance Guard," n.d., JLC Papers.

12. Harbord[3], p. 76.

13. Pershing[9], 1:45; Harbord[8], pp. 21–22.

14. Pershing[9], 1:45–46; Cable P-2, 6/8/17, Ser. 482, Box 2456, RG 120, NA.

15. Broun[2], p. 7; Gibbons[3], p. 31; E. Crozier, pp. 191–92.

16. Pershing[9], 1:46.

17. Harbord[8], p. 23.

18. Ibid., p. 24.

19. Ibid., p. 22.

20. Pershing[9], 1:27 & 46–47; George V diary, 6/9/17, George V Papers; "Life's Dream Realized," p. 7.

21. Pershing[9], 1:334.

22. Ibid., p. 48. On Page, see both J. M. Cooper and Gregory.

23. Ambrose[2], p. 29; Pershing[9], 1:48 & 55.

24. Mangum intvw, 7/10/63; Pershing[9], 1:48; ABMC, p. 451. On Sims, see Morison[1] and Sims's *Victory at Sea*.

25. Pershing[9], 1:49–50; Harbord[8], pp. 28–29.

26. "Pershing Kept Busy," p. 2. Quotation is from draft of Pershing's *My Experiences in the World War*, chap. 4, PP #364.

27. Pershing[9], 1:51; *Louisville Times*, 1/16/31; *Baltimore Sun*, 1/17/31.

28. Bonham-Carter, xv; Harbord[8], p. 36; Pershing[9], 1:51–52.

29. Hughes intvw.

30. "General Pershing Sees British," p. 5; JLH diary, 6/12/17, Hines Papers, USAMHI.

31. Curtin intvw, 4/1/70; *NYT*, 4/13/17; Pershing[9], 1:54–55.

32. F. Palmer[3], p. 155.

3. First Days in France (June 1917)

All the maps in this book, except the first map in Chapter 12, are from American Battle Monuments Commission, American Armies and Battlefields in Europe, Washington, D.C., 1938.

1. Film H-1320, RG 111; JMP-wife, 6/16/17, JMP Papers; Broun[2], p. 10; R. Reynolds, p. 70; Hubbard, p. 13.

2. Harbord[8], p. 41.

3. Ibid., pp. 42 and 153; Harbord[3], pp. 78–79; Mott, pp. 290–91.

4. Harbord[3], p. 79.

5. Pershing[9], 1:58; CBS diary, 6/13/17, Shaw Papers; Grasty in *CH*, 7/15/17, in PP #387.

6. Ribot, p. 152; Pershing[9], 1:58; Harbord[8], p. 43.

7. Herbillon, 2:102; Gibbons[1], pp. 55–57; Film H-1320, RG 111; Harbord[3], p. 80.

8. CBS diary, 6/13/17, Shaw Papers; Forrest[2], p. 86; JMP-wife, 6/13/17, JMP Papers; Sharp, p. 194; Harbord[3], p. 80; Poincaré[1], 9:164; R. Reynolds, p. 70; Pershing[9], 1:58–59.

9. "Gibbons' Audience," p. 16.

10. Pershing[9], 1:59–60; Hunter[2], p. 133; *Deutsche Warte* (Berlin), 6/26/17, in PP #387.

11. Mitchell[3], pp. 140–41; "Honor General Pershing," pp. 1275 & 1282; Harbord[8], p. 86; Pershing[9], 1:60.

12. JLC diary, 6/16/17, JLC Papers; May Birkhead-JGH, 7/8/35, JGH Papers, NYHS; Grasty[2], p. 65.

13. Grasty-EMH, 6/16/17, EMH Papers; Grasty[2], pp. 65–66; Harbord[8], pp. 85, 91 & 99; FF-NDB, 8/15/17, NDB #1.

14. Fisher-JJP, 6/15/17, PP #74; Pershing[9], 1:70; Blake, p. 55; Harbord[8], p. 47.

15. Painlevé, pp. 55–90; Pershing[9], 1:67, 69–70 & 113; W. Churchill, pp. 272–96.

16. Painlevé, pp. 129–75; Barnett, p. 222; Gilbert, pp. 24–41; HPP-Minister of War, 5/29/17, File 28042, Entry 6, No. 8121, RG 120; Pershing[9], 1:70 & 113. Details of the mutinies are in Pedroncini[2].

17. Barnett, pp. 227–32 & 239; *USAWW*, 2:1–2; Spears, pp. 69–128; Pershing[19], p. 82.

18. J.H. Perkins-Grayson Murphy, n.d., PP #352; Pershing[9], 1:142; FF-NDB, 8/15/17, NDB #1.

19. Barnett, pp. 59 & 197–98; R. Griffiths, pp. 91–93; Mott, pp. 221–22.

20. Harbord[8], pp. 47, 49, 120–21 & 180; Pershing[9], 1:63; Harbord[9], p. 54.

21. Boatner corres; Reilly intvw.

22. Harbord[3], p. 141.

23. Harbord[3], p. 89; Pershing[9], 1:79.

24. Harbord[3], pp. 88–90.

25. Harbord[6], p. 6.

26. Pershing[9], 1:71; Harbord[3], pp. 90–91.

27. Harbord[8], p. 124; Andrews, p. 92.

28. C. Smith, p. 302; JJP-JP, 7/6/17, FWP Papers.

29. HJR-JJP, 9/19/28, PP #353.

30. Millett[1], p. 312.

31. GHQ War Diary, 7/14/17, Entry, 272, Box 31, RG 120; Cable A-79, 8/4/17, WD Cables, Box 22, RG 94.

32. E. Roosevelt, pp. 84–85.

33. Text, 8/10/17, PP #347.

34. Mary Edie-JJP, n.d., loaned to author by Henry Castor.

35. Harbord[8], pp. 124–25.

36. Ibid., pp. 125–26 & 280.

37. Ibid., p. 126; McKelvie[2], pp. 69–72.

38. Coffman[2], pp. 75–76; Pershing[9], 1:79–86; *USAWW*, 2:42–43, 91–92; FC AWC talk, 1/6/25, p. 1; W. Williams[2], pp. 323–26; Tardieu, p. 166.

39. Pershing[9], 1:81–82, 109–10.

40. Harbord[3], p. 136.

41. *USAWW*, 2:5; GCM talk to Ordnance Assoc, 10/11/39, GCM Papers.

42. HAD diary, July 16–19, 1917, HAD Papers; G. Marshall[3], pp. 8, 13–14, 19, 38; N. D. Baker[1], pp. 314–15.

43. Gibbons[1], pp. 66–67; GCM talk to Ordnance Assoc, 10/11/39, and talk at Brunswick, Md., 11/6/38, GCM Papers.

44. Pershing[9], 1:130.

45. Ibid., p. 88; Millett[1], p. 310; Harbord[8], pp. 81–82.

46. G. Marshall[3], pp. 243–45; Bullard[3], pp. 164–65.

47. FF-NDB, 8/15/17, NDB #1; Harbord[8], pp. 116–17.

48. MacArthur, pp. 53–54; MHT diary, 11/13/17, MHT Papers.

49. JJP remarks to the Institute of France, 7/1/36, PP #105.

50. Pétain speech on occasion of JJP election to the Institute of France, 7/1/36, PP #105.

51. DeWeerd, p. 214; *USAWW*, 3:241–42; Lonergan, p. 266; Pershing[9], 1:265. On AEF training, see Rainey.

52. D. James, 1:197.

53. PBM-JJP, 1/8/24, PP #352; Pershing[9], 1:154–55, 259. Details of the schools are in Vandiver[1], 2:770–72.

54. Kaspi, pp. 135–36; Pershing[9], 1:74; JLC diary, 6/23/17, JLC Papers; Blake, pp. 246–47.

55. JD-WW, n.d., WW Papers, ser. 2, #165.

56. *USAWW*, 2:81; Harbord[8], pp. 54 & 95; WHP-WW, 6/22/17, WW Papers, ser. 2, #163.

57. Proces-verbal, 2d sess., SWC, 12/1/17, NDB #15; Whitlock, 2:443; Harbord[8], p. 77.

58. Sylvester, p. 20; WHP-WW, 6/22/17, WW Papers, ser. 2. #163.

59. Resco intvw, 8/8/65; *Sunday Times* (London), 8/5/17, p. 7.

4. Getting Organized (July-August 1917)

1. Pershing[9], 1:91; Coffman[9], pp. 3–4; Film H-1349, RG 111.

2. Singleton corres, 3/15/61.

3. Gleaves, p. 53; Broun[1], pp. 30–34; Blumenson[2], pp. 403–04; Harbord[8], pp. 87–88, 92.

4. Pershing[9], 1:92–93; "Lafayette," p. 2. Stanton's text is in PP #159.

5. Whitlock diary, 7/4/17, Whitlock Papers #4.

6. *USAWW*, 16:13–24; USAWC[2], 1:5, 11–12.

7. A. Andrews, p. 151.

8. March, p. 226; JEM 1921 recollection of Nolan, JEM Papers; Forbes, 1:238.

9. Coffman[9], pp. 266–67; Eisenhower, pp. 185–87.

10. WDC AWC talk, 11/3/31, p. 17; JGH-LW, 10/11/17, JGH Papers, LC.

11. USWD[3], pp. 9–10.

12. Harbord[3], pp. 205–07; Harbord[6], p. 4.

13. Hughes intvw; Clarke intvw; Villaret intvw, 7/6/60; Herron intvw; WDC AWC talk, 2/18/28, p. 3.

14. Coffman[3], pp. 35–43; Nenninger, pp. 134–51; JJP jotting no. 18, n.d., PP #355; JGH AWC talk, 2/8/29, p. 16; Harbord[3], pp. 29–30, 98.

15. Pershing[9], 1:103; Cable A-29, 7/9/17, #22, RG 94.

16. *USAWW*, 2:17; Pershing[9], 1:118.

17. *USAWW*, 1:55; DeWeerd[4], p. 205; Harbord[3], pp. 100–01.

18. *USAWW*, 1:56; Chauncey Baker-JJP, 6/7/17, PP #18.

19. *USAWW*, 1:108.

20. Pratt[1], pp. 248–49, 252, 258–59; JGH AWC talk, 4/29/33, p. 6; CPS-TAG, 7/21/17, Entry 1564, folder 46, RG 120; JJP-THB, 7/9/17, PP #26; Harbord[3], p. 101.

21. THB rept to SWC, 2/6/20, PP #355.

22. JJP jotting on CPS, n.d., FWP Papers.

23. *USAWW*, 1:93–106.

24. Pershing[9], 1:101. More details are in Millett[1], pp. 336–37.

25. F. Conner, p. 166.

26. Harbord[6], p. 10; HAD-JGH, 7/20/34, JGH Papers, NYHS.

27. F. Connor, p. 167; *USAWW*, 2:406–12.

28. Liddell Hart[9], p. 208; March, p. 251.

29. Fuller[2], p. 379; Millett[1], pp. 336 & 347.

30. F. Palmer[9], 1:253–57; Hill, pp. 263–65. After the war Pershing recommended a much smaller division of about 17,000 men. JJP-NDB, 7/9/20, RG 200, NA.

31. Marshall-Cornwall[2], xi–xii; Blake, pp. 28–29, 51; Harbord[8], p. 266.

32. Charteris[1], p. 235; Blake, p. 245; Duncan, p. 59.

33. Charteris[1], p. 235. Details of the visit to Haig are in Vandiver[1], 2:744–55.

34. AG, AEF-CG, 1st Div., 8/7/17, Entry 6, no. 951, RG 120; Gibbons[4], pp. 60–61.

35. JJP-JFB, 9/13/17, PP #23; Kennett, p. 6; *USAWW*, 16:56.

36. JJP-CG, 1st Div., 8/7/17, Entry 6, no. 951, RG 120; F. Palmer[8], p. 11.

37. S. L. A. Marshall[4], pp. 138–56.

38. Blumenson[2], 1:410.

39. FF-NDB, 8/15/17, NDB #1.

40. Blumenson[2], 1:410; Harbord[8], p. 129.

41. Cable P-78, 8/7/17, Box 40, RG 94, NA.

42. Harbord[8], p. 125; Pershing[9], 1:161.

43. Cable P-119, 8/23/17, PP #353.

44. WHP-WW, 8/14/17, Series 2, WW #366; Harbord[8], p. 136.

45. Hurst intvw (Fries's daughter); Pershing[9], 1:167.

46. Edward N. Johnson-JGH, 7/30/19, PP #351; Harbord[3], p. 223.

47. Fries-JJP, 1/3/24, PP #351; Edward N. Johnson-JGH, 7/30/19, PP #351.

48. Pershing[9], 1:96 & 110; Harbord[3], pp. 120–21, 382; *USAWW*, 16:52–53; DCS-JJP, 9/3/30, PP #182.

49. Pershing[9], 1:147-48; JGH AWC talk, 4/29/33, p. 7.

50. Pershing[9], 1:148; Dawes[4], 1:27.

51. *USAWW*, 16:57; J. Chambrun, pp. 355–56.

52. JGH AWC talk, 4/29/33, p. 7; Harbord[3], pp. 125–26. On the Dawes-Pershing relationship, see Goedeken.

53. Curtin intvw, 7/19/60; Cleveland *Plain Dealer*, 1/8/31.

54. Harbord[3], p. 127; Dawes[5], pp. 131–32; Timmons[2], pp. 171–72, 175–77, 179; Harbord[8], pp. 353–56; Griscom, pp. 412, 416–17, 419–20.

55. Bowditch intvw.

56. Curtin intvws, 7/19/60 & 7/22/63; Bowditch intvw; Mott., p. 295; B. Dawes corres, 1/16/61; Hughes intvw; Hughes corres, 11/19/64.

57. JMP, 1939–1940 chap. notes, vol. 20, JMP Papers; Dawes[4], 1:99; H. Dawes corres; Bowditch intvw; Eller intvw.

58. Frier intvw, 1/20/70; Forrest[2], p. 101.

59. Pershing[9], 1:145; F. Palmer[5], p. 130.

60. Pershing[9], 1:123; Cable P-51, 7/18/17, Box 40, RG 94; Henry S. Graves-JJP, 3/6/23, PP #353.

61. Pershing[9], 1:90 & 145.

5. Chaumont (September 1917)

1. JLC diary, 7/16/17, JLC Papers.

2. Pershing[9], 1:126 & 163; Film H-1319, RG 111.

3. Stoddard remin, p. 83.

4. Blumenson[2], 1:416. I have retained Patton's awkward spelling and punctuation. In May 1918 Pershing moved his residence from Chaumont to a place called Val des Écoliers, a tasteful chateau built on the foundations of an old monastery.

5. Harbord[3], p. 166.

6. Pershing[9], 1:164–65, 180; Kaspi, p. 98.

7. Poincaré[2], 1:213; Pershing[9], 1:163–64; Pogue[2], pp. 151–52; Buck, pp. 163–66.

8. Pershing[9], 1:157–58, 224; Pattullo[1], 4/29/22, p. 5.

9. Coffman[6], p. 44; Pershing[9], 1:225–26.

10. Pershing[9], 1:229.

11. Ibid.; Coffman[6], pp. 44 & 47.

12. FP-JJP, 1/10/34, PP #153; Coffman[9], p. 168. When Bliss came to die in 1930, he wanted his grave in Arlington to be in a low spot, so that if Pershing were later buried there, he would be higher, as befitted a field commander. F. Palmer[3], pp. 264–65.

13. PCM-NDB, 1/7/35, NDB Papers #155; Bullard[3], pp. 20–25, 73–74.

14. JGH-JJP, 3/16/18, JGH Papers, LC; Harbord[3], p. 181.

15. Pershing[9], 1:182–83.

16. Ibid., 1:146; Coffman[9], pp. 198–99; WM autobiog, p. 75, WM #21.

17. Pershing[9], 1:183; Cable P-115, 8/20/17, WD Cables, Box 40, RG 94, NA; GVHM-Clarence C. Williams, 5/10/28, PCM #23.

18. March, pp. 49–50.

19. Cable P-211, 10/10/17, Entry 482, RG 120.

20. Cable P-171, 9/21/17, Entry 482, Box 2457, RG 120; Pershing[9], 1:121–22, 183.

21. Cable P-125, 8/25/17, WD Cables, Box 40, RG 94.

22. Cable P-37, 7/11/17, Series 482, Box 2456, RG 120.

23. Cable P-157, 9/12/17, Box 40, and Cable A-176, 9/14/17, Box 22, WD Cables, RG 94.

24. Taylor cable to Chief of Engineers, 8/6/17, in PP #351.

25. Cable P-201, 10/4/17, WD Cables, Box 50, RG 94.

26. Drum diary, Oct. 15–23,1917, HAD Papers; J. W. McConaughy-NDB, 10/26/17, NDB #3.

27. Cable P-116 (8/22/17), P-126 (8/29/17), and P-175 (9/23/17), WD Cables, Box 40, RG 94; unidentified clipping, 9/1/17, Scrpbk 7, p. 170, PP #387; W. C. Brown-JJP, 2/21/31, W. C. Brown Papers; W. C. Brown-GWG, 4/3/18, PP #28; Repington[2], 2:88.

28. Pershing[9], 1:210–11; Harbord[8], p. 149; Harbord[3], p. 183.

29. Pershing[9], 1:185.

30. Ibid., 1:210.

31. F. Palmer[1], p. 149.

32. JJP-BB, 2/23/30, BB Papers; Harbord[3], p. 19; Coffman[6], p. 42.

33. M. Watson[5], pp. 4–6; NDB-PCM, 3/1/31, PCM #32.

34. M. Watson[5], p. 5.

35. March, pp. 207, 283–84; F. Palmer[9], 2:16–18.

36. USAWW, 12:183; F. Palmer[9], 2:18.

37. Cable A-222, 9/27/17, WD Cables, Box 22, RG 94; Memo, CofS-CinC, AEF, 10/29/17, with attached Chauncey Baker memo, 11/2/17, Project Files, AG 573.51EE, Box 325, RG 407.

38. Pershing[9], 1:185.

39. M. Watson[5], p. 4; NDB-FP, 3/10/31, NDB #184.

40. FP-NDB, 3/12/31, NDB #184.

6. Into the Lines (October 1917)

1. Pershing[9], 1:225.
2. Ibid., 1:190–91 & 193–94; Coffman[1], p. 188; JJP-NDB, 11/13/17, PP #19.
3. Coffman[9], p. 249.
4. Ibid., pp. 249–51; Bullard[3], pp. 143–44.
5. Pogue[2], pp. 152–53; GCM-Edwin T. Cole, 2/24/39, GCM Papers; Pershing[19], p. 82; Wilhelm, p. 463; Harriman, p. 267.
6. JJP jotting, n.d., FWP Papers.
7. JJP-NDB, 10/4/17, PP #19.
8. JJP-THB, 10/4/17, PP #26.
9. D. James, 1:147–48; JJP-NDB, 11/13/17, PP #19.
10. Wiener, p. 31; JJP diploma, PP #419; JJP-MP, 11/9/17, FWP Papers.
11. Film H-1258, RG 111; *USAWW*, 3:447–56; Pershing[9], 1:201–02.
12. Cable P-228, 10/20/17, WD Cables, Box 50, RG 94; Pershing[9], 1:201–02; JLH diary, 11/1/17 to 1/1/18, JLH Papers, USAMHI.
13. Azan, pp. 162–63; Barnett, pp. 254–55; Pershing[9], 1:202–04.
14. DeWeerd[4], p. 196; *USAWW*, 2:265–66; Pershing[9], 206–07.
15. Buchan, 4:183; *USAWW*, 3:335–36, 378–79; G. Marshall[3], pp. 61–62.
16. Carver, pp. 132 & 82.
17. Dawes[4], 1:34–35.
18. Pershing[9], 1:206 & 209; Charteris[2], p. 261; DEN critique of JJP MS, 4/7/30, Chap. 12, PP #354.
19. Pershing[9], 1:207–08; Harbord[3], p. 162.
20. Harbord[8], pp. 191–92; Pershing[9], 1:207 & 211; Blumenson[2], 1:418.
21. MMP diary, 10/31/17 & 11/5/17, MMP Papers; Harbord[8], p. 201.
22. Blatchford-JJP, 9/30/22, PP #26.
23. JJP-Blatchford, 9/21/22, PP #26.
24. Coffman[9], p. 139.
25. Ibid., p. 140; Hoehling, pp. 152–75; C. Smith, pp. 310–11; Frye, pp. 132–34.
26. "Town Crier," *Detroit Free Press*, 5/26/61.
27. G. Marshall[3], pp. 49–50; Pershing[9], 1:217–18.

7. Bleak Prospects (November 1917)

1. Pershing[9], 1:213 & 217.
2. Foch[2], p. 238.
3. Rapallo Agreement, 11/7/17, Entry 1562, Box 23, RG 120; *USAWW*, 2:60; U. S. Grant III, pp. 295–340; Pershing[9], 1:214. On the SWC, see Shumate. On General Wilson, see Collier.
4. N. Maurice, p. 53; F. Palmer[3], p. 228; *USAWW*, 2:180; Robertson, p. 324; LCG AWC talk.
5. Robertson, pp. 328, 333, 336–37; Harbord[3], 175–78, 419; Pershing[9], 1:216; JGH AWC talk, 4/29/33; Callwell, 2:18, 31, 40–41.
6. *USAWW*, 2:77–79 and 3:666–70; MacArthur, p. 53.
7. Reilly, pp. 25–26; F. Palmer[9], 1:356–57; Coffman[9], pp. 149–50; USWD[2], p. 51.
8. D. James, 1:148.
9. Ibid., 1:133; *USAWW*, 3:669–70.
10. *USAWW*, 3:667–68; Ayres, pp. 33 & 102.

11. D. James, 1:149; MacArthur, p. 53; Hunt, pp. 70–71; HAD diary, 11/2/17 to 11/30/17, HAD Papers; Herron intvw, 6/25/60.

12. *USAWW*, 3:670; JJP-FC, 10/14/40, PP #52.

13. Blake, pp. 277–78; Pershing[9], 1:243; Wolff, pp. 252–53.

14. Pershing[9], 1:243–45, 252; C. Smith, p. 304.

15. D. Cooper, 2:185; Pershing[9], 1:220 & 242.

16. *USAWW*, 2:68; Coffman[9], pp. 168–69.

17. Pershing[9], 1:233.

18. Ibid., 1:95, 118, 233–34; D. Lloyd George, 5:3011; F. Palmer[3], p. 203.

19. D. Lloyd George, 5:3005–06.

20. THB-NDB, 12/23/17, THB #74.

21. Pershing[9], 1:221–22, 238.

22. *USAWW*, 2:63 & 65; Pershing[9], 1:229.

23. *USAWW*, 2:138–39, 149–50, 157; Pershing[9], 1:145, 286–87, 298–99.

24. Dawes[4], 1:58–59; Lonergan, p. 65; MMP diary, 11/13/17, MMP Papers.

25. Pershing[9], 1:221–22; Cable P-232, 10/20/17, WD Cables, Box 50, RG 94.

26. *USAWW*, 2:65.

27. Mary Roberts Rinehart-NDB, 12/5/17, NDB #3; LW-JGH, 9/14/17, JGH Papers, LC; Beaver[1], pp. 79–109; Kreidberg and Henry, pp. 318–23.

28. JT-WW, 12/29/17, Series 2, WW Papers; LW diary, Dec. 7–8, 1917, LW #9; Coffman[9], p. 160.

8. Valley Forge (December 1917)

1. Coffman[9], p. 141; Cheatham, p. 6; Duffy, p. 51; MacArthur, pp. 53–54; Knightley, p. 130.

2. G. Marshall[3], p. 53.

3. *USAWW*, 2:74; GHQ War Diary, 11/22/17, PP #365.

4. Cheatham, p. 6; MHT diary, 11/13/17 and 11/18/17, MHT Papers; GVHM diary, Oct. 23–24, 1917, GVHM #1.

5. F. Palmer[1], pp. 127, 129, 131, 133.

6. C. Smith, pp. 293–94, 300–13; Smith intvw.

7. Cheatham, p. 6; JLC diary, 12/25/17, JLC Papers.

8. Pershing[9], 1:269–70; *USAWW*, 2:126.

9. Harbord[8], pp. 201–03.

10. Pershing[9], 1:199–200; USAWC[2], 2:1.

11. HAD-JJP, 1/9/30, PP #354; Clark, pp. 160–70; Pogue[2], p. 159.

12. JLC diary, 5/2/19, JLC Papers; JLH memo, "Meeting with New Division Commander," 12/15/17, JLH #41; "Robert Lee Bullard," p. 2.

13. RLB diary, 10/20/17, 11/11/17, 11/25/17, RLB #2; Bullard[3], p. 91.

14. Bullard[3], pp. 92 & 115.

15. HTA diary, 12/23/17, HTA Papers.

16. *USAWW*, 2:88 and 3:4 & 33; Fuller[2], p. 376; WS-wife, 1/2/18, WS Papers.

17. Barnett, p. 239; F. Maurice[2], p. 597; Hancock, p. 484.

18. "British Feeling about America," 12/6/17, PP #19; Repington[2], 2:160.

19. Kaspi, pp. 174 & 176; DeWeerd[2], p. 167; Pattullo, *SEP*, 5/6/22, p. 98.

20. Harbord[8], pp. 122–23; Harbord[3], p. 190; Hankey[2], 2:744; Williamson in PP #359. On amalgamation, see DeFrancisco.

21. Serrigny, pp. 167–68; Lonergan, pp. 9–10.

22. Harbord³, p. 190; JGH AWC talk, 4/11/32, p. 14.

23. Pershing⁹, 1:75; JJP Jotting No. 19 & 25, n.d., PP #355.

24. *USAWW*, 2:88.

25. Coffman⁹, p. 10; Blake, pp. 46–47; JGH AWC talk, 4/11/32, p. 8.

26. *USAWW*, 3:4; Lonergan, p. 33.

27. Seymour³, 3:309–10.

28. R.S. Baker¹, 7:417; D. Lloyd George, 5:3018.

29. R.S. Baker¹, 7:417.

30. Pershing⁹, 1:255; Sharp, p. 280.

31. Pershing⁹, 1:254–55; Seymour³, 3:269 & 301.

32. Harbord³, p. 190.

33. *USAWW*, 2:132.

34. Ibid.

35. Ibid., 3:268; Pershing⁹, 1:291; Pattullo, *SEP*, 5/13/22, p. 14.

36. Pershing⁹, 2:228.

37. *USAWW*, 2:491.

38. Pershing⁹, 1:12, 152, 265–66.

39. Ibid., 1:153–54, 181; *USAWW*, 2:562; Cable P-228, 10/20/17, WD Cables, Box 50, RG 94; Fiske, p. 8; O'Ryan, 1:121.

40. Leonard M. Thomas-*NYT*, 3/29/31, PP #31; Alexander, pp. 2–3.

41. Seymour³, 3:268–69; Kaspi, pp. 169–75.

42. Harbord⁸, pp. 207 & 214; *USAWW*, 2:81 & 117 and 3:8; Pershing⁹, 1:256–57; EMH diary, 12/5/17, EMH Papers; GCM-Thomas G. Frothingham, 10/25/27, PP #79.

9. The Robertson Proposal (January 1918)

1. *USAWW*, 2:156; USWD², 2:7.

2. Coffman⁹, p. 144; Pogue², 1:159.

3. G. Marshall³, pp. 59–60.

4. Ibid.; JCH diary, 1/31/18, JCH Papers; Coffman⁹, pp. 144–45.

5. Edgar Russel-JJP, 1/10/24, PP #351.

6. HAD diary, 1/30/18, HAD Papers; Bullard³, p. 140.

7. WRR-JJP, 1/10/18, PP #353.

8. Ibid.; Lonergan, pp. 46–50 & 58–60; Hankey², 2:745.

9. Pershing⁹, 1:242, 288–89.

10. D. Lloyd George, 5:3006, 3019–20, 3024; H. Hoover, 1:255–57.

11. F. Maurice², p. 600; F. Maurice³, pp. 225–26; Liddell Hart⁹, pp. 197–98.

12. Cable P-487, 1/13/18, PP #353.

13. *USAWW*, 3:22, 30 & 36; Pershing⁹, 1:295; NDB-WW, 1/19/18, NBD #8.

14. Cable P-487, 1/13/18, PP #353; Pershing⁹, 1:295.

15. *USAWW*, 3:18–19; Robertson, pp. 324, 342–43.

16. NDB-WW, 1/19/18 and WW-NDB, 1/20/18, NDB #8.

17. *USAWW*, 3:22.

18. Harbord⁸, p. 218; Pershing⁹, 1:297.

19. THB-NDB, 1/22/18, THB #74. Derby was British War Minister; Andrew Bonar Law was Chancellor of the Exchequer and leader of the House of Commons.

20. Ibid.; Hyde, p. 240.

21. *USAWW*, 2:165 and 3:23; Pershing⁹, 1:296.

22. *USAWW*, 3:18–19; D. Lloyd George, 5:3025; WRR-THB, 1/27/18, PP #198; THB-NDB, 2/2/18, THB #74; THB-TAG, 1/27/18, Series 2, WW Papers.

23. Lonergan, pp. 278–82; D. Lloyd George, 5:3024.

24. Pershing[9], 1:304; Dawes[4], 1:71.

25. Harbord[8], p. 220; Pershing[9], 1:304–05.

26. *USAWW*, 3:25–26.

27. Pershing[9], 1:305, 314.

28. Resco intvw, 8/25/65.

29. Callwell, 2:54; *USAWW*, 3:32; Edmonds[1] (1918), 1:65.

30. Pattullo, *SEP*, 4/29/22, p. 34.

31. Pershing[9], 1:308.

32. Ibid., 1:331.

33. D. Lloyd George, 5:3026–27.

34. Pershing[9], 1:309–10; Hankey[2], 2:764–65; *USAWW*, 3:32, 37–39, 44–46.

35. *USAWW*, 3:40.

10. Leonard Wood (February 1918)

1. Foch[2], pp. 240–41; *USAWW*, 2:189–90, 194–95; F. Palmer[3], pp. 237–41.

2. Mordacq[3], 1:152–53; *USAWW*, 2:81; SWC Proces Verbaux, 2/2/18, THB #82.

3. *USAWW*, 2:218–19, 228, 233–34, 238–39; Blake, pp. 290–92; W. Griffiths, pp. 113–19.

4. Clemenceau, p. 37; *USAWW*, 2:207–08.

5. Pershing[9], 1:327–29; *USAWW*, 2:220–21.

6. Pershing[9], 1:319, 325, and passim.

7. Rublee remin, p. 173; MMP diary, 2/20/18, MMP Papers.

8. Harbord[3], p. 212; [WDC]-JGH, 5/6/35, JGH Papers, NYHS; *USAWW*, 2:103, 204–06.

9. Harbord[2], pp. 214–16; Pershing[9], 1:321–22; USWD[2], 1:6, 12–13; Film H-1448, RG 111.

10. JJP-NDB, 2/24/28, PP #19; PCM-NDB, 3/4/31, NDB #154.

11. JJP-FEW, 2/4/18, FWP Papers.

12. FEW-JJP, 7/3/19, FWP Papers; Whitlock, 2:614; Williams remin, p. 435; Hagedorn, 2:264–65.

13. R. S. Baker[1], 7:417.

14. EMH diary, 1/30/18, EMH Papers; William Wiseman Cable 523 to Drummond and Balfour, 2/4/18, Wiseman Papers; FEW-JJP, 5/18/18, FEW Papers, Laramie; Bowditch intvw; Mathews corres; FLP-JGH, 11/21/34, NDB #113.

15. JGH-William Phillips, 1/31/35, JGH Papers, NYHS; JWW remin, pp. 182–90; WS-wife, 1/30/18, WS Papers.

16. LW diary, 1/11/18, LW #10.

17. LW diary, 2/2/18, LW #10.

18. THB-NDB, 1/22/18, THB #74.

19. Ibid.; LW diary, 2/26/18, LW #10; Cronin, p. 277; Daniels[3], p. 290; JJP-CGD, 3/5/18, PP #59; memo of intvw of NDB by RSB and A. Howard Meneely, 4/6/28, RSB #20, Series 1 (cited as Baker-Meneely memo).

20. JJP-FEW, 2/4/18, FWP Papers; LW diary, 1/29/18, LW #10; Pershing[9], 1:308; Hagedorn, 2:259–61; March, p. 60.

21. JJP-NDB, 2/24/18, PP #19.

22. Ibid. Pershing's memo to the Chief of Staff was substantially the same.

23. LW diary, Jan. 1, 16 & 23, 1918, LW #10; Hagedorn, 2:267 and 271–72; JJP-JGH, 2/15/18, JGH Papers, LC; LW-Major Shannon, 2/26/18, LW #10; JJP-LW, 2/28/18, PP #215; Cable A-837, JGH Papers, NYHS; GVHM intvw, 9/12/60.

24. Baker-Meneely memo; Bliss Cable 38, 2/26/18, THB #201; FEW-JJP, 6/12/18, FWP Papers.

25. Baker-Meneely memo; JWW remin, pp. 188–89.

26. Pershing[9], 1:334; PHC-Major Rozet, 2/15/18, PHC Papers.

27. *USAWW*, 3:600–02; HAD diary, Jan. 1–29, 1918, HAD Papers; PLS diary, Jan. 27 & 29, Feb. 6 & 17, 1918, PLS Papers.

28. USAWC[2], 2:272 & 277; JLC diary, 2/13/18, JLC Papers.

29. USAWC[2], 2:27; Pershing[9], 1:335.

30. Press Review 107, 4/15/18, JLC Papers.

11. Peyton C. March (March 1918)

1. March, pp. 34–36; JJP-FEW, 2/4/18, FWP Papers; Pershing[9], 1:314; Coffman[6], pp. 39–51.

2. Coffman[6], pp. 52–53; JJP diary, Feb. 2 & 4, 1918, PP #4; March, p. 36; Pershing[9], 1:314.

3. JCH intvw; JLC diary, 2/2/18, JLC Papers.

4. THB-JJP, 3/17/21, PP #26.

5. Carter, p. 48; March, p. 50; Semsch, pp. 16–27. The command hierarchy suffered no such obfuscation in World War II. Eisenhower, the field commander, was clearly under Marshall, the Chief of Staff in Washington.

6. JGH AWC talk, 4/29/33, pp. 9–10.

7. NDB-JGH, 12/14/34, NDB #113; Frothingham, xxii–xxiii.

8. Hewes[1], p. 23.

9. Coffman[6], p. 123; EHC-JJP, 1/19/18, PP #56.

10. Snow, p. 175; Coffman[6], p. 64; Coffman[9], p. 163.

11. March, pp. 51–52, 56, 66–67; Coffman[6], 62 & 144; Coffman[4], pp. 1–10.

12. March, p. 76; Ayres, p. 37.

13. March, pp. 3, 69–70, 75–76, 93–94, 101; Coffman[6], pp. 65, 73, 84, 88–89; Coffman[9], pp. 227 & 231; E. Hurley, p. 122.

14. March, pp. 362–63.

15. Baruch, p. 57; Coffman[6], p. 189; Cramer, p. 128; Pogue[2], p. 207; Virden intvw, 3/8/61.

16. Ginnetti intvw.

17. FP-NDB, 11/3/34, NDB #184; Coffman[1], pp. 192–93; NDB AWC talk; memo of intvw of NDB by RSB and A. Howard Meneely, 4/6/28, RSB #20, Series 1.

18. Cable A-995, 3/27/18, JGH Papers, NYHS; Cable P-834 & P-954, Apr. 1 & 19, 1918, WD Cables, RG 407; Coffman[6], pp. 58–59.

19. *USAWW*, 2:342.

20. Cable A-1159, 4/23/18, PP #19.

21. JJP-PCM, 4/23/18, PP #123; Pershing[9], 1:350–51; Harbord[3], p. 224; Coffman[6], pp. 58 & 81.

22. Mitchell[3], p. 134; F. Palmer[1], pp. 66–67; Mott, p. 119; *USAWW*, 16:56; JJP-NDB, 7/11/19, PP #19.

23. *USAWW*, 17:74; March, p. 175; Cable A-1317, 5/15/18, JGH Papers, NYHS; Stallings[2], p. 177; Cable P-1172, 5/23/18, RG 120; JGH-LW, 2/4/19, JGH Papers, LC; NDB-JJP, 8/3/19, PP #19.

24. E. Lowry[2], pp. 256–58; Cable A-1317, 5/15/18, JGH Papers, NYHS; NDB-JJP, 8/3/19, PP #19.

25. Coffman[6], pp. 117–18; Smythe[19], pp. 53–62; Coffman[9], p. 186.

26. March intvw, Mar. 11 & 16, 1961; PCM-JJP, 5/10/18, PP #123; Cable A-915, 3/14/18, JGH Papers, NYHS.

27. JGH-JJP, 3/16/18, JGH Papers, LC.

28. *USAWW*, 2:244–45; Cable A-956, 3/21/18, JGH Papers, NYHS.

29. JGH-JJP, 3/16/18, JGH Papers, LC.

30. Coffman[6], p. 61; JJP-PCM, 5/5/18, and PCM-JJP, May [June] 6, 1918, PP #123.

31. Blumenson[2], 1:499; JJP-NDB, 7/27/17, PP #19; NDB-FP, 3/17/31, NDB #184; JJP diary, 3/17/18, PP #4. .ON PRINT

32. Film H-1444, RG 111; Pershing[9], 1:342–51; Harbord[3], pp. 229–37; Harbord[8], pp. 246–47; Hayes, *passim*; F. Palmer[9], 2:89–103; JLC-GEA, 3/18/27, JLC Papers.

33. JJP-FEW, 4/15/18, FWP Papers.

34. *USAWW*, 2:245; DeWeerd[4], p. 259.

35. Blake, p. 291; Hankey[2], 2:760; Riddell, p. 362; Terraine[2], pp. 398–99.

12. The German March Offensive (March 1918)

1. Foch[2], p. 248; Summary of Intelligence No. 29, 2/8/18, JLC Papers; Coffman[9], p. 154.

2. DeWeerd[4], pp. 263–64 & 267; Terraine[3], pp. 234–43; Foch[2], pp. 248–49; Fuller[1], p. 160; D. James, p. 161; S. L. A. Marshall[1], pp. 267–77. As a sort of psychological warfare, the Germans coupled their March offensive with the appearance of "Big Bertha," an extraordinary gun which shelled Paris from seventy-five miles away.

3. F. Palmer[9], 2:131; JLC diary, 9/18/18, JLC Papers.

4. Foch[2], pp. 257–58; Pershing[9], 1:354–55; *USAWW*, 3:121; Wales[2].

5. Clark's 1934 Preface to his collection of wartime letters to GHQ, USMA.

6. Pershing[9], 1:356; JJP diary, 3/25/18, PP #4.

7. *USAWW*, 3:273–77, 288–89; Pershing[9], 1:356–57; PHC-GHQ6 3/8/18, PHC Papers.

8. R. Griffiths, pp. 70–75; Blake, p. 298; Clemenceau, p. 41.

9. Clemenceau, p. 39.

10. Ibid.

11. Coffman[9], p. 130; Ralph H. Graves-PCM, 3/31/32, PCM #23.

12. Blake, p. 298; Wrench, pp. 340 & 342; *USAWW*, 2:254; Hendrick, 2:366; Mordacq[3], 1:243–45; Bliss[2], pp. 1–30; JJP MS, Folder 9, PP #353; Pershing[9], 1:323. See also Bonasso.

13. F. Palmer[3], p. 224; *USAWW*, 2:255–56.

14. *USAWW*, 2:257.

15. Ibid., 2:258.

16. Ibid.; Pershing[9], 1:360; F. Palmer[3], p. 224; *USAWW*, 2:279.

17. LCG-JJP, 7/16/18, PP #85; F. Maurice[2], p. 602; Seymour[3], 3:444.

18. Clemenceau, pp. 63–65, 75; WSS-Opnav, enclosure in JD-WW, c. 3/27/18, WW Papers, Series 2.

19. *USAWW*, 2:261–62.

20. Pershing[9], 1:363–65; JJP diary, 3/28/18, PP #4; Suarez, 2:232; Conquet, p. 244; Belcher, p. 411; Foch[2], p. 270.

21. Pershing[9], 1:382.

22. Williams-JJP, 5/21/23, PP #351.

23. Clemenceau, p. 65.

24. *USAWW*, 3:486; Pogue[2], pp. 162–63; Coffman[9], p. 155.

25. DeWeerd[4], p. 268; *USAWW*, 1:11.

26. *USAWW*, 2:263; DLG-LR, 3/28/18, WW Papers, Series 2; DLG-LR, 3/29/18, EMH Papers; Hyde, pp. 249–50 & 252. On Reading, see Jackson.

27. W. Churchill, 2:196; Bridges, pp. 202–03.

28. LR-DLG, 3/30/18, William Wiseman Papers; Jusserand, p. 137; Reading, 2:92–93 & 96.

29. WW-NDB, 4/6/18, PP #193.

30. PR 106, 4/14/18, JLC Papers.

13. The London Agreement (April 1918)

1. *USAWW*, 2:277.

2. Pershing[9], 1:375–76.

3. Hunter[1], pp. 33–52; C. Grant[2], p. 333; Recouly[1], pp. 19–21, 58–60; Bugnet, pp. 250–52.

4. Dawes[4], 1:84–90, 96–97, 109–11; Pershing[9], 1:398–99; Bruun, p. 158; F. Maurice[6], p. 151; JGH-JJP, 4/13/18, PP #87.

5. DeWeerd[4], p. 280; Pershing[9], 1:395–96.

6. Pershing[9], 1:396–97.

7. MacArthur, p. 47.

8. Pershing[9], 1:391–95; *USAWW*, 3:489–90; Folliard, p. B-3.

9. JLH diary, 4/16/18, JLH Papers, USAMHI.

10. *USAWW*, 3:615; Coffman[9], pp. 148–49; E. Taylor, pp. 122–24.

11. E. Taylor, pp. 129–30; *USAWW*, 3:613–17; Coffman[9], p. 149.

12. Watson corres; DLG-LR, 5/4/18, William Wiseman Papers.

13. GCM-JJP, 11/24/30, PP #354.

14. Harbord[3], p. 199; *USAWW*, 2:413.

15. LR-DLG, 4/18/18, Drawer 90, File 3, Wiseman Papers; DLG-LR, 3/29/18, EMH Papers.

16. *USAWW*, 2:336–37.

17. JJP penciled note on Baker memo of 4/19/18, PP #19; Pershing[9], 2:8; *USAWW*, 2:283–85.

18. DEN-JJP, 4/7/30, PP #354; Memo "E," DEN-JJP, pp. 17–18, n.d., PP #352; *USAWW*, 2:351–52.

19. Harbord[8], pp. 270–71.

20. *USAWW*, 2:340; JGH memo, n.d. (probably April 1918), JGH Papers, LC.

21. Pershing[9], 2:6; *USAWW*, 2:340; Harbord[3], pp. 254 & 259; JGH AWC talk, 4/11/32, pp. 11–12.

22. D. Lloyd George, 5:3046–48 & 3051–52; *USAWW*, 2:342–43; Pershing[9], 2:6–9; Harbord[8], pp. 275–76; Lonergan, pp. 172–75.

23. *USAWW*, 2:342–43.

24. Pershing[9], 1:396–97; NDB-WW, 4/29/18, NDB #8.

25. NDB-JJP, 6/6/18, PP #19; Coffman[5], p. 83.

26. PHC-GHQ, ltr 54, 4/25/18, PHC Papers; *USAWW*, 2:345–48.

27. *USAWW*, 3:93.

28. F. Palmer³, pp. 253–54; Charteris¹, p. 300.

29. LCG-EMH, 8/16/18, PP #85.

30. DH-CIGS, 10/18/17, PP #86; *NY Tribune*, 4/20/31; *NYT*, 4/7/18, sec. 5, p. 2; HAD diary, Apr. 1–30, 1918, HAD Papers; *USAWW*, 2:337–39.

31. Viereck¹, pp. 296–300; PLS diary, Apr. 18 & 25, 1918, PLS Papers.

32. Pétain-Foch, 4/24/18, PP #355; *USAWW*, 3:283 & 4:266; PHC-GHQ, ltr 39, 4/10/18, PHC Papers.

33. PHC-GHQ, ltr 80, 5/27/18, PHC Papers; *USAWW*, 3:292–93.

34. Lonergan, p. 304; Blake, pp. 307 & 311; *USAWW*, 2:322.

14. Abbeville (May 1918)

1. Harbord³, p. 260; *USAWW*, 2:258, 355, 358, 360–61; Clemenceau, p. 66; F. Palmer³, p. 262; PHC-GHQ, ltr 56, 4/27/18, PHC Papers.

2. JJP-PCM, 5/5/18, PP #123; Coffman⁹, p. 173; F. Palmer³, p. 262.

3. *USAWW*, 2:361–62; Pershing⁹, 2:21; JJP-NDB, 5/9/18, PP #19.

4. Pershing⁹, 2:22; *USAWW*, 2:261–62, 264; JJP-NDB, 5/9/18, PP #19; AF-SS, 5/1/18, EMH Papers. I have truncated the dialogue for the sake of brevity and to highlight the clash of personalities. Thus I have omitted people who interrupt, go off on tangents, etc.

5. AF-SS, 5/1/18, EMH Papers; Pershing⁹, 2:23–24; *USAWW*, 2:363.

6. Summaries of the May 1 Abbeville meeting are in Pershing⁹, 2:24–29; *USAWW*, 2:360–65 & 3:303; AF-SS, 5/1/18, EMH Papers; LE Notes on Abbeville, PP #193; Clemenceau, p. 64; Coffman⁹, pp. 213–14; D. Lloyd George, 5:3053; Roskill, 1:536; *NYT*, 2/20/31; Eller intvw; Hershey intvw.

7. *USAWW*, 2:269–72, 394, & 404; Pershing⁹, 2:30–33; *FR, 1918*, Sup. 1, 1:225; LE Notes on Abbeville, PP #193; JJP-NDB, 5/9/18, PP #19.

8. Wiseman-LR, 5/8/18, Wiseman Papers; Wiseman-EMH, 5/11/18, EMH Papers. On Wiseman, see Fowler's fine biography.

9. AF-SS, 5/6/18, EMH Papers; Wiseman-EMH, 5/11/18, EMH Papers; Coffman⁶, p. 277; D. Lloyd George, 5:3054; Willert, p. 144; Trask³, pp. 77, 84–85.

10. Pershing⁹, 2:33–34; *USAWW*, 2:379; D. Lloyd George, 6:3053–54; Foch², p. 308.

11. ME-FLP, 5/3/18, FLP Papers.

12. *USAWW*, 2:380 & 403–04; Pershing⁹, 2:35.

13. *USAWW*, 2:404.

14. Roskill, 1:536; Blake, p. 307; Hyde, p. 259; DH diary, 5/1/18, DH Papers.

15. Clemenceau, pp. 69–71; Reading, 2:99; Mordacq³, 2:6–7; AF-SS, 5/5/18, EMH Papers.

16. DLG-LR, 5/4/18, William Wiseman Papers; Clemenceau, pp. 71–72; Lonergan, pp. 180 & 186.

17. Seymour³, 3:447–48; EMH-WW, 5/20/18, EMH Papers.

18. *USAWW*, 2:399.

19. Ibid.

15. The Removal of Leonard Wood (May 1918)

1. Harbord³, pp. 262–63.

2. Ibid., p. 264; Holcomb intvw.

3. Harbord[3], p. 263; MLH-JJP, 5/16/21, PP #93.

4. FEW-JJP, 3/27/18, FWP Papers; LW diary, 2/26/18, LW #11; USAWC[2], 2:400 & 403, *NYT*, 3/26/18, pp. 1 & 4.

5. FEW-JJP, 6/12/18, FWP Papers.

6. JJP-FWP, 4/15/18, FWP Papers.

7. Wadsworth remin, pp. 188–89; Marvin remin, pp. 35–36; March, pp. 63–64; NDB-JJP, 6/6/18, PP #19.

8. F. Palmer[9], 2:236–37; USAWC[2], 2:403; Hagedorn, 2:283. Wadsworth remin, pp. 189–90.

9. NDB-JJP, 6/6/18, PP #19; NDB-WAW, 3/30/29, RSB #20, Series 1; LW diary, 5/23/18, LW #11.

10. Marvin remin, p. 36; Hagedorn, 2:284; EMH diary, 5/26/18, EMH Papers.

11. March, pp. 65–66; PCM-NDB, 4/5/32, NDB #155; LW-CRE, 10/1/18, CRE #10.

12. Hagedorn, 2:284–88; LW diary, May 27–28, 1918, LW #11.

13. Marvin remin, p. 36; NDB-JJP, 6/6/18, PP #19; NDB-Thomas H. Barry, 6/6/18, PP #19; NDB-HH, 11/2/29, HH Papers; FEW-JJP, 6/12/18, FWP Papers; F. Palmer[9], 2:244–45.

14. Hagedorn, 2:290–92; LW diary, 5/28/18, LW #11; FEW-JJP, June 12 & 25, 1918, FWP Papers; NDB-JJP, 6/6/18, PP #19; Mrs. FEW-JJP, 6/26/18, FWP Papers; Marvin remin, p. 38; F. Palmer[9], 2:244–45; Tumulty, p. 291.

15. Hagedorn, 2:296–98 & 316; Williams remin, pp. 424–25; JD diary, 5/28/18, JD #1.

16. Hagedorn, 2:295.

17. Williams remin, pp. 431 & 438; LW diary, 6/1/18, LW #11.

18. Longworth intvws, Mar. 7 & 15, 1961.

19. JJP-FEW, 6/14/18, FWP Papers; MR intvw, 8/9/65.

20. NDB-JJP through AF, 6/1/18, and NDB-JJP, 6/6/18, both in PP #19; JJP-NDB through AF, 6/12/18, EMH Papers.

16. Cantigny and Chemin des Dames (May 1918)

1. Pershing[9], 2:70. Documents on the Cantigny operation are in *USAWW*, 4:259–347.

2. Ely lecture to students of Army Center of Artillery Studies, 3/10/19, p. 2, HEE Papers; Pogue[2], p. 165.

3. Parker, p. 28; Millett[1], pp. 361–62; Pershing[9], 2:59.

4. Buck, p. 172; Ely, pp. 202–03; Stallings[2], p. 59.

5. Millett[1], pp. 361–62; *Infantry in Battle*, pp. 155–56.

6. Ely, p. 204; Millett[1], 361–62.

7. T. Johnson[2], 57–62; Evarts, pp. 1–93.

8. Buck, p. 174; Ely lecture, 3/10/19, p. 3, HEE Papers; Film H-1264, RG 111; Coffman[9], p. 156; Millett[1], pp. 363–64.

9. Hopper (10/12/18), p. 23; Ely lecture, 3/10/19, p. 3.

10. JJP-RLB, 5/28/18, PP #36; JJP diary, 5/28/18, PP #4.

11. Millett[1], p. 364.

12. Ely, "The Attack on Cantigny," p. 5, n.d., HEE Papers; Ely lecture, 3/10/19, p. 3, HEE Papers; Millett[1], p. 365.

13. Joseph M. Hanson, "Heroes of the West on the Field of France," *Common Sense*, n.d., p. 23, HEE Papers; Ely, "Attack on Cantigny," pp. 5–6, HEE Papers; Coffman[9], p. 157.

14. Buck, p. 176; Ely, "Attack on Cantigny," p. 6, HEE Papers.

15. Ely lecture, 3/10/19, p. 3., HEE Papers.

16. *USAWW*, 4:319; Ely AWC talk, 2/3/38, p. 6.

17. Ely AWC talk, 2/3/38, p. 13.

18. H. Holt, p. 185; Welcome P. Waltz, "Operations of Company C, 3d Machine Gun Battalion, at Cantigny," pp. 28–29, Waltz Papers.

19. Ely AWC talk, 2/3/38, pp. 13–14; Coffman[9], pp. 157–58; Millett[1], pp. 366–67.

20. Ely, "Attack on Cantigny," p. 6, HEE Papers; G. Marshall[3], p. 97. Translations of German orders and reports on the Cantigny fight are in the Battle of Cantigny Papers, USAMHI.

21. Coffman[9], p. 158; Smith corres, 6/26/63; D. C. Fisher-Henry Castor, 7/30/53, Fisher Papers, c/o Franklin Watts. The context of the Fisher quotation indicates that it refers to Cantigny.

22. *USAWW*, 2:434.

23. Pershing[9], 2:65–66; Smith corres, 6/26/63.

24. *NYES*, 5/31/18.

25. DeWeerd[4], pp. 277 & 288–90; Edmonds[1], 3:20; F. Palmer[3], p. 283; France, État-Major de l'Armée, Tome 6, Vol. 2, p. 8.

26. Pitt, pp. 139–40; Hubbard, pp. 222–33; Liddell Hart[3], pp. 177–81; Pershing[9], 2:61–62; DeWeerd[4], pp. 289–90.

27. DeWeerd[4], pp. 289–91; F. Palmer[3], p. 284; PHC-GHQ, ltr 80, 5/27/18, PHC Papers.

28. F. Palmer[3], p. 283; Pierrefeu, pp. 268–69.

29. Harbord[3], p. 269; Pershing[9], 2:61.

30. F. Palmer[9], 2:217; Coffman[9], p. 213.

31. JJP diary, 5/30/18, PP #4.

32. Pershing[9], 2:65.

33. PHC-GHQ, ltrs 83 & 84, both 5/30/18, PHC Papers.

34. Pershing[9], 2:65.

35. Ibid., 2:62–63; Pogue[2], p. 167.

17. Versailles and Belleau Wood (June 1918)

1. F. Palmer[3], pp. 269–72; *USAWW*, 2:438, 442–43.

2. Pershing[9], 2:71-72; JJP diary, 6/1/18, PP #4.

3. *USAWW*, 2:399. For Haig's hostile reaction to the news, see Haig diary, 6/1/18, Haig Papers.

4. JWM-JJP, 11/3/20, PP #353.

5. *USAWW*, 2:438–39.

6. JWM-JJP, 11/3/20, PP #353.

7. Ibid.; *USAWW*, 2:439; JJP diary, 6/1/18, PP #4.

8. Pershing[9], 2:73.

9. Ibid., 2:28 & 73; D. Lloyd George, 5:3058; Hankey[2], 2:811.

10. JJP jotting, "Versailles," n.d., PP #50.

11. *USAWW*, 2:440.

12. Ibid., 2:440–41; Pershing[9], 2:76–77; JJP diary, 6/2/18, PP #4.

13. Mangin[2], p. 304; Blake, pp. 307 & 315; Wm. Wiseman-Eric Drummond, 5/30/18, Wiseman Papers; *USAWW*, 2:403.

14. JJP diary, 6/2/18, PP #4.

15. Smuts, 3:661–63.

16. W. Williams[3], p. 289; C. Grant[1], pp. 264–65; Bugnet, pp. 115–24; Pershing[9], 2:78.

17. *USAWW*, 2:445; Pershing[9], 2:78–79; JJP diary, 6/2/18, PP #4.

18. Hagood, pp. 312–20.

19. S. L. A. Marshall[1], p. 277.

20. Pershing[9], 2:62–63.

21. S. L. A. Marshall[1], p. 277.

22. Pershing[9], 2:62–63.

23. Harbord[8], p. 288.

24. Ibid., pp. 288–89; Harbord[3], p. 287.

25. Harbord[3], pp. 274 & 284; Harbord[8], p. 289.

26. MHT diary, 6/13/18, MHT Papers; W. Churchill, 2:178.

27. Harbord[3], p. 283; Coffman[9], p. 217; MHT diary, 6/13/18, MHT Papers.

28. Pogue[2], p. 167; DeWeerd[4], pp. 291 & 293.

29. Harbord[3], p. 298.

30. Pierrefeu, p. 272; F. Palmer[3], p. 282; Kahn, pp. 9–10; Seymour[2], p. 14.

31. Gibbons[1], p. 304; Heinl, pp. 201–02.

32. Harbord[3], pp. 286, 295–97; Coffman[9], pp. 217–21; Dawes[4], 1:147; Bellamy, pp. 34–38; Otto, pp. 940–62; Asprey, *passim*.

33. S. L. A. Marshall[1], p. 281.

34. Coffman[9], pp. 221–22; Dickman, pp. 270–72.

35. Harbord[3], p. 261.

36. Coffman[9], p. 219.

37. Ibid.; "Candid Comment on the American Soldier," 6/12/18, JLC Papers.

38. Millett[2], p. 304.

39. SI No. 103, 7/12/18, JLC Papers.

40. Watson AWC talk, p. 4; DEN-JJP, n.d., PP #352; Bullard[3], pp. 208–09.

41. Gibbons[2], pp. 34–35, 143–48; Lejeune, p. 294.

42. MWI-JJP, 5/16/23, PP #351; Trader corres.

43. Pershing[9], 2:195.

44. "War Nurse Tells of Maimed Doughboy and 'Black Jack,' " *Cleveland Plain Dealer*, n.d., PP #29.

45. Dawes[1], pp. 7–8.

18. The 100-Division Program (June-July 1918)

1. Bullard[3], p. 198.

2. Pershing[9], 2:189; *USAWW*, 3:324.

3. *USAWW*, 3:95; Pershing[9], 2:45–46.

4. Coffman[9], pp. 285–86; LCG-EMH, 6/7/18, EMH Papers.

5. *USAWW*, 2:446 & 453; *USAWW*, 3:312; Lonergan, pp. 213–14 & 218.

6. *USAWW*, 2:467; Pershing[9], 2:95.

7. Chap. 29 draft, PP #366; Pershing[9], 1:333; Coffman[9], p. 195; Foulois, pp. 156–71.

8. Mitchell[3], p. 146; Harbord[8], p. 120; Coffman[9], p. 198.

9. WM-BDF, 4/1/18, PP #351; Mitchell[3], pp. 165–66, 177.

10. BDF-WM, 3/19/18, PP #351; Mitchell[3], pp. 182–83.

11. BDF-JJP, 3/13/24, PP #351; MMP diary, 3/11/18, MMP Papers; Foulois, pp. 167–71.

12. Patrick, pp. 3–8; *USAWW*, 16:331–32.

13. BDF-JJP, 3/13/24, PP #351; BDF-JJP, 6/4/18, PP #77.

14. BDF-JJP, 6/4/18, PP #77; PLS diary, 6/4/18, PLS Papers; Foulois, pp. 172–74.

15. JWM-BDF. 6/8/18; BDF-JWM, 6/10/18; BDF-MMP, 1/29/19—all PP #77; Foulois, pp. 172–79.

16. DeWeerd[4], pp. 294 & 315.

17. Pershing[9], 2:93–94.

18. JJP diary, 6/9/18, PP #4.

19. Pershing[9], 2:99 & 124; JJP diary, June 17 & 23, 1918, PP #4; PHC-GHQ, ltr 105, PHC Papers; USAWW, 2:469.

20. JJP-PCM, 6/19/18, PP #123; Pershing[9], 2:111.

21. USAWW, 3:324 & 326–27.

22. JJP-EMH, 6/19/18, PP #97; Pershing[9], 2:108 & 111; JJP-TR, 6/27/18, PP #177.

23. Pershing[9], 2:104, 107, 110–13; USAWW, 2:476–79 & 3:324.

24. USAWW, 2:482–83; JJP diary, 6/23/18, PP #4.

25. Pershing[9], 2:111-12; JJP-PCM, 6/19/18, PP #123.

26. Pershing[9], 2:121.

27. Ibid., 2:80 & 106; Coffman[9], p. 179.

28. USAWW, 2:482.

29. USAWW, 2:489; NDB-JJP, 6/6/18, PP #19.

30. JJP-EHC, 6/28/18, PP #56; USAWW, 2:489; NDB-JJP, 6/6/18, PP #19.

31. USAWW, 2:497–98; March, p. 102; Coffman[9], p. 179; GWG, "Report on Military Program 1918–1919 to the Chief of Staff," 7/12/18, EE 570, TAG, RG 94.

32. JJP-PCM, 7/19/18, PP #123; USAWW, 2:544; Coffman[9], p. 180.

33. USAWW, 2:519-21; Pershing[9], 2:143–45.

34. JJP diary, 7/10/18, PP #4.

35. Harbord[6], p. 13; USAWW, 2:518–19, 528, 530–31; Pershing[9], 2:144–47.

36. A good critique against Foch's proposal is in USAWW, 2:529–31.

37. JJP diary, 7/21/18, PP #4.

38. Harbord[8], p. 313; Chaffin, p. 50; D. James, 1:173–74.

39. MacArthur, p. 57; D. James, p. 174; Stallings[2], p. 119.

40. Viereck, pp. 145–48; ABMC, pp. 35, 330–31; Bullard[1], pp. 49–50.

41. Duffy, p. 130; D. James, 1:177.

42. MacArthur, p. 58; Liggett[1], pp. 98–99; ABMC, pp. 331–32; D. James, 1:178.

43. Infantry in Battle, pp. 335–36 & 340; Pershing[9], 2:153; Dickman, p. 112. See also McArthur.

44. Pershing[4], p. 35; Coffman[9], p. 227.

45. Coffman[9], p. 224.

46. D. James, 1:181.

47. ABMC, p. 36.

19. Soissons: The Turn of the Tide (July 1918)

1. Foch[2], p. 340; ABMC, pp. 36 & 103; Coffman[9], pp. 234–36; Bullard[3], pp. 136–37; Pershing[9], 2:65.

2. JJP diary, 6/9/18, PP #4; PLS diary, 7/6/18, PLS Papers; Mrs. Wainwright intvw. For the Belfort Ruse, see Smythe[20], pp. 34–38.

3. Harbord[3], p. 317; Pershing[9], 2:158.

4. MHT diary, 7/24/18, MHT Papers; Harbord[3], pp. 322–26; Harbord[8], pp. 321–24.

5. Harbord[3], pp. 322, 324–25; Harbord[8], pp. 322–23; MHT diary, 7/24/18, MHT Papers.

6. HEE lecture to students of Army Center of Artillery Studies, 3/10/19, p. 4, HEE Papers; MHT diary, July 14 and 24, 1918, MHT Papers; Thomason[2], p. 94; Pershing[9], 2:163–64; Coffman[9], pp. 236–37.

7. Rickenbacker[1], pp. 243–44.

8. Films H-1368, M-103 & M-348, RG 111; BHB diary, July 14 & 18, 1918, BHB Papers; MHT diary, 7/24/18, MHT Papers.

9. MHT diary, 7/24/18, MHT Papers.

10. Ibid.

11. Bolté intvw; BHB, "Foot Soldiers," p. 93, BHB Papers.

12. BHB diary, 7/19/18, BHB Papers.

13. MHT diary, 7/24/18, MHT Papers.

14. Ibid.; Coffman[9], pp. 238 & 241.

15. Young, pp. 367–68; Harbord[3], p. 333; Harbord[8], p. 327.

16. MWI-JJP, 5/16/23, PP #351.

17. S. Thomas, pp. 56–57; Berdoulat-JGH, 6/29/25, JGH Papers, NYHS.

18. BHB diary, 7/19/18, BHB Papers; MHT diary, July 18 & 24, 1918, MHT Papers.

19. Coffman[9], pp. 204–05.

20. MHT diary, 7/24/18, MHT Papers; Harbord[3], pp. 336–37; Harbord[8], pp. 325 & 329–30; Millett[2], pp. 305–06.

21. Pershing[9], 2:167.

22. Patch, p. 37.

23. E. Roosevelt, p. 103.

24. Coffman[9], pp. 244–45.

25. PHC-GHQ, ltr 143, 7/18/18, and ltr 243, 11/11/18, PHC Papers; Mangin[2], pp. 284–85.

26. Hindenburg, 2:208.

27. Harbord[3], xiv.

28. "Pershing's Story Thrills Educator," *NYT*, 3/20/31, PP #359.

29. S. Thomas, p. 114; Miller, p. 26.

30. Duffy, p. 206; MacArthur, pp. 59–60.

31. MacArthur, pp. 60–61.

32. Film M-50, RG 111; E. James, pp. 401–10; Coffman[9], pp. 250–61.

33. Young, p. 370; Taber, 2:58–60; *USAWW*, 2:568–69; PHC-GHQ, ltr 156, 7/31/18, PHC Papers.

34. PHC-GHQ, ltr 159, 8/4/18, PHC Papers; Viereck[1], pp. 162–63 & 165; Notes by AEF IG, n.d., p. 21, folder 4, PP #352.

35. Viereck[1], pp. 123–24; Teilhard de Chardin, p. 218; Kaspi, pp. 295, 298–99.

36. Coffman[9], pp. 234–61.

37. D. James, 1:191; JJP-TR, 7/27/18, PP #177.

38. TR-JJP, 8/19/18, PP #177:

39. Bishop, 2:458.

20. The Goethals Proposal (July 1918)

1. *USAWW*, 2:549–53; Pershing[9], 2:171–73; Foch[2], pp. 369–74.

2. Pershing[9], 2:139 & 175; Harbord[3], pp. 347–48; NDB-JGH, 2/8/35, JGH Papers, LC.

3. JJP-PCM, 7/19/19, PP #123; Pershing[9], 2:140 & 177.

4. Coffman[6], p. 272.

5. FEW-JJP, 6/25/18, FWP Papers; EMH diary, 5/23/18, EMH Papers; Wiseman-EMH, 5/11/18, EMH Papers.

6. EMH-JJP, 6/19/18 & 7/4/18, PP #97.

7. EMH-WW, 6/3/18, EMH Papers.

8. PCM-JJP, 7/5/18, PP #123; LCG-JJP, 7/20/18, PP #85.

9. NDB-WW, 6/8/18, NDB #8.

10. JJP-FEW, 2/4/18, FWP Papers; DCS-JJP, 9/4/30, PP #182; Beaver[3], pp. 95–109.

11. Pershing[9], 2:185–86.

12. Ibid., 2:180–81.

13. NDB-JJP, 7/30/18, PP #19.

14. PCM-NDB, 2/26/32, NDB #155; JJP-JGH, 12/21/29, JGH Papers, NYHS.

15. MLH-JJP, 5/30/21, PP #93.

16. Harbord[3], pp. 345–52; Harbord[8], pp. 338–40.

17. *USAWW*, 2:553; Pershing[9], 2:177.

18. JJP-NDB, 7/27/18, PP #19.

19. Pershing[9], 2:190-91; JJP-NDB, 7/28/18, PP #19.

20. NDB-JJP, 7/30/18, PP #19.

21. Harbord[3], pp. 353, 356, 367, 372.

22. Ibid., pp. 376–77; Pershing[9], 1:345–46; Film H-1370, RG 111.

23. JJP-NDB, 8/17/18, PP #19; Pershing[9], 2:192–204; Wilgus[2], pp. 130–33. Sample JJP speeches to stevedores are in PP #342.

24. JJP-NDB, 8/7/18, PP #19.

25. Beaver[1], p. 166; JJP-EMH, 8/7/18, PP #97; EMH diary, 8/17/18, EMH Papers.

26. Harbord[3], pp. 385, 485–510; JGH AWC talk, 4/29/33, p. 10.

27. DCS-JJP, 9/4/30, PP #182; Connor AWC talk, 2/18/28, p. 8; DCS-JGH, n.d., but received 3/18/35, JGH Papers, NYHS; Hagood, pp. 72, 75, 221–35.

28. JGH-JMP, 8/21/18, JMP Papers.

29. Harbord[8], pp. 349–51; Harbord[3], pp. 348–51, 380–81; L. Thomas, 2:345–50.

30. Harbord[3], p. 381; AWB-JJP, 1/19/24, PP #352; FG-JJP, 6/2/21, PP #81.

31. A. Andrews, pp. 142–43; Pershing[9], 2:197.

32. Harbord[3], pp. 391–92; Cornebise, p. 117.

33. FEW-JJP, 8/27/18, FWP Papers; Harbord[8], p. 339.

34. Leighton & Coakley, pp. 242–43.

35. JJP-EMH, 8/7/18, EMH Papers.

36. JJP-NDB, 7/28/18, PP #19.

37. Harbord[8], p. 310; Harbord[3], p. 304; Coffman[6], p. 110; JJP-PCM, 7/15/18, PP #19.

38. JJP diary, 8/22/18, PP #4.

39. Harbord[3], p. 304; Harbord[8], p. 310.

40. JGH-JJP, 7/17/18, PP #87.

41. PCM-JJP, 7/2/18, PP #123.

42. JJP-NDB, 7/28/18, PP #19; Pershing[9], 2:223.

43. March, pp. 266–67.

44. Ibid., p. 50.

45. Watson[2], p. 61.

21. The American First Army (August 1918)

1. JLC diary, 8/20/18, JLC Papers; PLS diary, 8/4/18, PLS Papers; Film H-1402, RG 111; Freidel, p. 194.

2. Dawes[4], 1:153.

3. Albert Thomas-GC, 8/22/18, PP #196; *USAWW*, 3:354–55; Pershing[9], 2:218.

4. Lonergan, pp. 234–37; *USAWW*, 3:303; Pershing[9], 2:190.

5. *USAWW*, 3:324 & 331; Pershing[9], 2:113–14.

6. *USAWW*, 2:554 and 3:349.

7. Notes on Foch-JJP conversation, 8/24/18, PP #50; Pershing[9], 2:237–38.

8. Edmonds[2], pp. 344–45; Baldwin, p. 147; Goerlitz, p. 377; Ludendorff, 2:326–28.

9. Edmonds[2], pp. 344–45; DeWeerd[4], pp. 327–28; Ludendorff, 2:328–34.

10. *USAWW*, 2:518; Pershing[9], 2:143, 214–15; JJP diary, 8/12/18, PP #4.

11. JJP diary, 8/12/18, PP #4; Pershing[9], 2:216–17; AF-JJP, 10/5/36, PP #78; Blake, pp. 323 & 325; DH-JJP, 8/27/18, DH Papers.

12. Pershing[9], 2:230.

13. Ibid., 2:229–31; *USAWW*, 2:583–85.

14. AB-LR, 7/11/18, Wm. Wiseman Papers; *USAWW*, 2:566–67, 574.

15. *USAWW*, 2:573. For an interesting conspiracy theory concerning the British actions, see Parson[2], pp. 140ff.

16. WW-NDB, 8/9/18, NDB #8.

17. *USAWW*, 2:482–83, 544, 566; Pershing[9], 2:224.

18. *USAWW*, 2:579–80.

19. Ibid., 2:613–14.

20. Ibid., 2:588 & 610.

21. Ibid., 2:580, 588, 610.

22. Ibid., 2:489; Coffman[9], p. 179; Foch[2], p. 345.

23. Pershing[9], 2:174–75, 212; Foch[2], p. 397. See also Historical Section, Army War College, *The Genesis of the American First Army*. After the reduction of the St. Mihiel salient, the AEF planned to advance against the German stronghold at Metz.

24. PHC-GHQ, ltr 164, 8/9/18, PHC Papers.

25. Pershing[9], 2:238.

26. Haig's concept of the whole western front as a massive salient had its limitations. Eliminating a salient by a pincer's movement against its shoulders demands a certain swiftness that the size of the western front made impossible. As things worked out, the massive salient was never closed. In practice, the Allies made local flanking attacks which compelled German withdrawal or, in the case of the Americans in the Meuse-Argonne region, pushed the Germans back with frontal attacks, taking great casualties.

27. Foch[2], pp. 398–99; Weygand[3], 1:597, 601–02; Pershing[9], 2:243; Coffman[9], pp. 270–71; USAWC[1], pp. 53–54, 77–78; Foch-JJP, 8/30/18, PP #50; Notes on Foch-JJP conversation, 8/30/18, PP #50.

28. Pershing[9], 2:244–45. On Degoutte, see Millett[1], pp. 384–88, and Stallings[2], pp. 90, 100, 119, 201, 204.

29. Pershing[9], 2:246–48; Dawes[4], 1:163; *USAWW*, 2:461; TBM-JJP, 12/4/29, PP #354; Notes on Foch-JJP conversation 8/30/18, PP #50.

30. *NYHT*, 8/11/54.

31. JJP diary, 8/30/18, PP #4; JJP memo No. 5, n.d., PP #355.

32. Pershing[9], 2:248–50; JJP diary, 8/31/18, PP #4.

33. JJP diary, Aug. 30–31, 1918, PP #4; Pershing[9], 2:251–53; Notes on JJP-HPP conversation, 8/31/18, PP #50.

34. *USAWW*, 2:589–92; Foch-JJP, 9/1/18, PP #75; Pershing[9], 2:253–55; Coffman[9], pp. 271–72; F. Maurice[5], p. 187; JJP diary, 9/2/18, PP #4.

35. Foch[2], pp. 401, 404–05.

22. St. Mihiel (September 12–16, 1918)

1. Foch[1], p. 1: D. Johnson, pp. 402–03; DeWeerd[4], pp. 330; Coffman[9], pp. 263–64; *USAWW*, 2:211.

2. HEE, "Training Management & Instructional Methods," Ft. Belvoir, Va. lecture, 1937, p. 3, author's file; Pershing[9], 2:262–63; Harbord[3], p. 421.

3. Keller, p. 2C; English, pp. 129–30; HEE, "Lecture to students of Army Center of Artillery Studies," 3/10/19, p. 7, HEE Papers.

4. W. Thornton, p. 432; LCG-EMH, 9/21/18, PP #85; JLC diary, 9/15/18, JLC Papers; Recouly[1], p. 22; Roskill, 1:596; NDB-JGH, 4/10/35, JGH Papers, LC.

5. G. Marshall[3], pp. 124–28, 133–34; Coffman[9], pp. 266–69.

6. DEN-JJP, n.d., PP #352; Pershing[9], 2:260; Harbord[3], p. 414.

7. Pershing[9], 2:260–61; D. James, 1:198; Mitchell[3], pp. 234–48. See also Mitchell[1].

8. Coffman[9], pp. 277–78; Pershing[9], 2:260–61.

9. Sherwood, p. 120; Amerine, p. 173.

10. Pershing[9], 2:265–66.

11. Ibid., 2:226 & 265; Coffman[9], pp. 273–76; Bullard[2], pp. 1–10.

12. HAD-JJP, 9/24/30, PP #354.

13. SDR-JJP, 1/21/24, PP #352; Blumenson[2], 1:568–69, 574, 581, 592; Pershing[9], 2:261; SDR, "Tanks," Dec. 1926, p. 8, PP #352.

14. JJP diary, 9/10/18, PP #4; EFM-HAD, 9/10/18, G-3 files, AEF, 122.04, Box 3385, RG 120, NA; G. Marshall[3], pp. 134–36.

15. JJP diary, Sept. 10–11, 1918, PP #4; Pershing[9], 2:265; Coffman[9], p. 278; Duffy, pp. 233–34.

16. Harbord[3], p. 422; Langer, p. 32; DeWeerd[4], p. 335.

17. Pershing[9], 2:267.

18. Ibid., 2:266–67; Coffman[9], pp. 278–79.

19. GMC, "Accomplishments of AEF," 4/20/19, AGO 370.24 EE, RG 94, NA; PHC-GHQ, ltr 199, 9/15/18, PHC Papers.

20. Duffy, p. 236; Pershing[9], 2:268.

21. Coffman[9], pp. 280–81; Liggett[1], pp. 153–54.

22. JJP-JTD, 4/4/26, PP #64; Weygand[3], 1:610–11; Liddell Hart[7], pp. 485–86.

23. JLC diary, 9/12/18, JLC Papers; Film M-50, RG 111; Coffman[9], pp. 282–83; Pershing[9], 2:269–72.

24. PR 224, 9/28/18, JLC Papers.

25. *CN*, 3/9/31, PP #359; Coffman[9], p. 283.

26. Young, pp. 372–73; JJP diary, 9/13/18, PP #4; Pershing[9], 2:271.

27. Eller intvw; Curtin intvw, 7/17/63; DEN-JGH, 2/10/34, JGH Papers, NYHS; "Greetings to America's General," p. 40. By a coincidence the victory came on Sept. 13, the day Pershing celebrated as his birthday. Noting that Pershing would be 58 on the 13th, one female admirer pointed out that the two digits (5 and 8) added up to 13, an unlucky number for Kaiser Wilhelm, whose name had 13 letters in it.

28. Moseley intvw, 9/13/60.

29. DLG-JJP, 9/14/18 and JJP-DLG, 9/17/18, PP #81.

30. JGH-JJP, 9/13/18 and JJP-JGH, 9/19/18, JGH Papers, LC.

31. PR 224, 9/28/18 and SE 166, 9/14/18, JLC Papers.

32. SI 250, 1/11/19, p. 11, JLC Papers; Coffman[9], p. 283.

33. Williamson, pp. 46–49; *USAWW*, 8:312.

34. MacArthur, pp. 63–64.

35. Ibid., p. 64; Pershing[9], 2:270.

36. Liddell Hart[8], p. 312; D. James, 1:210.

37. Liggett[1], p. 159.

38. CC, pp. 6–10, JLC Papers; Willey Howell, "2d Section, GS, 1st Army, in St. Mihiel & Meuse-Argonne Operations," 1/6/19, p. 13, Folder 191-58, 1st Army Historical, Box 76, RG 120, NA (cited as Howell rept); NRO No. 3, 1918, pp. 8–12, JLC Papers; Notes by AEF IG, n.d., pp. 1, 23–24, 26, 28, PP #352; G. Marshall[4], p. 36.

39. Blumenson[2], 1:593; Walton, p. 193; Clemenceau, pp. 75–76; Martet, p. 87.

40. Howell rept, p. 14.

23. Meuse-Argonne: September 26, 1918

1. GCM, "On Active Service," 4/2/19, p. 16, GCM Papers; Pogue[2], 1:179; Pershing[9], 2:291–92, 321; SOW, 9/25/18, JLC Papers; Esposito[2], Map 69; PHC-GHQ, ltrs 207 & 209, Sept. 27 & 30, 1918, PHC Papers; Seldes, pp. 35–37. For an extended treatment of the Meuse-Argonne, see F. Palmer[10] and the excellent dissertation by Braim; for the German side, see Giehrl[2].

2. Essame, p. 166; DeWitt AWC talk, p. 9; Coffman[9], pp. 299–300; Ormsby, pp. 129–30, 333–34; photos in USAMHI.

3. Harbord[3], p. 433; Pershing & Liggett, pp. 38–39.

4. Oury corres; *Infantry in Battle*, pp. 199–200; Pershing[9], 2:278, 286–87, 290; Coffman[9], pp. 301 & 305; Notes by AEF IG, n.d., p. 28, PP #352.

5. Pershing[9], 2:287; GCM-JJP, 10/24/30, PP #354.

6. Film M-346, RG 111; G. Marshall[3], pp. 137–42, 149–58; *USAWW*, 9:64–66; Coffman[9], pp. 303–04.

7. F. Palmer[5], p. 303; *USAWW*, 9:64–66.

8. Pershing[9], 2:286.

9. Ibid., 2:292–93; *USAWW*, 9:82–88; Coffman[9], p. 301; HAD-JJP, 9/24/18, PP #354.

10. Alexander, p. 162; FC, NOO-D, n.d., p. 3, JLC Papers; Giehrl[2], p. 132; SI 193, 10/11/18, JLC Papers.

11. Pershing[9], 2:294.

12. Ibid., 2:290–91, 295; USAWC[2], 1:281.

13. Pershing[9], 2:290; Blumenson[2], 1:607. See also Mitchell[2].

14. JLC diary, 9/25/18, JLC Papers; Oviatt intvw, 1/27/70; ADD diary, 9/25/18, ADD Papers; JCH diary, 9/26/18, JCH Papers; Rickenbacker[1], p. 212.

15. "War Flyer Recalls Battle's Splendor," NYT, 3/24/31.

16. PR, 10/25/18, p. 1, and JLC diary, 9/26/18, both JLC Papers.

17. GCM-Lloyd N. Winters, 2/26/31, GCM Papers.

18. Ibid.; PLS diary, 9/26/18, PLS Papers; NRO No. 3, pp. 16–20, JLC Papers; Notes by AEF IG, n.d., p. 8; GMC, "On Active Service," 4/2/19, p. 17, GCM Papers; Viereck[1], pp. 38–41, 50–51, 246, 286; SI 191 & 202, 10/9/18 & 10/20/18, JLC Papers; Woods, pp. 3–5; PHC-GHQ, ltr 217, 10/11/18, PHC Papers.

19. Millett[1], pp. 402–05; Bach & Hall, p. 174; Coffman[9], pp. 308–10; BAP memoirs, 1927, pp. 17–18, BAP Papers, Bolté Collection; HAD-GCM, 12/9/20, HAD Papers.

20. PLS diary, 9/26/18, PLS Papers; RA-JJP, 3/20/31, PP #28.

21. Gallwitz-T. M. Johnson, 3/20/28, PP #353.

22. Stallings[2], pp. 225 & 271; WSM lecture at First Army Hq, 12/23/18, First Army Hist. File 191-58, Box 76, RG 120, NA (cited as WSM lecture).

23. PLS diary, 9/28/18, PLS Papers.

24. Pershing[9], 2:301–02; Coffman[9], pp. 321–22.

25. JJP diary, 9/27/18, PP #4; PSL diary, 9/28/18, PLS Papers; Coffman[9], p. 311.

26. DEN-JJP, 1/1/18, PP #352; JJP diary, 9/28/18, PP #4.

27. CFF-JJP, 2/27/19, CFF Papers.

28. Ibid.; WSM lecture; Notes by AEF IG, n.d., p. 7. PP #352; Cheseldine, p. 245; Breckinridge remin, pp. 264–65; NRO No. 3, 1918, p. 22, JLC Papers.

29. USAWW, 9:138–40; JJP diary, 9/28/18, PP #4.

30. USAWW, 9:522; Wm. H. Johnston-JJP, 6/19/31, PP #360; PLS diary, 9/29/18, PLS Papers.

31. N. Hall & Schultz, p. 12; R. McCormick, pp. 171–75; Coffman[9], p. 312; PLS diary, Sept. 26–30, 1918, PLS Papers.

32. USAWW, 9:148.

33. Pershing[9], 2:301–03; JJP diary, 9/29/18, PP #4; Film H-1405, RG 111.

34. Weygand[3], 1:617; F. Maurice[7]; Mordacq[1], p. 160; T. Johnson[3], p. 185; Mangin[1], p. 207; H. W. Allen, pp. 28–36.

35. PHC-GHQ, ltrs 210 & 212–14, Oct. 1 & 3–5, 1918, PHC Papers; JJP diary, 10/1/18, PP #4.

36. Mordacq[3], 2:244.

37. G. Marshall[3], pp. 162–63; Pershing[9], 2:304.

38. Marenches-JJP, 12/14/23, PP #353; Pershing[9], 2:303–04; RAC diary, 9/29/18, RAC Papers.

24. Meuse-Argonne: October 4, 1918

1. Pershing[9], 2:293 & 300.

2. Foch[2], pp. 212, 410–11; Recouly[1], p. 63; Falls[2], viii-x.

3. Pershing[9], 2:280; Foch[2], p. 408.

4. Marshall-Cornwall[2], p. 288. On October 3 the 2d Division (Lejeune), loaned to the French XXI Corps, performed brilliantly in storming and capturing dominating German positions on Blanc Mount Ridge, enabling the French Fourth Army (Gouraud), which had been held up there, to move forward. Lejeune, pp. 336–66.

5. PHC-GHQ, ltr 217, 10/11/18, PHC Papers; Blake, pp. 329–30; Foch[2], p. 412.

6. Foch[2], p. 412; Weygand[3], 1:618; USAWW, 2:617–18; JJP diary, 10/2/18, PP #4; Pershing[9], 2:306–07; Repington[2], 2:458–59.

7. Pershing[9], 2:307; JJP diary, 10/2/18, PP #4; JJP annotation to F. Maurice[2], p. 604, PP #359.

8. USAWW, 2:619.

9. JJP diary, 10/3/18, PP #4.

10. Pershing[9], 1:213.

11. JJP diary, Oct. 3 & 8, 1918, PP #4.

12. Pershing[9], 2:321–23.

13. Coffman[9], p. 333.

14. Ibid., pp. 335–36; Stallings[2], p. 294; JJP diary, 10/4/18, PP #4.

15. Mitchell[3], p. 260; PLS diary, 10/8/18, PLS Papers; Wecter[2], p. 328.

16. Liggett[1], pp. 186–97; Coffman[9], pp. 323–25; T. Johnson & Pratt, pp. 219–85; Skeyhill, pp. 217–69; McCarthy, pp. 86–91 & 93.

17. Pershing[9], 2:331–32; Coffman[9], pp. 326–27.

18. ABMC, p. 249 and endpaper map.

19. Pershing[9], 2:320; JCH diary, 10/7/18, JCH Papers; Sherwood, pp. 160–61; Rickenbacker[1], p. 241.

20. Walton, p. 194; ABMC, pp. 175–76.

21. JJP diary, 10/13/18, PP #4; Mordacq², p. 150; Notes on Foch-JJP conversation, 10/13/18, PP #50.

22. Kaspi, p. 343.

23. *USAWW*, 2:594, 603, 620, 630, 634, 637–39; Pershing⁹, 2:312, 328, 341.

24. Coffman⁶, p. 141; F. Palmer⁹, 2:365–66; Pershing⁹, 2:327.

25. Pershing⁹, 2:310.

26. Ibid., 2:22 & 308; *USAWW*, 2:602–03 & 619; Coffman⁶, pp. 139–40.

27. *USAWW*, 3:353 & 12:184–85.

28. JJP-Foch, 9/24/18, PP #75; JJP-GC, 10/11/18 and GC-JJP, 10/18/18, PP #47; *USAWW*, 2:621 & 625.

29. *USAWW*, 2:622–24.

30. DEN-AEF CofS, 9/10/18, PP #123; JJP diary, 9/5/18, PP #4.

31. AF-EMH, 9/12/18, EMH Papers; JJP diary, 10/6/18, PP #4; Coffman⁶, p. 113; Mrs. Ely intvw, 7/4/61.

32. MR intvw, 8/25/65.

33. Bothwell, p. 7.

34. R. O'Connor, p. 182.

35. JLC diary, 10/12/18, JLC Papers; AF-SS, 10/5/18, EMH Papers.

36. HTA diary, 10/17/18, HTA #2; Simonds², p. 18.

37. GCM-JJP, 10/24/30, PP #354; Pogue⁴, p. 13.

38. Lippmann remin, p. 118.

39. JLC diary, Sep. 19–20, 1918, JLC Papers; Harbord⁸, pp. 363 & 367.

40. JGH-JJP, 9/23/18, PP #87. Baker later told Frederick Palmer that he considered Liggett, Summerall, and Harbord as possible successors to Pershing, with Harbord as his first choice. F. Palmer⁹, 2:369.

41. *USAWW*, 2:566–67, 598–99; Harbord³, p. 400.

42. Pershing⁹, 2:311–14; Harbord³, pp. 427–28; *USAWW*, 2:611.

43. *USAWW*, 2:482–83, 544, 579, 588.

44. Ibid., 2:610, 613–14; March, p. 304.

45. *USAWW*, 2:618.

46. Ibid., pp. 625–26.

47. JJP-Mrs. GSP, 10/10/18, PP #155.

48. Foch², xxv.

49. NDB-FP, 7/18/31, NDB #184.

50. JGH AWC talk, 4/11/32, p. 13.

25. Meuse-Argonne: October 14, 1918

1. Coffman⁹, pp. 329–30; USAWC², 1:193, 237, 268. Hines was the only American officer in World War I to command a regiment, brigade, division, and corps in combat. For details on Summerall, see Dupuy & Dupuy¹, pp. 248–52.

2. Pershing⁹, 2:338; Coffman⁹, p. 327.

3. Taber, pp. 160 & 168.

4. Pershing⁹, 2:339; JJP diary, 10/14/18, PP #4.

5. JJP diary, 10/15/18, PP #4; JLH diary, 10/15/18, JLH Papers, Bolté Collection.

6. SI 201, 10/19/18, JLC Papers; Fitzgerald, p. 125.

7. Smythe & Pocek, pp. 26–27.

8. Film H-1411, RG 111; PLS diary, Oct. 15 & 17, 1918, PLS Papers.

9. MacArthur, p. 67; Haan, pp. 15-26.

10. Pershing[9], 2:340-41.

11. Buck-JJP, 4/27/21 & JJP-Buck, 5/3/21, PP #36; JJP diary, 10/15/18, PP #4; JWM-Buck, 10/20/18, PP #36.

12. JJP diary, 10/15/18, PP #4; PLS diary, June 3 and Sept. 9 & 14, 1918, PLS Papers; Pershing[9], 2:272. Pershing does not identify McMahon in the incident, but it was probably he whom he had in mind.

13. Albertine, pp. 303-04; PLS diary, 3/16/19, PLS Papers; WDC-JGH, 4/7/31, JGH Papers, NYHS; MC-HAD, 12/8/20, HAD Papers; EB-CRE, 5/8/18, with enclosure, PP #69; HL-AG AEF, 8/13/18, CRE Papers; Stallings[2], pp. 155-56.

14. Bowditch intvw.

15. JJP jotting, n.d., FWP Papers.

16. PLS diary, 10/20/18, PLS Papers; Coffman[9], pp. 330-31; JWM-CRE, 10/19/18, CRE Papers, #10.

17. EMH diary, 10/27/18, EMH Papers. For a defense of Edwards, see the Kelly articles in the Bibliography.

18. Riddell, p. 369; Harriman, pp. 291-92.

19. EMH diary, 10/26/18, and EMH-WW, 10/27/18, EMH Papers; Liddell Hart[2], p. 379.

20. Clemenceau, pp. 81-87, 92; Foch[2], pp. 434-36; Poincaré[1], 10:368-73; Translation of Poincaré article in *Excelsior*, 4/14/30, PP #353.

21. Recouly[1], pp. 25-26; Foch[2], pp. 437-48. It was undoubtedly this tactic of increasing the ten and diminishing the twenty that Foch had in mind in ordering Pershing on Sept. 30 to send two or three American divisions to the French XVII Corps and one or two divisions to the French XXXVIII Corps.

22. USAWC[2], 1:150-55; Pershing[9], 2:335-36.

23. J.P. DuCane-CIGS, 10/19/18, PP #354; PLS diary, Oct. 17-22 & Nov. 11, 1918, PLS Papers; E. Johnson, p. 343; Pershing[9], 2:328 & 358; Coffman[9], pp. 332-33; JJP-CHM, 10/24/18, PP #142; HAD-JWM, 10/19/18, HAD Papers; USAWW, 15:304-05; Liggett[1], pp. 207-08; Bridges, p. 218; Notes by AEF IG, n.d., pp. 27-28, PP #352.

24. HAD-JWM, 10/19/18, HAD Papers; PLS diary, Oct. 13, 18, 22-24, 1918, PLS Papers; Coffman[9], p. 332.

25. PLS diary, Oct. 14-17, 1918, PLS Papers.

26. Coffman[9], pp. 340-41.

27. Ibid., pp. 337-38; Pershing[9], 2:340-41 & 357; Notes on JJP-Foch conversation, 10/13/18, PP #50; SI 262, 10/19/18, JLC Papers; Liggett[1], pp. 2-3; G. Marshall[3], p. 159; J.P. DuCane-CIGS, 10/19/18, PP #354; T. Johnson[3], pp. 290-91; Maximilian, 2:294 & 301; Howland, 2:map 136.

28. Liddell Hart[2], pp. 385-86; Viereck[1], pp. 272-73; USAWW, 10:frontispiece map.

29. C. Grant[1], pp. 286-87; *Preliminary History*, pp. 139-40.

30. Pershing[9], 2:342.

31. Ludendorff, 2:398.

32. Coffman[9], p. 336.

33. Ibid., p. 337; USAWW, 9:133.

34. PR, 11/3/18, JLC Papers.

35. USAWW, 11:455, 459, 464.

36. TBM-JJP, 12/4/29, PP #354.

37. USAWW, 10:20; Seymour[3], 4:121; Blake, p. 333; unsigned statement, n.d., PP #353. Haig later apologized for his remark about the American Army. DH-JJP, 10/27/18, PP #86.

38. *USAWW*, 10:21.

39. Ibid.

40. Ibid., 10:22–23; Pershing[9], 2:362–63.

41. *USAWW*, 10:29; Pershing[9], 2:368–69.

42. Pershing[9], 2:360 & 363; NDB-JJP, 10/27/18, NDB #8.

43. JJP diary, Oct. 26–30, 1918, PP #4; EMH diary, 10/27/18, EMH Papers; GA diary, 10/29/18, GA Papers.

44. JJP diary, 10/30/18, PP #4; GA diary, 10/30/18, GA Papers; EMH annotations on JJP-SWC, 10/30/18, EMH Papers; U.S. Dept. of State[2], 2:169–70.

45. EMH diary, 10/30/18, EMH Papers; AF-JJP, 11/16/38, PP #78.

46. JJP diary, 10/30/18, PP #4; GA diary, 10/30/18, GA Papers; JJP-EMH, 10/30/18, EMH Papers.

47. EMH diary, 10/30/18, EMH Papers.

48. TBM-JJP, 12/4/29, PP #354; JJP diary, 10/30/18, PP #4.

49. Foch[2], pp. 462–63; Seymour[3], 4:91.

50. Seymour[3], 4:95.

51. EMH diary, 11/2/18, EMH Papers.

52. NDB-WW, 10/31/18, WW Papers, Series 2, Reel 101; RL diary, 10/31/18, RL #65.

53. A different interpretation of Pershing's motives is in B. Lowry's excellent article and Bonsal's book, pp. 9–11.

54. Pershing[9], 2:364-65.

55. JJP diary, 11/3/18, PP #4; WW-NDB, 11/5/18, WW Papers, Series 2, Box 187. The Baker letter to Pershing, dated 11/5/18, has disappeared from the Baker Papers at the Library of Congress, but Prof. Bullitt Lowry graciously loaned me a copy of it from his notes.

26. Meuse-Argonne: November 1, 1918

1. PLS diary, 10/25/18, PLS Papers; JJP-JWM, 10/28/18, PP #126; JJP to JTD, JLH, & CPS, 10/28/18, PP #64, #94, & #193 respectively.

2. Pershing[9], 2:264, 291, 370–73; *USAWW*, 9:371; G. Marshall[3], pp. 178–80; Harbord[3], p. 451.

3. Gallwitz-T. M. Johnson, 3/20/28, PP #353.

4. G. Marshall[3], p. 183; Pershing[9], 2:374.

5. Coffman[9], pp. 344–45.

6. Ibid.; Pershing[9], 2:373–74.

7. Jacks, pp. 294–95.

8. Pratt[2], pp. 41–42; Coffman[9], p. 345.

9. Liggett[1], pp. 221–24; Pershing[9], 2:374–75.

10. Pershing[9], 2:375–76; Liggett[1], pp. 222–23.

11. Coffman[9], p. 346.

12. *Infantry in Battle*, pp. 7–10.

13. PHC-GHQ, ltr 237, 11/4/18, PHC Papers.

14. T. Johnson[3], p. 333.

15. PHC-GHQ, ltr 234, 11/1/18, PHC Papers.

16. *USAWW*, 9:576.

17. Coffman[9], p. 354; Pershing[9], 2:379.

18. Viereck[1], pp. 281–82; Coffman[9], pp. 354-55.

19. JEM intvw, 7/10/63; JJP-EMH, 11/6/18, EMH Papers.

20. Foch[2], pp. 437–38, 445–46; JJP diary, 11/7/18, PP #4; Pattullo[1] (5/20/22), pp. 89 & 92; Pershing[2], 2:386–87; FC memo for AEF CofS, 4/2/19, JGH Papers, NYHS.

21. Palmer & Colton, pp. 536–37; JJP diary, 11/3/18, PP #4; Smythe[1], pp. 134–49.

22. In World War II the United Nations diplomatically let the French recapture Paris.

23. JJP diary, Nov. 3 & 6, 1918, PP #4; Pershing[9], 2:381.

24. Pershing[9], 2:381; FC-JGH, July 11 & Aug. 3, 1935, JGH Papers, LC.

25. JJP-JTD, 4/4/26, PP #64; HAD-JGH, 8/8/35, JGH Papers, NYHS.

26. Dickman, p. 190. In fairness to Summerall, he did tell the 1st Division commander to send a message to I Corps informing it of the 1st Division's line of march.

27. Smythe[1], p. 142.

28. Ibid., p. 143.

29. Ibid., pp. 143–45.

30. Ibid., p. 146.

31. Ibid., pp. 146–48; Society of First Division, p. 366, Pershing[9], 2:381.

32. USAWW, 2:640–41; Harbord[3], p. 401; G. Marshall[3], p. 192; MWI-JJP, 5/16/23, PP #351; Wilgus[1], pp. 73–75.

33. Foch[2], pp. 466–69.

34. Ibid., p. 473.

35. Ibid., pp. 473–74; Pershing[9], 2:394–95; Payot AWC talk, pp. 3–4.

36. Foch[2], pp. 471–72.

37. USAWC[2], 1:159–61; Pershing[9], 2:183–85; I Corps SI 115, 11/7/18, Frank Parker Papers; Seymour[3], 4:141.

38. Griscom, p. 443.

39. "Sherburne Places Blame," Boston Transcript, 1/8/20, CRE Papers; Powell, p. 50.

40. Foch[2], pp. 476–77, 486–87.

41. Freidel, pp. 344–47; PLS diary, 11/11/18, PLS Papers; JJP-JTD, 4/4/26, PP #64; FP-JJP, 1/22/19, PP #155.

42. LCG-mother, 11/11/18, LCG #1.

43. Wadsworth remin, pp. 231–34; Shaeffer intvw; Markey, p. 39.

44. USAWW, 11:475 (author's italics); Zabriskie, p. 131; Gibbs[2], p. 241.

45. JMP, Chapter Notes, Vol. 10, 1939–40, JMP Papers.

46. Wythe, p. 130; RMB diary, 11/11/18, RMB Papers.

47. Rickenbacker[1], pp. 284–85.

48. Fisher, pp. 139–47.

49. Pershing[9], 2:395–96.

50. C. Smith, p. 316; CLS corres, 6/26/63.

51. Pershing[9], 2:397.

52. JGH, AWC talk, 4/11/32, p. 15.

53. Palmer & Colton, p. 687; Holley, p. 131; Coffman[9], p. 206; Pogue[2], p. 203; AEF Chief Ordnance Officer-JGH, n.d., enclosing table of 1/7/19, JGH Papers, NYHS; JGH, "Penalties of Pacifism," 1/24/24, PP #88; JJP-FDR, 11/25/38, PP #177.

54. Pattullo[1] (5/20/22), p. 83; Ayres, p. 149.

55. Pershing[9], 2:294, 388–90.

56. Maximilian, 1:320; Kaspi, p. 343.

57. PHC-GHQ, ltr 243, 11/11/18, PHC Papers.

58. W. Thornton, p. 27.

59. DEN-JGH, 2/10/34, JGH Papers, NYHS.

60. Liddell Hart[8], p. 316.

61. JJP-GCM, 3/7/23, Series 3, Box 5, RG 316, NA.

62. Pershing[9], 1:153; Lt. Carlisle V. Allan's comment on the quotation in an early draft of Pershing's memoirs, PP #365.

63. F. Palmer[9], 2:122.

64. Liddell Hart[8], pp. 314–15.

65. DeWeerd[4], pp. 215 & 397.

66. S. L. A. Marshall, a military authority who fought in World War I, said that the rifle was used very little by Americans and that in practice we did not put more emphasis on it than did the French or British. Marshall intvw, 6/13/61.

67. F. Maurice[3], p. 223; Simonds[1], 5:315; S. Thomas, p. 55; Carver, p. 61.

68. *USAWW*, 10:frontispiece map.

69. G. Marshall[4], p. 37; Liddell Hart[9], p. 198; Liggett[1], p. 137.

70. Drew, p. 30; DeWeerd[2], p. 179; Liddell Hart[7], p. 406; DeWeerd[4], pp. 380 & 397.

71. Seldes, pp. 35–37; Hindenburg, 2:270–71.

27. Portrait of Pershing (1917–1948)

1. "Old Soldier," p. 56.

2. Dupuy corres; Thomas corres, 6/20/60; RLB diary, 5/9/18, RLB Papers.

3. "Pershing, 70, Glad He's Only Soldier," NY World, 9/14/30, PP #403; Chase, pp. 19–28; M. James, p. 5; Smythe[9], pp. 66–72; Smythe[15], pp. 202–03; Smythe[16], pp. 41–43.

4. Mangum corres, 8/31/68 & 4/11/65; Harbord[6], p. 6.

5. E. Crozier, p. 151.

6. J. Mangum intvw, 7/10/63; Reilly corres, 6/19/60.

7. Curtin intvw, 7/17/63; JJP-Bess Pershing, 9/10/28, FWP Papers; T. Johnson[1], p. 82; Vandiver[4], pp. 1–21.

8. E. Crozier, p. 149.

9. Blumenson[2], 1:422 & 425–26; Harbord[8], p. 160.

10. Oviatt intvw, 1/27/60; Criswell intvw; Lippmann remin, p. 117; Kass intvw; Blumenson[2], 1:482; Fries intvw; Shaeffer intvw.

11. Resco intvw, 8/6/65; F. W. Pershing intvw, 5/26/60; Mangum intvw, 7/10/63; Shaeffer intvw; Holle intvw; Curtin intvw, 7/17/63.

12. Mangum corres, 8/30/68.

13. Mangum corres, 4/11/65.

14. Robinett intvw; Mangum corres, 4/11/65 & 10/31/68; Harbord[6], p. 6; JLC diary, 2/5/18 & 4/12/19, JLC Papers.

15. Eller intvw; Harriman intvw; Butz corres.

16. Hughes intvw; Roberts corres.

17. Resco intvw, 8/8/65; T. Johnson[1], p. 84; NYT, 8/14/17, PP #387; Eisenhower, p. 260.

18. Curtin intvw, 7/22/63; Schneider intvw, 3/17/61; North intvw, 3/14/61.

19. Watson corres; Dawes[1], p. 1; Ely intvw, 4/11/61.

20. JLC-Don Wharton, 7/17/39, JLC Papers; Holle intvw.

21. JMP-wife, Nov. 4 [or 14], 1917, Chapter Notes, Vol. 8, JMP Papers; JLC diary, 10/12/18, JLC Papers; JJP-FL, 10/13/17, FL Papers; JLC-FP, 6/17/39, JLC Papers; Bowditch intvw; Eller intvw; Barbee, pp. 1–2; JJP 201 File, 7/29/55, JJP Papers, NPRC.

22. Smith intvw; Mrs. F. Allen intvw; Reilly intvw.

23. Ely intvw, 4/11/61; F. W. Pershing intvw, 5/26/60; Hughes intvw.

24. JJP 201 File, 7/29/55, JJP Papers, NPRC. Other interesting yarns are in McKelvie[1], p. 155, and C. Smith, p. 309.

25. Colby intvw; Hughes intvw; F. W. Pershing intvw, 5/26/60; JJP-DCF, Sept. 2 [about 1922], DCF Papers, U of Vt.

26. Resco intvw, 8/8/65; F. W. Pershing intvw, 5/26/60; Reilly intvw; Heiberg intvw, 4/10/61; Harriman intvw, Hughes intvw.

27. Harbord[8], p. 193.

28. Pershing[9], 1:171 & 270; Hughes intvw; Curtin intvw, 8/1/63; Resco intvw, 8/11/65; Purdon intvw; Hershey intvw.

29. F. W. Pershing intvw, 5/26/60; North intvw, 3/14/61; Eller intvw; Blumenson[2], 1:431; Curtin intvw, 7/22/63; Resco intvw, 8/6/65.

30. Resco intvw, 8/6/65.

31. North intvw, 3/14/61; F. W. Pershing intvw, 5/26/60; J. Mangum intvw, 7/10/63; Eller intvw; Oviatt intvw, 1/2/70.

32. Curtin intvw, 4/24/71.

33. Resco intvw, 8/8/65; Hughes intvw; Eller intvw; Curtin intvw, 7/22/63; Whiting intvw; Dawes[4], 1:65; JJP diary, 7/7/18, PP #4; "How Pershing Lived Behind the Front," NYT, 1/11/31, PP #359.

34. Blumenson[2], 1:431.

35. JJP diary, Jan. 12 & 16, 1918, PP #4; NYT, 1/11/31; Whitley intvw; Hughes intvw; Hershey intvw.

36. Sherwood, p. 128; Whiting intvw; Chriswell intvw; Virden intvw, 3/24/61; JCH diary, Feb. 14 & 18, 1918, JCH Papers; Marshall intvw, 6/13/61; Salt Lake (Utah) Tribune, 8/1/48; S.L.A. Marshall[1], p. 205.

37. Curtin intvw, 7/22/63; Robinett intvw; MR intvw, 8/30/65.

38. JJP diary, 7/13/18, PP #4.

39. Bothwell, p. 7.

40. Smythe[7], p. 214; Curtin intvw, 7/17/63; J. Mangum intvw, 7/30/63; Resco intvw, 8/8/63; Harriman intvw.

41. Cobb, pp. 408–09; Ely intvw, 4/11/61; Holle intvw; Smith corres, 6/26/63.

42. JJP diary, 2/27/19, PP #4; JJP-NDB, 2/1/19, PP #19; GEA-Chicago Tribune, 5/7/28, PP #42; "General John J. Pershing," p. 325. He was not, however, above quietly seeking to have a movie made about himself. See Smythe[12], pp. 34–38.

43. Eller intvw.

44. Villaret intvw, 7/8/60; Ely intvw, 4/11/61; Dawes[4], 1:163; Moseley intvw, 9/12/60; Moseley corres, 9/22/60.

45. Simonds[2], p. 1.

46. Curtin intvw, 7/22/63.

28. Peace (December 1918-April 1919)

1. JJP-CEM, 4/19/19, PP #121; JLC diary, Feb. 10, Mar. 5, Apr. 4, 1919; JLC Papers; JLC-Hugh S. Stewart, 1/16/19, JLC Papers.

2. USAWC[2], 1:170–73; PLS diary, Nov. 17, 1918, Mar. 20 & Apr. 9, 1919, PLS Papers.

3. Nelson, pp. 33–35; SI 286, 11/24/18, JLC Papers.

4. JJP-JTD, 12/22/18, PP #64; Dickman, pp. 217–18.

5. JJP diary, Jan. 12 & 20, 1919, PP #4; PHC-JJP, 1/2/19, PHC Papers; Villard, p. 389; Woolcott, pp. 490–98; JJP-JTD, 12/22/18, PP #64; Cornebise, pp. 132–34.

6. Tardieu[3], p. 238; Walworth[1], pp. 108–09; JJP-Foch correspondence, Nov. 1918-Jan. 1919, PP #75; JJP diary, 11/25/18, PP #4.

7. JJP diary, Nov. 29–30 & Dec. 8–9, 1918, PP #4; *USAWW*, 10:91, 169, 171–72, 223–25, 262, 264–65; *USAWW*, 14:56; Mott, p. 250–51.

8. JJP diary, 5/13/19, PP #4.

9. JJP diary, Jan. 12, 23, 24, 26, 30, 23, 26 and May 7, 9, 19, 22, 24, 1919; King, pp. 84–89; R. S. Baker[2], 2:87; Pattullo (5/27/22), pp. 128–29; *USAWW*, 10:331–33, 368–69, 483, 569–70; *USAWW*, 14:57–58.

10. Pattullo (5/20/22), p. 92. Pattullo deleted the phrase "and even criminal" in his published version.

11. JJP diary, 1/24/19, PP #4; Galpin remin, p. 5.

12. DEN-JJP ("Important Conversations"), n.d., Folder 5, PP #352; JJP diary, Dec. 16 & 25, 1918, PP #4; JJP-LCG, 12/11/37, PP #85; Oviatt intvw, 12/27/70; JLC diary, 12/25/18, JLC Papers.

13. Blake, p. 61.

14. DEN AWC talk, pp. 16–17; Andrews, pp. 259–60; Pogue[2], p. 193; DEN-JJP, 1/1/19, PP #352; Dickman, p. 209; E. Crozier, pp. 236–37.

15. J. Mangum intvw, 7/10/63; GCM, "Battle Actions Engaged in by American Troops," 4/20/19, GCM Papers; JJP diary, 4/29/19, PP #4; Pogue[2], pp. 193, 196–97.

16. Pogue[2], pp. 224–25.

17. Ibid., pp. 225–26; GCM-Edwin T. Cole, 2/24/39, GCM Papers.

18. Pogue[2], p. 394.

19. Winterich, pp. 223–25; W. Williams[1], xv-xvi; Paxton[2], p. 7; Sullivan, 5:477–78.

20. AWB-JJP, 1/19/24, PP #352; JJP-CEM, 4/19/19, PP #121; JGH AWC talk, 4/29/33, pp. 15–16; Pershing[9], 2:390; Cornebise, pp. 159–60.

21. Eisenhower, p. 152.

22. D. James, 1:250–51; Pogue[2], pp. 190–91; Fosdick, p. 181.

23. Fosdick, pp. 179 & 181; Pogue[2], p. 194.

24. Helmick AWC talk, p. 11; APT diary, 9/29/18, APT Papers; Pogue[2], p. 194.

25. Herron intvw; Dawes[2], p. 270; F. Palmer[8], pp. 10–11; RF-FPK, 1/21/19, Passports No. 1100, CofS File, RG 165, NA; Raymond to ?, rept of 1/5/19, and Gaines rept of 1/4/19, CRE #10; Coffman[6], p. 188.

26. C. Smith, pp. 325–26.

27. RF-NDB, 4/16/19, PP #19; ABMC, pp. 492–93; Erskine, pp. 302–04; Mayo, pp. 253–66; JJP diary, 4/26/19, PP #4; Cornebise, p. 203.

28. JJP-FP, 5/8/19, PP #153. For an amusing slip of the tongue during Pershing's visit to Tours, see Robert Beaudry, "Thank You, Ladies," *Army*, March 1971, p. 27.

29. Clarke, p. 126; Bach & Hall, p. 239; Junor corres; Stacy corres.

30. S. L. A. Marshall[3], pp. 12–13; Marshall intvws, 6/13/61 & 10/23/70.

31. Harriman, pp. 319–20; JJP-ME, 4/8/19, PP #69; Cochran corres; Junor corres.

32. P. Mueller intvw; JJP-NDB, 2/1/19, PP #12; Dickman, p. 247; JJP 201 File, NPRC. See also George Walker and Smythe[21].

33. Young, p. 341; Harbord[3], pp. 146–47.

34. Brest speech, 1/31/19, PP #100. The texts of Pershing's speeches to various units are in PP #100 & 101.

35. JLC diary, Mar. 13 & 24, 1919, JLC Papers; JJP diary, 2/4/19, PP #4; JJP-ME, 4/8/19, PP #69; Brabson corres; Kerll corres; Stacy corres.

36. John corres; S. L. A. Marshall[5], pp. 144–45; Marshall intvw, 6/13/61.

37. Donald F. Walker-CGD, 4/1/28, PP #60. It is perhaps significant that when I put a query in newspapers, asking for recollections of Pershing, many wrote concerning this

farewell inspection. For most, if not all, it was the only time they had seen the AEF commander, but it was such a memorable experience that many remarked on what a fine figure of a man he was and how impressed they were with seeing him.

38. FP-JJP, n.d. [spring 1919], PP #153.

39. Ibid.; NDB-JJP, 1/20/19 & 2/3/19, PP #19; JJP-NDB, 3/12/19, PP #19; *NYT*, 1/14/19, p. 6 & 2/19/19, p. 8; ME-JJP, 1/24/19, PP #69; EBH diary, 12/5/18, EBH #1.

40. FP-JGH, 3/21/19, JGH Papers, LC; *NYT*, 1/14/19, p. 6 & 2/19/19, p. 8; Hagedorn, 2:357; Coffman⁶, p. 168.

41. JJP-FEW, 3/12/19, FWP Papers; JJP-NDB, 3/12/19, PP #19.

42. FEW-JJP, 1/21/19, FWP Papers; NDB-JJP, 1/20/19 & 1/27/19, PP #19; JJP-NDB, 2/23/19, PP #19; ME-JJP, 1/24/19, PP #69.

43. FEW-JJP, 1/21/19, FWP Papers; *CR*, 65th Cong., 3d sess., vol. 57, pt. 4, p. 3218.

44. JJP diary, Apr. 5 & 14, 1919, PP #4; JLC diary, Apr. 18–19, 1919, JLC Papers; JGH-LW, 2/4/19, JGH Papers, LC; Harbord³, pp. 553–54.

45. Braynard², 1:242; JJP diary, 4/14/19, PP #4; JJP-Edythe P. Corbin, 5/2/19, Mrs. HCC Papers; FEW-JJP, Mar. 22, Apr. 1 & 16, 1919, FWP Papers.

46. Eller intvw.

47. JJP-MP, 9/11/17, FWP Papers.

48. JJP-JP, 2/27/18; JJP-FEW, 4/15/18; FEW-JJP, 8/27/18—all FWP Papers.

49. Brabson corres.

50. JJP diary, 12/31/18, PP #4; *USAWW*, 2:644, 647–48; JJP-FEW, 1/11/19, FWP Papers; Cable P-2176, 11/12/18, RG 120, NA; "Commissioned Personnel in the AEF, 1917–1919," pp. 199–205, JJP Papers, RG 316, NA.

51. Cables A-2300 & A-2397, 12/10/18 & 1/3/19, RG 120, NA.

52. Cable A-2557, 1/28/19, RG 120, NA; JJP-FEW, 1/11/19, FWP Papers; C. Roberts corres.

53. JJP-FEW, 1/11/19, FWP Papers.

54. Ely intvw, 4/11/61; CDR diary, 8/23/19, CDR Papers.

55. Coffman⁶, p. 165.

29. The Return Home (May–November 1919)

1. Film H-1348, RG 111; Weygand⁴, pp. 111–28; Pogue², p. 187. Details of the parade are in PP #203.

2. Singleton corres, 3/15/61; Harbord³, p. 564.

3. JJP-NDB, 7/11/19, PP #19; JJP diary, 7/14/19, PP #4.

4. Mangum corres, 8/17/63; JJP diary, 7/14/19, PP #4; Pogue², pp. 197–98; Bach & Hall, p. 255; JJP-NDB, 7/11/19, PP #19; Harbord³, pp. 561 & 564; " 'Corps d'Élite,' " pp. 6–7, 15. On the Army Band ("Pershing's Own") see Bodeau, Blumenson³, and David McCormick.

5. Harbord³, p. 564; JJP diary, 7/14/19, PP #4.

6. Pogue², pp. 198–99.

7. JJP diary, 7/19/19, PP #4; GPE diary, July 18–19, 1919, GPE Papers. Details are in Vandiver¹, 2:1027–28 and PP #119.

8. FEW-JJP, 7/27/18 & JJP-FEW, 8/17/18, both FWP Papers; G. Marshall³, pp. 213–25.

9. CGD speech at Mississippi Dept. of American Legion Convention, 7/28/27, JGH Papers, NYHS.

10. JJP diary, May 27 & 30, 1919, PP #4; JJP Romagne speech, 5/30/19, PP #4. On the AEF cemeteries and war memorials in Europe, see Pershing[5], Pershing[11], Pershing[15], Pershing[20], and Smythe[8].

11. Film H-1336, RG 111; *Transport Ace*, 9/2/19, pp. 1–2, JEM Papers; TBM-JJP, 11/8/19, PP #141; CBS diary, 9/1/19, CBS Papers.

12. Braynard[1], 1:258–59; Film H-1336, RG 111; Pogue[2], p. 201; JJP diary, Sept. 8–9, 1919, PP #4; JJP-FEW, 8/15/19, FWP Papers.

13. "General Pershing's Homecoming," pp. 1–2; JJP diary, 9/8/19, PP #4.

14. Wiener, pp. 31–32; Coffman[6], pp. 189–90, 192; JLC diary, 3/22/19, JLC Papers; *NYT*, 7/19/19, p. 5; PB-JGH, 7/19/19, forwarded by JGH to JJP, 8/4/19, PP #87.

15. March, pp. 350–51; Coffman[6], p. 195.

16. JJP-FEW, 8/15/19, FWP Papers.

17. JJP commission in PP #419; Watson[4], p. A-1; "Pershing Created General," p. 14.

18. Wiener, pp. 31–34, 45–47.

19. Film H-1124, RG 111; "Welcome to General Pershing," p. 54; *NYT*, 9/11/19, pp. 1–2; Souvenir Program of NY Parade, 9/10/19, PP #147; JJP diary, 9/10/19, PP #4.

20. JJP diary, Sept. 8–11, 1919, PP #4; Vandiver, 2:1039–41. Details on the Philadelphia Victory Parade are in Morley, pp. 137–42.

21. Daniels[3], p. 174; *WP*, 9/18/19, pp. 1–2, 5; Souvenir Program, PP #147; *CR*, 66th Cong., 1st sess (1919), vol. 58, pt. 5, p. 4465.

22. *CR*, 66th Cong., 1st sess (1919), vol. 58, pt. 6, p. 5562.

23. Pogue[2], p. 391; V. Conner, pp. 88–93; Vandiver[1], 2:1044–45.

24. USWD[1], vol. 1, pt. 1, pp. 61–68; U.S. Congress[3], pp. 3–12; March, pp. 333–41.

25. *CR*, 65th Cong., 3d sess, vol. 57, pt. 3, pp. 2418–19; U.S. Congress[7] (1919), 1:8 & 55.

26. U.S. Congress[7] (1919), 2:1177; J.M. Palmer[1], p. 168; J.M. Palmer[4], xii–xv. See also U.S. Congress[4]. On Palmer, see J. M. House, pp. 11–18, and Holley's excellent biography.

27. JMP-JWW, 3/11/40, JWW #21; NDB-JWW, 8/3/19, CofS Gen. Corres. file, Box 11, Folder 72, RG 165.

28. "Army Reorganization—Interviews," JJP Papers, Box 25, Entry 25, RG 200, NA.

29. JWW-JMP, 3/8/40, JMP Papers; U.S. Congress[7] (1919), 2:1571–72, 1578.

30. U.S. Congress[7] (1919), 2:1572 & 1782.

31. Ibid., 1:1580–81.

32. Ibid., 2:1572, 1592, 1581, 1675.

33. JWW-JMP, 3/8/40, JMP Papers. Pershing's whole testimony is in U.S. Congress[7] (1919), 2:1571–1704.

34. Pogue[2], p. 210; J. M. Palmer[4], xiv.

30. Marking Time (December 1919-June 1920)

1. "General Pershing's Washington Staff," p. 111.

2. Pershing[4], pp. 35, 63, 76, 92–93; U. S. Grant, pp. 3–77; *NY Evening Post*, 1/2/20. Pershing's appreciation of airpower increased after Billy Mitchell sank a battleship from the air in 1922. See Pershing[8], pp. 71 & 145.

3. Schneider intvw, 3/17/61; Moseley intvw, 9/12/60; Vandiver[1], 2:1047–51; GVHM, "One Soldier's Journey," 2:13, GVHM Papers. The itinerary is in PP #102–104.

4. Brabson corres; Pogue[2], p. 211.

5. JJP rept of inspection, 3/23/20, PP #172; JGH-NDB, Feb. 21 & Apr. 5, 1920, JGH Papers, LC.

6. USDA[1], p. 61; *Columbus* (Ga.) *Enquirer*, 9/12/60.

7. Moseley intvw, 9/12/60.

8. DCF-Henry Castor, 7/20/53, DCF Papers, Castor Collection.

9. Moseley intvw, 9/12/60.

10. Schneider, p. 72.

11. Wheaton corres; Schwerke corres; Trim corres; Fitchett corres.

12. Bruel corres.

13. Milliken remin, p. 46.

14. JJP rept of inspection, 3/23/20, PP #172; JJP-NDB, 11/26/19, PP #19.

15. JJP-NDB, 11/26/19, PP #19.

16. *CR*, 66th Cong., 2d sess, vol. 59, pt. 4, p. 4033; Pogue[2], p. 213; Coffman[6], pp. 207–08.

17. Boylan, pp. 115–28; *CR*, 66th Cong., 2d sess, vol. 59, pt. 8, pp. 7813–33; Pogue[2], pp. 213–14.

18. Pogue[2], p. 214; G. Marshall[5], p. 177.

19. USWD[1] (1920), 1:162; D. James, 1:285; Weigley[2], p. 401.

20. USWD[1] (1920), 1:240; NDB-JJP, 7/29/20, PP #19.

21. Coffman[6], p. 215.

22. JLC diary, 3/22/19, JLC Papers.

23. *NYT*, 1/22/20, p. 21; NDB-JJP, 4/17/20, PP #19.

24. NDB-JJP, 4/17/20, PP #19; U.S. Congress[8], (1/21/20), pp. 11–12; G. Ryan, p. 218.

25. JJP-TBM, 5/25/20, PP #141; JJP-TBM, 6/26/20, FWP Papers.

26. JJP-NDB, 6/7/20, PP #19; JJP-C. R. Cameron, 6/9/20, PP #38; JJP-TBM, 5/25/20, PP #141; *WP*, 6/8/20, pp. 1 & 3; Pogue[2], p. 215.

31. Pershing for President (1920)

1. In addition to presidents, a number of military heroes had been nominees, like Winfield Scott, or contenders, like Leonard Wood. For details, see Somit.

2. *NY American*, 6/10/17.

3. FEW-JJP, 7/11/17, FWP Papers.

4. JJP-FEW, 6/7/17, 7/7/17, 7/31/17, FWP Papers.

5. JJP-JP, 9/27/17 & 5/16/18, FWP Papers; JJP-Mrs. JP, 8/18/17, FWP Papers.

6. FEW-JJP, 11/27/18 & 12/4/18, FWP Papers; Carl Boyd-International News Service, 1/4/19, PP #163; JJP-J. Bourne, Jr., 5/4/19, PP #163; JJP-James E. Ferguson, 1/16/19, PP #163; Charles B. Elliott-JJP, 4/7/19, PP #163; E. Mont Reily-JJP, 11/24/18, PP #163; *NYT*, 11/26/18, p. 3; Elmer J. Burkett-JJP, 11/18/18, PP #163.

7. FEW-JJP, 11/27/18 & 12/4/18, FWP Papers.

8. JJP-JP, 11/27/18, 12/27/18, 3/9/19, FWP Papers.

9. FEW-JJP, 12/4/18, FWP Papers; FEW-Charles Dick, 11/27/18, FWP Papers.

10. GSP-JJP, 6/14/19, PP #155. Details on the Wood campaign are in J. Lane, pp. 240–49.

11. FEW-JJP, 3/22/19, and JJP-FEW, 5/2/19, FWP Papers; JJP-Anne Boyd, 6/20/19, PP #69.

12. *CR*, 66th Cong., 1st sess (1919), vol. 58, pt. 5, p. 4467.

13. LCG memo of conversation with EMH, 8/6/19, PP #85.

14. CGD-JLC, 10/15/19, JLC Papers; Frier intvw, 1/20/70, quoting Frier's mother.

15. JJP-FEW, 1/11/19, FWP Papers; Curtin intvw, 7/19/60.

16. Elmer J. Burkett-JJP, 9/24/19 & 11/28/19, PP #37; L. Murray, pp. 225–27, 232.

17. Dupuy corres; Pogue², pp. 210–12.

18. ADC-John R. Shellady, 2/18/20, PP #163; L. Murray, p. 236; Griscom remin, pp. 80–83.

19. L. Murray, pp. 234, 238, 250–51.

20. Ibid., p. 251; *WP*, 4/15/20, p. 1; JJP diary, 4/14/20, PP #4.

21. L. Murray, pp. 241–42.

22. Ibid., pp. 237–38, 246–47.

23. "Digest's Nation-Wide Presidential Poll," (4/10/20), pp. 21–22; (4/24/20), pp. 6–7; (5/1/20) pp. 22–23; (5/8/20), pp. 28–29; (5/15/20), pp. 24–25; (5/22/20), pp. 20–21; (5/29/20), pp. 16–17; (6/5/20), pp. 24–25.

24. L. Murray, pp. 234, 243–44.

25. JJP-NDB, 6/7/20, PP #19.

26. L. Murray, p. 245; Bowditch intvw; Shaeffer intvw.

27. JJP-Eleanor P. Cushman, 7/1/20, PP #154; "General Pershing Denies Political Aspiration," p. 1303.

28. JJP-MP, 3/8/21, FWP Papers.

29. JJP-JGH, 3/12/21, PP #88; *NYHT* (Paris ed.), 1/25/21, in PP #69.

30. FC-JJP, 4/9/21, PP #52; *NYT*, 4/22/21, pp. 1 & 4; "Pershing to Command Army G.H.Q.," p. 932.

31. "General Pershing's New G.H.Q.," p. 9; JGH-JJP, 3/20/21, PP #88.

32. "General Pershing To Be Chief of Staff," p. 997.

32. Chief of Staff (1921–1924)

1. "Changes in Army Uniform," p. 1206; Pogue², p. 218; *ANJ*, 4/30/21, p. 957.

2. Hammond, pp. 119–20; Cline, pp. 20–21, 30–31; U.S. Congress⁵, pp. 571–77; J. M. Palmer³, p. 1365; Coffman⁶, p. 228; *ANJ*, 5/14/21, p. 997; Craven & Cate, pp. 258–59.

3. D. James, 1:261, 264–83; MacArthur, p. 77. See also Ganoe².

4. MLH-JJP, 6/14/22, PP #93.

5. JJP-DM, 11/22/21, PP #121; D. James, 1:293 & 668; JJP-Fred Sladen, 5/5/23, PP #185, Ambrose¹, pp. 282–83.

6. Hunt, pp. 110–11; D. James, 1:319–20; Lee & Henschel, p. 48; Lehr, pp. 278–79; C. Wright¹, pp. 128–29; Manchester, pp. 129–30; Hughes intvw; Shaeffer intvw; Harriman intvw.

7. Lait & Mortimer, p. 143; Lea & Henschel, p. 49; Manchester, p. 127.

8. Lea & Henschel, p. 49; *NYT*, 4/20/64, p. 9; "Account of Rivalry," p. 20; Heiberg intvw, 3/9/61.

9. JJP-DM, 11/22/21, PP #121.

10. Pogue⁵, p. 62.

11. *NYT*, 2/10/22, p. 3.

12. D. James, 1:322.

13. Curtin intvw, 7/19/60; Schneider intvw, 3/17/61; Resco intvw, 8/9/65; BB-DM, 11/11/53, DM Papers; D. James, 1:343; J. R. M. Wilson, p. 45; Lohbeck, pp. 101–02; Hunt, p. 148; DM-JJP, 2/15/42, PP #121.

14. Ely intvw, 4/11/61; Curtin intvw, 7/17/63; Smith intvw.

15. Boatner corres; Moseley corres, 9/22/60; Heiberg intvws, 3/9/61 & 4/10/61; JJP-JCO, 6/10/37, PP #150.

16. JJP-Mrs. Mary B. Dawes, 1/27/21, Charles G. Slack Papers; JJP-W. E. Borah, 12/10/26, PP #81.

17. JJP-Mrs. John Edie, 3/2/22, PP #69; Ward, pp. 59–61; Pershing[3], pp. 3–4, 111–14; "National Defense: A Composite," pp. 3–8, JEM Papers; Simpich, pp. 34 & 68; "National Position in Readiness," pp. 1169–70; "Gen. Pershing Attacks Pacifists," p. 1086; Wadsworth remin, p. 319. See also Pershing[10], Pershing[12], and Pershing[13].

18. JJP-Mrs. J. Borden Harriman, 5/2/23, PP #90; JJP remarks at Horse Association Banquet, 12/6/22, PP #96.

19. WMW-JJP, 6/23/21, PP #217; U.S. Congress[2], pp. 598 & 604.

20. JGH, "Penalties of Pacifism," p. 5, PP #88; JJP statement to Nat. Press Club, 3/20/22, Box 4, Series 3, RG 316, NA; JMP-JJP, 7/21/22, RG 316, NA; Pogue[2], p. 219; Ganoe[1], pp. 483–84.

21. J. M. Palmer[1], pp. 188–89; J. M. Palmer[4], pp. 161–66; J. M. Palmer[5], pp. 367–70; JMP-JJP, 7/21/22, RG 316, NA.

22. Pogue[2], pp. 220 & 393; JMP-JJP, 1/16/22, Vol. 18, & JMP memo to JJP, 2/1/22, JMP Papers; JMP-GCM, 11/2/44, GCM Papers.

23. JMP-GCM, 11/2/44, GCM Papers; U.S. Congress[2], p. 601; Pogue[2], pp. 214 & 220.

24. CGD-JGH, 8/12/22, JGH Papers, NYHS; Colby intvw; Pogue[2], p. 219; JJP-JLH ltrs, Nov. 1923-Apr. 1924, PP #94.

25. JJP-Clara Warren, 11/27/23, FWP Papers; JJP-MTH, 10/11/23, PP #93; "General Pershing Elected Member of the Institute," *La Vie Française*, 3/1/36, translation in PP #105.

26. JJP-WDC, 9/29/24, PP #52; U.S. Congress[2], P. 601.

27. Dupuy corres.

28. Watson corres; Watson[4], p. A-1. Pershing was also the first Army Chief of Staff to get legislation to send officers to private schools for special studies, e.g., to Harvard University, where he sent his aide, J. Thomas Schneider, for a law degree.

33. In Retirement (1924–1930)

1. JJP-JGH, 4/28/23, JGH Papers, NYHS.

2. JJP-BP, 8/22/24, FWP Papers; Damon Runyon, "It's a Great Life," 9/30/24, FL Papers; Mangum intvw, 7/30/63.

3. Eller intvw; *NYT*, 9/10/24, p. 25; JJP-Annie Boyd, 10/1/19, PP #69.

4. Schneider, p. 74; Robinett intvw; I. Hoover, p. 249; B. Dawes corres, 4/6/61.

5. JJP-D. F. Bailey, 4/24/22, PP #163; JJP statement to the press, 4/24/24, PP #163.

6. JJP-JP, 3/23/25 & JJP-BP, 7/7/25, FWP Papers. For background, see Colby. The best account is Joe F. Wilson.

7. Ellis, p. 87; C. R. Cameron-JJP, 3/16/20, PP #38. Details of Pershing's work in Tacna-Arica are in PP #333–341 & FR (1925) 1:304–431 and (1926) 1:260–76. See also Vandiver[1], 2:1074–83.

8. J. F. Wilson, pp. 59–63; Dodds remin, pp. 86 & 89.

9. Dodds corres; JJP-Wm. C. Dennis, 6/10/26, PP #64; Dodds remin, pp. 86–88; JJP-JGH, 9/13/25, PP #88; J. F. Wilson, pp. 69–71; JJP diary, Aug. 5–6, 1925, PP #334.

10. JJP-F. C. Hicks, 11/13/25, PP #93.

11. Parker corres, 10/9/60; Curtin intvw, 7/17/63; JJP-ME, 12/22/25, PP #70; Dodds remin, p. 87.

12. Dodds remin, p. 87; O'Laughlin, pp. 101–02.

13. Dodds remin, p. 91; Dodds corres; Curtin intvw, 7/17/63; M. A. Santiago rept, 11/24/25, 2657-0-37, WD Gen Staff MID, 1917–1941, Box 2160, RG 165, NA.

14. JJP-BP, 12/22/25, FWP Papers; Dennis, pp. 247–53; JJP-MTH, 3/25/26, PP #93; *FR* (1926), 1:274–530.

15. *FR* (1929), 1:732–803; Dodds remin, p. 87.

16. WM-JJP, 6/13/17, in WM Memoirs, p. 76, WM #21. On Mitchell, see the biographies by Gauvreau, Levine, and A. Hurley.

17. D. James, 1:306–07; O'Connor, p. 364; Patrick, p. 181; A. Hurley, pp. 101 & 104; "Colonel Mitchell's Charges," p. 25.

18. U.S. War Dept.[1] (1919), vol. 1, pt. 1, pp. 68–70; JJP-DWM, 10/17/25, PP #8; JJP-CTM, 1/12/25, PP #8; JJP-ME, 12/22/25, PP #70.

19. O'Connor, pp. 392–93; A. Hurley, p. 46; Weigley[2], p, 413.

20. JJP-BP, 2/23/26, FWP Papers.

21. JJP-BP, 3/2/26, FWP Papers.

22. GEA-FWP, 11/8/27, FWP Papers; FWP expense account for Feb. 1928, FWP Papers.

23. JJP-FWP, 2/10/30, FWP Papers.

24. O'Connor, pp. 374–75.

25. *NYHT*, 6/15/31; *NYT*, 6/16/31; JJP-FWP, 5/12/33, FWP Papers.

26. JJP-George C. Dyer, 3/23/25, PP #163; *Nashville Banner*, 12/9/27; *NY Sun*, 12/8/27.

27. Ginnetti intvw.

28. Curtin intvw, 7/17/63. Confirmed by Shaw intvw, 7/25/63.

29. CGD-JGH, 12/20/27, JGH Papers, NYHS; O'Laughlin, iv-v.

30. L. Murray, p. 246.

31. JJP-BP, 6/18/28, FWP Papers.

32. "Pershing, 70, Glad He's Only Soldier," in PP #403.

33. JJP-CGD, 3/28/29, PP #60.

34. JJP-JGH, 1/24/29, PP #88.

35. JJP-JGH, 1/31/29, PP #88.

36. JGH-JJP, 2/2/29, PP #88.

34. *My Experiences in the World War* (1931)

1. John Macrae-JJP, 10/22/30, PP #358; Jones intvw.

2. JJP-FP, 1/10/21, PP #153; DCF-JJP, 11/18/19, PP #74; *NYT*, 12/15/30.

3. *NYT*, 12/15/30; JJP-MR, 1/24/24, MR Papers; JJP-BP, 1/2/24 & 2/1/24, FWP Papers; JJP-DCF, Sep. 2 [1922?], DCF Papers, U of VT; MR intvw, 8/8/62.

4. Dawes[3], p. 178; *NYT*, 12/15/30; "Gen. Pershing Elected Member of the Institute," *La Vie Française*, 3/1/36, translation in PP #105 (cited as "Gen. Pershing Elected"); Harriman intvw; J. Mangum intvw, 7/30/63.

5. JJP-NDB, 11/21/28, PP #19; Allan intvw; Shaw intvws; North intvw, 3/24/61.

6. JJP-Mrs. HCC, 8/9/29, HCC Papers.

7. "Gen. Pershing Elected"; Assorted letters from publishers to JJP, PP #358; FAS-JJP, 5/17/30 and JJP-FAS, 8/30/30, PP #358; JNW-JJP, 12/1/30, PP #148; Wheeler[2], p. 36; MAD-JJP, 9/8/30, FWP Papers; FAS-JJP, 1/12/31, PP #191; JJP-MR, 3/19/31, MR Papers; *NYT*, Jan. 12-Mar. 29, 1931.

8. JGH-CGD, 9/19/33, JGH Papers, NYHS; PCM-NDB, 6/25/31, NDB #154; FP-NDB, 6/10/31, NDB #184; MAD-GEA, 6/29/32, PP #191; MAD-JJP rc Pulitzer Prize,

n.d., PP #191. Stokes closed out the Pershing account with a debit balance of $13,693.22 in 1943. FAS-JJP, 6/22/43, PP #191.

9. JJP-ME, 2/3/30, FWP Papers; Eisenhower, pp. 208–09.

10. X. H. Price-JJP, Jan. 7 & 30, 1939, PP #354.

11. JJP diary, 6/18/17, PP #4.

12. Pershing[9], 1:64.

13. JJP-MR, 2/7/31, MR Papers.

14. "Synopsis of Units Mentioned," n.d., PP #354; GCM-JJP, 11/24/30, PP #354.

15. Unnamed person-JJP concerning Chapter 50, n.d., PP #367; CGM-JJP, 11/24/30, PP #354.

16. T. H. Thomas, pp. 341–43.

17. HLS-NDB, 1/7/31, NDB #204; NDB-HLS, 2/26/31, NDB #204; NDB-FP, Mar. 17 & 28, 1931, NDB #184; NDB-PCM, 3/1/31, PCM #23. The lawnmower reference is to the incident mentioned in Pershing[9], 1:185. As for the incident of sawing off pilings to get them into ships (Pershing[9], 1:210), Baker frankly didn't believe it. NDB-Grote Hutchinson, 7/11/31, NDB #123.

18. GEA-MAD, 12/8/30, PP #191; GCM-JJP, 11/24/30, PP #354.

19. Pershing[9], 1:174, 229, 314, 388.

20. PCM-NDB, 3/4/31, NDB #154; Smythe[3], pp. 30–32.

21. PCM-NDB, 3/4/31 & 6/25/31, NDB #154.

22. NDB-FP, 3/17/31, NDB #184.

23. NDB-PCM, 10/27/31, NDB #154.

24. PCM-NDB, 2/17/32, NDB #155; Russell Doubleday-PCM, 4/28/32 & Mrs. PCM notation on this ltr, 3/25/54, PCM #1.

25. PCM-Ralph H. Graves, 4/2/32 & Ralph H. Graves-PCM, 7/5/32, PCM #23; Watson[6], pp. 1–3; Harry Emerson Wildes review of The Nation at War, PPL, 9/21/32, PCM #11.

26. March, pp. 243–99.

27. Curtin intvw, 8/3/63; JJP-JGH, 9/10/32, JGH Papers, NYHS.

28. JCO-JJP, 8/23/32, PP #150; JGH-NDB, 10/2/34, NDB #113; Curtin intvw, 7/17/63.

29. JJP-JGH, 2/10/34, JGH Papers, NYHS; Smythe[11], pp. 173–83.

30. JGH-DEN, 12/10/34, JGH Papers, NYHS; JGH-NDB, 5/11/34 and 12/31/34, NDB #113; JGH-JJP, 3/1/34, JGH Papers, NYHS.

31. NDB-JGH, 9/27/34, NDB #113.

32. PCM-Little Brown, & Co., 2/28/36, NDB #115.

35. Micheline Resco (1917–1948)

1. JLC diary, 5/17/17, JLC Papers; Totten corres; Curtin intvw, 7/22/63; Blumenson[2], 1:389; PCM-JJP, 11/23/17, PP #123; Seydell, pp. 10–13; Wales[1], pp. 6–7; C. Wright[2], pp. 6 & 13.

2. Resco intvws, Aug. 11, 24, & 28, 1965; Cutler intvw; Whitley intvw; Curtin intvw, 8/1/63; I. Mangum intvw, 7/10/63; S. Hinman intvw, 4/7/61; Immaculée corres; C. Wright[1], p. 131; Isabel Mangum biographical sketch of MR for Catholic Art Assoc., 12/42, author's file.

3. C. Wright[1], pp. 131–33; Resco intvws, Aug. 2, 11, 13, 1965 & Apr. 19, 1966; JJP-MR, 7/4/17; 9/5/17; 11/20/17; 3/19/18; 6/13/18, MR Papers.

4. JJP-MR, 1/4/18, MR Papers; Eller intvw; B. Dawes corres, 1/16/61.

5. Cutler intvw; JJP-MR, 8/16/19, FWP Papers; Resco intvw, 8/25/65.

6. Mitchell[3], p. 124; Resco intvw, 4/19/66.

7. JJP-Mrs. Walter O. Boswell, 11/18/18, PP #32.

8. JJP-MR, Oct. 27 & Nov. 15, 1919, MR Papers; JJP-TBM, 6/26/20, FWP Papers.

9. JJP-MR, 2/13/20, MR Papers.

10. Resco intvw, 8/26/65.

11. JJP identical ltrs to Bullard, Harbord, and others, all 1/6/23, FWP Papers.

12. MR-VF, 8/18/64, MR Papers; Resco intvw, 8/12/65.

13. MR-VF, 8/18/64, MR Papers; Resco intvws, Aug. 6 & 11, 1965; C. Wright[1], pp. 144, 149–50; Wood intvw; Hayes intvw.

14. Carol Cutler notes on MR, 7/14/64, author's file; Cutler intvw; Resco intvw, 8/12/65; MR-VF, 8/18/64, MR Papers.

15. Curtin intvw, 7/17/63.

16. Wood intvw; Harriman intvw; March intvw, 3/16/61; Cabell intvw, 7/5/60; Shaeffer intvw; Hughes intvw.

17. Resco intvw, 4/14/66.

18. GEA-MR, 2/19/39, FWP Papers; JJP-MR, 12/16/26, MR Papers; Indenture of trust, 7/23/38, attached to report form TFR-300, Series B (1941), FWP Papers.

19. JJP-MR, 10/10/26, MR Papers.

20. JJP-MR, 5/16/38, FWP Papers; explanation of code in author's file.

21. Resco intvw, 8/11/65; Resco corres, 5/18/61; Cutler intvw.

22. Resco intvw, 8/8/65.

23. Resco intvws, 8/30/65 & 4/19/66.

24. Curtin intvws, 7/17/63 & 4/24/71; Harriman intvw; JJP-MR, 8/7/28, 12/15/30, 12/10/32, 11/12/34, 5/20/36, 10/29/36, 11/8/37, MR Papers.

25. JJP-MR, 1/24/38, MR Papers.

26. JJP-MR, 12/20/29, MR Papers; Resco intvw, 5/21/65.

36. Awaiting the Bugle's Call (1932–1948)

1. JJP-Wm. H. Carter, 9/11/21, PP #40; JJP-Ernest C. Brown, 9/11/21, PP #114; JJP-MP, 9/11/21, FWP Papers; JJP-C. L. DeGaugue, 9/11/21, PP #114; JJP autobiography, 1934-1935, chap. 6, p. 10, PP #377; Schneider, p. 72; JJP-MR, 3/8/33, MR Papers; JJP-JCO, 1/25/36, JCO #57; JJP-Mrs. HCC, 2/11/36, Mrs. HCC Papers; Woolf, pp. 290-91; JJP-Louis L. Ludlow, 10/19/37, PP #120.

2. Moginier intvw; Mathews corres; JGH-CGD, 10/3/38, JGH Papers, NYHS.

3. JJP-GCM, 10/6/27, PP #124.

4. GCM-JJP, 10/14/27, PP #124.

5. K. Marshall, p. 4; Pogue[2], p. 267; K. Marshall corres.

6. Pogue[2], pp. 298, 314-15, 319, 330; FWP intvw, 5/26/60.

7. On Pershing's near-fatal illness, see "John J. Pershing: Twilight of His Life," pp. 16–17; "General of the Armies Wins Another Victory," pp. 9–12; Smythe[4], pp. 50–55.

8. JJP-GEA, 6/28/39, ABMC Papers; Resco intvw, 8/9/65.

9. JJP-CGD, 9/6/39, PP #60.

10. JJP-BB, 10/31/39, BB Papers.

11. JJP-BB, 5/3/40 & 6/4/40, BB Papers; JJP-CGD, July 30, Oct. 8 and Dec. 30, 1940, PP #60; JJP-TBM, 7/11/40, PP #141.

12. Clayton corres; Agar corres; Lippman remin, pp. 174–76; Clayton remin, pp. 126–28.

13. Lippman corres; Lippmann remin, pp. 174–76; JJP-MP, 8/28/40, FWP Papers; Steel, p. 385; Chadwin, pp. 86, 89–91; text of radio address, PP #167; Recording 200–726, RG 117.

14. JJP-MR, 12/5/37 & 1/13/38, MR Papers; JJP-CGD, 10/24/40, PP #60; JJP-TBM, 10/15/40, PP #141; JJP-MWI, 4/1/41, PP #106.

15. FDR-JJP, 11/13/40 & JJP-FDR, 11/16/40, PP #177; JJP-JLC, 1/9/41, PP #49.

16. JJP-CSF, 9/22/41, author's file. For a humorous incident while at Walter Reed, see "The General Went A.W.O.L."

17. CGD-JGH, 6/10/41 & JGH-CGD, 6/18/41, JGH Papers, NYHS.

18. "Old Soldier," p. 55; Marietta intvw; Holle intvw; McCrary intvw; Cummings intvw.

19. McCrary intvw; Marietta corres.

20. JJP-FDR, 12/10/41 & FDR-JJP, 12/10/41, PP #177; JJP-WMW, 9/29/41, PP #217.

21. JMP-GEA, 3/26/43 & GEA-JMP, 3/29/43, PP #153; JJP-FDR, 9/16/43, PP #177; NYT, 11/12/42, pp. 1 & 20.

22. McClary corres; Smythe[13], pp. 10–13; Blumenson[2], 2:26, 256–57, 848.

23. Farago, pp. 195–96; Blumenson[2], 2:93; Totten corres; Codman, pp. 146–47.

24. Pogue[4], pp. 267, 365–66, 483; Henry L. Stimson diary, Sept. 13–14, 1944, Stimson Papers; JWW-JGH, 2/11/44, JWW #22.

25. Siefert intvw; Cummings intvw; JGH-CGD, 10/20/44 & 12/27/44, JGH Papers, NYHS.

26. Cummings intvw.

27. DDE-GCM, 5/8/45, DEE Papers. The schools are respectively infantry, artillery, cavalry, and command & general staff.

28. Ibid.; Hughes intvw.

29. King intvw; Cummings intvw; Siefert intvw.

30. JGH-CGD, 7/18/42 and CGD-JGH, 7/18/42, 7/22/43, 7/28/43, JGH Papers, NYHS.

31. King intvw.

32. McClary corres.

33. Siefert intvw; Cummings intvw.

34. Cummings intvw; Siefert intvw.

35. C. Wright[1], pp. 302–03; Resco intvw, 8/10/65.

36. Carol Cutler notes on MR, 8/27/65, author's file; Cutler intvw; Resco intvw, 8/27/65.

37. Fr. Baisnée statement, 9/3/46, MR Papers; Resco intvw, 8/6/65; Immaculée corres.

38. Wales[3], p. 6; JGH-CGD, 6/5/45, JGH Papers, NYHS; JGH-JJP, 4/11/46, PP #89; JGH eulogy of JJP, filed with 9/11/43 papers, JGH Papers, NYHS.

39. C. Mueller intvws; Marietta intvw.

40. Mossman & Stark, pp. 28–44; "Pershing's Funeral," p. 23; WP, 7/19/48, pp. 1 & 3.

41. Washington Times-Herald, 7/19/48, p. 4.

42. WS, 7/18/48.

43. Virden corres, 3/24/61; WS, 7/20/48, p. B1; WP, 7/20/48.

44. "Pershing's Funeral," p. 22; Virden intvw, 3/22/61. Eisenhower, p. 210, presents a slightly different version.

45. "General Pershing's Funeral," pp. 1287, 1319–20; March intvw, 4/14/61; Kelly corres; PI, 7/20/48.

46. GEA-L. D. Gasser, 10/4/44, JJP 201 file, NPRC; "I Want To Stand Up," p. A3.

47. WP, 7/20/48, p. 1.

BIBLIOGRAPHY

Manuscripts

Allen, Henry T.—Library of Congress.
American Battle Monuments Commission—ABMC Office, Paris, France.
Auchincloss, Gordon—Yale University.
Baker, Newton D.—Library of Congress.
_____.—Baker and Hostetler, Inc., Cleveland.
Baker, Ray Stannard—Library of Congress.
Baruch, Bernard M.—Mr. Baruch's Office, New York City.
Belmont, August—Columbia University.
Belmont, Mrs. August—Yale University.
Belmont, Eleanor Robson—Columbia University.
Battle of Argonne—USAMHI.
Battle of Cantigny—USAMHI.
Bernheisel, Benjamin H.—Cantigny War Museum, Wheaton, Ill.
Bliss, Tasker H.—Library of Congress.
Boardman, Charles Ruggles—State Historical Society of Wisconsin, Madison.
Boardman, Mabel T.—Library of Congress.
Bolles, Stephen—State Historical Society of Wisconsin, Madison.
Breckinridge, Henry—Library of Congress.
Brent, Charles H.—Library of Congress.
Brown, Ralph M.—Library of Congress.
Brown, William Cary—University of Colorado, Boulder.
Bryan, William Jennings—Library of Congress.
Bullard, Robert L.—Library of Congress.
Butler, Nicholas Murray—Columbia University.
Canfield, James H.—Columbia University.
Clark, Arthur Elliott—Minnesota Historical Society, St. Paul.
Clark, Paul H.—Library of Congress.
Collins, James L.—USAMHI.
Corbin, Henry C.—Library of Congress.
Corbin, Mrs. Henry C.—Georgetown University.
Cosulich, Bernice—Arizona Pioneers Historical Society, Tucson.
Curtin, Ralph A.—Mrs. Frances Curtin, Washington, D.C.
Daniels, Josephus—Library of Congress.
Dawes, Charles G.—Library of Congress.
Decatur House—Library of Congress.
DeShon, George D.—USAMHI.
Dewees, A. Draper—USAMHI.
Doremus, Frank E.—Detroit Public Library.
Drum, Hugh A.—Hugh Drum Johnson, Closter, N.J.

Duncan, George B.—Henry T. Duncan, Lexington, Ky.
Edwards, Clarence R.—Massachusetts Historical Society, Boston.
Eisenhower, Dwight D.—Eisenhower Library, Abilene, Kansas.
Eller, George P.—George P. Eller, Bronx, N.Y.
Ely, Hanson E.—Mrs. Judith Ely Glocker, Jacksonville, Fla.
Erskine, John—Columbia University.
Farnsworth, Charles F.—Huntington Library, San Marino, Cal.
Fisher, Dorothy Canfield—Henry Castor, c/o Franklin Watts, Inc., New York City.
———.—University of Vermont, Burlington.
Fisher, Irving—Yale University.
Forbes, William Cameron—Harvard University.
———.—Library of Congress.
Foulois, Benjamin D.—Library of Congress.
Franklin, Robert J.—George C. Marshall Library, Lexington, Va.
George V—Windsor Castle, England.
Gleaves, Albert—Library of Congress.
Goethals, George W.—Library of Congress.
Griscom, Lloyd C.—Library of Congress.
Hagedorn, Hermann—Library of Congress.
Haig, Douglas—National Library of Scotland, Edinburgh.
Harbord, James G.—Library of Congress.
———.—New York Historical Society, New York City.
Harriman, Florence J.—Library of Congress.
Helm, Edith B.—Library of Congress.
Henry, Guy V., Jr.—USAMHI.
———.—U.S. Military Academy.
Hines, John L.—Library of Congress.
———.—USAMHI.
Hodges, Courtney H.—Eisenhower Library, Abilene, Kansas.
House, Edward M.—Yale University.
Hughes, John C.—Lawrence Hughes, c/o William Morrow and Co., New York City.
Hyde, James H.—New York Historical Society, New York City.
Kean, Jefferson R.—University of Virginia, Charlottesville.
Keenan, T. J.—Massachusetts Historical Society, Boston.
King, Campbell—Duke University.
Lanckton, Frank—Mrs. Myrtle Lanckton Montgomery, Falls Church, Va.
Langan, Manus A.—James Langan, Cleveland.
Lansing, Robert—Library of Congress.
Lejeune, John A.—Library of Congress.
Lenihan, Michael J.—USAMHI.
Logan Family—Yale University.
Louthan, Henry T.—University of Virginia, Charlottesville.
MacArthur, Douglas—MacArthur Memorial, Norfolk, Va.
McCormick, Vance C.—Yale University.
McCoy, Frank R.—Library of Congress.
McKelvie, Samuel R.—Nebraska State Historical Society, Lincoln.
McReynolds, James C.—University of Virginia, Charlottesville.
Mangum, James E.—Mrs. Isabel Mangum, Washington, D.C.
March, Peyton C.—Library of Congress.

Marriner, J. Theodore—Columbia University.
Marshall, George C.—George C. Marshall Library, Lexington, Va.
Mayo, Katherine—Yale University.
Meiklejohn, George D.—Nebraska State Historical Society, Lincoln.
Meloney, Mrs. William Brown—Columbia University.
Miscellaneous Manuscripts—Library of Congress.
Mitchell, William—Library of Congress.
Morrow, Dwight W.—Amherst College.
Moseley, George Van Horn—Library of Congress.
National Archives—RG 94, 111, 112, 117, 120, 165, 200, 407.
Nevins, Allan—Columbia University.
O'Laughlin, John Callan—Library of Congress.
Palmer, John McAuley—Library of Congress.
Palmer, Paul—Yale University.
Parker, Frank—University of North Carolina.
Parsons, William Barclay—Columbia University.
Patrick, Mason—U.S. Air Force Academy, Colorado.
Patterson, Robert P.—Library of Congress.
Patton, George S.—Library of Congress.
Pershing, F. Warren—Micheline Resco, Paris, France.
Pershing, John J.—Author's possession.
_____.—Center of Military History, Washington, D.C.
_____.—Chicago Historical Society.
_____.—F. Warren Pershing, Southampton, N.Y.
_____.—Library of Congress.
_____.—National Personnel Records Center, St. Louis.
_____.—Nebraska State Historical Society, Lincoln.
_____.—New York Public Library.
_____.—USAMHI.
_____.—U.S. Military Academy.
_____.—Wellesley College.
Pershing Family Papers—Pershing Boyhood Home, Laclede, Mo.
Personal Papers: Miscellaneous—Library of Congress.
Polk, Frank L.—Yale University.
Poore, Benjamin A.—Charles L. Bolté, Alexandria, Va.
_____.—USAMHI.
Reilly, Henry J.—USAMHI.
Resco, Micheline—Author's possession.
Rhodes, Charles D.—Library of Congress.
Roosevelt, Theodore—Harvard University.
_____.—Library of Congress.
_____.—New York Historical Society.
Russell, Edgar—Mrs. Marion Woldridge, Breckenridge, Mo.
Scott, Hugh L.—Library of Congress.
Shaeffer, Crawford—Edgewater, Fla.
Sharpe, Henry G.—USAMHI.
Shaw, Charles B.—Russell B. Shaw, Washington, D.C.
Sheffield, James R.—Yale University.
Simonds, George S.—Library of Congress.

Sims, William S.—Library of Congress.
Slack, Charles G.—Marietta College.
Sladen, Fred W.—USAMHI.
Stackpole, Pierpont L.—George C. Marshall Library, Lexington, Va.
Stimson, Henry L.—Yale University.
Straight, Willard—Cornell University.
Summerall, Charles P.—Library of Congress.
Swift, Eben, Jr.—U.S. Military Academy.
Taylor, Marvin H.—Marvin H. Taylor, Jr., Lexington, Mass.
Terry, Arthur P.—George C. Marshall Library, Lexington, Va.
Wadsworth, James W., Jr.—Library of Congress.
Waltz, Welcome P.—Infantry School, Fort Benning, Ga.
War Cabinet Minutes—Public Record Office, London, England.
War Office Papers Relating to the AEF—Public Record Office, London, England.
Warren, Francis E.—New York Public Library.
———.—University of Wyoming, Laramie.
Whitlock, Brand—Columbia University.
———.—Library of Congress.
Wilgus, William J.—New York Public Library.
Wilson, James H.—Library of Congress.
Wilson, Woodrow—Library of Congress.
Wiseman, William—Yale University.
Wood, Leonard—Library of Congress.

Interviews

Allan, Carlisle V.   Washington, D.C., July 11, 1960.
Allen, Mrs. Frank A., Jr.   Washington, D.C., June 10, 1968.
Andel, John.   Washington, D.C., May 10, 1961.
Ashby, Eugene K.   Apr. 28, 1960.
Baskett, G. Noel.   Laclede, Mo., June 10, 1971.
Baukhage, Mrs. H. R.   Washington, D.C., July 26, 1966.
Bliss, Edward G.   Washington, D.C., July 27, 1966.
Blumenson, Martin.   Washington, D.C., Apr. 18, 1977.
Boatner, Mark M., III.   Arlington, Va., June 19 and July 17, 1967.
Bolté, Charles L.   Alexandria, Va., July 28, 1969.
Boone, Joel T.   Washington, D.C., Apr. 28, 1961.
Bowditch, Edward.   New York City, Dec. 29, 1960.
Brause, Jacob.   Washington, D.C., Sept. 28, 1960.
Cabell, Edith M.   Washington, D.C., June 25 and July 22, 1960.
Cassou, Mrs. Berten E.   Washington, D.C., Apr. 26, 1971; June 9 and July 13, 1972.
Chambers, James J.   University Hts., Ohio, Jan. 22, 1972.
Clarke, Carter W.   Washington, D.C., Feb. 10, 1960.
Cochrun, Mrs. James L.   Akron, Ohio, Sept. 23, 1970.
Colby, Elbridge.   Washington, D.C., Apr. 10, 1973.
Collins, James L.   Alexandria, Va., July 31 and Dec. 29, 1962.
Corrigan, Peter J.   Cleveland, Ohio, Oct. 28, 1972.

Criswell, Robert L.   Martinsburg, W. Va., Feb. 10, 1961.

Cummings, Margaret.   Washington, D.C., Dec. 30, 1962.

Curtin, Ralph A.   Washington, D.C., Mar. 28 and July 19, 1960; July 15, 17, and 22 and Aug. 1, 1963; Mar. 20, Apr. 1 and 19, 1970; and Apr. 24, 1971.

Cutler, Carol.   Washington, D.C., July 22, 1970.

Davies, John M.   Washington, D.C., May 3, 1961.

Dupuy, R. Ernest.   Arlington, Va., Mar. 7, 1971.

Ebner, Roy.   Wheaton, Md., Apr. 5, 1961.

Egan, Mrs. Martin.   New York City, Apr. 24, 1961.

Eller, George P.   New York City, Dec. 28, 1960.

Elliott, Dabney O.   Washington, D.C., Apr. 13, 1961.

Ely, Mrs. Hanson E.   Washington, D.C., Apr. 11, 1961; Blue Ridge Summit, Pa., July 4, 1961; Woodstock, Md., Aug. 15, 1963.

Epstein, Harold.   New York City, Dec. 29, 1960; Oct. 29, 1964.

Frank, Walter H.   Washington, D.C., July 14, 1960.

Frier, James H., Jr.   Cleveland, Ohio, Jan. 20 and 28, 1970.

Fries, Amos A.   Washington, D.C., May 14, 1960.

Ginnetti, Ernest.   Washington, D.C., May 3, 1961.

Hains, John P.   Washington, D.C., Apr. 17, 1961.

Harriman, Mrs. J. Borden.   Washington, D.C., Apr. 18, 1961.

Hart, Franklin A.   Washington, D.C., Mar. 21, 1961.

Hayes, Margaret A.   Chicago, Ill., Apr. 29, 1967.

Heiberg, Louise Cromwell Brooks MacArthur Atwill.   Washington, D.C., Mar. 9, Apr. 5 and 10, 1961.

Herron, Charles D.   Bethesda, Md., June 25, 1960.

Heister, John H.   Washington, D.C., Apr. 11, 1961.

Hershey, Burnet.   New York City, Dec. 29, 1966.

Hinman, George W.   Washington, D.C., July 22, 1960; Mar. 26, 1961; June 7, 1972.

Hinman, Sylvana.   Washington, D.C., Apr. 7 and 10, 1961; Mar. 27, 1966.

Holcomb, Thomas.   Washington, D.C., Mar. 21, 1961.

Holle, Charles G.   Washington, D.C., July 20, 1960.

Horgan, John L.   Washington, D.C., May 5, 1961.

Horkan, George A.   Washington, D.C., July 19, 1972.

Horkan, Mrs. George A.   Washington, D.C., July 27, 1972.

Hughes, John C.   New York City, Oct. 30, 1964.

Hurst, Elizabeth.   Washington, D.C., May 9, 1960.

Ingram, Ralph C.   Washington, D.C., July 9, 1973.

Jones, Richard S.   Washington, D.C., July 28, 1961.

Kass, Garfield I.   Washington, D.C., Apr. 7, 1961.

Kauffman, Benjamin F.   Washington, D.C., Mar. 24, 1960.

Kelly, Charles C.   Washington, D.C., Nov. 14, 1962.

Kelly, Thomas J.   Miami, Fla., Nov. 14, 1962.

Kennedy, Eugene, S.J.   Washington, D.C., Jan. 15, 1961.

Kines, Louis B., S.J.   New York City, Dec. 29, 1960.

King, John T.   Baltimore, Md., May 15, 1961.

Lanckton, Myrtle.   Washington, D.C., May 2, 1961.

Longworth, Alice Roosevelt.   Washington, D.C., Mar. 7 and 15, 1961.

McCoy, Mrs. Frank.   Washington, D.C., Apr. 5, 1961.

McCrary, Martha E.   Mayfield Hts., Ohio, Dec. 20, 1972.

McDonnell, Mary F. Washington, D.C., Aug. 4, 1967.

McNeil, Edwin C. Washington, D.C., Mar. 17, 1961.

Mangum, James E. Washington, D.C., July 10 and 30, 1963; Apr. 23, 1971.

Mangum, Isabel. Washington, D.C., July 10, 1963; Apr. 23, 1971; July 1, 1975.

March, Mrs. Peyton C. Washington, D.C., Dec. 11, 1960; Mar. 11 and 16, Apr. 10 and 14, 1961.

Marietta, Shelly. Washington, D.C., July 2, 1960.

Marshall, S. L. A. Arlington, Va., June 13, 1961; Oct. 23, 1970.

Montgomery, Myrtle Lanckton. Washington, D.C., July 19, 1970.

Moginier, Celia. Paris, France, Aug. 26, 1965.

Moseley, George Van Horn. Washington, D.C., Sep. 12–13, 1960.

Mueller, Charles R. Washington, D.C., Apr. 9 and 12, 1961.

Mueller, Paul J. Washington, D.C., July 31, 1963.

North, Thomas. Washington, D.C., Mar. 14, 1961; Feb. 26 and Mar. 2, 1973; Feb. 11, 1976.

Oviatt, Douglas G. Richmond Hts., Ohio, Jan. 2 and 27, 1970.

Pershing, Eli R. Washington, D.C., May 8, 1961.

Pershing, F. Warren. New York City, May 26, 1960; Southampton, N.Y., Aug. 14, 1966.

Potter, Georgia W. Brookfield, Mo., Dec. 3, 1977.

Pratt, H. Conger. Washington, D.C., May 1, 1960.

Purdon, Mrs. Eric. Washington, D.C., June 25, 1960.

Reilly, Henry J. New York City, May 26, 1960.

Resco, Micheline. Paris, France, May 21, Aug. 3, 6, 8–14, 16, 24–30, 1965; Apr. 12-May 1, 1966.

Reynolds, Russel B. Washington, D.C., June 25, 1960; Apr. 28, 1961.

Robinett, Paul McD. Washington, D.C., Apr. 13, 1961.

Runk, William. Washington, D.C., May 7, 1960.

Schneider, J. Thomas. Washington, D.C., Mar. 17, 1961; Apr. 4, 1974.

Schroth, Raymond, S.J. Woodstock, Md., Nov. 16, 1964.

Schuyler, Edwin C. Washington, D.C., Apr. 6, 1961.

Shaeffer, Crawford. Washington, D.C., Feb. 16, 1964.

Shaw, Charles B. Washington, D.C., July 25, 1963; May 5, 1970.

Siefert, George J., Jr. Washington, D.C., Apr. 6, 1961.

Skilton, John. Fairfield, Conn., Apr. 24, 1961.

Smith, Corinna Lindon. New York City, June 27, 1963.

Stathis, Getty. Alexandria, Va., May 6, 1961.

Totten, Ruth Patton. South Hamilton, Mass., Apr. 14, 1977.

Twitchell, Heath. Camp Springs, Md., Aug. 7, 1970.

Villaret, Gustav. Chevy Chase, Md., July 6 and 8, 1960.

Virden, John M. Washington, D.C., Mar. 6, 8, 22 and July 31, 1962.

Wainwright, John D. Washington, D.C., May 12, 1961.

Wainwright, Mrs. John D. Washington, D.C., May 12, 1961.

Wedemeyer, Albert C. Washington, D.C., Aug. 3, 1970.

Whiting, Lawrence. Chicago, Ill., Apr. 28, 1967.

Whitley, George R. Arlington, Va., July 30, 1966.

Wood, Mrs. John S. Washington, D.C., Apr. 7, 1961.

Correspondence

Agar, Herbert. Petworth, Sussex, England, Nov. 19, 1963.
Allen, Hugh. New York, N.Y., Sept. 28 and Oct. 11, 1960.
Andrews, Hugh P. Portland, Ore., Apr. 9, 1961.
Army Records Center. St. Louis, Mo., May 9, 1960.
Bechely, Francis C. Los Angeles, Cal., Mar. 22, 1961.
Bettison, William T. Wynnewood, Pa., Aug. 4, 1960.
Bliss, Edward Goring. Washington, D.C., July 27, 1966.
Boatner, Mark, Jr. Jackson, La., May 23, 1961.
Boehs, Charles J. San Antonio, Tex., May 31, 1961.
Booth, C. C. Dallas, Tex., Mar. 20 and July 20, 1960.
Boswell, James O. San Francisco, Cal., Feb. 28, 1963.
Boswell, John P. San Francisco, Cal., Sept. 12, 1963.
Boswell, William O. Cairo, United Arab Republic, May 18, 1963.
Brabson, F. W. Staunton, Va., Sept. 25, 1960.
Breul, Mrs. Harold. Chillicothe, Ohio, Feb. 4, 1970.
Brewer, B. E. Lexington Park, Ky., July 12, 1960.
Brimberry, John H. San Jose, Cal., Mar. 19, 1960.
Butz, Bright B. St. Petersburg, Fla., June 30, 1961.
Cabell, Edith M. Washington, D.C., July 5, 20, and 25, 1960.
Chudly, Mrs. Edward. Lincoln, Neb., Apr. 2, 1960.
Clark, Charles B. St. Petersburg, Fla., Aug. 1, 1960.
Clayton, W. L. Houston, Tex., Sept. 4, 1963.
Clinton, Edward. Baltimore, Md., Feb. 7, 1960.
Cochran, Paul. Mann's Choice, Pa., Feb. 10, 1960.
Coleman, Miles. Outwood, Ky., Mar. 14, 1960.
Collins, James L. Alexandria, Va., Dec. 29, 1962; Jan. 16 and Mar. 28, 1963.
Confidential Source No. 2. Apr. 1 and May 1, 1961; Feb. 8 and Mar. 14, 1963.
Conklin, H. W. El Paso, Tex., Nov. 21, 1962.
Coop, Basil C. Belmont, Cal., Mar. 19, 1960.
Craven, Thomas, Jr. Scranton, Pa., Mar. 29, 1961.
Crivello, William A. Alton, Ill., Mar. 14, 1960.
Cronin, Gerald. St. Petersburg, Fla., Nov. 3, 1961.
Curtin, Ralph A. Washington, D.C., Aug. 16, 1963; Jan. 9, 1964.
Davenport, Erwin R. Miami Beach, Fla., June 14, 1960.
Davison, Roland. Paget West, Bermuda, Jan. 28 and Feb. 19, 1963.
Dawes, Beman Gates, Jr. Cincinnati, Ohio, Jan. 16 and Apr. 6, 1961.
Dawes, C. Burr. Columbus, Ohio, May 30 and June 6, 1961.
Dawes, Henry. Hartford, Conn., May 8, 1961.
Demarest, Mrs. Glenn. Brookfield, Mo., July 15, 1960.
Dodds, Harold W. Princeton, N.J., Aug. 2, 1960.
Doherty, James F. Mill Valley, Cal., Mar. 21, July 30, and Oct. 10, 1960.
Downs, Mrs. Norton. Bryn Mawr, Pa., Mar. 8, 1960.
Dunn, Mrs. Cary. Miami, Fla., Nov. 8, 1961.
Dupuy, R. Ernest. Arlington, Va., Apr. 10, 1961.
Eidson, H. H. Tulsa, Okla., Dec. 15, 1961.
Ennis, William P. Vineyard Haven, Mass., Aug. 2, 1960.

Farnsworth, Robert J.   Los Angeles, Cal., Nov. 20, 1962.
Fitchett, P. V., Jr.   Norfolk, Va., Nov. 24, 1969.
Fletcher, Robert H.   Leesburg, Va., May 23, 1961.
Fulbright, Sen. J. W.   Washington, D.C., June 21, 1960.
Furnos, Sally L.   Oakland, Cal., June 10 and July 24, 1961.
Gates, John M.   Wooster, Ohio, Jan. 7, 1971.
Gerhart, Charles I.   Lawrenceville, Ill., Mar. 26, 1960.
Goldsmith, Myron B.   San Francisco, Cal., Aug. 17, 1961.
Good, Arthur.   Kansas City, Kans., Mar. 19, 1960.
Green, Mrs. Roy M.   Lincoln, Neb., Nov. 19, 1962.
Greene, Paul.   State Dept. of Education, Jefferson City, Mo., Feb. 18, 1960.
Greer, Allen J.   San Clemente, Cal., Sept. 19, 1960.
Grendon, Arthur de.   St. Louis, Mo., Mar. 12, 1960.
Gutleben, Dan.   Walnut Creek, Cal., Oct. 14, 1960.
Hanes, Murray S.   Springfield, Ill., Oct. 5, 1960.
Harts, William W.   Madison, Conn., July 20, 1960.
Hartshonn, Elizabeth P.   New Hope, Pa., Apr. 17, 1961.
Henry, Guy V.   Chevy Chase, Md., Aug. 31, 1960.
Herring, Grover.   N.p., Sept. 25 and Dec. 6, 1970.
Herron, Charles D.   Bethesda, Md., Aug. 1, 1960; Nov. 13, 1962.
Hoffmann, Charles W.   Santa Barbara, Cal., Oct. 27 and 30, 1969.
Holiday, John.   Los Angeles, Cal., Jan. 28, 1971.
Humphrey, Evan H.   San Antonio, Tex., Aug. 4, 1960.
Hughes, John C.   New York, N.Y., Nov. 19, 1964.
Immaculée, Sister.   St. Mary of the Woods, Ind., Jan. 18, 1963.
John, William H.   St. Louis, Mo., Nov. 21, 1969.
Jones, Everett N.   Kansas City, Mo., Mar. 19, 1960.
Jorgenson, O. M.   Manhattan, Kans., Mar. 17, 1960.
Junor, J. B.   Los Angeles, Cal., Mar. 3, 1970.
Kass, Garfield I.   Washington, D.C., Apr. 21, 1961.
Kassel, Mrs. Murray M.   Middletown, N.Y., Feb. 8, 1960.
Kelly, Mrs. D. T.   New York, N.Y., Feb. 22, 1960.
Kenedy, Eugene L., S.J.   New York, N.Y., Jan. 28 and Feb. 8, 1961.
Kerll, R. H.   Kansas City, Mo., Mar. 28, 1960.
Ketterman, C. W.   Bloomington, Ind., May 1, 1967.
Kilcullen, Gerald.   Jamaica, N.Y., Nov. 13, 1960.
Lambert, John H.   Washington, D.C., Sept. 26, 1960.
Lamme, Mrs. T. T.   Laclede, Mo., Mar. 17, 1960.
Larkin, William.   Los Angeles, Cal., Aug. 23, 1960.
Lear, Ben.   Memphis, Tenn., Feb. 10 and 18, 1960.
Lee, Walter R., Sr.   Jackson, Miss., Sept. 26, 1960.
Lipkin, Florence.   New York, N.Y., Apr. 29, 1960.
Lippmann, Walter.   Washington, D.C., Sept. 14, 1964.
Long, John D.   Baltimore, Md., Aug. 27, 1960.
Lynn, Miles R., Jr.   Emlenton, Pa., Nov. 20, 1961.
MacAdam, Mrs. George.   Scarsdale, N.Y., May 12, 1960.
MacArthur, Douglas.   New York, N.Y., Sept. 17 and Oct. 13, 1960.
McClary, G. R. N.   Miami, Fla., July 25, 1961.
McFarland, E. L.   Rock Island, Ill., Mar. 25, 1960.

McKay, James V.   Washington, D.C., May 24, 1961.
McKinstry, C. H.   Santa Barbara, Cal., Sept. 17, 1960.
Magruder, L. B.   Rumson, N.J., July 11 and 17, 1961.
Maguire, C. L.   Wickenburg, Ariz., Aug. 9, 1960.
Mahoney, Tom.   New York, N.Y., Feb. 14, 1960.
Mangum, James E.   Washington, D.C., Aug. 17 and Dec. 14, 1963; Apr. 11, 1965; Aug. 30–31, 1968.
Marietta, Shelley U.   Washington, D.C., Sept. 25, 1960.
Marsh, Ralph E.   Kansas City, Mo., Mar. 16, 1960.
Marshall, Katherine Tupper.   Southern Pines, N.C., Apr. 26, 1961.
Marshall, S. L. A.   Birmingham, Mich., Jan. 19, 1963.
Mathews, William R.   Tucson, Ariz., Feb. 12, 1960.
Mauer, Charles A.   Blythe, Cal., Aug. 15, 1961.
Merrill, Adelbert.   Portland, Me., Feb. 7 and 21, 1960.
Miller, Harvey W.   Syracuse, N.Y., Aug. 9, 1960.
Moginier, Celia S.   Paris, France, Sept. 15, 1965.
Molski, John A.   Chicago, Ill., May 1, 1960.
Montfort, Harold de.   New Orleans, La., Nov. 24, 1961.
Moore, Lafayette.   Laclede, Mo., June 2, Sept. 22, and Oct. 20, 1960.
Morgan, Harold A.   Merrill, Wis., Mar. 29, 1961.
Moseley, George Van Horn.   Atlanta, Ga., July 19, Aug. 10, Sept. 22, and Nov. 7, 1960.
Mulloney, D. H.   Columbus, O., Apr. 30, 1961.
Munday, Charles V.   San Antonio, Tex., Aug. 26, 1961.
O'Connell, Mrs. Frank B.   Lincoln, Neb., Aug. 2, 1960.
O'Donnell, Joseph M.   Archivist, USMA, West Point, N.Y., Mar. 10 and Aug. 18, 1960; Feb. 24, 1967.
Otwell, Curtis W.   Palo Alto, Cal., Aug. 4, 1960.
Oury, William H.   Apr. 13, 1961.
Parker, F. Lej.   Charleston, S.C., Sept. 24 and Oct. 9, 1960.
Parr, Perry.   Colorado Springs, Colo., Sept. 5, 1961.
Patton, George S.   Washington, D.C., Nov. 25, 1966.
Pegler, Westbrook.   New York, N.Y., Dec. 16, 1960.
Pepper, K. L.   Port Richey, Fla., Oct. 27 and Dec. 10, 1960.
Perkins, George T.   Morgan Hill, Cal., Mar. 27, 1963.
Reid, L. Leon.   Pittsburgh, Pa., Sept. 16, 1960.
Reilly, Henry T.   New York, N.Y., June 19, July 7, and Sept. 13, 1960; May 3, 1961.
Resco, Mlle. Micheline.   Paris, France, May 18, 1961; Aug. 18 and Oct. 21, 1964; Sept. 15, 1965.
Rickenbacker, Eddie.   New York, N.Y., July 20, 1960.
Rinard, Claude.   Milwaukee, Wis., Oct. 17, 1960.
Roberts, Charles D.   Chevy Chase, Md., Oct. 1, 1960.
Roberts, E. A.   Carlsbad, N.M., July 16, Sept. 25, Nov. 3, Dec. 3, 1961.
Ryle, Walter.   Kirksville, Mo., Jan. 20, 1960.
Scott, Ernest D.   Miami, Fla., Aug. 12 and Nov. 7, 1960.
Schmidt, C. J.   Blair, Neb., Oct. 4, 1960.
Schneider, J. Thomas.   Washington, D.C., May 28, 1963.
Schwerke, Irving.   Appleton, Wis., Nov. 1, 1970.
Shapland, Lester B.   Hettinger, N.D., May 11 and 22, 1963.
Shepherd, Lemuel C., Jr.   Warrenton, Va., Mar. 18, 1961.

Shinkle, Edward.   San Francisco, Cal., Aug. 3, 1960.

Siefert, George J., Jr.   Washington, D.C., June 18, 1961.

Simons, Marji.   Pres., Agora Society, Wellesley College, Feb. 8 and Mar. 5, 1963.

Singleton, Ann.   Orlando, Fla., Mar. 15, 1960; July 19, 1961.

Skilton, John D.   Fairfield, Conn., Nov. 23, 1982.

Smith, Corinna Lindon.   Norman, Okla., Jan. 23, 1961; Dublin, N.H., June 25–26, 29 and
     Aug. 28, 1963.

Stacy, Barney H.   Weatherford, Tex., Oct. 19, 1960.

Stephens, Mrs. Flecta M.   State Historical Society, Columbia, Mo., June 29, 1960.

Straw, Harry J.   Muncie, Ind., Oct. 21, 1960.

Sunderland, A. H.   Hampton, Va., Aug. 3, 1960.

Surgner, Stanley G.   Philadelphia, Pa., July 26, 1960.

Sweeney, Walter C.   San Francisco, Cal., Oct. 10, 1960.

Taylor, John M.   Arlington, Va., June 17, 1961.

Thomas, Floyd E.   Tucson, Ariz., June 20 and July 7, 1960.

Totten, Ruth Patton.   Washington, D.C., Nov. 5, 1966.

Trader, John J.   Battle Creek, Mich., May 27, 1961.

The Tribune-Herald.   Waco, Tex., July 25, 1960.

Trim, Wallis.   Tacoma, Wash., Mar. 25, 1961.

Turner, Marion.   DeSoto, Mo., Mar. 14, 1960.

Vance, John R.   Corte Madera, Cal., Sept. 13, 1960.

Virden, John M.   Chevy Chase, Md., Mar. 24, June 12, and July 17, 1961.

Wade, T. R. Sec.,   Cypress Lodge No. 227, A.F. and A.M., Brookfield, Mo., May 16, 1960.

Watson, Mark S.   Baltimore, Md., May 5, 1961.

Weeks, Sinclair.   Lancaster, N.H., July 30, 1960.

Wenger, Samuel S.   Lancaster, Pa., Jan. 23, 1961.

West, Eugene R.   Washington, D.C., Aug. 30, 1960.

Wheaton, James W.   Hingham, Mass., Jan. 3, 1970.

Whipp, Mrs. Elmer.   Frederick, Md., Apr. 5, 1962.

Wilkinson, J. P.   Asst. Director for Libraries, Univ. of Nebraska, Lincoln, Neb., July 8,
     1960.

Williams, Irvin.   Sumner, Mo., Mar. 27, 1960.

Willis, George G.   Greenville, S.C., Mar. 23, 1965.

Winkler, Arthur E.   Pastor, Methodist Church. Laclede, Mo., Feb. 19, 1960.

Winslow, Mabel E.   Washington, D.C., May 11, 1961.

Withers, W. R.   Greensboro, Ala., Sept. 27, 1960.

Wood, Robert E.   Chicago, Ill., Aug. 12, 1960.

Woodruff, J. A.   Coronado, Cal., Aug. 18, 1960.

Yates, Halsey E.   San Francisco, Cal., May 24, 1962.

Youngberg, Gilbert A.   Jacksonville, Fla., Aug. 5, 1960.

Reminiscences

(At the Oral History Research Office, Columbia University.)

Albright, Horace M.   Browning, Gordon.
Bakhmeteff, Boris Alexander.   Bruere, Henry.
Breckinridge, Henry.   Cahill, Holger.

Chambers, Reed M.
Clayton, William Lockhart.
Cumberland, William Wilson.
Davis, Charles C.
Dodds, Harold.
Emerson, Guy.
Emerson, Haven.
Foulois, Benjamin D.
Frey, John P.
Galpin, Perrin.
Giesecke, Albert A.
Griscom, Lloyd C.
Harkness, William E.
Irvin, Leslie.
Lehman, Herbert H.

Lippmann, Walter.
Kelland, Clarence B.
Manship, Paul.
Marvin, Langdon P.
Meyer, Eugene.
Milliken, Carl E.
O'Ryan, John F.
Page, Arthur W.
Poole, DeWitt Clinton.
Rublee, George.
Stoddard, Francis R.
Wadsworth, James W.
Wagoner, Clyde D.
Williams, James T., Jr.
Windels, Paul.

Army War College Talks

(Filed at Army War College, Carlisle Barracks, Pa.)

Baker, Newton D. "The Secretary of War During the World War." May 11, 1929.
Bliss, Tasker H. "The Supreme War Council." May 22, 1929.
Conner, Fox. "G-4 from a G-3 A.E.F. Point of View." Jan. 6, 1925.
———. "Organization and Functioning of G-3, A.E.F." Sept. 18, 1931.
Connor, William D. "Duties of the A.C. of S., G-4, G.H.Q." Nov. 14, 1928.
———. "G-4, G.H.Q. and the S.O.S." Mar. 19, 1936.
———. "Logistics and Its Relation to the Commander-in-Chief in the Field." Feb. 18, 1928.
———. "Supply of the A.E.F. in France During the World War." Nov. 3, 1931.
DeWitt, J. L. "The Duties of the Assistant Chief of Staff, G-4, of an Army." Nov. 8–9, 1929.
Ely, Hanson E. "The Commander-in-Chief of the Field Forces." May 6, 1924.
———. "Graduation Address." June 26, 1934.
———. "Leadership and Morale in War." Feb. 3, 1938.
Griscom, Lloyd C. "Liaison." Apr. 30, 1940.
Harbord, James G. "Personalities and Personal Relationships in the American Expeditionary Forces." Apr. 29, 1933.
———. "The Preservation of American Identity in the World War." Apr. 11, 1932.
———. "The Services of Supply from July 1918 to May 1919." Mar. 14, 1930.
———. "A Year as Chief of Staff, A.E.F." Feb. 8, 1929.
Helmick, Eli A. "The Relation of Psychology to Leadership." Mar. 26, 1925.
March, Peyton C. "Further Reminiscences of a Wartime Chief of Staff." Feb. 3, 1931.
Marshall, George C. "The Development of the War Department General Staff." Sept. 3, 1921.
Nolan, D. E. "The Military Intelligence Division of the General Staff." Sept. 6, 1921.
Payot, Charles. "Supply and Transportation at the Front." Nov. 3, 1921.

Watson, Mark. "Press Relations and Censorship in the A.E.F." Jan. 7, 1927.

Films and Recordings

Record Group 111 (National Archives).
H-1124. "General Pershing's Return, and the 1st Division."
H-1258. "Occupation of the Sommerviller Sector, October 21-Nov. 20, 1917, First Division."
H-1264. "Occupation of Cantigny Sector (Picardy), April-June, 1918, 1st Division."
H-1319. "The American GHQ Moves from Paris to Chaumont, and Scenes of Chaumont."
H-1320. "General Pershing and Party Go to France, June, 1917."
H-1336. "Pershing's Farewell to France."
H-1348. "Celebrations in Paris, Bastille Day, 1919."
H-1349. "Celebrations in Paris, July 4, 1917."
H-1368. "Champagne-Marne Operations, July 15-18, 1918."
H-1370. "The Intermediate Zone, Quartermaster Activities at Gievres."
H-1402. "General Pershing, General Bliss, and Famous Visitors to the American GHQ."
H-1405. "Meuse-Argonne Offensive, Sept. 26-Nov. 11, 1918, Scenes of Traffic Conditions."
H-1411. "Meuse-Argonne Offensive, Sept. 26-Nov. 11, 1918, Corps and Army Headquarters."
H-1444. "Base Section No. 1 (St. Nazaire), Prominent Visitors."
H-1448. "Activities and Reviews at Headquarters SOS, Tours, France, 1918-1919."
M-50. "Flashes of Action."
M-103. "The Turn of the Tide" (Soissons).
M-346. "Meuse-Argonne Offensive."
M-348. "Château-Thierry and the Aisne-Marne Operation."

Record Group 117 (National Archives).
Film 117.1. "America Honors Her Dead."
Recording: "Addresses at the Dedication of the Meuse-Argonne War Memorial," Aug. 1, 1937.

Record Group 200 (National Archives).
Film 200.144. "General Pershing Receives Medal from President Roosevelt, 1940."
Recording 200-726. John J. Pershing. "Security of the Americas," Aug. 4, 1940.
Recording: "Addresses on Defense Test Day, Sept. 12, 1924; General John J. Pershing's Retirement."
U.S. Department of the Army, Office of the Chief of Information, Military District of Washington. "Tribute to General John J. Pershing." A Washington, D.C., radio broadcast over Station WRC on Sept. 12, 1960, featuring interviews with Ralph A. Curtin, J. Thomas Schneider, and James L. Collins.
U.S. Department of Defense, Office of Armed Forces Information and Education. "The Pershing Story" (1960 film).

Newspapers

General Pershing subscribed to a clipping service, with the result that the Pershing Papers in the Library of Congress contain more than a score of scrapbooks, each two hundred pages, bulging with press clippings. Many of these are repetitive, covering the same event in different newspapers. Because of this, and because a list would be impossibly long, no formal listing of newspapers based on the Pershing Papers appears here.

Books, Articles, Theses, and Dissertations

(Because an enumeration of all the works consulted would be very long, I list mainly those to which footnotes refer.)

"An Account of Rivalry between Two Famous Generals." *U.S. News and World Report*, May 4, 1964, 20. JK1.U65.

Albertine, Connell. *The Yankee Doughboy*. Boston, 1968. D570.3/26th/A8.

Alexander, Robert. *Memories of the World War, 1917–1918*. New York, 1931. D570.A6.

Allen, H. Warner. "The American Military Achievement: A British View." *Living Age*, July 5, 1919, 28–36. AP2.L65.

Ambrose, Stephen E. *Duty, Honor, Country: A History of West Point*. Baltimore, 1966. U410.L1A7. (Ambrose[1]).

———. "Seapower in World Wars I and II." *Naval War College Review* 22 (Mar. 1970):26–40. V1.U48. (Ambrose[2]).

American Battle Monuments Commission. *American Armies and Battlefields in Europe: A History, Guide, and Reference Book*. Washington, D.C., 1938. D528.U5/1938. (ABMC)

Amerine, William H. *Alabama's Own in France*. New York, 1919.

Andrews, Avery DeLano. *My Friend and Classmate, John J. Pershing; with Notes from My War Diary*. Harrisburg, Pa., 1939. E181.P42.

Army List and Directory, April 20, 1917. Washington, D.C., 1917.

Asprey, Robert B. *At Belleau Wood*. New York, 1965. D545.B4A8.

Ayres, Leonard P. *The War With Germany: A Statistical Summary*. Washington, D.C., 1919. D570.1.A5/1919.

Azan, Paul. *Franchet d'Esperey*. Paris, 1949. DC373.F7A9.

Bach, Christian A. and Henry Noble Hall. *The Fourth Division: Its Services and Achievements in the World War*. New York, 1920. D570.3/4th/B3.

Baldwin, Hanson W. *World War I: An Outline History*. New York, 1962. D522.5.B3.

Baker, Newton D. *Frontiers of Freedom*. New York, 1918. D619.B27. (N. D. Baker[1]).

———. *War in the Modern World*. Boston, 1935. JX1952.B24. (N. D. Baker[2]).

Baker, Ray Stannard. *Woodrow Wilson: Life and Letters*. Vol. 7: *War Leader: April 6, 1917–February 28, 1918* and Vol. 8: *Armistice: March 1-November 11, 1918*. Garden City, N.Y., 1939. E767.B16. (R. S. Baker[1]).

———. *Woodrow Wilson and World Settlement*. 3 vols. Garden City, N.Y., 1922. D644.B27. (R. S. Baker[2]).

Barbee, David Rankin. "Exit 'Black Jack': Enter 'Uncle John.' " *The Washington Post*, Sept. 14, 1930, Mag Sec, 1–2.

Barnett, Correlli. *The Swordbearers: Supreme Command in The First World War*. New York, 1964. D530.B26.

Baruch, Bernard M. *Baruch: The Public Years*. New York, 1960. E748.B32A3.

Beaver, Daniel R. *Newton D. Baker and the American War Effort, 1917–1919*. Lincoln, 1966. E748.B265B4. (Beaver[1]).

———. "The Problem of American Military Supply, 1890–1920." In *War, Business, and American Society: Historical Perspectives on the Military-Industrial Complex*. Edited by Benjamin Franklin Cooling. Port Washington, N.Y., 1977. HC110.D4W34. (Beaver[2]).

———., ed. *Some Pathways in Twentieth-Century History*. Detroit, 1969. D414.S57. (Beaver[3]).

Belcher, William Henry and Joseph Warren. *The Belcher Family in England and America*. Detroit, 1941. CS71.B445/1941.

Bellamy, David. "A Marine at the Front." *American History Illustrated* 5 (Feb. 1971):30–42. E171.A574.

Bishop, Joseph B. *Theodore Roosevelt and His Time*. 2 vols. New York, 1920. E757.B625.

Blake, Robert, ed. *The Private Papers of Douglas Haig, 1914–1919*. London, 1952. D544.A2H29.

Bland, Larry, and Sharon R. Ritenour, eds. *The Papers of George Catlett Marshall*. Vol. 1: *The Soldierly Spirit, December 1880-June 1939*. Baltimore, 1981.

Bliss, Tasker H. "The Armistices." *American Journal of International Law* 16 (Oct. 1922):509–22. JX1.A6. (Bliss[1]).

———. "The Evolution of the Unified Command." *Foreign Affairs* 1 (Dec. 1922):1–30. D410.F6. (Bliss[2]).

———. "The Strategy of the Allies." *Current History* 29 (Nov. 1928):197–211. D410.C8. (Bliss[3]).

Blumenson, Martin. "The Outstanding Soldier of the A.E.F." *American History Illustrated* 1 (Feb. 1967):4–13, 50–54. E171.A574. (Blumenson[1]).

———. *The Patton Papers*. 2 vols. Boston, 1972–1974. E745.P3B55. (Blumenson[2]).

———. "Pershing's Own." *Army* 31 (May 1981):26–31. U1.A893. (Blumenson[3]).

Bodeau, Vivienne. "Army Band Pershing's Own." *The Pentagram News* (Washington, D.C.), Sept. 22, 1960.

Bonasso, Russell P. "The Evolution of the Supreme War Council, the Unified Command, and the First American Army in World War I." M.A. thesis, Georgetown University, 1951. D544.B55.

Bonham-Carter, Victor. *Soldier True: The Life and Times of Field-Marshal Sir William Robertson*. London, 1963. DA69.3.R6B6.

Bonsal, Stephen. *Suitors and Suppliants: The Little Nations at Versailles*. New York, 1946. D645.B6.

Bothwell, Dick. "Armistice Day with Pershing." *Sunday: St. Petersburg Times Magazine*, Nov. 5, 1961, 6–7.

Boylan, Bernard L. "Army Reorganization, 1920: The Legislative Story." *Mid-America* 49 (Apr. 1967):115–28. BX1415.I3M5.

Braim, Paul F. "The Test of Battle: The American Expeditionary Forces in the Meuse-Argonne Campaign, 26 September-11 November 1918." Ph.D. dissertation, University of Delaware, 1983.

Braynard, Frank O. "A Movable Feast Aboard *Leviathan*, Our Prize of War." *Smithsonian* 4 (Nov. 1973):50–56. AS30.S6. (Braynard[1]).

———. *World's Greatest Ship: The Story of the Leviathan*. Vol. 1. New York, 1972. VM383.L3B7/1. (Braynard[2]).

Bridges, Tom. *Alarms and Excursions*. New York, 1939. DA69.3.B7A3/1939.

Broun, Heywood. *The A.E.F.: With General Pershing and the American Forces*. New York, 1918. D570.9.B8. (Broun[1]).

————. *Our Army at the Front*. Vol. 5 of *America in the War*. New York, 1918. D570.A2A8/ v.5. (Broun[2]).

Bruun, Geoffrey. *Clemenceau*. Cambridge, Mass., 1943. DC342.8.C6B7.

Buchan, John. *A History of the Great War*. 4 vols. Boston, 1923. D521.B82/1923.

Buck, Beaumont B. *Memories of Peace and War*. San Antonio, Tex., 1935. E181.B92.

Bugnet, Charles. *Foch Speaks*. New York, 1929. DC342.8.F6B8/1929.

Bullard, Robert Lee. *American Soldiers Also Fought*. New York, 1936. D570.B78. (Bullard[1]).

————. *Fighting Generals: Illustrated Biographical Sketches of Seven Major Generals in World War I*. Ann Arbor, Mich., 1944. D507.B8. (Bullard[2]).

————. *Personalities and Reminiscenses of the War*. Garden City, N.Y., 1925. D570.B8. (Bullard[3]).

Callwell, Charles E. *Field-Marshal Sir Henry Wilson: His Life and Diaries*. 2 vols. New York, 1927. DA69.3.W5C3.

Carter, William Harding. *Creation of the American General Staff*. Washington, D.C., 1924. UB233.C3.

Carver, Michael, ed. *The War Lords: Military Commanders of the Twentieth Century*. Boston, 1976. U51.W32/1976.

Chadwin, Mark Lincoln. *The Hawks of World War II*. Chapel Hill, N.C., 1968. D753.C52.

Chaffin, A. D. "Strategy of the Central Powers in the World War." *Infantry Journal*. Sept.-Oct., Nov.-Dec., 1931; Jan.-Feb., 1932. UD1.I6.

Chambrun, Jacques and Charles de Marenches. *The American Army in the European Conflict*. New York, 1919. D570.C4.

"Changes in Army Uniform." *Army and Navy Journal*, July 9, 1921, 1206. U1.A66.

Charteris, John. *At G.H.Q.* London, 1931. D546.C5. (Charteris[1]).

————. *Field-Marshal Earl Haig*. New York, 1929. DA69.3.H3C5. (Charteris[2]).

————. *Haig*. New York, 1933. DA69.3.H3C54. (Charteris[3]).

Chase, Joseph Cummings. *Soldiers All: Portraits and Sketches of the Men of the A.E.F.* New York, 1920. D609.U6C5/1920.

Cheatham, B. F. "Reminiscences of the World War." *The Quartermaster Review* 8 (Mar.-Apr. 1929):5–7. UC34.Q8.

Cheseldine, Raymond M. *Ohio In the Rainbow: Official History of the 166th Infantry, 42nd Division, in the World War*. Columbus, Ohio, 1924. D570.33/166th/C5.

Churchill, Winston. *The World Crisis, 1916–1918*. 2 vols. New York, 1927. D521.C5/ 1923a.

Clark, Edward B. *William L. Sibert: The Army Engineer*. Philadelphia, 1930. UG128.S5C6.

Clarke, William F. *Over There with O'Ryan's Roughnecks*. Seattle, 1969. D570.9.C47.

Clemenceau, Georges. *Grandeur and Misery of Victory*. New York, 1930. D521.C58.

Cline, Ray S. *Washington Command Post: The Operations Division*. In *United States Army In World War II. The War Department*. Washington, D.C., 1951. D769.A533/Vol. 4, Pt. 2.

Cobb, Irvin S. *The Glory of the Coming*. New York, 1918. D570.9.C55.

Codman, Charles R. *Drive*. Boston, 1957. D811.C5856.

Coffman, Edward M. "American Command and Commanders in World War I." In *New Dimensions in Military History*, 177–95. Edited by Russell F. Weigley. San Rafael, Cal., 1975. U39.N47. (Coffman[1]).

————. "The American Military and Strategic Policy in World War I." In *War Aims and Strategic Policy in the Great War, 1914–1918*, 67–84. Edited by Barry Hunt and Adrian Preston. Totowa, N.J., 1977. (Coffman[2]).

———. "The American Military Generation Gap: The Leavenworth Clique in World War I." In *Command and Commanders in Modern Warfare*. Edited by William Geffen. USAF Academy, 1971. UB210.M54/1968. (Coffman³).

———. "The Battle Against Red Tape: Business Methods of the War Department General Staff, 1917–1918." *Military Affairs* 26 (Spring 1962):1–10. E181.M55. (Coffman⁴).

———. "Conflicts in American Planning: An Aspect of World War I Strategy." *Military Review* 43 (June 1963):78–90. Z6723.U35. (Coffman⁵).

———. *The Hilt of the Sword: The Career of Peyton C. March*. Madison, Wis., 1966. U53.M35C6. (Coffman⁶).

———. "John J. Pershing, General of the Armies." In *Essays in Some Dimensions of Military History*, Vol. 4, 48–61. Edited by B. F. Cooling III, Carlisle Barracks, Pa., 1976. (Coffman⁷).

———. Review of *Memoirs of My Services in the World War, 1917–1918*, by George C. Marshall, and *Black Jack: The Life and Times of John J. Pershing*, by Frank E. Vandiver. *Reviews in American History* 6 (1978):243–48. (Coffman⁸).

———. *The War To End All Wars: The American Military Experience in World War I*. New York, 1968. D570.C6. (Coffman⁹).

Coffman, Edward M., and Peter F. Herrly. "The American Regular Army Officer Corps Between the World Wars: A Collective Biography." *Armed Forces and Society* 4 (Fall 1977). (Coffman¹⁰).

Colby, Elbridge. "The Tacna-Arica Dispute." *Georgetown Law Journal* 13 (May 1925):343–66.

Collier, Basil. *Brasshat: A Biography of Field-Marshal Sir Henry Wilson*. London, 1961. DA69.3.W5C6.

"Colonel Mitchell's Charges May Lead to Trial by Court-Martial." *Army and Navy Journal*, Sept. 12, 1925, 25 & 27. U1.A66.

Conner, Fox. "Divisional Organization." *Infantry Journal* (May-June 1933), 165–68. UD1.I6.

Conner, Virginia. *What Father Forbad*. Philadelphia, 1951. CT275.C7637A3.

Conquêt, Alfred. *Auprès du Maréchal Pétain*. Paris, 1970. DC342.8.P4C598.

Cooper, Duff. *Haig*. 2 vols. London, 1936. DA69.3.H3C65.

Cooper, John Milton, Jr. *Walter Hines Page: The Southerner as American, 1855–1918*. Chapel Hill, N.C., 1977. E664.P15C66.

Cornebise, Alfred E. *The Stars and Stripes: Doughboy Journalism in World War I*. Westport, Conn., 1984. D501.S725C67 1984.

" 'Corps d'Élite': The A.E.F. Composite Regiment." *United States Army Recruiting News* 21 (Jan. 1939):6–7, 15. UA23.A1A88.

"Correspondence of Theodore Roosevelt and the Secretary of War." *Metropolitan* 46 (Aug. 1917):22–25, 62–65. AP2.M5.

Cramer, Clarence H. *Newton D. Baker: A Biography*. Cleveland, 1961. E748.B265C7.

Craven, Wesley Frank and James Lea Cate. *The Army Air Forces in World War II*. Vol I: *Plans and Early Operations: January 1939 to August 1942*. Chicago, 1948. D790.A47.

Cronin, E. David, ed. *The Cabinet Diaries of Josephus Daniels, 1913–1921*. Lincoln, Neb., 1963. E766.D29/1963.

Crozier, Emmet. *American Reporters on the Western Front, 1914–1918*. New York, 1959. D632.C72.

Daniels, Josephus. *The Life of Woodrow Wilson, 1856–1924*. Philadelphia, 1924. E767.D18 (Daniels¹).

———. *The Wilson Era: Years of Peace, 1910–1917*. Chapel Hill, N.C., 1944. E766.D3. (Daniels²).

_____. *The Wilson Era: Years of War and After, 1917–1923*. Chapel Hill, N.C., 1946. E766.D33. (Daniels[3]).

Davenport, Samuel R. "Pershing in World War II: His Stature Potent Weapon." *Army* 33 (Jan. 1983):55–57.

Davis, Burke. *The Billy Mitchell Affair*. New York, 1967. UG633.M45D3.

Dawes, Charles G. *Address of Charles G. Dawes at the Meeting Held in Honor of General John J. Pershing Under the Auspices of the City of Chicago at the Auditorium Theater, Sunday Evening, December 21st, 1919*. n.p.,n.d. (Dawes[1]).

_____. *Journal as Ambassador to Great Britain*. New York, 1939. E183.8.G7D27. (Dawes[2]).

_____. *A Journal of Reparations*. London, 1939. D649.G3A5/1939. (Dawes[3]).

_____. *A Journal of the Great War*. 2 vols. Boston, 1921. D570.D3. (Dawes[4]).

_____. *Notes as Vice President*. Boston, 1935. E748.D22D22. (Dawes[5]).

DeFrancisco, Joseph E. "Amalgamation: A Critical Issue in British-American Command Relations, 1917–1918." M.A. thesis, Rice University, 1973.

Dennis, William Jefferson. *Documentary History of the Tacna-Arica Dispute*. Port Washington, N.Y., 1971. F3097.3.DA/1971.

DeWeerd, Harvey A. "The American Adoption of French Artillery, 1917–1918." *Journal of the American Military Institute* 3 (Summer 1939):104–16. E181.M55. (DeWeerd[1])

_____. *Great Soldiers of the Two World Wars*. New York, 1941. D507.D4. (DeWeerd[2]).

_____. "Pershing and the Anvil Chorus." *Infantry Journal* 43 (Mar.-Apr. 1936):99–103. UD1.I6. (DeWeerd[3]).

_____. *President Wilson Fights His War: World War I and the American Intervention*. New York, 1968. D570.D4. (DeWeerd[4]).

Dickman, Joseph T. *The Great Crusade: A Narrative of the World War*. New York, 1927. D570.3/3d/D4.

"The Digest's Nation-Wide Presidential Poll." *Literary Digest* 65 (Apr. 10, 1920), 21–22; (Apr. 24), 6–7; (May 1), 22–23; (May 8), 28–29; (May 15), 24–25; (May 22), 20–21; (May 29), 16–17; (June 5), 24–25. AP2.L58.

Drew, George A. "The Truth About the War." *MacLean's*, July 1, 1928, 3–5, 30, 32, 34, 38, 40. AP5.M2.

Duffy, Francis P. *Father Duffy's Story*. New York, 1919. D570.9.D8.

Duncan, George S. *Douglas Haig as I Knew Him*. London, 1966. DA69.3.H3D8.

Dupuy, R. Ernest, and Trevor N. Dupuy. *Brave Men and Great Captains*. New York, 1959. E181.D77. (Dupuy & Dupuy[1]).

_____. *Military Heritage of America*. Revised edition. Arlington, Va., 1984. (Dupuy & Dupuy[2]).

Editors of the *Army Times*. *The Yanks Are Coming: The Story of General John J. Pershing*. New York, 1960. E181.P423.

Edmonds, James E., ed. *Military Operations, France and Belgium: 1917*. 3 vols; *1918*. 5 vols. London, 1935–1948. D521.E45. (Edmonds[1]).

_____. *A Short History of World War I*. London, 1951. D521.E457. (Edmonds[2]).

Edwards, Frederick T. *Fort Sheridan to Montfaucon*. DeLand, Fla., 1954. D640.E424.

Eisenhower, Dwight D. *At Ease: Stories I Tell to Friends*. Garden City, N.Y., 1967. E836.A3.

Ely, Hanson E. "The Attack on Cantigny." *National Service* 7 (Apr. 1920):201–08. UA23.A1N5.

English, George H., Jr. *History of the 89th Division, U.S.A.* Denver, 1920. D570.3/89th/E5.

Erskine, John. *The Memory of Certain Persons*. Philadelphia, 1947. PS3509.R5Z5.

Esposito, Vincent J. *A Concise History of World War I*. New York, 1964. D521.E49. (Esposito[1]).

————. *The West Point Atlas of American Wars.* 2 vols. New York, 1959. G1201.SiU5/ 1959. (Esposito²).

Essame, Hubert. *The Battle for Europe, 1918.* New York, 1972. D530.E77.

Evarts, Jeremiah M. *Cantigny: A Corner of the War.* n.p., 1938. D570.9.È8.

Falls, Cyril. *The Great War.* New York, 1959. D521.F25. (Falls¹).

————. *Marshal Foch.* London, 1939. DC342.8.F6F35. (Falls²).

Farago, Ladislas. *Patton: Ordeal and Triumph.* New York, 1965. E745.P3F3.

Fisher, Dorothy Canfield. *The Day of Glory.* New York, 1919. D640.F55.

Fiske, H. B. "General Pershing and His Headquarters in France." *Military Review* 20 (Sept. 1940):5–9. Z6723.U35.

Fitzgerald, F. Scott. *Tender Is the Night.* Revised version. Harmondsworth, England, 1948. PZ3.F5754Te9.

Foch, Ferdinand. "La Victoire Finale." *Le Figaro* (Paris), Sept. 30, 1928. (Foch¹).

————. *The Memoirs of Marshal Foch.* Tranlated by T. Bentley Mott. New York, 1931. D530.F55. (Foch²).

Folliard, Edward T. "Pershing's Illness Spurs Rare Tribute from Army and Public." *The Washington Post,* Mar. 6, 1938, B-3.

Forbes, William Cameron. *The Philippine Islands.* 2 vols. Boston, 1928.

Forrest, Wilbur. "A.E.F. Unhinged 'Swinging Door' in Last Drive." *New York Herald Tribune,* Mar. 15, 1931. (Forrest¹).

————. *Behind the Front Page: Stories of Newspaper Stories in the Making.* New York, 1934. PN4874.F57A3. (Forrest²).

Fosdick, Raymond B. *Chronicle of a Generation: An Autobiography.* New York, 1958. E748.F69A3.

Foulois, Benjamin D. *From the Wright Brothers to the Astronauts: The Memoirs of Benjamin D. Foulois.* New York, 1968. U53.F6A3.

Fowler, Wilton B. *British-American Relations, 1917–1918: The Role of Sir William Wiseman.* Princeton, 1969. E183.8.G7F58.

France. État-Major de l'Armée. Service Historique. *Les Armées Françaises dans la grande guerre.* Tomes 5–7, with annexes. Paris, 1923–1938. D548.A2.

Freidel, Frank. *Over There: The Story of America's First Great Overseas Crusade.* Boston, 1964. D570.F69.

Frothingham, Thomas G. *The American Reinforcements in the World War.* Freeport, N.Y., 1971. D570.F7/1971.

Frye, William. *Marshall: Citizen Soldier.* Indianapolis, 1947. E745.M37F7.

Fuller, J. F. C. *The Conduct of War, 1789–1961.* New Brunswick, N.J., 1961. U39.F8. (Fuller¹).

————. *Decisive Battles of the U.S.A.* New York, 1942. E181.F95. (Fuller²).

Ganoe, William A. *The History of the United States Army.* New York, 1942. E181.G17/ 1942. (Ganoe¹).

————. *MacArthur Close-Up: Much Then and Some Now.* New York, 1962. E745.M3G3. (Ganoe²).

Gauss, Christian. "The Education of General Harbord." *The Saturday Evening Post,* July 30, 1932, 28–29, 62–63. AP2.S2.

Gauvreau, Emile, and Lester Cohen. *Billy Mitchell: Founder of Our Air Force and Prophet without Honor.* New York, 1942. UG633.M45G3.

"General John J. Pershing." *The American Society Legion of Honor Magazine* 19 (Winter 1948–1949):313–25. CR5061.U6A3.

"General of the Armies Wins Another Victory." *Life,* May 2, 1938, 9–12. AP2.L547.

"Gen. Pershing Attacks Pacifists in Speech." *Army and Navy Journal*, July 8, 1922, 1086. U1.A66.

"General Pershing Denies Political Aspirations." *Army and Navy Journal*, June 19, 1920, 1303. U1.A66.

"General Pershing in France." *Current History* 6 (July 1917):6–11. D410.C8.

"General Pershing Sees British in Training." *New York Times*, June 13, 1917, 5.

"General Pershing To Be Chief of Staff." *Army and Navy Journal*, May 14, 1921, 997. U1.A66.

"General Pershing's Funeral." *Army and Navy Journal*, July 24, 1948, 1287, 1319–20.

"General Pershing's Homecoming." *Current History* 11 (Oct. 1919):1–9. D410.C8.

"General Pershing's New G.H.Q." *Literary Digest*, May 7, 1921, 9. AP2.L58.

"General Pershing's Washington Staff." *Army and Navy Journal*, Sept. 27, 1919, 111. U1.A66.

"The General Went A.W.O.L." *Reader's Digest* 67 (Oct. 1955), 29. AP2.R255.

Gibbons, Floyd. *And They Thought We Wouldn't Fight*. New York, 1918. D570.9.G5. (Gibbons[1]).

_____. "The Hottest Four Hours I Ever Went Through." *American Magazine* 87 (Mar. 1919):34–35, 143–48. AP2.A346. (Gibbons[2]).

_____. "Lafayette, We Are Here." *Liberty*, Dec. 13, 1930, 30–36. AP2.L541. (Gibbons[3]).

_____. "Through the School of War." *Liberty*, Dec. 27, 1930, 58–62. AP2.L541. (Gibbons[4]).

Gibbs, Philip. *Now It Can Be Told*. New York, 1920. (Gibbs[1]).

_____. *The Pageant of the Years: An Autobiography*. London, 1946. PN5123.G5A33. (Gibbs[2]).

Giehrl, Hermann von. "Battle of the Meuse-Argonne." *Infantry Journal* 19 (Aug., Sept., Oct., Nov. 1921):131–38, 264–70, 377–84, 534–40. UD1.16.

Gilbert, Bently B., and Paul P. Bernard. "French Army Mutinies of 1917." *Historian* 22:24–41.

Ginsburgh, Robert. "Pershing as His Orderlies Know Him." *American Legion Monthly* 5 (Nov. 1928):12–15, 52–57; (Dec. 1928):14–15, 57–61. D570.A1A32.

Gleaves, Albert. *A History of the Transport Service*. New York, 1921. D570.72.G6.

Goedeken, Edward. "The Dawes-Pershing Relationship During World War I." *Nebraska History* (Spring 1984):108–29.

Goerlitz, Walter, ed. *The Kaiser and His Court: The Diaries, Note Books and Letters of Admiral Georg Alexander von Muller, Chief of the Naval Cabinet, 1914–1918*. New York, 1964. D531.M773/1964.

Goldhurst, Richard. *Pipe Clay and Drill—John J. Pershing: The Classic American Soldier*. New York, 1977. E181.P4695/1977.

Grant, C. J. C. "Marshall Foch: 26th of March to the 11th of November, 1918." *Army Quarterly* 1 (Jan. 1921):263–89. U1.A85. (C. Grant[1]).

_____. "Recollections of Marshal Foch in 1918." *Army Quarterly* 18 (July, 1929):325–34. U1.A85. (C. Grant[2]).

Grant, U. S. *Report of Lieutenant-General U. S. Grant of the Armies of the United States—1864-'65*. New York, 1866. E470.U562.

Grant, U. S., III. "America's Part in the Supreme War Council during the World War." *Records of the Columbia Historical Society* 29–30 (1928):295–340. F191.C72.

Grasty, Charles H. "Britain Fears No Famine." *New York Times*, June 12, 1917, 1 & 3. (Grasty[1]).

_____. *Flashes from the Front*. New York, 1918. D64.G685. (Grasty[2]).

_____. "Pershing's Staff Works Busily Over War Problems on Voyage." *New York Times*, June 9, 1917, 1–2. (Grasty[3]).

"Greetings to America's General on His Birthday Anniversary." *Army and Navy Journal*, Sept. 8, 1934, 25–54. U1.A66.

Gregory, Ross. *Walter Hines Page: Ambassador to the Court of St. James*. Lexington, Ky., 1970. E664.P15G7.

Griffiths, Richard M. *Pétain*. New York, 1972. DC342.8.P4G7/1972.

Griffiths, William R. "Coalition for Total War: Field-Marshal Sir Douglas Haig and Entente Military Cooperation, 1916–1918." M.A. thesis, Rice University, 1970.

Griscom, Lloyd C. *Diplomatically Speaking*. Boston, 1940. E183.7.G76.

Haan, William G. *The Division as a Fighting Machine*. N.p., 1920. D570.3/32d/H3.

Hagedorn, Hermann. *Leonard Wood, a Biography*. 2 vols. New York, 1931. E181.W83.

Hagood, Johnson. *The Services of Supply: A Memoir of the Great War*. Boston, 1927. D570.75.H3.

Haig, Douglas. *Sir Douglas Haig's Dispatches: December 1915-April 1919*. Edited by J. H. Boraston. London, 1919.

Hall, Norman S., and Sigrid Schultz. "Five Red Days." *Liberty*, May 14, 1927, 9–14. AP2.L541.

Halsey, Francis W. *Balfour, Viviani, and Joffre: Their Speeches in America, and Those of Italian, Belgian, and Russian Commissions During the Great War*. New York, 1917.

Hammond, Paul Y. *Organizing for Defense: The American Military Establishment in the 20th Century*. Princeton, 1961. UB23.H3.

Hancock, William K. *Smuts: The Sanguine Years, 1870–1919*. Cambridge, 1962. DT779.8.S6H28.

Hankey, Maurice. *Diplomacy by Conference*. London, 1920. D504.H3. (Hankey[1]).

———. *The Supreme Command*. 2 vols. London, 1961. D546.H43. (Hankey[2]).

Harbord, James G. *Address by Major General James G. Harbord, Delivered at the Dedication of the Monument at Hill 204, Near Château-Thierry, France, Erected in Memory of the American Soldiers Who Died in the Aisne-Marne Salient During the World War. October 7, 1937*. [n.p., 1937]. (Harbord[1]).

———. *America in the World War*. Boston, 1933. D570.H27. (Harbord[2]).

———. *The American Army in France, 1917–1919*. Boston, 1936. D570.H275. (Harbord[3]).

———. *The American Expeditionary Forces: Its Organization and Accomplishments*. Evanston, Ill., 1929. D570.H28. (Harbord[4]).

———. "The American General Staff." *Saturday Evening Post*, Mar. 13, 1926, 31, 189–90, 193–94, 197–98, 201. AP2.S2. (Harbord[5]).

———. *A Chief of Staff in the Theater of Operations*. New York, 1939. D570.25.H3. (Harbord[6]).

———. "General Pershing Tells His Story of the War." *New York Herald Tribune*, Apr. 26, 1931. (Harbord[7]).

———. *Leaves from a War Diary*. New York, 1925. D570.H3. (Harbord[8]).

———. "Pershing: A Close-Up." *American Legion Monthly* 13 (Sept. 1932):14–15, 53–55. D570.A1A32. (Harbord[9]).

———. *Serving with Pershing. An Address Delivered before the University Club of Port Chester, Port Chester, N.Y., May 26, 1944*. n.d., n.p. (Harbord[10]).

———. "The Story of the Roosevelt Division." *American Legion Monthly* 16 (Apr. 1934):9–13, 40–42. D570.A1A32. (Harbord[11]).

———. "Universal Military Training." *U.S. Infantry Journal* 18 (Jan. 1921). UD1.I6. (Harbord[12]).

Harriman, Mrs. J. Borden. *From Pinafores to Politics*. New York, 1923. E748.H34H34.

Hayes, Ralph A. *Secretary Baker at the Front*. New York, 1918. D570.9.H3.

Heinl, Robert Debs, Jr. *Soldiers of the Sea*. Annapolis, 1962. VE23.H4.

Hendrick, Burton J. *The Life and Letters of Walter H. Page.* 3 vols. Garden City, N.Y., 1925–1926. E664.P15H4.

Herbillon, Émile. *Souvenirs d'un officier de liaison pendant la guerre mondiale.* 2 vols. Paris, 1930. D640.H3842.

Hewes, James E., Jr. *From Root to McNamara: Army Organization and Administration, 1900–1963.* Washington, D.C., 1975. UA25.H55. (Hewes[1]).

———. "The United States Army General Staff, 1900–1917." *Military Affairs* 38 (Apr. 1974):67–71. E181.M55. (Hewes[2]).

Hill, Jim Dan. *The Minute Man in Peace and War: A History of the National Guard.* Harrisburg, 1964. UA42.H5.

Hindenburg, Paul von. *Out of My Life.* 2 vols. New York, 1921. D531.H5/1921.

Historical Section, Army War College. *The Genesis of the American First Army.* Washington, D.C., 1938. D570.2.A5.

Hoehling, A. A. *The Fierce Lambs.* Boston, 1960. D570.H48. (Hoehling[1]).

———. "John J. Pershing—the Human Side." *Army Information Digest* 16 (Oct. 1960):2–7. (Hoehling[2]).

Holley, I. B. *General John M. Palmer, Citizen Soldier and the Army of Democracy.* Westport, Conn., 1982. (Holley[1]).

———. *Ideas and Weapons.* New Haven, 1953. UG633.H6. (Holley[2]).

Holt, Hamilton. "The Black Snakes: A Visit to Bullard's Boys at Cantigny." *The Independent,* Aug. 3, 1918, 184–85, 197–98, 200. AP2.I53.

"Honor General Pershing." *Army and Navy Journal,* July 17, 1948, 1274–75, 1282–83. U1.A66.

Hoover, Herbert. *Memoirs: Years of Adventure, 1874–1920.* New York, 1951. E802.H7.

Hoover, Irwin H. *Forty-two Years in the White House.* Boston, 1934. E176.1.H78.

Hopper, James. "Our First Victory." *Collier's* (Aug. 24, 1918), 6–7, 28–29; (Sept. 7, 1918), 5–8, 34–35; (Oct. 12, 1918), 9–10, 23–24. AP2.C65.

House, Edward M. *The Intimate Papers of Colonel House.* 4 vols. Edited by Charles Seymour. Boston, 1926–28. E766.H852.

House, Jonathan M. "John McAuley Palmer and the Reserve Components." *Parameters* 12 (Sept. 1982):11–18.

Howland, C. R. *A Military History of the World War.* 2 vols. Fort Leavenworth, Kansas, 1923. D521.H65.

Hubbard, Samuel T. *Memoirs of a Staff Officer, 1917–1919.* Tuckahoe, N.Y. 1959. D640.H88.

Hunt, Frazier. *The Untold Story of Douglas MacArthur.* New York, 1954. E745.M3H8.

Hunter, Thomas M. "Foch and Eisenhower: A Study in Allied Supreme Command." *Army Quarterly* 87 (1963):33–52. (Hunter[1]).

———. *Marshal Foch: A Study in Leadership.* Ottawa, 1961. U55.F6H8. (Hunter[2]).

Hurley, Alfred F. *Billy Mitchell: Crusader for Air Power.* New York, 1964. UG633.M45H8/1975.

Hurley, Edward N. *The Bridge to France.* Philadelphia, 1927. VM23.H8.

Hyde, H. Montgomery. *Lord Reading: The Life of Rufus Isaacs, First Marquis of Reading.* London, 1967. DA566.9.R3H9.

In the Matter of the Arbitration Between the Republic of Chile and the Republic of Peru, with Respect to the Unfulfilled Provisions of the Treaty of Peace of October 20, 1883, Under the Protocol and Supplementary Act Signed at Washington July 20, 1922: Opinion and War Award of the Arbitrator. Washington, D.C., 1925.

Infantry in Battle. 2d ed. Washington, D.C., 1939. UD157.U53/1939.

"I Want To Stand Up with My Soldiers, Pershing Said of Grave." *Evening Star* (Washington, D.C.), July 15, 1948, A3.

Jacks, L. V. *Service Record by an Artilleryman*. New York, 1928. D570.9.J23.

Jackson, Stanley. *Rufus Isaacs: First Marquess of Reading*. London, 1936. DA566.9.R3J3.

Jacobs, Bruce. "July 4, 1918." *National Guardsman* 32 (July 1978):16–18, 38–39.

James, D. Clayton. *The Years of MacArthur*. 3 vols. Boston, 1970–1985. E745.M3J3.

James, Edwin L. "America's Part in a Historic Battle." *Current History* 8 (Sept. 1918):398–413. D410.C8.

James, Marquis. "Pershing." *American Legion Weekly*, Sept. 5, 1924, 5–7, 16–18. D570.A1A32.

Joffre, Joseph. *Personal Memoirs*. 2 vols. New York, 1932. D530.J62.

"John J. Pershing: Twilight of His Life Finds Him Fighting Still." *Newsweek*, Mar. 7, 1938, 16–17. AP2.N6772.

Johnson, Douglas W. *Battlefields of the World War—Western and Southern Fronts: A Study in Military Geography*. New York, 1921. D528.J6.

Johnson, Elliott L. "The Military Experiences of General Hugh A. Drum from 1898–1918." Ph.D. dissertation, University of Wisconsin, 1975.

Johnson, Thomas M. "Boys, We Had Him Wrong!" *American Magazine* 105 (May, 1928):11–13, 78, 80, 82, 84, 86, 88. AP2.A346. (Johnson[1]).

———. "First American Offensive a Success." *Current History* 8 (July 1918):57–62. D410.C8. (Johnson[2]).

———. *Without Censor: New Light on Our Greatest World War Battles*. Indianapolis, 1928. D570.J6. (Johnson[3]).

Johnson, Thomas M., and Fletcher Pratt. *The Lost Battalion*. Indianapolis, 1938. D570.33/308th/J6.

Jusserand, Jean Jules. *Le sentiment américain pendant la guerre*. Paris, 1931. D570.1.J8.

Kahn, Otto H. *When the Tide Turned*. [Boston, 1918?]. D570.9.K3.

Kaspi, André. *Le temps des Américains: le concours Américain à la France en 1917–1918*. Paris, 1976.

Keller, Victor. "A German Reply to General Pershing's War Story." *New York Times*, May 3, 1931.

Kelly, T. Howard. "Why General Edwards Was Sent Home." *McClure's* 61 (Oct. 1928):10–13, 98–101; (Nov. 1928):54–55, 120–26. AP2.M2.

Kennedy, David M. *Over Here: The First World War and American Society*. New York, 1980. D570.1.K43.

Kennett, Lee. "A.E.F. through French Eyes." *Military Review* 52 (Nov. 1972):3–11. Z6723.U35.

Keppel, Frederick P. "The General Staff." *Atlantic Monthly* 125 (Apr. 1920):539–49. AP2.A8. (Keppel[1]).

———. "Newton D. Baker." *Foreign Affairs* 16 (Apr. 1938):503–14. D410.F6. (Keppel[2]).

King, Jere C. *Foch versus Clemenceau: France and German Dismemberment, 1918–1919*. Cambridge, Mass., 1960. D650.M5K5.

Knightley, Phillip. *The First Casualty*. New York, 1975. PN4823.K5.

Kraft, Barbara S., and Donald Smythe. "How T.R. Tried in Vain To Fight in World War I." *Smithsonian* 4 (Oct. 1973):54–62. AS30.S6.

Kreidberg, Marvin A., and Merton G. Henry. *History of Military Mobilization in the United States Army, 1775–1945*. Washington, D.C., 1955. U15.U64.

"Lafayette, We Are Here." *Washington Post*, Sept. 19, 1960, 2.

Lait, Jack, and Lee Mortimer. *Washington Confidential*. New York, 1951. F196.L3/1951.

Lane, Jack C. *Armed Progressive: General Leonard Wood*. San Rafael, Cal., 1978. E181.W854.

Langer, William L. *Gas and Flame in World War I*. New York, 1965. D570.9.L3/1965.

Lansing, Robert. *War Memoirs of Robert Lansing*. Indianapolis, 1935. D619.L347.

Leary, John J., Jr. *Talks with T.R.* Boston, 1920. E757.L42.

Lee, Clark, and Richard Henschel. *Douglas MacArthur.* New York, 1952. E745.M3L4.

Lehr, Elizabeth D. *"King Lehr" and the Gilded Age.* Philadelphia, 1935. CT275.L355D4/1935a.

Leighton, Richard M., and Robert W. Coakley. *The War Department: Global Logistics and Strategy, 1940-1943. United States Army in World War II.* Washington, D.C., 1955. D769.A533/Vol. 4, Pt. 4.

Lejeune, John A. *Reminiscences of a Marine.* Philadelphia, 1930. E182.L53.

Levine, Isaac Don. *Mitchell: Pioneer of Air Power.* New York, 1943. UG633.M45L4.

Liddell Hart, B. H. "America at War." *The Fighting Forces* 10 (June 1933):127-36. U1.F5. (Liddell Hart[1]).

_____. *Foch: The Man of Orleans.* Boston, 1932. DC342.8.F6L5/1932. (Liddell Hart[2]).

_____. "The Inner Story of the Aisne, 1918." *Fortnightly Review* 135 (Feb. 1931):170-82. AP2.F7. (Liddell Hart[3]).

_____. "Pershing." *Atlantic Monthly* 140 (Aug. 1927):166-77. AP2.A8. (Liddell Hart[4]).

_____. "Pershing and His Critics." *Current History* 37 (Nov. 1932):135-40. D410.C8. (Liddell Hart[5]).

_____. "Pershing and the World War." *New York Times Book Review,* Apr. 26, 1931, Sec. 4, pp. 1 and 26. AP2.N658. (Liddell Hart[6]).

_____. *The Real War, 1914-1918.* London, 1930. D521.L48/1930. (Liddell Hart[7]).

_____. *Reputations: Ten Years After.* Boston, 1928. D507.L5. (Liddell Hart[8]).

_____. *Through the Fog of War.* London, 1938. D521.L483/1938. (Liddell Hart[9]).

"Life's Dream Realized, King Tells Pershing." *New York Times,* June 10, 1917, 1 and 7.

Liggett, Hunter. *A.E.F.: Ten Years Ago in France.* New York, 1928. D570.L5. (Liggett[1]).

_____. *Commanding an American Army: Recollections of the World War.* Boston, 1925. D570.27/1st/L5. (Liggett[2]).

Link, Arthur S., et al. *The Papers of Woodrow Wilson.* Vols. 42-49. Princeton, 1983-1985. E660.W717.

Livermore, Seward W. *Politics Is Adjourned: Woodrow Wilson and the War Congress, 1916-1918.* Middletown, Conn., 1966. E780.L5.

Lloyd George, David. *War Memoirs of David Lloyd George.* 6 vols. London, 1933-37. D546.L5.

Lohbeck, Don. *Patrick J. Hurley.* Chicago, 1956. E748.H96L6.

Lonergan, Thomas C. *It Might Have Been Lost: A Chronicle from Alien Sources of the Struggle To Preserve the National Identity of the A.E.F.* New York, 1929. D570.L6.

Lowry, Bullitt. "Pershing and the Armistice." *Journal of American History* 55 (Sept. 1968):281-91. E171.J86.

Lowry, Edward G. "The Emerging Mr. Baker." *Collier's,* Oct. 6, 1917, 6-7, 35-36. AP2.C65. (E. Lowry[1]).

_____. *Washington Close-ups.* Boston, 1921. E663.L9. (E. Lowry[2]).

Ludendorff, Erich von. *Ludendorff's Own Story: August 1914-November 1918.* 2 vols. New York, 1919. D531.L8/1920.

McArthur, C. N. "Rock of the Marne." *U.S. Infantry Journal* 17 (Sept. 1920). UD1.16.

MacArthur, Douglas. *Reminiscences.* New York, 1965. E745.M3A34.

McCarthy, Joe. "The Lost Battalion." *American Heritage* 28 (Oct. 1977):86-91, 93. E171.A43.

McCormick, David C. "A History of the United States Army Band to 1946." Ph.D. dissertation, Northwestern University, 1970.

McCormick, Robert. *The Army of 1918.* New York, 1920. D570.M25.

McFarland, Keith D. *Harry H. Woodring: A Political Biography of FDR's Controversial Secretary of War.* Lawrence, Kansas, 1975. E748.W79M32.

McKelvie, Martha Groves. *The Journey*. Philadelphia, 1962. PS3525.A2554Z5. (McKelvie[1]).

———. *Presidents, Politicians & People I Have Known*. Philadelphia, 1971. E747.M27. (McKelvie[2]).

Malcolm, Ian. *Lord Balfour: A Memory*. London, 1930. DA566.9.B2M3.

Manchester, William. *American Caesar: Douglas MacArthur, 1880–1964*. Boston, 1978. E745.M3M27.

Mangin, Charles. *Comment finir la guerre*. Paris, 1920. D521.M33. (Mangin[1]).

———. *Lettres de guerre, 1914–1918*. Paris, 1950. D548.M33. (Mangin[2]).

March, Peyton C. *The Nation at War*. Garden City, N.Y., 1932. D570.M35/1932a.

Markey, D. John. "That Was Pershing." *American Legion Magazine* 46 (Jan. 1949):28–29, 34–36, 38–39. D570.A1A32.

Marshall, George C. "John Joseph Pershing." *Assembly* 8 (Apr. 1940):6–8. U410.K55. (G. Marshall[1]).

———. "How Pershing Met Crisis in Offensive of Meuse-Argonne." *Atlanta Constitution*, Jan. 18, 1931. (G. Marshall[2]).

———. *Memoirs of My Services in the World War, 1917–1918*. Boston, 1976. D570.9.M37/1976. (G. Marshall[3]).

———. "Profiting by War Experience." *Infantry Journal* 18 (Jan. 1921):34–37. UD1.I6. (G. Marshall[4]).

———. "Some Lessons of History." *Maryland Historical Magazine* 40 (Sept. 1945):175–84. F176.M18. (G. Marshall[5]).

Marshall, Katherine Tupper. *Together: Annals of an Army Wife*. New York, 1946. E745.M37M3.

Marshall, S. L. A. *The American Heritage History of World War I*. New York, 1964. D521.M412. (S. L. A. Marshall[1]).

———. *Bringing Up the Rear: A Memoir*. Edited by Cate Marshall. San Rafael, Cal., 1979. D15.M34A32. (S. L. A. Marshall[2]).

———. *The Last Refuge: Three Public Addresses in the Spring, 1969*. N.p., n.d. (S. L. A. Marshall[3]).

———. *Men Against Fire*. New York, 1947. UB210.M26. (S. L. A. Marshall[4]).

———. *The Officer as a Leader*. Harrisburg, Pa., 1966. UB210.M27. (S. L. A. Marshall[5]).

———. "Pershing Guided by Two Rules: Keep Cool and Obey Orders!" *Detroit News*, July 15, 1948, 48. (S. L. A. Marshall[6]).

———. "Pershing Howled Down But Stood Up for His Men." *Detroit News*, Jan. 9, 1931. (S. L. A. Marshall[7]).

Marshall-Cornwall, James H. *Foch as Military Commander*. London, 1972. DC342.8.F6M34/1976b. (Marshall-Cornwall[1]).

———. *Haig as Military Commander*. New York, 1973. (Marshall-Cornwall[2]).

Martet, Jean. *Clemenceau*. London, 1930. DC342.8.C6A3/1930.

Maurice, Frederick B. *The Armistices of 1918*. D642.M36. (Maurice[1]).

———. "General Pershing and the A.E.F." *Foreign Affairs* 9 (July 1931):592–604. D410.F6. (Maurice[2]).

———. "General Pershing and the American Expeditionary Force." *19th Century* 110 (Aug. 1931):222–31. AP2.N6778. (Maurice[3]).

———. *Intrigues of War*. Boston, 1922. (Maurice[4]).

———. *The Last Four Months: How the War Was Won*. Boston, 1919. D544.M35/1919a. (Maurice[5]).

———. *Lessons of Allied Co-operation: Naval, Military and Air, 1914–1918*. London, 1942. D521.M46. (Maurice[6]).

_____. "Pershing's Censures." *The Morning Post* (London), June 20, 1931. (Maurice[7]).

Maurice, Nancy, ed. *The Maurice Case*. Hamden, Conn., 1972. D517.M383/1972.

Maximilian, Prince of Baden. *The Memoirs of Prince Max of Baden*. 2 vols. London, 1928. DD231.M3A4.

Mayo, Katherine. *"That Damn Y."* Boston, 1920. D639.Y7M35.

Miller, Henry Russell. *The First Division*. Pittsburgh, 1924. D570.3/1st/M5.

Millett, Allan R. *The General: Robert L. Bullard and Officership in the United States Army, 1881-1925*. Westport, Conn., 1975. U53.B78M54. (Millett[1]).

_____. *Semper Fidelis: The History of the United States Marine Corps*. New York, 1980. VE23.M54. (Millett[2]).

Mitchell, William. "The Air Service at St. Mihiel." *World's Work* 38 (Aug. 1919):360-70. AP2.W8. (Mitchell[1]).

_____. "The Air Service at the Argonne-Meuse." *World's Work* 38 (Sept. 1919):552-60. AP2.W8. (Mitchell[2]).

_____. *Memoirs of World War I*. New York, 1960. D606.M5. (Mitchell[3]).

Mordacq, Jean Jules Henri. *Clemenceau*. Paris, 1939. DC342.8.C6M52. (Mordacq[1]).

_____. *Le Commandement unique: Comment il fut réalisé*. Paris, 1929. D544.M55. (Mordacq[2]).

_____. *Le Ministère Clemenceau: Journal d'un témoin*. 4 vols. Paris, 1930-1931. DC342.8.C6M55. (Mordacq[3]).

Morison, Elting E. *Admiral Sims and the Modern American Navy*. Boston, 1942. E748.S52M6. (Morison[1]).

_____., ed. *The Letters of Theodore Roosevelt*. 8 vols. Cambridge, Mass., 1951-1954. E757.R7958. (Morison[2]).

Morley, Christopher. *Pipefuls*. New York, 1920. PS3525.071P5/1920.

Moseley, Leonard. *Marshall: Hero for Our Times*. New York, 1982.

Mossman, B. C., and M. W. Stark. *The Last Salute: Civil and Military Funerals, 1921-1969*. Washington, D.C., 1971. GT3203.M67.

Mott, T. Bentley. *Twenty Years as Military Attaché*. New York, 1937. D413.M6A3.

Mowrer, Edgar Ansel. "War Foe Says Pershing Broke German Morale." *Chicago News*, Mar. 9, 1931.

Murray, Lawrence L. "General John J. Pershing's Bid for the Presidency in 1920." *Nebraska History* 53 (Summer 1972):216-52. F661.N22.

"A National Position in Readiness." *Army and Navy Journal*, July 29, 1922, 1169-70. U1.A66.

Nelson, Keith L. *Victors Divided: America and the Allies in Germany, 1918-1923*. Berkeley, 1975. D650.M5N44.

Nenninger, Timothy K. *The Leavenworth Schools and the Old Army: Education, Professionalism, and the Officer Corps of the United States Army, 1881-1918*. Westport, Conn., 1978. U415.N46.

"Newton D. Baker, the Mayor-Idealist of Cleveland, Becomes the New Secretary of War." *Current Opinion* 60 (Apr. 1916):246-48. AP2.C95.

Notes d'un témoin. *Les grands jours de France en Amérique*. Paris, 1917. D570.8.M6F5.

O'Connor, Richard. *Black Jack Pershing*. Garden City, N.Y., 1961. E181.P487.

O'Laughlin, John Callan. *Pershing*. New York, 1928. E181.P49.

"Old Soldier." *Time*, Nov. 15, 1943, 55-56, 58, 60. AP2.T37.

Ormsby, Helen. *France: A Regional and Economic History*. New York, 1931. HC276.07.

O'Ryan, John F. *The Story of the 27th Division*. 2 vols. New York, 1921. D570.3/27th.

Otto, Ernst. "The Battles for the Possession of Belleau Woods, June, 1918." *U.S. Naval Institute Proceedings* 54 (Nov. 1928):940-62. V1.U8.

"A Pacifist Secretary of War." *Literary Digest*, Mar. 9, 1916, 701. AP2.L58.

Painlevé, Paul. *Comment j'ai nommé Foch et Pétain*. Paris, 1924. D548.P3/1924.

Palmer, Frederick. *America in France*. New York, 1919. D570.P3. (F. Palmer[1]).

———. "America's Part in the Titanic Conflict." *New York Times Magazine*, July 29, 1934, 8–9, 15. AP2.N6575. (F. Palmer[2]).

———. *Bliss, Peacemaker: The Life and Letters of General Tasker Howard Bliss*. New York, 1934. E181.B68. (F. Palmer[3]).

———. "Heroes Then and Now." *Scribner's* 84 (Nov. 1928):580–86. AP2.S4. (F. Palmer[4]).

———. *John J. Pershing, General of the Armies: A Biography*. Harrisburg, Pa., 1948. E181.P512. (F. Palmer[5]).

———. "John J. Pershing—Plower." *Collier's*, May 3, 1919, 5–6, 30, 32, 34, 36–37. AP2.C65. (F. Palmer[6]).

———. "Looking Back on the World War." *World's Work* 53 (Apr. 1927):587–93. AP2.W8. (F. Palmer[7]).

———. "Looking Back with Pershing Ten Years After." *Saturday Evening Post*, Apr. 2, 1927, 10–11, 197–209. AP2.S2. (F. Palmer[8]).

———. *Newton D. Baker: America at War*. 2 vols. New York, 1931. D570.P32. (F. Palmer[9]).

———. *Our Greatest Battle*. New York, 1919. D545.A63P2. (F. Palmer[10]).

———. "Pershing at 75: The Story of a Soldier." *New York Times Magazine*, Sept. 8, 1935, 4–5, 13. AP2.N6575. (F. Palmer[11]).

———. "Pershing Finds Ambition Met in Leading U.S. Army." *Washington Star*, Jan. 11, 1931. (F. Palmer[12]).

Palmer, John McAuley. *America in Arms: The Experience of the United States with Military Organization*. New Haven, 1941. UA25.P27. (J. M. Palmer[1]).

———. "Permanent Military Policy for the U.S. Is at Last Provided by Act of Congress." *Washington (D.C.) Sunday Star*, Aug. 14, 1921. (J. M. Palmer[2]).

———. "Reorganization of the War Department." *Army and Navy Journal*, Aug. 27, 1921, 1365. U1.A66. (J. M. Palmer[3]).

———. *Statesmanship or War*. Garden City, N.Y., 1927. UA23.P26/1927. (J. M. Palmer[4]).

———. *Washington, Lincoln, Wilson: Three War Statesmen*. Garden City, N.Y., 1930. E181.P17. (J. M. Palmer[5]).

Palmer, R. R., and Joel Colton. *A History of the Modern World*. 3d ed. New York, 1965.

Parker, Frank. "Memories of France in the Summer of 1914 and of Cantigny in France in 1918." *Town Topics of the Mohawk Valley* (Utica, N.Y.), Sept. 1929, 13, 21, 24, 28.

Parson, Edward B. "Why the British Reduced the Flow of American Troops to Europe in August-October 1918." *Canadian Journal of History* 12 (Dec. 1977). (Parson[1]).

———. *Wilsonian Diplomacy: Allied-American Rivalries in War and Peace*. St. Louis, 1978. D619.P33. (Parson[2]).

Patch, Joseph D. *A Soldier's War*. Corpus Christi, Texas, 1966. D570.3/1st/P3.

Patrick, Mason M. *The United States in the Air*. Garden City, N.Y., 1928. TL521.P3/1928.

Pattullo, George. "The Inside Story of the A.E.F." *Saturday Evening Post* (Apr. 29, 1922), 3–5, 30, 32, 34, 36; (May 6, 1922), 10–11, 98, 101–02, 104, 107, 109–10; (May 13, 1922), 14–15, 116, 119, 122–23; (May 20, 1922), 10–11, 83, 86, 89, 92; (May 27, 1922), 23, 128–30. AP2.S2. (Pattullo[1]).

———. "The Second Elder Gives Battle." *Saturday Evening Post*, Apr. 26, 1919, 3–4, 71, 73–74. AP2.S2. (Pattullo[2]).

Paxson, Frederic L. *America at War, 1917–1918*. Boston, 1939. D619.P42. (Paxson[1]).

———. *Postwar Years: Normalcy, 1918–1923*. Berkeley, 1948. D619.P42. (Paxson[2]).

Peake, Louis A. "West Virginia's Best Known General Since 'Stonewall Jackson': John L. Hines." *West Virginia History* 38 (Apr. 1977):226–35.

Pédroncini, Guy. *Le haut commandement français de mai 1917 à novembre 1918.* Paris, 1972. (Pédroncini[1]).

_____. *Les mutineries de 1917.* Paris, 1967. D548.P42. (Pédroncini[2]).

Pershing, John J. "The Citizen Army." *Infantry Journal* 27 (Dec. 1925):621–23. UD1.I6. (Pershing[1]).

_____. "Dear War Mothers." *McCall's* 55 (Nov. 1927):5, 113–14. TT500.M2. (Pershing[2]).

_____. "A Discussion of National Defense." *Saturday Evening Post,* Mar. 10, 1923, 3–4, 111–14. AP2.S2. (Pershing[3]).

_____. *Final Report of General John J. Pershing, Commander-in-Chief, American Expeditionary Forces.* Washington, D.C., 1920. D570.P35/1920. (Pershing[4]).

_____. "Forever America." *American Legion Monthly* 2 (May, 1927):14–17, 84. D570.A1A32. (Pershing[5]).

_____. "Lest We Forget." *Reserve Officer* 11 (Sept. 1934):5–6. (Pershing[6]).

_____. "The Meuse-Argonne." *Foreign Service* 15 (Aug. 1927), 6–7; (Sept. 1927), 8–9; (Oct. 1927), 12-13. E181.F7. (Pershing[7]).

_____. "Military Aviation." *Aeronautical Digest* 2 (Feb. 1923):71 and 145. TL501.A292. (Pershing[8]).

_____. *My Experiences in the World War.* 2 vols. New York, 1931. D570.P44. (Pershing[9]).

_____. "Our National Military Policy." *Scientific American* 127 (Aug. 1922):83, 142. T1.S5. (Pershing[10]).

_____. "Our National War Memorials in Europe." *National Geographic* 65 (Jan. 1934):1–36. G1.N27. (Pershing[11]).

_____. "Our Plans for the National Defense." *American Legion Weekly,* May 12, 1922, 5–6, 28–29. D570.A1A3. (Pershing[12]).

_____. "Peace-time Patriotism." *Women's Home Companion* 51 (July 1924):4 and 60. AP2.W714. (Pershing[13]).

_____. "Practical Patriotism." *Quartermaster Review* (July-Aug. 1923):3–4. UC34.Q8. (Pershing[14]).

_____. "The Rejected War Memorial." *Good Housekeeping* 100 (Apr. 1935):41. TX1.G7. (Pershing[15]).

_____. *Report of General John J. Pershing, U.S.A., Commander-in-Chief, American Expeditionary Forces, Cabled to the Secretary of War, November 20, 1918, Corrected January 16, 1919.* N.p., n.d. D570.P35/1919a. (Pershing[16]).

_____. "Stand by the Soldier." *National Geographic* 31 (May 1917):457–59. G1.N27. (Pershing[17]).

_____. "Statement on 'Defense Test' for September 12, 1924." *Infantry Journal* 25 (Sept. 1924):351–54. UD1.I6. (Pershing[18]).

_____. "The Thing We Need Today." *American Magazine* 114 (Dec. 1932):18–19, 82, 84. AP2.A346. (Pershing[19]).

_____. "To the Ages." *American Legion Magazine* 16 (June 1934):7–11, 40. D570.A1A32. (Pershing[20]).

_____. "We Are at War." *American Magazine* 113 (June 1932):15–17, 72, 74. AP2.A346. (Pershing[21]).

Pershing, John J., and Hunter Liggett. *Report of the First Army, American Expeditionary Forces: Organization and Operations.* Fort Leavenworth, Kansas, 1923.

"Pershing Created General." *Army and Navy Journal,* Sept. 6, 1919, 14. U1.A66.

"Pershing in London, Eager for Service; England Warmly Greets Our General, Who Hopes America Can Play Big Part." *New York Times,* June 9, 1917, 1–2.

"Pershing Kept Busy by British Hosts." *New York Times,* June 12, 1917, 2.

"Pershing, 70, Glad He's Only Soldier." *New York World*, Sept. 14, 1930.

"Pershing Tells How Secret Telegram Called Him from Here to France." *San Antonio Express*, Jan. 13, 1922.

"Pershing to Command Army G.H.Q." *Army and Navy Journal*, Apr. 23, 1921, 932–33. U1.A66.

"Pershing's Funeral." *Life*, Aug. 2, 1948, 22–23. AP2.L547.

Pierrefeu, Jean de. *French Headquarters, 1915–1918*. London, 1924. D548.P53.

Pitt, Barrie. *1918, The Last Act*. New York, 1962. D530.P5.

Pogue, Forrest C. "General Marshall and the Pershing Papers." *Quarterly Journal of the Library of Congress* 21 (Jan. 1964):1–11. Z881.U49A3. (Pogue[1]).

———. *George C. Marshall: Education of a General, 1880–1939*. New York, 1963. E745.M37P6/Vol. I. (Pogue[2]).

———. *George C. Marshall: Ordeal and Hope, 1939–1942*. New York, 1966. E745.M37P6/Vol. 2. (Pogue[3]).

———. *George C. Marshall: Organizer of Victory, 1943–1945*. New York, 1973. E745.M37P6/Vol. 3. (Pogue[4]).

———. "The Military in a Democracy." *International Security* 3 (Spring 1979):58–80. (Pogue[5]).

Poincaré, Raymond. *Au Service de la France*. 11 vols. Vol. 9: *L'Année Trouble, 1917*; Vol. 10: *Victoire et armistice, 1918*. Paris, 1932–1933. DC385.A6. (Poincaré[1]).

———. *Messages, Discours et Allocutions*. Vol. I. Paris, 1919. D505.F5/1919. (Poincaré[2]).

Powell, Ernest F. "The Last Man Killed in World War I." *American History Illustrated* 4 (June 1969):50. E171.A574.

Pratt, Fletcher. *Eleven Generals: Studies in American Command*. New York, 1949. E181.P79/1949. (Pratt[1]).

———. "Then Came Summerall." *American Legion Magazine* 26 (Mar. 1939):18–19, 40–42. D570.A1A32. (Pratt[2]).

Preliminary History of the Armistice: Official Documents Published by the German National Chancellery by Order of the Ministry of State. New York, 1924. D641.A3G4.

Rainey, James W. "Training of the American Expeditionary Force in World War I." M.A. thesis, Temple University, 1981.

Reading, Gerald R. *Rufus Isaacs, First Marquess of Reading*. 2 vols. New York, 1942–1945. DA566.9.R3R4.

Recouly, Raymond. *Foch: My Conversations with the Marshal*. New York, 1929. DC342.8.F6R45. (Recouly[1]).

———. *Foch: The Winner of the War*. New York, 1920. DC342.8.F6R4. (Recouly[2]).

Reilly, Henry J. *Americans All: The Rainbow at War*. Columbus, Ohio, 1936. D570.3/42d/R4.

Repington, Charles. "America's Effort: A Tribute." *London Morning Post*, Dec. 9, 1918. (Repington[1]).

———. *The First World War*. 2 vols. Boston, 1920. D544.R43. (Repington[2]).

Reynolds, Ruth. "First To Go Over There." *Sunday News* (New York), May 26, 1940, 50–52; June 9, 1940, 70–72.

Ribot, Alexandre. *Journal d'Alexandre Ribot et correspondances inédites, 1914–1922*. Paris, 1936. DC342.8.R5A27.

Rickenbacker, Edward V. *Fighting the Flying Circus*. Garden City, N.Y., 1965. D606.R5/1965. (Rickenbacker[1]).

———. *Rickenbacker*. Englewood Cliffs, N.J., 1967. E748.R4A3. (Rickenbacker[2]).

Riddell, George A. *Lord Riddell's War Diary, 1914–1918*. London, 1933. D546.R5.

"Robert Lee Bullard." *United States Army Recruiting News* 31 (July 1939):2–3, 18. UA23.A1A88.

Robertson, William R. *From Private to Field-Marshal.* London, 1921. DA69.3.R6A3.

Roosevelt, Eleanor B. *Day Before Yesterday: The Reminiscences of Mrs. Theodore Roosevelt, Jr.* Garden City, N.Y., 1959. E748.R68R6.

Ropp, Theodore. *War in the Modern World.* Durham, N.C., 1959. U39.R6.

Roskill, Stephen. *Hankey: Man of Secrets.* 3 vols. Vol I: *1877–1918.* London, 1970. DA566.9.H286R6.

Ryan, Garry D. "Disposition of AEF Records of World War I." *Military Affairs* 30 (Winter 1966–1967):212–19. E181.M55.

Schneider, J. Thomas. "General Pershing and I." *Saturday Evening Post*, Apr. 27, 1963, 70, 72, 74. AP2.S2.

Scott, Hugh Lenox. *Some Memories of a Soldier.* New York, 1928. E181.S4.

Second Section, General Staff, General Headquarters, American Expeditionary Forces. *Summary of Information.* 12 vols. [Chaumont, France], 1917–1919. D570.A2A617.

Seldes, George. *You Can't Print That!* New York, 1929. D443.S45.

Semsch, Philip L. "Elihu Root and the General Staff." *Military Affairs* 27 (Spring 1963):16–27. E181.M55.

Serrigny, Bernard. *Trente ans avec Pétain.* Paris, 1959. DC342.8.P4S4.

Seydell, Mildred. "It Began in Paris: The Friendship Between Micheline Resco and John J. Pershing." *Seydell Quarterly* 7 (Spring 1977):10–13.

Seymour, Charles. "Foch and Pershing." *Yale Review.* N.s. 20 (June 1931):805–09. AP2.Y2. (Seymour[1]).

———. *Letters from the Paris Peace Conference.* New Haven, Conn., 1965. D644.S47. (Seymour[2]).

———., ed. *The Intimate Papers of Colonel House.* 4 vols. Boston, 1928. E766.H852. (Seymour[3]).

Sharp, William Groves. *War Memoirs.* London, 1931. D570.S5.

Sherwood, Elmer. *Diary of a Rainbow Veteran.* Terre Haute, Ind., 1929. D570.9.S46.

Simonds, Frank H. *History of the World War.* 5 vols. New York, 1917–1920. D521.S55. (Simonds[1]).

———. *They Won the War.* New York, 1931. D507.S5. (Simonds[2]).

Simpich, Frederick. "Pershing's Last Job." *Saturday Evening Post* (Feb. 2, 1924), 34, 68. AP2.S2.

Simpson, Albert F., ed. *The World War I Diary of Col. Frank P. Lahm, Air Service, A.E.F.* Maxwell AFB, Alabama, 1970. D570.9.L25.

Sims, William S. and Burton J. Hendrich. *The Victory at Sea.* Garden City, N.Y., 1920. D589.U6S6/1920a.

Skeyhill, Tom, ed. *Sergeant York: His Own Life Story and War Diary.* New York, 1928. D570.9.Y7A5/1928.

Smith, Corinna Lindon. *Interesting People: Eighty Years with the Great and Near-Great.* Norman, Okla., 1962. ND237.S6S5.

Smythe, Donald. "A.E.F. Snafu at Sedan." *Prologue* 5 (Sept. 1973):134–49. CB3020.P75. (Smythe[1]).

———. "The Baltic Society." *Army* 28 (Feb. 1978):41–42. U1A893. (Smythe[2]).

———. "The Battle of the Books: Pershing v. March." *Army* 22 (Sept. 1972):30–32. U1.A893. (Smythe[3]).

———. "The Battle Pershing Almost Lost." *Army* 33 (Feb. 1983):50–55. U1.A893. (Smythe[4]).

———. "Five Days in June: General Pershing Arrives in England, 1917." *Army Quarterly and Defence Journal* 104 (Jan. 1974):193–202. U1.A85. (Smythe[5]).

_____. "General of the Armies John J. Pershing." In *The War Lords*, 160–75. Edited by Michael Carver. Boston, 1976. U51.W32/1976. (Smythe[6]).

_____. *Guerrilla Warrior: The Early Life of John J. Pershing*. New York, 1973. E181.P518. (Smythe[7]).

_____. "Honoring the Nation's Dead: General Pershing's American Battle Monuments Commission." *American History Illustrated* 16 (May 1981):26–33. E171.A574. (Smythe[8]).

_____. "John J. Pershing: A Study in Paradox." *Military Review* 49 (Sept. 1969):66–72. Z6723.U35. (Smythe[9]).

_____. "A Kibitzer's Guide to Winning a War." *Army* 19 (July 1968):22–23. U1.A893. (Smythe[10]).

_____. "Literary Salvos: James G. Harbord and the Pershing-March Controversy." *Mid-America* 57 (July 1975):173–83. BX1415.I3M5. (Smythe[11]).

_____. " 'Over There': The Pershing Story." *Army* 30 (Dec. 1980):34–38. U1.A893. (Smythe[12]).

_____. "Patton and Pershing." *Family*, Jan. 30, 1974, 10–13. (Smythe[13]).

_____. "Pershing and Gen. J. Franklin Bell, 1917–1918." *Mid-America* 54 (Jan. 1972):34–51. BX1415.I3M5. (Smythe[14]).

_____. "Pershing and the Canoeists." *Yankee* 34 (Sept. 1970):202–03. (Smythe[15]).

_____. "Pershing and the Roosters." *Military Review* 51 (Nov. 1971):41–43. Z6723.U35. (Smythe[16]).

_____. "Pershing Goes 'Over There': The *Baltic* Trip." *American Neptune* 34 (Oct. 1974):262–77. (Smythe[17]).

_____. "Pershing Lays Down the Law." *Military Chaplain* 44 (Nov.-Dec. 1971):8 and 10. (Smythe[18]).

_____. "The Pershing-March Conflict in World War I." *Parameters* 11 (Dec. 1981):53–62. U1.P32. (Smythe[19]).

_____. "The Ruse at Belfort." *Army* 22 (June 1972):34–38. U1.A893. (Smythe[20]).

_____. "Venereal Disease: The AEF's Experience." *Prologue* 9 (Summer 1977):64–74. CB3020.P75. (Smythe[21]).

_____. "When General Pershing Missed the Chance To Make a Million, Solve Unemployment, Become President, Save the World, and Do Everything Else That Needed Doing." *Army* 20 (Nov. 1970):18–21. U1A893. (Smythe[22]).

_____. " 'Your Authority in France Will Be Supreme': The Baker-Pershing Relationship in World War I." *Parameters* 9 (Sept. 1979):38–45. U1P32. (Smythe[23]).

Smythe, Donald, and Daniel S. Pocek, "The Sordid Side of War." *Mankind* 4 (no.9, 1974):26–27. D1.M3. (Smythe[24]).

Smuts, Jan Christian. *Selections from the Smuts Papers*. Edited by W. K. Hancock and Jean von der Poel. 7 vols. Cambridge, 1966–1973. DT779.8.S6A25.

Snow, William J. *Signposts of Experience: World War Memoirs*. Washington, D.C., 1941. UF23.S56.

Society of the First Division. *History of the First Division during the World War, 1917–1919*. Philadelphia, 1922. D570.3.1st.A5.

Somit, Albert. "The Military Hero as Presidential Candidate." *Public Opinion Quarterly* 12 (Summer 1948):192–200. HM261.A1P8.

"Son Reveals General Pershing Almost Hit Marshal Foch," *New York Herald Tribune*, Aug. 11, 1954.

Spears, Edward. *Two Men Who Saved France: Pétain and de Gaulle*. New York, 1966. DC342.8P463.

Spector, Ronald. "You're Not Going to Send Soldiers Over There Are You!": The American Search for an Alternative to the Western Front." *Military Affairs* 36 (Feb. 1972):1–4. E181.M55.

Stallings, Laurence. "The Book of the Day." *New York Sun*, Apr. 25, 1931. (Stallings[1]).
———. *The Doughboys: The Story of the AEF, 1917-1918*. New York, 1963. D570.S75. (Stallings[2]).
———. "The War to End All War." *American Heritage* 10 (Oct. 1959):4-17, 84-85. E171.A43. (Stallings[3]).
Steel, Ronald. *Walter Lippmann and the American Century*. Boston, 1980. PN4874.L45S8.
Stokesbury, James L. "The Aisne-Marne Offensive." *American History Illustrated* (July 1980):8-17. E171.A574. (Stokesbury[1]).
———. *A Short History of World War I*. New York. (Stokesbury[2]).
Suarez, Georges. *Clemenceau*. 2 vols. Paris, 1932. DC342.8.C6S8/1933.
Sullivan, Mark. *Our Times: The United States, 1900-1925*. Vol. 5: *Over Here, 1914-1918*. New York, 1933. E741.S9.
Sylvester, Albert J. *The Real Lloyd George*. London, 1947. DA566.9.L559.
Taber, John H. *The Story of the 168th Infantry*. 2 vols. Iowa City, Iowa, 1925. D570.33.168th.T3.
Tansill, Charles C. *America Goes to War*. Boston, 1938.
Tardieu, André. *France and America: Some Experiences in Cooperation*. Boston, 1927. DC59.8.U6T3. (Tardieu[1]).
———. "John J. Pershing." *Gringoire*, Mar. 4, 1938. (Tardieu[2]).
———. *Notes de semaine, 1938: L'année de Munich*. Paris, 1939. DC389.T33. (Tardieu[3]).
Teilhard de Chardin, Pierre. *The Making of a Mind: Letters from a Soldier-Priest*. New York, 1961. QE707.T4A393.
Terraine, John. "The Aftermath of Nivelle: The Allied Offensive in Spring 1917 Promised Victory...." *History Today* 27 (July 1977):426-33. D1.H818. (Terraine[1]).
———. *Douglas Haig, the Educated Soldier*. London, 1963. DA69.3.H3T4/1963a. (Terraine[2]).
———. "The March Offensive, 1918." *History Today* 18 (Apr., 1968):234-43. D1.H818. (Terraine[3]).
Tessan, François de. *La mission Joffre-Viviani: Notes d'un témoin*. Paris, 1917.
Thomas, Lowell. *Old Gimlet Eye: The Adventures of Smedley D. Butler*. New York, 1933. E182.B975.
Thomas, Shipley. *S-2 in Action*. Harrisburg, Pa., 1940. UB250.T5.
Thomas, T. H. Review of *My Experiences in the World War*, by John J. Pershing. *American Historical Review* (Jan. 1932):341-43. E171.A57.
Thomason, John W., Jr. "Crossing the Line with Pershing." *Scribner's Magazine* 80 (Aug. 1926):115-24. AP2.S4. (Thomason[1]).
———. *Fix Bayonets!*. New York, 1926. D570.348.5th.T5. (Thomason[2]).
Thornton, Earl L. "75,000 Miles with Pershing." *American Legion Monthly* 14 (May 1933): 10-11, 53-54. D570.A1A32.
Thornton, Willis. *Newton D. Baker and His Books*. Cleveland, 1954. Z989.B18T5.
Timmons, Bascom N. "Centennial of Great American." *Houston Chronicle*. Sept. 13, 1960. (Timmons[1]).
———. *Portrait of an American: Charles G. Dawes*. New York, 1953. E748.D22T55. (Timmons[2]).
Toland, John. *No Man's Land: 1918, The Last Year of the Great War*. Garden City, N.Y., 1980. D521.T6
Towne, Charles H. *The Balfour Visit: How America Received Her Distinguished Guests*. New York, 1917. D570.8.M6B6.
Trask, David F. *Captains and Cabinets: Anglo-American Naval Relations, 1917-1918*. Columbia, Mo., 1972. D611.T73. (Trask[1]).

_____. "General Tasker Howard Bliss and the 'Sessions of the World,' 1919." *Transactions of the American Philosophical Society.* New Series. 56 (Dec. 1966):3–74. Q11.P6. (Trask²).

_____. *The United States and the Supreme War Council: American War Aims and Inter-Allied Strategy, 1917–1918.* Middletown, Conn., 1961. D544.T7. (Trask³).

Tumulty, Joseph P. *Woodrow Wilson as I Know Him.* Garden City, N.Y., 1921. E767.T9.

Twichell, Heath, Jr. *Allen: The Biography of an Army Officer, 1859–1930.* New Brunswick, N.J., 1974. U53.A44T94.

U.S. Army. American Expeditionary Forces. General Staff, G-2. *Candid Comment on the American Soldier of 1917–1918 and Kindred Topics, by Germans.* Chaumont, 1919.

U.S. Army War College. Historical Section. *The Genesis of the American First Army.* Washington, D.C., 1938. D570.2.A5/1938. (U.S. Army War College¹).

_____. *Order of Battle of the United States Land Forces in the World War.* 3 vols. Washington, D.C., 1931–1949. D570.A353. (U.S. Army War College²).

U.S. Congress. *Congressional Record.* J11.R5. (U.S. Congress¹).

_____. House. Committee on Armed Services. *The National Defense Program—Unification and Strategy. Hearings before the Committee on Armed Services.* 81st Cong., 1st sess., 1949. UA23.A4/1949j. (U.S. Congress²).

_____. House. Committee on Military Affairs. *Army Reorganization. Hearings before the Committee on Military Affairs on H.R. 14560.* 65th Cong., 3d sess., 1919. UA24.A7/1919f. (U.S. Congress³).

_____. *Army Reorganization. Hearings on H.R. 8287, 8068, 7925, and 8870.* 66th Cong., 1st and 2d sess., 1919–1920. 2 vols. UA24.A7/1919j. (U.S. Congress⁴).

_____. *The National Defense. Hearings before the Committee on Military Affairs. Historical Documents Relating to the Reorganization Plans of the War Department and to the Present National Defense Act.* 69th Cong., 2d sess., 1927. UA23.A4/1927a. (U.S. Congress⁵).

_____. Senate. Committee on Military Affairs. *Army Reorganization Bill. Analytical and Exploratory Statement of the Bill (S. 2715) . . . by Senator George E. Chamberlain of Oregon, September 5, 1919.* 66th Cong., 1st sess., 1919. UA24.A7/1919k. (U.S.Congress⁶).

_____. *Reorganization of the Army. Hearings before the Subcommittee of the Committee on Military Affairs on S. 2691, 2693 and 2715.* 66th Cong., 1st and 2d sess., 1919–1920. 2 vols. UA24.A7/1919k. (U.S. Congress⁷).

_____. *Reorganization of the Army. Hearings before the Committee on Military Affairs on S. 3792. Statement of Hon. Newton D. Baker, Secretary of War.* 66th Cong., 2d sess., 1920. UA24.A7/1920j. (U.S. Congress⁸).

_____. Senate. Remarks on the Bill to Increase the Military Establishment. S. Res. 1871, 65th Cong., 1st sess., Apr. 23, 1917. *Congressional Record*, vol. 55, 932–52. J11.R5. (U.S. Congress⁹).

U.S. Department of the Army. *General of the Armies John J. Pershing Centennial, 1860–1960: Press Reports.* N.p., 1960. (U.S. Department of the Army¹).

_____. Historical Division. *United States Army in the World War, 1917–1919.* 17 vols. Washington, D.C., 1948. D570.A4A45. (U.S. Department of the Army²).

U.S. Department of State. *Papers Relating to the Foreign Relations of the United States:* 1917, 1918, 1925, 1926, 1929. JX233.A3. (U.S. Department of State¹).

_____. *Papers Relating to the Foreign Relations of the United States. The Lansing Papers, 1914–1920.* 2 vols. Washington, D.C., 1939–1940. E766.U43. (U.S. Department of State²).

U.S. War Department. *Annual Reports:* 1917–1924. UA24.A1. (U.S. War Department¹).

_____. *Annual Report of the Secretary of War, 1917.* Washington, D.C., 1917. UA24.A11. (U.S. War Department²).

_____. *Staff Manual, United States Army, 1917.* Washington, D.C., 1917. UB223.A38/ 1917. (U.S. War Department[3]).

Vandiver, Frank E. *Black Jack: The Life and Times of John J. Pershing.* 2 vols. College Station, Texas, 1977. E181.P575. (Vandiver[1]).

_____. "Commander-in-Chief—Commander Relationships: Wilson and Pershing." *Rice University Studies* 57 (Winter 1971):69–76. AS36.W65. (Vandiver[2]).

_____. *John J. Pershing.* Morristown, N.J., 1967. U53.P4V3. (Vandiver[3]).

_____. *John J. Pershing and the Anatomy of Leadership.* U.S. Air Force Academy, Colo., 1963. (Vandiver[4]).

Viereck, George S. *As They Saw Us.* Garden City, N.Y., 1929. D570.V5/1929. (Viereck[1]).

_____. *The Strangest Friendship in History: Woodrow Wilson and Colonel House.* New York, 1932. E767.V35. (Viereck[2]).

Villard, Oswald G. *Fighting Years: Memoirs of a Liberal Editor.* New York, 1939. E664.V65V5.

Viviani, René. *La mission française en Amérique.* Paris, 1917. D570.8.M6F4.

Wales, Henry. "Pershing and the Lovely Parisienne." *Chicago Sunday Tribune*, Nov. 30, 1952, Mag. Sec., 6–7. (Wales[1]).

_____. "Pershing—A Personal Reminiscence." *Sunday World-Herald Magazine* (Omaha), Oct. 10, 1948. (Wales[2]).

_____. "Pershing, at 87, 'Forgotten Man' of World War I." *Chicago Sunday Tribune*, Sept. 28, 1947, pt. 1, p. 6. (Wales[3]).

Walker, George. *Venereal Disease in the American Expeditionary Forces.* Baltimore, 1922. RC201.4.W3.

Walton, Robert C. *Over There: European Reactions to Americans in World War I.* Itasca, Ill., 1971. D505.W35.

Walworth, Arthur. *America's Movement: 1918—American Diplomacy at the End of World War I.* New York, 1977. E768.W34/1977. (Walworth[1]).

_____. *Woodrow Wilson.* 2 vols. New York, 1958. E767.W34. (Walworth[2]).

Ward, Robert D. "Against the Tide: The Preparedness Movement of 1923–1924." *Military Affairs* 38 (Apr. 1974):59–61. E181.M55.

Watson, Mark. "At the Front with General Harbord." *Baltimore Sun*, Mar. 8, 1936, 11. (Watson[1]).

_____. *Chief of Staff: Prewar Plans and Preparations.* In *United States Army in World War II. The War Department.* Washington, D.C., 1950. D769.A533/vol. 4, pt. 1. (Watson[2]).

_____. "An Estimate of What the A.E.F. Did." *Baltimore Sun*, Apr. 26, 1931. (Watson[3]).

_____. "Pershing—Nation's Greatest Soldier." *Baltimore Sun*, Aug. 28, 1960. (Watson[4]).

_____. "The War as Seen from the Home Sector." *Baltimore Sun*, July 5, 1931, 4–6. (Watson[5]).

_____. "Who Won the War? Still at Issue." *The Sun* (Baltimore), Sept. 25, 1932, Mag. Sec., 1–3. (Watson[6]).

Wecter, Dixon. *The Hero in America: A Chronicle of Hero Worship.* New York, 1941. E176.W4/1942. (Wecter[1]).

_____. *When Johnny Comes Marching Home.* Boston, 1944. E181.W43. (Wecter[2]).

Weigley, Russell F. *The American Way of War: A History of United States Military Strategy and Policy.* New York, 1973. E181.W45. (Weigley[1]).

_____. *The History of the United States Army.* New York, 1967. UA25.W35. (Weigley[2]).

_____. *Towards an American Army: Military Thought from Washington to Marshall.* New York, 1962. UA25.W4. (Weigley[3]).

"Welcome to General Pershing." *Army and Navy Journal*, Sept. 13, 1919, 54. U1.A66.

Weygand, Maxime. *Foch.* Paris, 1947. DC342.8.F6W39. (Weygand[1]).

———. "Le Maréchal Foch et l'armistice." *Revue des Deux Mondes*, Nov. 1, 1938, 5–29. AP20.R3. (Weygand[2]).

———. *Mémoires.* Vol. 1: *Idéal Vécu.* Paris, 1953. DC373.W4A3. (Weygand[3]).

———. *Le 11 Novembre.* Paris, 1932. D641.W4. (Weygand[4]).

Wheeler, John N. "Pershing Didn't Tell All." *Boston Transcript*, Nov. 28, 1931. (Wheeler[1]).

———. "They Never Tell—All." *American Magazine* (Dec. 1931):36–38, 80. AP2.A346. (Wheeler[2]).

Whitlock, Brand. *The Letters and Journal of Brand Whitlock.* 2 vols. New York, 1936. PS3545.H75Z53/1936.

Wiener, Frederick B. "How Many Stars for Pershing?" *Army* 20 (Dec. 1970):28–34; 21 (Jan. 1971):42–48. U1.A893.

Wildes, Harry Emerson. Review of *The Nation at War*, by Peyton C. March. *Philadelphia Public Ledger.* Sept. 21, 1932.

Wilgus, William J. *Transporting the A.E.F. in Western Europe: 1917–1918.* New York, 1931. D570.72.W5. (Wilgus[1]).

———. *War Diary, 1917–1919.* n.p., 1922. D570.72.W52. (Wilgus[2]).

Wilhelm, Donald. "If He Were President." *Independent* Sept. 27, 1919, 444–45, 462–65. AP2.I53.

Willert, Arthur. *The Road to Safety.* New York, 1953. E183.8.G7W6/1953.

Williams, T. Harry. *Americans at War: The Development of the American Military System.* N.p., 1960. E181.W63. (T. H. Williams[1]).

———. *The History of American Wars.* New York, 1981. E181.W64/1981. (T. H. Williams[2]).

Williams, Wythe. *Dusk of Empire.* New York, 1937. D443.W534. (W. Williams[1]).

———. "An Eyewitness in Devastated France." *Current History* 6 (May 1917):323–26. D410.C8. (W. Williams[2]).

———. *The Tiger of France: Conversations with Clemenceau.* New York, 1949. DC342.8.C6W5. (W. Williams[3]).

Williamson, S. T. "The War that Was Fought behind the War." *New York Times*, Mar. 22, 1931.

Wilson, Joe F. *The United States, Chile and Peru in the Tacna and Arica Plebiscite.* Washington, D.C., 1979. F3097.3.W54.

Wilson, John R. M. "The Quaker and the Sword: Herbert Hoover's Relations with the Military." *Military Affairs* 38 (Apr. 1974):41–47. E181.M55.

Winterich, John T. *Squads Write!* New York, 1931. D501.S725A3.

Wolff, Leon. *In Flanders Fields: The 1917 Campaign.* New York, 1958. D541.W7.

Woods, William S. *Colossal Blunders of the War.* New York, 1930. D521.W6.

Woolcott, Alexander. "Them Damned Frogs." *North American* 210 (Oct. 1919):490–98. AP2.N7.

Woolf, Samuel Johnson. *Drawn From Life.* New York, 1932. CT120.W6.

Wrench, Evelyn. *Alfred Lord Milner, the Man of No Illusions.* London, 1958. DA566.9.M5W7.

Wright, Cobina. *I Never Grew Up.* New York, 1952. CT275.W755A3. (Wright[1]).

———. "The Story of General Pershing's Secret Romance." *Sunday Mirror* (New York), May 11, 1952, 6 and 13. (Wright[2]).

Wythe, George. *A History of the 90th Division.* n.p., 1920. D570.3/90th/W9.

Young, Hugh. *Hugh Young: A Surgeon's Autobiography.* New York, 1940. R154.Y63A3.

Zabriskie, Alexander C. *Bishop Brent: Crusader for Christian Unity.* Philadelphia, 1948. BX5995.B75Z3.

INDEX